THE CRICKETERS'
WHO'S WHO
1987

GW00691966

THE
CRICKETERS'
WHO'S WHO
1987

compiled and edited by
IAIN SPROAT

associate editor
RALPH DELLOR

WILLOW BOOKS
Collins
8 Grafton Street, London W1
1987

Willow Books
William Collins Sons & Co. Ltd
London · Glasgow · Sydney · Auckland
Toronto · Johannesburg

First published in Great Britain in 1987 by
William Collins Sons & Co Ltd, 8 Grafton Street
London W1X 3LA in association with The
Cricketers' Who's Who Limited
© Iain Sproat 1987

British Library Cataloguing in Publication Data
The Cricketers' who's who – 8th ed.
1. Cricket players – Biography
I. Sproat, Iain
796.35′8′0922   GV915.A1
ISBN 0-00-218272-6 hardback
ISBN 0-00-218262-9 paperback

Cover photographs of Neil Foster and Graham Hick by
Adrian Murrell/All-Sport
Portraits by Bill Smith

Typeset by Rowland Phototypesetting Ltd,
Bury St Edmunds, Suffolk
Printed and bound in Great Britain by
Butler and Tanner Ltd, Frome, Somerset

PREFACE

EACH YEAR, I try to find something new to add to the *Cricketers' Who's Who*. This year – the eighth successive season – the latest improvement is to add biographies of the first-class umpires – something that has been requested by many readers, but which, previously, pressures of space, and consequently price, had prevented me from doing. Any suggestions from readers for further improvement would be gratefully received.

Incidentally, I have been enabled to clear up a minor cricketing mystery since I mentioned in one of my last year's Quiz Questions that Sir P. G. Wodehouse, creator of the famous Jeeves, and Sir Arthur Conan Doyle, creator of the famous Sherlock Holmes, had once taken part together in a stand of 50 at Lord's. I had at the time no more information than I put in the question, and asked readers if they could tell me more. Subsequently, that great authority on the works of Wodehouse, Richard Usborne, directed my attention to an essay by Alec Waugh, older brother of Evelyn, in which he says that, as a schoolboy, he saw The Authors play The Publishers at Lord's in August 1910. The Authors were captained by Conan Doyle (who also by the way, played for the MCC, scored a century in his first match at Lord's, and once clean bowled W. G. Grace); Wodehouse, according to Waugh, went in first wicket down for The Authors and 'made over sixty runs'. The match was a draw. Waugh kept his score-card for many years, but it is now in the library of Haverford College. It would be interesting to see more details from that score card. As a schoolboy, Wodehouse himself was a member of the Dulwich College cricket XI for two years.

The cricketers listed in this volume include all those who played for their county at least once last season, either in the county championship, John Player Special League, Benson & Hedges or NatWest matches. The statistics are accurate up to the end of the last English season – with one exception: it has proved impossible to guarantee the accuracy of the statistics of certain matches, classified as first-class, in India and Pakistan. However, Test match figures in those countries have been included. Figures about 50 wickets and 1000 runs, etc. in a season refer to matches in England only. First-class figures do not include figures for Test matches which are listed separately.

The following abbreviations apply: * means not out; JPL means John Player Special League and B&H means Benson & Hedges. Where there are two lines of bowling figures, the top line refers to eight ball overs, the bottom line to six. Normally there is only one line, referring to six ball overs. The figures for batting and bowling averages refer to 1986 followed in brackets by the 1985 figures. Inclusion in the first-class batting averages depends on a minimum of eight innings, and an average of at least 10 runs; a bowler has had to have taken at least 10 wickets in at least 10 innings.

Readers will notice certain occasional differences in the way the same kind of information about cricketers is presented. This is because I have usually tried to follow the way in which the cricketers themselves have provided the relevant information.

I should like to acknowledge with particular gratitude the very wide-ranging help I have had from Mr Ralph Dellor, the cricket broadcaster, journalist and NCA staff coach. Once again I am indebted to Mr Robert Brooke for his splendidly professional work in the collection of the statistics, and to Mr Bill Smith, FRPS who personally took most of the photographs. I should also like to thank Mr Laurence Gretton for contributing the question about the 1938 Test records.

Above all I am grateful to the cricketers themselves without whose support this book could not have been compiled.

Iain Sproat
January 1987

ABRAHAMS, J.　　　　Lancashire

Full Name: John Abrahams
Role: Left-hand bat, right-arm
off-break bowler
Born: 21 July 1952, Cape Town,
South Africa
Height: 5′ 7″ **Weight:** 10st 4lbs
Nickname: Abey
County debut: 1973
County cap: 1982
1000 runs in a season: 4
1st-Class 50s scored: 50
1st-Class 100s scored: 12
1st-Class 200s scored: 1
One-day 50s: 17
One-day 100s: 1
Place in batting averages: 45th
av. 40.35 (1985 134th av. 26.63)
1st-Class catches 1986: 13
(career: 155)
Parents: Cecil John and Cynthia Jean
Marital status: Single
Education: Heywood Grammar School (later became Heywood Senior High
School)
Qualifications: 9 O-levels, A-level Biology, NCA Preliminary Coaching
Certificate
Jobs outside cricket: Shop manager and representative, Beaverwise Plant
Hire, Oldham
Family links with cricket: Father was professional with Milnrow and Radcliffe
in Central Lancashire League. Brothers Basil and Peter have both pro'd in the
Leagues
Overseas teams played for: Player-coach for Mowbray CC, Tasmania
1980–81; Western Creek CC, Canberra 1983–84, 1984–85
Cricketers particularly learnt from: Jack Bond and Peter Lever
Cricketers particularly admired: Clive Lloyd and Mike Brearley
Other sports played: Badminton, golf
Other sports followed: Watching rugby union on TV
Relaxation: 'Listening to pop music: Rod Stewart, Fleetwood Mac, for
example'
Extras: Has lived in UK since 1962. Substitute for England in place of Brian
Rose in Fifth Test against West Indies at Headingley in August 1980. 'Would
very much like to be a physiotherapist when I retire.' Gold award winner in
1984 B & H final. Captain 1984 and 1985
Best batting performance: 201* Lancashire v Warwickshire, Nuneaton 1984

Best bowling performance: 3-27 Lancashire v Worcestershire, Old Trafford 1981

LAST SEASON: BATTING

	I.	N.O.	R.	H.S.	AV.
TEST					
1ST-CLASS	38	7	1251	189*	40.35
INT					
JPL	12	2	334	103*	33.40
NAT.W.	5	1	188	67*	47.00
B & H	4	0	90	39	22.50

CAREER: BATTING

	I.	N.O.	R.	H.S.	AV.
TEST					
1ST-CLASS	371	51	9476	201*	29.61
INT					
JPL	115	23	2375	103*	25.81
NAT.W.	24	3	491	67*	23.38
B & H	27	5	573	66*	26.04

LAST SEASON: BOWLING

	O.	M.	R.	W.	AV.
TEST					
1ST-CLASS	44.5	5	175	3	58.33
INT					
JPL	24	3	103	5	20.60
NAT.W.	19	3	64	2	32.00
B & H	24	2	95	1	—

CAREER: BOWLING

	O.	M.	R.	W.	AV.
TEST					
1ST-CLASS	925.1	195	2746	54	50.85
INT					
JPL	81.2	6	420	11	38.18
NAT.W.	44	6	176	5	35.20
B & H	31	2	134	2	67.00

ACFIELD, D. L. Essex

Full Name: David Laurence Acfield
Role: Right-hand bat, right-arm off-break bowler
Born: 24 July 1947, Chelmsford
Height: 5′ 9½″ **Weight:** 12st 1lb
Nickname: Ackers
County debut: 1966
County cap: 1970
Benefit: 1981 (£42,788)
50 wickets in a season: 7
1st-Class 5 w. in innings: 34
1st-Class 10 w. in match: 4
Place in bowling averages: 47th
av. 27.63 (1985 106th av. 40.83)
1st-Class catches 1986: 5
(career: 137)
Parents: Robert and Ena
Wife and date of marriage: Helen, 27 October 1973
Children: Clare Louise, 10 December 1977; Rosemary Helen, 16 March 1982
Education: Brentwood School; Christ's College, Cambridge
Qualifications: MA (Cantab) History
Jobs outside cricket: Schoolmaster
Family links with cricket: Late elder brother, Ian 1944–68, member of MCC,

Incogniti, Cambridge University Crusaders, etc.

Overseas tours: With MCC to East Africa 1973–74

Cricketers particularly learnt from: All spinners

Off-season 1986–87: Working for Barwell & Jones, Wine Merchants

Other sports played: Fencing (sabre), British Olympic team 1968 and 1972. Commonwealth Games Gold Medal (team event) 1970, British champion 1969–72. Cambridge Blue for fencing

Relaxations: Bird-watching; films, especially Westerns; wine

Extras: Cambridge cricket Blue 1967, 1968

Best batting performance: 42 Cambridge University v Leicestershire, Leicester 1967

Best bowling performance: 8-55 Essex v Kent, Canterbury 1981

LAST SEASON: BATTING

	I.	N.O.	R.	H.S.	AV.
TEST					
1ST-CLASS	19	10	52	11	5.77
INT					
JPL	1	0	2	2	–
NAT.W.	1	1	4	4*	–
B & H					

LAST SEASON: BOWLING

	O.	M.	R.	W.	AV.
TEST					
1ST-CLASS	401.3	107	912	33	27.63
INT					
JPL	71	3	356	10	35.60
NAT.W.	17	1	73	1	–
B & H					

CAREER: BATTING

	I.	N.O.	R.	H.S.	AV.
TEST					
1ST-CLASS	417	212	1677	42	8.18
INT					
JPL	48	32	81	9*	5.06
NAT.W.	8	7	8	4*	–
B & H	4	3	15	8*	–

CAREER: BOWLING

	O.	M.	R.	W.	AV.
TEST					
1ST-CLASS	11267.2	3220	26800	950	28.21
INT					
JPL	815.2	74	3284	127	25.85
NAT.W.	112.3	22	357	11	32.45
B & H	142	18	502	14	35.86

---

1. Who was Man of the Match in the 1986 Nat West Final?

2. Which current Hampshire cricketer bowls with his left hand and throws with his right?

AFFORD, J. A. Nottinghamshire

Full Name: John Andrew Afford
Role: Right-hand bat, slow left-arm bowler
Born: 12 May 1964, Crowland, Nr. Peterborough
Height: 6′ 2″ **Weight:** 12st 8lbs
Nickname: Aff
County debut: 1984
1st-Class 5 w. in innings: 3
1st-Class 10 w. in match: 1
Place in bowling averages: 67th av. 32.33
1st-Class catches 1986: 4 (career: 7)
Parents: Jill
Marital status: Single
Education: Spalding Grammar School; Stamford College for Further Education
Qualifications: 5 O-levels, NCA Coaching Certificate

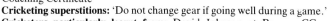

Cricketing superstitions: 'Do not change gear if going well during a game.'
Cricketers particularly learnt from: David Johnson at Bourne CC and everyone at Nottinghamshire, especially Eddie Hemmings
Cricketers particularly admired: Richard Hadlee, Bishen Bedi, Derek Underwood
Off-season 1986–87: Playing and coaching for Upper Hutt CC, Wellington, New Zealand
Other sports followed: 'Will give anything a whirl, but nothing too serious.

LAST SEASON: BATTING

	I.	N.O.	R.	H.S.	AV.
TEST					
1ST-CLASS	12	7	19	9*	3.80
INT					
JPL	–	–	–	–	–
NAT.W.					
B & H					

CAREER: BATTING

	I.	N.O.	R.	H.S.	AV.
TEST					
1ST-CLASS	13	7	21	9*	3.50
INT					
JPL	–	–	–	–	–
NAT.W.					
B & H					

LAST SEASON: BOWLING

	O.	M.	R.	W.	AV.
TEST					
1ST-CLASS	492.4	132	1455	45	32.33
INT					
JPL	8	0	27	1	–
NAT.W.					
B & H					

CAREER: BOWLING

	O.	M.	R.	W.	AV.
TEST					
1ST-CLASS	606.1	169	1788	54	33.11
INT					
JPL	8	0	27	1	–
NAT.W.					
B & H					

Able to watch most things – just can't fathom out people's fascination for horse racing.'

Relaxations: Enjoys listening to music, plays bass guitar, and 'a few quiet ones in the TBI'.

Injuries 1986: 'Every rash under the sun.'

Best batting performance: 9* Nottinghamshire v Essex, Chelmsford 1986

Best bowling performance: 6-81 Nottinghamshire v Kent, Trent Bridge 1986

AGNEW, J. P.   Leicestershire

Full Name: Jonathan Philip Agnew
Role: Right-hand bat, right-arm fast bowler, outfielder
Born: 4 April 1960, Macclesfield, Cheshire
Height: 6′ 4″ **Weight:** 12st 7lbs
Nickname: Spiro (after former US Vice-President Spiro Agnew)
County debut: 1978
County cap: 1984
Test debut: 1984
No. of Tests: 3
No. of One-Day Internationals: 3
50 wickets in a season: 3
1st-Class 50s scored: 1
1st-Class 5 w. in innings: 12
1st-Class 10 w. in match: 2
Place in batting averages: 222nd av. 12.92 (1985 253rd av. 10.08)
Place in bowling averages: 49th av. 27.78 (1985 35th av. 27.49)
1st-Class catches 1986: 2 (career: 45)
Parents: Philip and Margaret
Wife and date of marriage: Beverley, 8 October 1983
Children: Jennifer, 31 October 1985
Education: Uppingham School
Qualifications: 9 O-levels, 2 A-levels
Jobs outside cricket: Cricket Coach. Spent 1981–82 off-season coaching at Sindia High School, Zimbabwe. Production control at T. L. Bennett's Windows Ltd
Cricketing superstitions: 'I never use a bowling marker so am never popular with groundsmen!'
Cricketers particularly learnt from: Ken Higgs, Andy Roberts, Frank Tyson, Peter Willey
Cricketers particularly admired: Imran Khan

Off-season 1986–87: Freelance journalist with BBC Radio Leicester
Family links with cricket: First cousin, Mary Duggan, Captain of England's Women's XI in 1960s
Overseas tours: Young England tour of Australia, 1978–79; Leicestershire CCC to Zimbabwe, 1981; England to India and Australia, 1984–85; England B to Sri Lanka, 1986
Overseas teams played for: Whitbread scholarship, playing for Essendon CC, Melbourne, 1978, 1980; Alexander CC, Harare, Zimbabwe, 1981–82; Central Cumberland District Cricket Club, Sydney, 1982–83
Other sports played: Hockey, badminton, squash, table-tennis
Injuries 1986: Sprained both ankles within a fortnight
Relaxations: Music (all kinds). Playing piano and tuba. Coaching cricket. 'I became very interested in game viewing in Zimbabwe. I spent days driving around to study and photograph – particularly elephants.'
Extras: Played for Surrey 2nd XI 1976–77. Back trouble in 1979 season.
Opinions on cricket: 'Over-rate required is still far too high and the rate stipulated must come down to encourage a decent standard of cricket.'
Best batting performance: 56 Leicestershire v Worcestershire, Worcester 1982
Best bowling performance: 9-70 Leicestershire v Kent, Leicester 1985

LAST SEASON: BATTING

	I.	N.O.	R.	H.S.	AV.
TEST					
1ST-CLASS	20	6	181	35*	12.92
INT					
JPL	2	0	2	2	1.00
NAT.W.	1	1	5	5*	–
B & H	1	0	2	2	–

LAST SEASON: BOWLING

	O.	M.	R.	W.	AV.
TEST					
1ST-CLASS	522.5	118	1528	55	27.78
INT					
JPL	43.1	0	173	8	21.62
NAT.W.	17	7	42	1	–
B & H	22	3	96	3	32.00

CAREER: BATTING

	I.	N.O.	R.	H.S.	AV.
TEST	4	3	10	5	–
1ST-CLASS	115	21	914	56	9.72
INT	1	1	2	2*	–
JPL	10	5	31	13*	6.20
NAT.W.	3	2	14	5*	–
B & H	7	2	31	23*	6.20

CAREER: BOWLING

	O.	M.	R.	W.	AV.
TEST	92	22	373	4	93.25
1ST-CLASS	2895.4	558	9776	339	28.83
INT	21	0	120	3	40.00
JPL	216.4	10	1079	32	33.71
NAT.W.	67	12	205	8	25.62
B & H	175.2	26	667	26	25.65

3. Who won the first and last John Player League titles?
4. In which season did the Sunday League come into being?

ALDERMAN, T. M.   Kent

Full Name: Terence Michael Alderman
Role: Right-hand bat, right-arm
fast bowler, slip fielder
Born: 12 June 1956, Subiaco,
Western Australia
Height: 6' 2½" **Weight:** 13½st
Nickname: Clem, Snagger
County debut: 1984
County cap: 1984
Test debut: 1981
No of Tests: 22
No. of One-Day Internationals: 23
50 wickets in a season: 2
1st-Class 50s scored: 1
1st-Class 5 w. in innings: 34
1st-Class 10 w. in match: 7
Place in bowling averages: 7th
av. 19.20

1st-Class catches 1986: 9 (career: 124)
Parents: William and Joan
Wife and date of marriage: Jane, 16 December 1977
Children: Kate, 6 April 1986
Education: Aquinas College, Perth; Churchlands College of Advanced Education
Qualifications: Teacher's Certificate
Jobs outside cricket: Business Development Officer with Town & Country WA Building Society
Family links with cricket: Father played State Colts, sister (Denise) played for Australian Women
Overseas tours: Australia – England, Sri Lanka 1981; New Zealand 1982; West Indies 1984; Pakistan 1982; South Africa (Rebels) 1984
Overseas teams played for: Watsonians (Scotland) 1980
Cricketers particularly learnt from: Dennis Lillee, Rod Marsh
Off-season 1986–87: 'In South Africa and at home with my feet up.'
Other sports played: Golf
Relaxations: Golf, antiques, old cars, gardening
Injuries 1986: Right arm
Best batting performance: 52* Kent v Sussex, Hastings 1984
Best bowling performance: 8-46 Kent v Derbyshire, Derby 1986

LAST SEASON: BATTING

	I.	N.O.	R.	H.S.	AV.
TEST					
1ST-CLASS	20	7	102	25	7.86
INT					
JPL					
NAT.W.					
B & H					

LAST SEASON: BOWLING

	O.	M.	R.	W.	AV.
TEST					
1ST-CLASS	610	139	1882	98	19.20
INT					
JPL					
NAT.W.					
B & H					

CAREER: BATTING

	I.	N.O.	R.	H.S.	AV.
TEST	33	15	113	23	6.27
1ST-CLASS	132	60	660	52*	9.16
INT	9	3	27	9*	–
JPL	5	4	21	11	–
NAT.W.	–	–	–	–	–
B & H	2	1	4	4*	–

CAREER: BOWLING

	O.	M.	R.	W.	AV.
TEST	895.3	202	2597	79	32.87
1ST-CLASS	952.2	176	11027	500	22.05
INT	215	31	803	29	27.69
JPL	105	9	477	21	22.71
NAT.W.	57	10	222	10	22.20
B & H	40	7	113	7	16.14

ALIKHAN, R. K.   Sussex

Full Name: Rehan Kebal Alikhan
Role: Right-hand bat
Born: 28 December 1962, London
Height: 6′ 1½″ **Weight:** 13st
Nickname: Prince, Oily, Pretty
Polly, Munch
County debut: 1986
1st-Class 50s scored: 7
Place in batting averages: 73rd
av. 35.12
1st-Class catches 1986: 7
(career: 7)
Parents: Akbar and Farida
Marital status: Single
Education: King's College School,
Wimbledon
Qualifications: 2 A-levels, 8 O-levels
Jobs outside cricket: Insurance broker
Cricketing superstitions: 'I never bat
with a cap on.'
Overseas tours: King's College School, Wimbledon tours to Holland 1978 and
1980; Surrey Schools U-19 tour to Australia 1979–80; Club Cricket Conference tour to Kenya 1985
Overseas teams played for: Mosman Middle Harbour District Cricket Club
1982–83 and 1983–84
Cricketers particularly learnt from: Imran Khan, Paul Parker, Monty Lynch
Cricketers particularly admired: Zaheer Abbas, Imran Khan, Viv Richards,
Greg Chappell

Off-season 1986–87: Playing cricket in Pakistan
Other sports played: Squash, soccer, rugby
Other sports followed: American football, Aussie rules, hockey, golf, tennis
Injuries 1986: 'I tore the ligaments in my right ankle playing rugby before the start of the season which stopped me playing until June.'
Relaxations: Reading, music, theatre, watching sport
Best batting performance: 72 Sussex v Derbyshire, Eastbourne 1986

LAST SEASON: BATTING

	I.	N.O.	R.	H.S.	AV.
TEST					
1ST-CLASS	28	4	843	72	35.12
INT					
JPL	1	0	10	10	–
NAT.W.	5	1	61	41	15.25
B & H					

LAST SEASON: BOWLING

	O.	M.	R.	W.	AV.
TEST					
1ST-CLASS	10	0	65	0	–
INT					
JPL					
NAT.W.					
B & H					

CAREER: BATTING

	I.	N.O.	R.	H.S.	AV.
TEST					
1ST-CLASS	28	4	843	72	35.12
INT					
JPL	1	0	10	10	–
NAT.W.	5	1	61	41	15.25
B & H					

CAREER: BOWLING

	O.	M.	R.	W.	AV.
TEST					
1ST-CLASS	10	0	65	0	–
INT					
JPL					
NAT.W.					
B & H					

ALLEYNE, M. W. Gloucestershire

Full Name: Mark Wayne Alleyne
Role: Right-hand bat, cover fielder
Born: 23 May 1968, Tottenham
Height: 5' 10" **Weight:** 12st 3lbs
Nickname: Boo-Boo
County debut: 1986
1st-Class 50s scored: 1
1st-Class 100s scored: 1
Place in batting averages: 102nd
av. 30.54
1st-Class catches 1986: 4
(career: 4)
Parents: Euclid Clevis and
Hyacinth Cordeilla
Marital status: Single
Education: Harrison College,
Barbados and Cardinal Pole School, E London
Qualifications: 5 O-levels, NCA senior coaching award

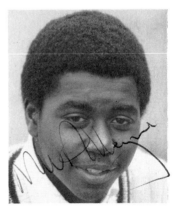

Family links with cricket: Brother plays for Gloucestershire 2nd XI and father played club cricket in Barbados
Overseas tours: South of England YC to Bermuda
Cricketers particularly learnt from: Seymour Nurse (former coach)
Cricketers particularly admired: Gordon Greenidge, Viv Richards
Other sports played: Basketball, football
Other sports followed: Football, snooker
Injuries 1986: Slight groin strain
Relaxations: Watching films and sport; listening to music
Extras: Youngest player to score a century for Gloucestershire
Best batting performance: 116* Gloucestershire v Sussex, Bristol 1986

LAST SEASON: BATTING

	I.	N.O.	R.	H.S.	AV.
TEST					
1ST-CLASS	16	5	336	116*	30.54
INT					
JPL	2	0	47	46	23.50
NAT.W.					
B & H					

CAREER: BATTING

	I.	N.O.	R.	H.S.	AV.
TEST					
1ST-CLASS	16	5	336	116*	30.54
INT					
JPL	2	0	47	46	23.50
NAT.W.					
B & H					

ALLOTT, P. J. W.   Lancashire

Full Name: Paul John Walter Allott
Role: Right-hand bat, right-arm fast-medium bowler
Born: 14 September 1956, Altrincham, Cheshire
Height: 6′ 4″ **Weight:** 14st
County debut: 1978
County cap: 1981
Test debut: 1981
No. of Tests: 13
No. of One-Day Internationals: 13
50 wickets in a season: 3
1st-Class 50s scored: 4
1st-Class 5 w. in innings: 23
Place in batting averages: 129th av. 27.28 (1985 205th av. 17.43)
Place in bowling averages: 29th av. 24.48 (1985 10th av. 22.89)
1st-Class catches 1986: 9 (career: 52)
Parents: John Norman and Lillian Patricia
Wife and date of marriage: Helen, 27 October 1979
Education: Altrincham Grammar School; Bede College, Durham

Qualifications: Qualified teacher; cricket coach

Jobs outside cricket: Teacher; cricket coach for Manchester Education Committee; coach in Tasmania for Tasmanian Cricket Association

Family links with cricket: Father was dedicated club cricketer for 20 years with Ashley CC and is now active with Bowdon CC (Cheshire County League) as a selector, administrator and junior organiser

Overseas tours: With England to India 1981–82; India and Australia 1984–85; to Jamaica with International XI 1982–83

Cricketers particularly learnt from: Dennis Lillee, Steve Murrills

Other sports played: Golf, football, squash, rugby, tennis

Relaxations: Playing golf, watching all sports, listening to music, eating out, photography

Extras: Played as goalkeeper for Cheshire schoolboys. Took part in 10th wicket record partnership for England with Bob Willis, 70, v India, at Lord's, June 1982. Wears contact lenses. Forced by injury to return early from Indian tour in 1984–85

Best batting performance: 78 Lancashire v Gloucestershire, Bristol 1985

Best bowling performance: 8-48 Lancashire v Northamptonshire, Northampton 1981

LAST SEASON: BATTING

	I.	N.O.	R.	H.S.	AV.
TEST					
1ST-CLASS	19	5	382	65	27.28
INT					
JPL	7	2	68	20	13.60
NAT.W.	2	0	4	4	2.00
B & H	4	2	44	23*	22.00

LAST SEASON: BOWLING

	O.	M.	R.	W.	AV.
TEST					
1ST-CLASS	405.1	106	1053	43	24.48
INT					
JPL	83.3	8	291	13	22.38
NAT.W.	59	12	181	10	18.10
B & H	42	8	138	10	13.80

CAREER: BATTING

	I.	N.O.	R.	H.S.	AV.
TEST	18	3	213	52*	14.20
1ST-CLASS	143	40	1740	78	16.89
INT	6	1	15	8	3.00
JPL	39	20	283*	32*	14.89
NAT.W.	8	3	40	19*	8.00
B & H	15	5	92	23*	9.20

CAREER: BOWLING

	O.	M.	R.	W.	AV.
TEST	370.5	75	1084	26	41.69
1ST-CLASS	3817.5	1039	9984	410	24.35
INT	136.3	19	552	15	36.80
JPL	585.2	55	2306	97	23.72
NAT.W.	178.4	36	535	34	15.73
B & H	295.1	49	944	39	24.20

5. Which long-serving county cricketer is renowned for his connoisseurship of fish and chips?

6. How much money did the winners and losers get in the 1986 Nat West Final?

AMISS, D. L.   Warwickshire

Full Name: Dennis Leslie Amiss
Role: Right-hand bat, slow left-arm
chinaman bowler, slip fielder
Born: 7 April 1943, Harborne,
Birmingham
Height: 5′ 11″ **Weight:** 13st
Nickname: Sacka
County debut: 1960
County cap: 1965
Benefit: 1975 (£34,947)
Testimonial: 1985 (when part of
proceeds went to schools'
cricket in Warwickshire)
Test debut: 1966
No. of Tests: 50
No. of One-Day Internationals: 18
1000 runs in a season: 22
1st-Class 50s scored: 207
1st-Class 100s scored: 97
1st-Class 200s scored: 3
One-day 50s: 73
One-day 100s: 13
Place in batting averages: 64th av. 37.17 (1985: 47th av. 39.87)
1st-Class catches 1986: 12 (career: 410)
Wife: Jill
Children: Paul, Becca
Jobs outside cricket: Director of Officescape Ltd (office interior space planning and design consultancy)
Family links with cricket: Father, A. F. Amiss, played good club cricket

LAST SEASON: BATTING

	I.	N.O.	R.	H.S.	AV.
TEST					
1ST-CLASS	45	6	1450	110	37.17
INT					
JPL	14	1	375	60	28.84
NAT.W.	3	0	87	77	29.00
B & H	4	0	151	73	37.75

LAST SEASON: BOWLING

	O.	M.	R.	W.	AV.
TEST					
1ST-CLASS					
INT					
JPL					
NAT.W.					
B & H					

CAREER: BATTING

	I.	N.O.	R.	H.S.	AV.
TEST	88	10	3612	262*	46.31
1ST-CLASS	1005	113	38511	232*	43.17
INT	18	0	859	137	47.72
JPL	230	19	6861	117*	32.51
NAT.W.	52	5	1861	135	39.59
B & H	64	6	2012	115	34.68

CAREER: BOWLING

	O.	M.	R.	W.	AV.
TEST					
1ST-CLASS	213.1	32	718	18	39.88
INT					
JPL	3	0	23	1	
NAT.W.	12.1	0	67	1	–
B & H	0.2	0	4	0	–

Overseas tours: Pakistan 1966–67; India, Pakistan and Sri Lanka 1972–73; West Indies 1973–74; Australia, New Zealand 1974–75; India, Sri Lanka and Australia 1976–77; South Africa (Rebel tour) 1982
Overseas teams played for: World Series Cricket 1978–79
Other sports played: Golf, tennis
Other sports followed: Soccer, rugby
Relaxations: Bridge, gardening
Extras: Scored two centuries in one match, 155* and 112 v Worcestershire at Birmingham 1978. Slipped a disc at 17 playing football and the injury means he still has to take precautionary exercise every day. 'There is still a stiffness in the back which takes three or four minutes loosening-up work to get rid of.' Banned from Test cricket for three years for playing for England rebels in South Africa, 1982
Best batting performance: 262* England v West Indies, Kingston 1973–74
Best bowling performance: 3-21 Warwickshire v Middlesex, Lord's 1970

ANDERSON, I. S.   Derbyshire

Full Name: Iain Stuart Anderson
Role: Right-hand opening bat, off-break bowler
Born: 24 April 1960, Derby
Height: 6′ 0″ **Weight:** 11st 2lbs
Nickname: Tommy, Tom
County debut: 1978
County cap: 1985
1000 runs in a season: 1
1st-Class 50s scored: 24
1st-Class 100s scored: 2
One-day 50s: 4
One-day 100s: 1
Place in batting averages: 180th av. 20.40 (1985 128th av. 27.37)
1st-Class catches 1986: 6 (career: 100)
Parents: May and Norman

Wife and date of marriage: Linda, 28 September 1985
Education: Dovecliff Grammar School; Wulfric School, Burton
Qualifications: 8 O-levels, 3 A-levels, Preliminary Coaching Certificate
Family links with cricket: Father and brother (Kenny) played club cricket
Overseas tours: England Young Cricketers Tour to Australia 1979
Overseas teams played for: Bergvliet, Cape Town, 1979–80 and 1980–81;

Kew, Melbourne, 1982; Ellerslie, Auckland, 1982; Boland, South Africa, 1983–84
Other sports played: Soccer, squash
Relaxations: Eating, listening to music, sleeping
Best batting performance: 112 Derbyshire v Kent, Chesterfield 1983
Best bowling performance: 4-35 Derbyshire v Australia, Derby 1981

LAST SEASON: BATTING

	I.	N.O.	R.	H.S.	AV.
TEST					
1ST-CLASS	23	1	449	93	20.40
INT					
JPL	8	1	163	63	23.28
NAT.W.	2	0	134	134	67.00
B & H	5	0	117	42	23.40

LAST SEASON: BOWLING

	O.	M.	R.	W.	AV.
TEST					
1ST-CLASS					
INT					
JPL					
NAT.W.					
B & H					

CAREER: BATTING

	I.	N.O.	R.	H.S.	AV.
TEST					
1ST-CLASS	204	25	4319	112	24.12
INT					
JPL	42	4	869	64	22.86
NAT.W.	6	0	219	134	36.50
B & H	6	0	149	42	24.83

CAREER: BOWLING

	O.	M.	R.	W.	AV.
TEST					
1ST-CLASS	355.5	67	1290	20	64.50
INT					
JPL	7.1	2	28	2	14.00
NAT.W.					

ANDREW, S. J. W. Hampshire

Full Name: Stephen Jon Walter Andrew
Role: Right-hand bat, right-arm medium bowler
Born: 27 January 1966, London
Height: 6′ 3″ **Weight:** 13st
Nickname: Rip
County debut: 1984
1st-Class 5 w. in innings: 1
Place in bowling averages: 61st av. 29.92 (1985 68th av. 33.06)
1st-Class catches 1986: 3 (career: 9)
Parents: Jon Trevor and Victoria Julia Maud
Marital status: Single
Education: Hordle House Prep. School; Milton Abbey Public School
Qualifications: 3 O-levels

Overseas teams played for: Pirates CC, Durban, South Africa, 1983–84; South African Police CC, 1984
Off-season 1986–87: Coaching in Durban
Overseas tours: Young England to West Indies 1985
Cricketers particularly learnt from: Peter Sainsbury, Malcolm Marshall
Cricketers particularly admired: D. K. Lillee, Malcolm Marshall
Other sports played: Squash, golf
Other sports followed: Interested in most sports
Relaxations: Listening to music
Extras: Youngest bowler to have opened bowling for Hampshire
Best batting performance: 7 Hampshire v Kent, Southampton 1986
Best bowling performance: 6-43 Hampshire v Gloucestershire, Bournemouth 1985

LAST SEASON: BATTING

	I.	N.O.	R.	H.S.	AV.
TEST					
1ST-CLASS	5	2	15	7	5.00
INT					
JPL					
NAT.W.					
B & H					

LAST SEASON: BOWLING

	O.	M.	R.	W.	AV.
TEST					
1ST-CLASS	141.2	32	419	14	29.92
INT					
JPL					
NAT.W.					
B & H					

CAREER: BATTING

	I.	N.O.	R.	H.S.	AV.
TEST					
1ST-CLASS	16	10	36	7	6.00
INT					
JPL					
NAT.W.	–	–	–	–	–
B & H	1	1	1	1*	–

CAREER: BOWLING

	O.	M.	R.	W.	AV.
TEST					
1ST-CLASS	587.4	128	1941	55	35.29
INT					
JPL					
NAT.W.	10	1	28	1	–
B & H	18	1	60	6	10.00

7. Which fair-haired player wore a long black wig during part of the 1986 Nat West Final?

8. What was special about John Wright's 119 for New Zealand v England at The Oval in 1986?

ASIF DIN, M. Warwickshire

Full Name: Mohamed Asif Din
Role: Right-hand bat, leg-break bowler
Born: 21 September 1960, Kampala, Uganda
Height: 5′ 10″ **Weight:** 10st
Nickname: Gunga and many others
County debut: 1981
1st-Class 50s scored: 15
1st-Class 100s scored: 1
1st-Class 5 w. in innings: 1
One-day 50s: 7
One-day 100s: 1
Place in batting averages: 90th av. 32.83 (1985 68th av. 36.11)
1st-Class catches 1986: 10 (career: 50)
Parents: Jamiz and Mumtaz
Marital status: Single
Education: Ladywood Comprehensive School, Birmingham
Qualifications: CSEs and O-levels
Jobs outside cricket: Argos Distributors Limited
Family links with cricket: Brothers Khalid and Abid play in Birmingham League
Cricketing superstitions: 'Mixing my batting gloves around every time.'
Overseas tours: East Africa 1981 with MCC; Bangladesh 1980–81 with MCC; Barbados with Dennis Amiss 1985
Overseas teams played for: Rugby Union CC, Bathurst, New South Wales, 1984–85; Blayney CC, Blayney, New South Wales, 1985–86

LAST SEASON: BATTING

	I.	N.O.	R.	H.S.	AV.
TEST					
1ST-CLASS	38	14	788	69*	32.83
INT					
JPL	14	3	302	108*	27.45
NAT.W.	3	1	55	38*	27.50
B & H	4	1	79	52*	26.33

LAST SEASON: BOWLING

	O.	M.	R.	W.	AV.
TEST					
1ST-CLASS	103.4	13	409	5	81.80
INT					
JPL	43	0	30	1	–
NAT.W.	1.1	0	5	1	–
B & H					

CAREER: BATTING

	I.	N.O.	R.	H.S.	AV.
TEST					
1ST-CLASS	150	27	3356	102	27.28
INT					
JPL	65	1	1362	108*	25.22
NAT.W.	10	3	182	45	26.00
B & H	17	3	350	52*	25.00

CAREER: BOWLING

	O.	M.	R.	W.	AV.
TEST					
1ST-CLASS	558.5	99	2261	39	57.97
INT					
JPL	15.3	1	90	3	30.00
NAT.W.	1.1	0	5	1	–
B & H	2	0	20	0	–

Cricketers particularly admired: Zaheer Abbas, Majid Khan
Off-season 1986–87: Working at Argos
Other sports played: Squash, badminton, golf, snooker
Other sports followed: American football, basketball
Relaxations: Staying in
Opinions on cricket: 'Too much cricket, would like to see 16 4-day matches.'
Best batting performance: 102 Warwickshire v Middlesex, Coventry 1982
Best bowling performance: 5-100 Warwickshire v Glamorgan, Edgbaston 1982

ASLETT, D. G. Kent

Full Name: Derek George Aslett
Role: Right-hand bat, leg-break bowler
Born: 12 February 1958, Dover
Height: 6′ **Weight:** 12st
Nickname: Spacko and variations
County debut: 1981
County cap: 1983
1000 runs in a season: 2
1st-Class 50s scored: 22
1st-Class 100s scored: 10
1st-Class 200s scored: 1
One-day 50s: 7
One-day 100s: 1
Place in batting averages: 172nd av. 22.47 (1985 88th av. 33.27)
1st-Class catches 1986: 17 (career: 69)
Parents: George and Jean
Wife and date of marriage: Bernadine, 17 November 1984
Education: Dover Grammar School; Leicester University
Qualifications: BA (Hons) History
Jobs outside cricket: Postman, orderly, window cleaner for Jim Day International
Family links with cricket: Father played club cricket for Dover
Overseas teams played for: West Perth CC 1981 and 1982, Bayswater CC 1983–84 on Whitbread Scholarship
Cricketers particularly learnt from: Father, Nigel Sutton, Andy Froude, Graham Mart, and senior Kent players
Cricketers particularly admired: Mark Benson, Bob Woolmer, C. B. Fry
Other sports played: Rugby, hurling, tennis, diving

Relaxations: Reading, yoga, music
Extras: Scored 146 on debut v Hampshire, 1981; scored 168 and 119 in same match v Derbyshire, 1983. Wears spectacles
Best batting performance: 221* Kent v Sri Lanka, Canterbury 1984
Best bowling performance: 4-119 Kent v Sussex, Hove 1982

LAST SEASON: BATTING

	I.	N.O.	R.	H.S.	AV.
TEST					
1ST-CLASS	23	0	517	63	22.42
INT					
JPL	6	1	82	31	16.40
NAT.W.					
B & H					

LAST SEASON: BOWLING

	O.	M.	R.	W.	AV.
TEST					
1ST-CLASS	35	3	187	4	46.75
INT					
JPL					
NAT.W.					
B & H					

CAREER: BATTING

	I.	N.O.	R.	H.S.	AV.
TEST					
1ST-CLASS	159	12	5159	221*	35.09
INT					
JPL	45	2	1097	100	25.51
NAT.W.	12	0	274	67	22.83
B & H	11	1	262	49	26.20

CAREER: BOWLING

	O.	M.	R.	W.	AV.
TEST					
1ST-CLASS	192	20	918	15	61.20
INT					
JPL					
NAT.W.	0.5	0	0	1	–
B & H					

ATHEY, C. W. J.   Gloucestershire

Full Name: Charles William Jeffrey Athey
Role: Right-hand bat, right-arm medium bowler
Born: 27 September 1957, Middlesbrough
Height: 5′ 10″ **Weight:** 12st 3lbs
Nickname: Bumper, Wingnut, Ath
County debut: 1976 (Yorkshire), 1984 (Gloucestershire)
County cap: 1980 (Yorkshire), 1985 (Gloucestershire)
Test debut: 1980
No. of Tests: 8
No. of One-Day Internationals: 3
1000 runs in a season: 5
1st-Class 50s scored: 57
1st-Class 100s scored: 22
One-day 50s: 40
One-day 100s: 5
Place in batting averages: 42nd av. 41.10 (1985 27th av. 46.52)
1st-Class catches 1986: 21 (career: 253)

Parents: Peter and Maree

Wife and date of marriage: Janet Linda, 9 October 1982

Education: Linthorpe Junior School; Stainsby Secondary School; Acklam Hall High School

Qualifications: 4 O-levels, some CSEs, National Cricket Association Coaching Certificate

Jobs outside cricket: Barman, building labourer, sports shop assistant

Family links with cricket: 'Father played league cricket in North Yorkshire and South Durham League for 29 years, 25 of them with Middlesbrough. President of Middlesbrough CC since 1975. Brother-in-law Colin Cook played for Middlesex, other brother-in-law (Martin) plays in Thames Valley League. Father-in-law deeply involved in Middlesex Youth cricket.'

Overseas tours: D. H. Robins XI to Canada 1976; South America 1979; Australasia 1980; England U-19 to West Indies 1976; England to West Indies 1981; Barbican XI to Gulf States

Overseas teams played for: Manly Warringah, Sydney, Australia, 1977–78, 1978–79, 1979–80; Balmain, Sydney, 1980–81; Schoeman Park, Bloemfontein, South Africa, 1981–82; Papatoetoe, Auckland, New Zealand, 1983–84

Cricketers particularly learnt from: D. Padgett

Cricketers particularly admired: G. Greenidge, M. Marshall, C. L. Smith

Off-season 1986–87: In Australia with England

Other sports played: Squash, tennis, soccer

Other sports followed: Most sports

Relaxations: Music, good films, good food

Extras: Played for Teeside County Schools U-16s at age 12. Made debut in 1972 North Yorkshire and South Durham League. Played for Yorkshire Colts 1974. Played for North of England Young Cricketers XI v West Indies Young Cricketers at Old Trafford in 1974. Played football for Middlesbrough Schools U-16 XI 1972–74. Played for Middlesbrough Juniors 1974–75. Offered but declined apprenticeship terms with Middlesbrough FC. Captained North Riding U-19 XI 1975–76.

LAST SEASON: BATTING

	I.	N.O.	R.	H.S.	AV.
TEST	9	0	216	55	24.00
1ST-CLASS	22	1	1017	171*	48.42
INT	1	1	142	142*	–
JPL	11	0	381	74	34.63
NAT.W.	2	0	6	4	3.00
B & H	4	0	123	78	30.75

LAST SEASON: BOWLING

	O.	M.	R.	W.	AV.
TEST					
1ST-CLASS	18	5	60	1	–
INT					
JPL	5	0	35	1	–
NAT.W.	1.1	0	14	0	–
B & H	4	0	24	0	–

CAREER: BATTING

	I.	N.O.	R.	H.S.	AV.
TEST	15	0	233	55	15.53
1ST-CLASS	385	34	11508	184	32.78
INT	3	1	225	142*	112.50
JPL	126	12	4039	121*	35.42
NAT.W.	22	3	696	115	36.63
B & H	38	6	891	94*	27.84

CAREER: BOWLING

	O.	M.	R.	W.	AV.
TEST					
1ST-CLASS	433.2	83	1437	33	43.54
INT					
JPL	95.4	1	545	21	25.95
NAT.W.	19.1	1	106	1	–
B & H	56.4	4	242	13	18.61

Injuries 1986: Played for last 10 weeks of season with broken finger
Opinions on cricket: 'Tighten up on "qualifying for England" rules; too many overseas players.'
Best batting performance: 184 England B v Sri Lanka XI, Gulf 1985–86
Best bowling performance: 3-3 Gloucestershire v Hampshire, Bristol 1985

ATKINSON, J. C. M.   Somerset

Full Name: Jonathon Colin Mark Atkinson
Role: Right-hand bat, right-arm medium bowler
Born: 10 July 1968, Butleigh
Height: 6′ 3″ **Weight:** 13st 7lbs
Nickname: Atko, Sprog
County debut: 1985
1st-Class 50s scored: 1
Parents: Colin R. M. and Shirley
Marital status: Single
Education: Millfield School
Qualifications: 11 O-levels
Family links with cricket: Father Captain of Somerset CCC 1965–67; President of Somerset CCC
Cricketers particularly learnt from: Father, Gerry Wilson (Millfield pro.), Martin Crowe
Cricketers particularly admired: I. V. A. Richards, I. T. Botham (admire their competitive natures)

LAST SEASON: BATTING

	I.	N.O.	R.	H.S.	AV.
TEST					
1ST-CLASS	6	2	71	16*	17.75
INT					
JPL					
NAT.W.	–	–	–	–	–
B & H					

LAST SEASON: BOWLING

	O.	M.	R.	W.	AV.
TEST					
1ST-CLASS	34	7	132	2	66.00
INT					
JPL					
NAT.W.	6	2	16	1	–
B & H					

CAREER: BATTING

	I.	N.O.	R.	H.S.	AV.
TEST					
1ST-CLASS	11	3	238	79	29.75
INT					
JPL					
NAT.W.	–	–	–	–	–
B & H					

CAREER: BOWLING

	O.	M.	R.	W.	AV.
TEST					
1ST-CLASS	99	16	382	4	95.50
INT					
JPL					
NAT.W.	6	2	16	1	–
B & H					

Other sports played: Rugby, hockey, basketball
Relaxations: Music tapes (Bob Dylan, Dire Straits)
Best batting performance: 79 Somerset v Northamptonshire, Weston 1985
Best bowling performance: 2-80 Somerset v India, Taunton 1986

AUSTIN, I. D. — Lancashire

Full Name: Ian David Austin
Role: Left-hand bat, right-arm medium bowler
Born: 30 May 1966, Haslingden, Lancashire
Height: 5′ 10″ **Weight:** 14st 5lbs
Nickname: Oscar, School Bully
County debut: 1986
Parents: Jack and Ursula
Marital status: Single
Education: Haslingden High School
Family links with cricket: Father opened batting for Haslingden CC
Overseas tours: NCA North U-19 to Bermuda 1985
Cricketers particularly learnt from: Hartley Alleyne, Robby Bentley
Cricketers particularly admired: I. T. Botham, Collis King, Mudassar Nazar
Off-season 1986–87: Having a break until November and then doing a bit of work i.e. labouring, carpet fitting or coaching

LAST SEASON: BATTING

	I.	N.O.	R.	H.S.	AV.
TEST					
1ST-CLASS					
INT					
JPL	1	0	4	4	–
NAT.W.					
B & H					

LAST SEASON: BOWLING

	O.	M.	R.	W.	AV.
TEST					
1ST-CLASS					
INT					
JPL	8	1	25	0	–
NAT.W.					
B & H					

CAREER: BATTING

	I.	N.O.	R.	H.S.	AV.
TEST					
1ST-CLASS					
INT					
JPL	1	0	4	4	–
NAT.W.					
B & H					

CAREER: BOWLING

	O.	M.	R.	W.	AV.
TEST					
1ST-CLASS					
INT					
JPL	8	1	25	0	–
NAT.W.					
B & H					

Other sports played: Football, squash, snooker
Other sports followed: Golf
Relaxations: Listening to music, playing snooker
Extras: Hold Lancashire League record for highest individual score for amateur since limited overs (149*)
Opinions on cricket: 'I think the game would benefit from playing 4-day county games, it would cut down the number of games played and save the clubs money in the long run, making results more possible and therefore more enjoyable to watch.'

BABINGTON, A. M. Sussex

Full Name: Andrew Mark Babington
Role: Left-hand bat, right-arm fast medium bowler
Born: 22 July 1963, London
Height: 6' 2" **Weight:** 12st 4lbs
Nickname: Hagar, Reggie, Shilts
County debut: 1986
Place in bowling averages: 18th av. 23.20
1st-Class catches 1986: 4 (career: 4)
Parents: Roy and Maureen
Marital status: Single
Education: Reigate Grammar School; Borough Road PE College
Qualifications: 5 O-levels, 2 A-levels; Member of Institute of Legal Executives
Jobs outside cricket: Work for my father's firm of solicitors
Family links with cricket: Father played club cricket
Cricketing superstitions: Always put my kit on in a certain order
Overseas tours: Australia 1980 with Surrey Schools Cricket Association
Cricketers particularly learnt from: Bob Cottam, the staff at Sussex CCC
Cricketers particularly admired: Dennis Lillee, John Snow, Andy Roberts
Off-season 1986–87: Working for my father's firm of solicitors and continuing my studies to become a fully qualified legal executive
Other sports played: Football, squash, golf
Other sports followed: Motor racing
Relaxations: Watching TV, social drink with friends, playing golf, reading, listening to music
Extras: Took a hat-trick against Gloucestershire (Bainbridge, Curran,

Lloyds), my 2nd, 3rd and 4th championship wickets in my 3rd championship game, 1986

Opinions on cricket: 'Players should be able to do their job, ie play cricket, in any part of the world without recriminations, if they choose to play abroad.'

Injuries 1986: Back injury, out for 3 weeks

Best batting performance: 1 Sussex v Gloucestershire, Bristol 1986

Best bowling performance: 4-18 Sussex v Gloucestershire, Bristol 1986

LAST SEASON: BATTING

	I.	N.O.	R.	H.S.	AV.
TEST					
1ST-CLASS	3	1	1	1	0.50
INT					
JPL	1	0	0	0	–
NAT.W.	1	1	4	4*	–
B & H					

LAST SEASON: BOWLING

	O.	M.	R.	W.	AV.
TEST					
1ST-CLASS	117.5	16	348	15	23.20
INT					
JPL	19	2	100	1	–
NAT.W.	13	0	54	4	13.50
B & H					

CAREER: BATTING

	I.	N.O.	R.	H.S.	AV.
TEST					
1ST-CLASS	3	1	1	1	0.50
INT					
JPL	1	0	0	0	–
NAT.W.	1	1	4	4*	–
B & H					

CAREER: BOWLING

	O.	M.	R.	W.	AV.
TEST					
1ST-CLASS	117.5	16	348	15	23.20
INT					
JPL	19	2	100	1	–
NAT.W.	13	0	54	4	13.50
B & H					

BAIL, P. A. C.   Somerset

Full Name: Paul Andrew Clayden Bail

Role: Right-hand bat

Born: 23 June 1965, Burnham-on-Sea

Height: 5′ 11″ **Weight:** 11st 7lbs

Nickname: Pac-man

County debut: 1985

1st-Class 50s scored: 2

1st-Class 100s scored: 1

One-Day 50s: 1

Place in batting averages: 135th av. 26.50

1st-Class catches 1986: 5 (career: 5)

Parents: John Clayden and Erica

Marital status: Single

Education: Berrow Primary; King Aldred's Highbridge; Blue School, Wells; Millfield School, Street; Downing College, Cambridge University

Qualifications: 10 O-levels, 3 A-levels

Family links with cricket: Father captained local cricket side; President of Somerset League

Cricketing superstitions: Always puts left pad on first

Overseas tours: Somerset to Barbados, March 1985

Cricketers particularly learnt from: Gerry Wilson (Millfield), Somerset coaches and players, Graham Saville (Cambridge Coach 1986)

Cricketers particularly admired: 'Too many to mention.'

Off-season 1986–87: Cambridge University and 2 week tour to Barbados

Other sports played: Soccer, hockey

Relaxations: Rock music, concerts, videos, reading, films, pubs

Extras: 200 v Lancashire IIs 1984; 2nd in Minor County averages 1984; represented England Schools U-19s 1984; English Public Schools soccer team 1983 and 1984

Opinions on cricket: 'Every effort should be made to make the game more attractive to the spectators.'

Injuries 1986: Broken finger

Best batting performance: 174 Cambridge University v Oxford University, Lord's 1986

LAST SEASON: BATTING

	I.	N.O.	R.	H.S.	AV.
TEST					
1ST-CLASS	20	0	530	174	26.50
INT					
JPL	1	0	18	18	–
NAT.W.					
B & H	4	0	132	59	33.00

LAST SEASON: BOWLING

	O.	M.	R.	W.	AV.
TEST					
1ST-CLASS	4	0	28	0	–
INT					
JPL					
NAT.W.					
B & H	4	0	20	1	–

CAREER: BATTING

	I.	N.O.	R.	H.S.	AV.
TEST					
1ST-CLASS	29	2	657	174	24.33
INT					
JPL	1	0	18	18	–
NAT.W.					
B & H	4	0	132	59	33.00

CAREER: BOWLING

	O.	M.	R.	W.	AV.
TEST					
1ST-CLASS	8	2	32	0	–
INT					
JPL					
NAT.W.					
B & H	4	0	20	1	–

9. How many players did the English selectors name for Test service against India and New Zealand in 1986?

10. Which all-rounder retired at the end of the 1986 season, being the only man to take 300 wickets and score 3000 runs in the John Player League?

BAILEY, R. J. — Northamptonshire

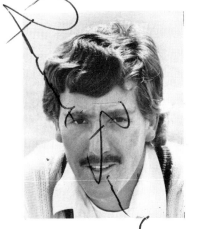

Full Name: Robert John Bailey
Role: Right-hand bat, off-break bowler
Born: 28 October 1963, Biddulph, Stoke-on-Trent
Height: 6′ 3″ **Weight:** 14st
Nickname: Bailers
County debut: 1982
County cap: 1985
No. of One-Day Internationals: 1
1000 runs in a season: 3
1st-Class 50s scored: 23
1st-Class 100s scored: 8
1st-Class 200s scored: 2
One-Day 50s: 15
One-Day 100s: 2
Place in batting averages: 6th av. 56.32 (1985 52nd av. 38.52)
1st-Class catches 1986: 23 (career: 48)
Parents: John and Marie
Marital status: Single
Education: Biddulph High School
Qualifications: 6 CSEs, 1 O-level
Jobs outside cricket: Worked for three winters in electrical trade
Family links with cricket: Father played in North Staffordshire League for 30 years for Knypersley and Minor Counties cricket for Staffordshire as wicket-keeper
Overseas tours: England to Sharjah 1985 for Rothmans 1-day International tournament
Overseas teams played for: Rhodes University, Grahamstown, 1982–83; Witenhage CC, South Africa, 1983–84, 1984–85; Fitzroy CC, Melbourne 1985–86
Cricketers particularly learnt from: My father, Stan Crump
Other sports played: Badminton, football, golf
Other sports followed: 'Like to see Port Vale and Stoke City doing well.'
Relaxations: Listening to music
Extras: Played for Young England v Young Australia, 1983. Scored 2 hundreds in match v Middlesex II 1984
Best batting performance: 224* Northamptonshire v Glamorgan, Swansea 1986
Best bowling performance: 3-33 Northamptonshire v Cambridge University, Cambridge 1983

LAST SEASON: BATTING	I.	N.O.	R.	H.S.	AV.
TEST					
1ST-CLASS	43	9	1915	224*	56.32
INT					
JPL	15	1	641	118*	45.78
NAT.W.	1	0	34	34	–
B & H	5	0	147	86	29.40

CAREER: BATTING	I.	N.O.	R.	H.S.	AV.
TEST					
1ST-CLASS	134	25	4624	224*	42.42
INT	1	1	41	41*	–
JPL	47	8	1460	118*	37.43
NAT.W.	8	3	186	56*	37.20
B & H	12	1	479	86	43.54

LAST SEASON: BOWLING	O.	M.	R.	W.	AV.
TEST					
1ST-CLASS	15.5	7	47	2	23.30
INT					
JPL					
NAT.W.					
B & H	3	3	0	0	–

CAREER: BOWLING	O.	M.	R.	W.	AV.
TEST					
1ST-CLASS	54.5	18	143	6	23.83
INT	6	0	25	0	–
JPL	5	0	49	0	–
NAT.W.	2	0	16	1	–
B & H	7	3	22	1	–

BAINBRIDGE, P.   Gloucestershire

Full Name: Philip Bainbridge
Role: Right-hand bat, right-arm medium bowler
Born: 16 April 1958, Stoke-on-Trent
Height: 5′ 10″ **Weight:** 11st 13lbs
Nickname: Bains, Robbo
County debut: 1977
County cap: 1981
1000 runs in a season: 6
1st-Class 50s scored: 50
1st-Class 100s scored: 12
1st-Class 5 w. in innings: 5
One-Day 50s: 10
One-Day 100s: 1
Place in batting averages: 128th av. 27.30 (1985 12th av. 56.69)
Place in bowling averages: 46th av. 27.55 (1985 51st av. 30.00)
1st-Class catches 1986: 12 (career: 84)
Parents: Leonard George and Lilian Rose
Wife and date of marriage: Barbara, 22 September 1979
Children: Neil, 11 January 1984; Laura, 15 January 1985
Education: Hanley High School; Stoke-on-Trent Sixth Form College; Borough Road College of Education
Qualifications: 9 O-levels, 2 A-levels, BEd, MCC Coaching Certificate

Jobs outside cricket: PE Lecturer, Marketing Executive Gloucs CCC
Family links with cricket: Cousin, Stephen Wilkinson, played for Somerset 1969–72
Overseas tours: Holland with NCA North of England Youth team 1976; Barbados, Trinidad and Tobago with British Colleges 1978; Barbados 1980 with Gloucestershire CCC; Pakistan 1983 for two Zaheer Abbas benefit matches; Zimbabwe 1985 with English Counties XI; Barbados 1986 with David Graveney Benefit Tour; Sri Lanka 1987 with Gloucestershire
Cricketers particularly learnt from: All senior players at Gloucestershire – and county coach
Cricketers particularly admired: Mike Procter
Off-season 1986–87: Working in the marketing department of Gloucs CCC
Other sports played: Football, rugby, squash, golf
Relaxations: Photography, wine-making, beer-making, listening to music, 'walking in the country with my Golden Retriever dog and my wife, entertaining my children.'
Extras: Played for four 2nd XIs in 1976 – Gloucestershire, Derbyshire, Northamptonshire and Warwickshire. Played for Young England v Australia 1977. Won Commercial Union U-23 Batsman of the Year 1981. Scored first century for Stoke-on-Trent aged 14. 'I am producing a cricket calendar for 1987 with photographer David Munden. Provided engraved glass trophies for our beneficiary, David Graveney.'
Opinions on cricket: 'We play too much cricket; the game should be restructured in some way. How this will be done I'm not sure at present.'
Best batting performance: 151* Gloucestershire v Derbyshire, Derby 1985
Best bowling performance: 8-53 Gloucestershire v Somerset, Bristol 1986

LAST SEASON: BATTING

	I.	N.O.	R.	H.S.	AV.
TEST					
1ST-CLASS	43	4	1065	105	27.30
INT					
JPL	14	2	363	106*	30.25
NAT.W.	2	0	38	24	19.00
B & H	4	1	37	10	12.33

LAST SEASON: BOWLING

	O.	M.	R.	W.	AV.
TEST					
1ST-CLASS	414.1	89	1185	43	27.55
INT					
JPL	89	2	451	13	34.69
NAT.W.	11	2	45	2	22.50
B & H	29.1	4	99	4	24.75

CAREER: BATTING

	I.	N.O.	R.	H.S.	AV.
TEST					
1ST-CLASS	298	47	8234	151*	32.00
INT					
JPL	93	15	1433	106*	18.57
NAT.W.	13	2	403	75	36.63
B & H	25	7	457	80	25.38

CAREER: BOWLING

	O.	M.	R.	W.	AV.
TEST					
1ST-CLASS	2237	525	6671	184	36.25
INT					
JPL	607.1	18	3091	99	31.22
NAT.W.	139	17	453	18	25.16
B & H	202.3	23	714	24	29.75

Full Name: David Leslie Bairstow
Role: Right-hand bat, wicket-keeper, occasional medium pacer
Born: 1 September 1951, Bradford
Height: 5′ 10″ **Weight:** 14st 7lbs
Nickname: Bluey
County debut: 1970
County cap: 1973
Benefit: 1982 (£56,913)
Test debut: 1979
No. of Tests: 4
No. of One-Day Internationals: 21
1000 runs in a season: 3
1st-Class 50s scored: 67
1st-Class 100s scored: 7
One-Day 50s: 13
One-Day 100s: 1
Place in batting averages: 127th av. 27.44 (1985 24th av. 47.24)
Wife: Gail Lesley
Children: Andrew David, Claire Louise
Education: Hanson Grammar School, Bradford
Qualifications: O and A-levels
Jobs outside cricket: Sales representative
Family links with cricket: Father, Lesley, played cricket for Laisterdyke
Cricketing superstitions: 'I will pat the ground three times or fiddle with my gloves three times. It is ridiculous but I do not want to stop it. I was in a pub a couple of days before the Leeds Test, and a lad I had never seen before gave me a medallion, and told me to keep it in my pocket for luck. Many people would have forgotten completely, but that medallion went into the pocket of my flannels, and stayed there for the whole match.'
Overseas tours: Australia 1978–79 and 1979–80; West Indies 1981
Overseas teams played for: Griqualand West 1966–67 and 1977–78 as Captain
Cricketers particularly learnt from: Laurie Bennett, maths and sports master at school; Mike Fearnley
Relaxations: Gardening
Other sports played: Golf
Extras: Turned down an offer to play for Bradford City FC. Played for MCC Schools at Lord's in 1970. First Yorkshire wicket-keeper to get 1000 runs in a season (1982) since Arthur Wood in 1935. Set Yorkshire record of seven catches v Derbyshire at Scarborough, 1982. 133 consecutive John Player League matches. His 145 for Yorkshire v Middlesex is the highest score by a

Yorkshire wicket-keeper. Allowed to take an A-level at 6 am at school in order to make Yorkshire debut. Published *A Yorkshire Diary – a year of crisis* 1984. Captain 1984–86

Best batting performance: 145 Yorkshire v Middlesex, Scarborough 1980
Best bowling performance: 3-62 Griqualand West v Transvaal B, Johannesburg 1976–77

LAST SEASON: BATTING

	I.	N.O.	R.	H.S.	AV.
TEST					
1ST-CLASS	33	4	796	88	27.44
INT					
JPL	12	3	210	83*	23.33
NAT.W.	2	0	11	8	5.50
B & H	3	0	59	31	19.66

CAREER: BATTING

	I.	N.O.	R.	H.S.	AV.
TEST	7	1	125	59	20.83
1ST-CLASS	569	110	12137	145	26.44
INT	20	6	206	23*	14.71
JPL	191	45	3016	83*	20.65
NAT.W.	24	5	424	92	22.31
B & H	47	9	677	103*	17.81

LAST SEASON: BOWLING

	O.	M.	R.	W.	AV.
TEST					
1ST-CLASS	5	2	7	0	–
INT					
JPL					
NAT.W.					
B & H					

CAREER: BOWLING

	O.	M.	R.	W.	AV.
TEST					
1ST-CLASS	84	18	254	6	42.33
INT					
JPL					
NAT.W.					
B & H	3	0	17	0	–

LAST SEASON: WICKET-KEEPING

	C.	ST.			
TEST					
1ST-CLASS	40	3			
INT					
JPL	9	–			
NAT.W.	1	1			
B & H	3	1			

CAREER: WICKET-KEEPING

	C.	ST.			
TEST	12	1			
1ST-CLASS	843	131			
INT	17	4			
JPL	196	19			
NAT.W.	29	3			
B & H	95	5			

11. Which Test Match umpire was awarded the MBE in 1986, saying it was the proudest day of his life?

12. Which captain of Kent scored a century for Repton v Uppingham, won the Public Schools Lawn Tennis Cup, won a Blue at Cambridge for cricket and soccer, scored a century on his Test debut and was awarded the MC for bravery in the Second World War?

BAKKER, P.-J. Hampshire

Full Name: Paul-Jan Bakker
Role: Right-hand bat, right-arm medium pace bowler. Fields: 'As far away from the bat as possible.'
Born: 19 August 1957, Vlaardingen, Holland
Height: 6′ **Weight:** 14st 2lbs
Nickname: Nip, Grandad, Peech
County debut: 1986
No. of One-Day Internationals: 17 for Holland
Parents: Hubertus Antonius Bakker, Wilhelmina Hendrika Bakker-Goos
Marital status: Single
Education: I^e VCL and Hugo de Groot College, The Hague, Holland
Qualifications: 'We have a different school system but finished my HAVO schooling.' Ski-instructor
Family links with cricket: Father is the scorer for the first team of my club in The Hague
Cricketing superstitions: I need coffee before a game
Overseas tours: South Africa 1978 with Klaas Vervelde XI; since 1974 toured England almost every summer with touring sides; since 1983 invited to play for the Dutch 'MCC', the Flamingo Touring Club
Overseas teams played for: Green Point CC, Cape Town 1981–86; Flamingo Touring Club, Kent and Essex 1983; Holland, Gloucester, Essex and MCC 1984 and ICC trophy 1986
Cricketers particularly learnt from: Laddy Oudtshoorn, Hylton Ackerman
Cricketers particularly admired: Michael Holding, Malcolm Marshall
Off-season 1986–87: 'I'll be working for a band (The Clarks) during the winter and as a PRO for a firm and some skiing.'
Other sports played: 'I ski, play a bit of golf and like to drive fast.'
Other sports followed: Grand Prix motor racing, tennis, football and most other sports
Relaxations: Social visits to pubs, bars and restaurants; films and newspapers
Extras: First ever Dutch player to play professional cricket
Opinions on cricket: 'A great game.'
Injuries 1986: A slipped disc in my neck while brushing my teeth in August: 10 days off with a stiff neck

Best batting performance: 3* Hampshire v Gloucestershire, Bournemouth 1986
Best bowling performance: 2-15 Hampshire v Cambridge University, Cambridge 1986

LAST SEASON: BATTING

	I.	N.O.	R.	H.S.	AV.
TEST					
1ST-CLASS	2	1	6	3*	–
INT					
JPL	–	–	–	–	–
NAT.W.					
B & H	–	–	–	–	–

LAST SEASON: BOWLING

	O.	M.	R.	W.	AV.
TEST					
1ST-CLASS	66.5	20	220	6	36.62
INT					
JPL	13	0	66	2	33.00
NAT.W.					
B & H	11	5	19	2	9.50

CAREER: BATTING

	I.	N.O.	R.	H.S.	AV.
TEST					
1ST-CLASS	2	1	6	3*	–
INT					
JPL	–	–	–	–	–
NAT.W.					
B & H	–	–	–	–	–

CAREER: BOWLING

	O.	M.	R.	W.	AV.
TEST					
1ST-CLASS	66.5	20	220	6	36.62
INT					
JPL	13	0	66	2	33.00
NAT.W.					
B & H	11	5	19	2	9.50

BALDERSTONE, J. C.   Leicestershire

Full Name: John Christopher Balderstone
Role: Right-hand bat, slow left-arm bowler, slip fielder
Born: 16 November 1940, Huddersfield
Height: 6′ 2″ **Weight:** 12st 7lbs
Nickname: Baldy, Chris, Dad
County debut: 1961 (Yorkshire), 1971 (Leicestershire)
County cap: 1973 (Leicestershire)
Testimonial: 1984 (£64,470)
Test debut: 1976
No. of Tests: 2
1000 runs in a season: 11
1st-Class 50s scored: 102
1st-Class 100s scored: 32
1st-Class 5 w. in innings: 5
One-Day 50s: 32
One-Day 100s: 5
Place in batting averages: 189th av. 18.63 (1985 63rd av. 36.31)
1st-Class catches 1986: 3 (career: 210)
Parents: Frank and Jenny

Wife and date of marriage: Madeline, April 1962
Children: Sally Victoria, 15 September 1970; Michael James, 3 January 1973
Education: Paddock County School, Huddersfield
Qualifications: Advanced cricket coach, soccer coach
Jobs outside cricket: Professional footballer with Huddersfield Town, Carlisle United, Doncaster Rovers, Queen of the South, Enderby Town. Representative for a sports shop
Overseas tours: With Leicester to Zimbabwe March 1981 and to Oman 1984
Cricketers particularly learnt from: 'Everyone.'
Off-season 1986–87: Coaching
Other sports played: Golf, professional football
Relaxations: Do-it-yourself, golf, reading, and watching all sports
Extras: Played for Yorkshire 1961–70. Once played first-class cricket match and a league football match on the same day, 15 September 1975 (Leicestershire v Derbyshire at Chesterfield 11.30 am to 6.30 pm and Doncaster Rovers v Brentford at Doncaster 7.30 pm to 9.10 pm). Former Chairman of Cricketers' Association. Appointed as Cricket Development Officer in Leicestershire 1986
Best batting performance: 181* Leicestershire v Gloucestershire, Leicester 1984
Best bowling performance: 6-25 Leicestershire v Hampshire, Southampton 1978

LAST SEASON: BATTING

	I.	N.O.	R.	H.S.	AV.
TEST					
1ST-CLASS	23	1	410	115	18.63
INT					
JPL	3	0	90	47	30.00
NAT.W.	2	0	111	66	55.50
B & H					

LAST SEASON: BOWLING

	O.	M.	R.	W.	AV.
TEST					
1ST-CLASS	45	9	143	2	71.50
INT					
JPL					
NAT.W.					
B & H					

CAREER: BATTING

	I.	N.O.	R.	H.S.	AV.
TEST	4	0	39	35	9.75
1ST-CLASS	615	61	18995	181*	34.28
INT					
JPL	125	23	2673	96	26.20
NAT.W.	32	2	891	119*	29.70
B & H	57	12	2059	113*	45.76

CAREER: BOWLING

	O.	M.	R.	W.	AV.
TEST	16	0	80	1	–
1ST-CLASS	3187	957	8080	309	26.14
INT					
JPL	58.3	2	296	12	24.66
NAT.W.	48	12	176	11	16.00
B & H	30	4	103	5	20.60

13. Of whom did John Arlott say that he 'wasn't the least bit interested in batting, only in making runs'?

Full Name: Eldine Ashworth
Elderfield Baptiste
Role: Right-hand bat, right-arm
fast-medium bowler
Born: 12 March 1960, Liberta,
Antigua
Height: 6′ 1″ **Weight:** 12st
Nickname: Soca or Bapo
County debut: 1981
County cap: 1983
Test debut: 1983–84
No. of Tests: 9
No. of One-Day Internationals: 29
50 wickets in a season: 2
1st-Class 50s scored: 17
1st-Class 100s scored: 3
1st-Class 5 w. in innings: 7
One-Day 50s: 3
Place in batting averages: 78th
av. 34.12 (1985 99th av. 31.36)
Place in bowling averages: — (1985 44th av. 28.64)
1st-Class catches 1986: 1 (career: 53)
Parents: Gertrude and Samuel
Children: Forbes, David
Education: Liberta Primary; All Saints Secondary School
Jobs outside cricket: Sports officer in the Sports Department of the Ministry of
Education
Family links with cricket: Father played for Liberta 1940–48. Brother,
Rowan, played for Liberta at School level
Cricketing superstitions: The numbers 49 and 13
Overseas tours: With Leeward Youths to Barbados 1978; to Australia, St
Lucia, St Kitts, St Thomas and Montserrat with Antigua National team in
1979; to England with Antigua Youth in 1979; with West Indies to India 1983,
England 1984, Australia 1984–85
Overseas teams played for: Geelong CC, Australia, 1985–86. Leeward
Islands 1981–86
Cricketers particularly learnt from: Guy Yearwood, Viv Richards, Andy
Roberts, Malcolm Marshall
Other sports played: Football, tennis, volleyball
Other sports followed: Boxing
Relaxations: Watching movies, music – especially calypso – and meeting
people
Extras: Awarded Viv Richards Schools Cricket Trophy for the Most Out-

standing Cricketer 1979. Sportsman of the Year in Antigua 1979
Best batting performance: 136* Kent v Yorkshire, Sheffield 1983
Best bowling performance: 6-42 Kent v Northamptonshire, Northampton 1985

LAST SEASON: BATTING

	I.	N.O.	R.	H.S.	AV.
TEST					
1ST-CLASS	8	0	273	113	34.12
INT					
JPL	11	0	161	52	14.63
NAT.W.	1	0	4	4	–
B & H	6	1	74	25*	14.80

CAREER: BATTING

	I.	N.O.	R.	H.S.	AV.
TEST	10	1	224	87*	24.89
1ST-CLASS	144	22	3501	136*	28.69
INT	10	2	119	28*	14.88
JPL	43	4	689	60	17.66
NAT.W.	9	1	64	22	8.00
B & H	12	2	148	43*	14.80

LAST SEASON: BOWLING

	O.	M.	R.	W.	AV.
TEST					
1ST-CLASS	146	40	351	13	27.00
INT					
JPL	101.2	2	507	22	23.04
NAT.W.	18	3	62	2	31.00
B & H	70	4	304	10	30.40

CAREER: BOWLING

	O.	M.	R.	W.	AV.
TEST	204	55	485	15	32.33
1ST-CLASS	2251.5	502	6827	253	26.98
INT	246	17	989	27	36.63
JPL	350.2	14	1581	62	25.50
NAT.W.	115	18	385	14	27.50
B & H	129	13	504	18	28.00

BARCLAY, J. R. T. Sussex

Full Name: John Robert Troutbeck Barclay
Role: Right-hand bat, off-break bowler, slip fielder
Born: 22 January 1954, Bonn, West Germany
Height: 5′ 10″ **Weight:** 12st
Nickname: Trout
County debut: 1970, aged 16 yrs 6 mths, while still at school
County cap: 1976
Benefit: 1986
1000 runs in a season: 4
50 wickets in a season: 1
1st-Class 50s scored: 46
1st-Class 100s scored: 9
1st-Class 5 w. in innings: 9
1st-Class 10 w. in match: 1
One-Day 50s: 6
Place in batting averages: — (1985 163rd av. 23.36)
Place in bowling averages: — (1985 48th av. 29.45)
1st-Class catches 1986: 1 (career: 216)
Parents: C. F. R. Barclay, Mrs J. B. Denman

Wife and date of marriage: Mary Louise, 16 September 1978
Children: Georgina Clare, 9 January 1981
Education: Summerfields School, Oxford; Eton College
Jobs outside cricket: Marketing Executive with International Factors Ltd
Family links with cricket: Great uncle, F. J. J. Ford, played for Middlesex
Overseas tours: India 1970–71 with England Schools' Cricket Association
(Vice-Captain); England Young Cricketers to West Indies 1972 as Captain.
Overseas teams played for: Orange Free State, 1978–79; Waverley CC,
Sydney, 1981
Cricketers particularly learnt from: Vic Cannings
Cricketers particularly admired: David Steele
Other sports played: Golf
Relaxations: Fishing
Extras: Sussex Captain 1981–86, when forced to give up cricket through
prolonged injury
Best batting performance: 119 Sussex v Leicestershire, Hove 1980
Best bowling performance: 6-61 Sussex v Sri Lanka, Hove 1979

LAST SEASON: BATTING

	I.	N.O.	R.	H.S.	AV.
TEST					
1ST-CLASS	3	0	36	28	12.00
INT					
JPL	2	1	21	15	–
NAT.W.					
B & H	2	1	12	9	–

LAST SEASON: BOWLING

	O.	M.	R.	W.	AV.
TEST					
1ST-CLASS	13	2	65	0	–
INT					
JPL	2	0	20	0	–
NAT.W.					
B & H					

CAREER: BATTING

	I.	N.O.	R.	H.S.	AV.
TEST					
1ST-CLASS	434	44	9677	119	24.81
INT					
JPL	103	35	1261	48	18.54
NAT.W.	22	2	340	48	17.00
B & H	44	5	1095	93*	28.07

CAREER: BOWLING

	O.	M.	R.	W.	AV.
TEST					
1ST-CLASS	3497.2	845	9936	324	30.66
INT					
JPL	587	27	2721	105	25.91
NAT.W.	128.3	17	425	23	18.48
B & H	274.5	33	1010	36	28.05

14. Which non-league soccer team did Viv Richards sign to play for
in 1986?

15. Which Test Match commentator won school caps at Cranbrook
for cricket, rugby, hockey, athletics and fives, but was stopped
from playing any more games at 19 because of back injury, and
retired from cricket commentating after 40 years in 1986?

BARLOW, G. D.   Middlesex

Full Name: Graham Derek Barlow
Role: Left-hand bat, right-arm medium bowler
Born: 26 March 1950, Folkestone
Height: 5′ 10″ **Weight:** 12st 12lbs
Nickname: Ed
County debut: 1969
County cap: 1976
Benefit: 1984
Test debut: 1976–77
No. of Tests: 3
No. of One-Day Internationals: 6
1000 runs in a season: 7
1st-Class 50s scored: 58
1st-Class 100s scored: 26
One-Day 50s: 33
One-Day 100s: 5
Place in batting averages:—
(1985 22nd av. 47.96)
1st-Class catches 1986: 2 (career: 136)
Parents: Derek Albert and Millicent Louise (Betty)
Education: Woolverstone Hall; Ealing Grammar School; Loughborough College of Education
Qualifications: Certificate of Education for Physical Education and English, NCA Coach
Jobs outside cricket: PE teacher, Brentside School, Greenford 1973–74. Coach to Wynberg Boys' School, Cape Town 1975–76. Printing representative for Hildesley Ltd 1974–75. Abbey Life Assurance Co Ltd
Family links with cricket: 'Negligible. Distant great-uncle played good club cricket, but that's it.'
Overseas tours: India, Sri Lanka and Australia 1976–77
Overseas teams played for: Greenpoint CC, Cape Town, 1977–78, 1979–80; St Kilda, Melbourne, 1978–79; Subiaco Floreat CC, Perth, 1982–83
Cricketers particularly learnt from: Peter Parfitt
Other sports played: General fitness and particularly squash and running, especially when away in the winter. Played rugby for Loughborough
Relaxations: 'Music – cross-section of taste from Beethoven and particularly Sibelius to "Yes" on the "heavier" side. Reading when time permits, likewise cinema and, to a lesser extent, theatre.'
Extras: Played rugby union for Loughborough Colleges, Leicestershire, England U-23 and, briefly, Rosslyn Park. Played in MCC Schools matches in

1968. Ran pre-season training for Middlesex. Forced to retire from the game through injury during 1986
Best batting performance: 177 Middlesex v Lancashire, Southport 1981

LAST SEASON: BATTING

	I.	N.O.	R.	H.S.	AV.
TEST					
1ST-CLASS	6	1	194	107	38.80
INT					
JPL	3	0	78	45	26.00
NAT.W.					
B & H	4	0	93	48	23.25

LAST SEASON: BOWLING

	O.	M.	R.	W.	AV.
TEST					
1ST-CLASS					
INT					
JPL					
NAT.W.					
B & H					

CAREER: BATTING

	I.	N.O.	R.	H.S.	AV.
TEST	5	1	17	7*	4.25
1ST-CLASS	399	58	12370	177	36.27
INT	6	1	149	80*	29.80
JPL	150	14	3840	114	28.23
NAT.W.	29	3	884	158	34.00
B & H	50	4	1076	129	23.39

CAREER: BOWLING

	O.	M.	R.	W.	AV.
TEST					
1ST-CLASS	19.1	2	68	3	22.66
INT					
JPL	15.3	0	91	4	22.75
NAT.W.					
B & H	4	0	18	1	—

BARNETT, K. J. Derbyshire

Full Name: Kim John Barnett
Role: Right-hand bat, leg-break or seam bowler, cover fielder
Born: 17 July 1960, Stoke-on-Trent
Height: 6′ 1″ **Weight:** 13st
Nickname: Wristy
County debut: 1979
County cap: 1982
1000 runs in a season: 4
1st-Class 50s scored: 51
1st-Class 100s scored: 17
1st-Class 5 w. in innings: 1
One-Day 50s: 9
One-Day 100s: 3
Place in batting averages: 65th av. 36.76 (1985 46th av. 40.21)
Place in bowling averages: —
(1985 53rd av. 30.24)
1st-Class catches 1986: 24
(career: 121)
Parents: Derek and Doreen
Wife and date of marriage: Nancy, 30 September 1984
Education: Leek High School, Staffs
Qualifications: 7 O-levels

Jobs outside cricket: Bank clerk, National Westminster Bank 1978
Overseas tours: With England Schools to India 1977; Young England to Australia 1978–79; Derrick Robins XI to New Zealand and Australia 1979–80; England B to Sri Lanka 1986 (vice-captain)
Overseas teams played for: Boland, South Africa, 1982–83, 1984–85
Cricketers particularly learnt from: Eddie Barlow
Off-season 1986–87: Resting
Other sports played: Football (has played soccer semi-professionally for Cheshire League side, Leek Town FC), tennis
Other sports followed: Horse-racing
Extras: Played for Northants 2nd XI when aged 15. Played one Minor County match for Staffordshire; also for Warwickshire 2nd XI. Became youngest captain of a first-class county when appointed in 1983
Opinions on cricket: 'Would like to see the introduction of 4-day cricket to the County Championship with each team played only once; also one overseas player per side as soon as possible.'
Best batting performance: 144 Derbyshire v Middlesex, Derby 1984
Best bowling performance: 6-115 Derbyshire v Yorkshire, Bradford 1985

LAST SEASON: BATTING

	I.	N.O.	R.	H.S.	AV.
TEST					
1ST-CLASS	45	3	1544	143	36.76
INT					
JPL	16	3	700	92	53.84
NAT.W.	2	0	73	47	36.50
B & H	5	0	141	62	28.20

LAST SEASON: BOWLING

	O.	M.	R.	W.	AV.
TEST					
1ST-CLASS	104	20	359	6	50.83
INT					
JPL					
NAT.W.	11.1	3	34	3	11.33
B & H					

CAREER: BATTING

	I.	N.O.	R.	H.S.	AV.
TEST					
1ST-CLASS	303	29	9415	143	34.36
INT					
JPL	107	20	2899	131*	33.32
NAT.W.	15	2	475	88	36.53
B & H	28	1	535	86	19.81

CAREER: BOWLING

	O.	M.	R.	W.	AV.
TEST					
1ST-CLASS	732.5	141	2543	46	55.28
INT					
JPL	42.3	2	278	7	39.71
NAT.W.	11.1	3	34	3	11.33
B & H	9	2	33	2	16.50

16. Which three Lancashire wicket-keepers have played for England?

17. Who was the youngest batsman to score a hundred hundreds and at what age?

BARTLETT, R. J.   Somerset

Full Name: Richard James
Bartlett
Role: Right-hand bat
Born: 8 October 1966, Ash
Priors, Somerset
Height: 5′ 9″
County debut: 1986
1st-Class 100s scored: 1
Place in batting averages: 32nd
av. 43.85
1st-Class catches 1986: 4 (career: 4)
Education: Taunton School;
Swansea University
Other sports played:
Represented Somerset
at U-21 hockey
Extras: First Somerset player
to score a century on first-
class debut since Harold

Gimblett. Won Gray-Nicholls Trophy 1985 as most improved schools
cricketer. Represented England Schools and England Young Cricketers
Best batting performance: 117* Somerset v Oxford University, Oxford 1986

LAST SEASON: BATTING

	I.	N.O.	R.	H.S.	AV.
TEST					
1ST-CLASS	9	2	307	117*	43.85
INT					
JPL					
NAT.W.					
B & H	2	0	4	4	2.00

CAREER: BATTING

	I.	N.O.	R.	H.S.	AV.
TEST					
1ST-CLASS	9	2	307	117*	43.85
INT					
JPL					
NAT.W.					
B & H	2	0	4	4	2.00

18. Who in 1938 beat the record for the highest Test score in
England against Australia, and what was the score(s)?

19. Which New Zealander has taken the second most Test wickets,
after Richard Hadlee, and how many?

BARWICK, S. R.   Glamorgan

Full Name: Stephen Royston Barwick
Role: Right-hand bat, right-arm medium bowler
Born: 6 September 1960, Neath
Height: 6′ 2″ **Weight:** 13st 2lbs
Nickname: Baz
County debut: 1981
50 wickets in a season: 1
1st-Class 5 w. in innings: 5
Place in bowling averages: 89th av. 37.07 (1985 94th av. 38.62)
1st-Class catches 1986: 3 (career: 21)
Parents: Margaret and Roy
Marital status: Single
Education: Cwrt Sart Comprehensive School; Dwr-y-Felin Comprehensive School
Qualifications: 'Commerce, human biology, mathematics, English.'
Jobs outside cricket: Ex-steel worker
Family links with cricket: 'My uncle David played for Glamorgan 2nd XI.'
Other sports played: Badminton, squash, table-tennis, football
Other sports followed: Watching Swansea City
Extras: Made debut on 25 April 1981 v Oxford University, and took 4 wickets in 1st innings
Injuries 1986: Knee operation (cartilage)
Best batting performance: 29 Glamorgan v Somerset, Cardiff 1985
Best bowling performance: 8-42 Glamorgan v Worcestershire, Worcester 1983

LAST SEASON: BATTING

	I.	N.O.	R.	H.S.	AV.
TEST					
1ST-CLASS	8	2	33	9	5.50
INT					
JPL	4	3	34	29*	–
NAT.W.					
B & H					

CAREER: BATTING

	I.	N.O.	R.	H.S.	AV.
TEST					
1ST-CLASS	71	30	372	29	9.07
INT					
JPL	14	9	57	29*	11.40
NAT.W.	4	2	13	6	6.50
B & H	10	6	40	18	10.00

LAST SEASON: BOWLING

	O.	M.	R.	W.	AV.
TEST					
1ST-CLASS	296.4	61	964	26	37.07
INT					
JPL	37.3	2	146	3	48.66
NAT.W.					
B & H					

CAREER: BOWLING

	O.	M.	R.	W.	AV.
TEST					
1ST-CLASS	1768.3	412	5285	162	32.62
INT					
JPL	278.1	17	1250	33	37.87
NAT.W.	46.2	9	131	10	13.10
B & H	106.1	16	366	19	19.26

BASE, S. J.   Glamorgan

Full Name: Simon John Base
Role: Right-hand bat, right-arm medium bowler
Born: 2 January 1960, Maidstone
Height: 6′ 2″ **Weight:** 13st 5lbs
Nickname: Basey
County debut: 1986
Place in bowling averages: 87th av. 36.85
1st-Class catches 1986: 3 (career: 3)
Parents: Christine and Peter
Marital status: Single
Education: Fish Hoek Primary School, Fish Hoek High School, Cape Town, South Africa
Qualifications: High School, School Certificate. Refrigeration and air conditioning technician
Jobs outside cricket: Hall-Thermotank in South Africa as a technician and S.A. Sea Products. G.S.P.K. Electronics in North Yorkshire, England
Overseas teams played for: Western Province 'B' 1982–83
Cricketers particularly learnt from: Stuart Leary, Graham Gooch, Kevin Lyons, Martin Stovold
Cricketers particularly admired: Stuart Leary, Graham Gooch
Off-season 1986–87: Hopefully playing cricket in Cape Town, South Africa
Other sports played: Football, golf, wind-surfing
Other sports followed: Golf, tennis, snooker

LAST SEASON: BATTING

	I.	N.O.	R.	H.S.	AV.
TEST					
1ST-CLASS	11	4	53	15*	7.57
INT					
JPL	1	0	1	1	–
NAT.W.	1	0	2	2	–
B & H	2	1	8	4*	–

CAREER: BATTING

	I.	N.O.	R.	H.S.	AV.
TEST					
1ST-CLASS	13	5	55	15*	6.87
INT					
JPL	1	0	1	1	–
NAT.W.	1	0	2	2	–
B & H	2	1	8	4*	–

LAST SEASON: BOWLING

	O.	M.	R.	W.	AV.
TEST					
1ST-CLASS	222.5	39	774	21	36.85
INT					
JPL	25	0	122	5	24.40
NAT.W.	12	0	49	2	24.50
B & H	19	1	104	2	52.00

CAREER: BOWLING

	O.	M.	R.	W.	AV.
TEST					
1ST-CLASS	265.5	58	835	26	32.11
INT					
JPL	25	0	122	5	24.40
NAT.W.	12	0	49	2	24.50
B & H	19	1	104	2	52.00

Relaxations: Wind-surfing and golf. Reading science fiction, watching films and music
Injuries 1986: Trapped sciatic nerve
Best batting performance: 15* Glamorgan v Somerset, Taunton 1986
Best bowling performance: 4-74 Glamorgan v Yorkshire, Scarborough 1986

BENJAMIN, W. K. M.   Leicestershire

Full name: Winston Keithroy
Matthew Benjamin
Role: Right-hand bat, right-arm
fast bowler
Born: 31 December 1964, All
Saints, Antigua
County debut: 1986
1st-Class 50s scored: 3
1st-Class 5 w. in innings: 4
Place in batting averages: 44th
av. 40.40
Place in bowling averages: 75th
av. 33.50
1st-Class catches 1986: 9 (career: 11)
Education: All Saints School
Overseas teams played for:
Leeward Islands since 1985

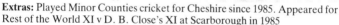

Extras: Played Minor Counties cricket for Cheshire since 1985. Appeared for Rest of the World XI v D. B. Close's XI at Scarborough in 1985
Best batting performance: 95* Leicestershire v India, Leicester 1986
Best bowling performance: 6-33 Leicestershire v Nottinghamshire, Leicester 1986

LAST SEASON: BATTING

	I.	N.O.	R.	H.S.	AV.
TEST					
1ST-CLASS	20	10	404	95*	40.40
INT					
JPL	10	4	88	13*	14.66
NAT.W.	1	0	5	5	–
B & H	3	2	23	19*	–

LAST SEASON: BOWLING

	O.	M.	R.	W.	AV.
TEST					
1ST-CLASS	465.3	89	1541	46	33.50
INT					
JPL	95.1	5	408	17	24.00
NAT.W.	21	2	51	3	17.00
B & H	41.4	8	127	11	11.54

CAREER: BATTING

	I.	N.O.	R.	H.S.	AV.
TEST					
1ST-CLASS	29	12	515	95*	30.29
INT					
JPL	10	4	88	13*	14.66
NAT.W.	1	0	5	5	–
B & H	3	2	23	19*	–

CAREER: BOWLING

	O.	M.	R.	W.	AV.
TEST					
1ST-CLASS	645	131	2002	69	29.01
INT					
JPL	95.1	5	408	17	24.00
NAT.W.	21	2	51	3	17.00
B & H	41.4	8	127	11	11.54

BENSON, M. R.   Kent

Full Name: Mark Richard Benson
Role: Left-hand bat, right-arm
off-break bowler
Born: 6 July 1958, Shoreham,
Sussex
Height: 5′ 10″ **Weight:** 12st 7lbs
Nickname: Benny
County debut: 1980
County cap: 1981
Test debut: 1986
No. of Tests: 1
No. of One-Day Internationals: 1
1000 runs in a season: 5
1st-Class 50s scored: 47
1st-Class 100s scored: 17
One-Day 50s: 20
One-Day 100s: 1
Place in batting averages: 52nd
av. 39.48 (1985 59th av. 37.53)
1st-Class catches 1986: 5 (career: 60)
Parents: Frank and Judy

Wife and date of marriage: Sarah, 20 September 1986
Education: Sutton Valence School
Qualifications: O- and A-levels and 1 S-level; Qualified tennis coach
Jobs outside cricket: Marketing assistant with Shell UK Oil
Family links with cricket: Father played for Ghana
Overseas teams played for: Balfour Guild CC, 1979–80; Johannesburg Municipals, 1980–81; Port Adelaide CC, 1981–82
Cricketers particularly learnt from: Derek Aslett

LAST SEASON: BATTING

	I.	N.O.	R.	H.S.	AV.
TEST	2	0	51	30	25.50
1ST-CLASS	37	2	1410	128	40.28
INT	1	0	24	24	–
JPL	12	0	244	63	20.33
NAT.W.	2	0	50	36	25.00
B & H	7	1	220	65	36.66

LAST SEASON: BOWLING

	O.	M.	R.	W.	AV.
TEST					
1ST-CLASS	7	0	55	2	27.50
INT					
JPL					
NAT.W.					
B & H					

CAREER: BATTING

	I.	N.O.	R.	H.S.	AV.
TEST	2	0	51	30	25.50
1ST-CLASS	222	20	7751	162	38.37
INT	1	0	24	24	–
JPL	70	1	1981	97	28.71
NAT.W.	17	1	699	113*	43.68
B & H	26	5	589	65	28.04

CAREER: BOWLING

	O.	M.	R.	W.	AV.
TEST					
1ST-CLASS	40.2	1	265	3	88.33
INT					
JPL					
NAT.W.					
B & H					

Off-season 1986–87: Trying to build up career outside cricket
Other sports played: Golf
Other sports followed: Rugby
Extras: Scored 1000 runs in first full season; record for most runs in career and season at Sutton Valence School
Opinions on cricket: 'We play too much cricket, thus breeding mediocrity.'
Best batting performance: 162 Kent v Hampshire, Southampton 1985

BERRY, P. J. Yorkshire

Full Name: Philip John Berry
Role: Right-hand bat, right-arm
off-break bowler
Born: 28 December 1966, Saltburn,
Cleveland
Height: 6' **Weight:** 11st
Nickname: 'Chuck, Goose, Bill
and anymore they can think of.'
County debut: 1986
1st-Class catches 1986: 2 (career: 2)
Parents: John and Beryl
Marital status: Single
Education: Saltscar
Comprehensive; Longlands
College of Further Education
Qualifications: 1 O-level, City and
Guilds passes in Recreational
Management

Jobs outside cricket: Worked for Redcar Racecourse Co as a groundsman
Family links with cricket: Brother plays for Saltburn in North Yorkshire and South Durham Cricket League
Cricketing superstitions: Put left pad on first. Try to change in same place in a changing room if I have done well from that place before
Overseas tours: NCA North U-19 to Bermuda in July 1985 for the International Youth Tournament
Cricketers particularly learnt from: 'Steve Oldham, Doug Padgett and Brian Bainbridge, who taught me everything about the game, when I joined Middlesbrough.'
Cricketers particularly admired: Brian Bainbridge for showing keenness at 53 years old, turning out for Middlesbrough 1st Team every week
Off-season 1986–87: Working on the racecourse and keeping fit for coming season
Other sports played: Snooker, badminton, football

Other sports followed: Rugby union, Middlesbrough Football Club
Relaxations: Reading, snooker, rugby, listening to music
Extras: Played for young Young England in the Final Test against Sri Lanka at Trent Bridge which England won by 6 wkts to win series 1–0

LAST SEASON: BATTING

	I.	N.O.	R.	H.S.	AV.
TEST					
1ST-CLASS	1	1	4	4*	—
INT					
JPL					
NAT.W.					
B & H					

LAST SEASON: BOWLING

	O.	M.	R.	W.	AV.
TEST					
1ST-CLASS	39	13	83	1	—
INT					
JPL					
NAT.W.					
B & H					

CAREER: BATTING

	I.	N.O.	R.	H.S.	AV.
TEST					
1ST-CLASS	1	1	4	4*	—
INT					
JPL					
NAT.W.					
B & H					

CAREER: BOWLING

	O.	M.	R.	W.	AV.
TEST					
1ST-CLASS	39	13	83	1	—
INT					
JPL					
NAT.W.					
B & H					

BICKNELL, M. P.   Surrey

Full Name: Martin Paul Bicknell
Role: 'Right-hand bat with L-plates', right-arm fast medium bowler
Born: 14 January 1969, Guildford
Height: 6' 3½" **Weight:** 13½st
Nickname: Bickers, Spandau
County debut: 1986
Place in bowling averages: 11th av. 22.22 (1985 — av. —)
1st-Class catches 1986: 4 (career: 4)
Parents: Valerie and Victor
Marital status: Single
Education: Robert Haining Secondary, Mychett, Surrey
Qualifications: 2 O-levels, 5 CSEs
Family links with cricket: Brother just signed for Surrey
Cricketing superstitions: 'Left pad on first, not that it helps!'
Overseas tours: Surrey Young Cricketers to Australia 1985–86
Cricketers particularly learnt from: Geoff Arnold, Mickey Stewart

Cricketers particularly admired: Richard Hadlee, Dennis Lilee
Off-season 1986–87: Running up sand hills to get fit and possibly going on tour with Young England to Sri Lanka
Other sports played: Football, golf
Other sports followed: Anything except horse racing
Relaxations: Listening to Dire Straits, playing golf
Extras: Youngest player to play for Surrey since David Smith. On County debut first two overs were maidens. Scored four successive ducks in June!! Played in successful series win for Young England against Sri Lanka. Finished 11th in National Bowling Averages. 1986 won Supporters Young Player of the Year, also George Brittain Young Player of the Year
Opinions on cricket: 'Championship should be 16 4-Day games. Bad light should be offered only when it is dangerous.'
Injuries 1986: Severely strained side; out for a month
Best batting performance: 9* Surrey v Nottinghamshire, Trent Bridge 1986
Best bowling performance: 3-27 Surrey v Leicestershire, The Oval 1986

LAST SEASON: BATTING

	I.	N.O.	R.	H.S.	AV.
TEST					
1ST-CLASS	10	2	21	9*	2.62
INT					
JPL	2	1	13	13	–
NAT.W.	3	2	5	2*	–
B & H					

LAST SEASON: BOWLING

	O.	M.	R.	W.	AV.
TEST					
1ST-CLASS	196	43	600	27	22.22
INT					
JPL	35	1	138	4	34.50
NAT.W.	37	6	105	5	21.00
B & H					

CAREER: BATTING

	I.	N.O.	R.	H.S.	AV.
TEST					
1ST-CLASS	10	2	21	9*	2.62
INT					
JPL	2	1	13	13	–
NAT.W.	3	2	5	2*	–
B & H					

CAREER: BOWLING

	O.	M.	R.	W.	AV.
TEST					
1ST-CLASS	196	43	600	27	22.22
INT					
JPL	35	1	138	4	34.50
NAT.W.	37	6	105	5	21.00
B & H					

20. When Dennis Amiss hit his 100th first-class 100 in 1986, how many others had done the feat before him?

21. England and Surrey cricketer and manager, Mickey Stewart, also played serious soccer. Name one of his clubs.

BIRCH, J. D. — Nottinghamshire

Full Name: John Dennis Birch
Role: Right-hand bat, right-arm medium bowler, slip fielder
Born: 18 June 1955, Nottingham
Height: 6′ 1″ **Weight:** 13st
Nickname: Bonk
County debut: 1973
County cap: 1981
1000 runs in a season: 2
1st-Class 50s scored: 41
1st-Class 100s scored: 5
1st-Class 5 w. in innings: 1
One-Day 50s: 15
Place in batting averages: 77th av. 34.19 (1985 140th av. 25.56)
1st-Class catches 1986: 24 (career: 157)
Parents: Bill and Mavis
Wife and date of marriage: Linda, 23 May 1980
Children: Nathalie and Daniel (twins), 21 January 1981
Education: William Crane Bilateral School
Qualifications: O-levels
Jobs outside cricket: Runs a small building firm with a friend and brothers
Family links with cricket: Father was a local cricketer
Cricketers particularly learnt from: Clive Rice
Cricketers particularly admired: Clive Rice, Richard Hadlee, Geoffrey Boycott
Other sports played: Soccer (player/manager of local team), golf, snooker

LAST SEASON: BATTING

	I.	N.O.	R.	H.S.	AV.
TEST					
1ST-CLASS	28	7	718	79*	34.19
INT					
JPL	6	1	110	66	22.00
NAT.W.					
B & H	5	3	130	48*	65.00

CAREER: BATTING

	I.	N.O.	R.	H.S.	AV.
TEST					
1ST-CLASS	303	52	6983	125	27.82
INT					
JPL	121	28	2403	92	25.83
NAT.W.	13	2	133	32	12.09
B & H	36	7	636	85	21.93

LAST SEASON: BOWLING

	O.	M.	R.	W.	AV.
TEST					
1ST-CLASS	11	1	24	1	–
INT					
JPL					
NAT.W.					
B & H					

CAREER: BOWLING

	O.	M.	R.	W.	AV.
TEST					
1ST-CLASS	505.5	72	1927	39	49.41
INT					
JPL	152	12	719	20	35.95
NAT.W.	14	1	73	1	–
B & H	59	7	237	8	29.62

Other sports followed: Watching any other sports
Relaxations: 'Gardening and fishing.'
Extras: 'Would like to thank Frank Woodhead for giving me the chance to play for Notts and all who have helped me at the club.'
Best batting performance: 125 Nottinghamshire v Leicestershire, Trent Bridge 1982
Best bowling performance: 6-64 Nottinghamshire v Hampshire, Bournemouth 1975

BLACKETT, M.   Leicestershire

Full Name: Mark Blackett
Role: Right-hand bat, short-leg fielder
Born: 3 February 1964, Edmonton, Middlesex
Height: 5′ 7″ **Weight:** 12st 7lbs
Nickname: Little Gatt, Dumpy, Blackers
County debut: 1985
Parents: Frederick Albert and Audrey Betty
Marital status: Single
Education: Edmonton County School
Qualifications: Senior Coaching Award
Jobs outside cricket: Working in sports shop
Family links with cricket: Father played club cricket
Cricketing superstitions: Always put right pad on first
Cricketers particularly learnt from: Don Wilson, Ken Higgs, Brian Taylor
Cricketers particularly admired: David Gower, Viv Richards, Chris Balderstone (for his professional attitude and approach to the game)
Other sports played: Snooker

LAST SEASON: BATTING

	I.	N.O.	R.	H.S.	AV.
TEST					
1ST-CLASS					
INT					
JPL	2	1	20	17	–
NAT.W.					
B & H					

CAREER: BATTING

	I.	N.O.	R.	H.S.	AV.
TEST					
1ST-CLASS					
INT					
JPL	5	3	53	21*	26.50
NAT.W.					
B & H					

Relaxations: Listening to music, playing snooker
Extras: Spent two years on the MCC ground staff at Lord's (1983–84) and three years playing for Middlesex 2nds and U-25s (1982–84)
Best batting performance: 28* Leicestershire v Worcestershire, Leicester 1985

BLAKEY, R. J. *Yorkshire*

Full Name: Richard John Blakey
Role: Right-hand bat, occasional wicket-keeper
Born: 15 January 1967, Huddersfield
Height: 5′ 9″ **Weight:** 11st 7lbs
Nickname: Dick, Mutley
County debut: 1985
1st-Class 50s scored: 2
Place in batting averages: —
(1985 136th av. 25.90)
1st-Class catches 1986: 4 (career 16)
Parents: Brian and Pauline
Marital status: Single
Education: Rastrick Grammar School
Qualifications: 4 O-levels, NCA Coaching Certificate
Family links with cricket: Father played local cricket

Overseas tours: Young England to West Indies 1985
Overseas teams played for: Waverley CC, Melbourne 1985–86
Cricketers particularly learnt from: My father Brian, Doug Padgett, Steve Oldham
Cricketers particularly admired: Ian Botham, Martyn Moxon
Off-season 1986–87: In Melbourne playing and coaching
Other sports played: Golf, squash, snooker, football
Relaxations: Music, sleeping and watching Leeds United FC
Extras: Made record 2nd XI score – 273* v Northamptonshire 1986
Opinions on cricket: 'In our climate I would like to see 16 4-day matches. With 3-day fixtures you seem to spend the first 2½ days jockeying for position, using declaration bowlers, forfeits etc, in order to try to manufacture a result.'
Best batting performance: 90 Yorkshire v Somerset, Headingley 1985

LAST SEASON: BATTING

	I.	N.O.	R.	H.S.	AV.
TEST					
1ST-CLASS	7	0	143	46	20.42
INT					
JPL	1	0	3	3	–
NAT.W.	–	–	–	–	–
B & H					

LAST SEASON: BOWLING

	O.	M.	R.	W.	AV.
TEST					
1ST-CLASS	10.3	1	68	1	–
INT					
JPL					
NAT.W.					
B & H					

CAREER: BATTING

	I.	N.O.	R.	H.S.	AV.
TEST					
1ST-CLASS	29	2	661	90	24.48
INT					
JPL	1	0	3	3	–
NAT.W.	–	–	–	–	–
B & H					

CAREER: BOWLING

	O.	M.	R.	W.	AV.
TEST					
1ST-CLASS	10.3	1	68	1	–
INT					
JPL					
NAT.W.					
B & H					

LAST SEASON: WICKET-KEEPING

	C.	ST.			
TEST					
1ST-CLASS					
INT					
JPL					
NAT.W.	3	–			
B & H					

CAREER: WICKET-KEEPING

	C.	ST.			
TEST					
1ST-CLASS					
INT					
JPL					
NAT.W.	3	–			
B & H					

BLITZ, R. J.   Somerset

Full Name: Rayner John Blitz
Role: Right-hand bat,
wicket-keeper
Born: 25 March 1968, Watford
Height: 5′ 4″
County debut: 1986
1st-Class catches 1986: 8 (career: 8)
Education: Gaynes School,
Upminster
Extras: Played for Essex 2nd XI in
1985. Left Somerset at end of 1986
Best batting performance: 18
Somerset v Hampshire,
Bournemouth 1986

	I.	N.O.	R.	H.S.	AV.
TEST					
1ST-CLASS	5	0	33	18	6.60
INT					
JPL	1	0	1	1	–
NAT.W.					
B & H					

LAST SEASON: WICKET-KEEPING

	C.	ST.			
TEST					
1ST-CLASS	8	–			
INT					
JPL	1	–			
NAT.W.					
B & H					

CAREER: BATTING

	I.	N.O.	R.	H.S.	AV.
TEST					
1ST-CLASS	5	0	33	18	6.60
INT					
JPL	1	0	1	1	–
NAT.W.					
B & H					

CAREER: WICKET-KEEPING

	C.	ST.			
TEST					
1ST-CLASS	8	–			
INT					
JPL	1	–			
NAT.W.					
B & H					

BOON, T. J. Leicestershire

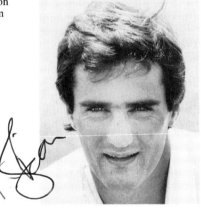

Full Name: Timothy James Boon
Role: Right-hand bat, right-arm medium bowler
Born: 1 November 1961, Doncaster
Height: 6′ 0″ **Weight:** 12st
Nickname: 'Ted Moon, Cod, amongst others.'
County debut: 1980
1000 runs in a season: 2
1st-Class 50s scored: 13
1st-Class 100s scored: 5
Place in batting averages: 56th av. 38.57
1st-Class catches 1986: 12 (career: 31)
Parents: Jeffrey and Elizabeth
Marital status: Single
Education: Mill Lane Primary; Edlington Comprehensive; three months at Doncaster Art School
Qualifications: 1 A-level, 6 O-levels, Coaching qualifications
Family links with cricket: Father played club cricket
Cricketing superstitions: 'Constantly changing.'
Overseas tours: Toured the Caribbean with England Young Cricketers 1980, as captain; Leicestershire CCC tour of Zimbabwe, March 1981
Overseas teams played for: Old Hararians, Zimbabwe, 1980–81; Ceylon CC, Colombo, 1981–82; Pirates CC, Durban, 1982–83, 1984–85

Cricketers particularly learnt from: The late Mike Fearnley, Ken Higgs, Chris Balderstone, Peter Willey

Other sports played: 'Enjoy playing and watching all sports.'

Relaxations: Sleeping

Extras: Captain England Young Cricketers Tour West Indies 1980; Captain England Young Cricketers v Indian Young Cricketers 1981; Most Promising Schoolboy Cricketer 1979. Missed 1985 season due to broken leg sustained in a car crash in South Africa the previous winter

Best batting performance: 144 Leicestershire v Gloucestershire, Leicester 1984

Best bowling performance: 3-40 Leicestershire v Yorkshire, Leicester 1986

LAST SEASON: BATTING

	I.	N.O.	R.	H.S.	AV.
TEST					
1ST-CLASS	36	10	1003	117	38.57
INT					
JPL	13	2	265	49*	24.00
NAT.W.	2	1	29	19	–
B & H	2	0	53	43	26.50

CAREER: BATTING

	I.	N.O.	R.	H.S.	AV.
TEST					
1ST-CLASS	136	22	3386	144	29.70
IN I					
JPL	43	9	675	49*	19.85
NAT.W.	5	3	55	22*	27.50
B & H	5	2	95	43	31.66

LAST SEASON: BOWLING

	O.	M.	R.	W.	AV.
TEST					
1ST-CLASS	30.3	2	170	5	34.00
INT					
JPL					
NAT.W.	1	0	2	0	–
B & H					

CAREER: BOWLING

	O.	M.	R.	W.	AV.
TEST					
1ST-CLASS	46.3	7	227	5	45.40
INT					
JPL	2	0	14	0	–
NAT.W.	1	0	2	0	–
B & H					

22. Which current county cricketer is nicknamed Bud?

23. Which current county cricketer is nicknamed Animal?

24. What was unusual about the umpires in the Eton v Harrow match in 1986?

BORDER, A. R.   Essex

Full Name: Allan Robert Border
Role: Left-hand bat, slow
left-arm bowler
Born: 27 July 1955, Cremorne,
Sydney
Height: 5′ 9″
Nickname: A.B., Herby
(from Herbaceous)
County debut: 1977 (Gloucestershire),
1986 (Essex)
Test debut: 1978–79
No. of Tests: 81
No. of One-Day Internationals: 130
1000 runs in a season: 2
1st-Class 50s scored: 71
1st-Class 100s scored: 36
1st-Class 200s scored: 1
One-Day 50s: 23
One-Day 100s: 3
Place in batting averages: 13th av. 49.46
1st-Class catches 1986: 17 (career: 180)
Overseas tours: With Australia to England 1980, 1981, 1985; West Indies 1983–84; New Zealand 1981–82, 1986; India 1979–80, 1986, Pakistan 1979–80, 1982–83; Sri Lanka 1982–83
Overseas teams played for: NSW 1976–80, Queensland 1980–86
Extras: Played one match for Gloucestershire in 1977. Captain of Queensland since 1983–84; captain of Australia since 1985. Joined Essex on 2-year

LAST SEASON: BATTING

	I.	N.O.	R.	H.S.	AV.
TEST					
1ST-CLASS	32	4	1385	150	49.46
INT					
JPL	13	1	330	75	27.50
NAT.W.	2	0	29	23	14.50
B & H	5	0	81	31	16.20

LAST SEASON: BOWLING

	O.	M.	R.	W.	AV.
TEST					
1ST-CLASS	26	3	120	1	–
INT					
JPL	5	0	66	3	8.66
NAT.W.	2	0	11	0	–
B & H	·				

CAREER: BATTING

	I.	N.O.	R.	H.S.	AV.
TEST	143	24	6199	196	52.09
1ST-CLASS	181	24	8621	200	54.91
INT	121	17	3254	127*	31.28
JPL	13	1	330	75	27.50
NAT.W.	2	0	29	23	14.50
B & H	5	0	81	31	16.20

CAREER: BOWLING

	O.	M.	R.	W.	AV.
TEST	49 202.3	55	626	15	41.73
1ST-CLASS	243.6 255.3	58	1487	40	37.17
INT	166	6	791	23	34.39
JPL	5	6	26	3	8.66
NAT.W.	2	0	11	0	–
B & H					

contract but returned to Australia in August 1986 and will not complete original term

Best batting performance: 200 New South Wales v Queensland, Brisbane 1979–80

Best batting performance: 4–61 Queensland v New South Wales, Sydney 1980–81

BOTHAM, I. T. Worcestershire

Full Name: Ian Terrence Botham
Role: Right-hand bat, right-arm fast-medium bowler, slip fielder
Born: 24 November 1955, Heswall, Cheshire
Height: 6′ 2″ **Weight:** 15st 5lbs
Nickname: Guy, Both, Beefy
County debut: 1974 (Somerset)
County cap: 1976 (Somerset)
Benefit: 1984 (£90,822)
Test debut: 1977
No. of Tests: 85
No. of One-Day Internationals: 78
1000 runs in a season: 4
50 wickets in a season: 7
1st-Class 50s scored: 70
1st-Class 100s scored: 31
1st-Class 200s scored: 2
1st-Class 5 w. in innings: 52
1st-Class 10 w. in match: 7
One-Day 50s: 23
One-Day 100s: 4

Place in batting averages: 19th av. 47.94 (1985 4th av. 69.54)
Place in bowling averages: 102nd av. 41.72 (1985 58th av. 31.27)
1st-Class catches 1986: 8 (career: 260)
Parents: Les and Marie
Wife and date of marriage: Kathryn, 31 January 1976
Children: Liam James, 26 August 1977; Sarah Lianne, 3 February 1979; Rebecca Kate, 13 November 1985
Education: Millford Junior School; Buckler's Mead Secondary School, Yeovil
Family links with cricket: Father played for Navy and Fleet Air Arm; mother played for VAD nursing staff
Overseas tours: Pakistan and New Zealand 1977–78; Australia 1978–79;

Australia and India, 1979–80; West Indies 1981 as Captain; India 1981–82; Australia and New Zealand 1982–83; West Indies 1986

Cricketers particularly learnt from: Brian Close

Cricketers particularly admired: Viv Richards, David Gower, Allan Border

Off season 1986–87: Touring Australia with England

Other sports played: Captained school soccer team, and has played for Scunthorpe United, making debut as striker v Bournemouth in March 1980. Offered terms by Crystal Palace. Now plays for Yeovil Town. U-16 Somerset champion, badminton doubles

Relaxations: Golf, shooting, fishing (salmon and trout). Has learned to fly

Extras: Captain of England 1980–81. Took five Australian wickets in his first day of Test Match cricket aged 21. Played for County 2nd XI 1971. On MCC staff 1972–73. Played for county in last two John Player League matches 1973. Honorary townsman of Epworth, South Humberside, where he lives, and Freeman of Yeovil, Somerset. Subject of 'This is Your Life' television programme in November 1981. Was Best Man at Viv Richards' wedding in March 1981 in Antigua. Published *The Incredible Tests 1981*. Voted BBC TV Sportsview Sporting Personality of 1981. Having a go at baseball in Los Angeles in September 1981 easily exceeded the striking rate of established American baseball stars: he complained that Americans could not pitch the ball fast enough. Scored fastest 100 of 1982 and 1985 seasons. Scored 200 in 272 minutes for England v India at The Oval, 9 July 1982, third fastest Test double century by an Englishman, after Walter Hammond (240 mins v New Zealand in 1932) and Denis Compton (245 mins v Pakistan in 1954). Crashed two £12,000 sports cars at 100 mph in same afternoon in May 1982. Among the books he chose to take a desert island was Jack Fingleton's book on the great Australian cricketer *The Immortal Victor Trumper*. First cricketer since W. G. Grace to have painting commissioned by National Portrait Gallery. Captain of Somerset 1984–85. Holds record for having scored 1000 runs and taken 100 wickets in fewest Test matches. First player to score a century and take 8 wickets in an innings in a Test Match, v Pakistan at Lord's in 1978. Most

LAST SEASON: BATTING

	I.	N.O.	R.	H.S.	AV.
TEST	1	1	59	59*	–
1ST-CLASS	19	1	804	139	44.66
INT					
JPL	7	3	331	175*	82.75
NAT.W.					
B & H	4	1	197	126*	65.66

LAST SEASON: BOWLING

	O.	M.	R.	W.	AV.
TEST	26	4	82	3	27.33
1ST-CLASS	285.1	61	961	22	43.68
INT					
JPL	40	0	235	7	33.57
NAT.W.					
B & H	28	6	107	7	15.28

CAREER: BATTING

	I.	N.O.	R.	H.S.	AV.
TEST	136	4	4636	208	35.12
1ST-CLASS	314	29	10043	228	35.23
INT	69	8	1299	72	21.29
JPL	124	21	3185	175*	30.92
NAT.W.	28	6	825	96*	37.50
B & H	48	7	1039	126*	25.34

CAREER: BOWLING

	O.	M.	R.	W.	AV.
TEST	259.4 2880	42 651	9663	357	27.06
1ST-CLASS	190.3 7168.5	43 1655	15008	579	25.92
INT	38.7 626.4	2 80	2761	103	26.80
JPL	899.1	41	3964	148	26.78
NAT.W.	341.3	56	1162	41	28.34
B & H	554	108	1890	88	21.47

sixes in a first-class season and most instances of 5 wickets in a Test innings (both 1985). Leading wicket-taker in Test cricket. Left Somerset at the beginning of 1987 to join Worcestershire after Somerset had decided not to renew the contracts of Richards and Garner

Opinions on cricket: 'Too many people live in the past.'
Best batting performance: 228 Somerset v Gloucestershire, Taunton 1980
Best bowling performance: 8-34 England v Pakistan, Lord's 1978

BOWLER, P. D.   Leicestershire

Full Name: Peter Duncan Bowler
Role: Right-hand bat, off-spinner
Born: 30 July 1963, Plymouth
Height: 6′ 1″ **Weight:** 13st
County debut: 1986
1st-Class 50s scored: 1
1st-Class 100s scored: 1
One-Day 50s: 1
Place in batting averages: 150th av. 24.90
1st-Class catches 1986: 2 (career: 2)
Parents: Peter and Etta
Marital status: Single
Education: Canberra, Australia (Daramalan College)
Qualifications: Australian Yr 12 Certificate
Overseas teams played for:
Australia Manly CC 1982; Westbury CC 1983, 1984, 1985
Cricketers particularly learnt from: Rob Jeffery, Bill Carracher, Gus Valence

LAST SEASON: BATTING

	I.	N.O.	R.	H.S.	AV.
TEST					
1ST-CLASS	11	1	249	108*	24.90
INT					
JPL	10	1	164	55	18.22
NAT.W.					
B & H					

LAST SEASON: BOWLING

	O.	M.	R.	W.	AV.
TEST					
1ST-CLASS	25.4	10	57	0	–
INT					
JPL					
NAT.W.					
B & H					

CAREER: BATTING

	I.	N.O.	R.	H.S.	AV.
TEST					
1ST-CLASS	11	1	249	100*	24.90
INT					
JPL	10	1	164	55	18.22
NAT.W.					
B & H					

CAREER: BOWLING

	O.	M.	R.	W.	AV.
TEST					
1ST-CLASS	25.4	10	57	0	–
INT					
JPL					
NAT.W.					
B & H					

Cricketers particularly admired: Greg Chappell, Richard Hadlee, Jeff Thomson
Off-season 1986–87: Coaching and playing in Australia
Other sports played: Rugby union, rugby league
Relaxations: Music, reading, papers. Watching sports other than cricket
Extras: First Leicestershire player to score a first-class hundred on debut (100* v Hampshire 1986)
Best batting performance: 100* Leicestershire v Hampshire, Leicester 1986

BOYCOTT, G. Yorkshire

Full Name: Geoffrey Boycott
Role: Right-hand opening bat, right-arm medium bowler
Born: 21 October 1940, Fitzwilliam, Yorkshire
Height: 5′ 10″ **Weight:** 11st 7lbs
Nickname: Fiery or Boycs (or Thatch, 'but only from Ian Botham')
County debut: 1962
County cap: 1963
Benefit: 1974 (£20,639), 1984 (£147,000)
Test debut: 1964
No. of Tests: 108 (Captain in 4)
No. of One-Day Internationals: 36
1000 runs in a season: 23
1st-Class 50s scored: 238
1st-Class 100s scored: 141
1st-Class 200s scored: 10
One-Day 50s: 71
One-Day 100s: 7
Place in batting averages: 9th av. 52.21 (1985 2nd av. 75.32)
1st-Class catches: 3 (career: 263)
Marital status: Single
Education: Hemsworth Grammar School
Qualifications: 7 O-levels
Jobs outside cricket: Was civil servant, worked for Yorkshire Electricity Board
Family links with cricket: Brothers Peter and Tony both played cricket, but father did not play at all
Overseas tours: South Africa 1964–65; Australia, New Zealand 1965–66 and

1970–71, returning home early with broken arm; West Indies 1967–68 and 1973–74; Pakistan and New Zealand 1977–78 as Vice-Captain; Australia 1978–79 and 1979–80; West Indies; India 1981–82

Overseas teams played for: Northern Transvaal 1971–72

Players particularly learnt from: 'At the start of every season and before I go on tour I visit Johnny Lawrence who has coached me since I was nine years old.'

Other sports played: Golf, tennis

Relaxations: Reading, theatre, cinema. Watching television programmes (thrillers). Enjoys classical ballet – 'I don't understand modern ballet'. Favourite reading includes World Wildlife Fund magazines. 'I am a member of the Fund because I believe strongly that we should conserve nature. To me, life, whether human or animal is precious. I've been to most of the major game parks in Africa. They are marvellous places to visit.'

Extras: Finished top of the batting averages 1971 with an average of 100.12, the only English batsman ever to have an average of over 100 for a season. Repeated 1979 with average of 102.53. Captained Hemsworth Grammar School and the local Schools XI; at 13, played for Ackworth in Yorkshire Council League; at 15, played for Yorkshire Schoolboys' and Barnsley. Before playing for Yorkshire for first time at age 21, he was top of batting averages for Leeds, Yorkshire Colts and Yorkshire 2nd XI. Plays in contact lenses. Wears cap when bowling. Scored two centuries in a match (103 and 105) v Nottinghamshire at Sheffield in 1966, and 160* and 116 for England v the Rest at Worcester in 1974. On exhibition at Madame Tussaud's. Bowled in the Lord's Test v West Indies 1980 wearing his cap back to front. Awarded OBE in 1980. Rarely drinks alcohol. Published *Put to the Test*, 1979; *Opening Up*, 1980; *In the Fast Lane*, 1981 and *Master Class*, 1982. Also *Geoffrey Boycott's Book for Young Cricketeers*. Banned from Test cricket for three years in 1982 for playing for an England XI in South Africa. Elected to Yorkshire committee in 1984, the sixth man to serve with the club as player and committee member. Not offered new playing contract for 1987 season

LAST SEASON: BATTING

	I.	N.O.	R.	H.S.	AV.
TEST					
1ST-CLASS	20	1	992	135*	52.21
INT					
JPL					
NAT.W.	1	0	31	31	–
B & H	2	1	82	55	–

LAST SEASON: BOWLING

	O.	M.	R.	W.	AV.
TEST					
1ST-CLASS					
INT					
JPL					
NAT.W.					
B & H					

CAREER: BATTING

	I.	N.O.	R.	H.S.	AV.
TEST	193	23	8114	246*	47.73
1ST-CLASS	821	139	40312	261*	59.10
INT	34	4	1082	105	36.06
JPL	157	24	5051	108*	37.97
NAT.W.	39	4	1378	146	39.37
B & H	55	9	2052	142	44.60

CAREER: BOWLING

	O.	M.	R.	W.	AV.
TEST	28 120.3	4 41	382	7	54.57
1ST-CLASS	28.4 434.2	2 134	1057	38	27.81
INT	28	1	105	5	21.00
JPL	151.5	11	611	14	43.64
NAT.W.	78	15	238	8	29.75
B & H	63	4	227	2	113.50

Injuries 1986: Broken bone in left hand
Best batting performance: 261* MCC v Presidents XI, Bridgetown 1973–74
Best bowling performance: 4-14 Yorkshire v Lancashire, Leeds 1979

BOYD-MOSS, R. J.   Northamptonshire

Full Name: Robin James
Boyd-Moss
Role: Right-hand bat, slow left-
arm bowler
Born: 16 December 1959, Hatton,
Sri Lanka
Height: 5′ 10″ **Weight:** 12st 9lbs
Nickname: Mossy, Mouse
County debut: 1980
County cap: 1984
1000 runs in a season: 3
1st-Class 50s scored: 40
1st-Class 100s scored: 13
1st-Class 5 w. in innings: 1
One-Day 50s: 8
Place in batting averages: 101st
av. 30.56 (1985 129th av. 27.36)
1st-Class catches 1986: 7 (career: 58)
Parents: Michael and Shelagh
Wife and date of marriage: Deborah, 21 December 1985
Education: Bedford School; Cambridge University
Qualifications: 3 A-levels, BA in Land Economy

LAST SEASON: BATTING

	I.	N.O.	R.	H.S.	AV.
TEST					
1ST-CLASS	42	3	1192	155	30.56
INT					
JPL	12	2	244	86	24.40
NAT.W.					
B & H	5	1	145	58	36.25

CAREER: BATTING

	I.	N.O.	R.	H.S.	AV.
TEST					
1ST-CLASS	244	19	6850	155	30.44
INT					
JPL	50	6	1010	99	22.95
NAT.W.	6	2	179	88*	44.75
B & H	20	1	360	58	18.94

LAST SEASON: BOWLING

	O.	M.	R.	W.	AV.
TEST					
1ST-CLASS	80.1	19	232	7	33.14
INT					
JPL	1	0	11	0	–
NAT.W.					
B & H					

CAREER: BOWLING

	O.	M.	R.	W.	AV.
TEST					
1ST-CLASS	617.5	143	2111	50	42.20
INT					
JPL	1	0	11	0	–
NAT.W.	12	1	47	3	15.66
B & H	12	1	49	0	–

Off-season 1986–87: Coaching/teaching in Kenya at Banda School and working for the Nairobi Provincial Cricket Assn
Other sports played: Rugby football. Played centre for Cambridge v Oxford in 100th Varsity Match. Double Blue. Golf, squash
Relaxations: Wildlife, photography
Injuries 1986: Back injury
Best batting performance: 155 Northamptonshire v Lancashire, Northampton 1986
Best bowling performance: 5-27 Cambridge University v Oxford University, Lord's 1983

BREDIN, A. M.   Sussex

Full Name: Andrew Michael Bredin
Role: Right-hand bat, slow left-arm bowler; gully fielder
Born: 12 January 1962, Wimbledon
Height: 5′ 11″ **Weight:** 11st 10lbs
Nickname: Bovis, Jumble
County debut: 1986
1st-Class catches 1986: 1 (career: 1)
Parents: John Joseph and Patricia Ann
Marital status: Single
Education: King's College School, Wimbledon
Qualifications: 5 O-levels, qualified cricket coach
Family links with cricket: Father played club cricket for Wimbledon CC
Cricketing superstitions: Click my fingers during run up
Overseas tours: Surrey YCs to Australia, 1980–81
Overseas teams played for: Perth CC, Australia, 1981–82
Cricketers particularly learnt from: Chris Waller, Colin Wells
Cricketers particularly admired: Dennis Amiss, Paul Parker, Tony Pigott
Off-season 1986–87: Coaching at the Surrey indoor school, East Molesey
Other sports played: Most sports
Other sports followed: Rugby
Relaxations: Drinking and socialising, listening to music
Extras: 'Released at end of 1986 season after having taken twice as many wickets as any other bowler in the 2nd XI.'

Opinions on cricket: 1) I should have taken up golf earlier. 2) Counties should do more to encourage spin bowlers.
Injuries 1986: 'Hit on head by ball that I thought was short from Tony Gray!'
Best batting performance: 8* Sussex v Leicestershire, Hove 1986
Best bowling performance: 2-50 Sussex v Essex, Ilford 1986

LAST SEASON: BATTING

	I.	N.O.	R.	H.S.	AV.
TEST					
1ST-CLASS	6	2	26	8*	6.50
INT					
JPL					
NAT.W.					
B & H					

LAST SEASON: BOWLING

	O.	M.	R.	W.	AV.
TEST					
1ST-CLASS	115	25	385	7	55.00
INT					
JPL					
NAT.W.					
B & H					

CAREER: BATTING

	I.	N.O.	R.	H.S.	AV.
TEST					
1ST-CLASS	6	2	26	8*	6.50
INT					
JPL					
NAT.W.					
B & H					

CAREER: BOWLING

	O.	M.	R.	W.	AV.
TEST					
1ST-CLASS	115	25	385	7	55.00
INT					
JPL					
NAT.W.					
B & H					

BRIERS, N. E.   Leicestershire

Full Name: Nigel Edwin Briers
Role: Right-hand bat, right-arm medium bowler, cover fielder
Born: 15 January 1955, Leicester
Height: 6′ 0″ **Weight:** 12st 5lbs
Nickname: Kudu
County debut: 1971 (aged 16 yrs 104 days)
County cap: 1981
1000 runs in a season: 3
1st-Class 50s scored: 33
1st-Class 100s scored: 9
1st-Class 200s scored: 1
One-Day 50s: 25
One-Day 100s: 3
Place in batting averages: —
(1985 166th av. 23.04)
1st-Class catches 1986: 1 (career: 75)
Parents: Leonard Arthur Roger and Eveline
Wife and date of marriage: Suzanne Mary Tudor, 3 September 1977

Children: Michael Edward Tudor, 25 March 1983; Andrew James Tudor, 30 June 1986

Education: Lutterworth Grammar School; Borough Road College

Qualifications: Qualified teacher (Certificate of Education), BEd Hons, MCC Advanced Coach

Jobs outside cricket: Lecturer in Physical Education at Leicester Polytechnic

Family links with cricket: Father was captain and wicket-keeper of Narborough and Littlethorpe Cricket Club, first division of Leicestershire League, for 15 years. Mother was scorer for team. Father was Captain of South Leicestershire Representative XI and played for the Royal Marines in the same team as Trevor Bailey. Cousin, Norman Briers, played for Leicestershire once in 1967

Off-season 1986–87: Teaching PE and history at Ludgrove School

Injuries 1986: Broken arm in June kept him out for the rest of the season

Best batting performance: 201* Leicestershire v Warwickshire, Edgbaston 1983

Best bowling performance: 4-29 Leicestershire v Derbyshire, Leicester 1985

LAST SEASON: BATTING

	I.	N.O.	R.	H.S.	AV.
TEST					
1ST-CLASS	7	1	223	83	37.16
INT					
JPL	5	1	206	60*	51.50
NAT.W.					
B & H	3	0	52	37	17.33

LAST SEASON: BOWLING

	O.	M.	R.	W.	AV.
TEST					
1ST-CLASS	13	0	60	2	30.00
INT					
JPL	21	0	116	1	–
NAT.W.					
B & H	17	0	83	1	–

CAREER: BATTING

	I.	N.O.	R.	H.S.	AV.
TEST					
1ST-CLASS	301	31	7471	201*	27.67
INT					
JPL	112	17	3343	119*	35.18
NAT.W.	17	2	291	59	19.40
B & H	29	2	436	71*	16.14

CAREER: BOWLING

	O.	M.	R.	W.	AV.
TEST					
1ST-CLASS	331.5	69	970	32	30.31
INT					
JPL	80.2	5	384	10	38.40
NAT.W.	14	0	75	6	12.50
B & H	55	3	266	3	88.60

25. Who was New Zealand's first Test captain?

26. What was the only song that Surrey and England batsman Laurie Fishlock (who died in 1986) could play on his banjo?

BROAD, B. C.   Nottinghamshire

Full Name: Brian Christopher Broad
Role: Left-hand bat, right-arm medium bowler
Born: 29 September 1957, Bristol
Height: 6' 4" **Weight:** 14st 7lbs
Nickname: Walter, Broodie
County debut: 1979 (Gloucestershire), 1984 (Nottinghamshire)
County cap: 1981 (Gloucestershire), 1984 (Nottinghamshire)
Test debut: 1984
No. of Tests: 5
1000 runs in a season: 6
1st-Class 50s scored: 60
1st-Class 100s scored: 18
One-Day 50s: 26
One-Day 100s: 3
Place in batting averages: 49th av. 39.82 (1985 45th av. 40.59)

1st-Class catches 1986: 19 (career: 88)
Parents: Nancy and Kenneth
Wife and date of marriage: Carole Ann, 14 July 1979
Children: Gemma Joanne, 14 January 1984; Stuart Christopher John, 24 June 1986
Education: Colston's School, Bristol; St Paul's College, Cheltenham
Qualifications: 5 O-levels, NCA advanced coach
Family links with cricket: Father and grandfather both played local cricket. Father member of Gloucestershire Committee until retired
Cricketing superstitions: Puts left pad on first
Overseas tours: Gloucestershire CCC tour of Malawi 1978 and Barbados 1980; British Colleges to Trinidad and Barbados 1979
Overseas teams played for: Orange Free State 1985–86 (Captain)
Cricketers particularly learnt from: Reg Sinfield, Sadiq Mohammed
Cricketers particularly admired: Graham Gooch, Richard Hadlee
Off-season 1986–87: Touring Australia with England
Other sports played: Played rugby for English Colleges, Bristol United, St Paul's College, and now plays for Clifton
Relaxations: 'Playing any sport, spending time with my family.'
Extras: Ended 1979 with a century (129) in last match for Gloucestershire v Northamptonshire and hit a century (120) for Gloucestershire v Oxford University in first match of 1980. With Gloucestershire 1979–83

Best batting performance: 171 Nottinghamshire v Derbyshire, Derby 1985
Best bowling performance: 2-14 Gloucestershire v West Indies, Bristol 1980

LAST SEASON: BATTING

	I.	N.O.	R.	H.S.	AV.
TEST					
1ST-CLASS	42	2	1593	122	39.82
INT					
JPL	15	2	701	104*	53.92
NAT.W.	3	0	139	73	46.33
B & H	6	0	171	70	28.50

LAST SEASON: BOWLING

	O.	M.	R.	W.	AV.
TEST					
1ST-CLASS	7	1	41	0	–
INT					
JPL					
NAT.W.					
B & H					

CAREER: BATTING

	I.	N.O.	R.	H.S.	AV.
TEST	9	0	281	86	31.22
1ST-CLASS	293	21	10016	171	36.82
INT					
JPL	92	3	2770	104*	31.12
NAT.W.	16	0	555	98	34.68
B & H	31	0	776	122	25.03

CAREER: BOWLING

	O.	M.	R.	W.	AV.
TEST					
1ST-CLASS	265.5	60	1002	16	52.81
INT					
JPL	111.3	4	602	19	31.68
NAT.W.					
B & H	50.4	2	282	5	56.40

BROWN, A. M. Derbyshire

Full Name: Andrew Mark Brown
Role: Left-hand opening bat, off-break bowler ('very occasionally'), cover fielder
Born: 6 November 1964, Heanor, Derbyshire
Height: 5′ 9″ **Weight:** 10st
Nickname: Brownie
County debut: 1985
1st-Class 50s scored: 1
1st-Class catches 1986: 1 (career: 4)
Parents: John Derek and Marion
Marital status: Single
Education: Aldercar Comprehensive; South-East Derbyshire College of PE
Qualifications: 8 O-levels, 1 A-level, NCA Coaching Certificate
Family links with cricket: Father is County Coaching Organiser for Derbyshire and was also a good league player. Brother Stephen played for Derbyshire U-13 – U-19. Sister Helen played for club junior boys' sides
Overseas teams played for: Pukekohe CC and Counties Association, New

Zealand, 1983–84, Old Boys Hastings and Hawkes Bay Association, New Zealand, 1984–85, 1985–86
Cricketers particularly learnt from: My father, John Wright, John Wiltshire
Cricketers particularly admired: John Wright, Geoff Boycott, Dennis Lillee
Off-season 1986–87: Coaching and playing in Hawkes Bay
Other sports played: 'Football, tennis (very badly).'
Other sports followed: 'Follow football and most other sports but I don't like wrestling.'
Relaxations: Enjoys watching Nottingham Forest play, listening to music, playing computer games
Extras: Made senior debut in JPL game against Nottinghamshire at Heanor only about 200 yards from where he was born
Best batting performance: 74 Derbyshire v Warwickshire, Chesterfield 1985

LAST SEASON: BATTING

	I.	N.O.	R.	H.S.	AV.
TEST					
1ST-CLASS	3	1	53	23	26.50
INT					
JPL					
NAT.W.					
B & H					

CAREER: BATTING

	I.	N.O.	R.	H.S.	AV.
TEST					
1ST-CLASS	6	0	146	74	24.33
INT					
JPL					
NAT.W.					
B & H					

BROWN, G. E. Surrey

Full Name: Graham Elliott Brown
Role: Batsman, wicket-keeper
Born: 11 October 1966, Balham
Height: 5' 7" **Weight:** 9½st
Nickname: Browny, Stumper, Pipsqueek
County debut: 1986
Parents: Alan and Dorothy
Wife and date of marriage: Pamela Campbell, engaged to be married in January 1987
Education: Spencer Park School, Wandsworth; South London College, West Norwood
3 O-levels in English, Maths, Economics; postman, photographer and sports coach

Jobs outside cricket: Worked at Cecil Gee in London last winter

Family links with cricket: Father and uncles avid watchers

Cricketing superstitions: Left keeping pad on first; left inner glove on first; being first out onto the middle to get new ball off umpire

Overseas tours: Jamaica in 1983 with London Schools U-16s

Cricketers particularly learnt from: Jack Richards, Ray Jackson, Ron Brown

Cricketers particularly admired: 'Jack Richards only from the age of 13 until now.'

Off-season 1986–87: Working at an Insurance Brokers

Other sports played: Football, athletics

Relaxations: 'Reading, travelling, listening to Saxon Studio, Coxsone Hi-Power, and seeing my fiancee, plus a good plotting. Also listening to David Ward talking on life.'

Injuries 1986: Bruised little finger, out for one week

Best batting performance: 2* Surrey v Kent, The Oval 1986

LAST SEASON: BATTING

	I.	N.O.	R.	H.S.	AV.
TEST					
1ST-CLASS	2	2	2	2*	–
INT					
JPL					
NAT.W.					
B & H					

CAREER: BATTING

	I.	N.O.	R.	H.S.	AV.
TEST					
1ST-CLASS	2	2	2	2*	–
INT					
JPL					
NAT.W.					
B & H					

LAST SEASON: WICKET-KEEPING

	C.	ST.			
TEST					
1ST-CLASS	4	1			
INT					
JPL					
NAT.W.					
B & H					

CAREER: WICKET-KEEPING

	C.	ST.			
TEST					
1ST-CLASS	4	1			
INT					
JPL					
NAT.W.					
B & H					

27. What was the title of Mike Gatting's first book, published in 1986?

28. What is Brian Close's first name?

BROWN, G. K.   Middlesex

Full Name: Gary Kevin Brown
Role: Right-hand bat, right-arm medium bowler, gully fielder
Born: 16 June 1965, Welling, Kent
Height: 6′ **Weight:** 13st 2lb
Nickname: Browny
County debut: 1986
1st-Class catches 1986: 2 (career: 2)
Parents: Kenneth William and Margaret Sonia
Marital status: Single
Education: Lavender Infant and Junior; Chance Secondary School
Qualifications: 3 O-levels
Jobs outside cricket: Coaching, commercial office work
Family links with cricket: Father played, brother Keith also with Middlesex
Cricketing superstitions: Always put left pad on first
Overseas teams played for: Spent winter of 1984 in New Zealand, playing for the Marist Club and Manawatu in Palmerston North
Cricketers particularly learnt from: Father, brother Keith, John Snow
Cricketers particularly admired: Ian Botham, Viv Richards
Off-season 1986–87: Coaching and commercial office work
Other sports played: Rugby, golf, snooker
Other sports followed: Boxing, athletics
Relaxations: Listening to music, pint down the local
Extras: Represented Essex and Eastern Counties at Rugby; played South of England U-19 cricket
Best batting performance: 14 Middlesex v Nottinghamshire, Trent Bridge 1986

LAST SEASON: BATTING

	I.	N.O.	R.	H.S.	AV.
TEST					
1ST-CLASS	2	0	17	14	8.50
INT					
JPL					
NAT.W.					
B & H					

CAREER: BATTING

	I.	N.O.	R.	H.S.	AV.
TEST					
1ST-CLASS	2	0	17	14	8.50
INT					
JPL					
NAT.W.					
B & H					

BROWN, K. R.   Middlesex

Full Name: Keith Robert Brown
Role: Right-hand bat, wicket-keeper
Born: 18 March 1963, Edmonton
Height: 5' 11" **Weight:** 13st 7lbs
Nickname: Browny, Gloves, Scarface
County debut: 1984
1st-Class 50s scored: 3
1st-Class 100s scored: 1
Place in batting averages: 138th
av. 26.4 (1985 84th av. 33.11)
1st-Class catches 1986: 8 (career: 17)
Parents: Kenneth William and
Margaret Sonia
Wife and date of marriage: Marie,
3 November 1984
Education: Chance Boys' School,
Enfield

Qualifications: French O-level; Senior Cricket Coach
Jobs outside cricket: Plasterer, light engineering, painter, decorator
Family links with cricket: Brother Gary is on Middlesex staff as well; father is qualified umpire
Cricketing superstitions: 'I bite my gloves when keeping'; the number 111
Overseas tours: NCA tour to Denmark in 1981. Played for South of England. Pre-season trips to La Manga 1985–86
Cricketers particularly learnt from: Father, Don Bennett
Cricketers particularly admired: Clive Radley
Off-season 1986–87: 'Plastering, looking forward to fatherhood in the New Year.'
Other sports played: Rugby, tennis, snooker
Other sports followed: All of them, especially boxing and football
Relaxations: Exercising Golden Retriever, decorating house, beer tasting
Extras: Had promising boxing career but gave it up in order to concentrate on cricket. Picked to play rugby for Essex
Opinions on cricket: '4-day cricket may benefit county players with a view to representing their country.'
Best batting performance: 102 Middlesex v Australia, Lord's 1985

	I.	N.O.	R.	H.S.	AV.
TEST					
1ST-CLASS	16	2	367	66	26.21
INT					
JPL	2	0	10	6	5.00
NAT.W.					
B & H					

LAST SEASON: BOWLING

	O.	M.	R.	W.	AV.
TEST					
1ST-CLASS	0.4	0	10	0	–
INT					
JPL					
NAT.W.					
B & H					

CAREER: BATTING

	I.	N.O.	R.	H.S.	AV.
TEST					
1ST-CLASS	28	4	671	102	27.95
INT					
JPL	5	0	68	33	13.60
NAT.W.					
B & H					

CAREER: BOWLING

	O.	M.	R.	W.	AV.
TEST					
1ST-CLASS	1.4	1	10	0	–
INT					
JPL					
NAT.W.					
B & H					

BULLEN, C. K.   Surrey

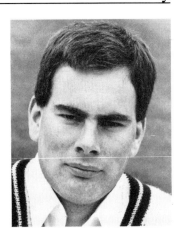

Full Name: Christopher Keith Bullen
Role: Right-hand bat, off-break bowler, slip fielder
Born: 5 November 1962, Clapham
Height: 6′ 5″ **Weight:** 14st
Nickname: CB, Jasper, Bullo, Roadrunner
County debut: 1985
1st-Class catches 1986: 2 (career: 2)
Parents: Keith Thomas and Joan
Marital status: Single
Education: Glenbrook Primary; Chaucer Middle; Rutlish School
Qualifications: 6 O-levels
Jobs outside cricket: Worked on a building site, car washer
Family links with cricket: 'Parents are enthusiastic cricket watchers. Father claims he played cricket at a high standard, but there's no evidence!'
Cricketing superstitions: Always puts left things on first, ie socks, shoes, batting gloves
Overseas tours: Surrey Schools U-19 to Australia 1980–81
Overseas teams played for: Claremont Cottesloe, Perth, 1984–85, 1985–86
Cricketing particularly learnt from: Mickey Stewart, Geoff Arnold, Chris Waller

Cricketers particularly admired: Pat Pocock, Jim Laker

Off-season 1986–87: Staying at home to have a break from cricket

Other sports played: Golf, rugby

Other sports followed: Watches soccer

Relaxations: Listening to music, leisurely walk after a golf ball. 'I like to wear colourful or rather "different" style of clothes.'

Extras: Spends free time playing club cricket for Wimbledon who won the league and cup for the second successive year. Captain of Surrey U-25 side which won Warwick Trophy in 1986

Opinions: '4-day county games; uncovered wickets; English registration is given too freely; more should be done by clubs to look after their players during the winter, especially those staying in this country.'

Injuries 1986: Chipped finger – out for 3 weeks

Best batting performance: 19 Surrey v Gloucestershire, The Oval 1985

Best bowling performance: 2-36 Surrey v Cambridge University, Cambridge, 1985

LAST SEASON: BATTING

	I.	N.O.	R.	H.S.	AV.
TEST					
1ST-CLASS					
INT					
JPL	3	2	1	1*	–
NAT.W.					
B & H					

LAST SEASON: BOWLING

	O.	M.	R.	W.	AV.
TEST					
1ST-CLASS					
INT					
JPL	32	5	81	4	20.25
NAT.W.					
B & H					

CAREER: BATTING

	I.	N.O.	R.	H.S.	AV.
TEST					
1ST-CLASS	4	0	53	19	13.25
INT					
JPL	5	2	20	10	6.66
NAT.W.					
B & H					

CAREER: BOWLING

	O.	M.	R.	W.	AV.
TEST					
1ST-CLASS	37	11	104	2	52.00
INT					
JPL	38	5	116	4	29.00
NAT.W.					
B & H					

29. Which England cricket captain was knighted in 1986?

30. What was unusual about the University of East Anglia's matches against Earlham Lodge and Cromer in June 1986?

BURNS, N. D.   Somerset

Full Name: Neil David Burns
Role: Left-hand bat,
wicket-keeper
Born: 19 September 1965,
Chelmsford
Height: 5′ 10″ **Weight:** 11½st
Nickname: Burnsie, George
County debut: 1986 (Essex)
Parents: Roy and Marie
Marital status: Engaged to Susan
Anne Clark; wedding planned for
26 September 1987
Education: Mildmay Junior,
Moulsham High School
Qualifications: 5 O-levels;
Advanced Cricket Coach
Jobs outside cricket: Worked in a
sports shop one winter

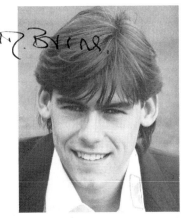

Family links with cricket: Father Roy played club cricket for Finchley CC;
brother Ian captained Essex U-19 and plays for Chelmsford CC and Stock
Exchange CC
Cricketing superstitions: Must go through a particular warm-up and practice
before every day's play; always keep wicket in a cap
Overseas tours: Young England to West Indies 1985
Overseas teams played for: Northerns-Goodwood CC, Cape Town, 1984–85,
1985–86; Western Province 'B' in Saab Castle Bowl, 1985–86
Cricketers particularly learnt from: Ray East, Graham Saville, Keith Pont,
Alan Knott, John Childs, Robin Jackman, Hylton Ackerman, Graham
Gooch, Keith Fletcher
Cricketers particularly admired: Alan Knott, Bob Taylor, Rod Marsh,
Graham Gooch, Keith Fletcher, Ken McEwan, John Childs
Off-season 1986–87: Keeping fit, coaching and relaxing at home
Other sports played: Soccer, squash, badminton, golf, tennis, snooker
Other sports followed: Most sports particularly soccer and West Ham United
FC
Relaxations: Relaxing at home, music, theatre, watching and playing sport,
TV, sleeping
Extras: Former schoolboy footballer with Spurs and Orient FC; joining
Somerset for 1987 on two-year contract to further career after spending 4
years at Essex; once took 8 stumpings in match v Kent 2nd XI at Dartford
1984; second XI cap 1984; Essex Young Player of Year 1984
Opinions on cricket: 'Should be a regular overseas tour in the winter of an
England Under 25 or 'B' team to bridge gap between young England and the

full side. More should be done by clubs to encourage players to work for the club in winter months in some promotional capacity. Would like to play on uncovered pitches for a season or two to see if fewer "contrived" matches take place. 2nd XI competition to be 16 3-day games playing each County once with venues switching alternate seasons. Better quality pitches at 2nd XI level and one 1st-class umpire to stand to raise umpiring level. All grounds should have top quality grass practice pitches available.'

Best batting performance: 29 Essex v Middlesex, Chelmsford 1986

LAST SEASON: BATTING

	I.	N.O.	R.	H.S.	AV.
TEST					
1ST-CLASS	3	0	54	29	18.00
INT					
JPL	–	–	–	–	–
NAT.W.					
B & H					

LAST SEASON: WICKET-KEEPING

	C.	ST.		
TEST				
1ST-CLASS	2	2		
INT				
JPL				
NAT.W.				
B & H				

CAREER: BATTING

	I.	N.O.	R.	H.S.	AV.
TEST					
1ST-CLASS	8	0	84	29	10.50
INT					
JPL	–	–	–	–	–
NAT.W.					
B & H					

CAREER: WICKET-KEEPING

	C.	ST.		
TEST				
1ST-CLASS	10	2		
INT				
JPL				
NAT.W.				
B & H				

BURROWS, D. A.   Gloucestershire

Full Name: Dean Andrew Burrows
Role: Right-hand bat, right-arm quick bowler
Born: 20 June 1966, Easington, Co Durham
Height: 6' 3" **Weight:** 13st 5lbs
Nickname: Deano
County debut: 1984
Parents: Michael Alec John and Barbara Michelle
Marital status: Single
Education: Shotton Hall School, Peterlee, Co Durham
Qualifications: 5 O-levels
Cricketers particularly learnt from: Dennis Lillee had everything

Cricketers particularly admired: Dennis Lillee, Bob Willis, Michael Holding
Off-season 1986–87: Playing for Hamilton in Auckland, New Zealand
Other sports played: Soccer, swimming, some tennis
Relaxations: 'Enjoy watching films, videos etc. I also love music.'
Extras: Represented Durham County in the Minor Counties when 17

LAST SEASON: BATTING

	I.	N.O.	R.	H.S.	AV.
TEST					
1ST-CLASS					
INT					
JPL	1	1	1	1*	
NAT.W.					
B & H					

LAST SEASON: BOWLING

	O.	M.	R.	W.	AV.
TEST					
1ST-CLASS					
INT					
JPL	8	0	38	1	
NAT.W.					
B & H					

CAREER: BATTING

	I.	N.O.	R.	H.S.	AV.
TEST					
1ST-CLASS	1	0	0	0	–
INT					
JPL	2	2	1	1*	–
NAT.W.					
B & H					

CAREER: BOWLING

	O.	M.	R.	W.	AV.
TEST					
1ST-CLASS	15	0	76	0	–
INT					
JPL	13	0	70	2	35.00
NAT.W.					
B & H					

BUTCHER, A. R. Glamorgan

Full Name: Alan Raymond Butcher
Role: Left-hand bat, slow left-arm and medium bowler
Born: 7 January 1954, Croydon
Height: 5′ 8″ **Weight:** 11st 7lbs
Nickname: Butch, Budgie
County debut: 1972 (Surrey)
County cap: 1975 (Surrey)
Test debut: 1979
No. of Tests: 1
No. of One-Day Internationals: 1
1000 runs in a season: 7
1st-Class 50s scored: 69
1st-Class 100s scored: 28
1st-Class 200s scored: 1
1st-Class 5 w. in innings: 1
One-Day 50s: 40
One-Day 100s: 4
Place in batting averages: 142nd av. 25.36 (1985 87th av. 32.72)

Place in bowling averages: — (1985 122nd av. 44.90)
1st-Class catches 1986: 6 (career: 132)
Parents: Raymond and Jackie
Wife and date of marriage: Elaine, 27 September 1972
Children: Mark, Gary, Lisa
Education: Heath Clark Grammar School
Qualifications: 5 O-levels, 1 A-level
Jobs outside cricket: Football coach, PE master, Cumnor House School, South Croydon, Surrey
Family links with cricket: Brother, Martin, an MCC Young Professional; Brother, Ian, joined Leicestershire in 1979, making debut v Surrey in John Player League
Other sports played: Football
Relaxations: Most sport, rock music, reading
Extras: Scored a century before lunch v Glamorgan at The Oval, 1980. Released by Surrey after 1986 season and joined Glamorgan
Best batting performance: 216 Surrey v Cambridge University, Cambridge 1980
Best bowling performance: 6-48 Surrey v Hampshire, Guildford 1972

LAST SEASON: BATTING

	I.	N.O.	R.	H.S.	AV.
TEST					
1ST-CLASS	25	0	634	157	25.36
INT					
JPL	11	0	283	64	25.72
NAT.W.	3	0	65	38	21.66
B & H	4	0	126	65	31.50

LAST SEASON: BOWLING

	O.	M.	R.	W.	AV.
TEST					
1ST-CLASS	111	28	305	13	23.46
INT					
JPL	20.2	0	71	4	17.75
NAT.W.	19	3	57	2	28.50
B & H	7	2	23	2	11.50

CAREER: BATTING

	I.	N.O.	R.	H.S.	AV.
TEST	2	0	34	20	17.00
1ST-CLASS	488	43	14700	216*	33.03
INT	1	0	14	14	–
JPL	164	17	4233	113*	28.79
NAT.W.	25	3	615	86*	27.95
B & H	51	4	1203	80	25.59

CAREER: BOWLING

	O.	M.	R.	W.	AV.
TEST	2	0	9	0	–
1ST-CLASS	1515.2	316	4799	126	38.08
INT					
JPL	323.2	22	1420	36	39.44
NAT.W.	67.2	10	249	5	49.80
B & H	168.3	30	507	24	21.12

31. How many England captains have been Middlesex players, and who were they?

32. Who was the last Gloucestershire player to play for England before Bill Athey in 1986, and when?

BUTCHER, I. P.   Leicestershire

Full Name: Ian Paul Butcher
Role: Right-hand bat, slip fielder
Born: 1 July 1962, Farnborough, Kent
Height: 6′ 0″ **Weight:** 13st 7lbs
Nickname: Butch, Dog
County debut: 1980
County cap: 1984
1000 runs in a season: 2
1st-Class 50s scored: 17
1st-Class 100s scored: 9
One-Day 50s: 5
One-Day 100s: 2
Place in batting averages: 210th av. 15.16 (1985 83rd av. 33.11)
1st-Class catches 1986: 11 (career: 72)

Parents: Ray and Jackie
Wife and date of marriage: Marie, 12 March 1983
Education: John Ruskin High School
Jobs outside cricket: Football coach, Cumnor House School, South Croydon. Asst Sports Director, Leicester University.
Family links with cricket: Brother, Alan, Surrey CCC and England. Brother, Martin, MCC Young Pros
Cricketing superstitions: 'I have many! . . . If I score runs I like to do everything (if possible) the same, the following day. I always wear a sweat-band on left wrist while batting.'
Overseas tours: England Young Cricketers tour of West Indies 1980
Cricketers particularly learnt from: Brian Davison, Graham Gooch, Chris Balderstone
Other sports played: Football, golf. 'I try my hand at anything!'
Relaxations: Sleeping, good beer, good food
Extras: Made his debut for Leicestershire CCC in the John Player League 1979 v Surrey, the team for which his brother, Alan Butcher, played. Made his county debut 1980 v Oxford University. Scored century on championship debut at Grace Road
Best batting performance: 139 Leicestershire v Nottinghamshire, Leicester 1983

LAST SEASON: BATTING

	I.	N.O.	R.	H.S.	AV.
TEST					
1ST-CLASS	19	1	273	58	15.16
INT					
JPL	5	1	100	43	25.00
NAT.W.					
B & H	3	1	115	103*	57.50

CAREER: BATTING

	I.	N.O.	R.	H.S.	AV.
TEST					
1ST-CLASS	141	9	4025	139	30.49
INT					
JPL	47	3	843	71	19.15
NAT.W.	6	0	170	81	28.33
B & H	14	1	547	103*	42.07

LAST SEASON: BOWLING

	O.	M.	R.	W.	AV.
TEST					
1ST-CLASS	2	0	4	0	–
INT					
JPL					
NAT.W.					
B & H					

CAREER: BOWLING

	O.	M.	R.	W.	AV.
TEST					
1ST-CLASS	8	2	24	1	–
INT					
JPL	1	0	4	0	–
NAT.W.	0.3	0	6	1	–
B & H					

BUTCHER, R. O.   Middlesex

Full Name: Roland Orlando Butcher
Role: Right-hand bat, right-arm medium bowler
Born: 14 October 1953, East Point, St Philip, Barbados
Height: 5′ 7″ **Weight:** 12st
Nickname: Butch
County debut: 1974
County cap: 1979
Test debut: 1980–81
No. of Tests: 3
No. of One-Day Internationals: 3
1000 runs in a season: 4
1st-Class 50s scored: 58
1st-Class 100s scored: 14
One-Day 50s: 20
One-Day 100s: 1
Place in batting averages: 99th
av. 30.78 (1985 56th av. 37.81)
1st-Class catches 1986: 15 (career: 244)
Parents: Robert and Doreen
Wife: Cheryl Denise
Children: Paul Nicholas Roland, 2 January 1979; Michelle Denise, 11 November 1982
Education: Secondary
Qualifications: Advanced Cricket Coaching Certificate, Football Association

Preliminary Coaching Certificate

Jobs outside cricket: Coaching. Played semi-professional soccer for Biggles-
wade and Stevenage. Football coach. Insurance salesman

Family links with cricket: Cousin is Basil Butcher, of Guyana and West Indies

Overseas teams played for: Barbados 1974–75 in Shell Shield Competition.
Spent 1979–80 off season playing cricket in Barbados

Other sport played: Football

Relaxations: Television, horse-racing, cinema

Extras: Arrived in England aged 13. Does work for Inter-Action Group in
deprived areas of London. A devout member of the Anglican church

Best batting performance: 197 Middlesex v Yorkshire, Lord's 1982

LAST SEASON: BATTING

	I.	N.O.	R.	H.S.	AV.
TEST					
1ST-CLASS	37	4	1016	171	30.78
INT					
JPL	11	1	138	42*	13.80
NAT.W.	2	1	40	30	–
B & H	6	0	128	65	21.33

LAST SEASON: BOWLING

	O.	M.	R.	W.	AV.
TEST					
1ST-CLASS	13.4	2	49	2	24.30
INT					
JPL	0.4	0	1	0	–
NAT.W.					
B & H					

CAREER: BATTING

	I.	N.O.	R.	H.S.	AV.
TEST	5	0	71	32	14.20
1ST-CLASS	348	35	9972	197	31.85
INT	3	0	58	52	19.33
JPL	125	11	2501	100	21.93
NAT.W.	21	3	319	59	17.72
B & H	22	2	455	85	22.75

CAREER: BOWLING

	O.	M.	R.	W.	AV.
TEST					
1ST-CLASS	45.4	9	171	4	42.75
INT					
JPL	1.2	0	5	0	–
NAT.W.	2	0	18	1	–
B & H					

33. Which England cricket captain is descended from the poet
Robert Browning?

34. What was significant about Gavaskar playing for India in
England at Edgbaston in 1986?

35. How many players did England play in the 3-match Test Series
in India in 1986?

36. Who kept wicket for England v New Zealand at Lord's in July
1986?

37. Which countries were the finalists in the 1986 ICC Trophy?

BYAS, D. Yorkshire

Full Name: David Byas
Role: Left-hand bat, right-arm
medium bowler, slip or cover fielder
Born: 26 August 1963, Kilham,
Driffield
Height: 6′ 4″ **Weight:** 13st 7lbs
Nickname: Billy, Bingo
County debut: 1985
1st-Class catches 1986: 1 (career: 1)
Parents: Richard and Anne
Marital status: Single
Education: Scarborough College
Qualifications: 1 O-level (Engineering)
Jobs outside cricket: Farmer
Cricketers particularly learnt from:
'Too numerous to say.'
Coached by F. S. Trueman, Don
Wilson

Cricketers particularly admired: D. Gower, I. Botham, V. Richards
Other sports played: Hockey, squash
Relaxations: Game shooting, watching rallies
Injuries 1986: Bad disc strain in lower spine
Extras: Scarborough Cricket Club captain. Only player to score 200 (n.o.) in Yorkshire League, most runs in Yorkshire League (broke M. Crowe's record). 2nd XI cap 1986

LAST SEASON: BATTING

	I.	N.O.	R.	H.S.	AV.
TEST					
1ST-CLASS	1	0	0	0	–
INT					
JPL	1	0	10	10	–
NAT.W.					
B & H					

LAST SEASON: BOWLING

	O.	M.	R.	W.	AV.
TEST					
1ST-CLASS	2	0	15	0	–
INT					
JPL					
NAT.W.					
B & H					

CAREER: BATTING

	I.	N.O.	R.	H.S.	AV.
TEST					
1ST-CLASS	1	0	0	0	–
INT					
JPL	2	0	25	15	12.50
NAT.W.					
B & H	1	0	2	2	–

CAREER: BOWLING

	O.	M.	R.	W.	AV.
TEST					
1ST-CLASS	2	0	15	0	–
INT					
JPL					
NAT.W.					
B & H					

CANN, M. J. Glamorgan

Full Name: Michael James Cann
Role: Left-hand bat, right-arm
off-break bowler
Born: 4 July 1965, Cardiff
Height: 5′ 9″ **Weight:** 11½st
Nickname: Tin, Canny
County debut: 1986
Parents: Leslie and Catherine
Marital status: Single
Education: St Illtyds College,
Cardiff; Swansea University
Qualifications: 10 O-levels,
3 A-levels (Physics, Chemistry
and Biology)
Cricketers particularly learnt from:
Tom Cartwright, Alan Jones,
Tony Cordle
Cricketers particularly admired:
Barry Lloyd
Off-season 1986–87: Doing final year at university (Biochemistry degree)
Other sports played: Squash, cards, snooker
Other sports followed: Football (Cardiff City), American football on TV
Relaxations: Playing cards (3 card brag), general socialising, going out for meals
Opinions on cricket: 'Quicker wickets with more even bounce would benefit the game as bowlers would be more effective and batters could also play their shots. Wrong to go back to uncovered wickets.'

LAST SEASON: BATTING

	I.	N.O.	R.	H.S.	AV.
TEST					
1ST-CLASS	1	1	16	16*	–
INT					
JPL					
NAT.W.					
B & H					

LAST SEASON: BOWLING

	O.	M.	R.	W.	AV.
TEST					
1ST-CLASS	1	1	0	0	–
INT					
JPL					
NAT.W.					
B & H					

CAREER: BATTING

	I.	N.O.	R.	H.S.	AV.
TEST					
1ST-CLASS	1	1	16	16*	–
INT					
JPL					
NAT.W.					
B & H					

CAREER: BOWLING

	O.	M.	R.	W.	AV.
TEST					
1ST-CLASS	1	1	0	0	–
INT					
JPL					
NAT.W.					
B & H					

CAPEL, D. J.   Northamptonshire

Full Name: David John Capel
Role: Right-hand bat, right-arm
medium bowler
Born: 6 July 1963, Northampton
Height: 6′ **Weight:** 12st 6lbs
Nickname: Capes
County debut: 1981
County cap: 1986
50 wickets in a season: 1
1st-Class 50s scored: 17
1st-Class 100s scored: 1
1st-Class 5 w. in innings: 4
One-day 50s: 4
Place in batting averages: 108th
av. 29.41 (1985 147th av. 24.96)
Place in bowling averages: 68th
av. 32.44 (1985 64th av. 31.68)
1st-Class catches 1986: 11
(career: 48)
Parents: John and Angela Janet
Wife and date of marriage: Debbie, 21 September 1985
Education: Roade Primary and Roade Comprehensive School
Qualifications: 3 O-levels, 5 CSEs, NCA Coaching Certificate
Jobs outside cricket: Hand-made surgical shoemaker off-season when 16–17
Family links with cricket: Father and brother Andrew played in local league
cricket
Overseas tours: Dubai with *The Cricketer XI*, 1983
Overseas teams played for: Latrobe, Tasmania, 1982–83; Westview CC, Port
Elizabeth, 1983–85; Grey School and Eastern Province, 1985–86

LAST SEASON: BATTING

	I.	N.O.	R.	H.S.	AV.
TEST					
1ST-CLASS	36	7	853	111	29.41
INT					
JPL	13	1	423	61	35.25
NAT.W.	1	0	13	13	–
B & H	5	2	84	43*	28.00

LAST SEASON: BOWLING

	O.	M.	R.	W.	AV.
TEST					
1ST-CLASS	633.1	131	2044	63	32.44
INT					
JPL	92	3	371	12	30.91
NAT.W.	12	1	29	1	–
B & H	45	10	116	5	23.20

CAREER: BATTING

	I.	N.O.	R.	H.S.	AV.
TEST					
1ST-CLASS	151	28	3452	111	28.06
INT					
JPL	52	14	994	79	26.15
NAT.W.	8	3	106	27	21.20
B & H	13	4	194	43*	21.55

CAREER: BOWLING

	O.	M.	R.	W.	AV.
TEST					
1ST-CLASS	1422.2	259	4907	134	36.61
INT					
JPL	232	7	1165	44	26.47
NAT.W.	34	2	138	4	34.50
B & H	89	15	285	12	23.75

Cricketers particularly learnt from: Brian Reynolds (coach) and many others
Cricketers particularly admired: Barry Richards, Richard Hadlee
Off-season 1986–87: Playing and coaching overseas
Other sports played: Golf
Relaxations: Enjoys swimming and eating out at restaurants
Extras: Played for Young England 1982
Best batting performance: 111 Northamptonshire v Leicestershire, Northampton 1986
Best bowling performance: 7-86 Northamptonshire v Derbyshire, Derby 1986

CARR, J. D.   Middlesex

Full Name: John Donald Carr
Role: Right-hand bat, right-arm off-break bowler, slip fielder
Born: 15 June 1963, St John's Wood
Height: 6' **Weight:** 11st 10lbs
Nickname: Carsi
County debut: 1983
1st-Class 50s scored: 9
1st-Class 100s scored: 4
1st-Class 5 w. in innings: 3
One-day 50s: 3
Place in batting averages: 79th av. 34.00 (1985: 94th av. 31.60)
Place in bowling averages: —
(1985 84th av. 36.24)
1st-Class catches 1986: 11 (career: 31)
Parents: Donald and Stella
Education: The Hall School, Repton School and Oxford University (Worcester College)
Qualifications: BA Hons (Philosophy, Politics and Economics)
Jobs outside cricket: Taught for one term at St George's School, Windsor; worked briefly at DHSS in Oxford
Family links with cricket: Father, D. B. Carr, is secretary of TCCB and played for Oxford University, Derbyshire and England, captaining all three at some stage
Overseas tours: Australia with Repton Pilgrims 1982–83; La Manga with Hertfordshire 1983; Australia and Hong Kong with Oxbridge 1985–86
Overseas teams: Sydney University, 1986
Crickets particularly admired: Viv Richards, Ian Botham

Off-season 1986–87: Coaching and playing for Weston Creek CC in Canberra, Australia

Other sports played: Eton fives, golf, squash, soccer

Injuries 1986: Split webbing between thumb and forefinger on left hand – out for 10 days

Relaxations: Eating, sleeping, reading, TV and cinema

Extras: Played for Oxford in Varsity Match 1984. Secretary of University in 1984. Came on as substitute fielder for Middlesex in the 1983 Benson and Hedges Cup Final, holding a vital catch to help his side defeat Essex. Received special clearance to play in the match having previously appeared for Combined Universities in the same competition

Best batting performance: 123 Oxford University v Lancashire, Oxford 1984

Best bowling performance: 6-61 Middlesex v Gloucestershire, Lord's 1985

LAST SEASON: BATTING

	I.	N.O.	R.	H.S.	AV.
TEST					
1ST-CLASS	26	3	782	84*	34.00
INT					
JPL	9	3	186	45*	31.00
NAT.W.					
B & H					

LAST SEASON: BOWLING

	O.	M.	R.	W.	AV.
TEST					
1ST-CLASS	93.2	17	284	1	–
INT					
JPL	21	1	103	3	34.33
NAT.W.					
B & H					

CAREER: BATTING

	I.	N.O.	R.	H.S.	AV.
TEST					
1ST-CLASS	76	8	1791	123	26.33
INT					
JPL	11	4	190	45*	27.14
NAT.W.					
B & H	9	1	269	67	33.63

CAREER: BOWLING

	O.	M.	R.	W.	AV.
TEST					
1ST-CLASS	855.3	225	2261	49	46.14
INT					
JPL	21	1	103	3	34.33
NAT.W.					
B & H	79.2	9	318	7	45.42

38. Whose autobiography is entitled 'Flat Jack'?

39. When did Graham Gooch make his Test debut?

40. Which England captain won a DSO and a MC in the Second World War?

41. Who was the first Englishman to reach 1000 runs in the 1986 English season?

CARRICK, P.   Yorkshire

Full Name: Phillip Carrick
Role: Right-hand bat, slow left-arm
bowler, slip fielder
Born: 16 July 1952, Leeds
Height: 6′ 0″ **Weight:** 14st
Nickname: Fergie
County debut: 1970
County cap: 1976
Benefit: 1985
50 wickets in a season: 7
1st-Class 50s scored: 26
1st-Class 100s scored: 3
1st-Class 5 w. in innings: 5
One-day 50s: 2
Place in batting averages: 154th
av. 24.50 (1985 162nd av. 23.48)
Place in bowling averages: 109th
av. 43.05 (1985 49th av. 29.59)
1st-Class catches 1986: 11 (career: 159)
Parents: Arthur (deceased) and Ivy
Wife and date of marriage: Elspeth, 2 April 1977
Children: Emma Elizabeth, 6 May 1980; Phillipa Louse, 11 January 1982
Education: Bramley CS, Intake CS, Park Lane College of Further Education
Qualifications: 2 O-levels, 8 CSEs, NCA Coaching Certificate
Jobs outside cricket: Company Director, coach
Family links with cricket: 'Father and brother useful league players.'
Cricket superstitions: Left pad on first
Overseas tours: Toured with Derrick Robins XI to South Africa 1975–76; Far
East 1977

LAST SEASON: BATTING

	I.	N.O.	R.	H.S.	AV.
TEST					
1ST-CLASS	32	6	637	51	24.50
INT					
JPL	12	3	157	39*	17.44
NAT.W.	2	0	54	54	27.00
B & H	2	0	24	14	12.00

CAREER: BATTING

	I.	N.O.	R.	H.S.	AV.
TEST					
1ST-CLASS	390	72	7003	131*	22.02
INT					
JPL	89	27	879	43*	14.17
NAT.W.	15	2	206	54	15.84
B & H	22	4	230	53	12.77

LAST SEASON: BOWLING

	O.	M.	R.	W.	AV.
TEST					
1ST-CLASS	621.3	186	1550	36	43.05
INT					
JPL	100.1	3	449	19	23.63
NAT.W.	36	3	69	5	13.80
B & H	36.4	2	135	6	22.50

CAREER: BOWLING

	O.	M.	R.	W.	AV.
TEST					
1ST-CLASS	9094.2	2916	22780	756	30.13
INT					
JPL	615	27	2718	86	31.60
NAT.W.	146.5	30	389	14	27.78
B & H	272.3	38	927	28	33.10

Overseas teams played for: Eastern Province in 1976–77 Currie Cup Competition; Northern Transvaal 1982–83
Cricketers particularly learnt from: Geoff Boycott, Ray Illingworth, Mike Fearnley
Off-season 1986–87: In England
Other sports played: Golf
Other sports followed: Rugby
Extras: Appointed Yorkshire captain for 1987
Best batting performance: 131* Yorkshire v Northamptonshire, Northampton 1980
Best bowling performance: 8-33 Yorkshire v Cambridge University, Cambridge 1973

CHADWICK, M. R. Lancashire

Full Name: Mark Robert Chadwick
Role: Right-hand bat, right-arm off-break bowler
Born: 9 February 1963, Rochdale
Height: 6' 1" **Weight:** 13st
Nickname: Chad
County debut: 1983
1st-Class 50s scored: 5
1st-Class 100s scored: 1
One-day 50s: 1
Place in batting averages: 158th av. 23.50 (1985 137th av. 25.63)
1st-Class catches 1986: 6 (career: 14)
Parents: Robert and Kathleen
Education: Moorhouse County Primary School, Milnrow; Roch Valley High School, Milnrow
Qualifications: 2 O-levels
Jobs outside cricket: Storeman for diesel engine firm; window cleaner

Family links with cricket: 'Father club cricketer and now umpires in C Lancashire League. Mother washes all my kit and is very good critic but knows nothing about the game.'
Cricketing superstitions: 'Trying not to make a habit of fielding at short leg.'
Overseas tours: Barbados 1984 with Lancashire
Overseas teams played for: In Queensland, 1985–86
Cricketers particularly learnt from: Picked up lots of helpful tips from all the staff at Lancashire

Cricketers particularly admired: Geoffrey Boycott – powers of concentration while at the crease, Viv Richards – domination of bowlers
Other sports played: Football, table-tennis, badminton, golf
Other sports followed: Very keen rugby league fan
Relaxations: Listening to music
Extras: Central Lancashire League record run scorer for amateur. 1267 runs for Milnrow CC in 1983, beating the previous record of 1205 from 1915. Won gold award in first B & H match (1984 semi-final)
Best batting performance: 132 Lancashire v Somerset, Old Trafford 1985

LAST SEASON: BATTING

	I.	N.O.	R.	H.S.	AV.
TEST					
1ST-CLASS	18	0	423	61	23.50
INT					
JPL					
NAT.W.					
B & H					

LAST SEASON: BOWLING

	O.	M.	R.	W.	AV.
TEST					
1ST-CLASS	5	0	51	0	–
INT					
JPL					
NAT.W.					
B & H					

CAREER: BATTING

	I.	N.O.	R.	H.S.	AV.
TEST					
1ST-CLASS	51	1	1128	132	22.56
INT					
JPL	3	0	16	10	5.33
NAT.W.	1	0	43	43	–
B & H	1	0	87	87	–

CAREER: BOWLING

	O.	M.	R.	W.	AV.
TEST					
1ST-CLASS	7	0	71	0	–
INT					
JPL					
NAT.W.					
B & H					

CHILDS, J. H. Essex

Full Name: John Henry Childs
Role: Left-hand bat, slow left-arm orthodox bowler
Born: 15 August 1951, Plymouth
Height: 6′ 0″ **Weight:** 12st 6lbs
Nickname: Charlie
County debut: 1975 (Gloucestershire), 1985 (Essex)
County cap: 1977 (Gloucestershire), 1986 (Essex)
Testimonial match: 1985
50 wickets in a season: 3
1st-Class 5 w. in innings: 26
1st-Class 10 w. in match: 5
Place in batting averages: 218th av. 13.37
Place in bowling averages: 3rd av. 16.28

1st-Class catches 1986: 4 (career: 68)
Parents: Sydney and Barbara (both deceased)
Wife and date of marriage: Jane Anne, 11 November 1978
Children: Lee Robert, 28 November 1980; Scott Alexander, 21 August 1984
Education: Audley Park Secondary Modern, Torquay
Qualifications: Advanced Cricket Coach
Jobs outside cricket: Signwriter
Overseas tours: Zambia, 1977; Barbados, 1983
Overseas teams played for: Spent winter 1979–80 coaching in Gisborne, New Zealand and 1982–83 in Auckland for Howice-Pakuranga
Cricketers particularly admired: G. Sobers, M. Procter
Other sports played: Most ball games
Relaxations: 'Watching rugby, decorating at home, walking on moors and beaches. My family.'
Extras: Played for Devon 1973–74. Released by Gloucestershire at end of 1984 and joined Essex. Granted Testimonial Match by Gloucestershire v Essex in 1985
Best batting performance: 34* Gloucestershire v Nottinghamshire, Cheltenham 1982
Best bowling performance: 9-56 Gloucestershire v Somerset, Bristol 1981

LAST SEASON: BATTING

	I.	N.O.	R.	H.S.	AV.
TEST					
1ST-CLASS	23	7	214	34	13.37
INT					
JPL					
NAT.W.					
B & H					

LAST SEASON: BOWLING

	O.	M.	R.	W.	AV.
TEST					
1ST-CLASS	640.1	212	1449	89	16.28
INT					
JPL					
NAT.W.					
B & H					

CAREER: BATTING

	I.	N.O.	R.	H.S.	AV.
TEST					
1ST-CLASS	178	80	766	34*	7.81
INT					
JPL	19	10	74	16*	8.22
NAT.W.	4	3	22	14*	–
B & H	7	5	25	10	12.50

CAREER: BOWLING

	O.	M.	R.	W.	AV.
TEST					
1ST-CLASS	5811.5	1712	15445	515	29.99
INT					
JPL	318.1	17	1444	39	37.02
NAT.W.	60	12	180	7	25.71
B & H	156	35	466	14	33.29

42. Which three New Zealanders all hit their highest Test score in the Second Test v England at Trent Bridge in August 1986?

43 Which legendary England cricketer told Victor Trumper that 'he would never make a batsman'?

CLARKE, S. T.　　　　　　　　Surrey

Full Name: Sylvester Theophilus Clarke
Role: Right-hand bat, right-arm fast bowler, gully fielder
Born: 11 December 1955, Lead Vale, Christchurch, Barbados
Height: 6′ 2″ **Weight:** 15st
Nickname: Silvers
County debut: 1979
County cap: 1980
Test debut: 1977–78
No. of Tests: 11
No. of One-Day Internationals: 10
50 wickets in a season: 4
1st-Class 50s scored: 4
1st-Class 100s scored: 1
1st-Class 5 w. in innings: 46
1st-Class 10 w. in match: 6
Place in batting averages: 197th av. 17.33

Place in bowling averages: 4th av. 16.79
1st-Class catches 1986: 9 (career: 110)
Parents: Marjorie and Ashton
Children: Desiree, 8 December 1974; Dawn, 18 August 1976; Shelly, 2 July 1978
Education: St Bartholomew Boys' School
Jobs outside cricket: Carpenter
Family links with cricket: Half-brother Damien is professional at Todmorden
Overseas tours: Toured with West Indies to India and Sri Lanka, 1978–79; Pakistan 1980–81; Australia 1981; and South Africa 1982–83 and 1983–84
Overseas teams played for: Local club in Barbados Cricket League, Transvaal, 'Rebel' West Indians in S Africa
Cricketers particularly learnt from: V. Holder
Other sports played: Football
Other sports followed: Watch tennis
Relaxations: 'Music and parties.'
Extras: Made fastest century of the 1981 season in 62 mins v Glamorgan. Took championship hat-trick in 1980 season v Nottinghamshire
Best batting performance: 100* Surrey v Glamorgan, Swansea 1981
Best bowling performance: 7-34 West Indies XI v South Africa, Johannesburg 1983–84

	I.	N.O.	R.	H.S.	AV.
TEST					
1ST-CLASS	13	4	156	32*	17.33
INT					
JPL	3	2	31	15	–
NAT.W.	3	1	55	23	27.50
B & H	2	0	4	4	2.00

CAREER: BATTING

	I.	N.O.	R.	H.S.	AV.
TEST	16	5	172	35*	15.64
1ST-CLASS	199	35	2522	100*	15.37
INT	8	2	60	20	10.00
JPL	46	11	436	34*	12.45
NAT.W.	11	4	159	45*	22.71
B & H	23	4	172	39	9.05

LAST SEASON: BOWLING

	O.	M.	R.	W.	AV.
TEST					
1ST-CLASS	341.3	95	806	48	16.79
INT					
JPL	52.1	2	211	8	26.37
NAT.W.	30.3	13	47	6	7.83
B & H	33	3	86	3	28.66

CAREER: BOWLING

	O.	M.	R.	W.	AV.
TEST	412.5	79	1171	42	27.88
1ST-CLASS	5523	1443	14083	716	19.66
INT	87.2	13	245	13	18.85
JPL	471.3	44	1858	77	24.12
NAT.W.	189.2	50	432	25	17.28
B & H	326.4	73	866	53	16.33

CLIFT, P. B.   Leicestershire

Full Name: Patrick Bernard Clift
Role: Right-hand bat, right-arm medium bowler
Born: 14 July 1953, Salisbury, Rhodesia
Height: 6′ 1″ **Weight:** 14st
Nickname: Paddy, Paddles
County debut: 1975
County cap: 1976
50 wickets in a season: 6
1st-Class 50s scored: 27
1st-Class 100s scored: 2
1st-Class 5 w. in innings: 23
1st-Class 10 w. in match: 2
One-day 50s: 4
Place in batting averages: 152nd av. 24.66 (1985 161st av. 23.57)
Place in bowling averages: 12th av. 22.26 (1985 55th av. 30.76)
1st-Class catches 1986: 13 (career: 152)
Parents: George Neville and Ivy Susan
Wife and date of marriage: Penelope Anne, 18 May 1978
Children: Robert William Patrick, 16 September 1982; Josephine Anne, 10 May 1984
Education: St Michael's; Hartmann House, St George's College
Qualifications: O-level
Jobs outside cricket: Accounting, insurance

Overseas tours: Rhodesia Ridgebacks 1974 UK tour
Overseas teams played for: Rhodesia, Natal
Cricketers particularly learnt from: Robin Jackman, Mike Procter, Duncan Fletcher, Jack Birkenshaw, Roger Tolchard, Ken Higgs, Jim Cornford, school coach at St George's College
Other sports played: Squash, golf, tennis, jogging
Relaxations: Stamp collecting, reading, listening to records
Extras: Debut for Rhodesia 1971–72. Took 8 wickets for 17 in opening match in 1976 season v MCC. Performed hat-trick in 1976 at Grace Road v Yorkshire. Suffered from injury in 1981 and 1982 season. Rhodesian 7th wicket partnership record of 174 with Howie Gardiner v Western Province, and Rhodesian 9th wicket partnership of 154 with Robin Jackman v Eastern Province, both in Currie Cup Competition, South Africa
Best batting performance: 106 Leicestershire v Essex, Chelmsford 1985
Best bowling performance: 8-17 Leicestershire v MCC, Lord's 1976

LAST SEASON: BATTING

	I.	N.O.	R.	H.S.	AV.
TEST					
1ST-CLASS	16	1	370	49	24.66
INT					
JPL	5	1	43	13*	10.75
NAT.W.	–	–	–	–	–
B & H	3	1	32	25*	16.00

CAREER: BATTING

	I.	N.O.	R.	H.S.	AV.
TEST					
1ST-CLASS	414	87	7671	106*	23.45
INT					
JPL	85	27	1163	51*	20.05
NAT.W.	16	5	244	48*	22.18
B & H	25	4	389	91	18.52

LAST SEASON: BOWLING

	O.	M.	R.	W.	AV.
TEST					
1ST-CLASS	413.3	120	1002	45	22.26
INT					
JPL	58	4	251	8	31.57
NAT.W.	12	1	39	2	19.50
B & H	40	5	147	5	29.40

CAREER: BOWLING

	O.	M.	R.	W.	AV.
TEST					
1ST-CLASS	8018.3	2115	20236	816	24.79
INT					
JPL	862.3	64	3561	158	22.53
NAT.W.	171.3	20	613	19	32.26
B & H	370.4	51	1255	47	26.70

44. Which current England player's wife had twin daughters in the same week as he hit a Test century?

45. What was special about Derek Pringle's first innings in the Lord's Test v India in June 1986?

46. Which England Test cricketer pulled a muscle by sneezing?

47. Which England Test cricketer pulled a muscle writing a letter?

CLINTON, G. S.　　　　　　　　　Surrey

Full Name: Graham Selvey Clinton
Role: Left-hand bat, right-arm
medium bowler
Born: 5 May 1953, Sidcup
Nickname: Clint
County debut: 1974 (Kent),
1979 (Surrey)
County cap: 1980 (Surrey)
1000 runs in a season: 5
1st-Class 50s scored: 49
1st-Class 100s scored: 15
One-day 50s: 19
One-day 100s: 3
Place in batting averages: 87th
av. 33.12 (1985 25th av. 47.11)
1st-Class catches 1986: 10
(career: 69)
Education: Chislehurst and
Sidcup Grammar School
Family links with cricket: Younger brothers Neil and Tony are regular
members of the Blackheath team
Overseas tours: West Indies with England Young Cricketers 1972
Extras: Formerly played for Kent, where he made his debut 1974. Left after
1978 season to join Surrey. Renowned as a dressing-room wit. At age 11, he
played for Kemnal Manor, Kent. Later played club cricket for Sidcup and for
Blackheath
Best batting performance: 192 Surrey v Yorkshire, The Oval 1984
Best bowling performance: 2-8 Kent v Pakistan, Canterbury 1978

LAST SEASON: BATTING

	I.	N.O.	R.	H.S.	AV.
TEST					
1ST-CLASS	35	4	1027	117	33.12
INT					
JPL	14	2	567	92*	47.25
NAT.W.	4	0	88	49	22.00
B & H	3	0	82	47	27.33

LAST SEASON: BOWLING

	O.	M.	R.	W.	AV.
TEST					
1ST-CLASS	3	1	12	0	–
INT					
JPL					
NAT.W.					
B & H					

CAREER: BATTING

	I.	N.O.	R.	H.S.	AV.
TEST					
1ST-CLASS	319	39	9054	192	32.33
INT					
JPL	60	9	1670	105*	32.74
NAT.W.	17	1	526	146	32.87
B & H	33	1	976	106*	30.50

CAREER: BOWLING

	O.	M.	R.	W.	AV.
TEST					
1ST-CLASS	26	2	185	4	46.25
INT					
JPL					
NAT.W.	4	2	2	0	–
B & H	1.2	0	10	0	–

Full Name: Russell Alan Cobb
Role: Right-hand bat, slow left-arm bowler, short-leg fielder – 'great!'
Born: 18 May 1961, Leicester
Height: 5′ 11″ **Weight:** 11st 5lbs
Nickname: Cobby
County debut: 1980
County cap: 1986
1000 runs in a season: 1
1st-Class 50s scored: 17
Place in batting averages: 118th av. 28.23 (1985 92nd av. 31.65)
1st-Class catches 1986: 9 (career: 46)
Parents: Alan and Betty
Wife and date of marriage: Sharon, 30 March 1985
Education: Woodbank School, Leicester; Trent College, Nottingham
Qualifications: 7 O-levels, NCA Advanced Coaching Certificate
Jobs outside cricket: Clerk for British Shoe Corporation, Leicester. Worked on promotion for Leicestershire CCC
Family links with cricket: Father a club cricketer. Godfather, Maurice Hallam, former Leicestershire captain
Cricketing superstitions: 'Always put my left pad on first. Must wear some sort of headgear.'
Overseas tours: Australia with Young England in 1979; West Indies with Young England in 1980; Zimbabwe with Leicestershire in 1981

LAST SEASON: BATTING

	I.	N.O.	R.	H.S.	AV.
TEST					
1ST-CLASS	41	3	1092	91	28.73
INT					
JPL	2	2	11	10*	–
NAT.W.	3	0	57	26	19.00
B & H	2	0	26	22	13.00

LAST SEASON: BOWLING

	O.	M.	R.	W.	AV.
TEST					
1ST-CLASS	10	3	41	0	–
INT					
JPL					
NAT.W.					

CAREER: BATTING

	I.	N.O.	R.	H.S.	AV.
TEST					
1ST-CLASS	132	8	3028	91	24.41
INT					
JPL	6	4	60	24	30.00
NAT.W.	3	0	57	26	19.00
B & H	2	0	26	22	13.00

CAREER: BOWLING

	O.	M.	R.	W.	AV.
TEST					
1ST-CLASS	14	5	46	0	–
INT					
JPL					
NAT.W.					

Overseas teams played for: Glenelg, Adelaide, South Australia, 1980–81; Teachers Training College, Pretoria, 1983–84, 1984–85
Cricketers particularly learnt from: Jack Birkenshaw, Chris Balderstone
Cricketers particularly admired: 'All who have played top class cricket for a number of years.'
Off-season 1986–87: Working for the club on advertising and promotion
Other sports played: Squash, badminton
Other sports followed: Watching rugby and football
Relaxations: 'A little gardening, walking, eating out.'
Best batting performance: 91 Leicestershire v Northamptonshire, Leicester 1986

CONNOR, C. A.   Hampshire

Full Name: Cardigan Adolphus Connor
Role: Right-hand bat, right-arm fast-medium bowler
Born: 24 March 1961, West End, Anguilla
Height: 5′ 10″ **Weight:** 11st 6lbs
Nickname: 'Christy, Cardy and many more.'
County debut: 1984
1st-Class 5 w. in innings: 2
Place in batting averages: —
(1985 231st av. 13.00)
Place in bowling averages: 71st av. 32.97 (1985 110th av. 41.91)
1st-Class catches 1986: 3
(career: 19)
Parents: Ethleen Snagg
Marital status: Single
Education: Valley Secondary School, Anguilla; Langley College
Qualifications: Engineer
Jobs outside cricket: Timko Engineering, Slough Trading Estate
Cricketing superstitions: Never changes before the end of the day's play
Overseas tours: CCC tour of Hong Kong, Singapore, New Zealand and Australia, 1983
Overseas teams played for: Merriweather CC, Newcastle, Australia, 1983–85; West End CC, Anguilla, 1973–76
Cricketers particularly learnt from: Tim Tremlett
Cricketers particularly admired: Viv Richards, Andy Roberts, Richard Hadlee

Other sports played: Most other sports
Other sports followed: Football, boxing, tennis
Relaxations: Music, wine bars, meeting people
Extras: Played for Buckinghamshire in Minor Counties before joining Hampshire. First Anguillan-born player to appear in the County Championship
Best batting performance: 36 Hampshire v Northamptonshire, Northampton 1985
Best bowling performance: 7-37 Hampshire v Kent, Bournemouth 1984

LAST SEASON: BATTING

	I.	N.O.	R.	H.S.	AV.
TEST					
1ST-CLASS	13	5	41	16	5.12
INT					
JPL	–	–	–	–	–
NAT.W.	1	0	5	5	–
B & H	1	1	4	4*	–

LAST SEASON: BOWLING

	O.	M.	R.	W.	AV.
TEST					
1ST-CLASS	541.4	123	1616	49	32.97
INT					
JPL	111.5	3	502	17	29.52
NAT.W.	23.3	4	53	4	13.25
B & H	33.5	1	142	7	20.28

CAREER: BATTING

	I.	N.O.	R.	H.S.	AV.
TEST					
1ST-CLASS	47	18	171	36	5.89
INT					
JPL	3	3	2	2*	–
NAT.W.	2	1	8	5	–
B & H	2	1	4	4*	–

CAREER: BOWLING

	O.	M.	R.	W.	AV.
TEST					
1ST-CLASS	1652.2	369	5032	146	34.46
INT					
JPL	313.2	13	1405	57	24.64
NAT.W.	71.5	10	231	8	28.87
B & H	80.1	7	301	16	18.81

COOK, G.   Northamptonshire

Full Name: Geoffrey Cook
Role: Right-hand bat, slow left-arm bowler
Born: 9 October 1951, Middlesbrough
Height: 6′ 0″ **Weight:** 12st 10lbs
Nickname: Geoff
County debut: 1971
County cap: 1975
Benefit: 1985
Test debut: 1981–82
No. of Tests: 7
No. of One-Day Internationals: 6
1000 runs in a season: 11
1st-Class 50s scored: 98
1st-Class 100s scored: 30
One-day 50s: 42
One-day 100s: 3

Place in batting averages: 39th av. 41.69 (1985 56th av. 38.09)
1st-Class catches 1986: 16 (career: 384)
Parents: Harry and Helen
Wife and date of marriage: Judith, 22 November 1975
Children: Anna, 21 May 1980
Education: Middlesbrough High School
Qualifications: 6 O-levels, 1 A-level
Jobs outside cricket: Has taught at Spratton Hall Prep. School
Family links with cricket: Father and brother, David, very keen club cricketers. 'Father was virtually "Mr Cricket" in Middlesbrough cricket in the 1960s. (President, Secretary, Chairman, of various leagues.)'
Overseas tours: With England to India 1981–82 and Australia 1982–83
Overseas teams played for: Eastern Province, 1978–81
Cricketers particularly learnt from: Wayne Larkins
Cricketers particularly admired: Clive Rice
Other sports played: 'All sports when given opportunity.' Football with Wellingborough in the Southern League
Relaxations: Walking, reading, crosswords
Extras: 'Great believer in organised recreation for young people. Would enjoy time and scope to carry my beliefs through.' Captain since 1981. Chairman of the Cricketers' Association
Best batting performance: 183 Northamptonshire v Lancashire, Northampton 1986
Best bowling performance: 3-47 England XI v South Australia, Adelaide 1983–84

LAST SEASON: BATTING

	I.	N.O.	R.	H.S.	AV.
TEST					
1ST-CLASS	30	4	1084	183	41.69
INT					
JPL	11	4	86	15*	12.28
NAT.W.	1	0	57	57	–
B & H	5	0	101	37	20.20

CAREER: BATTING

	I.	N.O.	R.	H.S.	AV.
TEST	13	0	203	66	15.61
1ST-CLASS	661	51	19794	183	32.44
INT	6	0	106	32	17.67
JPL	194	17	4274	98	24.14
NAT.W.	33	1	1272	130	39.75
B & H	54	4	1357	96	27.14

LAST SEASON: BOWLING

	O.	M.	R.	W.	AV.
TEST					
1ST-CLASS	17	4	38	1	–
INT					
JPL					
NAT.W.					
B & H	48	7	165	2	82.50

CAREER: BOWLING

	O.	M.	R.	W.	AV.
TEST	7	3	27	0	–
1ST-CLASS	181.1	36	686	15	45.73
INT					
JPL	1	0	6	0	–
NAT.W.					
B & H					

Full Name: Nicholas Grant Billson Cook
Role: Right-hand bat, slow left-arm bowler, backward short-leg fielder
Born: 17 June 1956, Leicester
Height: 6' 0" **Weight:** 12st
Nickname: Beast, Rag'ead
County debut: 1978 (Leicestershire), 1986 (Northamptonshire)
County cap: 1982 (Leicestershire)
Test debut: 1983
No. of Tests: 9
No. of One-Day Internationals: 1
50 wickets in a season: 5
1st-Class 50s scored: 2
1st-Class 5 w. in innings: 22
1st-Class 10 w. in match: 3
Place in batting averages: 212th av. 14.62 (1985 235th av. 12.67)
Place in bowling averages: 60th av. 29.53 (1985 121st av. 44.40)
1st-Class catches 1986: 21 (career: 123)
Parents: Peter and Cynthia
Wife and date of marriage: Janet Elizabeth, 3 November 1979
Education: Stokes Croft Junior; Lutterworth High; Lutterworth Upper
Qualifications: 7 O-levels, 1 A-level, advanced cricket coach
Jobs outside cricket: Has worked for Leicestershire CCC on promotions, organising lotteries, sponsored walks, general fund-raising projects. Also coaching
Family links with cricket: Father played club cricket
Overseas tours: Whitbread Scholarship to Perth, Australia, 1980–81; Far East tour with MCC to Bangkok, Singapore, Hong Kong, 1981; Australia and New Zealand with Derrick Robins XI, 1980; Zimbabwe with Leicestershire CCC, 1981; Dubai with Barbican XI, 1982; America with MCC 1982–83; Kuwait with MCC 1983; New Zealand and Pakistan with England 1983–84; Sri Lanka with England B, 1986
Overseas teams played for: Claremont-Cottesloe CC, Perth, 1980–81
Cricketers particularly learnt from: Jack Birkenshaw, Roger Tolchard
Other sports followed: Soccer, rugby, horse-riding
Off-season 1986–87: 'Looking for work.'
Relaxations: Crosswords; watching horse-racing and football, especially Leicester City, and most sporting events; reading, especially Wilbur Smith; good comedy programmes and good food

Extras: Played for ESCA 1975. Played for Young England v Young West Indies 1975. Played for MCC v Middlesex at start of 1981 season. Played for England B Team v Pakistan, August 1982. Left Leicestershire to join Northamptonshire for 1986 season

Opinions on cricket: 'Overseas players should be limited to one per county team. Loopholes in TCCB rules should be tightened to prevent overseas players becoming "English". To play for England you should be brought up and educated in England and have at least a father who has been through the same process.'

Best batting performance: 75 Leicestershire v Somerset, Taunton 1980
Best bowling performance: 7-63 Leicestershire v Somerset, Taunton 1982

LAST SEASON: BATTING

	I.	N.O.	R.	H.S.	AV.
TEST					
1ST-CLASS	27	3	351	45	14.62
INT					
JPL	7	4	41	13*	13.66
NAT.W.	1	0	13	13	–
B & H	2	1	33	19	–

CAREER: BATTING

	I.	N.O.	R.	H.S.	AV.
TEST	15	1	101	26	7.21
1ST-CLASS	193	55	1773	75	12.84
INT	–	–	–	–	–
JPL	18	8	94	13*	9.40
NAT.W.	1	0	13	13	–
B & H	5	2	62	23	20.66

LAST SEASON: BOWLING

	O.	M.	R.	W.	AV.
TEST					
1ST-CLASS	870.2	290	1890	64	29.53
INT					
JPL	109	3	442	21	21.04
NAT.W.	6	0	38	0	–
B & H	48	7	165	2	82.50

CAREER: BOWLING

	O.	M.	R.	W.	AV.
TEST	498.2	162	1212	40	30.30
1ST-CLASS	5523	1789	15057	515	29.43
INT	8	0	34	1	–
JPL	281.2	20	1203	42	28.64
NAT.W.	42	8	169	4	42.25
B & H	115	18	389	6	64.83

48. Who is the only current England Test cricketer to wear a watch while playing?

49. When Geoffrey Boycott first opened the batting for England, who was his partner?

50. Which England captain won an Olympic Gold Medal for boxing?

51. What is a King Pair?

52. Whose nickname is the Little Master?

COOMBS, R. V. J. Somerset

Full Name: Robert Vincent Jerome
Coombs
Role: Right-hand bat, slow
left-arm bowler
Born: 20 July 1959, Barnet, Herts
Height: 6′ 4″ **Weight:** 13st 12lbs
Nickname: Coombsee
County debut: 1985
1st-Class 5 w. in innings: 1
Place in bowling averages: 120th
av. 52.75
1st-Class catches 1986: 3 (career: 3)
Parents: John Michael and Dena
Marjorie
Marital status: Single
Education: King's College Taunton;
St Luke's College, University of
Exeter
Qualifications: 10 O-levels,
2 A-levels, BEd
Jobs outside cricket: Motor claims negotiator, Norman Frizzell
Family links with cricket: Brother a devoted club cricketer
Cricketers particularly learnt from: Many school, club and county colleagues
Cricketers particularly admired: Derek Underwood
Other sports played: Hockey
Other sports followed: Enjoy watching most sports
Relaxations: Watching television, meeting friends, cricket coaching
Extras: NCA coaching award. On first-class debut v Middlesex returned
figures of 5-58. 1985 held dual registration with Dorset for whom he debuted

LAST SEASON: BATTING

	I.	N.O.	R.	H.S.	AV.
TEST					
1ST-CLASS	6	3	31	18	10.33
INT					
JPL					
NAT.W.					
B & H					

LAST SEASON: BOWLING

	O.	M.	R.	W.	AV.
TEST					
1ST-CLASS	256.5	58	844	16	52.75
INT					
JPL					
NAT.W.					
B & H					

CAREER: BATTING

	I.	N.O.	R.	H.S.	AV.
TEST					
1ST-CLASS	9	3	32	18	5.33
INT					
JPL					
NAT.W.					
B & H					

CAREER: BOWLING

	O.	M.	R.	W.	AV.
TEST					
1ST-CLASS	349.5	75	1112	32	34.75
INT					
JPL					
NAT.W.					
B & H					

in 1979. Plays club cricket for Bournemouth CC. Played with Hampshire II 1982
Best batting performance: 18 Somerset v Gloucestershire, Bristol 1986
Best bowling performance: 5-58 Somerset v Middlesex, Weston 1985

COOPER, K. E.   Nottinghamshire

Full Name: Kevin Edwin Cooper
Role: Left-hand bat, right-arm fast-medium bowler
Born: 27 December 1957, Sutton-in-Ashfield
Height: 6′ 1″ **Weight:** 12st 4lbs
Nickname: Henry
County debut: 1976
County cap: 1980
50 wickets in a season: 5
1st-Class 5 w. in innings: 15
Place in batting averages: 220th av. 13.12 (1985 245th av. 11.58)
Place in bowling averages: 26th av. 23.86 (1985 22nd av. 25.67)
1st-Class catches 1986: 4 (career: 62)
Parents: Gerald Edwin and Margaret
Wife and date of marriage: Linda Carol, 14 February 1981
Children: Kelly Louise, 8 April 1982; Tara Amy, 22 November 1984
Education: Secondary Modern

LAST SEASON: BATTING

	I.	N.O.	R.	H.S.	AV.
TEST					
1ST-CLASS	13	5	105	19	13.12
INT					
JPL	3	1	6	5	3.00
NAT.W.	1	0	0	0	–
B & H	–	–	–	–	–

CAREER: BATTING

	I.	N.O.	R.	H.S.	AV.
TEST					
1ST-CLASS	186	45	1357	46	9.62
INT					
JPL	35	11	116	31	4.83
NAT.W.	5	1	29	11	7.25
B & H	13	8	62	25*	12.40

LAST SEASON: BOWLING

	O.	M.	R.	W.	AV.
TEST					
1ST-CLASS	410.5	106	1026	43	23.86
INT					
JPL	72	11	200	7	28.57
NAT.W.	12	3	48	1	–
B & H	55	15	166	4	41.50

CAREER: BOWLING

	O.	M.	R.	W.	AV.
TEST					
1ST-CLASS	4823.3	1329	12893	475	27.14
INT					
JPL	722.2	49	3268	95	34.40
NAT.W.	183.2	43	514	23	22.34
B & H	389.4	75	1359	42	32.35

Jobs outside cricket: Has been warehouseman and maintenance man, also PR in free trade department of local brewery
Family links with cricket: Father played local cricket
Overseas tours: Toured Australasia with Derrick Robins U-23 XI 1979–80
Off-season 1986–87: 'On dole.'
Other sports played: Football, golf, shooting
Injuries 1986: Missed 4 weeks due to car crash, 3 weeks with torn hamstring
Extras: On 23 June 1974, playing for Hucknall Ramblers CC, took 10 wickets for 6 runs in one innings against Sutton Coll. in the Mansfield and District League
Best batting performance: 46 Nottinghamshire v Middlesex, Trent Bridge 1985
Best bowling performance: 8-44 Nottinghamshire v Middlesex, Lord's 1984

COTTEY, P. A. Glamorgan

Full Name: Phillip Anthony Cottey
Role: Right-hand bat
Born: 2 June 1966, Swansea
Height: 5' 4"
County debut: 1986
1st-Class catches 1986: 2 (career: 2)
Education: Bishopston Comprehensive School
Other sports played: Plays football for Swansea City
Best batting performance: 9* Glamorgan v New Zealand, Swansea 1986

LAST SEASON: BATTING

	I.	N.O.	R.	H.S.	AV.
TEST					
1ST-CLASS	5	1	24	9*	6.00
INT					
JPL	3	0	5	2	1.66
NAT.W.					
B & H					

CAREER: BATTING

	I.	N.O.	R.	H.S.	AV.
TEST					
1ST-CLASS	5	1	24	9*	6.00
INT					
JPL	3	0	5	2	1.66
NAT.W.					
B & H					

COWANS, N. G.   Middlesex

Full Name: Norman George Cowans
Role: Right-hand bat, right-arm fast-medium bowler
Born: 17 April 1961, Enfield St Mary, Jamaica
Height: 6' 3" **Weight:** 14st
Nickname: Flash
County debut: 1980
County cap: 1984
Test debut: 1982–83
No. of Tests: 19
No. of One-Day Internationals: 23
50 wickets in a season: 3
1st-Class 50s scored: 1
1st-Class 5 w. in innings: 16
Place in batting averages: 206th av. 15.92 (1985 254th av. 10.00)
Place in bowling averages: 25th av. 23.79 (1985 12th av. 22.95)
1st-Class catches 1986: 4 (career: 42)
Parents: Gloria and Ivan
Marital status: Single
Education: Park High Secondary, Stanmore, Middlesex
Qualifications: Qualified coach
Jobs outside cricket: Squash and real tennis professional. Glassblower with Whitefriars hand-made glass
Overseas tours: Young England tour to Australia 1979; Middlesex tour to Zimbabwe 1980; *Cricketer* tour to Dubai 1981; England to Australia and New Zealand 1982–83 and New Zealand and Pakistan 1983–84; International tour to Jamaica 1983; India and Australia with England 1984–85; England B to Sri Lanka 1986
Overseas teams played for: Claremont-Cottesloe CC, Perth, Australia
Cricketers particularly learnt from: Dennis Lillee, Michael Holding, Wayne Daniel. 'The aggression of Lillee, the power of Daniel, and the smoothness of Holding.'
Off-season 1986–87: Due to play Grade Cricket in Australia but returned to England early when there was a contractual dispute
Other sports played: Basketball, squash, table-tennis, swimming, tennis, real tennis
Relaxations: Dancing, reading, being with friends, listening to music. Reggae. Arsenal FC
Extras: Two Young England Tests, one One-Day Youth International. Has

won athletics championship in sprinting and javelin throwing
Best batting performance: 66 Middlesex v Surrey, Lord's 1984
Best bowling performance: 6-31 Middlesex v Leicestershire, Leicester 1985

LAST SEASON: BATTING

	I.	N.O.	R.	H.S.	AV.
TEST					
1ST-CLASS	21	7	223	44*	15.92
INT					
JPL	4	2	17	13	8.50
NAT.W.	1	0	1	1	–
B & H	1	1	0	0*	–

LAST SEASON: BOWLING

	O.	M.	R.	W.	AV.
TEST					
1ST-CLASS	436.2	95	1380	58	23.79
INT					
JPL	70	4	274	8	34.25
NAT.W.	18	4	59	4	14.75
B & H	55	11	136	11	12.36

CAREER: BATTING

	I.	N.O.	R.	H.S.	AV.
TEST	29	7	175	36	7.96
1ST-CLASS	92	18	710	66	9.59
INT	8	3	13	4	2.60
JPL	13	6	78	20	11.14
NAT.W.	10	2	33	12*	4.12
B & H	5	2	16	6	5.33

CAREER: BOWLING

	O.	M.	R.	W.	AV.
TEST	575.2	113	2003	51	39.27
1ST-CLASS	2158	431	6913	302	22.89
INT	213.4	17	913	23	39.70
JPL	246.2	12	1068	35	30.51
NAT.W.	147	23	497	22	22.59
B & H	149.2	21	481	29	16.58

53. Who sponsored the Test series, England against India and New Zealand, in 1986?

54. A Bombay duck is
   a) an exotic Oriental bird whose mating call is thought by some to sound like ball on bat; or
   b) a kind of dried fish; or
   c) when an Indian is out first ball?

COWDREY, C. S. Kent

Full Name: Christopher Stuart
Cowdrey
Role: Right-hand bat, right-arm
medium bowler
Born: 20 October 1957,
Farnborough, Kent
Height: 6′ 0″ **Weight:** 14st
Nickname: Cow, Woody
County debut: 1977
County cap: 1979
Test debut: 1984
No. of Tests: 5
No. of One-Day Internationals: 3
1000 runs in a season: 3
1st-Class 50s scored: 41
1st-Class 100s scored: 11
1st-Class 5 w. innings: 1
One-day 50s: 24
One-day 100s: 2
Place in batting averages: 112th av. 29.10 (1985 88th av. 32.70)
Place in bowling averages: 76th av. 33.51 (1985 129th av. 50.40)
1st-Class catches 1986: 31 (career: 205)
Parents: Michael Colin and Penelope Susan
Marital status: Single
Education: Wellesley House, Broadstairs; Tonbridge School
Jobs outside cricket: Representative for Stuart Canvas Products, Warrington,
Cheshire
Family links with cricket: Grandfather, Stuart Chiesman, on Kent Commit-
tee, 12 years as Chairman. Pavilion on Kent's ground at Canterbury named
after him. Father played for Kent and England, brother made Kent debut
1984
Overseas tours: Captained Young England to West Indies, 1976; with Derrick
Robins XI to Far East, South America and Australasia, 1979–80; India and
Australia with England, 1984–85
Overseas teams played for: Avendale CC, Cape Town, 1983–84; Cumberland
CC, Sydney, 1978–79 and 1982–83
Cricketers particularly learnt from: Asif Iqbal, Allan Lamb
Cricketers particularly admired: David Gower
Off-season 1986–87: Writing. Touring and working for Stuart Canvass
Other sports played: Golf, tennis, backgammon
Other sports followed: All sports
Relaxations: Dining at Silks Restaurant with Richard Scott and taking Blaise
Craven's money at backgammon

Extras: Played for Kent 2nd XI at age 15. Vice-captain 1984. Captain 1985
Best batting performance: 159 Kent v Surrey, Canterbury 1985
Best bowling performance: 5-69 Kent v Hampshire, Canterbury 1986

LAST SEASON: BATTING

	I.	N.O.	R.	H.S.	AV.
TEST					
1ST-CLASS	33	3	873	100	29.10
INT					
JPL	13	1	311	59	25.91
NAT.W.	2	1	63	62*	–
B & H	6	2	193	89*	48.25

CAREER: BATTING

	I.	N.O.	R.	H.S.	AV.
TEST	6	1	96	38	19.20
1ST-CLASS	308	43	8230	159	31.05
INT	3	1	51	46*	25.50
JPL	122	16	2489	95	23.48
NAT.W.	23	4	617	122*	32.47
B & H	38	6	951	114	29.71

LAST SEASON: BOWLING

	O.	M.	R.	W.	AV.
TEST					
1ST-CLASS	266.2	45	905	27	33.51
INT					
JPL	96	1	461	18	25.61
NAT.W.	9	0	43	0	–
B & H	60	1	284	3	94.66

CAREER: BOWLING

	O.	M.	R.	W.	AV.
TEST	61	2	288	4	72.00
1ST-CLASS	1374.5	247	4590	120	38.25
INT	8.4	0	55	2	27.50
JPL	406.3	5	1924	64	30.06
NAT.W.	126	13	470	20	23.50
B & H	165	3	748	15	49.86

COWDREY, G. R.   Kent

Full Name: Graham Robert Cowdrey
Role: Right-hand bat, right-arm medium bowler, cover fielder
Born: 27 June 1964, Farnborough, Kent
Height: 5′ 10″ **Weight:** 12st
Nickname: Van
County debut: 1984
1st-Class 50s scored: 5
One-day 50s: 3
Place in batting averages: 200th av. 17.00
1st-Class catches 1986: 10 (career: 16)
Parents: Michael Colin and Penelope Susan
Marital status: Single
Education: Wellesley House, Broadstairs; Tonbridge School; Durham University
Qualifications: 8 O-levels, 3 A-levels, University entrance

Family links with cricket: Father and brother Chris played for England and Kent

Overseas tours: Australia with Tonbridge School in 1980; 'Christians in Sport' India tour, 1985–86

Overseas teams played for: Avendale CC, Cape Town, 1983–84; Mosman CC, Sydney, 1985–86

Cricketers particularly learnt from: Mark Benson, Chris Tavaré

Cricketers particularly admired: Richard Hadlee, Chris Cowdrey

Off-season 1986–87: In Sydney

Other sports played: Most sports, particularly golf and tennis

Other sports followed: Racing

Relaxations: Music (particularly Van 'The Man' Morrison)

Extras: Played for Young England and Australia. 1000 runs for Kent II first season on staff, captain of Kent II in 1984. Very interested in psychology of cricket. Broke 2nd XI record with 1300 runs in 26 innings in 1985

Best batting performance: 75 Kent v Northamptonshire, Canterbury 1986

LAST SEASON: BATTING

	I.	N.O.	R.	H.S.	AV.
TEST					
1ST-CLASS	26	1	425	75	17.00
INT					
JPL	14	3	249	48	22.63
NAT.W.	1	0	22	22	–
B & H	6	1	232	65	46.40

LAST SEASON: BOWLING

	O.	M.	R.	W.	AV.
TEST					
1ST-CLASS	10	3	27	1	–
INT					
JPL					
NAT.W.	11	2	30	1	–
B & H					

CAREER: BATTING

	I.	N.O.	R.	H.S.	AV.
TEST					
1ST-CLASS	36	3	674	75	20.42
INT					
JPL	16	3	290	48	22.30
NAT.W.	1	0	22	22	–
B & H	6	1	232	65	46.40

CAREER: BOWLING

	O.	M.	R.	W.	AV.
TEST					
1ST-CLASS	17	3	49	2	24.50
INT					
JPL					
NAT.W.	11	2	30	1	–
B & H					

55. What was remarkable about Dilip Vengsarkar's first innings in the First Test against England at Lord's in June 1986?

56. Which Test Match commentator has, as a catchphrase, the words 'My dear old thing!'

COWLEY, N. G. — Hampshire

Full Name: Nigel Geoffrey Cowley
Role: Right-hand bat, right-arm
off-break bowler
Born: 1 March 1953, Shaftesbury,
Dorset
Height: 5′ 7″ **Weight:** 12st 5lbs
Nickname: Dougall
County debut: 1974
County cap: 1978
1000 runs in a season: 1
50 wickets in a season: 5
1st-Class 50s scored: 28
1st-Class 100s scored: 2
1st-Class 5 w. in innings: 5
One-day 50s: 5
Place in batting averages: 140th
av. 25.71 (1985 178th av. 21.30)
Place in bowling averages: 36th
av. 26.50 (1985 39th av. 27.95)
1st-Class catches 1986: 5 (career: 90)
Parents: Geoffrey and Betty
Wife: Susan

Children: Mark and Darren
Education: Mere Dutchy Manor, Mere, Wiltshire
Family links with cricket: Father played good club cricket, 2 sons play for
Hampshire under 13 and under 11 teams
Overseas tours: Sri Lanka 1977; West Indies 1980
Overseas teams played for: Paarl CC (Cape Town) 1981–83
Cricketers particularly learnt from: Peter Sainsbury

LAST SEASON: BATTING

	I.	N.O.	R.	H.S.	AV.
TEST					
1ST-CLASS	21	7	360	78*	25.71
INT					
JPL	8	3	96	23	19.20
NAT.W.	2	0	12	8	6.00
B & H	2	1	26	21*	–

LAST SEASON: BOWLING

	O.	M.	R.	W.	AV.
TEST					
1ST-CLASS	385.2	78	1060	40	26.50
INT					
JPL	96.3	5	515	16	32.18
NAT.W.	24	3	55	3	18.33
B & H	34	2	159	3	53.00

CAREER: BATTING

	I.	N.O.	R.	H.S.	AV.
TEST					
1ST-CLASS	337	53	6340	104*	22.32
INT					
JPL	123	26	1890	74	19.48
NAT.W.	20	3	315	63*	18.52
B & H	35	3	440	59	13.75

CAREER: BOWLING

	O.	M.	R.	W.	AV.
TEST					
1ST-CLASS	4690.5	1233	12851	392	32.78
INT					
JPL	813.4	45	3890	128	30.39
NAT.W.	212.1	31	612	25	24.48
B & H	301.3	48	973	25	38.92

Off-season 1986–87: Working for Austin Reed in Southampton
Other sports played: Golf – 9 handicap
Injuries 1986: 3 weeks out with pulled side muscle
Extras: In charge of pre-season and match day training
Best batting performance: 109* Hampshire v Somerset, Taunton 1977
Best bowling performance: 6-48 Hampshire v Leicestershire, Southampton 1982

CURRAN, K. M. — Gloucestershire

Full Name: Kevin Malcolm Curran
Role: Right-hand bat, right-arm fast-medium bowler
Born: 7 September 1959, Rusape, Zimbabwe
Height: 6′ 2″ **Weight:** 13st 9lbs
Nickname: KC
County debut: 1985
County cap: 1985
No. of One-Day Internationals: 6
1000 runs in a season: 1
50 wickets in a season: 1
1st-Class 50s scored: 15
1st-Class 100s scored: 4
1st-Class 5 w. in innings: 2
One-day 50s: 7
Place in batting averages: 33rd av. 43.64 (1985 152nd av. 24.58)
Place in bowling averages: —
(1985 14th av. 23.26)
1st-Class catches 1986: 29 (career: 43)
Parents: Kevin Patrick
Marital status: Single
Education: Marandelias High School
Qualifications: 6 O-levels, 2 M-levels
Jobs outside cricket: Tobacco buyer/farmer
Family links with cricket: Father played for Rhodesia 1949–53
Overseas tours: Sri Lanka 1982; World Cup 1983 with Zimbabwe
Overseas teams played for: Zimbabwe 1981–85 (Harare SC)
Cricketers particularly learnt from: Brian Davison, Duncan Fletcher, Richard Hadlee
Cricketers particularly admired: Brian Davison, Mike Procter, Graeme Pollock, Barry Richards, John Traicos

Other sports played: Rugby, squash and tennis, gym work and running

Injuries 1986: Stress fracture in shoulder meant no bowling for the whole season

Relaxations: 'Tiger fishing, big game hunting and being away from everything in the bush; relaxing at home, listening to music, good food.'

Extras: Qualified to play in England by virtue of an Irish passport. Appeared for Zimbabwe in the 1982 ICC Trophy, and then took part in the 1983 Prudential Cup. Had appeared in League cricket in Lancashire as professional for Rawtenstall before joining Gloucestershire

Opinions on cricket: 'The rule about slow over rates should be closely reviewed. Gloucestershire, for instance, paid fines in the region of £8000 and £6000 for 1985 and 1986 seasons. On several occasions we finished first-class games inside 2 days – and still got fined. Where is the logic? You play positive cricket, win games which the public come to see, and end up transforming your bonus into fines. Most quick bowlers have pressure on them to get the overs in, restrict their run-ups, and bowl medium pace. No wonder England have no genuine quick bowlers – what incentive is there?'

Best batting performance: 117* Gloucestershire v Nottinghamshire, Cheltenham 1986

Best bowling performance: 5-35 Gloucestershire v Australia, Bristol 1985

LAST SEASON: BATTING

	I.	N.O.	R.	H.S.	AV.
TEST					
1ST-CLASS	39	8	1353	117*	43.64
INT					
JPL	13	2	376	71*	34.18
NAT.W.	2	0	59	38	29.50
B & H	3	0	100	47	33.33

LAST SEASON: BOWLING

	O.	M.	R.	W.	AV.
TEST					
1ST-CLASS	33	8	83	0	–
INT					
JPL	12	0	59	1	–
NAT.W.					
B & H					

CAREER: BATTING

	I.	N.O.	R.	H.S.	AV.
TEST					
1ST-CLASS	106	17	2785	117*	31.29
INT	6	0	212	73	35.33
JPL	29	6	745	71*	32.39
NAT.W.	5	0	140	38	28.00
B & H	6	2	184	53*	46.00

CAREER: BOWLING

	O.	M.	R.	W.	AV.
TEST					
1ST-CLASS	892.5	191	2802	114	24.58
INT	88.2	3	274	5	54.80
JPL	102.5	6	514	27	19.03
NAT.W.	34	10	77	6	12.83
B & H	43.5	4	169	8	21.12

57. Which England player made his Test debut as captain?

58. Which two legendary England Test cricketers died within one day of each other in April 1986?

CURTIS, T. S.   Worcestershire

Full Name: Timothy Stephen Curtis
Role: Right-hand bat, right-arm
leg-break bowler
Born: 15 January 1960, Chislehurst,
Kent
Height: 5′ 11″ **Weight:** 12st 5lbs
Nickname: TC, Duracell,
Professor
County debut: 1979
County cap: 1984
1000 runs in a season: 3
1st-Class 50s scored: 38
1st-Class 100s: 6
One-day 50s: 14
One-day 100s: 1
Place in batting averages: 11th
av. 49.93 (1985 91st av. 31.75)
1st-Class catches 1986: 9
(career: 52)
Parents: Bruce and Betty
Wife and date of marriage: Philippa, 21 September 1985
Education: The Royal Grammar School, Worcester; Durham University;
Cambridge University
Qualifications: 12 O-levels, 4 A-levels, BA (Hons) English, and postgraduate
certificate in Education in English and Games
Family links with cricket: Father played good club cricket in Bristol and
Stafford
Overseas tours: NCA U-19 tour of Canada 1979
Cricketers particularly learnt from: Glenn Turner

LAST SEASON: BATTING

	I.	N.O.	R.	H.S.	AV.
TEST					
1ST-CLASS	40	10	1498	153	49.93
INT					
JPL	12	0	442	102	36.83
NAT.W.	4	1	181	94	60.33
B & H	2	1	43	40*	–

CAREER: BATTING

	I.	N.O.	R.	H.S.	AV.
TEST					
1ST-CLASS	189	26	5672	153	34.79
INT					
JPL	45	9	1197	102	33.25
NAT.W.	11	2	473	94	52.55
B & H	14	1	356	75	27.38

LAST SEASON: BOWLING

	O.	M.	R.	W.	AV.
TEST					
1ST-CLASS					
INT					
JPL					
NAT.W.					
B & H					

CAREER: BOWLING

	O.	M.	R.	W.	AV.
TEST					
1ST-CLASS	54.3	9	194	4	48.50
INT					
JPL					
NAT.W.					
B & H	0.2	0	4	0	–

Off-season 1986–87: Teaching
Other sports played: Rugby, tennis, squash, golf
Injuries 1986: Only minor ones
Extras: Captained Durham University at cricket
Opinions on cricket: '16 4-day matches would seem to be the best combination for championship cricket, with one-day competitions taking place at the weekends. This would reduce the amount of cricket played and place a greater emphasis on the quality of the cricket. It would also avoid the lottery which I feel uncovered wickets would produce.'
Best batting performance: 153 Worcestershire v Somerset, Worcester 1986
Best bowling performance: 2-58 Cambridge University v Nottinghamshire, Cambridge 1983

DALE, C. S. Kent

Full Name: Christopher Stephen Dale
Role: Right-hand bat, right-arm off-spinner, gully fielder
Born: 15 December 1961, Canterbury
Height: 6′ 2″ **Weight:** 12½st
Nickname: Arther, Emma, Daley
County debut: 1984 (Gloucestershire), 1986 (Kent)
1st-Class catches 1986: — (career: 1)
Parents: David and Doreen
Marital status: Engaged to Tessa
Education: Sir William Nottige, Thanet College
Qualifications: 6 O-levels, 1 A-level, NCA coaching award
Jobs outside cricket: Fitter for a couple of refrigeration companies, one in England, one in Australia. Technician in gold laboratory, Australia. Bar work, coaching, driving etc.
Family links with cricket: Father played many seasons with Whitstable CC
Overseas teams played for: Scarborough CC 1983–84 and 1984–85
Cricketers particularly learnt from: David Allen (Gloucestershire)
Cricketers particularly admired: John Emburey, John Childs, Derek Underwood
Off-season 1986–87: Looking for a job in sales
Other sports played: Squash, badminton, long-distance running
Other sports followed: Snooker, golf, athletics

Injuries 1986: 'Pulled muscle in back, which affected me for about a month longer than it should have because I was asked to play and carry the injury.'
Relaxations: All sports. Whisky and American with plenty of ice!!
Opinions on cricket: 'I was not good enough or maybe I was not encouraged enough to make a career out of cricket. I am concerned that the next off-spinner that comes to Kent will not get the encouragement and most important the bowling, i.e. 400 overs plus in a season. At the moment seam bowling is dominating the game because of uncovered wickets or maybe 4-day games would be better on covered pitches. Young cricketers generally seem to be getting louder, giving umpires a particularly hard time with unnecessary appealing.'
Best batting performance: 49 Gloucestershire v Yorkshire, Bradford 1984
Best bowling performance: 3-10 Gloucestershire v Oxford University, Oxford 1984

LAST SEASON: BATTING

	I.	N.O.	R.	H.S.	AV.
TEST					
1ST-CLASS	3	1	18	16	9.00
INT					
JPL	–	–	–	–	–
NAT.W.					
B & H					

LAST SEASON: BOWLING

	O.	M.	R.	W.	AV.
TEST					
1ST-CLASS	34	5	142	0	–
INT					
JPL	–	–	–	–	–
NAT.W.					
B & H					

CAREER: BATTING

	I.	N.O.	R.	H.S.	AV.
TEST					
1ST-CLASS	11	3	118	49	14.75
INT					
JPL	1	0	0	0	–
NAT.W.					
B & H					

CAREER: BOWLING

	O.	M.	R.	W.	AV.
TEST					
1ST-CLASS	159.1	27	609	9	87.00
INT					
JPL	23	0	139	2	69.50
NAT.W.					
B & H					

59. With which three counties was the great England Test bowler Jim Laker most connected in cricketing terms?

Full Name: Wayne Wendell Daniel
Role: Right-hand bat, right-arm
fast bowler
Born: 16 January 1956, St Philip,
Barbados
Nickname: Diamond
County debut: 1977
County cap: 1977
Benefit: 1985
Test debut: 1975–76
No. of Tests: 10
No. of One-Day Internationals: 18
50 wickets in a season: 10
1st-Class 50s scored: 2
1st-Class 5 w. in innings: 31
1st-Class 10 w. in innings: 7
Place in batting averages: 216th
av. 14.00
Place in bowling averages: 15th av. 22.37 (1985 30th av. 26.72)
1st-Class catches 1986: 3 (career: 58)
Marital status: Single
Relaxations: Enjoys listening to soul music
Extras: Toured England with West Indies Schoolboys team 1974. Played for
Middlesex 2nd XI 1975. Debut for Barbados 1975–76. Toured with West
Indies to England 1976. Spent 1979–80 off-season in Barbados playing island
cricket. Best bowling record for Benson & Hedges Competition 1978 with 7
for 12 v Minor Counties East at Ipswich
Best batting performance: 53* Middlesex v Yorkshire, Lord's 1981
Best bowling performance: 9-61 Middlesex v Glamorgan, Swansea 1982

LAST SEASON: BATTING

	I.	N.O.	R.	H.S.	AV.
TEST					
1ST-CLASS	16	6	140	33	14.00
INT					
JPL	2	1	5	4	–
NAT.W.	1	1	1	1*	–
B & H	–	–	–	–	–

CAREER: BATTING

	I.	N.O.	R.	H.S.	AV.
TEST	11	4	46	11	6.57
1ST-CLASS	216	94	1474	53*	12.08
INT	5	4	49	16*	–
JPL	38	15	93	14	4.04
NAT.W.	17	9	39	14	4.88
B & H	17	5	56	20*	4.66

LAST SEASON: BOWLING

	O.	M.	R.	W.	AV.
TEST					
1ST-CLASS	402.1	52	1387	62	22.37
INT					
JPL	47	4	211	6	35.16
NAT.W.	24	3	73	6	12.16
B & H	65	3	255	9	28.33

CAREER: BOWLING

	O.	M.	R.	W.	AV.
TEST	292	61	910	36	25.28
1ST-CLASS	6021.1	1184	17268	797	21.66
INT	152	17	595	23	25.87
JPL	796	76	2909	157	18.52
NAT.W.	340.3	58	990	65	15.23
B & H	418	71	1282	82	15.63

DAVIES, T.   Glamorgan

Full Name: Terry Davies
Role: Right-hand bat,
wicket-keeper
Born: 25 October 1960, St Albans
Height: 5′ 6″ **Weight:** 10st 8lbs
Nickname: Sid
County debut: 1979
County cap: 1985
1st-Class 50s scored: 6
Place in batting averages: 177th
av. 21.06 (1985 115th av. 29.54)
Parents: Harry and Peggy
Wife and date of marriage: Noelle,
26 November 1983
Education: Townsend Secondary
School, St Albans
Jobs outside cricket: Civil servant
with NSW Public Service,
PRO for a building society
Family links with cricket: Brother playing club cricket in Sydney, Australia.
'Father a fantastic back-garden bowler!'
Overseas teams played for: Bankstown Canterbury 1980–81; Bathurst
1981–82; Canberra 1982–83; Mosman 1983–86
Cricketers particularly learnt from: Bob Taylor, Alan Knott
Off-season 1986–87: Playing and coaching in Sydney for Mosman CC
Other sports played: Squash, football
Relaxations: Music, TV
Extras: Played soccer for Hertfordshire U-16 and for Watford and West Ham
Youths in the South-East Counties League. Had trials with West Ham FC,

LAST SEASON: BATTING

	I.	N.O.	R.	H.S.	AV.
TEST					
1ST-CLASS	28	13	316	41	21.06
INT					
JPL	10	4	49	16*	8.16
NAT.W.	2	1	46	30*	–
B & H	3	0	22	11	7.33

CAREER: BATTING

	I.	N.O.	R.	H.S.	AV.
TEST					
1ST-CLASS	121	36	1775	75	20.88
INT					
JPL	33	17	288	46*	18.00
NAT.W.					
B & H	10	1	92	23	10.22

LAST SEASON WICKET-KEEPING

	C.	ST.
TEST		
1ST-CLASS	31	8
INT		
JPL	11	1
NAT.W.	4	2
B & H	1	1

CAREER: WICKET-KEEPING

	C.	ST.
TEST		
1ST-CLASS	164	27
INT		
JPL	43	18
NAT.W.	10	2
B & H	13	5

Tottenham Hotspur and Luton. Trained with Watford for a season. On Lord's ground staff 1977–78. Equalled Bob Taylor's record for dismissals in a Nat West Trophy match (4 c, 2 st)
Opinions on cricket: '16 four-day matches with weekends for one-day cricket would be an interesting introduction.'
Best batting performance: 75 Glamorgan v Middlesex, Cardiff 1985

DAVIS, M. R. Somerset

Full Name: Mark Richard Davis
Role: Left-hand bat, left-arm fast-medium bowler, outfielder
Born: 26 February 1962, Kilve, Somerset
Height: 5' 11½" **Weight:** 13st
Nickname: Pooch
County debut: 1982
50 wickets in a season: 1
1st-Class 50s scored: 1
1st-Class 5 w. in innings: 4
1st-Class 10 w. in match: 1
Place in batting averages: 207th av. 15.75 (1985 171st av. 22.50)
Place in bowling averages: 125th av. 57.36 (1985 52nd av. 52.04)
1st-Class catches 1986: 2 (career: 25)
Parents: Penelope and Robert Ernest Charles
Wife: Elizabeth Rebecca
Education: Kilve Primary School; Williton First and Middle School; West Somerset School; Bridgwater College
Qualifications: 4 O-levels, NCA Senior Coaching Award
Jobs outside cricket: Self employed in building trade
Family links with cricket: 'Father and relatives all play for my local club side, Kilve.'
Overseas tours: Zimbabwe with English Counties XI
Cricketers particularly admired: I. Botham, M. Crowe, V. Richards, J. Garner
Off-season 1986–87: 'Working for my father's firm and doing a lot of cricket coaching.'
Other sports played: Squash
Other sports followed: Football

Injuries 1986: 2 broken fingers while bowling (2 breaks in 3 balls)
Relaxations: 'Skittles, my local pub.'
Opinions on cricket: '4-day matches (or 3-day on uncovered pitches); more positive result wickets required from batsmen captains.'
Best batting performance: 60* Somerset v Glamorgan, Taunton 1984
Best bowling performance: 7-55 Somerset v Northamptonshire, Northampton 1984

LAST SEASON: BATTING

	I.	N.O.	R.	H.S.	AV.
TEST					
1ST-CLASS	8	4	63	21*	15.75
INT					
JPL	4	3	7	6	–
NAT.W.					
B & H	1	0	7	7	–

LAST SEASON: BOWLING

	O.	M.	R.	W.	AV.
TEST					
1ST-CLASS	167.3	21	631	11	57.36
INT					
JPL	38.3	0	203	7	29.00
NAT.W.					
B & H	11	0	55	1	–

CAREER: BATTING

	I.	N.O.	R.	H.S.	AV.
TEST					
1ST-CLASS	71	23	746	60*	15.54
INT					
JPL	14	7	54	11	7.71
NAT.W.	2	1	6	6	–
B & H	7	0	67	28	9.57

CAREER: BOWLING

	O.	M.	R.	W.	AV.
TEST					
1ST-CLASS	1419.4	252	4803	138	34.80
INT					
JPL	230.4	10	996	28	35.57
NAT.W.	34	6	132	2	66.00
B & H	117	19	404	14	28.85

DAVIS, R. P.   Kent

Full Name: Richard Peter Davis
Role: Slow left-arm bowler, gully fielder
Born: 18 March 1966, Westgate
Height: 6′ 4″ **Weight:** 14st
Nickname: Dickie
County Debut: 1986
1st-Class catches 1986: 1 (career: 1)
Parents: Brian and Silvia
Marital status: Single
Education: King Ethelberts School, Birchington; Thanet Technical College, Broadstairs
Qualifications: CSEs
Jobs outside cricket: Carpenter
Overseas tours: Kent Schools CA U-17s Canadian Tour 1983

Cricketers particularly learnt from: Derek Underwood, Colin Page
Cricketers particularly admired: Derek Underwood
Off-season 1986–87: In New Zealand
Other sports played: Golf, badminton
Other sports followed: Football, American football
Relaxations: Reading, cards and TV
Opinions on cricket: 'Probably play too much cricket and would like to see uncovered wickets.'
Best bowling performance: 3-38 Kent v Warwickshire, Folkestone 1986

LAST SEASON: BATTING

	I.	N.O.	R.	H.S.	AV.
TEST					
1ST-CLASS	1	1	0	0*	–
INT					
JPL					
NAT.W.					
B & H					

LAST SEASON: BOWLING

	O.	M.	R.	W.	AV.
TEST					
1ST-CLASS	59.5	22	121	6	20.16
INT					
JPL					
NAT.W.					
B & H					

CAREER: BATTING

	I.	N.O.	R.	H.S.	AV.
TEST					
1ST-CLASS	1	1	0	0*	–
INT					
JPL					
NAT.W.					
B & H					

CAREER: BOWLING

	O.	M.	R.	W.	AV.
TEST					
1ST-CLASS	59.5	22	121	6	20.16
INT					
JPL					
NAT.W.					
B & H					

DEFREITAS, P. A. J.　　Leicestershire

Full Name: Phillip Anthony Jason DeFreitas
Role: Right-hand bat, right-arm fast-medium bowler, cover fielder
Born: 18 February 1966, Dominica
Height: 6′ **Weight:** 12st
Nickname: Daffy
County debut: 1985
County cap: 1986
50 wickets in a season: 1
1st-class 50s scored: 3
1st-class 100s scored: 1
1st-Class 5 w. in innings: 8
1st-Class 10 w. in match: 1
One-day 50s: 1
Place in batting averages: 167th av. 23.03 (1985 232nd av. 13.00)

Place in bowling averages: 16th av. 23.09 (1985 24th av. 26.04)
1st-Class catches 1986: 7 (career: 9)
Parents: Sybil and Martin
Marital status: Single
Education: Willesden High School
Qualifications: 2 CSEs
Family links with cricket: Father played in the Windward Is. All six brothers play
Overseas tours: Young England to West Indies 1985
Overseas teams played for: Port Adelaide CC 1985–86
Cricketers particularly learnt from: Don Wilson, Ken Higgs, Paddy Clift, Peter Willey and several others
Off-season 1986–87: In Australia with England
Other sports played: Football and golf
Opinions on cricket: 'Fines on over rates to be abolished. 2nd XI wickets ought to be much better.'
Best batting performance: 106 Leicestershire v Kent, Canterbury 1986
Best bowling performance: 7-44 Leicestershire v Essex, Southend 1986

LAST SEASON: BATTING

	I.	N.O.	R.	H.S.	AV.
TEST					
1ST-CLASS	30	2	645	106	23.03
INT					
JPL	10	2	109	32	13.62
NAT.W.	1	0	69	69	–
B & H	3	2	22	11	–

LAST SEASON: BOWLING

	O.	M.	R.	W.	AV.
TEST					
1ST-CLASS	743.3	133	2171	94	23.09
INT					
JPL	101.1	8	443	25	17.72
NAT.W.	26.4	6	92	3	30.66
B & H	40	6	123	5	24.60

CAREER: BATTING

	I.	N.O.	R.	H.S.	AV.
TEST					
1ST-CLASS	72	7	1407	106	21.64
INT					
JPL	17	4	152	32	11.69
NAT.W.	1	0	69	69	–
B & H	3	2	22	11	–

CAREER: BOWLING

	O.	M.	R.	W.	AV.
TEST					
1ST-CLASS	977.5	176	2874	121	23.75
INT					
JPL	158.1	9	758	38	19.94
NAT.W.	26.4	6	92	3	30.66
B & H	51	9	148	5	29.60

60. True or false; Denis Compton, perhaps the most infamous of runners-out of other batsmen among the great names of cricket, never once ran out his most famous partner, Bill Edrich?

DENNIS, S. J.   Yorkshire

Full Name: Simon John Dennis
Role: Right-hand bat, left-arm fast-medium bowler
Born: 18 October 1960, Scarborough
Height: 6′ 1″ **Weight:** 13st
Nickname: Donkey
County debut: 1980
County cap: 1983
50 wickets in a season: 1
1st-Class 50s scored: 1
1st-Class 5 w. in innings: 5
Place in batting averages: 239th av. 10.25
Place in bowling averages: 64th av. 30.65
1st-Class catches 1986: 4 (career: 17)
Parents: Margaret and Geoff
Marital status: Single
Education: Northstead County Primary School; Scarborough College
Qualifications: 7 O-levels, 1 A-level, City and Guilds Computer Literacy
Jobs outside cricket: Assistant groundsman at Scarborough CC. Furniture salesman
Family links with cricket: Father captained Scarborough for many years. Uncle, Frank Dennis, played for Yorkshire 1928–33. Uncle, Sir Leonard Hutton, Yorkshire and England
Cricketing superstitions: 'If I have a good day I try to do everything the same the next day before the game.'
Overseas tours: India 1978–79 with ESCA; Australia 1980 with Young England; with MCC to East and Central Africa, 1981 and to America, 1982; Gibraltar with Sheffield Cricket Lovers, 1983
Overseas teams played for: Orange Free State 1982–83; Durban Collegians 1985–86
Cricketers particularly learnt from: Doug Padgett, Don Wilson, Ray Illingworth
Cricketers particularly admired: Dennis Lillee, John Lever
Off-season 1986–87: In England working for 'Scarborough Fixings'
Other sports played: Rugby, hockey, squash, golf, American football, soccer
Relaxations: Car maintenance, wine- and beer-making. Photography and real ale. Home computer, video games. 'Also terrible snooker player.'
Extras: On debut for Yorkshire v Somerset, at Weston, 6 August 1980, got Gavaskar as his first wicket. Cap awarded 6 August 1983

Best batting performance: 53* Yorkshire v Nottinghamshire, Trent Bridge 1984
Best bowling performance: 5-35 Yorkshire v Somerset, Sheffield 1981

LAST SEASON: BATTING

	I.	N.O.	R.	H.S.	AV.
TEST					
1ST-CLASS	12	4	82	18*	10.25
INT					
JPL	6	5	17	10*	–
NAT.W.	–	–	–	–	–
B & H					

LAST SEASON: BOWLING

	O.	M.	R.	W.	AV.
TEST					
1ST-CLASS	407.3	81	1318	43	30.65
INT					
JPL	51.1	1	224	4	56.00
NAT.W.	12	3	39	0	–
B & H					

CAREER: BATTING

	I.	N.O.	R.	H.S.	AV.
TEST					
1ST-CLASS	63	24	395	53*	10.12
INT					
JPL	19	11	87	16*	10.87
NAT.W.	2	0	14	14	7.00
B & H	2	0	10	10	5.00

CAREER: BOWLING

	O.	M.	R.	W.	AV.
TEST					
1ST-CLASS	1741	347	5556	182	30.52
INT					
JPL	258	14	1172	27	43.40
NAT.W.	52.2	8	202	6	33.66
B & H	76	13	291	7	41.57

DERRICK, J. Glamorgan

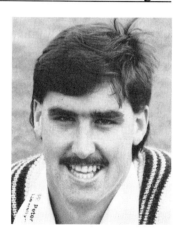

Full Name: John Derrick
Role: Right-hand bat, right-arm medium bowler
Born: 15 January 1963, Aberdare, South Wales
Height: 6′ 2″ **Weight:** 14st
Nickname: J.D., Bo
County debut: 1983
1st-Class 50s scored: 8
Place in batting averages: 71st av. 35.56 (1985 238th av. 12.21)
Place in bowling averages: 100th av. 40.77 (1985 130th av. 50.43)
1st-Class catches 1986: 3 (career: 15)
Parents: John Raymond and Megan Irene
Wife and date of marriage: Anne Irene, 20 April 1985
Education: Glynhafod and Blaengwawr Primary Schools; Blaengwawr Comprehensive School
Qualifications: School Certificate

Jobs outside cricket: Coaching cricket
Family links with cricket: Father and brother, Anthony, play club cricket for Aberdare
Overseas teams played for: Toombul CC, Brisbane, 1982–85; Te Puke CC & Bay of Plenty Red Team New Zealand 1985–86
Cricketers particularly learnt from: Tom Cartwright, Don Wilson, Andy Wagner and senior Glamorgan players and Lance Cairns and Andy Roberts in New Zealand
Cricketers particularly admired: Geoff Boycott, John Snow, Dennis Lillee
Off-season 1986–87: Coaching cricket in New Zealand (Te Puke CC)
Other sports played: Soccer, squash, golf
Other sports followed: Rugby
Relaxations: Swimming, TV, music, cooking
Injuries 1986: Back strain for last 2 weeks of season
Extras: Spent three years on MCC groundstaff 1980–82. Coached at Lord's in winter of 1981. Captained Welsh Schools U-11s on tour to Lancashire and Cheshire. Took 9 for 9 off 9 overs v Lancashire and 6 for 6 off 6 overs v Cheshire
Best batting performance: 78* Glamorgan v Derbyshire, Abergavenny 1986
Best bowling performance: 4-60 Glamorgan v Northamptonshire, Northampton 1985

LAST SEASON: BATTING

	I.	N.O.	R.	H.S.	AV.
TEST					
1ST-CLASS	24	8	569	78*	35.56
INT					
JPL	8	3	130	26	26.00
NAT.W.	–	–	–	–	. –
B & H	3	0	21	8	7.00

LAST SEASON: BOWLING

	O.	M.	R.	W.	AV.
TEST					
1ST-CLASS	265.2	47	897	22	40.77
INT					
JPL	85	1	460	13	35.38
NAT.W.	5.3	0	21	2	10.50
B & H	24	1	84	3	28.00

CAREER: BATTING

	I.	N.O.	R.	H.S.	AV.
TEST					
1ST-CLASS	59	20	1132	78*	29.02
INT					
JPL	24	8	242	26	15.12
NAT.W.	1	0	4	4	–
B & H	6	1	81	42	16.20

CAREER: BOWLING

	O.	M.	R.	W.	AV.
TEST					
1ST-CLASS	633.2	118	2075	44	47.15
INT					
JPL	210.3	3	1099	28	39.25
NAT.W.	28.3	6	62	6	10.33
B & H	52	5	192	5	38.40

61. Who in Denis Compton's view was the fastest bowler he ever played against, or saw?

DILLEY, G. R.　　　　　Worcestershire

Full Name: Graham Roy Dilley
Role: Left-hand bat, right-arm fast bowler
Born: 18 May 1959, Dartford
Height: 6′ 4″ **Weight:** 15st
Nickname: Picca
County debut: 1977 (Kent)
County cap: 1980 (Kent)
Test debut: 1979–80
No. of Tests: 22
No. of One-Day Internationals: 22
50 wickets in a season: 5
1st-Class 50s scored: 4
1st-Class 5 w. in innings: 15
1st-Class 10 w. in match: 2
Place in batting averages: 224th av. 12.11 (1985 250th av. 10.93)
Place in bowling averages: 33rd av. 25.93 (1985 72nd av. 33.59)
1st-Class catches 1986: 6 (career: 62)
Parents: Geoff and Jean
Wife and date of marriage: Helen, 6 November 1980
Education: Dartford West Secondary School
Qualifications: 3 O-levels
Jobs outside cricket: Diamond setter
Family links with cricket: Father and grandfather both played local cricket. His wife is his former Kent colleague Graham Johnson's sister
Overseas tours: With England to Australia 1979–80, West Indies 1981, India 1981–82, New Zealand and Pakistan 1983–84

LAST SEASON: BATTING

	I.	N.O.	R.	H.S.	AV.
TEST	5	1	35	17	8.75
1ST-CLASS	21	7	183	30	13.07
INT	2	1	8	6	–
JPL	3	1	4	2	2.00
NAT.W.	1	1	14	14*	–
B & H	1	1	4	4*	–

CAREER: BATTING

	I.	N.O.	R.	H.S.	AV.
TEST	33	9	365	56	15.20
1ST-CLASS	140	48	1279	81	13.90
INT	13	4	104	31*	11.55
JPL	26	8	252	33	14.00
NAT.W.	10	3	77	19	11.00
B & H	22	7	125	37*	8.33

LAST SEASON: BOWLING

	O.	M.	R.	W.	AV.
TEST	154.5	35	478	19	25.15
1ST-CLASS	350.3	51	1156	44	26.27
INT	42	3	191	5	38.20
JPL	52.5	2	201	7	28.71
NAT.W.	14.5	0	44	5	8.80
B & H	50	5	168	7	24.00

CAREER: BOWLING

	O.	M.	R.	W.	AV.
TEST	676.3	138	2073	69	30.04
1ST-CLASS	2933.5	639	8844	326	27.12
INT	204	17	786	23	34.17
JPL	380.2	29	1507	63	23.92
NAT.W.	129.4	21	393	21	18.71
B & H	289.5	35	986	47	20.97

Cricketers particularly learnt from: Dennis Lillee, John Snow
Off-season 1986–87: Touring Australia with England
Other sports played: Golf, squash, badminton
Relaxations: Music
Extras: Got sacked from his first job with a Hatton Garden diamond firm after taking time off to play for Kent 2nd XI. Suffered from glandular fever at end of 1980 season, causing him to miss Centenary Test. Voted Young Cricketer of the Year 1980 by Cricket Writers' Club. Missed 1984 season after suffering back injury on 1983–84 tour. Joined Worcestershire in 1987
Best batting performance: 81 Kent v Northamptonshire, Northampton 1979
Best bowling performance: 6-57 Kent v Lancashire, Canterbury 1986

D'OLIVEIRA, D. B. Worcestershire

Full Name: Damian Basil D'Oliveira
Role: Right-hand bat, right-arm off-spin bowler, fields anywhere 'except short leg!'
Born: 19 October 1960, Cape Town, South Africa
Height: 5′ 8″ **Weight:** 11st 8lbs
Nickname: Dolly
County debut: 1982
County cap: 1985
1000 runs in a season: 2
1st-Class 50s scored: 20
1st-Class 100s scored: 4
One-day 50s: 6
One-day 100s: 1
Place in batting averages: 117th av. 28.78 (1985 114th av. 29.62)
1st-Class catches 1986: 16 (career: 69)
Parents: Basil and Naomi
Wife and date of marriage: Tracey, 26 September 1983
Children: Marcus Damian, 27 April 1986
Education: St George's RC Primary School; Blessed Edward Oldcorne Secondary School
Qualifications: 3 O-levels, 5 CSEs
Family links with cricket: Father played for Worcestershire and England
Overseas tours: English Counties XI to Zimbabwe 1985
Overseas teams played for: West Perth CC, Western Australia, 1979–80; Christchurch Shirley 1982–83, 1983–84 on a Whitbread scholarship

Cricketers particularly admired: Greg Chappell, Viv Richards, Dennis Lillee, Malcolm Marshall, Richard Hadlee
Off-season 1986–87: Working for Duncan Fearnley Cricket Sales
Other sports played: Football
Other sports followed: Most others, but not horse-racing
Relaxations: Watching films, TV and eating out
Best batting performance: 146* Worcestershire v Gloucestershire, Cheltenham 1986
Best bowling performance: 2-17 Worcestershire v Gloucestershire, Cheltenham 1986

LAST SEASON: BATTING

	I.	N.O.	R.	H.S.	AV.
TEST					
1ST-CLASS	41	3	1094	146*	28.78
INT					
JPL	15	1	347	59	24.78
NAT.W.	4	0	181	99	45.25
B & H	6	0	135	66	22.50

LAST SEASON: BOWLING

	O.	M.	R.	W.	AV.
TEST					
1ST-CLASS	27.4	6	118	5	23.60
INT					
JPL					
NAT.W.	8	1	24	1	–
B & H	8	2	12	3	4.00

CAREER: BATTING

	I.	N.O.	R.	H.S.	AV.
TEST					
1ST-CLASS	167	11	4199	146*	26.91
INT					
JPL	59	3	1100	103	19.64
NAT.W.	11	1	298	99	29.80
B & H	17	2	306	66	20.40

CAREER: BOWLING

	O.	M.	R.	W.	AV.
TEST					
1ST-CLASS	225.4	44	776	20	38.80
INT					
JPL	39	2	232	7	33.14
NAT.W.	28	5	89	5	17.80
B & H	38	4	148	5	29.60

62. True or false: Bill Edrich, playing for Middlesex v Northamptonshire, was smashed in the face by a ferociously fast ball from Frank Tyson, was immediately taken off to hospital, was expected to stay there for several days, but returned to bat the next morning, and in his first over hooked Tyson off his face for six.

63. In June 1986, at the age of 77, the great Australian batsman, Sir Donald Bradman, cut his last official ties with cricket: what were they?

Full Name: Richard John Doughty
Role: Right-hand bat, right-arm fast-medium bowler
Born: 17 November 1960, Bridlington, Yorkshire
Height: 6′ **Weight:** 12½st
Nickname: Dick
County debut: 1981 (Gloucestershire), 1985 (Surrey)
1st-Class 50s scored: 1
1st-Class 5 w. in innings: 2
One-day 50s: 1
Place in batting averages: 168th av. 22.76 (1985 159th av. 23.90)
Place in bowling averages: 78th av. 34.50 (1985 19th av. 25.50)
1st-Class catches 1986: 12 (career: 22)
Parents: Mary and Trevor
Wife and date of marriage: Elizabeth, 2 April 1982
Education: Scarborough College, N Yorkshire
Qualifications: 3 O-levels, 4 CSEs
Jobs outside cricket: Ski technician
Cricketing superstitions: Putting left boot on first; changing chewing gum every hour when in the field
Overseas tours: 'The Leg Trap tour of South Africa 1981, a Canadian team for which I guested.'
Cricketers particularly learnt from: Don Wilson, Geoff Arnold, Trevor Jesty
Cricketers particularly admired: Richard Hadlee, Malcolm Marshall
Off-season 1986–87: Preparing for 1987 season
Other sports played: Golf, rugby, skiing, tennis, fishing
Other sports followed: Motor racing, athletics, American football, soccer
Relaxations: Music, eating, watching TV, films, painting and cooking
Injuries 1986: Split skin on big toe of left foot
Extras: 'After being released by Gloucestershire at the end of the 1984 season, I discovered in February 1985 that I had become a diabetic. With help and encouragement from my wife and friends I persisted in trying to carry on playing cricket and eventually won a place with Surrey. I hope this will encourage other diabetics to live a full life and an active sporting one.' Released by Surrey at end of 1986 season
Best batting performance: 65 Surrey v Derbyshire, Derby 1985
Best bowling performance: 6-33 Surrey v Warwickshire, The Oval 1985

LAST SEASON: BATTING

	I.	N.O.	R.	H.S.	AV.
TEST					
1ST-CLASS	19	2	387	48	22.76
INT					
JPL	8	2	98	36	16.33
NAT.W.					
B & H	3	0	53	30	17.66

CAREER: BATTING

	I.	N.O.	R.	H.S.	AV.
TEST					
1ST-CLASS	50	11	840	65	21.53
INT					
JPL	24	8	254	50*	15.87
NAT.W.	1	1	5	5*	–
B & H	7	0	122	31	17.42

LAST SEASON: BOWLING

	O.	M.	R.	W.	AV.
TEST					
1ST-CLASS	300	50	1104	32	34.50
INT					
JPL	71	3	293	6	48.83
NAT.W.					
B & H	33	4	166	3	55.33

CAREER: BOWLING

	O.	M.	R.	W.	AV.
TEST					
1ST-CLASS	789.5	126	2910	89	32.69
INT					
JPL	199.3	3	1097	20	54.85
NAT.W.	15	2	60	2	30.00
B & H	77	8	359	6	59.83

DOWNTON, P. R.   Middlesex

Full Name: Paul Rupert Downton
Role: Right-hand bat, wicket-keeper
Born: 4 April 1957, Farnborough, Kent
Height: 5′ 10″ **Weight:** 12st 4lbs
Nickname: Nobby
County debut: 1977 (Kent), 1980 (Middlesex)
County cap: 1979 (Kent), 1981 (Middlesex)
Test debut: 1980–81
No. of Tests: 27
No. of One-Day Internationals: 17
1st-Class 50s scored: 25
1st-Class 100s scored: 3
One-day 50s: 5
Place in batting averages: 62nd av. 37.70 (1985 51st av. 38.90)
Parents: George Charles and Jill Elizabeth
Wife and date of marriage: Alison, 19 October 1985
Education: Sevenoaks School; Exeter University
Qualifications: 9 O-levels, 3 A-levels; Law degree (LLB); NCA coaching course
Family links with cricket: Father kept wicket for Kent 1948–49
Overseas tours: England tour of Pakistan and New Zealand 1977. West Indies 1980–81 and 1986. India and Australia 1984–85. England Young Cricketers tour of West Indies (Vice-captain) 1976

Overseas teams played for: Sandgate, Redcliffe 1981–82; Stellenbosch University 1983–84
Cricketers particularly learnt from: Father, Alan Knott, Clive Radley
Cricketers particularly admired: Alan Knott, Rod Marsh
Off-season 1986–87: Working for James Capel & Co (stockbrokers)
Other sports played: Rugby (played in England U-19 squad 1975 and Exeter University 1st XV), golf, tennis
Other sports followed: American football
Relaxations: Reading
Extras: Made debut for Kent CCC in 1977, gaining cap in 1979. Played for Kent 2nd XI at age 16
Best batting performance: 104 Middlesex v Northamptonshire, Lord's 1985

LAST SEASON: BATTING

	I.	N.O.	R.	H.S.	AV.
TEST	2	0	34	29	17.00
1ST-CLASS	27	5	871	126*	39.59
INT	2	1	8	4*	–
JPL	9	1	280	50	35.00
NAT.W.	1	0	31	31	–
B & H	6	3	120	53*	40.00

LAST SEASON: WICKET-KEEPING

	C.	ST.		
TEST	1			
1ST-CLASS	43	5		
INT	2	–		
JPL	7	2		
NAT.W.	2	–		
B & H	6	–		

CAREER: BATTING

	I.	N.O.	R.	H.S.	AV.
TEST	43	7	701	74	19.47
1ST-CLASS	235	48	4487	126*	23.99
INT	14	4	193	44*	19.30
JPL	69	23	1052	70	22.86
NAT.W.	18	2	297	62	18.56
B & H	24	9	297	53*	19.80

CAREER: WICKET-KEEPING

	C.	ST.		
TEST	61	5		
1ST-CLASS	416	61		
INT	12	2		
JPL	97	29		
NAT.W.	31	4		
B & H	33	9		

64. Who was the England manager in the West Indies in 1986?

65. Which English counties has Alan Border played for, and when?

66. What have W. G. Grace, Len Hutton and Denis Compton got in common with Tim Robinson of Nottinghamshire and England?

DREDGE, C. H.   Somerset

Full Name: Colin Herbert Dredge
Role: Left-hand bat, right-arm
medium bowler
Born: 4 August 1954, Frome,
Somerset
Height: 6′ 5″ **Weight:** 14st 7lbs
Nickname: Herbie, Bert
County debut: 1976
County cap: 1978
Benefit: 1987
50 wickets in a season: 4
1st-Class 50s scored: 4
1st-Class 5 w. innings: 12
Place in batting averages: 226th
av. 12.61 (1985 182nd av. 20.67)
Place in bowling averages: 69th
av. 32.88 (1985 90th av. 37.16)
1st-Class catches 1986: 7 (career: 84)
Parents: Frederick and Kathleen
Wife and date of marriage: Mandy, 9 December 1978
Children: David, 13 November 1979; Mark, 6 July 1981; Neil, 27 June 1983
Education: Wesley Methodist School; Milk Street School; Oakfield School
Qualifications: Qualified toolmaker. Served apprenticeship Rolls Royce Ltd.,
Patchway, Bristol
Family links with cricket: One of ten children, eight boys and two girls; all the
brothers have played cricket for Frome CC
Jobs outside cricket: Toolmaker
Cricketers particularly learnt from: Peter White, Peter Robinson
Other sports played: Western League football for Welton Rovers. Played for

LAST SEASON: BATTING

	I.	N.O.	R.	H.S.	AV.
TEST					
1ST-CLASS	21	3	227	40	12.61
INT					
JPL	7	3	77	28*	19.25
NAT.W.	1	0	8	8	–
B & H	4	1	34	25	11.33

CAREER: BATTING

	I.	N.O.	R.	H.S.	AV.
TEST					
1ST-CLASS	218	68	2100	56*	14.00
INT					
JPL	54	29	317	28*	12.68
NAT.W.	9	4	28	9	5.60
B & H	21	11	99	25	9.90

LAST SEASON: BOWLING

	O.	M.	R.	W.	AV.
TEST					
1ST-CLASS	389	83	1151	35	32.88
INT					
JPL	74	1	352	8	44.00
NAT.W.	18	2	62	3	20.66
B & H	42.2	5	155	8	19.37

CAREER: BOWLING

	O.	M.	R.	W.	AV.
TEST					
1ST-CLASS	4666.5	1100	13113	440	29.80
INT					
JPL	889.1	41	3964	148	26.78
NAT.W.	254.3	34	868	39	22.25
B & H	397.4	46	1391	60	23.18

Bristol City Reserves 1974–76 and now for Frome Town AFC
Relaxations: 'Football, watching TV, playing with my children.'
Best batting performance: 56* Somerset v Yorkshire, Harrogate 1977
Best bowling performance: 6-37 Somerset v Gloucestershire, Bristol 1981

DYER, R. I. H. B.   Warwickshire

Full Name: Robin Ian Henry
Benbow Dyer
Role: Right-hand bat
Born: 22 December 1958, Hertford
Height: 6' 4" **Weight:** 13st
Nickname: Dobbin, Donkey, Tuft
County debut: 1981
1000 runs in a season: 2
1st-Class 50s scored: 18
1st-Class 100s scored: 3
One-day 50s: 2
One-day 100s: 1
Place in batting averages: 236th
av. 11.37 (1985 119th av. 28.88)
1st-Class catches 1986: 5 (career: 39)
Parents: Ian and Dee
Marital status: Single
Education: Wellington College,
Berkshire; Durham University

Qualifications: BA Hons in Politics; 3 A-levels
Jobs outside cricket: Returning to Wellington College as a schoolmaster
Family links with cricket: 'Father and mother gave me a lot of encouragement.'
Cricketing superstitions: 'I don't like changing my kit after scoring runs.'
Overseas tours: With English Schools to India 1977–78
Cricketers particularly learnt from: 'Learnt a lot from Fred Berry, the former Surrey player, who was coach at Wellington. Specially admired M. J. K. Smith and Dennis Amiss.'
Other sports played: Golf, squash
Other sports followed: Watches Rugby Union regularly
Relaxations: Listening to music (particularly Peter Gabriel), reading good books, watching films, theatre, eating and drinking in sociable situations, travelling
Extras: Captained Durham University. Wears spectacles. Released at end of 1986 season
Best batting performance: 109* Warwickshire v Zimbabwe, Edgbaston 1985

	I.	N.O.	R.	H.S.	AV.
TEST					
1ST-CLASS	10	2	91	28	11.37
INT					
JPL					
NAT.W.					
B & H	3	0	14	13	4.66

CAREER: BATTING

	I.	N.O.	R.	H.S.	AV.
TEST					
1ST-CLASS	116	11	2843	109*	27.07
INT					
JPL	22	2	357	50	17.85
NAT.W.	7	0	205	119	29.29
B & H	9	0	142	54	15.77

LAST SEASON: BOWLING

	O.	M.	R.	W.	AV.
TEST					
1ST-CLASS					
INT					
JPL					
NAT.W.					

CAREER: BOWLING

	O.	M.	R.	W.	AV.
TEST					
1ST-CLASS	6	0	41	0	–
INT					
JPL	2	0	18	0	–
NAT.W.					
B & H					

EAST, D. E.   Essex

Full Name: David Edward East
Role: Right-hand bat, wicket-keeper
Born: 27 July 1959, Clapton
Height: 5′ 10″ **Weight:** 12st 10lbs
Nickname: 'Various insults, but Ethel seems popular and Easty.'
County debut: 1981
County cap: 1982
1st-Class 50s scored: 12
1st-Class 100s scored: 3
Place in batting averages: 181st av. 20.27 (1985 75th av. 34.19)
Parents: Edward William and Joan Lillian
Wife and date of marriage: Jeanette Anne, 14 September 1984
Family links with cricket: Father played club cricket for Hadley CC, an Essex touring side
Education: Millfields Primary; Hackney Downs School; University of East Anglia
Qualifications: BSc Hons in Biological Sciences. Advanced Cricket Coach
Jobs outside cricket: Has worked for shipping, insurance and finance brokers, cricket coaching and now cricket administration
Overseas teams played for: Avondale CC, Cape Town, 1984–85

Cricketing superstitions: 'The number 111. Never take wicket-keeping pads off between sessions unless raining hard!'

Cricketers particularly learnt from: Alan Knott

Off-season 1986–87: Co-ordinating the County Benefit Season for 1987

Other sports played: Hockey, 'poor squash'

Other sports followed: Interested in most but loathes horse-racing

Relaxations: Playing the piano, listening to various types of music, video. Generally spending time at home; cooking (especially curry and Chinese)

Injuries 1986: 'Bruised thumb causing me to miss first 1st-Class match since my debut.'

Extras: Spent 1980 season with Northamptonshire 2nd XI. Played for Essex 2nd XI at 16. Gordon's Gin Wicket-keeper of the Year 1983

Cricketing opinions: 'I believe that the "bad light" law is far too ambiguous and that it is interpreted badly by a great number of umpires, particularly when tail-end batsmen are subjected to fast, often short-pitched, bowling.'

Best batting performance: 131 Essex v Gloucestershire, Southend 1985

LAST SEASON: BATTING

	I.	N.O.	R.	H.S.	AV.
TEST					
1ST-CLASS	40	4	730	100*	20.27
INT					
JPL	7	3	56	23	14.00
NAT.W.	2	0	28	28	14.00
B & H	4	1	33	16*	11.00

LAST SEASON: BOWLING

	O.	M.	R.	W.	AV.
TEST					
1ST-CLASS	0.2	0	1	0	–
INT					
JPL					
NAT.W.					
B & H					

CAREER: BATTING

	I.	N.O.	R.	H.S.	AV.
TEST					
1ST-CLASS	190	27	3433	131	21.06
INT					
JPL	38	14	290	43	12.08
NAT.W.	13	4	109	28	12.11
B & H	16	4	181	33	15.08

CAREER: BOWLING

	O.	M.	R.	W.	AV.
TEST					
1ST-CLASS	3.2	0	12	0	–
INT					
JPL					
NAT.W.					

LAST SEASON: WICKET-KEEPING

	C.	ST.			
TEST					
1ST-CLASS	64	19			
INT					
JPL	14	2			
NAT.W.	3	1			
B & H	8	–			

CAREER: WICKET-KEEPING

	C.	ST.			
TEST					
1ST-CLASS	361	43			
INT					
JPL	72	12			
NAT.W.	21	3			
B & H	38	–			

67. Who captained England B on their 1986 tour of Sri Lanka?

EDMONDS, P. H. Middlesex

Full Name: Phillippe Henri Edmonds
Role: Right-hand bat, slow left-arm bowler
Born: 8 March 1951, Lusaka
Height: 6' 2"
Nickname: Goat, Henry, Rommel
County debut: 1971
County cap: 1974
Benefit: 1983 (£80,000)
Test debut: 1975
No. of Tests: 41
No. of One-Day Internationals: 26
50 wickets in a season: 11
1st-Class 50s scored: 22
1st-Class 100s scored: 3
1st-Class 5 w. in innings: 47
1st-Class 10 w. in match: 9
One-day 50s: 2
Place in batting averages: 213th av. 14.42 (1985 229th av. 13.22)
Place in bowling averages: 56th av. 29.23 (1985 20th av. 25.55)
1st-Class catches 1986: 17 (career: 328)
Wife: Frances
Education: Gilbert Rennie High School, Lusaka; Skinner's School, Tunbridge Wells; Cranbrook School; Cambridge University
Jobs outside cricket: Has worked for sports promotion and finance company
Overseas tours: Pakistan and New Zealand 1977–78; Australia 1978–79; India and Australia 1984–85; West Indies 1986

LAST SEASON: BATTING

	I.	N.O.	R.	H.S.	AV.
TEST	8	2	77	20	12.83
1ST-CLASS	11	3	125	31	15.62
INT	–	–	–	–	–
JPL	3	2	24	14*	–
NAT.W.	1	0	0	0	–
B & H	2	1	24	15*	–

LAST SEASON: BOWLING

	O.	M.	R.	W.	AV.
TEST	186	59	390	15	26.00
1ST-CLASS	343	103	721	23	31.34
INT	22	2	91	2	45.50
JPL	48	2	198	6	33.00
NAT.W.	24	1	98	0	–
B & H	50.4	7	221	9	24.55

CAREER: BATTING

	I.	N.O.	R.	H.S.	AV.
TEST	53	10	765	64	17.79
1ST-CLASS	414	73	6583	142	19.30
INT	17	6	100	20	9.09
JPL	115	29	1283	52	14.91
NAT.W.	27	9	368	63*	20.44
B & H	39	9	506	44*	16.86

CAREER: BOWLING

	O.	M.	R.	W.	AV.
TEST	199 1385.1	48 451	3506	106	33.07
1ST-CLASS	287 11358	72 3520	26404	1079	24.47
INT	28 189.2	1 17	816	22	37.09
JPL	972	74	4064	175	23.22
NAT.W.	386.2	63	1169	43	27.18
B & H	663.1	84	1430	65	22.00

Overseas teams played for: Eastern Province in 1975–76 Currie Cup
Off-season 1986–87: With England in Australia
Other sports played: Rugby for Cambridge but missed blue. Squash
Relaxations: 'Read *Financial Times* avidly at breakfast.' Crosswords
Extras: Cambridge cricket blue 1971–72–73. Captain 1973. Vice-captain of Middlesex, 1980
Best batting performance: 142 Middlesex v Glamorgan, Swansea 1984
Best bowling performance: 8-53 Middlesex v Hampshire, Bournemouth 1984

ELLCOCK, R. M.　　　　Worcestershire

Full Name: Ricardo McDonald Ellcock
Role: Right-hand bat, right-arm fast bowler
Born: 17 June 1965, Barbados
Height: 5′ 11″ **Weight:** 13st
Nickname: Ricky
County debut: 1982
1st-Class catches 1986: — (career: 4)
Parents: Everson McDonald (deceased) and Ione Marian
Marital status: Single
Education: Welches Mixed School, Combermere, Barbados; Malvern College, England
Qualifications: 6 O-levels
Overseas tours: Around West Indies with Barbados

LAST SEASON: BATTING

	I.	N.O.	R.	H.S.	AV.
TEST					
1ST-CLASS	2	2	4	4*	–
INT					
JPL					
NAT.W.					
B & H					

CAREER: BATTING

	I.	N.O.	R.	H.S.	AV.
TEST					
1ST-CLASS	36	10	344	45*	13.23
INT					
JPL	5	2	6	5*	2.00
NAT.W.	1	0	6	6	–
B & H	2	1	16	12	–

LAST SEASON: BOWLING

	O.	M.	R.	W.	AV.
TEST					
1ST-CLASS	32	2	117	4	29.25
INT					
JPL					
NAT.W.					
B & H					

CAREER: BOWLING

	O.	M.	R.	W.	AV.
TEST					
1ST-CLASS	593.4	82	2128	67	31.76
INT					
JPL	61.3	4	235	13	18.08
NAT.W.	10	2	49	3	16.33
B & H	25	4	98	3	32.66

Overseas teams played for: Combined Schools, Barbados, 1980; Carlton and Barbados
Cricketers particularly learnt from: Malcolm Marshall
Cricketers particularly admired: Alvin Kallicharran, Michael Holding
Other sports played: Table-tennis and basketball
Other sports followed: Soccer and motor-racing
Relaxations: Movies, music, TV
Best batting performance: 45* Worcestershire v Essex, Worcester 1984
Best bowling performance: 4-34 Worcestershire v Glamorgan, Worcester 1984

ELLISON, R. M. Kent

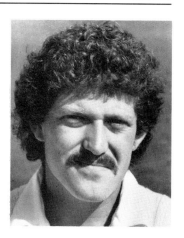

Full Name: Richard Mark Ellison
Role: Left-hand bat, right-arm medium bowler, outfielder
Born: 21 September 1959, Ashford, Kent
Height: 6′ 3″ **Weight:** 14st 5lbs
Nickname: Elly
County debut: 1981
County cap: 1983
Test debut: 1984
No. of Tests: 11
No. of One-Day Internationals: 14
50 wickets in a season: 3
1st-Class 50s scored: 11
1st-Class 100s scored: 1
1st-Class 5 w. in innings: 8
1st-Class 10 w. in match: 2
One-day 50s: 4
Place in batting averages: 157th av. 24.00 (1985 131st av. 26.98)
Place in bowling averages: 115th av. 47.95 (1985 1st av. 17.20)
1st-Class catches 1986: 5 (career: 40)
Parents: Peter (deceased) and Bridget
Wife and date of marriage: Fiona, 28 September 1985
Education: Friars Prep. School; Tonbridge School; St Luke's College, Exeter University
Qualifications: 8 O-levels, 2 A-levels, various teaching awards. BEd (teacher)
Family links with cricket: Grandfather played with the Grace brothers. Brother, Charles Christopher, played for Cambridge University in 1982
Overseas tours: With England to India and Australia 1984–85; Sharjah 1985; West Indies 1986

Overseas teams played for: University of Witwatersrand 1983–84, 1984–85
Cricketers particularly learnt from: Derek Underwood, Bob Woolmer, Ray Dovey
Cricketers particularly admired: R. Hadlee, M. Marshall
Off-season 1986–87: Playing for Tasmania
Other sports played: 'Hockey (UAU trial), snooker. Anything apart from horses and greyhounds.'
Relaxations: Music – Dire Straits, Chris de Burgh. Snooker and fruit machines with Chris Cowdrey
Extras: Public Schools Cricketer of the Year 1978. Invited to tour with MCC to Bangladesh (1980) and East and Central Africa (1981) but unable to go due to studies. Scored 55* on debut. 'Overweight, so Chris Cowdrey and Mark Benson keep telling me – but who are they to know?'
Injuries 1986: Ankle and achilles tendon
Opinions on cricket: 'Still too many overs leading to too late finishes. Fines for over-rates should be abolished.'
Best batting performance: 108 Kent v Oxford University, Oxford 1984
Best bowling performance: 7-87 Kent v Northamptonshire, Maidstone 1985

LAST SEASON: BATTING

	I.	N.O.	R.	H.S.	AV.
TEST	2	0	31	19	15.50
1ST-CLASS	27	6	521	62*	24.80
INT	2	0	22	12	11.00
JPL	7	3	85	33*	21.25
NAT.W.	1	0	9	9	–
B & H	5	2	74	34*	24.66

LAST SEASON: BOWLING

	O.	M.	R.	W.	AV.
TEST	35	11	80	1	–
1ST-CLASS	351.4	79	1023	22	46.50
INT	32	2	134	4	33.50
JPL	67.4	4	315	12	26.25
NAT.W.	10.4	2	46	2	23.00
B & H	76.5	17	245	13	18.84

CAREER: BATTING

	I.	N.O.	R.	H.S.	AV.
TEST	16	1	202	41	13.46
1ST-CLASS	135	35	2603	108	26.03
INT	12	4	87	24	10.88
JPL	46	19	720	84	26.66
NAT.W.	13	6	240	49*	34.28
B & H	16	3	279	74	21.46

CAREER: BOWLING

	O.	M.	R.	W.	AV.
TEST	377.2	90	1048	35	29.94
1ST-CLASS	471.5	563	5627	212	26.54
INT	116	9	510	12	42.50
JPL	373.2	26	1657	69	24.01
NAT.W.	145.4	28	456	24	19.00
B & H	197.4	39	615	29	21.20

68. Who was vice-captain of England B on their 1986 tour of Sri Lanka?

69. Who captained South Africa in their 1986 Test Matches v unofficial Australia?

EMBUREY, J. E.   Middlesex

Full Name: John Ernest Emburey
Role: Right-hand bat, right-arm off-break bowler, slip or gully fielder
Born: 20 August 1952, Peckham
Height: 6′ 2″ **Weight:** 13st 12lbs
Nickname: Embers, Ernie
County debut: 1973
County cap: 1977
Benefit: 1986
Test debut: 1978
No. of Tests: 37
No. of One-Day Internationals: 14
50 wickets in a season: 9
1st-Class 50s scored: 20
1st-Class 100s scored: 2
1st-Class 5 w. in innings: 47
1st-Class 10 w. in match: 8
One-day 50s: 1
Place in batting averages: 190th av. 18.63 (1985 126th av. 27.66)
Place in bowling averages: 13th av. 22.35 (1985 47th av. 29.44)
1st-Class catches 1986: 16 (career: 261)
Parents: John and Rose
Wife and date of marriage: Susie, 20 September 1980
Children: Clare, 1 March 1983; Chloe, 31 October 1985
Education: Peckham Manor Secondary School
Qualifications: O-levels, Advanced Cricket Coaching Certificate
Jobs outside cricket: 'No other jobs. Have been abroad coaching most years.'
Family links with cricket: Brother, Stephen, represented London Schools Colts in 1977
Overseas tours: With England to Australia 1978–79 and 1979–80 (following injury to Geoff Miller), West Indies 1981 and 1986, India 1981–82
Overseas teams played for: St Kilda CC, Melbourne, 1979–80, 1984–85; Prahran, Melbourne, 1977–78; Western Province 1982–83, 1983–84
Cricketers particularly learnt from: 'All.'
Cricketers particularly admired: K. Barrington
Off-season 1986–87: To Australia with England as vice-captain
Other sports: Golf, squash
Relaxations: Reading
Injuries 1986: Broken nose
Extras: Played for Surrey Young Cricketers 1969–70. Middlesex vice-captain since 1983. Banned from Test cricket for three years after playing for

England rebels in South Africa. Hit 6 sixes in 7 balls for Western Province v Eastern Province 1983–84 (52 n.o. in 22 balls)
Best batting performance: 133 Middlesex v Essex, Chelmsford 1983
Best bowling performance: 7-36 Middlesex v Cambridge University, Cambridge 1977

LAST SEASON: BATTING

	I.	N.O.	R.	H.S.	AV.
TEST	9	2	166	75	23.71
1ST-CLASS	13	1	188	49	15.66
INT	2	0	20	20	10.00
JPL	7	2	130	49	26.00
NAT.W.	1	0	7	7	–
B & H	4	2	60	28	30.00

LAST SEASON: BOWLING

	O.	M.	R.	W.	AV.
TEST	156.4	61	282	8	35.25
1ST-CLASS	316.5	110	590	31	19.03
INT	44	4	125	3	41.66
JPL	71	8	341	15	22.73
NAT.W.	24	1	78	3	16.00
B & H	66	12	179	10	17.90

CAREER: BATTING

	I.	N.O.	R.	H.S.	AV.
TEST	56	12	686	75	15.59
1ST-CLASS	299	63	5117	133	21.68
INT	12	2	73	20	7.30
JPL	101	35	1073	49	16.25
NAT.W.	19	6	281	36*	21.61
B & H	30	11	423	50	22.26

CAREER: BOWLING

	O.	M.	R.	W.	AV.
TEST	144.4 1340.3	49 422	2970	97	30.61
1ST-CLASS	155.1 8792.2	39 2644	19921	856	23.27
INT	153.3	20	540	11	49.09
JPL	1007.5	92	4215	194	21.72
NAT.W.	338	57	867	31	27.96
B & H	390.5	72	1051	39	26.94

EVANS, K. P.   Nottinghamshire

Full Name: Kevin Paul Evans
Role: Right-hand bat, right-arm medium bowler, slip fielder
Born: 10 September 1963, Calverton, Nottingham
Height: 6′ 2″ **Weight:** 12st 10lbs
Nickname: Ghost
County debut: 1984
1st-Class catches 1986: 1 (career: 5)
Parents: Eric and Eileen
Marital status: Single
Family links with cricket: Brother taken onto Nottinghamshire staff in 1985. Father played local cricket
Education: William Lee Primary; Colonel Frank Seely Comprehensive School, Calverton
Qualifications: 9 O-levels, 3 A-levels
Jobs outside cricket: Bank work
Cricketing superstitions: Putting left pad on first

Cricketers particularly learnt from: Mike Hendrick, Mike Bore, Bob White
Cricketers particularly admired: Richard Hadlee
Off-season 1986–87: Playing and coaching in New Zealand
Other sports played: Football, tennis, badminton, squash
Relaxations: Listening to music, reading
Injuries 1986: Operation on right elbow
Opinions on cricket: 'Review of the Championship points system. Maybe give points to the team with a first innings lead so that the Championship is not decided totally on declarations and weather.'
Best batting performance: 42 Nottinghamshire v Cambridge University, Trent Bridge 1984
Best bowling performance: 2-31 Nottinghamshire v Cambridge University, Trent Bridge 1984

LAST SEASON: BATTING

	I.	N.O.	R.	H.S.	AV.
TEST					
1ST-CLASS	3	0	15	14	5.00
INT					
JPL	3	1	12	8*	6.00
NAT.W.	2	0	11	10	5.50
B & H					

LAST SEASON: BOWLING

	O.	M.	R.	W.	AV.
TEST					
1ST-CLASS	51.2	8	218	1	–
INT					
JPL	36	1	195	4	48.75
NAT.W.	23	4	64	5	12.80
B & H					

CAREER: BATTING

	I.	N.O.	R.	H.S.	AV.
TEST					
1ST-CLASS	10	0	87	42	8.70
INT					
JPL	10	3	130	28	18.57
NAT.W.	3	0	19	10	6.33
B & H	2	1	22	20	–

CAREER: BOWLING

	O.	M.	R.	W.	AV.
TEST					
1ST-CLASS	129.2	24	460	4	115.00
INT					
JPL	81	2	507	13	39.00
NAT.W.	36	8	94	6	15.66
B & H	11	0	47	1	–

70. Who was England's number two wicket-keeper on their 1986 West Indies Tour?

71. Which current first-class player has turned out for Lancashire, Tasmania, Otago and West Indies?

72. Younis Ahmed has been capped by three counties. Which ones?

73. Name the England team that won the Ashes at The Oval in 1953 – and the 12th man.

Full Name: Russell John Evans
Role: Early order batsman, occasional off-spin bowler, gully or slip fielder
Born: 1 October 1965, Calverton, Nottingham
Height: 6′ **Weight:** 11st 11lbs
Nickname: Brains, G.C.
Parents: Eric and Eileen
Marital status: Single
Education: Colonel Frank Seely Comprehensive School, Calverton
Qualifications: 8 O-levels, 3 A-levels
Jobs outside cricket: Driving jobs, warehouse work
Family links with cricket: Brother Kevin on Nottinghamshire staff. Father played local cricket
Cricketing superstitions: Left pad on first
Cricketers particularly learnt from: M. K. Bore, NCA coaches
Cricketers particularly admired: R. T. Robinson, R. J. Hadlee, C. E. B. Rice, G. Gooch
Off-season 1986–87: Holiday in New Zealand and playing for Papakura Cricket Club near Auckland
Other sports played: Golf, football, snooker, squash
Other sports followed: American football
Relaxations: Music, videos, sleep, eating out, reading cricket books
Injuries 1986: Severely bruised thumb in right hand; sprained ankle
Opinions on cricket: 'Generally, second eleven wickets are not up to the standard required to play at this level of cricket. Not enough second eleven games are played on county grounds where the facilities are correct i.e. covers, groundsmen, wickets.'

LAST SEASON: BATTING

	I.	N.O.	R.	H.S.	AV.
TEST					
1ST-CLASS					
INT					
JPL	1	0	11	11	–
NAT.W.					
B & H					

CAREER: BATTING

	I.	N.O.	R.	H.S.	AV.
TEST					
1ST-CLASS					
INT					
JPL	2	0	31	20	15.50
NAT.W.					
B & H					

FAIRBROTHER, N. H.　　Lancashire

Full Name: Neil Harvey Fairbrother
Role: Left-hand bat, left-arm medium bowler
Born: 9 September 1963, Warrington, Cheshire
Height: 5′ 8″ **Weight:** 11st
Nicknames: Harvey, Farnsbarns, Little Ted
County debut: 1982
County cap: 1985
1000 runs in a season: 3
1st-Class 50s scored: 33
1st-Class 100s scored: 7
One-Day 50s: 6
Place in batting averages: 15th av. 48.68 (1985 48th av. 39.86)
1st-Class catches 1986: 11 (career: 50)
Parents: Leslie Robert and Barbara
Marital status: Single
Education: St Margaret's Church of England School, Oxford; Lymn Grammar School
Qualifications: 5 O-levels
Family links with cricket: Father and two uncles played local league cricket
Overseas tours: Denmark 1980 with North of England U-19
Overseas teams played for: Canberra, Australia 1985–86
Cricketers particularly learnt from: 'All the senior players at Old Trafford have been a great help.'

LAST SEASON: BATTING

	I.	N.O.	R.	H.S.	AV.
TEST					
1ST-CLASS	33	8	1217	131	48.68
INT					
JPL	15	3	386	79	32.16
NAT.W.	4	1	181	93*	60.33
B & H	4	0	115	47	28.75

CAREER: BATTING

	I.	N.O.	R.	H.S.	AV.
TEST					
1ST-CLASS	137	18	4572	164*	38.42
INT					
JPL	44	9	944	79	26.97
NAT.W.	9	2	332	93*	47.42
B & H	13	4	282	47	31.33

LAST SEASON: BOWLING

	O.	M.	R.	W.	AV.
TEST					
1ST-CLASS	23	9	48	0	—
INT					
JPL					
NAT.W.	3	0	16	0	
B & H					

CAREER: BOWLING

	O.	M.	R.	W.	AV.
TEST					
1ST-CLASS	56.1	19	144	2	72.00
INT					
JPL	2	0	15	0	—
NAT.W.	3	0	16	0	—
B & H					

Cricketers particularly admired: Clive Lloyd
Other sports played: Rugby, squash
Other sports followed: Football, rugby union, rugby league
Relaxations: Music and playing sport
Extras: 'I was named after the Australian cricketer Neil Harvey, who was my mum's favourite cricketer.' Three Tests and two U-19 one-day internationals v Young Australians 1983
Best batting performance: 164* Lancashire v Hampshire, Liverpool 1985

FALKNER, N. J. Surrey

Full Name: Nicholas James Falkner
Role: Right-hand bat, right-arm seamer; cover or midwicket fielder
Born: 30 September 1962, Redhill, Surrey
Height: 5′ 10½″ **Weight:** 12st 7lbs
Nickname: Beefy, Vulture, Falksi
County debut: 1984
1st-Class 50s scored: 2
1st-Class 100s scored: 2
Place in batting averages: 72nd av. 35.43
1st-Class catches 1986: 7 (career: 7)
Parents: John and Barbara
Marital status: Single
Education: Yardley Court and Reigate Grammar School
Qualifications: 5 O-levels
Jobs outside cricket: Assistant buyer for Balfour Beatty Int Construction; worked in insurance company
Family links with cricket: Father plays club cricket for Chipstead and Coulsdon
Cricketing superstitions: Always put left pad on first. One of the last to leave changing room
Overseas teams played for: Perth Cricket Club 1982–83, 1985–86
Cricketers particularly learnt from: Geoff Arnold, Les Smithers, David Gibson
Cricketers particularly admired: Vivian Richards
Off-season 1986–87: Playing grade cricket in Perth, West Australia for University CC

Other sports played: Squash, rugby and golf (badly)
Other sports followed: Any sports
Relaxations: Reading, playing chess and sleeping
Opinions on cricket: 'When the 110 overs are complete that should be it for the day even if all 110 overs are finished by 6.15 pm. Four-day games must come in, *i.e.* every County plays one another once during the season. One overseas player per County only!'
Injuries 1986: Knee injury, August; pulled hamstring, September
Best batting performance: 102 Surrey v Middlesex, Lord's 1986

LAST SEASON: BATTING

	I.	N.O.	R.	H.S.	AV.
TEST					
1ST-CLASS	18	2	567	102	35.43
INT					
JPL	1	0	31	31	–
NAT.W.	2	0	36	36	18.00
B & H					

CAREER: BATTING

	I.	N.O.	R.	H.S.	AV.
TEST					
1ST-CLASS	19	3	668	102	41.75
INT					
JPL	3	0	99	44	33.00
NAT.W.	2	0	36	36	18.00
B & H	1	0	2	2	–

LAST SEASON: BOWLING

	O.	M.	R.	W.	AV.
TEST					
1ST-CLASS	4	1	9	1	–
INT					
JPL					
NAT.W.					
B & H					

CAREER: BOWLING

	O.	M.	R.	W.	AV.
TEST					
1ST-CLASS	4	1	9	1	–
INT					
JPL					
NAT.W.					
B & H					

74. Who is the only man to have captained England at both cricket and soccer?

75. Which England opener christened his son after his England opening partner?

76. What was unusual about Matthew Maynard's innings for Glamorgan v Yorkshire on 27 August 1985?

FELTHAM, M. A. Surrey

Full Name: Mark Andrew Feltham
Role: Right-hand bat, right-arm
fast-medium bowler
Born: 26 June 1963, London
Height: 6′ 2″ **Weight:** 13st 2lbs
Nickname: Felts, Felpsi, Boff or
Douglas
County debut: 1983
1st-Class 50s scored: 1
1st-Class 5 w. in innings: 1
Place in batting averages: 137th
av. 26.33
Place in bowling averages: 63rd
av. 30.03
1st-Class catches 1986: 1 (career: 6)
Parents: Leonard William and
Patricia Louise
Marital status: Single
Education: Roehampton Church
School; Tiffin Boys' School
Qualifications: 7 O-levels; Advanced Cricket Coach
Family links with cricket: Mother involved in Ken Barrington Cricket Centre
Appeal; brother plays for Surrey Young Cricketers
Cricketing superstitions: Left pad on before right
Overseas tours: Australia, 1980, with Surrey Cricket Association U-19s;
Barbados, 1981, with MCC Young Professionals
Overseas teams played for: Glenwood High School Old Boys, Durban,
1984–85

LAST SEASON: BATTING

	I.	N.O.	R.	H.S.	AV.
TEST					
1ST-CLASS	14	5	237	76	26.33
INT					
JPL	7	3	67	37	16.75
NAT.W.	2	0	13	12	6.50
B & H	2	2	6	6*	–

LAST SEASON: BOWLING

	O.	M.	R.	W.	AV.
TEST					
1ST-CLASS	224	48	781	26	30.03
INT					
JPL	68	2	391	12	32.58
NAT.W.	22	3	78	4	19.50
B & H	31.5	3	160	1	–

CAREER: BATTING

	I.	N.O.	R.	H.S.	AV.
TEST					
1ST-CLASS	31	10	478	76	22.76
INT					
JPL	18	9	144	37	16.00
NAT.W.	3	0	17	12	5.66
B & H	6	3	51	22*	17.00

CAREER: BOWLING

	O.	M.	R.	W.	AV.
TEST					
1ST-CLASS	544.2	107	1911	60	31.85
INT					
JPL	162.2	7	924	24	38.50
NAT.W.	35	7	118	5	23.60
B & H	70.2	9	302	7	43.14

Cricketers particularly learnt from: Sylvester Clarke, Pat Pocock, Mickey Stewart, Geoff Arnold
Cricketers particularly admired: Ian Botham, David Gower, Graham Gooch
Other sports played: Football, snooker
Relaxations: Listening to music
Extras: Played for England Schools at U-15 and U-19 levels. On the MCC Young Professionals Staff 1981 and 1982 seasons
Best batting performance: 76 Surrey v Gloucestershire, The Oval 1986
Best bowling performance: 5-62 Surrey v Warwickshire, Edgbaston 1984

FELTON, N. A.   Somerset

Full Name: Nigel Alfred Felton
Role: Left-hand bat
Born: 24 October 1960, Guildford, Surrey
Height: 5′ 7″ **Weight:** 10st 7lbs
Nickname: Will, Twiglets
County debut: 1982
1000 runs in a season: 1
1st-Class 50s scored: 19
1st-Class 100s scored: 6
One-Day 50s: 7
Place in batting averages: 103rd av. 30.29 (1985 76th av. 34.15)
1st-Class catches 1986: 7 (career: 20)
Parents: Ralph and Enid
Marital status: Single
Education: Hawes Down Secondary School, West Wickham, Kent; Millfield School, Street, Somerset; Loughborough University
Qualifications: 6 O-levels, 2 A-levels, BSc(Hons), Cert of Education PE/Sports Sciences
Cricketing superstitions: Always put right pad on first
Overseas tours: English Schools Tour of India, 1976–77; Young England in Australia, 1978
Overseas teams played for: Waneroro CC, Perth, Western Australia 1985–86
Cricketers particularly learnt from: Peter Denning
Cricketers particularly admired: Alan Knott, Ian Botham, Viv Richards
Other sports: Most ball games
Relaxations: Music, reading, relaxing at home
Extras: Joined Somerset in July 1981. Played a season for Kent in 1980 after leaving Millfield and before going to Loughborough. Left Kent at pre-season

training 1981, due to the size of the staff. Joined Somerset at end of first year at Loughborough

Best batting performance: 173* Somerset v Kent, Taunton 1983

LAST SEASON: BATTING

	I.	N.O.	R.	H.S.	AV.
TEST					
1ST-CLASS	37	3	1030	156*	30.29
INT					
JPL	9	2	268	96	38.28
NAT.W.	2	1	73	59*	–
B & H	2	0	3	3	1.50

LAST SEASON: BOWLING

	O.	M.	R.	W.	AV.
TEST					
1ST-CLASS	1	0	3	0	–
INT					
JPL					
NAT.W.					
B & H					

CAREER: BATTING

	I.	N.O.	R.	H.S.	AV.
TEST					
1ST-CLASS	112	5	3173	173*	29.65
INT					
JPL	27	4	624	96	27.13
NAT.W.	7	2	295	87	59.00
B & H	2	0	3	3	1.50

CAREER: BOWLING

	O.	M.	R.	W.	AV.
TEST					
1ST-CLASS	1.1	0	7	0	–
INT					
JPL	1	0	7	0	–
NAT.W.					
B & H					

FERREIRA, A. M.   Warwickshire

Full Name: Anthonie Michal Ferreira
Role: Right-hand bat, right-arm medium bowler, slip or gully fielder
Born: 13 April 1955, Pretoria, South Africa
Height: 6′ 3″ **Weight:** 15st 5lbs
Nickname: Yogi – 'known as Anton'
County debut: 1979
County cap: 1983
50 wickets in a season: 3
1st-Class 50s scored: 32
1st-Class 100s scored: 4
1st-Class 5 w. in innings: 18
1st-Class 10 w. in match: 2
One-Day 50s: 2
Place in batting averages: 25th av. 45.88 (1985 122nd av. 28.75)
Place in bowling averages: 121st av. 53.20 (1985 40th av. 28.14)
1st-Class catches 1986: 8 (career: 108)
Parents: Anthonie and Eileen
Wife and date of marriage: Dalène, 28 March 1981
Education: Hillview High School, Pretoria; Pretoria University

Qualifications: BA(Ed) Psychology and geography
Jobs outside cricket: Employed by University of Pretoria as a full-time cricket coach and organiser
Cricket superstitions: 'When the score is 111, 222 or 333, hoping either for a wicket when fielding or a run when batting.'
Overseas tours: Toured UK with Pretoria University in 1975 and in 1978 with a group of young South African players sponsored by Barclays Bank. During tour played twice for Derrick Robins XI
Overseas teams played for: Northern Transvaal
Cricketers particularly admired: 'Tried to pick out sound advice from all team-mates and opponents throughout career and apply in own specific style.'
Cricketers particularly admired: Mike Procter, Clive Rice
Other sports played: 'I play golf, squash and tennis – provincial colours in boxing and soccer while still at school.' Once fought Gerry Coetzee – since world professional heavyweight champion (lost in 6th round)
Other sports followed: 'I watch all sports whenever possible (TV or live).'
Relaxations: 'Music, movies, videos and good restaurants.'
Extras: Released at end of 1986 season
Best batting performance: 112* Warwickshire v India, Edgbaston 1982
Best bowling performance: 8-38 Northern Transvaal v Transvaal B, Pretoria 1977–78

LAST SEASON: BATTING

	I.	N.O.	R.	H.S.	AV.
TEST					
1ST-CLASS	15	6	413	69*	45.88
INT					
JPL	6	2	135	32*	33.75
NAT.W.	2	2	59	32*	–
B & H					

LAST SEASON: BOWLING

	O.	M.	R.	W.	AV.
TEST					
1ST-CLASS	178	47	532	10	53.20
INT					
JPL	27.2	0	140	6	23.33
NAT.W.	19.3	2	52	4	13.00
B & H					

CAREER: BATTING

	I.	N.O.	R.	H.S.	AV.
TEST					
1ST-CLASS	316	63	7114	112*	28.11
INT					
JPL	70	18	1217	52	23.40
NAT.W.	13	6	166	32*	23.71
B & H	24	8	393	71	24.56

CAREER: BOWLING

	O.	M.	R.	W.	AV.
TEST					
1ST-CLASS	5566.4	1289	16283	538	30.26
INT					
JPL	634	25	3264	124	26.32
NAT.W.	168.3	26	565	28	20.17
B & H	298.4	29	1318	47	28.04

77. What was uniquely memorable about one ball bowled by C. J. Knott in the match between Hampshire and Gloucestershire at Portsmouth in 1951?

FERRIS, G. J. F.　　　　　　Leicestershire

Full Name: George John Fitzgerald Ferris
Role: Right-hand bat, right-arm fast bowler
Born: 18 October 1964, Urlings Village, Antigua
Height: 6′ 3″ **Weight:** 13st 7lbs
Nickname: Ferro
County debut: 1983
1st-Class 5 w. in innings: 3
1st-Class 10 w. in match: 1
Place in bowling averages: —
(1985 134th av. 55.07)
1st-Class catches 1986: 4 (career: 7)
Children: Imran
Education: Jenning's Secondary
Overseas tours: With Young West Indies to Zimbabwe 1983
Overseas teams played for: Leeward Islands; Matabeleland
Cricketers particularly learnt from: Andy Roberts (neighbour in Antigua)
Other sports: Soccer, tennis
Relaxations: Listening to music
Best batting performance: 26 Leeward Islands v Guyana, Nevis 1982–83
Best bowling performance: 7-42 Leicestershire v Glamorgan, Hinckley 1983

LAST SEASON: BATTING

	I.	N.O.	R.	H.S.	AV.
TEST					
1ST-CLASS	6	1	67	17*	13.40
INT					
JPL	1	1	2	2*	–
JPL	–	–	–	–	–
B & H					

LAST SEASON: BOWLING

	O.	M.	R.	W.	AV.
TEST					
1ST-CLASS	104	20	356	13	27.38
INT					
JPL	8	0	38	0	–
JPL	9	0	49	0	–
B & H					

CAREER: BATTING

	I.	N.O.	R.	H.S.	AV.
TEST					
1ST-CLASS	42	22	230	26	11.50
INT					
JPL	3	2	15	9*	–
NAT.W.	–	–	–	–	–
B & H	1	1	0	0*	–

CAREER: BOWLING

	O.	M.	R.	W.	AV.
TEST					
1ST-CLASS	907.1	161	3090	104	29.71
INT					
JPL	62.5	3	278	9	30.88
NAT.W.	15	1	58	0	–
B & H	40	3	209	6	34.83

FINNEY, R. J.   Derbyshire

Full Name: Roger John Finney
Role: Right-hand bat, left-arm
medium bowler
Born: 2 August 1960, Darley Dale,
Derbyshire
Height: 6′ 1″ **Weight:** 12st 10lbs
Nickname: Albert
County debut: 1982
County cap: 1985
50 wickets in a season: 2
1st-Class 50s scored: 9
1st-Class 5 w. in innings: 8
One-Day 50s: 1
Place in batting averages: 166th
av. 23.08 (1985 222nd av. 14.11)
Place in bowling averages: 92nd
av. 37.75 (1985 34th av. 27.42)
1st-Class catches 1986: 2 (career: 15)
Parents: Roy and Janet
Marital status: Single
Education: Lady Manners School, Bakewell
Qualifications: O-levels
Jobs outside cricket: Production clerk and sports salesman
Family links with cricket: Father played and captained local side for many
years
Cricket superstitions: 'Always put left pad on first.'
Overseas teams played for: Alexandrians, Pietermaritzburg, South Africa,
1980–82, 1984–85
Cricketers particularly learnt from: Phil Russell (Derbyshire coach), Don
Wilson (head coach at Lord's)

LAST SEASON: BATTING

	I.	N.O.	R.	H.S.	AV.
TEST					
1ST-CLASS	17	5	277	54	23.00
INT					
JPL	7	3	72	24*	18.00
NAT.W.	–	–	–	–	–
B & H	2	2	19	12*	–

CAREER: BATTING

	I.	N.O.	R.	H.S.	AV.
TEST					
1ST-CLASS	127	22	1934	82	18.60
INT					
JPL	37	10	469	50*	17.37
NAT.W.	2	1	19	14*	–
B & H	9	2	152	46	21.71

LAST SEASON: BOWLING

	O.	M.	R.	W.	AV.
TEST					
1ST-CLASS	318.4	62	1057	28	37.75
INT					
JPL	75	5	339	14	24.4
NAT.W.	6	0	25	1	–
B & H	37	7	108	3	36.00

CAREER: BOWLING

	O.	M.	R.	W.	AV.
TEST					
1ST-CLASS	164.8	318	5290	174	30.40
INT					
JPL	308.5	18	1524	49	31.10
NAT.W.	38	7	111	4	27.75
B & H	102.5	13	394	14	28.14

Other sports played: Rugby, football, golf
Relaxations: 'Music, movies, good beer, eating at a good restaurant.'
Extras: Before joining Derbyshire, spent two years with the MCC Young Professionals
Best batting performance: 82 Derbyshire v Gloucestershire, Derby 1985
Best bowling performance: 7-54 Derbyshire v Leicestershire, Leicester 1986

FLETCHER, K. W. R.   Essex

Full Name: Keith William Robert Fletcher
Role: Right-hand bat, right-arm leg-break bowler
Born: 20 May 1944, Worcester
Height: 5' 10" **Weight:** 10st 7lbs
Nickname: Gnome, Fletch
County debut: 1962
County cap: 1963
Test debut: 1968
No. of Tests: 59
No. of One-Day Internationals: 24
1000 runs in a season: 20
1st-Class 50s scored: 215
1st-Class 100s scored: 60
1st-class 200s scored: 2
1st-Class 5 w. in innings: 1
One-Day 50s: 61
One-Day 100s: 2

Place in batting averages: 84th av. 33.45 (1985 89th av. 32.38)
1st-Class catches 1986: 25 (career: 622)
Parents: Joseph and Doris
Wife and date of marriage: Susan Elizabeth, 22 March 1969
Children: Tamara Jane, 2 August 1970; Sara Jane, 19 December 1972
Jobs outside cricket: Has worked as oil representative
Overseas tours: Pakistan 1966–67; Ceylon and Pakistan 1968–69; Australia and New Zealand 1970–71 and 1974–75; India, Sri Lanka and Pakistan 1972–73; West Indies 1973–74; India, Sri Lanka and Australia 1976–77; India and Sri Lanka 1981–82 as Captain
Other sports played: Golf, fishing, 'Shooting partridge – my second favourite sport after cricket.'
Relaxations: Gardening
Extras: Played for Essex at age of 17. Captained Essex from 1974 and led

county to first county championship in 1979, second in 1983 and third in 1984. Also Benson & Hedges Cup in 1979 and John Player Special League in 1981, 1984 and 1985. Won NatWest Trophy in 1985 to become first captain to win all four domestic competitions. Scored two centuries in a match, 111 and 102* v Nottinghamshire, at Nottingham in 1976. Awarded OBE in 1985 New Year's honours list. Gave up captaincy at end of 1985 season, but frequently stood in for Graham Gooch to lead Essex in 1986 Championship winning season

Injuries 1986: Broken finger

Best batting performance: 228* Essex v Sussex, Hastings 1968

Best bowling performance: 5-41 Essex v Middlesex, Colchester 1979

LAST SEASON: BATTING

	I.	N.O.	R.	H.S.	AV.
TEST					
1ST-CLASS	28	6	736	91	33.45
INT					
JPL	11	3	176	62	22.00
NAT.W.					
B & H	5	1	143	51*	35.75

LAST SEASON: BOWLING

	O.	M.	R.	W.	AV.
TEST					
1ST-CLASS					
INT					
JPL					
NAT.W.					
B & H					

CAREER: BATTING

	I.	N.O.	R.	H.S.	AV.
TEST	96	14	3272	216	39.90
1ST-CLASS	1022	150	33165	228*	38.03
INT	22	3	757	131	39.84
JPL	220	38	5524	99*	30.35
NAT.W.	41	4	957	97	25.86
B & H	70	14	1953	101*	34.87

CAREER: BOWLING

	O.	M.	R.	W.	AV.
TEST	20 20.5	1 5	193	2	96.50
1ST-CLASS	64.3 365.3	6 52	2094	49	42.23
INT					
JPL	2.5	0	37	1	–
NAT.W.	10.3	1	43	2	21.50
B & H	4.4	0	30	1	–

78. On one day, 5 September 1985, Gloucestershire awarded their county caps to five players. Who were they?

79. Who, in his first season for Derbyshire, played in eight matches, with a batting average of 2.75, and bowling average of 53.75, and later remarked to an earnest enquirer: 'Other way round, now, and what a lad I'd have been!'

FLETCHER, S. D.   Yorkshire

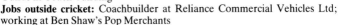

Full Name: Stuart David Fletcher
Role: Right-hand bat, right-arm medium bowler
Born: 8 June 1964, Keighley
Height: 5′ 10″ **Weight:** 12st
Nickname: Fletch, Godber, Norman Stanley, Dr Death, Ghostie
County debut: 1983
1st-Class 5 w. in innings: 1
Place in batting averages: —
(1985 242nd av. 12.00)
Place in bowling averages: 101st
av. 41.06 (1985 125th av. 48.19)
1st-Class catches 1986: 3 (career: 6)
Parents: Brough and Norma Hilda
Education: Woodhouse Primary; Reins Wood Secondary
Qualifications: O-level English and Woodwork; City and Guilds in Coach-building
Jobs outside cricket: Coachbuilder at Reliance Commercial Vehicles Ltd; working at Ben Shaw's Pop Merchants
Family links with cricket: Father played in league cricket
Overseas tours: Holland 1983 with National Cricket Association U-19s
Cricketers particularly learnt from: 'My father, Phil Carrick, Steve Oldham.'
Cricketers particularly admired: Ian Botham, Arnie Sidebottom
Other sports played: Snooker, golf, football.
Other sports followed: Watches Leeds United
Relaxations: Watching TV, snooker and golf

LAST SEASON: BATTING

	I.	N.O.	R.	H.S.	AV.
TEST					
1ST-CLASS	10	3	67	24	9.57
INT					
JPL	1	1	2	2*	–
NAT.W.	2	2	3	2*	–
B & H					

LAST SEASON: BOWLING

	O.	M.	R.	W.	AV.
TEST					
1ST-CLASS	414	82	1273	31	41.06
INT					
JPL	77.4	4	334	10	33.40
NAT.W.	35	4	128	6	21.33
B & H					

CAREER: BATTING

	I.	N.O.	R.	H.S.	AV.
TEST					
1ST-CLASS	29	13	152	28*	9.50
INT					
JPL	5	3	14	8	7.00
NAT.W.	2	2	3	2*	–
B & H	1	1	0	0*	–

CAREER: BOWLING

	O.	M.	R.	W.	AV.
TEST					
1ST-CLASS	977.3	172	3183	79	40.29
INT					
JPL	192.4	4	1040	28	37.14
NAT.W.	59	9	197	9	21.88
B & H	63.3	1	291	4	72.75

Extras: Played in the Yorkshire U-19s who were the first Yorkshire side to win the Cambridge and Oxford Festival, 1983
Best batting performance: 28* Yorkshire v Kent, Tunbridge Wells 1984
Best bowling performance: 5-90 Yorkshire v Middlesex, Leeds 1986

FOLLEY, I.   Lancashire

Full Name: Ian Folley
Role: Right-hand bat, slow left-arm bowler
Born: 9 January 1963
Height: 5′ 10″ **Weight:** 11st 7lbs
Nickname: Thatch, Vicar, Reverend
County debut: 1982
1st-Class 50s scored: 1
1st-Class 5 w. in innings: 3
Place in batting averages: —
(1985 225th av. 13.79)
Place in bowling averages: 84th
av. 36.06 (1983 61st av. 31.37)
1st-Class catches 1986: 10
(career: 32)
Parents: James and Constance
Wife and date of marriage: Julie,
27 September 1986
Education: Mansfield High School,
Nelson; Colne College
Qualifications: Business Studies diploma, 4 O-levels
Cricketers particularly learnt from: D. Bloodworth
Cricketers particularly admired: Clive Lloyd, Ian Botham
Overseas tours: Barbados 1982 with Lancashire; Denmark 1981 with NCA
Overseas teams played for: Glenorchy, Tasmania 1985–86
Other sports played: 'All, except anything to do with horses.'
Other sports followed: 'I'm a bad watcher.'
Extras: Represented Lancashire Schools U-15s and U-19s as captain. Represented Lancashire Federation 1979–81. Played for England U-19 v India U-19 in three 'Tests' in 1981. Young England v West Indies (three 'Tests') and two 1-day 'Internationals'. Debut for Lancashire v Cambridge University at Fenners. In 1984 changed from left-arm medium pace to slow left-arm bowler
Relaxations: Listening to Caribbean music, driving
Best batting performance: 69 Lancashire v Yorkshire, Old Trafford 1985
Best bowling performance: 6-8 Lancashire v Oxford University, Oxford 1985

157

	I.	N.O.	R.	H.S.	AV.
TEST					
1ST-CLASS	19	2	159	20*	9.35
INT					
JPL	–	–	–	–	–
NAT.W.	1	0	1	1	–
B & H					

LAST SEASON: BOWLING

	O.	M.	R.	W.	AV.
TEST					
1ST-CLASS	349	98	1046	29	36.06
INT					
JPL	10	0	70	2	35.00
NAT.W.	24	2	66	3	22.00
B & H					

CAREER: BATTING

	I.	N.O.	R.	H.S.	AV.
TEST					
1ST-CLASS	98	27	871	69	12.26
INT					
JPL	7	5	33	11*	16.50
NAT.W.	2	1	4	3*	–
B & H	5	5	21	11*	–

CAREER: BOWLING

	O.	M.	R.	W.	AV.
TEST					
1ST-CLASS	1679.3	433	4627	138	33.52
INT					
JPL	124	4	588	10	58.80
NAT.W.	39.3	4	114	7	16.28
B & H	84	17	215	14	15.36

FORDHAM, A.   Northamptonshire

Full Name: Alan Fordham
Role: Right-hand bat, occasional right-arm medium bowler
Born: 9 November 1964, Bedford
Height: 6' ½" **Weight:** 12st 7lbs
Nickname: Forders
County debut: 1986
Parents: Clifford Charles and Winifred Ruth
Marital status: Single
Education: Bedford Modern School, 1973–1983; Durham University 1984–1987
Qualifications: 8 O-levels, 3 A-levels
Overseas tours: Barbados in 1983 with Bedford Modern School
Overseas teams played for: Richmond CC, Melbourne, Australia 1983–84

Cricketers particularly learnt from: Andrew Curtis, Brian Reynolds, Bob Carter
Cricketers particularly admired: Allan Lamb, Bob Willis
Off-season 1986–87: Studying at Durham University for final exams in June for chemistry degree
Other sports played: Table tennis – have played for Bedford and for Bedfordshire, squash
Other sports followed: Rugby, anything on TV

Relaxations: Rock music, squash
Extras: Also play for Bedfordshire in the Minor County Championship (debut while still at school). Finished second in batting averages in 1985
Best batting performance: 17 Northamptonshire v Nottinghamshire, Trent Bridge 1986

LAST SEASON: BATTING

	I.	N.O.	R.	H.S.	AV.
TEST					
1ST-CLASS	3	0	26	17	8.66
INT					
JPL					
NAT.W.					
B & H					

CAREER: BATTING

	I.	N.O.	R.	H.S.	AV.
TEST					
1ST-CLASS	3	0	26	17	8.66
INT					
JPL					
NAT.W.					
B & H					

FOSTER, D. J.   Somerset

Full Name: Darren Joseph Foster
Role: Right-hand bat, right-arm fast medium bowler
Born: 14 March 1966, London
Height: 5′ 9″
County debut: 1986
Education: Somerset School; Southgate Technical College
Off-season 1986–87: Coach at Haringey Sports Centre
Extras: Appeared for Middlesex and Surrey 2nd XI's in 1985

LAST SEASON: BATTING

	I.	N.O.	R.	H.S.	AV.
TEST					
1ST-CLASS	1	0	0	0	–
INT					
JPL					
NAT.W.					
B & H					

LAST SEASON: BOWLING

	O.	M.	R.	W.	AV.
TEST					
1ST-CLASS	5	0	29	0	–
INT					
JPL					
NAT.W.					
B & H					

CAREER: BATTING

	I.	N.O.	R.	H.S.	AV.
TEST					
1ST-CLASS	1	0	0	0	–
INT					
JPL					
NAT.W.					
B & H					

CAREER: BOWLING

	O.	M.	R.	W.	AV.
TEST					
1ST-CLASS	5	0	29	0	–
INT					
JPL					
NAT.W.					
B & H					

FOSTER, N. A.   Essex

Full Name: Neil Alan Foster
Role: Right-hand bat, right-arm
fast-medium bowler, outfielder
Born: 6 May 1962, Colchester
Height: 6′ 4″ **Weight:** 13st
Nickname: Fozzy
County debut: 1980
County cap: 1983
Test debut: 1983
No. of Tests: 14
No. of One-Day Internationals: 14
50 wickets in a season: 4
1st-Class 50s scored: 4
1st-Class 5 w. in innings: 23
1st-Class 10 w. in match: 3
Place in batting averages: 185th
av. 19.91 (1985 208th av. 17.00)
Place in bowling averages: 14th
av. 22.37 (1985 56th av. 27.57)
1st-Class catches 1986: 11 (career: 42)
Parents: Jean and Alan
Wife and date of marriage: Rosemary Jane, 21 September 1985
Education: Broomgrove Infant & Junior Schools; Philip Morant Comprehensive, Colchester
Qualifications: 9 O-levels, 1 A-level, NCA Coaching Award
Jobs outside cricket: Played semi-pro football for some years
Family links with cricket: Father and brother both play local cricket
Overseas tours: NCA tour of Canada 1978; Young England XI tour of West Indies 1980; England tour of New Zealand and Pakistan 1983–84, India and Australia 1984–85, West Indies 1986
Overseas teams played for: Glenorchy (Tasmania) 1981–82 on Whitbread Scholarship
Cricketers particularly learnt from: All Essex players
Cricketers particularly admired: Dennis Lillee, Richard Hadlee
Off-season 1986–87: England tour to Australia
Other sports played: Nearly any sport and has had football trials with Colchester and Ipswich. Golf
Relaxations: 'My Boxer dog – Bertie; kennel name: Tropical Burlington Bertie.'
Extras: Was summoned from school at short notice to play for Essex v Kent at Ilford to open bowling. First ball went for 4 wides, but he went on to dismiss Woolmer, Tavaré and Ealham for 51 runs in 15 overs. Played for Young England v Young India 1981

Opinions on cricket: 'I'm fed up seeing all the critics always complaining about our performances. This does not just apply to cricket but all our sports with national sides. Those critics build people up to knock them down and I find it incredible that they get paid to do just that. It's about time we gave people a fair chance and showed them some loyalty.'

Best batting performance: 63 Essex v Lancashire, Ilford 1985

Best bowling performance: 6-30 England v Northern Districts, Hamilton 1983–84

LAST SEASON: BATTING

	I.	N.O.	R.	H.S.	AV.
TEST	3	0	25	17	8.33
1ST-CLASS	27	7	433	53*	21.65
INT	1	0	5	5	–
JPL	6	2	64	38	16.00
NAT.W.	2	0	26	20	13.00
B & H	3	1	12	8	6.00

CAREER: BATTING

	I.	N.O.	R.	H.S.	AV.
TEST	21	3	117	18*	6.50
1ST-CLASS	98	28	1450	63	20.71
INT	11	5	61	24	10.16
JPL	13	3	102	38	10.20
NAT.W.	4	0	29	20	7.25
B & H	8	3	50	23*	10.00

LAST SEASON: BOWLING

	O.	M.	R.	W.	AV.
TEST	91	25	210	5	42.00
1ST-CLASS	715.2	152	2139	100	21.39
INT	16	1	67	2	33.50
JPL	104	9	460	27	17.03
NAT.W.	24	3	61	5	12.20
B & H	55	4	243	9	27.00

CAREER: BOWLING

	O.	M.	R.	W.	AV.
TEST	503.5	105	1480	39	37.94
1ST-CLASS	2454.5	573	8064	345	23.37
INT	190.4	13	819	22	37.22
JPL	207.2	13	944	40	23.60
NAT.W.	112.2	20	317	20	15.85
B & H	206.1	17	789	38	20.76

80. What was noteworthy about the dismissal, stumped, of Sam Coe of Leicestershire at Lord's in July 1900?

FOWLER, G.   Lancashire

Full Name: Graeme Fowler
Role: Left-hand opening bat,
cover fielder, occasional wicket-
keeper
Born: 20 April 1957, Accrington
Height: 5′ 9″ **Weight:** 'Near 11st'
Nickname: Fow, Fox, Foxy
County debut: 1979
County cap: 1981
Test debut: 1982
No. of Tests: 21
No. of One-Day Internationals: 26
1000 runs in a season: 5
1st-Class 50s scored: 51
1st-Class 100s scored: 20
1st-Class 200s scored: 2
One-Day 50s: 22
One-Day 100s: 4
Place in batting averages: 55th
av. 38.76 (1985 207th av. 17.12)
1st-Class catches 1986: 9 (career: 72)
Education: Accrington Grammar School; Bede College, Durham University
Wife: Stephanie
Jobs outside cricket: Qualified teacher, swimming teacher, Advanced Cricket
Coach
Overseas tours: England tour of Australia and New Zealand 1982–83, New
Zealand and Pakistan 1983–84, India and Australia 1984–85
Overseas teams played for: Scarborough, Perth, Western Australia; Tasma-
nia, 1981–82

LAST SEASON: BATTING

	I.	N.O.	R.	H.S.	AV.
TEST					
1ST-CLASS	32	2	1163	180	38.76
INT	2	0	30	20	15.00
JPL	15	0	526	112	35.06
NAT.W.	5	0	61	24	12.20
B & H	4	0	86	76	21.50

LAST SEASON: BOWLING

	O.	M.	R.	W.	AV.
TEST					
1ST-CLASS	4	0	34	2	17.00
INT					
JPL					
NAT.W.					
B & H					

CAREER: BATTING

	I.	N.O.	R.	H.S.	AV.
TEST	37	0	1307	201	35.32
1ST-CLASS	218	11	7559	226	36.51
INT	26	2	744	81*	31.00
JPL	83	5	2166	112	27.76
NAT.W.	16	0	521	122	32.56
B & H	31	1	790	97	26.33

CAREER: BOWLING

	O.	M.	R.	W.	AV.
TEST	3	1	11	0	–
1ST-CLASS	23.2	2	117	4	29.25
INT					
JPL	1	0	1	0	–
NAT.W.					
B & H					

Extras: At 15 he was the youngest opener in the Lancashire League. Scored two consecutive centuries v Warwickshire in July 1982 with aid of a runner. Never played cricket until he was 12. Played for Accrington and Rawtenstall in Lancashire League. In 1975 and 1976 played for ESCA, NAYC, and MCC Schools and Young England
Best batting performance: 226 Lancashire v Kent, Maidstone 1984

FRASER, A. G. J.   Middlesex

Full Name: Alastair Gregory James Fraser
Role: Right-hand bat, right-arm fast-medium bowler
Born: 17 October 1967, Edgware
Height: 6′ 1″ **Weight:** 12st
Nickname: Junior
County debut: 1986
Parents: Don and Irene
Marital status: Single
Education: Gayton High School; John Lyon School; Harrow Weald Sixth Form College
Qualifications: 4 O-levels; NCA Coaching Certificate
Jobs outside cricket: Northwick Park Hospital (Harrow), winter 1985–86
Family links with cricket: Father played club cricket. Brother Angus on Middlesex staff
Overseas tours: NCA tour to Bermuda July 1986 for NCA (South)
Cricketers particularly learnt from: Don Bennett, Geoff Arnold, Gordon Jenkins
Cricketers particularly admired: Richard Hadlee, Malcolm Marshall
Off-season 1986–87: Playing and coaching at Plimmerton CC in New Zealand
Other sports played: Southern Amateur League for Old Lyonians at football. Plays most sports
Other sports followed: Football, rugby, golf, athletics etc.
Relaxations: Following Liverpool FC, watching TV, listening to music
Opinions on cricket: '1 four-day game per week, so players could have a day off each week. England should play South Africa, and politics should not mix with sport.'
Injuries 1986: Muscle pull in back, at start of season but only missed a week or so

Best batting performance: 19* Middlesex v Warwickshire, Uxbridge 1986
Best bowling performance: 3-46 Middlesex v New Zealand, Lord's 1986

LAST SEASON: BATTING

	I.	N.O.	R.	H.S.	AV.
TEST					
1ST-CLASS	3	2	32	19*	–
INT					
JPL	1	1	2	2*	–
NAT.W.					
B & H					

LAST SEASON: BOWLING

	O.	M.	R.	W.	AV.
TEST					
1ST-CLASS	56.4	15	165	8	20.62
INT					
JPL	21	0	80	2	40.00
NAT.W.					
B & H					

CAREER: BATTING

	I.	N.O.	R.	H.S.	AV.
TEST					
1ST-CLASS	3	2	32	19*	–
INT					
JPL	1	1	2	2*	–
NAT.W.					
B & H					

CAREER: BOWLING

	O.	M.	R.	W.	AV.
TEST					
1ST-CLASS	56.4	15	165	8	20.62
INT					
JPL	21	0	80	2	40.00
NAT.W.					
B & H					

FRASER, A. R. C.   Middlesex

Full Name: Angus Robert Charles Fraser
Role: Right-hand bat, right-arm fast-medium bowler, fine leg third-man fielder
Born: 8 August 1965, Billinge, Lancashire
Height: 6′ 6″ **Weight:** 15st 7lbs
Nickname: Gus, Gnat, Jacques Cousteau ('due to a bad round of golf in La Manga')
County debut: 1984
Parents: Don and Irene
Marital status: Single
Education: Gayton High School, Harrow; Orange High Senior High School, Edgware
Qualifications: 6 O-levels, coaching certificate
Jobs outside cricket: Worked at Makro in North Acton 1984–85; labouring for Norwest Holst Construction Ltd 1986–87
Family links with cricket: Father keen follower of cricket; brother Alastair on Middlesex staff

Overseas tours: Toured Barbados with Thames Valley Gentlemen in February 1985; La Manga with Middlesex in April 1985 and 1986
Overseas teams played for: Plimmerton CC, Wellington 1985–86
Cricketers particularly learnt from: Don Bennett, Don Wilson, Clive Desmond
Cricketers particularly admired: Dennis Lillee, Richard Hadlee
Off-season 1986–87: 'Getting fit for next season at RAF Training Camp and doing a labouring job.'
Other sports played: Rugby, golf, football
Relaxations: 'Playing other sport, watching Liverpool FC, playing for Stanmore CC.'
Extras: Took 3 wickets in 4 balls v Glamorgan in 1985.
Opinions on cricket: 'Bring back uncovered wickets and give the bowlers a chance.'
Injuries 1986: 'Stress fracture in back for most, if not all, of season.'
Best batting performance: 13 Middlesex v Worcestershire, Worcester 1986
Best bowling performance: 4-48 Middlesex v Cambridge University, Cambridge 1985

LAST SEASON: BATTING

	I.	N.O.	R.	H.S.	AV.
TEST					
1ST-CLASS	7	1	41	13	6.83
INT					
JPL	4	3	18	9*	–
NAT.W.					
B & H	–	–	–	–	–

LAST SEASON: BOWLING

	O.	M.	R.	W.	AV.
TEST					
1ST-CLASS	156	40	370	10	37.00
INT					
JPL	48	1	224	7	32.00
NAT.W.					
B & H	11	1	36	1	–

CAREER: BATTING

	I.	N.O.	R.	H.S.	AV.
TEST					
1ST-CLASS	8	1	42	13	6.00
INT					
JPL	7	3	26	9*	6.50
NAT.W.					
B & H	2	0	2	2	1.00

CAREER: BOWLING

	O.	M.	R.	W.	AV.
TEST					
1ST-CLASS	233.1	52	613	19	32.26
INT					
JPL	99	4	437	14	31.21
NAT.W.					
B & H	49	4	169	3	56.33

81. A great English poet had a grandson who captained England against Australia. Who was the poet and who was the cricketer?

FRASER-DARLING, D. Nottinghamshire

Full Name: David Fraser-Darling
Role: Right-hand bat, right-arm
medium bowler
Born: 30 September 1963, Sheffield
Height: 6′ 5″ **Weight:** 15st
Nickname: Meat
County debut: 1984
1st-Class 50s scored: 1
1st-Class 5 w. in innings: 1
1st-Class catches 1986: 1 (career: 6)
Parents: Alasdair and Mary
Marital status: Single
Education: Edinburgh University
Qualifications: 7 O-levels, 2 A-levels
Cricketing superstitions: Left sock,
shoe, pad, etc on first
Cricketers particularly learnt from:
David Stanley, Tony Dyer and all at
Nottinghamshire
Cricketers particularly admired: Mike Hendrick
Other sports played: Football; used to play rugby
Other sports followed: Watches any sport
Relaxations: Music, films, drinking
Extras: Played rugby for Scotland U-19 v England, Wales and Ireland 1981
Best batting performance: 61 Nottinghamshire v Northamptonshire, North-
ampton 1986
Best bowling performance: 5-84 Nottinghamshire v Northamptonshire,
Northampton 1986

LAST SEASON: BATTING

	I.	N.O.	R.	H.S.	AV.
TEST					
1ST-CLASS	4	0	142	61	35.50
INT					
JPL	3	1	13	9	6.50
NAT.W.					
B & H					

LAST SEASON: BOWLING

	O.	M.	R.	W.	AV.
TEST					
1ST-CLASS	120	16	461	12	38.41
INT					
JPL	33	2	157	7	22.42
NAT.W.					
B & H					

CAREER: BATTING

	I.	N.O.	R.	H.S.	AV.
TEST					
1ST-CLASS	8	1	175	61	25.00
INT					
JPL	4	1	20	9	6.66
NAT.W.					
B & H					

CAREER: BOWLING

	O.	M.	R.	W.	AV.
TEST					
1ST-CLASS	168	28	604	15	40.27
INT					
JPL	43	3	226	9	25.11
NAT.W.					
B & H					

FRENCH, B. N.   Nottinghamshire

Full Name: Bruce Nicholas French
Role: Right-hand bat, wicket-keeper
Born: 13 August 1959, Warsop,
Nottinghamshire
Height: 5′ 8″ **Weight:** 10st
Nickname: Frog
County debut: 1976, age 16 yrs
10 mths (youngest
Nottinghamshire player)
County cap: 1980
Test debut: 1986
No. of Tests: 5
No. of One-Day Internationals: 3
1st-Class 50s scored: 15
Place in batting averages: 184th
av. 20.05 (1985 211th av. 16.89)
Parents: Maurice and Betty
Wife and date of marriage: Ellen Rose,
9 March 1978
Children: Charles Daniel, 31 August 1978; Catherine Ellen, 28 December
1980
Education: Meden School, Warsop
Qualifications: O-level and CSE

LAST SEASON: BATTING

	I.	N.O.	R.	H.S.	AV.
TEST	7	2	55	21	11.00
1ST-CLASS	16	3	306	58	23.53
INT					
JPL	6	3	47	14*	15.66
NAT.W.	3	1	60	46	30.00
B & H	5	1	18	7	4.50

CAREER: BATTING

	I.	N.O.	R.	H.S.	AV.
TEST	7	2	55	21	11.00
1ST-CLASS	279	55	4120	98	18.39
INT	2	0	11	7	5.50
JPL	60	21	559	37	14.33
NAT.W.	14	5	249	49	27.66
B & H	26	5	216	49*	10.28

LAST SEASON: BOWLING

	O.	M.	R.	W.	AV.
TEST					
1ST-CLASS					
INT					
JPL					
NAT.W.					
B & H					

CAREER: BOWLING

	O.	M.	R.	W.	AV.
TEST					
1ST-CLASS	1	0	22	0	–
INT					
JPL					
NAT.W.					
B & H					

LAST SEASON WICKET-KEEPING

	I.	N.O.	R.	H.S.	AV.
TEST	12	–			
1ST-CLASS	39	4			
INT					
JPL	10	1			
NAT.W.	6	1			
B & H	2	–			

CAREER: WICKET-KEEPING

	I.	N.O.	R.	H.S.	AV.
TEST	12	–			
1ST-CLASS	488	55			
INT	3	1			
JPL	69	12			
NAT.W.	23	3			
B & H	36	8			

Jobs outside cricket: Warehouseman, window cleaner, bricklayer's labourer
Family links with cricket: Brothers, Neil, David, Charlie, Joe, play for Welbeck CC. Father, Treasurer Welbeck CC
Cricketing superstitions: Right pad on before left when keeping wicket
Cricketers particularly learnt from: Bob Taylor, Clive Rice
Off-season 1986–87: On tour with England to Australia
Other sports played: Rock climbing, fell walking and all aspects of mountaineering
Relaxations: Reading, pipe smoking and drinking Theakston's Ale
Extras: Equalled Nottinghamshire record for dismissals in match with 10 (7ct 3st), and dismissals in innings with 6 catches. New Nottinghamshire record for dismissals in a season with 87 (75ct 12st). Wicket-Keeper of the Year 1984
Injuries 1986: Hit on head while batting during Lord's Test v New Zealand
Best batting performance: 98 Nottinghamshire v Lancashire, Trent Bridge 1984

GARD, T. Somerset

Full Name: Trevor Gard
Role: Right-hand bat, wicket-keeper
Born: 2 June 1957, West Lambrook
Height: 5' 7" **Weight:** 10st 7lbs
Nickname: Gardy
County debut: 1976
County cap: 1983
1st-Class 50s scored: 3
Place in batting averages: 231st
av. 12.00 (1985 228th av. 13.36)
Parents: David and Brenda
Wife and date of marriage:
Amanda Kay, 29 September 1979
Education: Huish Episcopi
Comprehensive School
Qualifications: O-levels in English
and Technical Drawing;
Aircraft Engineer Turner

Jobs outside cricket: Engineering;
farm worker
Cricketing superstitions: 'Never keep wicket without wearing county cap.'
Overseas tours: Antigua 1981 with Somerset
Cricketers particularly learnt from: Derek Taylor, Bob Taylor
Other sports played: Field sports, snooker
Other sports followed: Watches soccer

Relaxations: Field sports (hunting, shooting and fishing), rearing pheasants
Injuries 1986: Twisted back – out for several weeks
Extras: Made debut for Somerset 2nd XI at 15
Best batting performance: 51* Somerset v India, Taunton 1979

LAST SEASON: BATTING

	I.	N.O.	R.	H.S.	AV.
TEST					
1ST-CLASS	25	6	228	36	12.00
INT					
JPL	4	0	24	19	6.00
NAT.W.	1	0	3	3	–
B & H	4	1	79	34	26.33

LAST SEASON: WICKET-KEEPING

	C.	ST.			
TEST					
1ST-CLASS	30	6			
INT					
JPL	5	1			
NAT.W.	1	1			
B & H	6	1			

CAREER: BATTING

	I.	N.O.	R.	H.S.	AV.
TEST					
1ST-CLASS	124	25	1349	51*	13.62
INT					
JPL	15	5	88	19	8.80
NAT.W.	5	2	27	17	9.00
B & H	12	5	125	34	17.85

CAREER: WICKET-KEEPING

	C.	ST.			
TEST					
1ST-CLASS	176	39			
INT					
JPL	28	7			
NAT.W.	10	4			
B & H	20	3			

GARNER, J. Somerset

Full Name: Joel Garner
Role: Right-hand bat, right-arm
fast bowler
Born: 16 December 1952, Barbados
Height: 6′ 8″ **Weight:** 17st
Nickname: Big Bird
County debut: 1977
County cap: 1979
Test debut: 1976–77
No. of Tests: 56
No. of One-Day Internationals: 85
50 wickets in a season: 2
1st-Class 50s scored: 7
1st-Class 100s scored: 1
1st-Class 5 w. in innings: 46
1st-Class 10 w. in match: 7
One-day 50s: 1
Place in batting averages: 203rd
av. 16.54 (1985 246th av. 11.50)
Place in bowling averages: 19th
av. 23.21 (1985 15th av. 23.84)
1st-Class catches 1986: 8 (career: 122)

Wife: Heather

Children: Jewel, 1983

Education: Boys' Foundation School, Christchurch, Barbados

Jobs outside cricket: Telegraph operator

Overseas tours: Toured with West Indies in Australia 1979–80; Pakistan 1980–81; Australia 1981–82; India 1982–83; England 1980 and 1984

Overseas teams played for: Made debut for Barbados in Shell Shield Competition in 1975–76

Other sports played: Football for Cable & Wireless team in Barbados, as goalkeeper

Relaxations: Sea-bathing, bird-watching, soul music, jazz, Manchester United

Extras: Has played as professional for Littleborough in Central Lancashire League. Takes size 16 in boots which are custom-built. Awarded MBE 1985. Released by Somerset at end of 1986 and joined Oldham in Lancashire League

Best batting performance: 104 West Indies v Gloucestershire, Bristol 1980

Best bowling performance: 8-31 Somerset v Glamorgan, Cardiff 1977

LAST SEASON: BATTING

	I.	N.O.	R.	H.S.	AV.
TEST					
1ST-CLASS	15	4	182	47	16.54
INT					
JPL	9	3	81	23	13.50
NAT.W.	1	0	8	8	–
B & H	3	2	20	14*	–

CAREER: BATTING

	I.	N.O.	R.	H.S.	AV.
TEST	65	14	661	60	12.96
1ST-CLASS	152	40	2139	104	19.09
INT	33	14	199	37	10.47
JPL	53	19	512	59*	15.05
NAT.W.	13	4	121	38*	13.44
B & H	10	5	70	17	14.00

LAST SEASON: BOWLING

	O.	M.	R.	W.	AV.
TEST					
1ST-CLASS	419	95	1091	47	23.21
INT					
JPL	105.5	14	362	14	25.85
NAT.W.	21	3	59	6	9.83
B & H	42	9	117	4	29.25

CAREER: BOWLING

	O.	M.	R.	W.	AV.
TEST	2117.5	558	5128	247	20.76
1ST-CLASS	4215.5	1190	10337	588	17.57
INT	771.2	122	2359	129	18.28
JPL	592	84	1918	101	18.99
NAT.W.	278.3	75	683	65	10.50
B & H	209.4	49	521	40	13.02

82. Which first-class cricketing Smith was nicknamed 'Round-the-corner Smith'?

GATTING, M. W. Middlesex

Full Name: Michael William
Gatting
Role: Right-hand bat, right-arm
medium bowler, slip fielder
Born: 6 June 1957, Kingsbury,
Middlesex
Height: 5′ 10″ **Weight:** 13st 8lbs
Nickname: Gatt
County debut: 1975
County cap: 1977
Test debut: 1977–78
No. of Tests: 48
No. of One-Day Internationals: 47
1000 runs in a season: 8
1st-Class 50s scored: 88
1st-Class 100s scored: 37
1st-Class 200s scored: 3
1st-Class 5 w. in innings: 2
One-day 50s: 37
One-day 100s: 5
Place in batting averages: 8th av. 54.55 (1985 11th av. 56.89)
Place in bowling averages: — (1985 27th av. 26.63)
1st-Class catches 1986: 13 (career: 254)
Parents: Bill and Vera
Wife and date of marriage: Elaine, September 1980
Children: Andrew, 21 January 1983; James, 11 July 1986
Education: Wykeham Primary School; John Kelly Boys' High School
Family links with cricket: Father used to play club cricket

LAST SEASON: BATTING

	I.	N.O.	R.	H.S.	AV.
TEST	11	2	463	183*	51.44
1ST-CLASS	12	1	628	158	57.09
INT	4	0	92	39	23.00
JPL	6	1	122	43	24.40
NAT.W.	2	1	126	118*	–
B & H	7	3	321	90*	80.25

LAST SEASON: BOWLING

	O.	M.	R.	W.	AV.
TEST	2	0	10	0	–
1ST-CLASS	72	24	186	8	23.25
INT					
JPL	21	0	113	1	–
NAT.W.	5	1	15	0	–
B & H	17	2	86	2	43.00

CAREER: BATTING

	I.	N.O.	R.	H.S.	AV.
TEST	83	12	2725	207	38.38
1ST-CLASS	347	57	14195	258	48.94
INT	44	10	1004	115*	29.52
JPL	118	13	3043	109	28.98
NAT.W.	34	8	1010	118*	38.84
B & H	48	15	1654	143*	50.12

CAREER: BOWLING

	O.	M.	R.	W.	AV.
TEST	1 56	0 12	177	2	88.50
1ST-CLASS	19.7 1111.2	3 263	3059	122	25.07
INT	41.2	14	214	6	35.66
JPL	394.1	12	1932	70	27.60
NAT.W.	136.3	21	503	16	31.43
B & H	178.4	14	707	35	20.20

Overseas tours: Toured West Indies with England Young Cricketers 1979–80; with England in West Indies 1981 and 1986; India 1981–82; New Zealand and Pakistan 1983–84
Overseas teams played for: Club cricket in Sydney, Australia 1979–80
Off-season 1986–87: With England in Australia
Cricketers particularly admired: Gary Sobers
Other sports: Football, table-tennis, tennis, swimming, golf
Other sports followed: Soccer (Spurs) and snooker
Relaxations: Reading (Tolkien), crosswords, cinema
Extras: Played for England Young Cricketers 1974. Young Cricketer of the Year 1981. Captain of Middlesex since 1983. Captain of England since 1986
Best batting performance: 258 Middlesex v Somerset, Bath 1984
Best bowling performance: 5-34 Middlesex v Glamorgan, Swansea 1982

GIFFORD, N. Warwickshire

Full Name: Norman Gifford
Role: Left-hand bat, slow left-arm bowler
Born: 30 March 1940, Ulverston, Cumbria
Height: 5′ 10″ **Weight:** 13st 7lbs
Nickname: Giff
County debut: 1960 (Worcestershire), 1983 (Warwickshire)
County cap: 1961 (Worcestershire), 1983 (Warwickshire)
Benefit: 1974 (£11,047)
Testimonial: 1981 (with Worcestershire)
Test debut: 1964
No. of Tests: 15
No. of One-Day Internationals: 2
50 wickets in a season: 22
1st-Class 50s scored: 3
1st-Class 5 w. in innings: 91
1st-Class 10 w. in match: 14
Place in bowling averages: 27th av. 23.88 (1985 71st av. 33.50)
1st-Class catches 1986: 2 (career: 316)
Qualifications: City & Guilds
Jobs outside cricket: Estimator, industrial decorating
Family links with cricket: Father played amateur cricket and football, and was also cricket umpire

Cricketers particularly learnt from: Charles Hallows (Worcestershire coach)
Overseas tours: Rest of World to Australia 1971–72; India, Pakistan and Sri Lanka 1972–73; Sharjah 1985 as captain
Other sports: Football, golf
Relaxations: Horse-racing
Extras: Was awarded MBE in 1979. Played in one match for Rest of World v Australia 1972. Suffers badly from the sun on overseas tours. Took 100 wickets in a season four times. Uncle, Harry Gifford, played rugby union for England. Released by Worcestershire at end of 1982 season. Debut 1960, cap 1961, captain 1971–80. England selector, and assistant manager of England side on tour. Appointed Warwickshire Captain 1985
Best batting performance: 89 Worcestershire v Oxford University, Oxford 1963
Best bowling performance: 8-28 Worcestershire v Yorkshire, Sheffield 1968

LAST SEASON: BATTING

	I.	N.O.	R.	H.S.	AV.
TEST					
1ST-CLASS	14	6	27	8	3.37
INT					
JPL	2	0	3	2	1.50
NAT.W.	1	0	0	0	–
B & H					

LAST SEASON: BOWLING

	O.	M.	R.	W.	AV.
TEST					
1ST-CLASS	564.3	158	1409	59	23.88
INT					
JPL	84	4	379	13	29.15
NAT.W.	8	1	29	2	14.50
B & H	42	7	116	2	58.00

CAREER: BATTING

	I.	N.O.	R.	H.S.	AV.
TEST	20	9	179	25*	16.27
1ST-CLASS	735	232	6633	89	13.18
INT	1	0	0	0	–
JPL	136	59	944	32*	12.25
NAT.W.	33	7	221	38	8.50
B & H	41	14	300	33	11.11

CAREER: BOWLING

	O.	M.	R.	W.	AV.
TEST	146.4 514	14 173	1026	33	31.09
1ST-CLASS	19810.2	6711	45608	1968	23.17
INT	20	1	50	4	12.50
JPL	1572.1	95	7086	268	26.44
NAT.W.	451	97	1328	54	24.59
B & H	677.3	101	2279	83	27.45

83. In the West Indies, Wilfred Rhodes said, 'Ay, a grand catch; but George shouldn't have done that'. Who was George, and what did he do?

84. What was unusual about David Gower's first ball in Test cricket, on 2 June 1978, at Edgbaston, from Liaquat Ali?

GILL, P. — Leicestershire

Full Name: Paul Gill
Role: Right-hand bat,
wicket-keeper
Born: 31 May 1963, Greenfield,
Manchester
Height: 5′ 7″
Education: Saddleworth and
Grange Schools
Extras: Has played in 2nd XI
since 1983
Best batting performance: 17
Leicestershire v Essex,
Southend 1986

LAST SEASON: BATTING

	I.	N.O.	R.	H.S.	AV.
TEST					
1ST-CLASS	11	4	68	17	9.71
INT					
JPL	2	1	5	3	–
NAT.W.					
B & H					

CAREER: BATTING

	I.	N.O.	R.	H.S.	AV.
TEST					
1ST-CLASS	11	4	68	17	9.71
INT					
JPL	2	1	5	3	–
NAT.W.					
B & H					

LAST SEASON: WICKET-KEEPING

	I.	N.O.	R.	H.S.	AV.
TEST					
1ST-CLASS	24	–			
INT					
JPL	1	–			
NAT.W.					
B & H					

CAREER: WICKET-KEEPING

	I.	N.O.	R.	H.S.	AV.
TEST					
fIST-CLASS	24	–			
INT					
JPL	1	–			
NAT.W.					
B & H					

---

85. What have the following batsmen (and a few others) in
common: K. W. R. Fletcher, J. M. Parks, D. Amiss, M. J. K.
Smith, D. Kenyon and G. Boycott?

GLADWIN, C.   Essex

Full Name: Christopher Gladwin
Role: Left-hand bat, right-arm
medium bowler, first slip or
cover fielder
Born: 10 May 1962, East Ham
Height: 6′ 2″ **Weight:** 14st
Nickname: Gladares, Guvnor
County debut: 1982
County cap: 1984
1000 runs in a season: 1
1st-Class 50s scored: 15
1st-Class 100s scored: 1
One-day 50s: 3
Place in batting averages: 221st
av. 13.00 (1985 144th av. 25.00)
1st-Class catches 1986: 4 (career: 26)
Parents: Edna and Ron
Wife and date of marriage: Julia,
20 September 1986
Education: Brampton Junior
and Landon Crescent
Qualifications: 5 CSEs
Jobs outside cricket: Pipe fitter, qualified cricket coach
Family links with cricket: Father and brother played club cricket
Overseas tours: England Schoolboys, West Indies 1977
Cricketers particularly learnt from: G. Gooch, K. Fletcher, A. Border
Off-season 1986–87: Playing overseas cricket
Other sports played: Football, snooker, athletics, table tennis, basketball,
golf

LAST SEASON: BATTING

	I.	N.O.	R.	H.S.	AV.
TEST					
1ST-CLASS	15	0	195	73	13.00
INT					
JPL	4	0	63	28	15.75
NAT.W.	1	0	10	10	–
B & H					

LAST SEASON: BOWLING

	O.	M.	R.	W.	AV.
TEST					
1ST-CLASS					
INT					
JPL					
NAT.W.					
B & H					

CAREER: BATTING

	I.	N.O.	R.	H.S.	AV.
TEST					
1ST-CLASS	97	5	2614	162	28.41
INT					
JPL	28	1	537	75	19.88
NAT.W.	4	0	26	15	6.50
B & H	7	0	178	41	25.43

CAREER: BOWLING

	O.	M.	R.	W.	AV.
TEST					
1ST-CLASS	21	1	71	0	–
INT					
JPL					
NAT.W.					
B & H					

Other sports followed: Snooker, football
Injuries 1986: Cracked ribs and dislocated thumb
Best batting performance: 162 Essex v Cambridge University, Cambridge 1984

GOOCH, G. A. Essex

Full Name: Graham Alan Gooch
Role: Right-hand bat, right-arm
medium bowler
Born: 23 July 1953, Leytonstone
Height: 6′ 0″ **Weight:** 13st
Nickname: Zap, Goochie
County debut: 1973
County cap: 1975
Benefit: 1985 (£153,906)
Test debut: 1975
No. of Tests: 59
No. of One-Day Internationals: 48
1000 runs in a season: 10
1st-Class 50s scored: 114
1st-Class 100s scored: 53
1st-Class 200s scored: 4
1st-Class 5 w. in innings: 3
One-day 50s: 67
One-day 100s: 19
Place in batting averages: 60th
av. 38.15 (1985 3rd av. 71.22)
Place in bowling averages: — (1985 28th av. 26.65)
1st-Class catches 1986: 22 (career: 328)
Parents: Alfred and Rose
Wife and date of marriage: Brenda, 23 October 1976
Children: Hannah, Megan, Sally
Education: Norlington Junior High School, Leytonstone
Qualifications: Four-year apprenticeship in toolmaking
Jobs outside cricket: Toolmaker
Family links with cricket: Father played local cricket for East Ham Corinthians. Second cousin, Graham Saville, played for Essex CCC and is now NCA coach for Eastern England
Overseas tours: West Indies with England Young Cricketers 1972; England to Australia 1978–79 and 1979–80; West Indies 1981 and 1986; India 1981–82
Overseas teams played for: Perth CC, Western Australia; Western Province, South Africa

Cricketers particularly admired: Bob Taylor, a model sportsman; Mike Procter for his enthusiasm; Barry Richards for his ability

Other sports played: Squash, soccer, golf. Trains in off-season with West Ham United FC

Relaxations: 'Relaxing at home.'

Extras: Published book (Pelham Books) entitled *Batting* in 1980. Wrote a diary of 1981 cricket year, published in April 1982 by Stanley Paul. *Out of the Wilderness* published by Collins in 1985. Hit a century before lunch v Leicester, 28 June 1981. Kept wicket for England v India in 2nd innings at Madras, 1982. Captained English rebel team in South Africa, 1982 and was banned from Test cricket for three years. Holds record one-day innings of 198* v Sussex, May 1982. Hit a hole in one at Tollygunge Golf Club during England's tour in India, 1981–82. Bowled both right and left handed in a Test match (v India at Calcutta, imitating Dilip Doshi). Shared in second wicket record partnership for county, 321 with K. S. McEwan v Northamptonshire, at Ilford in 1978. Holds record (jointly) for Essex for catches in match (6) and innings (5) v Gloucestershire, 1982. Essex captain 1986

Best batting performance: 227 Essex v Derbyshire, Chesterfield 1984

Best bowling performance: 7-14 Essex v Worcestershire, Ilford 1982

LAST SEASON: BATTING

	I.	N.O.	R.	H.S.	AV.
TEST	11	0	443	183	40.27
1ST-CLASS	21	0	778	151	37.04
INT	4	0	149	91	37.25
JPL	10	1	528	100	58.66
NAT.W.	2	0	92	48	46.00
B & H	5	0	195	73	39.00

LAST SEASON: BOWLING

	O.	M.	R.	W.	AV.
TEST	32	11	69	2	34.50
1ST-CLASS	137.4	34	329	7	47.00
INT	19	3	109	1	—
JPL	64	1	281	14	20.07
NAT.W.	24	5	74	4	18.50
B & H	33	5	113	3	37.67

CAREER: BATTING

	I.	N.O.	R.	H.S.	AV.
TEST	105	4	3746	196	37.08
1ST-CLASS	471	41	19089	227	44.39
INT	47	3	1665	129*	37.84
JPL	165	14	4805	176	31.82
NAT.W.	30	1	1226	133	42.27
B & H	65	4	2938	198*	48.16

CAREER: BOWLING

	O.	M.	R.	W.	AV.
TEST	6 228.3	1 66	546	13	42.00
1ST-CLASS	1 1923.4	0 480	5161	164	31.46
INT	165.5	10	791	19	41.63
JPL	610.1	32	2729	103	26.49
NAT.W.	191.1	28	583	19	30.68
B & H	349.5	36	1143	39	29.30

86. What kind of bowler was England Test captain, D. R. Jardine?

GOULD, I. J.   Sussex

Full Name: Ian James Gould
Role: Left-hand bat, wicket-keeper
Born: 19 August 1957, Taplow, Bucks
Height: 5′ 8″ **Weight:** 11st 10lbs
Nickname: Gunner
County debut: 1975 (Middlesex), 1981 (Sussex)
County cap: 1977 (Middlesex), 1981 (Sussex)
No. of One-Day Internationals: 18
1000 runs in a season: 1
1st-Class 50s scored: 28
1st-Class 100s scored: 2
One-day 50s scored: 11
Place in batting averages: 93rd av. 32.55 (1985 64th av. 36.24)
Parents: Doreen and George
Wife: Jo
Children: Gemma Louise, 30 June 1984
Education: Westgate School
Jobs outside cricket: Barman

LAST SEASON: BATTING

	I.	N.O.	R.	H.S.	AV.
TEST					
1ST-CLASS	24	6	586	78*	32.55
INT					
JPL	14	3	280	65*	25.45
NAT.W.	3	1	109	88	54.50
B & H	4	0	49	25	12.25

LAST SEASON: BOWLING

	O.	M.	R.	W.	AV.
TEST					
1ST-CLASS	22.3	0	110	2	55.00
INT					
JPL					
NAT.W.					

CAREER: BATTING

	I.	N.O.	R.	H.S.	AV.
TEST					
1ST-CLASS	294	48	5984	128	24.32
INT	14	2	155	42	12.91
JPL	121	20	1787	69*	17.69
NAT.W.	20	2	383	88	21.27
B & H	38	6	536	72	16.75

CAREER: BOWLING

	O.	M.	R.	W.	AV.
TEST					
1ST-CLASS	39	2	220	2	110.00
INT					
JPL					
NAT.W.					
B & H					

LAST SEASON: WICKET-KEEPING

	C.	ST.			
TEST					
1ST-CLASS	35	1			
INT					
JPL	14	–			
NAT.W.	11	–			
B & H	6	–			

CAREER: WICKET-KEEPING

	C.	ST.			
TEST					
1ST-CLASS	452	67			
INT	15	3			
JPL	120	21			
NAT.W.	26	6			
B & H	46	3			

Overseas tours: Toured West Indies with England Young Cricketers 1976; with England in Australia and New Zealand 1982–83
Overseas teams played for: Auckland, 1980
Other sports played: Amateur footballer for Slough Town FC at full-back; golf, swimming
Relaxations: Spending time with the family
Extras: Made debut for Middlesex in 1975, gaining cap in 1977. Was offered contract for 1981 by Middlesex but chose to join Sussex. Vice-captain in 1985. Took over captaincy during 1986 and officially appointed for 1987
Best batting performance: 128 Middlesex v Worcestershire, Worcester 1978

GOULDSTONE, M. R. Northamptonshire

Full Name: Mark Roger Gouldstone
Role: Opening bat, cover or short-leg fielder
Born: 3 February 1963, Bishops Stortford
Height: 5′ 11″ **Weight:** 11st 10lbs
Nickname: Bladder
County debut: 1986
Parents: Roy and Mary (deceased)
Marital status: Single
Education: Newport Grammar School; Braintree College of Further Education
Qualifications: 6 O-levels, coach
Jobs outside cricket: Coach
Family links with cricket: Father played village cricket
Cricketing superstitions: Left pad on first
Overseas teams played for: Penrith CC, Australia 1982–83, 1983–84; Uitenhage CC, South Africa 1985–86
Cricketers particularly learnt from: Bill Morris, Len Woolmer
Cricketers particularly admired: Wayne Larkins, Gordon Greenidge

LAST SEASON: BATTING

	I.	N.O.	R.	H.S.	AV.
TEST					
1ST-CLASS	1	0	35	35	–
INT					
JPL	1	0	4	4	–
NAT W					
B & H					

CAREER: BATTING

	I.	N.O.	R.	H.S.	AV.
TEST					
1ST-CLASS	1	0	35	35	–
INT					
JPL	1	0	4	4	–
NAT.W.					
B & H					

Off-season 1986–87: Working in England
Other sports played: Soccer, tennis
Other sports followed: Soccer
Relaxations: Reading, watching videos
Opinions on cricket: '4-day cricket playing every other team once, as 3-day cricket is not well supported. More chance of a natural result should rain intervene and less chance of a "rigged" game.'
Best batting performance: 35 Northamptonshire v New Zealand, Northampton 1986

GOWER, D. I.   Leicestershire

Full Name: David Ivon Gower
Role: Left-hand bat, right-arm off-break bowler
Born: 1 April 1957, Tunbridge Wells
Height: 5' 11" **Weight:** 11st 11lbs
Nickname: Stoat, Lubo, Lu
County debut: 1975
County cap: 1977
Benefit: 1987
Test debut: 1978
No. of Tests: 86
No. of One-Day Internationals: 85
1000 runs in a season: 6
1st-Class 50s scored: 86
1st-Class 100s scored: 36
1st-Class 200s scored: 2
One-day 50s: 35
One-day 100s: 17
Place in batting averages: 51st av. 39.52 (1985 14th av. 54.70)
1st-Class catches 1986: 25 (career: 184)
Parents: Richard Hallam and Sylvia Mary
Marital status: Single
Education: Marlborough House School; King's School, Canterbury; University College, London (did not complete law course)
Qualifications: 8 O-levels, 3 A-levels
Jobs outside cricket: Worked at Bostik Ltd
Family links with cricket: Father was club cricketer
Cricketing superstitions: 'They change every time they go wrong.'
Overseas tours: Toured South Africa with English Schools XI 1974–75 and West Indies with England Young Cricketers 1976; Derrick Robins XI to

Canada 1976 and to Far East 1977; with England to Australia 1978–79 and 1979–80, West Indies 1980–1, India 1981–82, Australia and New Zealand 1982–83, New Zealand 1983–84, India and Australia 1984–85, West Indies 1986

Overseas teams played for: Claremont-Cottesloe, Perth, Australia, 1977–78
Cricketers particularly learnt from: 'Ray Illingworth and Jack Birkenshaw, amongst many others whose advice has come my way.'
Cricketers particularly admired: Graeme Pollock and many others
Off-season 1986–87: England tour of Australia
Other sports played: Golf, squash, water and snow skiing. Rode in a British bobsled at Cervinia (Italy) in 1985
Relaxations: Music, photographs, beaches, vintage port and crosswords
Extras: Played for King's Canterbury 1st XI for three years. Has written *Anyone for Cricket* jointly with Bob Taylor about the 1978–79 Australian tour. Also *With Time to Spare*, an autobiography published in 1980. Published *Heroes and Contemporaries* (Collins) 1983, *A Right Ambition* (Collins) 1986. Writes regular column for *Wisden Cricket Monthly*. England captain 1984–86; Leicestershire captain 1984–86
Best batting performance: 215 England v Australia, Edgbaston 1985
Best bowling performance: 3-47 Leicestershire v Essex, Leicester 1977

LAST SEASON: BATTING

	I.	N.O.	R.	H.S.	AV.
TEST	9	0	394	131	43.77
1ST-CLASS	14	2	436	83	36.33
INT	4	0	108	81	27.00
JPL	8	3	160	51*	32.00
NAT.W.	3	1	135	121*	67.50
B & H	4	0	90	42	22.50

LAST SEASON: BOWLING

	O.	M.	R.	W.	AV.
TEST	1	0	5	0	–
1ST-CLASS					
INT					
JPL					
NAT.W.	0.3	0	4	0	–
B & H					

CAREER: BATTING

	I.	N.O.	R.	H.S.	AV.
TEST	148	11	6149	215	44.88
1ST-CLASS	313	29	10718	187	37.73
INT	82	7	2564	158	34.18
JPL	110	19	3581	135*	39.35
NAT.W.	25	4	1051	156	50.04
B & H	41	4	1021	114*	27.59

CAREER: BOWLING

	O.	M.	R.	W.	AV.
TEST	6	1	20	1	–
1ST-CLASS	36.1	4	191	3	63.66
INT	0.5	0	14	0	–
JPL					
NAT.W.	1.3	0	12	0	–
B & H					

87. Who said, 'If the batsman gets above himself, put one past his whiskers now and then'?

GRAVENEY, D. A. Gloucestershire

Full Name: David Anthony Graveney
Role: Right-hand bat, slow left-arm bowler
Born: 2 January 1953, Bristol
Height: 6′ 4″ **Weight:** 14st
Nickname: Gravity, Grav
County debut: 1972
County cap: 1976
Benefit: 1986
50 wickets in a season: 4
1st-Class 50s scored: 15
1st-Class 100s scored: 2
1st-Class 5 w. in innings: 28
1st-Class 10 w. in match: 4
One-day 50s: 1
Place in batting averages: 238th av. 10.44 (194th av. 19.00)
Place in bowling averages: 74th av. 33.30 (1985 18th av. 24.71)
1st-Class catches 1986: 20 (career: 171)
Parents: Ken and Jeanne (deceased)
Wife and date of marriage: Julie, 23 September 1978
Children: Adam, 13 October 1982
Education: Millfield School, Somerset
Jobs outside cricket: Company director. Accountant
Family links with cricket: Son of J. K. Graveney, Captain of Gloucestershire, who took 10 wickets for 66 runs v Derbyshire at Chesterfield in 1949, and nephew of Tom Graveney of Gloucestershire, Worcestershire and England.

LAST SEASON: BATTING

	I.	N.O.	R.	H.S.	AV.
TEST					
1ST-CLASS	18	9	94	30*	10.44
INT					
JPL	9	5	85	31	21.25
NAT.W.	2	2	11	11*	–
B & H	2	2	60	35*	–

LAST SEASON: BOWLING

	O.	M.	R.	W.	AV.
TEST					
1ST-CLASS	446	137	999	30	33.30
INT					
JPL	55	1	305	7	43.57
NAT.W.	22	6	39	3	13.00
B & H	24	2	68	1	–

CAREER: BATTING

	I.	N.O.	R.	H.S.	AV.
TEST					
1ST-CLASS	408	115	5447	119	18.59
INT					
JPL	121	44	1221	56*	15.85
NAT.W.	23	8	265	44	17.66
B & H	35	9	379	49*	14.57

CAREER: BOWLING

	O.	M.	R.	W.	AV.
TEST					
1ST-CLASS	7405.4	2215	19158	665	28.80
INT					
JPL	854.1	48	3992	124	32.19
NAT.W.	255.5	41	848	33	25.69
B & H	353.5	36	1272	44	28.90

Brother, John, selected for English Public Schools v English Schools at Lord's
Other sports played: Golf, soccer, squash
Relaxations: 'Playing sport, TV and cinema. Relaxing at a good pub.'
Extras: Treasurer of the County Cricketers' Association. Captain of Gloucestershire since 1981
Best batting performance: 119 Gloucestershire v Oxford University, Oxford 1980
Best bowling performance: 8-85 Gloucestershire v Nottinghamshire, Cheltenham 1974

GRAY, A. H. Surrey

Full Name: Anthony Hollis Gray
Role: Right-hand bat, right-arm fast bowler
Born: 23 May 1963, Belmont, Port of Spain, Trinidad
Height: 6' 6" **Weight:** 15st
Nickname: Big Man
County debut: 1985
County cap: 1985
No. of One-Day Internationals: 4
50 wickets in a season: 2
1st-Class 50s scored: 1
1st-Class 5 w. in innings: 14
1st-Class 10 w. in match: 3
Place in bowling averages: 6th av. 18.94 (1985 13th av. 22.99)
1st-Class catches 1986: 4 (career: 18)
Parents: Anthony and Merle
Education: Marlick Ser. Comprehensive; St Augustine Ser. Comprehensive

Qualifications: 3 O-levels, 1 CXC
Cricketing superstitions: Always bat with cap on
Cricketers particularly learnt from: Alf Gover
Cricketers particularly admired: Viv Richards, Mike Holding
Off-season 1986–87: Touring Pakistan with West Indies
Other sports played: Football, basketball, table-tennis
Other sports followed: Football
Relaxations: Watching sports, watching movies, music, going to the parks
Extras: The only son in a family of five. Trinidad and Tobago Player of the

Year 1985. Surrey CC Supporters' Association Player of the Year 1985.
Hat-trick v Yorkshire 1985
Best batting performance: 54* Trinidad v Leeward Islands, Bissetirre 1985–86
Best bowling performance: 8-40 Surrey v Yorkshire, Sheffield 1985

LAST SEASON: BATTING

	I.	N.O.	R.	H.S.	AV.
TEST					
1ST-CLASS	14	2	108	28	9.00
INT					
JPL	5	3	57	24*	28.50
NAT.W.	1	0	3	3	–
B & H	–	–	–	–	–

LAST SEASON: BOWLING

	O.	M.	R.	W.	AV.
TEST					
1ST-CLASS	342.3	69	966	51	18.94
INT					
JPL	56	2	211	18	11.72
NAT.W.	12	3	23	3	7.66
B & H	11	1	33	0	–

CAREER: BATTING

	I.	N.O.	R.	H.S.	AV.
TEST					
1ST-CLASS	52	8	486	54*	11.04
INT	1	1	7	7*	–
JPL	8	5	61	24*	20.33
NAT.W.	1	0	3	3	–
B & H	–	–	–	–	–

CAREER: BOWLING

	O.	M.	R.	W.	AV.
TEST					
1ST-CLASS	2221.3	239	4437	200	22.18
INT	22	5	82	2	41.00
JPL	126	3	513	33	15.54
NAT.W.	23	3	89	5	17.80
B & H	11	1	33	0	–

GREEN, A. M. Sussex

Full Name: Allan Michael Green
Role: Right-hand bat, right-arm
off-break bowler, short-leg fielder
Born: 28 May 1960, Pulborough
Height: 5′ 10″ **Weight:** 11st
Nickname: Gilbert, Greenie,
Wedgey
County debut: 1980
County cap: 1985
1000 runs in a season: 2
1st-Class 50s scored: 27
1st-Class 100s scored: 7
One-day 50s: 9
One-day 100s: 1
Place in batting averages: 96th
av. 31.23 (1985 38th av. 42.21)
1st-Class catches 1986: 12
(career: 62)
Parents: Sheila Cynthia and Basil
Michael
Wife and date of marriage: Kerry
Louise, 19 September 1986

Education: Knoll School, Hove; Brighton Sixth Form College
Qualifications: 5 O-levels
Jobs outside cricket: Sports shop assistant, labourer
Family links with cricket: Father played for Findon CC 'as a fielder'
Cricketing superstitions: 'Strap left pad on first and like to bat in same clothes, smell permitting.'
Overseas tours: *The Cricketer* tour to Dubai 1983
Overseas teams played for: Orange Free State, South Africa 1985–87
Cricketers particularly learnt from: Ian Thomson, Chris Waller, Roger Marshall, Tony Buss, Alvin Kallicharran
Off-season 1986–87: Playing and coaching in South Africa
Other sports played: Golf, snooker, football
Relaxations: 'Sleeping, going to concerts, eating, drinking and watching it rain!'
Opinions on cricket: Should play 16 4-day championship matches
Best batting performance: 179 Sussex v Glamorgan, Cardiff 1986
Best bowling performance: 4-59 Orange Free State v Northern Transvaal, Bloemfontein 1985–86

LAST SEASON: BATTING

	I.	N.O.	R.	H.S.	AV.
TEST					
1ST-CLASS	46	3	1343	179	31.23
INT					
JPL	13	0	283	69	21.76
NAT.W.	5	0	202	102	40.40
B & H	4	0	128	50	32.00

LAST SEASON: BOWLING

	O.	M.	R.	W.	AV.
TEST					
1ST-CLASS	174.1	25	583	7	83.28
INT					
JPL	1	0	7	0	–
NAT.W.					
B & H					

CAREER: BATTING

	I.	N.O.	R.	H.S.	AV.
TEST					
1ST-CLASS	211	13	6049	179	30.55
INT					
JPL	35	3	920	83	28.75
NAT.W.	10	0	335	102	33.50
B & H	12	0	268	50	22.33

CAREER: BOWLING

	O.	M.	R.	W.	AV.
TEST					
1ST-CLASS	450.5	72	1533	32	47.90
INT					
JPL	1	0	7	0	–
NAT.W.	1	0	7	0	–
B & H	6	2	26	1	–

88. When Yorkshire made 555 for the first wicket v Essex at Leyton in 1936, who were the two Yorkshire batsmen?

GREENIDGE, C. G.   Hampshire

Full Name: Cuthbert Gordon Greenidge
Role: Right-hand bat, right-arm medium bowler
Born: 1 May 1951, St Peter, Barbados
County debut: 1970
County cap: 1972
Benefit: 1983 (£28,648)
Test debut: 1974–75
No. of Tests: 71
No. of One-Day Internationals: 71
1000 runs in a season: 15
1st-Class 50s scored: 156
1st-Class 100s scored: 63
1st-Class 200s scored: 10
1st-Class 5 w. in innings: 1
One-day 50s: 71
One-day 108s: 24
Place in batting averages: 1st
av. 67.83 (1985 40th av. 41.20)

1st-Class catches 1986: 18 (career: 441)
Wife and date of marriage: Anita, September 1977
Children: Carl, born 1978
Education: Black Bess School; St Peter's Boys' School; Sutton Secondary School, Reading
Qualifications: Studied accountancy and book-keeping
Jobs outside cricket: Working for Sutton's Seeds, Reading; Dimplex, Southampton
Family links with cricket: Wife is cousin of West Indian and Leicestershire fast bowler Andy Roberts
Overseas tours: Toured with West Indies to India, Sri Lanka and Pakistan 1974–75; Australia 1975–76; England 1976, 1980 and 1984; Australia 1979–80; Pakistan 1980; Australia 1981–82; India 1983; Australia 1984–85
Overseas teams played for: Barbados
Other sports played: Soccer, rugby, golf
Extras: Could have played for either England or West Indies. Persuaded to join Hampshire by John Arlott after playing for Berkshire U-19s. Scored two centuries in one match (134 and 101) for West Indies v England at Manchester 1976, and v Kent at Bournemouth (136 and 120) in 1978. Shared in partnership of 285 for second wicket with D. R. Turner v Minor Counties South at Amersham in 1973, being the record partnership for all one-day competitions. Awarded MBE in 1985

Best batting performance: 273* D. H. Robins' XI v Pakistan, Eastbourne 1974
Best bowling performance: 5-49 Hampshire v Surrey, Southampton 1971

LAST SEASON: BATTING

	I.	N.O.	R.	H.S.	AV.
TEST					
1ST-CLASS	34	4	2035	222	67.83
INT					
JPL	12	1	493	125*	44.81
NAT.W.	1	0	18	18	–
B & H	4	1	148	83*	49.33

LAST SEASON: BOWLING

	O.	M.	R.	W.	AV.
TEST					
1ST-CLASS					
INT					
JPL					
NAT.W.					
B & H					

CAREER: BATTING

	I.	N.O.	R.	H.S.	AV.
TEST	117	13	5033	223	48.39
1ST-CLASS	626	71	26041	273*	46.92
INT	71	7	2988	115	46.68
JPL	174	12	6049	163*	37.33
NAT.W.	31	1	1262	177	42.06
B & H	53	3	1915	173*	38.30

CAREER: BOWLING

	O.	M.	R.	W.	AV.
TEST	1 3	1 2	4	0	–
1ST-CLASS	155.5	37	468	17	27.53
INT	10	0	45	1	–
JPL	18	0	89	1	–
NAT.W.					
B & H	12.1	1	57	0	–

GRIFFITHS, B. J. Northamptonshire

Full Name: Brian James Griffiths
Role: Right-hand bat, right-arm
medium bowler
Born: 12 June 1949, Wellingborough
Height: 6' 1" **Weight:** 14st 6lbs
Nickname: Jim
County debut: 1974
County cap: 1978
50 wickets in a season: 5
1st-Class 5 w. in innings: 13
Place in bowling averages: 80th
av. 35.28 (1985 45th av. 28.69)
1st-Class catches 1986: 2 (career: 36)
Parents: James and Muriel
Wife and date of marriage: Paula,
30 September 1972
Children: Rachel, 26 June 1973;
Leighton, 6 November 1975

Education: Irthlingborough Secondary School
Jobs outside cricket: Has worked for a haulage firm, and as a bank porter
Family links with cricket: Uncle played occasionally for Northamptonshire
Other sports played: Football, darts

Relaxations: Reading, quizzes and crosswords
Best batting performance: 16 Northamptonshire v Gloucestershire, Bristol 1982
Best bowling performance: 8-50 Northamptonshire v Glamorgan, Northampton 1981

LAST SEASON: BATTING

	I.	N.O.	R.	H.S.	AV.
TEST					
1ST-CLASS	6	3	18	7	6.00
INT					
JPL					
NAT.W.					
B & H					

LAST SEASON: BOWLING

	O.	M.	R.	W.	AV.
TEST					
1ST-CLASS	237.3	54	741	21	35.28
INT					
JPL					
NAT.W.					
B & H					

CAREER: BATTING

	I.	N.O.	R.	H.S.	AV.
TEST					
1ST-CLASS	138	51	290	16	3.33
INT					
JPL	27	14	61	11*	4.69
NAT.W.	4	2	2	1*	1.00
B & H	9	3	15	6	2.50

CAREER: BOWLING

	O.	M.	R.	W.	AV.
TEST					
1ST-CLASS	4521.5	1071	12899	444	29.05
INT					
JPL	782.4	63	3188	115	27.72
NAT.W.	180	22	703	27	26.04
B & H	301.2	41	1046	40	26.15

HADLEE, R. J.　　Nottinghamshire

Full Name: Richard John Hadlee
Role: Left-hand bat, right-arm fast bowler
Born: 3 July 1951, Christchurch, New Zealand
Height: 6′ 1″ **Weight:** 11st 9 lbs
Nickname: Paddles
County debut: 1978
County cap: 1978
Benefit: 1986
Test debut: 1972–73
No. of Tests: 66
No. of One-Day Internationals: 92
1000 runs in a season: 1
50 wickets in a season: 8
1st-Class 50s scored: 49
1st-Class 100s scored: 10
1st-Class 200s scored: 1
1st-Class 5 w. in innings: 76
1st-Class 10 w. in match: 13

One-Day 50s: 12
One-Day 100s: 1
Place in batting averages: 10th av. 50.81 (1985 86th av. 32.89)
Place in bowling averages: 2nd av. 15.98 (1985 2nd av. 17.39)
1st-Class catches 1986: 6 (career: 165)
Parents: Walter Arnold and Lillius Agnes
Wife and date of marriage: Karen Ann, 24 August 1973
Jobs outside cricket: Trainee manager, Woolworth's 1970; Dept. trainee manager, Bing Harris Sargood 1973; Sales manager, Shawn Sports, 1975. Employed by New Zealand CC; managed by International Management Group, contracted to Leopard Breweries and Armoured Security Services
Family links with cricket: Father played for New Zealand 1937–49, captaining New Zealand on tour of UK 1949. Brother, Dayle, played for New Zealand 1969–78. Brother Barry played for Canterbury. His father, Walter, has succeeded Gordon Burgess (father of former New Zealand Test captain, Mark) as president of the New Zealand Cricket Council
Overseas tours: With New Zealand to England 1973, 1978, 1983, 1986; Australia 1973–74, 1980–81, 1986; India, Pakistan 1976; World Cup in UK 1975, 1979, 1983
Overseas teams played for: Canterbury, New Zealand, 1971–; Tasmania 1979–80; World XI v Australia 1979, World Series Cricket
Cricketers particularly learnt from: 'My brother, Dayle; Dennis Lillee – I admire his approach to the game: competitive, inspires his team, great bowler.'
Cricketers particularly admired: Viv Richards, Gary Sobers, Greg Chappell, Abdul Qadir
Other sports played: Golf. Played goalkeeper for Rangers and for Woolston in New Zealand Southern League, 'but I never took it seriously.'
Other sports followed: Soccer, rugby, tennis, golf, snooker, etc.
Relaxations: 'Watching movies, music, writing weekly newspaper columns.'
Extras: Awarded MBE 1980. Hat-trick v Central Districts 1972 at Nelson.

LAST SEASON: BATTING

	I.	N.O.	R.	H.S.	AV.
TEST	3	0	93	68	31.00
1ST-CLASS	18	5	720	129*	55.38
INT	2	1	29	18*	–
JPL	9	3	151	34*	25.16
NAT.W.	3	0	81	55	27.00
B & H	5	1	131	61*	32.75

LAST SEASON: BOWLING

	O.	M.	R.	W.	AV.
TEST	152.5	42	390	19	20.52
1ST-CLASS	393.4	108	825	57	14.47
INT	20.2	1	63	2	31.50
JPL	87	7	344	10	34.40
NAT.W.	30	9	44	10	4.40
B & H	64.1	13	194	11	17.63

CAREER: BATTING

	I.	N.O.	R.	H.S.	AV.
TEST	106	13	2397	103	25.77
1ST-CLASS	292	57	7409	210*	31.52
INT	78	12	1259	79	19.07
JPL	73	20	1461	100*	27.56
NAT.W.	13	2	295	56	26.81
B & H	35	9	893	70	34.34

CAREER: BOWLING

	O.	M.	R.	W.	AV.
TEST	577.2 2094.3	68 548	7520	334	22.51
1ST-CLASS	1009 5166.5	163 1546	15046	887	16.96
INT	277.1 446.5	57 103	2619	127	20.62
JPL	599.2	67	2229	114	19.55
NAT.W.	149.3	39	359	26	13.80
B & H	396.4	83	1091	74	14.74

Only bowler to take 100 wickets in 1981 season. Top of English bowling averages 1980, 1981, 1982 and 1984. New Zealand Personality of the Year 1978 and nominated in final six on five occasions. New Zealand Bowler of the Year 1978–84. Has written autobiography *Hadlee*. Author of *Hadlee on Cricket, Hadlee's Humour* and *Hadlee Hits Out*. New Zealand records: (1) Most wickets in Test cricket. (2) Most numbers of 5 wickets in a Test innings. (3) Most wickets in a Test innings, and in a Test match, 15-123. (4) Best bowling in a Test match, 9-52 v Australia, 1985–86. (5) Most number of 10 wickets in a Test match, three times. (6) First New Zealand player to take Test double of 100 wickets and 1000 runs. In 1984 did 'double' of 1000 runs and 100 wickets in first-Class cricket – first time achieved since F. J. Titmus in 1967

Best batting performance: 210* Nottinghamshire v Middlesex, Lord's 1984
Best bowling performance: 9-52 New Zealand v Australia, Brisbane 1985–86

HARDEN, R. J.   Somerset

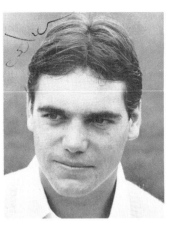

Full Name: Richard John Harden
Role: Right-hand bat, left-arm medium bowler
Born: 16 August 1965, Bridgwater
Height: 6' 0" **Weight:** 13st 3lbs
Nickname: Rich
County debut: 1985
1000 runs in a Season: 1
1st-Class 50s scored: 7
1st-Class 100s scored: 3
One-Day 50s: 1
Place in batting averages: 88th av. 33.12 (1985 109th av. 30.50)
1st-Class catches 1986: 12 (career: 21)
Parents: Chris and Ann
Marital status: Single
Education: Kings College, Taunton
Qualifications: 8 O-levels, 2 A-levels
Jobs outside cricket: Insurance clerk
Family links with cricket: Grandfather played club cricket for Bridgwater
Cricketers particularly learnt from: Roy Marshall
Cricketers particularly admired: V. Richards, D. Gower
Other sports played: Squash, hockey
Relaxations: Listening to music, eating good food and playing snooker or pool
Best batting performance: 108 Somerset v Sussex, Taunton 1986
Best bowling performance: 2-24 Somerset v Hampshire, Taunton 1986

LAST SEASON: BATTING

	I.	N.O.	R.	H.S.	AV.
TEST					
1ST-CLASS	36	3	1093	108	33.12
INT					
JPL	14	3	263	71	23.90
NAT.W.	1	0	17	17	–
B & H	2	0	24	24	12.00

CAREER: BATTING

	I.	N.O.	R.	H.S.	AV.
TEST					
1ST-CLASS	53	8	1459	108	32.42
INT					
JPL	17	3	284	71	20.28
NAT.W.	1	0	17	17	–
B & H	5	0	55	24	11.00

LAST SEASON: BOWLING

	O.	M.	R.	W.	AV.
TEST					
1ST-CLASS	54	5	208	4	52.00
INT					
JPL	0.1	0	0	0	–
NAT.W.					
B & H					

CAREER: BOWLING

	O.	M.	R.	W.	AV.
TEST					
1ST-CLASS	66.3	10	241	6	40.16
INT					
JPL	0.1	0	0	0	–
NAT.W.					
B & H					

HARDIE, B. R.   Essex

Full Name: Brian Ross Hardie
Role: Right-hand bat, right-arm medium bowler, bat/pad fielder
Born: 14 January 1950, Stenhousemuir
Height: 5′ 10″ **Weight:** 12st 7lbs
Nickname: Lager
County debut: 1973
County cap: 1974
Benefit: 1983 (£48,486)
1000 runs in a season: 10
1st-Class 50s scored: 73
1st-Class 100s scored: 20
One-Day 50s: 31
One-Day 100s: 5
Place in batting averages: 107th av. 29.43 (1985 66th av. 36.16)
1st-Class catches 1986: 19 (career: 282)
Parents: James Millar and Elspet
Wife and date of marriage: Fiona, 28 October 1977
Education: Stenhousemuir Primary School; Larbert High School
Qualifications: 7 O-levels, 3 H-levels, NCA Advanced Cricket Coach
Jobs outside cricket: Computer operator, bank clerk, shipping clerk
Family links with cricket: Father and brother, Keith, played for Scotland
Overseas teams played for: Two seasons in New Zealand club cricket 1980–81 and 1981–82
Cricketers particularly learnt from: 'Everyone has something to offer.'

Off-season 1986–87: Working with Essex CCC on promotions and sponsorships
Other sports played: Football, golf
Relaxations: Sport
Extras: Played for Stenhousemuir in East of Scotland League. Debut for Scotland 1970. Scored two centuries for Scotland v MCC at Aberdeen in 1971, but not then regarded as first-class match. Man of the Match in 1985 NatWest Final
Injuries 1986: Ankle ligaments, broken bone in hand
Best batting performance: 162 Essex v Warwickshire, Edgbaston 1975

LAST SEASON: BATTING

	I.	N.O.	R.	H.S.	AV.
TEST					
1ST-CLASS	35	5	883	113*	29.43
INT					
JPL	13	2	571	109	51.90
NAT.W.					
B & H	5	1	163	119*	40.75

LAST SEASON: BOWLING

	O.	M.	R.	W.	AV.
TEST					
1ST-CLASS	12	0	58	0	–
INT					
JPL					
NAT.W.					
B & H					

CAREER: BATTING

	I.	N.O.	R.	H.S.	AV.
TEST					
1ST-CLASS	501	63	14836	162	33.87
INT					
JPL	167	15	3961	109	26.05
NAT.W.	27	0	928	110	34.37
B & H	59	14	1331	119*	29.57

CAREER: BOWLING

	O.	M.	R.	W.	AV.
TEST					
1ST-CLASS	33	2	173	3	57.66
INT					
JPL	4.5	0	24	1	–
NAT.W.	8	1	16	1	–
B & H					

89. Who began his England career batting at Number 11 and worked his way up to open with Jack Hobbs?

90. How was His Highness Jam Sahib of Nawanagar better known to cricketers?

HARDY, J. J. E.   Somerset

Full Name: Jonathan James Ean
Hardy
Role: Left-hand bat
Born: 2 October 1960, Nakuru,
Kenya
Height: 6′ 3″ **Weight:** 13½st
Nickname: JJ
County debut: 1984 (Hampshire),
1986 (Somerset)
1st-Class 50s scored: 15
1st-Class 100s scored: 1
One-Day 50s: 2
Place in batting averages: 106th
av. 29.75 (1985 70th av. 35.33)
1st-Class catches 1986: 12
(career: 25)
Parents: Ray and Petasue
Marital status: Single
Education: Pembroke House, Gilgil,
Kenya; Canford School, Dorset
Qualifications: 10 O-levels, 3 A-levels (English, Economics, Geography)
Family links with cricket: Father played for Yorkshire Schools; related to
Nottinghamshire Gunn's
Overseas teams played for: Pirates, Durban 1981–85; Paarl CC 1985–86
Cricketers particularly admired: Graeme Pollock, Greg Chappell, Malcolm
Marshall
Off-season 1986–87: Coaching and playing in Cape Town
Other sports played: Hockey (capt Dorset U-19), rugby, squash
Relaxations: Photography, walking

LAST SEASON: BATTING

	I.	N.O.	R.	H.S.	AV.
TEST					
1ST-CLASS	29	0	863	79	29.75
INT					
JPL	8	0	83	40	10.37
NAT.W.	2	0	72	53	36.00
B & H	4	0	58	25	14.50

LAST SEASON: BOWLING

	O.	M.	R.	W.	AV.
TEST					
1ST-CLASS	1	0	5	0	–
INT					
JPL					
NAT.W.					
B & H					

CAREER: BATTING

	I.	N.O.	R.	H.S.	AV.
TEST					
1ST-CLASS	74	10	2118	107*	33.09
INT					
JPL	20	3	269	58	15.82
NAT.W.	4	1	74	53	24.66
B & H	5	0	62	25	12.40

CAREER: BOWLING

	O.	M.	R.	W.	AV.
TEST					
1ST-CLASS	2	0	8	0	–
INT					
JPL					
NAT.W.					
B & H					

Extras: Suffered from bilharzia, a tropical parasitic disease from 1980 to February 1986. Left Hampshire to join Somerset for 1986 season

Opinions on cricket: 'Would like to see an increasing role in Championship cricket for spinners and No.6 batsmen and a decreased one for continued finishes and attempts at under-prepared pitches. Uncovered wickets, perhaps?'

Best batting performance: 107* Hampshire v Essex, Southampton 1985

HARMAN, M. D. Somerset

Full Name: Mark David Harman
Role: Right-hand bat, right-arm off-spinner, 1st slip fielder
Born: 30 June 1964, Aylesbury
Height: 5' 11" **Weight:** 11st 12lbs
Nickname: Harmony, Basil
County debut: 1986
1st-Class catches 1986: 1 (career: 1)
Parents: Michael and Barbara
Marital status: Single
Education: Frome College; Loughborough University
Qualifications: 9 O-levels, 3 A-levels, BSc(Hons) Degree in Financial Management (completed in May 1987); cricket coaching awards
Jobs outside cricket: Chartered Accountancy
Family links with cricket: Father played club cricket
Cricketing superstitions: 'Always put socks on before shoes.'
Cricketers particularly learnt from: Many at Somerset CCC
Cricketers particularly admired: Viv Richards, Ian Botham, Vic Marks, John Emburey, Martin Crowe
Off-season 1986–87: Completing my degree
Other sports played: Soccer, golf, swimming, squash
Other sports followed: All sports through TV, media etc
Relaxations: Reading, listening to music, sleeping
Extras: Nearly run-out from first delivery in first-class cricket!
Opinions on cricket: '(1) England "B" Tours should become a regular feature of the winter season to help future Test cricketers bridge the gap between County and International cricket. (2) In order to gain more revenue from

advertising for Counties it may be necessary for limitations to be lifted on shirt/sweater advertising.'

Injuries 1986: Persistent lower back trouble over past two seasons

Best batting performance: 15 Somerset v Lancashire, Old Trafford 1986

LAST SEASON: BATTING

	I.	N.O.	R.	H.S.	AV.
TEST					
1ST-CLASS	5	2	27	15	9.00
INT					
JPL					
NAT.W.					
B & H					

LAST SEASON: BOWLING

	O.	M.	R.	W.	AV.
TEST					
1ST-CLASS	60.3	12	149	1	–
INT					
JPL					
NAT.W.					
B & H	·				

CAREER: BATTING

	I.	N.O.	R.	H.S.	AV.
TEST					
1ST-CLASS	5	2	27	15	9.00
INT					
JPL					
NAT.W.					
B & H					

CAREER: BOWLING

	O.	M.	R.	W.	AV.
TEST					
1ST-CLASS	60.3	12	149	1	–
INT					
JPL					
NAT.W.					
B & H					

HARPER, R. A.   Northamptonshire

Full Name: Roger Andrew Harper

Role: Right-hand bat, right-arm off-break bowler, slip fielder

Born: 19 March 1963, Georgetown, Guyana

Height: 6′ 5″ **Weight:** 14st 7lbs

Nickname: Juice ('I'm tee-total')

County debut: 1985

Test debut: 1983–84

No. of Tests: 16

No. of One-Day Internationals: 29

50 wickets in a season: 2

1st-Class 50s scored: 12

1st-Class 100s scored: 1

1st-Class 200s scored: 1

1st-Class 5 w. in innings: 14

1st-Class 10 w. in match: 1

One-Day 50s: 2

Place in batting averages: 69th av. 35.88 (1985 62nd av. 37.85)

Place in bowling averages: 45th av. 27.41 (1985 85th av. 36.53)

1st-Class catches 1986: 32 (career: 131)
Parents: Henry and Lynette
Marital status: Single
Education: Queen's College High School, Georgetown
Qualifications: 7 O-levels
Family links with cricket: Brother Mark plays for Guyana
Overseas tours: West Indies to India 1983, England 1984, Australia 1984–85, Pakistan 1985
Overseas teams played for: Guyana 1980–
Cricketers particularly learnt from: Brother Mark, Clive Lloyd
Cricketers particularly admired: Clive Lloyd, Gary Sobers
Off-season 1986–87: No off-season; playing in the West Indies
Other sports played: Tennis
Other sports followed: Tennis, athletics, boxing
Relaxations: Movies, music, good novels
Extras: Captain West Indies Youths on tour of England in 1982; County vice-captain 1986
Opinions on cricket: 'County Championship games should be four days, with each county playing each other once.'
Best batting performance: 234 Northamptonshire v Gloucestershire, Northampton 1986
Best bowling performance: 6-57 West Indies v England, Old Trafford 1984

LAST SEASON: BATTING

	I.	N.O.	R.	H.S.	AV.
TEST					
1ST-CLASS	30	4	933	234	35.88
INT					
JPL	14	6	344	57*	43.00
NAT.W.	1	0	1	1	–
B & H	5	0	118	56	23.60

LAST SEASON: BOWLING

	O.	M.	R.	W.	AV.
TEST					
1ST-CLASS	825.2	275	1700	62	27.41
INT					
JPL	113	5	449	16	28.06
NAT.W.	11	0	56	1	–
B & H	54	16	132	4	33.00

CAREER: BATTING

	I.	N.O.	R.	H.S.	AV.
TEST	20	3	303	60	17.82
1ST-CLASS	122	15	2958	234	27.64
INT	10	6	111	45*	27.75
JPL	23	7	416	57*	26.00
NAT.W.	2	0	1	1	0.50
B & H	5	0	118	56	23.60

CAREER: BOWLING

	O.	M.	R.	W.	AV.
TEST	462.4	139	1021	38	26.86
1ST-CLASS	3281.4	868	7847	284	27.63
INT	241	16	968	31	31.22
JPL	197	10	824	25	32.96
NAT.W.	20	4	69	1	–
B & H	76	17	217	7	31.00

91. Which father played Test cricket for one country and his son for another?

Full Name: Gordon Andrew Robert Harris
Role: Right-hand bat, right-arm fast medium bowler
Born: 11 January 1964, Tottenham
Height: 6′ 2½″
County debut: 1986
Education: Merchant Taylors' School, Northwood; Uxbridge Technical College; Leicester Polytechnic
Qualifications: BSc (Hons)
Family links with cricket: Father played for Northumberland in Minor Counties cricket
Off-season 1986–87: Temporary clerk

Other sport played: Represented Leicestershire at Under 21 hockey
Best batting performance: 6 Leicestershire v Worcestershire, Worcester 1986

LAST SEASON: BATTING

	I.	N.O.	R.	H.S.	AV.
TEST					
1ST-CLASS	2	1	6	6	–
INT					
JPL	–	–	–	–	–
NAT.W.					
B & H					

CAREER: BATTING

	I.	N.O.	R.	H.S.	AV.
TEST					
1ST-CLASS	2	1	6	6	–
INT					
JPL	–	–	–	–	–
NAT.W.					
B & H					

LAST SEASON: BOWLING

	O.	M.	R.	W.	AV.
TEST					
1ST-CLASS	8	1	34	0	–
INT					
JPL	8	2	27	1	–
NAT.W.					
B & H					

CAREER: BOWLING

	O.	M.	R.	W.	AV.
TEST					
1ST-CLASS	8	1	34	0	–
INT					
JPL	8	2	27	1	–
NAT.W.					
B & H					

92. Which famous captain of Yorkshire was not born in Yorkshire?

HARTLEY, P. J.   *Yorkshire*

Full Name: Peter John Hartley
Role: Right-hand bat, right-arm medium bowler
Born: 18 April 1960, Keighley
Height: 6′ 0″ **Weight:** 13st 2lbs
Nickname: Daisy, Jack
County debut: 1982 (Warwickshire), 1985 (Yorkshire)
1st-Class 50s scored: 4
1st-Class 5 w. in innings: 3
Place in batting averages: 80th av. 33.92 (1985 186th av. 19.98)
Place in bowling averages: 38th av. 26.70 (1985 93rd av. 37.90)
1st-Class catches 1986: 6 (career: 8)
Parents: Thomas and Molly
Marital status: Single
Education: Greenhead Grammar School; Bradford College
Qualifications: City & Guilds in Textiles
Jobs outside cricket: Textiles Supervisor
Family links with cricket: Father played village cricket
Overseas teams played for: Hamilton, Melville, New Zealand, 1983–84; Adelaide CC, 1985–86
Cricketers particularly learnt from: Phil Carrick, Steve Oldham, Mike Page
Cricketers particularly admired: Dennis Lillee, Richard Hadlee
Off-season 1986–87: Working at home in textile industry
Other sports played: Golf, tennis, football
Other sports followed: Follows Chelsea

LAST SEASON: BATTING

	I.	N.O.	R.	H.S.	AV.
TEST					
1ST-CLASS	17	4	441	87*	33.92
INT					
JPL	7	2	60	35	12.00
NAT.W.	1	0	23	23	–
B & H	2	1	29	29*	–

CAREER: BATTING

	I.	N.O.	R.	H.S.	AV.
TEST					
1ST-CLASS	32	8	631	87*	26.29
INT					
JPL	9	2	62	35	8.85
NAT.W.	1	0	23	23	–
B & H	2	1	29	29*	–

LAST SEASON: BOWLING

	O.	M.	R.	W.	AV.
TEST					
1ST-CLASS	321.1	49	1095	41	26.70
INT					
JPL	82	2	364	14	26.00
NAT.W.	24	4	96	6	16.00
B & H	41	1	185	8	23.14

CAREER: BOWLING

	O.	M.	R.	W.	AV.
TEST					
1ST-CLASS	694	100	2485	74	33.58
INT					
JPL	97	4	419	15	27.93
NAT.W.	24	4	96	6	16.00
B & H	41	1	185	8	23.12

Relaxations: Any sport, music
Injuries 1986: Torn rib muscles and groin
Best batting performance: 87* Yorkshire v Essex, Chelmsford 1986
Best bowling performance: 6-68 Yorkshire v Nottinghamshire, Sheffield 1986

HARTLEY, S. N.   Yorkshire

Full Name: Stuart Neil Hartley
Role: Right-hand bat, right-arm medium bowler, outfielder
Born: 18 March 1956, Shipley, West Yorkshire
Height: 5′ 11½″ **Weight:** 12st 3lbs
Nickname: Tommy
County debut: 1978
County cap: 1981
1st-Class 50s scored: 23
1st-Class 100s scored: 4
One-Day 50s: 12
Place in batting averages: 123rd av. 28.03 (1985 105th av. 30.78)
1st-Class catches 1986: 6 (career: 50)
Parents: Marjorie and Horace
Marital status: Divorced
Education: Beckfoot Grammar School, Bingley; Cannington High, Perth, Western Australia
Qualifications: 8 O-levels, 3 A-levels; exam passes in insurance
Jobs outside cricket: Trained insurance underwriter; National Sales Executive for R.B.S. (Financial Services) Ltd
Family links with cricket: Father played league cricket
Overseas tours: Captained North of England NCA team in Holland in 1975; Gibraltar 1981
Overseas teams played for: Orange Free State, 1981–82
Cricketers particularly learnt from: Doug Padgett and Mike Fearnley – Yorkshire County Cricket Club coaching staff
Cricketers particularly admired: Imran Khan, Clive Rice
Off-season 1986–87: Financial consultant
Other sports played: Golf
Extras: 'Started to play cricket in Perth, Western Australia, where I lived for 2½ years, 1967–69. I would like to live in Perth in the future.' Amateur football with Bradford City 1970–75. Rugby Union with Bingley RUFC. Has been acting captain of Yorkshire

Best batting performance: 114 Yorkshire v Gloucestershire, Bradford 1982
Best bowling performance: 4-51 Yorkshire v Surrey, The Oval 1985

LAST SEASON: BATTING

	I.	N.O.	R.	H.S.	AV.
TEST					
1ST-CLASS	30	2	785	87	28.03
INT					
JPL	15	1	254	57	18.14
NAT.W.	2	0	24	24	12.00
B & H	3	0	41	28	13.66

LAST SEASON: BOWLING

	O.	M.	R.	W.	AV.
TEST					
1ST-CLASS	48.4	9	206	4	51.50
INT					
JPL	22	0	120	2	60.00
NAT.W.					
B & H	8	0	30	1	–

CAREER: BATTING

	I.	N.O.	R.	H.S.	AV.
TEST					
1ST-CLASS	194	25	4309	114	25.49
INT					
JPL	90	15	1565	73	20.86
NAT.W.	10	0	239	69	23.90
B & H	19	5	401	65*	28.64

CAREER: BOWLING

	O.	M.	R.	W.	AV.
TEST					
1ST-CLASS	580	106	2107	46	48.80
INT					
JPL	204.3	3	1193	37	32.24
NAT.W.	26	2	102	1	–
B & H	81	3	311	12	25.92

HAYES, K. A.   Lancashire

Full Name: Kevin Anthony Hayes
Role: Right-hand bat, right-arm medium bowler
Born: 26 September 1962 Mexborough, Yorkshire
Height: 5′ 7″ **Weight:** 11st 7lbs
Nickname: Viking, Two-heads, Hazell, Crazy
County debut: 1980
1st-Class 50s scored: 7
1st-Class 100s scored: 2
1st-Class 5 w. in innings: 1
One-Day 50s: 1
1st-Class catches 1986: —
(career: 15)
Parents: Edward and Pam
Marital status: Single
Education: Queen Elizabeth's School, Blackburn; Merton College, Oxford
Qualifications: BA(Hons) Chemistry
Family links with cricket: Brother, David, played for Lancashire U-13 and U-15, and captained U-15 Schools
Cricketing superstitions: 111
Overseas teams played for: City District CC, Canberra 1984–85

Cricketers particularly admired: Richard Hadlee, Viv Richards
Other sports played: 'Any'
Relaxations: 'Listening to most types of music, crosswords.'
Extras: Oxford Blue – captain of University in 1984
Best batting performance: 152 Oxford University v Warwickshire, Oxford 1982
Best bowling performance: 6-58 Oxford University v Warwickshire, Edgbaston 1982

LAST SEASON: BATTING

	I.	N.O.	R.	H.S.	AV.
TEST					
1ST-CLASS	1	0	17	17	–
INT					
JPL NAT.W.					
B & H					

LAST SEASON: BOWLING

	O.	M.	R.	W.	AV.
TEST					
1ST-CLASS					
INT					
JPL NAT.W.					
B & H					

CAREER: BATTING

	I.	N.O.	R.	H.S.	AV.
TEST					
1ST-CLASS	71	4	1595	152	23.80
INT					
JPL	5	2	64	53	21.33
NAT.W.					
B & H	11	0	174	67	15.82

CAREER: BOWLING

	O.	M.	R.	W.	AV.
TEST					
1ST-CLASS	160.1	40	537	17	31.58
INT					
JPL	1	0	5	0	–
NAT.W.					
B & H	39	9	119	4	29.75

HAYHURST, A. N. — Lancashire

Full Name: Andrew Neil Hayhurst
Role: Right-hand bat, right-arm medium bowler
Born: 23 November 1962, Davyhulme, Manchester
Height: 6′ 0″ **Weight:** 13st
Nickname: Barney, The Piece
County debut: 1985
Place in batting averages: 237th av. 11.14
Place in bowling averages: 108th av. 42.90
1st-Class catches 1986: 2 (career: 2)
Parents: William and Margaret
Marital status: Single
Education: St Mark's Primary School; Worsley Wardley High; Eccles College; Carnegie College, Leeds

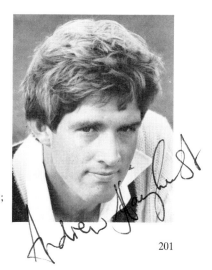

Qualifications: 8 O-levels, 3 A-levels, BA(Hons) Human Movement
Family links with cricket: Father played club cricket
Cricketers particularly learnt from: Father and Geoff Ogden (Worsley CC)
Cricketers particularly admired: Geoff Boycott, Ian Botham, Viv Richards
Off-season 1986–87: Teaching in Blackburn
Other sports played: Football, golf – all sports
Relaxations: Watching all sports, good food, company.
Extras: Scored a record 197 runs whilst playing for North of England v South, Southampton 1982. Represented NAYC v MCC 1982. Holds record number of runs for Lancashire Cricket Fed. U-19 (av. 105.00), 1982. Holds record number of runs in Manchester & District Cricket Association League, whilst playing for Worsley CC in 1984: 1193 runs (av. 70.17). Represented Greater Manchester U-19 County at football 1981–82
Opinions on cricket: '2nd XI cricket should be played on better pitches if that cricket is to be a successful grounding for future 1st XI players.'
Injuries 1986: Torn intercostal muscles
Best batting performance: 31 Lancashire v Somerset, Old Trafford 1986
Best bowling performance: 4-69 Lancashire v Yorkshire, Old Trafford 1986

LAST SEASON: BATTING

	I.	N.O.	R.	H.S.	AV.
TEST					
1ST-CLASS	14	0	156	31	11.14
INT					
JPL	5	1	65	34	16.25
NAT.W.	2	0	52	49	26.00
B & H					

LAST SEASON: BOWLING

	O.	M.	R.	W.	AV.
TEST					
1ST-CLASS	114.1	13	429	10	42.90
INT					
JPL	61	1	282	4	70.50
NAT.W.	35.5	3	130	6	21.66
B & H					

CAREER: BATTING

	I.	N.O.	R.	H.S.	AV.
TEST					
1ST-CLASS	15	0	173	31	11.53
INT					
JPL	6	2	77	34	19.25
NAT.W.	3	0	59	49	19.66
B & H					

CAREER: BOWLING

	O.	M.	R.	W.	AV.
TEST					
1ST-CLASS	127.1	17	466	13	35.84
INT					
JPL	66	1	313	4	78.25
NAT.W.	40.5	3	160	6	26.66
B & H					

93. Who are the only two brothers to have scored centuries for Cambridge University against Oxford?

HEGG, W. K. — Lancashire

Full Name: Warren Kevin Hegg
Role: Right-hand bat, wicket-keeper
Born: 23 February 1968, Radcliffe, Lancashire
Height: 5′ 10″ **Weight:** 11st 5lbs
Nickname: Chucky
County debut: 1986
Parents: Kevin and Glenda
Marital status: Single
Education: Unsworth High School; Stand College, Whitefield
Qualifications: 5 O-levels, 7 CSEs; qualified coach
Jobs outside cricket: Groundsman at Old Trafford; worked at warehouse (involved in textiles)
Family links with cricket: Father Kevin played in local leagues, as does brother Martin
Cricketing superstitions: 'Too many to mention.'
Overseas tours: Bermuda North England U-19's 1985
Cricketers particularly learnt from: Father Kevin and Jim Kenyon (old pro), Clive Lloyd
Cricketers particularly admired: Ian Botham, Bob Taylor, Alan Knott
Off-season 1986–87: Playing for Easts CC, Brisbane, Australia
Other sports played: County football, golf, tennis
Other sports followed: Football, golf
Relaxations: Watching TV, sleeping, walking dog, fishing

LAST SEASON: BATTING

	I.	N.O.	R.	H.S.	AV.
TEST					
1ST-CLASS	2	0	4	4	2.00
INT					
JPL					
NAT.W.					
B & H					

LAST SEASON: WICKET-KEEPING

	C.	ST.		
TEST				
1ST-CLASS	2	2		
INT				
JPL				
NAT.W.				
B & H				

CAREER: BATTING

	I.	N.O.	R.	H.S.	AV.
TEST					
1ST-CLASS	2	0	4	4	2.00
INT					
JPL					
NAT.W.					
B & H					

CAREER: WICKET-KEEPING

	C.	ST.		
TEST				
1ST-CLASS	2	2		
INT				
JPL				
NAT.W.				
B & H				

Extras: First player to make County debut from Lytham CC. Holds Lancashire Schools U-19 record for most dismissals in a match – 6 (previous holder Graeme Fowler)
Opinions on cricket: 'Every county should be allowed two overseas players to make things fair. Tea sessions should be ten minutes longer.'
Best batting performance: 4 Lancashire v Glamorgan, Lytham 1986

HEMMINGS, E. E.　　　Nottinghamshire

Full Name: Edward Ernest Hemmings
Role: Right-hand bat, right-arm off-break bowler
Born: 20 February 1949, Leamington Spa, Warwickshire
Height: 5′ 10″ **Weight:** 13st
Nickname: Eddie
County debut: 1966 (Warwickshire), 1979 (Nottinghamshire)
County cap: 1974 (Warwickshire), 1980 (Nottinghamshire)
Benefit: 1987
Test debut: 1982
No. of Tests: 5
No. of One-Day Internationals: 5
50 wickets in a season: 11
1st-Class 50s scored: 19
1st-Class 100s scored: 1
1st-Class 5 w. in innings: 52
1st-Class 10 w. in match: 12
One-Day 50s: 1
Place in batting averages: 195th av. 17.36 (1985 203rd av. 17.47)
Place in bowling averages: 57th av. 29.23 (1985 95th av. 38.24)
1st-Class catches 1986: 7 (career: 164)
Parents: Edward and Dorothy Phyliss
Wife and date of marriage: Christine Mary, 23 October 1971
Children: Thomas Edward, 26 July 1977; James Oliver, 9 September 1979
Education: Campion School, Leamington Spa
Family links with cricket: Father and father's father played Minor Counties and League cricket
Overseas tours: Derrick Robins XI tour to South Africa 1975; International XI to Pakistan 1981; England to Australia and New Zealand 1982–83
Cricketers particularly learnt from: J. A. Jameson

Cricketers particularly admired: R. T. Robinson

Other sport played: Golf

Relaxations: 'Watching football at any level – especially junior. Dining out with my wife.'

Extras: Debut for Warwickshire 1966, cap 1974. No longer wears glasses, plays in contact lenses. Started his career as a medium-pacer, and was thought of as a successor to Tom Cartwright. 'I was even known as "Tommy's Ghost" around Edgbaston.' Suffers from asthma. Took a hat-trick for Warwickshire in 1977 but had to wait four years to receive the inscribed match ball, when he had moved to Nottinghamshire. Hit first century – 127* v Yorkshire at Worksop, July 1982 – after 16 years in first-class game

Best batting performance: 127* Nottinghamshire v Yorkshire, Worksop 1982

Best bowling performance: 10-175 International XI v West Indies XI, Kingston 1982–83

LAST SEASON: BATTING

	I.	N.O.	R.	H.S.	AV.
TEST					
1ST-CLASS	23	4	330	54*	17.36
INT					
JPL	3	1	17	14	8.50
NAT.W.	2	1	7	4	–
B & H	2	2	28	26*	–

LAST SEASON: BOWLING

	O.	M.	R.	W.	AV.
TEST					
1ST-CLASS	818.3	259	2134	73	29.22
INT					
JPL	66	2	368	14	26.28
NAT.W.	33	8	80	2	40.00
B & H	33	9	101	0	–

CAREER: BATTING

	I.	N.O.	R.	H.S.	AV.
TEST	10	1	198	95	22.00
1ST-CLASS	471	103	7277	127*	19.77
INT	2	0	4	3	2.00
JPL	138	38	1363	44*	13.63
NAT.W.	22	5	207	31*	12.17
B & H	36	11	385	61*	15.40

CAREER: BOWLING

	O.	M.	R.	W.	AV.
TEST	244.4	71	558	12	46.50
1ST-CLASS	11290.2	3171	30314	1048	28.92
INT	41.5	4	175	5	35.00
JPL	1340	88	6237	222	28.09
NAT.W.	328.1	56	1070	28	38.21
B & H	594.4	79	1839	54	34.05

94. Who was the first Glamorgan player to represent England against Australia?

HENRIKSEN, S. Lancashire

Full Name: Søren Henriksen
Role: Right-hand bat, right-arm fast-medium bowler
Born: 1 December 1964, Copenhagen
Height: 6′ 3″ **Weight:** 14st 5lbs
Nickname: Herbie
County debut: 1985
1st-Class catches 1986: 1 (career: 2)
Parents: Anni and Bendt
Marital status: Single
Education: Trade School, Copenhagen
Qualifications: Trade exams
Jobs outside cricket: Office job in City Hall
Family links with cricket: Father played for Svanholm CC, Denmark
Overseas tours: Sweden 1979 with Svanholm CC; England 1981, 1982, 1984 with Danish Schools Teams; Kenya 1983 with Danish Sports Academic Club; Holland 1983 with Young Denmark; Barbardos 1985 with Forty Club, Denmark
Cricketers particularly learnt from: 'All Lancashire staff.'
Cricketers particularly admired: Ian Botham, Clive Lloyd
Other sports played: Badminton, table-tennis, handball
Other sports followed: Football, tennis
Relaxations: Music, TV, reading
Best batting performance: 10* Lancashire v Surrey, The Oval 1985

LAST SEASON: BATTING

	I.	N.O.	R.	H.S.	AV.
TEST					
1ST-CLASS	2	1	7	6*	–
INT					
JPL	–	–	–	–	–
NAT.W.					
B & H					

LAST SEASON: BOWLING

	O.	M.	R.	W.	AV.
TEST					
1ST-CLASS	17	2	61	1	–
INT					
JPL	4	0	7	0	–
NAT.W.					
B & H					

CAREER: BATTING

	I.	N.O.	R.	H.S.	AV.
TEST					
1ST-CLASS	4	3	17	10*	–
INT					
JPL	1	0	1	1	–
NAT.W.	1	1	1	1*	–
B & H	–	–	–	–	–

CAREER: BOWLING

	O.	M.	R.	W.	AV.
TEST					
1ST-CLASS	29	3	105	2	52.50
INT					
JPL	54	0	246	4	61.50
NAT.W.	10	1	51	2	25.50
B & H	7	0	32	0	–

HICK, G. A.   Worcestershire

Full Name: Graeme Ashley Hick
Role: Right-hand bat, right-arm
off-break bowler, slip and gully
fielder
Born: 23 May 1966, Salisbury,
Rhodesia
Height: 6′ 3″ **Weight:** 14½st
Nickname: Hicky, Hickery
County debut: 1984
County cap: 1986
1000 runs in a season: 2
1st-Class 50s scored: 18
1st-Class 100s scored: 9
1st-Class 200s scored: 3
One-Day 50s: 7
One-Day 100s: 2
Place in batting averages: 3rd

av. 64.64 (1985 19th av. 52.71)
1st-Class catches 1986: 29
(career: 62)
Parents: John and Eve
Marital status: Single
Education: Banket Primary; Prince Edward Boys' High School, Zimbabwe
Qualifications: 4 O-levels, NCA coaching award
Jobs outside cricket: Zimbabwe Cricket Union coach
Family links with cricket: Father connected with cricket administration since
1972 and in 1984 elected to Zimbabwe Cricket Union Board of Control
Cricketing superstitions: Left pad always put on first
Overseas tours: Zimbabwe XI 1983 World Cup; Zimbabwe v Sri Lanka in Sri
Lanka; Zimbabwe U-23 Triangular Tournament to Zambia; Zimbabwe to
UK 1985
Overseas teams played for: Old Harrarians, Zimbabwe, since 1982
Cricketers particularly learnt from: David Houghton, Basil D'Oliveira,
Father
Cricketers particularly admired: Duncan Fletcher (Zimbabwe captain) for
approach and understanding of the game
Off-season 1986–87: In Zimbabwe playing cricket
Other sports played: Golf, tennis, squash, indoor hockey
Other sports followed: Follows Liverpool FC
Relaxations: Watching movies, television, listening to music
Extras: Youngest player participating in 1983 Prudential World Cup (aged
17); youngest player to represent Zimbabwe. Scored 1234 runs in 1984
Birmingham League season; scored 964 runs in 1984 2nd XI for Worcester-

shire; scored 185 in Birmingham League – highest score since the War; scored 11 centuries (including six in a row) in both above competitions

Opinions on cricket: 'A little more time between games for players to get together and discuss coming games and relax. It may give better performances on the field.'

Best batting performance: 230 Zimbabwe v Oxford University, Oxford 1985
Best bowling performance: 3-39 Zimbabwe v Sri Lanka Board Presidents XI, Moratuwa 1983–84

LAST SEASON: BATTING

	I.	N.O.	R.	H.S.	AV.
TEST					
1ST-CLASS	37	6	2004	227*	64.64
INT					
JPL	16	1	507	68*	33.80
NAT.W.	4	1	37	27	12.33
B & H	6	2	345	103*	86.25

CAREER: BATTING

	I.	N.O.	R.	H.S.	AV.
TEST					
1ST-CLASS	91	11	4262	230	53.27
INT					
JPL	24	2	712	90	32.36
NAT.W.	4	1	37	27	12.33
B & H	6	2	345	103*	86.25

LAST SEASON: BOWLING

	O.	M.	R.	W.	AV.
TEST					
1ST-CLASS	28.4	5	109	3	36.33
INT					
JPL	14	0	70	2	35.00
NAT.W.	10	1	25	1	–
B & H	12	1	47	3	15.66

CAREER: BOWLING

	O.	M.	R.	W.	AV.
TEST					
1ST-CLASS	345.4	66	1161	21	55.28
INT					
JPL	24	0	136	5	27.20
NAT.W.	10	1	25	1	–
B & H	12	1	47	3	15.66

95. When did Glamorgan first win the county championship?
96. Which England Test cricketer had the nickname 'Farmer'?

HICKEY, D. J.   Glamorgan

Full Name: Denis Jon Hickey
Role: Right-hand bat, right-arm
fast-medium bowler
Born: 31 December 1964,
Melbourne, Australia
County debut: 1986
1st-Class 5 w. in innings: 3
1st-Class 10 w. in match: 1
Place in bowling averages: 113th
av. 45.91
1st-Class catches 1986: 3 (career: 4)
Overseas teams played for:
Victoria since 1985
Extras: Took 17 wickets in his
first four State matches. Came to
England on an Esso Scholarship
and used by Glamorgan as their
overseas player when Javed
Miandad left the county
Best batting performance: 9* Glamorgan v Kent, Maidstone 1986
Best bowling performance: 7-87 Victoria v South Australia, Adelaide 1985–86

LAST SEASON: BATTING

	I.	N.O.	R.	H.S.	AV.
TEST					
1ST-CLASS	9	5	19	9*	47.5
INT					
JPL	3	1	2	2*	–
NAT.W.	1	1	0	0*	–
B & H					

CAREER: BATTING

	I.	N.O.	R.	H.S.	AV.
TEST					
1ST-CLASS	11	6	27	9*	5.40
INT					
JPL	3	1	2	2*	1.00
NAT.W.	1	1	0	0*	–
B & H					

LAST SEASON: BOWLING

	O.	M.	R.	W.	AV.
TEST					
1ST-CLASS	281.5	39	1102	24	45.91
INT					
JPL	48.3	3	204	10	20.40
NAT.W.	9	0	64	1	–
B & H					

CAREER: BOWLING

	O.	M.	R.	W.	AV.
TEST					
1ST-CLASS	397.1	58	1465	41	35.73
INT					
JPL	48.3	3	204	10	20.40
NAT.W.	9	0	64	1	–
B & H					

HIGGS, K.   Leicestershire

Full Name: Kenneth Higgs
Role: Left-hand bat, right-arm
fast medium bowler
Born: 14 January 1937, Sandyford,
Stoke-on-Trent
Height: 6′ 0″
Nickname: Higgy
County debut: 1958 (Lancashire),
1972 (Leicestershire)
County cap: 1959 (Lancashire),
1972 (Leicestershire)
Benefit: £8,390 in 1968 (while at
Lancashire)
Test debut: 1965
No. of Tests: 15
1st-Class 5 w. in innings: 50
1st-Class 10 w. in match: 5
1st-Class catches 1986: 1 (career: 312)
Parents: James and Elsie
Wife and date of marriage: Mary, 14 December 1957
Children: Kenneth Paul, 31 August 1960; Terence, 1 October 1963
Education: Secondary Modern
Jobs outside cricket: None. In the past has been a professional footballer for
Port Vale FC and has worked for a Blackpool grocery firm
Overseas tours: Australia and New Zealand 1965–66, West Indies 1967–68
Other sports played: Squash
Relaxations: Gardening, watching all types of sport
Extras: Played for Staffordshire in 1957. Debut for Lancashire CCC in 1958,

LAST SEASON: BATTING

	I.	N.O.	R.	H.S.	AV.
TEST					
1ST-CLASS	2	1	11	8	–
INT					
JPL					
NAT.W.					
B & H					

LAST SEASON: BOWLING

	O.	M.	R.	W.	AV.
TEST					
1ST-CLASS	36	10	71	5	14.20
INT					
JPL					
NAT.W.					
B & H					

CAREER: BATTING

	I.	N.O.	R.	H.S.	AV.
TEST	19	3	185	63	11.69
1ST-CLASS	511	204	3463	98	11.28
INT					
JPL	32	21	142	17*	12.91
NAT.W.	20	9	96	25	8.73
B & H	15	9	60	10	10.00

CAREER: BOWLING

	O.	M.	R.	W.	AV.
TEST	30 645.2	6 187	1473	71	20.75
1ST-CLASS	249.3 13888	22 3401	34794	1465	23.75
INT					
JPL	1135.1	120	4089	217	18.84
NAT.W.	365.4	64	1055	52	20.30
B & H	502	91	1578	86	18.35

capped 1959. Retired after 1969 season. Debut for Leicestershire 1972, appointed Vice-Captain 1973 and County Captain 1979. In 1960 took 132 wickets at an average of 19.42. Coaches Leicestershire 2nd XI. Shared tenth wicket partnership for county, 228 with Ray Illingworth v Northants, at Leicester in 1977. Returned to the side in an emergency during 1986 and took 5-22 on reappearance

Best batting performance: 98 Leicestershire v Northamptonshire, Leicester 1977

Best bowling performance: 7-19 Lancashire v Leicestershire, Old Trafford 1965

HILL, A. Derbyshire

Full Name: Alan Hill
Role: Right-hand bat, right-arm off-break bowler
Born: 29 June 1950, Buxworth, Derbyshire
Height: 6' 0" **Weight:** 12st 4lbs
Nickname: Bud
County debut: 1972
County cap: 1976
Benefit: 1986
1000 runs in a season: 5
1st-Class 50s scored: 69
1st-Class 100s scored: 18
One-Day 50s: 15
One-Day 100s: 4
Place in batting averages: 38th av. 42.29 (1985 111th av. 30.27)
1st-Class catches 1986: 10 (career: 97)

Parents: Hilda and Jack
Wife and date of marriage: Linda, 18 March 1978
Children: Elizabeth Anne, Eleanor Jane, Laura Louise
Education: Buxworth Primary School; New Mill Grammar School; Chester College of Education
Qualifications: BEd Physical Education teacher, Advanced Cricket Coaching Award
Jobs outside cricket: Teaching posts, clerical work, promotional assistant
Family links with cricket: Father and brother both played local league cricket. Brother, Bernard, played for Derbyshire 2nd XI

Overseas teams played for: Orange Free State in 1976–77 Currie Cup Competition
Cricketers particularly admired: Sir Garfield Sobers
Other sports played: Soccer, rugby
Relaxations: Other sports, particularly football; music, reading
Extras: England Schoolboy cricketer 1968; also represented National Association of Young Cricketers. Went into semi-retirement after 1986 season. Will be 2nd XI captain/coach in 1987 and assistant to Commercial Manager at Derbyshire in winter. Might still play the odd game
Opinions on cricket: 'Would like to see the umpires receive greater backing from the authorities in their efforts to control the game.'
Best batting performance: 172* Derbyshire v Yorkshire, Sheffield 1986
Best bowling performance: 3-5 Orange Free State v North Transvaal, Pretoria 1976–77

LAST SEASON: BATTING

	I.	N.O.	R.	H.S.	AV.
TEST					
1ST-CLASS	40	6	1438	172*	42.29
INT					
JPL	15	1	296	50	21.14
NAT.W.	2	0	169	153	84.50
B & H	5	2	210	90*	70.00

LAST SEASON: BOWLING

	O.	M.	R.	W.	AV.
TEST					
1ST-CLASS	9	3	22	1	–
INT					
JPL					
NAT.W.	3	0	13	0	–
B & H					

CAREER: BATTING

	I.	N.O.	R.	H.S.	AV.
TEST					
1ST-CLASS	447	47	12356	172*	30.89
INT					
JPL	93	5	1924	120	21.86
NAT.W.	17	1	475	153	29.68
B & H	31	4	1096	107*	40.59

CAREER: BOWLING

	O.	M.	R.	W.	AV.
TEST					
1ST-CLASS	92.2	19	365	9	40.58
INT					
JPL	8	0	32	3	10.66
NAT.W.					
B & H					

97. Who was born in the West Indies but played for England, and had as his nickname the name of a fruit?

HINKS, S. G.   Kent

Full Name: Simon Graham Hinks
Role: Left-hand bat, bat/pad fielder
Born: 12 October 1960,
Northfleet, Kent
Height: 6′ 2″ **Weight:** 13st 7lbs
Nickname: Hinksy
County debut: 1982
County cap: 1985
1000 runs in a season: 1
1st-Class 50s scored: 13
1st-Class 100s scored: 3
One-Day 50s: 4
Place in batting averages: 139th
av. 26.00 (1985 77th av. 34.13)
1st-Class catches 1986: 14
(career: 43)
Parents: Mary and Graham
Marital status: Single
Education: Dover Road Infant and
Junior Schools, Northfleet; St George's C of E School, Gravesend
Qualifications: 5 O-levels, 1 A-level
Family links with cricket: Father captained Gravesend CC and is now
chairman. Brother Jonathan plays for Gravesend and Kent U-19s
Cricketing superstitions: 'Put gear on in set order.'
Overseas teams played for: Pirates, Johannesburg, 1981–82; University of
Tasmania, 1983–86
Cricketers particularly learnt from: 'Learnt from my father and members of
local club, Gravesend.'

LAST SEASON: BATTING

	I.	N.O.	R.	H.S.	AV.
TEST					
1ST-CLASS	38	2	936	131	26.00
INT					
JPL	12	0	356	99	29.66
NAT.W.	1	0	44	44	–
B & H	7	0	141	41	20.14

CAREER: BATTING

	I.	N.O.	R.	H.S.	AV.
TEST					
1ST-CLASS	114	6	2922	131	27.05
INT					
JPL	33	2	692	99	22.32
NAT.W.	4	0	188	95	47.00
B & H	12	0	235	49	19.58

LAST SEASON: BOWLING

	O.	M.	R.	W.	AV.
TEST					
1ST-CLASS	8	2	10	1	–
INT					
JPL	9	0	48	1	–
NAT.W.					
B & H	14	0	54	2	27.00

CAREER: BOWLING

	O.	M.	R.	W.	AV.
TEST					
1ST-CLASS	58.4	7	188	4	42.00
INT					
JPL	18	1	87	3	29.00
NAT.W.	12	0	59	1	–
B & H	14	0	54	2	27.00

Cricketers particularly admired: 'Admire Clive Loyd's style and power and anyone who has proved themselves over a long period.'
Off-season 1986–87: In England
Other sports played: Most ball games
Relaxations: TV, music, papers, books
Opinions on cricket: 'More should be done by administrators to help players find employment during the off-season. Too many players rely on coaching jobs abroad. Less travelling. Two one-day games at weekend and 16 three-day games midweek.'
Injuries: Suspected broken bone in wrist (missed last 3 games of season)
Best batting performance: 131 Kent v Hampshire, Canterbury 1986

HOLDING, M. A.   Derbyshire

Full Name: Michael Anthony Holding
Role: Right-hand bat, right-arm fast bowler
Born: 16 February 1954, Kingston, Jamaica
County debut: 1981 (Lancashire), 1983 (Derbyshire)
County cap: 1983 (Derbyshire)
Test debut: 1975–76
No. of Tests: 59
No. of One-Day Internationals: 96
50 wickets in a season: 2
1st-Class 50s scored: 4
1st-Class 5 w. in innings: 33
1st-Class 10 w. in match: 4
One-Day 50s: 4
Place in batting averages: 204th

av. 16.38 (1985 167th av. 22.94)
Place in bowling averages: 8th av. 20.09 (1985 9th av. 22.48)
1st-Class catches 1986: 7 (career: 76)
Overseas tours: With West Indies to Australia 1975–86, 1981–82; to England 1976, 1980, 1984; to India 1983–84; International team to Pakistan 1981–82
Overseas teams played for: Jamaica, Tasmania
Extras: Played for Lancashire in 1981
Best batting performance: 80 Derbyshire v Yorkshire, Chesterfield 1985
Best bowling performance: 8-92 West Indies v England, The Oval 1976

	I.	N.O.	R.	H.S.	AV.
TEST					
1ST-CLASS	20	2	295	36*	16.38
INT					
JPL	11	1	86	27	8.60
NAT.W.	1	0	0	0	–
B & H	3	0	75	69	25.00

LAST SEASON: BOWLING

	O.	M.	R.	W.	AV.
TEST					
1ST-CLASS	388.1	110	1045	52	20.09
INT					
JPL	111	14	435	21	20.71
NAT.W.	18	4	32	1	
B & H	48	9	136	7	19.42

CAREER: BATTING

	I.	N.O.	R.	H.S.	AV.
TEST	75	10	910	73	14.00
1ST-CLASS	139	18	1990	80	16.44
INT	38	10	217	64	7.75
JPL	34	3	324	58	15.42
NAT.W.	4	1	39	27	13.00
B & H	7	1	136	69	22.66

CAREER: BOWLING

	O.	M.	R.	W.	AV.
TEST	140.5 1888.5	15	5799	249	23.28
1ST-CLASS	56 2846.5	5 724	8264	363	22.76
INT	857.4	96	2872	135	23.27
JPL	253.4	32	998	47	21.23
NAT.W.	66	10	189	7	27.00
B & H	93	17	270	11	24.54

HOLMES, G. C.   Glamorgan

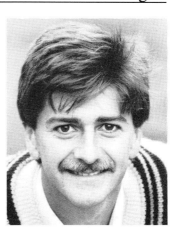

Full Name: Geoffrey Clark Holmes
Role: Right-hand bat, right-arm medium bowler, cover fielder
Born: 16 September 1958, Newcastle-on-Tyne
Height: 5′ 10″ **Weight:** 10st 10lbs
County debut: 1978
County cap: 1985
1000 runs in a season: 3
1st-Class 50s scored: 22
1st-Class 100s scored: 4
1st-Class 5 w. in innings: 1
One-Day 50s: 8
Place in batting averages: 121st av. 28.35 (1985 107th av. 30.51)
Place in bowling averages: 112th av. 45.36 (1985 99th av. 38.56)
1st-Class catches 1986: 19 (career: 59)
Parents: George and Rita
Wife: Christine
Education: West Denton High School
Qualifications: 6 O-levels, A-levels in Maths and Chemistry; Advanced Cricket Coach
Jobs outside cricket: Trainee estimator; has worked as milkman
Family links with cricket: Father played in the Northumberland League

Overseas teams played for: Villa CC, Antigua, 1980–81; Bathurst RUCC, New South Wales, 1983–84; Fish Hoek, South Africa, 1984–85
Cricketers particularly learnt from: Javed Miandad
Other sports played: Soccer, snooker
Relaxations: Reading, especially cricket books, TV, sport
Best batting performance: 112 Glamorgan v Leicestershire, Leicester 1985
Best bowling performance: 5-86 Glamorgan v Surrey, The Oval 1980

LAST SEASON: BATTING

	I.	N.O.	R.	H.S.	AV.
TEST					
1ST-CLASS	44	5	1106	107	28.35
INT					
JPL	15	2	365	65*	28.07
NAT.W.	2	0	58	45	29.00
B & H	4	0	59	30	14.75

LAST SEASON: BOWLING

	O.	M.	R.	W.	AV.
TEST					
1ST-CLASS	131	21	499	11	45.36
INT					
JPL	69	0	382	13	29.38
NAT.W.	24	4	60	3	20.00
B & H	20	0	101	3	33.67

CAREER: BATTING

	I.	N.O.	R.	H.S.	AV.
TEST					
1ST-CLASS	206	32	4670	112	26.83
INT					
JPL	70	13	1269	73	22.26
NAT.W.	7	0	106	45	15.14
B & H	14	2	284	70	23.67

CAREER: BOWLING

	O.	M.	R.	W.	AV.
TEST					
1ST-CLASS	816.4	166	2828	67	42.20
INT					
JPL	303.3	10	1580	62	25.48
NAT.W.	62	11	156	9	17.33
B & H	97.2	11	393	16	24.56

HOPKINS, J. A.   Glamorgan

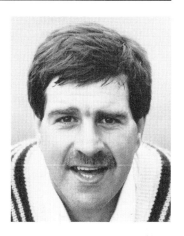

Full Name: John Anthony Hopkins
Role: Right-hand bat, occasional wicket-keeper
Born: 16 June 1953, Maesteg
Nickname: Ponty
County debut: 1970
County cap: 1977
1000 runs in a season: 7
1st-Class 50s scored: 56
1st-Class 100s scored: 17
1st-Class 200s scored: 1
One-Day 50s: 25
One-Day 100s: 2
Place in batting averages: 120th
av. 28.38 (1985 148th av. 24.81)
1st-Class catches 1986: 10
(career: 191)
Education: Trinity College of
Education, Carmarthen

Qualifications: Trained as a teacher
Jobs outside cricket: Teacher
Family links with cricket: Younger brother of J. D. Hopkins who appeared for Middlesex CCC and formerly on Glamorgan staff
Extras: Known as fine baritone singer and raconteur in the Glamorgan 'cabaret' act
Best batting performance: 230 Glamorgan v Worcestershire, Worcester 1977

LAST SEASON: BATTING

	I.	N.O.	R.	H.S.	AV.
TEST					
1ST-CLASS	26	0	738	142	28.38
INT					
JPL	15	0	440	89	29.33
NAT.W.	2	0	52	47	26.00
B & H	4	0	85	31	21.25

LAST SEASON: BOWLING

	O.	M.	R.	W.	AV.
TEST					
1ST-CLASS	2	0	12	0	—
INT					
JPL					
NAT.W.					
B & H					

CAREER: BATTING

	I.	N.O.	R.	H.S.	AV.
TEST					
1ST-CLASS	486	29	12857	230	28.08
INT					
JPL	157	13	3259	130*	22.63
NAT.W.	18	0	361	63	20.05
B & H	40	2	1046	103*	27.52

CAREER: BOWLING

	O.	M.	R.	W.	AV.
TEST					
1ST-CLASS	21.2	2	102	0	—
INT					
JPL					
NAT.W.					
B & H					

HUGHES, D. P. Lancashire

Full Name: David Paul Hughes
Role: Right-hand bat, slow left-arm bowler
Born: 13 May 1947, Newton-le-Willows
Height: 5′ 11″ **Weight:** 12st
Nickname: Yozzer
County debut: 1967
County cap: 1970
Testimonial: 1981
1000 runs in a season: 2
50 wickets in a season: 2
1st-Class 50s scored: 38
1st-Class 100s scored: 8
1st-Class 5 w. in innings: 20
1st-Class 10 w. in match: 2
One-Day 50s: 9
Place in batting averages: —
(1985 116th av. 29.36)

1st-Class catches 1986: — (career: 242)

Parents: Both deceased

Wife and date of marriage: Christine, March 1973

Children: James, July 1975

Education: Newton-le-Willows Grammar School

Qualifications: NCA Coaching Certificate

Family links with cricket: Father, Lloyd, a professional with Bolton League Club, Walkden, before and after Second World War

Overseas tours: With Derrick Robins to South Africa 1972–73; England Counties side to West Indies 1974–75

Overseas teams played for: Played for Tasmania while coaching there in 1975–76 and 1976–77

Cricketers particularly learnt from: 'At the start of my career I spoke to all the leading left-arm spin bowlers in the game for help.'

Relaxations: Golf

Extras: Coached in South Africa 1977–78; coached in Tasmania 1978–79 and 1979–80. Gillette Cup 'specialist'. Hit 24 runs off John Mortimer v Gloucestershire in penultimate over in Gillette semi-final in 1972. Hit 26 runs off last over of innings v Northamptonshire in Gillette Final at Lord's, 1976. Bowled 13 consecutive maiden overs v Gloucestershire at Bristol, 1980. John Player League 9th wicket partnership of 86 with P. Lever v Essex, Leyton 1973. Appointed Lancashire captain for 1987

Best batting performance: 153 Lancashire v Glamorgan, Old Trafford 1983

Best bowling performance: 7-24 Lancashire v Oxford University, Oxford 1970

LAST SEASON: BATTING

	I.	N.O.	R.	H.S.	AV.
TEST					
1ST-CLASS					
INT					
JPL	1	0	17	17	–
NAT.W.					
B & H	2	0	5	4	2.50

LAST SEASON: BOWLING

	O.	M.	R.	W.	AV.
TEST					
1ST-CLASS					
INT					
JPL	4	0	29	0	–
NAT.W.					
B & H	11	1	24	1	–

CAREER: BATTING

	I.	N.O.	R.	H.S.	AV.
TEST					
1ST-CLASS	463	84	8612	153	22.72
INT					
JPL	180	42	2556	92	18.52
NAT.W.	34	15	759	71	39.95
B & H	47	13	859	52	25.26

CAREER: BOWLING

	O.	M.	R.	W.	AV.
TEST					
1ST-CLASS	23 6701.1	3 2080	18254	610	29.92
INT					
JPL	790.1	62	3416	161	21.21
NAT.W.	300.2	29	1166	44	26.50
B & H	229.2	40	726	29	25.03

98. Who played Test cricket for both England and Australia – and also rugger for England?

HUGHES, S. P.   Middlesex

Full Name: Simon Peter Hughes
Role: Right-hand bat, right-arm
fast-medium bowler
Born: 20 December 1959, Kingston,
Surrey
Height: 5' 10" **Weight:** 11st 7lbs
Nickname: Yozzer, Spam, Yule
County debut: 1980
County cap: 1981
50 wickets in a season: 1
1st-Class 5 w. in innings: 8
Place in batting averages: 229th
av. 12.33 (1985 197th av. 18.80)
Place in bowling averages: 34th
av. 26.22 (1985 101st av. 38.83)
1st-Class catches 1986: 3 (career: 25)
Parents: Peter and Erica
Marital status: Single

Education: Latymer Upper School, Hammersmith; Durham University
Qualifications: 10 O-levels, 4 A-levels, BA Geography and Anthropology
Jobs outside cricket: Writes regular sports column in local weekly paper, and monthly for *The Cricketer*. Also contributes to *The Independent* (rugby)
Family links with cricket: Father very keen coach and player who owned indoor cricket school. 'Uncle once hit a ball over the school pavilion!'
Overseas tours: Personal overseas spell playing in Sri Lanka 1979; Middlesex CCC tour to Zimbabwe winter 1980; with Overseas XI (captained by J. M. Brearley) to Calcutta (v Indian XI) 1980–81; International Ambassadors tour to India 1985
Overseas teams played for: Colts CC, Colombo, Sri Lanka, and Sri Lanka Board President's XI; Northern Transvaal 1982–83; Grosvenor-Fynaland 1983–84; Auckland University 1984–85; Freemantle CC (Perth) 1985–86
Cricketers particularly learnt from: Father, Jack Robertson, Mike Brearley, Mike Selvey, G. O. Allen
Cricketers particularly admired: John Emburey, Clive Radley, Malcolm Marshall, Richard Hadlee
Off-season 1986–87: Journalism at home and then playing and coaching in Australia for Sydney University
Other sports played: Soccer (for university), tennis, golf
Relaxations: Travelling, slapstick films, jazz and blues piano, eating curry, broadcasting and journalism
Extras: Took 4-82 v Kent on Championship debut, plus played in County Championship and Gillette Cup winning sides (Lord's Final) in 1980 in first season. Selected for England U-25 XI v Sri Lanka (Trent Bridge) July 1981.

Awarded cap after only 20 matches. Middlesex/Austin Reed Player of the Year 1986. Won a free holiday as Middlesex leading wicket-taker 1986
Opinions on cricket: 'With declining public interest in county cricket it is time players adjusted their attitudes towards leaving the field for bad light, and umpires to take a stronger line on intimidatory bowling.'
Best batting performance: 47* Middlesex v Warwickshire, Uxbridge 1986
Best bowling performance: 7-35 Middlesex v Surrey, The Oval 1986

LAST SEASON: BATTING

	I.	N.O.	R.	H.S.	AV.
TEST					
1ST-CLASS	26	2	296	47	12.33
INT					
JPL	7	1	42	13	7.00
NAT.W.	1	0	3	3	–
B & H	1	1	4	4*	–

LAST SEASON: BOWLING

	O.	M.	R.	W.	AV.
TEST					
1ST-CLASS	530.4	123	1652	63	26.22
INT					
JPL	98	1	465	16	29.06
NAT.W.	23	1	91	5	18.20
B & H	26	3	96	4	24.00

CAREER: BATTING

	I.	N.O.	R.	H.S.	AV.
TEST					
1ST-CLASS	101	37	664	47	10.37
INT					
JPL	17	7	119	22*	11.90
NAT.W.	5	2	12	6	4.00
B & H	4	2	16	8*	8.00

CAREER: BOWLING

	O.	M.	R.	W.	AV.
TEST					
1ST-CLASS	2313.4	452	7573	271	27.94
INT					
JPL	274.1	5	1336	45	29.68
NAT.W.	116.2	16	445	19	23.42
B & H	57	7	205	6	34.17

HUMPAGE, G. W.   Warwickshire

Full Name: Geoffrey William Humpage
Role: Right-hand bat, wicket-keeper; can also bowl right-arm medium
Born: 24 April 1954, Birmingham
Height: 5' 9" **Weight:** 12st 7lbs
Nickname: Farsley
County debut: 1974
County cap: 1976
No. of One-Day Internationals: 3
1000 runs in a season: 9
1st-Class 50s scored: 71
1st-Class 100s scored: 26
1st-Class 200s scored: 2
One-Day 50s: 30
One-Day 100s: 3
Place in batting averages: 57th av. 38.47 (1985 58th av. 37.80)
Parents: Ernest and Mabel

Wife and date of marriage: Valerie Anne, 14 September 1983 (2nd marriage)
Children: Philip Andrew Guy, 16 November 1977
Education: Golden Hillock Comprehensive School, Birmingham
Jobs outside cricket: Former police cadet, then police constable, Birmingham City Police; Coach, Scarborough CC, Western Australia, 1978–79; sports executive for Pace Insurance Consultants, Birmingham
Other sports played: Soccer, squash, tennis, swimming, golf, snooker, table-tennis
Relaxations: Reading, listening to E.L.O.
Extras: Good impressionist, particularly of Frankie Howerd. Took part in record Warwickshire, and English first-class 4th wicket partnership of 470 v Lancashire at Southport, July 1982, with Kallicharran (230*). Humpage made 254* including 13 sixes. Previous 4th wicket record was 448 for Surrey at The Oval v Yorkshire in 1899, by R. Abel and T. W. Hayward. Joined England 'Rebels' in South Africa in 1982
Best batting performance: 254 Warwickshire v Lancashire, Southport 1982
Best bowling performance: 2-13 Warwickshire v Gloucestershire, Edgbaston 1980

LAST SEASON: BATTING

	I.	N.O.	R.	H.S.	AV.
TEST					
1ST-CLASS	42	4	1462	130	38.47
INT					
JPL	14	1	244	86	18.76
NAT.W.	3	0	79	70	26.33
B & H	4	0	54	21	13.50

LAST SEASON: BOWLING

	O.	M.	R.	W.	AV.
TEST					
1ST-CLASS					
INT					
JPL					
NAT.W.					
B & H					

CAREER: BATTING

	I.	N.O.	R.	H.S.	AV.
TEST					
1ST-CLASS	451	55	14700	254	37.12
INT	2	0	11	6	5.50
JPL	148	21	3187	109*	25.09
NAT.W.	26	4	600	77	27.27
B & H	48	7	1212	100*	29.56

CAREER: BOWLING

	O.	M.	R.	W.	AV.
TEST					
1ST-CLASS	130.1	17	444	10	44.40
INT					
JPL	94.5	2	527	15	35.13
NAT.W.					
B & H	27	2	123	3	41.00

LAST SEASON: WICKET-KEEPING

	C.	ST.			
TEST					
1ST-CLASS	42	8			
INT					
JPL	9	–			
NAT.W.	6	1			
B & H	5	–			

CAREER: WICKET-KEEPING

	C.	ST.			
TEST					
1ST-CLASS	514	64			
INT	2	–			
JPL	99	19			
NAT.W.	30	6			
B & H	56	2			

IGGLESDEN, A. P.   Kent

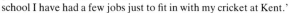

Full Name: Alan Paul Igglesden
Role: Right-hand bat, right-arm
fast bowler, outfielder
Born: 8 October 1964,
Farnborough, Kent
Height: 6′ 6″ **Weight:** 14st 4lbs
Nickname: Iggy
County debut: 1986
1st-Class catches 1986: 2 (career: 2)
Parents: Alan Trevor and Gillian
Catherine
Marital status: Single
Education: St Mary's Primary
School, Westerham; Hosey
School, Westerham; Churchill
Secondary School, Westerham
Qualifications: 9 CSEs
Jobs outside cricket: 'Since I left
school I have had a few jobs just to fit in with my cricket at Kent.'
Family links with cricket: Brother Kevin plays for same Kent league club
Cricketing superstitions: Like to be at the ground early
Overseas teams played for: Avendale 1985–86
Cricketers particularly learnt from: Terry Alderman, Bob Woolmer, Colin
Page, Stuart Leary and senior players at Kent
Cricketers particularly admired: Terry Alderman, Dennis Lillee, Ian Botham
Off-season 1986–87: Playing and coaching for Bob Woolmer's multi-racial
club, Avendale in Cape Town
Other sports played: Golf, football, snooker
Other sports followed: Football especially Crystal Palace, golf, tennis etc.

LAST SEASON: BATTING

	I.	N.O.	R.	H.S.	AV.
TEST					
1ST-CLASS	5	2	22	8*	7.33
INT					
JPL					
NAT.W.					
B & H					

LAST SEASON: BOWLING

	O.	M.	R.	W.	AV.
TEST					
1ST-CLASS	125	25	372	11	33.81
INT					
JPL					
NAT.W.					
B & H					

CAREER: BATTING

	I.	N.O.	R.	H.S.	AV.
TEST					
1ST-CLASS	5	2	22	8*	7.33
INT					
JPL					
NAT.W.					
B & H					

CAREER: BOWLING

	O.	M.	R.	W.	AV.
TEST					
1ST-CLASS	125	25	372	11	33.81
INT					
JPL					
NAT.W.					
B & H					

Relaxations: Listening to music, sleeping, watching sport on TV, crosswords
Injuries 1986: Torn muscle in left side of back
Extras: 'I didn't play any schools representative cricket.'
Opinions on cricket: 'I just feel sorry for the cricketers of South Africa, past and present. They surely would have been a tremendous force in Test cricket today.'
Best batting performance: 7 Kent v Surrey, The Oval 1986
Best bowling performance: 4-46 Kent v Surrey, The Oval 1986

ILLINGWORTH, R. K.   Worcestershire

Full Name: Richard Keith Illingworth
Role: Right-hand bat, slow left-arm bowler
Born: 1963, Bradford, Yorkshire
Height: 6′ **Weight:** 12st
Nickname: Illy, Lucy, Harry
County debut: 1982
County cap: 1986
50 wickets in a season: 1
1st-Class 50s scored: 1
1st-Class 5 w. in innings: 6
1st-Class 10 w. in match: 1
Place in batting averages: 196th av. 17.36 (1985 226th av. 13.75)
Place in bowling averages: 116th av. 48.60 (1985 42nd av. 28.27)
1st-Class catches 1986: 9 (career: 39)
Parents: Keith and Margaret
Wife and date of marriage: Anne, 20 September 1985
Education: Wrose Brow Middle and Salts Grammar School
Qualifications: 6 O-levels, senior coaching award holder
Jobs outside cricket: Civil servant
Family links with cricket: Father plays Bradford League cricket. Mother secretary Yorkshire CA Centre of Excellence nets
Overseas tours: Denmark Youth Tournament NAYC 1981; Whitbread scholarship playing for Colts CC, Brisbane 1982–83; Wisden Cricket XI, Barbados 1983
Cricketers particularly learnt from: Father, Keith Illingworth
Off-season 1986–87: Playing and coaching at University of St Heliers, Auckland, New Zealand
Other sports played: Golf, football

Other sports followed: Follows Leeds United and Bradford City
Relaxations: 'Listening to music, watching sport on TV, sampling my wife's wonderful cooking.'
Best batting performance: 55 Worcestershire v Leicestershire, Hereford 1973
Best bowling performance: 7-50 Worcestershire v Oxford University, Oxford 1985

LAST SEASON: BATTING

	I.	N.O.	R.	H.S.	AV.
TEST					
1ST-CLASS	15	4	191	39	17.36
INT					
JPL	8	4	50	14*	12.50
NAT.W.	1	0	8	8	–
B & H	2	2	22	17*	–

LAST SEASON: BOWLING

	O.	M.	R.	W.	AV.
TEST					
1ST-CLASS	564.2	189	1361	28	48.60
INT					
JPL	99	0	437	20	21.85
NAT.W.	4	1	12	0	–
B & H	42	5	148	4	37.00

CAREER: BATTING

	I.	N.O.	R.	H.S.	AV.
TEST					
1ST-CLASS	106	29	1166	55	15.14
INT					
JPL	29	15	128	21	9.14
NAT.W.	3	0	38	22	12.66
B & H	7	4	52	17*	17.33

CAREER: BOWLING

	O.	M.	R.	W.	AV.
TEST					
1ST-CLASS	2640.4	753	6920	188	36.80
INT					
JPL	277	18	1234	61	20.22
NAT.W.	59.1	9	179	3	59.66
B & H	127	17	462	17	27.17

IMRAN KHAN   Sussex

Full Name: Ahmad Khan Niazi Imran
Role: Right-hand bat, right-arm fast bowler
Born: 25 November 1952, Lahore, Pakistan
Height: 6' 0" **Weight:** 12st 12lbs
Nickname: Immie
County debut: 1971 (Worcestershire), 1977 (Sussex)
County cap: 1976 (Worcestershire), 1978 (Sussex)
Test debut: 1971
No. of Tests: 57
No. of One-Day Internationals: 65
1000 runs in a season: 3
50 wickets in a season: 6
1st-Class 50s scored: 80
1st-Class 100s scored: 25
1st-Class 5 w. in innings: 63

1st-Class 10 w. in match: 11
One-day 50s: 43
One-day 100s: 4
Place in batting averages: 16th av. 48.66 (1985 5th av. 68.46)
Place in bowling averages: 21st av. 23.40 (1985 6th av. 20.39)
1st-Class catches 1986: 1 (104)
Marital status: Single
Education: Aitchison College; Cathedral School, Lahore; Worcester Royal Grammar School; Keble College, Oxford University
Qualifications: BA Hons in politics and economics
Jobs outside cricket: 'I play cricket all the year round.'
Family links with cricket: Cousin of Pakistan cricketers, Majid Khan and Javed Burki
Overseas tours: Toured with Pakistan to England in 1971, 1974, 1982 and 1983 World Cup; Australia and West Indies 1976–77; India 1979–80; Australia 1981–82, 1983–84
Overseas teams played for: Various Lahore teams; New South Wales 1984–85
Cricketers particularly learnt from: John Snow, Basil D'Oliveira, Majid Khan
Other sports played: Squash, swimming, hockey
Relaxations: Shooting, listening to music (Western and Eastern)
Extras: Debut for Lahore A 1969–70. Debut for Worcestershire 1971, cap 1976. Left Worcestershire in 1977. Oxford cricket blue 1973–74–75. Captain in 1974. Scored two centuries in a match, 117* and 106, Oxford University v Nottinghamshire at Oxford in 1974. Had a match double of 111* and 13 for 99 v Lancashire at Worcester in 1976. Played World Series Cricket. Has bad scar on left arm resulting from falling off a slide in Lahore, and cannot fully extend his arm. Drinks no alcohol. Does not smoke. Captain of Pakistan for the first time 1982–83
Best batting performance: 170 Oxford v Northamptonshire, Oxford 1974
Best bowling performance: 8-34 Sussex v Middlesex, Lord's 1986

LAST SEASON: BATTING

	I.	N.O.	R.	H.S.	AV.
TEST					
1ST-CLASS	18	3	730	135*	48.66
INT					
JPL	14	0	347	89	24.78
NAT.W.	5	1	159	54	39.75
B & H	5	3	252	112*	126.00

LAST SEASON: BOWLING

	O.	M.	R.	W.	AV.
TEST					
1ST-CLASS	317.2	72	866	37	23.40
INT					
JPL	90	10	369	12	30.75
NAT.W.	53	7	128	11	11.63
B & H	46	4	153	5	30.60

CAREER: BATTING

	I.	N.O.	R.	H.S.	AV.
TEST	83	12	2140	123	30.14
1ST-CLASS	428	70	13308	170	37.17
INT	58	18	1212	102*	30.30
JPL	120	17	3220	104*	31.26
NAT.W.	29	6	763	114*	33.17
B & H	44	10	1410	112*	41.47

CAREER: BOWLING

	O.	M.	R.	W.	AV.
TEST	410 1782.5	68 435	5857	264	22.18
1ST-CLASS	713.4 6389.5	129 2310	19428	902	21.53
INT	454.4	61	1548	69	22.43
JPL	875.4	77	3262	166	19.65
NAT.W.	282.3	50	824	38	21.68
B & H	433.3	87	1235	61	20.24

INCHMORE, J. D.　　　Worcestershire

Full Name: John Darling Inchmore
Role: Right-hand bat, right-arm
fast-medium bowler
Born: 22 February 1949, Ashington,
Northumberland
Nickname: Inchers
County debut: 1973
County cap: 1976
Benefit: 1985 (£46,292)
50 wickets in a season: 2
1st-Class 50s scored: 7
1st-Class 100s scored: 1
1st-Class 5 w. in innings: 18
1st-Class 10 w. in match: 1
Place in batting averages: —
(1985 220th av. 14.29)
Place in bowling averages: 110th
av. 43.23 (1985 21st av. 25.58)
1st-Class catches 1986: 3 (career: 72)
Education: Ashington Grammar
School; St Peter's College, Saltley, Birmingham
Qualifications: BEd (physical education)
Overseas teams played for: Northern Transvaal in 1976–77 Currie Cup
Competition
Jobs outside cricket: Represents Allied Dunbar Assurance
Cricketers particularly learnt from: Vanburn Holder
Extras: Played for Northumberland 1970. Played for both Worcestershire and
Warwickshire 2nd XIs in 1972 and for Stourbridge in the Birmingham

LAST SEASON: BATTING

	I.	N.O.	R.	H.S.	AV.
TEST					
1ST-CLASS	8	2	55	23*	9.16
INT					
JPL	6	2	16	5*	4.00
NAT.W.	–	–	–	–	–
B & H	3	2	31	18*	–

CAREER: BATTING

	I.	N.O.	R.	H.S.	AV.
TEST					
1ST-CLASS	246	53	3137	113	16.25
INT					
JPL	96	28	992	45	14.58
NAT.W.	15	4	118	32*	10.73
B & H	38	12	352	49*	13.53

LAST SEASON: BOWLING

	O.	M.	R.	W.	AV.
TEST					
1ST-CLASS	221.1	48	562	13	43.23
INT					
JPL	81	2	381	9	42.33
NAT.W.	30	3	86	3	28.66
B & H	53	6	185	8	23.12

CAREER: BOWLING

	O.	M.	R.	W.	AV.
TEST					
1ST-CLASS	5031	992	14777	510	28.97
INT					
JPL	997.3	63	4240	169	25.08
NAT.W.	243.2	37	842	37	22.75
B & H	523.4	66	1811	71	25.50

League. Retired after 1986 season
Best batting performance: 113 Worcestershire v Essex, Worcester 1974
Best bowling performance: 8-58 Worcestershire v Yorkshire, Worcester 1977

JAMES, K. D. Hampshire

Full Name: Kevan David James
Role: Left-hand bat, left-arm fast-medium bowler. Fields 'anywhere but short leg'
Born: 18 March 1961, Lambeth, South London
Height: 6′ 0½″ **Weight:** 12st
Nickname: Jambo, Jaimo
County debut: 1980 (Middlesex), 1985 (Hampshire)
1st-Class 50s scored: 1
1st-Class 100s scored: 1
1st-Class 5 w. in innings: 3
One-day 50s: 1
Place in batting averages: 147th av. 25.00 (1985 54th av. 38.29)
Place in bowling averages: 70th av. 32.95 (1985 113th av. 42.33)
1st-Class catches 1986: 5 (career: 14)
Parents: David and Helen
Marital status: Single
Education: Edmonton County High School
Qualifications: 5 O-levels; qualified coach
Family links with cricket: Father and brother play club cricket in North London
Overseas tours: Young England tour of Australia, 1978–79; Young England tour of West Indies, 1979–80
Overseas teams played for: Canterbury Province U-23, New Zealand, 1980; Sydenham CC, Christchurch, New Zealand, 1980–81; Wellington, New Zealand, 1982–83, 1984–85
Cricketers particularly learnt from: Don Bennett (Middlesex coach)
Off-season 1986–87: Playing for Eden-Roskill in Auckland, New Zealand
Other sports played: Soccer
Other sports followed: Watches American football, follows Spurs
Relaxations: DIY and making money. Writes 2 columns, one in *The Club Cricketer*, the other in a local Southampton paper
Extras: Released by Middlesex at end of 1984 season and joined Hampshire

Best batting performance: 124 Hampshire v Somerset, Taunton 1985
Best bowling performance: 6-22 Hampshire v Australia, Southampton 1985

LAST SEASON: BATTING

	I.	N.O.	R.	H.S.	AV.
TEST					
1ST-CLASS	13	2	275	62	25.00
INT					
JPL	4	2	88	54*	44.00
NAT.W.	2	1	36	19	–
B & H					

LAST SEASON: BOWLING

	O.	M.	R.	W.	AV.
TEST					
1ST-CLASS	228.4	55	692	21	32.95
INT					
JPL	75.1	4	301	14	21.50
NAT.W.	17	1	91	3	30.33
B & H					

CAREER BATTING

	I.	N.O.	R.	H.S.	AV.
TEST					
1ST-CLASS	46	12	880	124	25.88
INT					
JPL	13	7	209	54*	34.83
NAT.W.	2	1	36	19	–
B & H	6	0	66	27	11.00

CAREER BOWLING

	O.	M.	R.	W.	AV.
TEST					
1ST-CLASS	762.2	195	2277	72	31.62
INT					
JPL	230.2	12	981	28	35.03
NAT.W.	29	1	122	3	40.66
B & H	77	11	261	9	29.00

JARVIS, K. B. S.   Kent

Full Name: Kevin Bertram Sidney Jarvis
Role: Right-hand bat, right-arm fast-medium bowler
Born: 23 April 1953, Dartford, Kent
Height: 6′ 3″ **Weight:** 13st
Nickname: Jarvo, Ferret, KJ
County debut: 1975
County cap: 1977
Benefit: 1987
50 wickets in a season: 7
1st-Class 5 w. in innings: 18
1st-Class 10 w. in match: 3
Place in bowling averages: 99th av. 40.58 (1985 51st av. 32.82)
1st-Class catches 1986: 2 (career 57)
Parents: Herbert John and Margaret Elsie
Wife and date of marriage: Margaret Anne, 16 September 1978
Children: Simon Martin, 16 April 1985
Education: Springhead School, Northfleet, Kent; Thames Polytechnic
Qualifications: 6 O-levels, 3 A-levels, NCA coach, ISMA, MAMSA
Jobs outside cricket: Accountancy, insurance, clerical

Family links with cricket: Son very keen; father played club cricket; Simon Hinks is a distant relative
Cricketing superstitions: 'I never hook before October and have a habit of not getting any runs.'
Overseas tours: Derrick Robins' XI to Far East 1977; Jamaica 1982
Overseas teams played for: Played and coached for South Melbourne, 1979 and 1981; Tooronga, 1978
Cricketers particularly learnt from: Derek Underwood, Bob Woolmer
Cricketers particularly admired: Richard Hadlee, Dennis Lillee
Off-season 1986–87: Looking for winter employment
Other sports played: Squash, badminton, tennis, football, hockey, darts
Other sports followed: Watches everything except synchronised swimming
Injuries 1986: Virus infection
Opinions on cricket: 'Play more one-day cricket and more exciting three-day cricket. Play on uncovered pitches (so D. Underwood can play forever!); four-day cricket will kill the championship as a spectator sport.'
Best batting performance: 19 Kent v Derbyshire, Maidstone 1984
Best bowling performance: 8-97 Kent v Worcestershire, Worcester 1978

LAST SEASON: BATTING

	I.	N.O.	R.	H.S.	AV.
TEST					
1ST-CLASS	6	4	9	4	4.50
INT					
JPL	6	5	4	3*	–
NAT.W.	–	–	–	–	–
B & H	1	0	0	0	–

LAST SEASON: BOWLING

	O.	M.	R.	W.	AV.
TEST					
1ST-CLASS	155.2	42	487	12	40.58
INT					
JPL	47	2	230	4	57.50
NAT.W.	9	1	27	1	–
B & H	22	4	82	4	20.50

CAREER: BATTING

	I.	N.O.	R.	H.S.	AV.
TEST					
1ST-CLASS	174	74	325	19	3.25
INT					
JPL	46	28	58	8*	3.22
NAT.W.	11	5	16	5*	2.66
B & H	24	15	16	4*	1.77

CAREER: BOWLING

	O.	M.	R.	W.	AV.
TEST					
1ST-CLASS	5685	1261	17879	606	29.50
INT					
JPL	933.1	79	3867	170	22.74
NAT.W.	236.5	29	874	37	23.62
B & H	526.2	82	1858	86	21.60

99. Which Australian Test cricketer said of the then England Test captain, Mike Brearley: 'He's the bloke with the degree in people'?

Full Name: Paul William Jarvis
Role: Right-hand bat, right-arm fast-medium bowler
Born: 29 June 1965, Redcar, North Yorkshire
Height: 5′ 11″ **Weight:** 12st 5lbs
Nickname: Jarv, Beaver
County debut: 1981
County cap: 1986
50 wickets in a season: 1
1st-Class 5 w. in innings: 10
1st-Class 10 w. in match: 2
Place in batting averages: 191st av. 18.30 (1985 251st av. 10.79)
Place in bowling averages: 10th av. 22.20 (1985 52nd av. 30.23)
1st-Class catches 1986: 10 (career: 57)
Parents: Malcolm and Marjorie
Marital status: Single
Education: Bydales Comprehensive School, Marske
Qualifications: 4 O-levels
Jobs outside cricket: Trainee groundsman, Marske Cricket Club
Family links with cricket: Father has played league cricket for 30 years with Marske CC; brother, Andrew, played for English Schools U-15s, and also had trials for Northamptonshire and Derbyshire
Cricketing superstitions: 'The number 111.'
Overseas tours: Channel Islands April 1986 and Ireland June 1986 with Yorkshire
Overseas teams played for: Mosman Middle Harbour CC, Sydney, 1984–85; Avendale CC, Cape Town 1985–86
Cricketers particularly learnt from: Maurice Hill, Phil Carrick, Geoff Boycott, Albert Padmore
Cricketers particularly admired: Dennis Lillee
Off-season 1986–87: Resting, training, looking for a job
Other sports played: Football, running and fitness, golf, squash
Other sports followed: Most sports
Injuries 1986: Lower back strain
Relaxations: Watching television, reading and cooking
Extras: Youngest player ever to play for Yorkshire 1st XI in John Player League and County Championships (16 years, 2 months, 1 day in John Player League, 16 years, 2 months, 13 days for County Championship). Youngest player to do hat-trick in JPL and Championship. Played for Young England

v West Indies 1982 and Australia 1983. Selected for TCCB XI v New Zealand 1986

Opinions on cricket: 'Only people actually born in England should be permitted to play for England. The English first-class season should be changed to 16 four-day matches.'

Best batting performance: 47 Yorkshire v Essex, Chelmsford 1986

Best bowling performance: 7-55 Yorkshire v Surrey, Leeds 1986

LAST SEASON: BATTING

	I.	N.O.	R.	H.S.	AV.
TEST					
1ST-CLASS	17	7	183	47	18.30
INT					
JPL	5	2	37	27*	12.33
NAT.W.	2	1	19	10	–
B & H	2	1	6	6*	–

LAST SEASON: BOWLING

	O.	M.	R.	W.	AV.
TEST					
1ST-CLASS	428.4	82	1332	60	22.20
INT					
JPL	82.5	7	369	11	33.54
NAT.W.	34.3	7	92	3	30.66
B & H	44	6	120	3	40.00

CAREER: BATTING

	I.	N.O.	R.	H.S.	AV.
TEST					
1ST-CLASS	55	18	520	47	14.05
INT					
JPL	18	9	79	27*	8.77
NAT.W.	3	1	35	16	17.50
B & H	4	1	29	20	9.66

CAREER: BOWLING

	O.	M.	R.	W.	AV.
TEST					
1ST-CLASS	1298.3	224	4440	147	30.20
INT					
JPL	261.5	14	1153	58	19.87
NAT.W.	68.3	9	269	6	44.83
B & H	81	10	270	14	19.28

JEAN-JACQUES, M.   Derbyshire

Full Name: Martin Jean-Jacques
Role: Right-hand bat, right-arm medium pace bowler
Born: 2 July 1960, Dominica
County debut: 1986
1st-Class 50s scored: 1
1st-Class 5 w. in innings: 1
1st-Class 10 w. in match: 1
Place in batting averages: 164th av. 23.11
Place in bowling averages: 41st av. 27.22
1st-Class catches 1986: 1 (career: 1)
Extras: Played Minor Counties cricket for Buckinghamshire since 1983. On debut for Derbyshire (v Yorkshire) put on 132 with A. Hill for the 10th wicket – a new Derbyshire record

Best batting performance: 73 Derbyshire v Yorkshire, Sheffield 1986
Best bowling performance: 8-77 Derbyshire v Kent, Derby 1986

LAST SEASON: BATTING

	I.	N.O.	R.	H.S.	AV.
TEST					
1ST-CLASS	12	3	208	73	23.11
INT					
JPL	2	0	1	1	0.50
NAT.W.	1	0	16	16	–
B & H					

LAST SEASON: BOWLING

	O.	M.	R.	W.	AV.
TEST					
1ST-CLASS	159	16	599	22	27.22
INT					
JPL	30	0	170	5	34.00
NAT.W.	17	1	57	4	14.25
B & H					

CAREER: BATTING

	I.	N.O.	R.	H.S.	AV.
TEST					
1ST-CLASS	12	3	208	73	23.11
INT					
JPL	2	0	1	1	0.50
NAT.W.	3	1	17	16	8.50
B & H					

CAREER: BOWLING

	O.	M.	R.	W.	AV.
TEST					
1ST-CLASS	159	16	599	22	27.22
INT					
JPL	30	0	170	5	34.00
NAT.W.	34	4	105	5	21.00
B & H					

JESTY, T. E. Surrey

Full Name: Trevor Edward Jesty
Role: Right-hand bat, right-arm medium bowler
Born: 2 June 1948, Gosport, Hampshire
Height: 5′ 9″ **Weight:** 11st 10lbs
Nickname: Jets
County debut: 1966 (Hampshire), 1985 (Surrey)
County cap: 1971 (Hampshire), 1985 (Surrey)
Benefit: 1982 (Hampshire)
No. of One-Day Internationals: 10
1000 runs in a season: 8
50 wickets in a season: 2
1st-Class 50s scored: 87
1st-Class 100s scored: 31
1st-Class 200s scored: 2
1st-Class 5 w. in innings: 18
One-day 50s: 37
One-day 100s: 7
Place in batting averages: 75th av. 34.41 (1985 35th av. 43.43)
Place in bowling averages: — (1985 88th av. 36.93)
1st-Class catches 1986: 10 (career: 242)

Parents: Aubrey Edward and Sophia
Wife and date of marriage: Jacqueline, 12 September 1970
Children: Graeme Barry, 27 September 1972; Lorna Samantha, 7 November 1976
Education: Privet County Secondary Modern, Gosport
Jobs outside cricket: Cricket coach in South Africa and New Zealand. Representative for wine company
Family links with cricket: Brother, Aubrey Jesty, wicket-keeper and left-hand bat. Could have joined Hampshire staff, but decided to continue with his apprenticeship
Overseas teams played for: Border in 1973–74, and Griqualand West in 1974–75 and 1975–76 in the Currie Cup Competition, South Africa
Cricketers particularly learnt from: Barry Richards
Other sports played: Soccer, golf
Relaxations: Watching soccer, gardening
Extras: Took him 10 years to score maiden first-class century. Missed most of 1980 season through injury. Made vice-captain of Hampshire in 1981. Considered to be most unlucky not to be chosen for England tour of Australia 1982–83 after brilliant 1982 season, then was called in as a replacement. Left Hampshire at end of 1984 when not appointed captain. Took over captaincy of Surrey in 1985
Best batting performance: 248 Hampshire v Cambridge University, Cambridge 1984
Best bowling performance: 7-75 Hampshire v Worcestershire, Southampton 1976

LAST SEASON: BATTING

	I.	N.O.	R.	H.S.	AV.
TEST					
1ST-CLASS	30	1	998	221	34.41
INT					
JPL	11	1	168	40*	16.80
NAT.W.	3	0	141	112	47.00
B & H	3	3	207	94*	–

LAST SEASON: BOWLING

	O.	M.	R.	W.	AV.
TEST					
1ST-CLASS	59	21	155	5	31.00
INT					
JPL	13	0	65	2	32.52
NAT.W.					
B & H	14	0	79	1	–

CAREER: BATTING

	I.	N.O.	R.	H.S.	AV.
TEST					
1ST-CLASS	650	84	18184	248	32.12
INT	10	4	127	52*	21.17
JPL	227	31	4926	166*	25.13
NAT.W.	30	2	886	118	31.64
B & H	60	8	1850	105	35.57

CAREER: BOWLING

	O.	M.	R.	W.	AV.
TEST					
1ST-CLASS	6027.3	1611	15737	574	27.41
INT	18	0	93	1	–
JPL	1287.3	76	6027	248	24.30
NAT.W.	299	50	984	38	25.89
B & H	473.4	60	1649	66	24.98

100. Which Test cricketer said: 'My attitude towards bouncers has been that if I'm playing well enough, three bouncers an over should be worth 12 runs to me'?

JOHNSON, P.   Nottinghamshire

Full Name: Paul Johnson
Role: Right-hand bat, right-arm
occasional bowler
Born: 24 April 1965, Newark
Height: 5′ 8″ **Weight:** 11st 7lbs
Nickname: Johno, Dwarf, Gus,
Ledge
County debut: 1982
County cap: 1986
1000 runs in a season: 1
1st-Class 50s scored: 18
1st-Class 100s scored: 7
One-day 50s: 5
One-day 100s: 1
Place in batting averages: 53rd
av. 39.06 (1985 100th av. 31.10)
1st-Class catches 1986: 24 (career: 53)
Parents: Donald Edward and Joyce
Marital status: Single
Education: Grove Comprehensive School, Newark
Qualifications: 9 CSEs, senior coaching certificate
Family links with cricket: Father played local cricket and is a qualified coach
Cricketing superstitions: Left pad on first

LAST SEASON: BATTING

	I.	N.O.	R.	H.S.	AV.
TEST					
1ST-CLASS	37	5	1250	128	39.06
INT					
JPL	14	1	355	90	27.30
NAT.W.	3	0	22	18	7.33
B & H	5	0	61	22	12.20

CAREER: BATTING

	I.	N.O.	R.	H.S.	AV.
TEST					
1ST-CLASS	120	13	3532	133	33.00
INT					
JPL	44	5	820	90	21.02
NAT.W.	7	1	168	101*	28.00
B & H	10	0	91	22	9.10

LAST SEASON: WICKET-KEEPING

	C.	ST.			
TEST					
1ST-CLASS					
INT					
JPL	3	–			
NAT.W.					
B & H					

LAST SEASON: BOWLING

	O.	M.	R.	W.	AV.
TEST					
1ST-CLASS	19	2	113	0	–
INT					
JPL					
NAT.W.					

CAREER: BOWLING

	O.	M.	R.	W.	AV.
TEST					
1ST-CLASS	49	6	288	3	96.00
INT					
JPL					
NAT.W.	1	0	5	0	–
B & H					

CAREER: WICKET-KEEPING

	C.	ST.			
TEST					
1ST-CLASS					
INT					
JPL	3	–			
NAT.W.					
B & H					

Cricketers particularly learnt from: Most of Nottinghamshire staff
Cricketers particularly admired: R. Hadlee, I. Botham, D. Lillee
Off-season 1986–87: Working and coaching in Nottingham
Other sports played: Football referee, golf (14 handicap)
Other sports followed: Watches ice-hockey (Nottingham Panthers), football (Forest and County)
Relaxations: Good films
Extras: Played for English Schools cricket in 1980–81 season. Youngest member ever to join the Nottinghamshire CCC staff. Hit 16 sixes in School County Cup game v Joseph Whittaker, 195*. Played for Young England U-19, 1982 and 1983. Made 235 for Nottinghamshire 2nd XI, July 1982, aged 17. Won man of match award in first NatWest game (101* v Staffordshire); missed 1985 final due to appendicitis
Opinions on cricket: 'Counties should make more effort to play 2nd XI games on first-class wickets.'
Best batting performance: 133 Nottinghamshire v Kent, Folkestone 1984

JONES, A. L.　　　　　　　Glamorgan

Full Name: Alan Lewis Jones
Role: Left-hand opening bat, slip fielder
Born: 1 June 1957, Alltwen, Swansea
Height: 5′ 9½″ **Weight:** 10st 4lbs
Nickname: Jonah, A.L.
County debut: 1973, at age of 16 years 99 days. Youngest player for Glamorgan
County cap: 1983
1000 runs in a season: 2
1st-Class 50s scored: 36
1st-Class 100s scored: 5
One-day 50s: 9
Place in batting averages: 145th av. 25.23 (1985 140th av. 25.44)
1st-Class catches 1986: 7 (career: 104)

Parents: Ieuan and Marian
Wife and date of marriage: Diane, 27 September 1980
Children: Rebecca Ellen, 29 December 1985
Education: Ystalyfera Grammar School; Cwmtawe Comprehensive School; Cardiff College of Education
Qualifications: 8 O-levels. Teacher training certificate. NCA staff coach

Jobs outside cricket: Working in chartered accountant's office training to be a certified accountant. Has worked as life assurance salesman and teacher

Family links with cricket: Father and grandfather local club cricketers

Cricketing superstitions: 'Put pads, gloves etc., on in a particular order. Don't like Nelson (111) and 13.'

Overseas tours: West Indies with England Young Cricketers 1976; Australasia with Derrick Robins' XI in 1980

Overseas teams played for: Hamilton-Wickham, Newcastle, Australia, 1978–79; Papatoetoe, Auckland, 1984–85

Cricketers particularly learnt from: Alan Jones

Cricketers particularly admired: Alan Jones, Gordon Greenidge, Andy Roberts

Off-season 1986–87: Works with Bristol and West Building Society

Other sports played: Rugby, soccer

Relaxations: Keeps up-to-date with previous biology studies; keep-fit enthusiast

Injuries 1986: Recurring dislocating right shoulder

Extras: Made debut for Glamorgan 2nd XI in 1972, aged 15. Played for Briton Ferry Town in 1979 in South Wales League

Opinions on cricket: 'Would like to see a two-year trial period for 16 4-day matches, with an improvement of pace and bounce of first-class pitches.'

Best batting performance: 132 Glamorgan v Hampshire, Cardiff 1984

LAST SEASON: BATTING

	I.	N.O.	R.	H.S.	AV.
TEST					
1ST-CLASS	21	4	429	50	25.23
INT					
JPL					
NAT.W.					
B & H	4	0	50	32	12.50

CAREER: BATTING

	I.	N.O.	R.	H.S.	AV.
TEST					
1ST-CLASS	278	24	6548	132	25.77
INT					
JPL	78	3	1642	82	21.89
NAT.W.	3	1	87	60*	43.50
B & H	5	0	54	32	10.80

LAST SEASON: BOWLING

	O.	M.	R.	W.	AV.
TEST					
1ST-CLASS					
INT					
JPL					
NAT.W.					
B & H					

CAREER: BOWLING

	O.	M.	R.	W.	AV.
TEST					
1ST-CLASS	15.5	0	152	1	–
INT					
JPL	0.4	0	5	0	–
NAT.W.					
B & H					

101. When did South Africa play their last fully recognised Test match and against whom?

JONES, A. N.   Somerset

Full Name: Adrian Nicholas Jones
Role: Left-hand bat, right-arm
fast bowler, outfielder
Born: 22 July 1961, Woking
Height: 6′ 2″ **Weight:** 13st 10lbs
Nickname: Quincy, Jonah
County debut: 1981 (Sussex)
County cap: 1986 (Sussex)
1st-Class 5 w. in innings: 2
Place in batting averages: —
(1985 181st av. 20.75)
Place in bowling averages: 59th
av. 29.52 (1985 114th av. 42.40)
1st-Class catches 1986: 5 (career: 10)
Parents: William Albert and Emily
Doris
Education: Forest Grange
Preparatory School; Seaford College

Qualifications: 8 O-levels, 2 A-levels,
NCA coaching qualifications, Consumer Credit Licence
Jobs outside cricket: Financial Consultant/Advisor
Family links with cricket: Father and brother, Glynne, both fine club
cricketers
Cricketing superstitions: 'Always salute a magpie.'
Overseas teams played for: Old Selbournians and Bohemians, South Africa,
1981–82; Border 1981–82; Red and White CC, Haarlem, Holland, 1980;
Orange Free State, 1986
Cricketers particularly learnt from: Geoff Arnold, Imran Khan, Duke Eaton
Cricketers particularly admired: Imran Khan, Geoff Arnold, Geoff Boycott,
Richard Hadlee, Ian Botham
Off-season 1986–87: Knee operation and then working as Financial Advisor
Other sports played: 'Golf badly; hockey slightly better; rugby like an
animal.'
Relaxations: 'UB40, watching Laurel and Hardy films, walking, eating, good
wine and port.'
Injuries 1986: Acute knee injury, split 3 toes
Extras: Played for Young England in 1981. Left Sussex to join Somerset at
end of 1986
Opinions on cricket: 'There should be an alternative system for the awarding
of a benefit than the present haphazard method. Perhaps an endowment
scheme taken out when the player is capped.'
Best batting performance: 35 Sussex v Middlesex, Hove 1984
Best bowling performance: 5-29 Sussex v Gloucestershire, Hove 1984

LAST SEASON: BATTING

	I.	N.O.	R.	H.S.	AV.
TEST					
1ST-CLASS	10	3	55	13	7.85
INT					
JPL	4	4	33	17*	–
NAT.W.	–	–	–	–	–
B & H	2	1	21	20	–

LAST SEASON: BOWLING

	O.	M.	R.	W.	AV.
TEST					
1ST-CLASS	171	26	620	21	29.52
INT					
JPL	90	6	397	27	14.70
NAT.W.	30	3	99	6	16.50
B & H	39	3	171	10	17.10

CAREER: BATTING

	I.	N.O.	R.	H.S.	AV.
TEST					
1ST-CLASS	46	20	284	35	10.92
INT					
JPL	5	5	34	17*	–
NAT.W.	1	1	3	3*	–
B & H	4	1	27	20	9.00

CAREER: BOWLING

	O.	M.	R.	W.	AV.
TEST					
1ST-CLASS	840.2	136	2953	95	31.08
INT					
JPL	169.2	11	770	48	16.04
NAT.W.	40	4	148	7	21.14
B & H	42.2	3	193	10	19.30

KALLICHARRAN, A. I.   Warwickshire

Full Name: Alvin Isaac Kallicharran
Role: Left-hand bat, right-arm off-spin bowler
Born: 21 March 1949, Guyana
Height: 5′ 4″
Nickname: Kalli
County debut: 1971
County cap: 1972
Benefit: 1983 (£34,094)
Test debut: 1971–72
No. of Tests: 66
No. of One-Day Internationals: 31
1000 runs in a season: 12
1st-Class 50s scored: 150
1st-Class 100s scored: 77
1st-Class 200s scored: 6
1st-Class 5 w. in innings: 1
One-day 50s: 50
One-day 100s: 11
Place in batting averages: 7th av. 55.83 (1985 90th av. 31.85)
1st-Class catches 1986: 13 (career: 299)
Marital status: Married
Children: One son, Rohan
Family links with cricket: Brother, Derek Isaac, played for Guyana
Overseas tours: With West Indies to New Zealand 1971; England in 1973 and 1976; India, Sri Lanka and Pakistan, 1974–75; Australia 1975–76 and 1979–80; India and Sri Lanka, 1978–79 as Captain; Pakistan, 1980

Overseas teams played for: Guyana 1966–67 in Shell Shield Competition; Queensland in 1977–78 Sheffield Shield Competition. Transvaal and Orange Free State in South Africa

Extras: Scored 100* and 101 in first two innings in Test matches v New Zealand in 1971. Signed for World Series Cricket but resigned before playing. He has made his home in England. With Geoff Humpage took part in record – for Warwickshire and for all English counties – 4th wicket stand of 470 v Lancashire at Southport in July 1982. Kallicharran made 230*, Humpage 254*. Previous record was 448 by Abel and Hayward for Surrey v Yorkshire at The Oval in 1899. Top of Warwickshire batting averages in 1982 and 1983. Banned from playing in West Indies for going to South Africa

Best batting performance: 243* Warwickshire v Glamorgan, Edgbaston 1983

Best bowling performance: 5-45 Transvaal v Western Province, Cape Town 1982–83

LAST SEASON: BATTING

	I.	N.O.	R.	H.S.	AV.
TEST					
1ST-CLASS	23	5	1005	163*	55.83
INT					
JPL	9	1	379	101	47.37
NAT.W.	2	0	138	99	69.00
B & H					

LAST SEASON: BOWLING

	O.	M.	R.	W.	AV.
TEST					
1ST-CLASS	9	0	65	2	32.50
INT					
JPL					
NAT.W.					
B & H					

CAREER: BATTING

	I.	N.O.	R.	H.S.	AV.
TEST	109	10	4399	187	44.43
1ST-CLASS	653	72	26377	243*	45.39
INT	28	4	826	78	34.41
JPL	155	17	4204	102*	30.46
NAT.W.	25	2	1169	206	50.82
B & H	51	6	1882	122*	41.82

CAREER: BOWLING

	O.	M.	R.	W.	AV.
TEST	3.1 63.3	1 13	158	4	39.50
1ST-CLASS	13.3 918.1	0 132	3350	73	45.89
INT	17	3	64	3	21.33
JPL	161.1	5	880	14	62.85
NAT.W.	80.4	9	277	14	19.78
B & H	34	0	153	0	–

102. Who introduced Graham Gooch to the music of Vivaldi and Tchaikovsky?

KERR, K. J.   Warwickshire

Full Name: Kevin John Kerr
Role: Right-hand bat, right-arm
off-break bowler
Born: 11 September 1961, Airdrie,
Scotland
Height: 5′ 11″
County debut: 1986
1st-Class 50s scored: 1
Place in batting averages: 198th
av. 17.14
Place in bowling averages: 96th
av. 39.79
1st-Class catches 1986: 6 (career: 46)
Education: Sandown High School,
Wits University
Extras: Left cricket at end of 1986 to
concentrate on his career in
chartered accountancy
Best batting performance: 74 Transvaal B v Western Province B, Cape Town
1985–86
Best bowling performance: 5-27 Transvaal B v Natal B, Durban 1978–79

LAST SEASON: BATTING

	I.	N.O.	R.	H.S.	AV.
TEST					
1ST-CLASS	12	5	120	45*	17.14
INT					
JPL	4	2	9	5*	4.50
NAT.W.	2	0	16	13	8.00
B & H					

LAST SEASON: BOWLING

	O.	M.	R.	W.	AV.
TEST					
1ST-CLASS	316	52	955	24	39.79
INT					
JPL	40	4	156	4	39.00
NAT.W.	24	3	74	3	24.66
B & H					

CAREER: BATTING

	I.	N.O.	R.	H.S.	AV.
TEST					
1ST-CLASS	53	16	535	74	14.45
INT					
JPL	4	2	9	5*	4.00
NAT.W.	2	0	16	13	8.00
B & H					

CAREER: BOWLING

	O.	M.	R.	W.	AV.
TEST					
1ST-CLASS	1261.5	327	3467	118	29.38
INT					
JPL	40	4	156	4	39.00
NAT.W.	24	3	74	3	24.66
B & H					

103. Which legendary Australian cricketer played an important part
in introducing Rugby League to Australia?

LAMB, A. J.   Northamptonshire

Full Name: Allan Joseph Lamb
Role: Right-hand bat
Born: 20 June 1954, Langebaanweg,
Cape Province, South Africa
Height: 5′ 8″ **Weight:** 12st 12lbs
Nickname: Lambie, Legger
County debut: 1978
County cap: 1978
Test debut: 1982
No. of Tests: 46
No. of One-Day Internationals: 51
1000 runs in a season: 7
1st-Class 50s scored: 103
1st-Class 100s scored: 45
One-Day 50s: 43
One-Day 100s: 10
Place in batting averages: 4th
av. 59.08 (1985 41st av. 41.04)
1st-Class catches 1986: 14
(career: 203)
Parents: Michael and Joan
Wife and date of marriage: Lindsay St Leger, 8 December 1979
Education: Wynberg Boys' High School; Abbotts College
Qualifications: Matriculation
Jobs outside cricket: Timber representative. Promotions and selling
Family links with cricket: Father played in the Boland League; brother played for Western Province 'B'. Brother-in-law, Tony Bucknall, won 10 caps for England at rugger
Cricketing superstitions: 'Try to use the same batting shirt which I have scored runs in.'
Overseas tours: With England to Australia and New Zealand 1982–83; New Zealand and Pakistan 1983–84; India and Australia 1984–85; West Indies 1986
Overseas teams played for: Western Province in Currie Cup Competition, 1972–81
Cricketers particularly learnt from: 'Everyone.'
Off-season 1986–87: Playing for England in Australia
Other sports played: Squash, golf. Rode in a British bobsled at Cervinia (Italy) in 1985
Other sports followed: Most sports
Relaxations: Shooting, fishing
Extras: Made first-class debut for Western Province in 1972–73 Currie Cup. Applied to be registered as English in 1980 but application deferred. Was top

of batting averages 1980. Was primarily a bowler when first played schoolboy cricket in South Africa. Missed two years of first-class cricket because of military training. Qualified to play for England 1982

Best batting performance: 178 Northamptonshire v Leicestershire, Leicester 1979

LAST SEASON: BATTING

	I.	N.O.	R.	H.S.	AV.
TEST	5	0	65	39	13.00
1ST-CLASS	22	4	1294	160*	71.88
INT	4	0	106	45	26.50
JPL	10	1	340	97	37.77
NAT.W.	1	0	80	80	–
B & H	5	0	220	106	44.00

LAST SEASON: BOWLING

	O.	M.	R.	W.	AV.
TEST					
1ST-CLASS	2	2	0	0	–
INT					
JPL					
NAT.W.					
B & H					

CAREER: BATTING

	I.	N.O.	R.	H.S.	AV.
TEST	79	6	2500	137*	34.24
1ST-CLASS	378	69	15699	178	50.80
INT	50	8	1755	118	41.78
JPL	99	17	3299	132*	40.23
NAT.W.	22	1	758	101	36.09
B & H	36	5	1538	106*	43.16

CAREER: BOWLING

	O.	M.	R.	W.	AV.
TEST	4	1	23	1	–
1ST-CLASS	31.2	9	100	4	25.00
INT					
JPL					
NAT.W.	1.2	0	12	1	–
B & H					

LAMPITT, S. R.   Worcestershire

Full Name: Stuart Richàrd Lampitt
Role: Right-hand bat, right-arm medium pace bowler, slip fielder
Born: 29 July 1966, Wolverhampton
Height: 5′ 11″ **Weight:** 12st 10lbs
Nickname: Louie
County debut: 1985
Parents: Joseph Charles and Muriel-Ann
Marital status: Single
Education: Kingswinford School; Dudley College of Technology
Qualifications: 7 O-levels
Jobs outside cricket: Steel shearers' mate
Cricketing superstitions: Always check guard when new bowler comes on

Overseas tours: NCA tour to Bermuda with England South, 1985
Overseas teams played for: Mangere CC, South Auckland 1986–87
Cricketers particularly learnt from: Ron Headley, Basil D'Oliveira

Cricketers particularly admired: Viv Richards, Ian Botham
Off-season 1986–87: Playing and coaching in New Zealand
Other sports played: Football, golf, snooker
Other sports followed: Every sport
Relaxations: Sleeping, listening to music, watching TV
Extras: Took five wickets in first appearance at Lord's, helping my club side Stourbridge to win National Club Knockout in 1986
Opinions on cricket: 'Politics should not enter into cricket or any sport.'
Best batting performance: 11* Worcestershire v Sussex, Worcester 1986

LAST SEASON: BATTING

	I.	N.O.	R.	H.S.	AV.
TEST					
1ST-CLASS	1	1	11	11*	–
INT					
JPL					
NAT.W.					
B & H					

LAST SEASON: BOWLING

	O.	M.	R.	W.	AV.
TEST					
1ST-CLASS	7	1	21	0	–
INT					
JPL					
NAT.W.					
B & H					

CAREER: BATTING

	I.	N.O.	R.	H.S.	AV.
TEST					
1ST-CLASS	2	1	11	11*	–
INT					
JPL					
NAT.W.					
B & H					

CAREER: BOWLING

	O.	M.	R.	W.	AV.
TEST					
1ST-CLASS	8	1	22	0	–
INT					
JPL					
NAT.W.					
B & H					

LARKINS, W.   Northamptonshire

Full Name: Wayne Larkins
Role: Right-hand bat, right-arm medium bowler
Born: 22 November 1953
Height: 5' 11" **Weight:** 12st
Nickname: Ned
County debut: 1972
County cap: 1976
Benefit: 1986
Test debut: 1979–80
No. of Tests: 6
No. of One-Day Internationals: 6
1000 runs in a season: 8
1st-Class 50s scored: 66
1st-Class 100s scored: 35
1st-Class 200s scored: 2
1st-Class 5 w. in innings: 1
One-Day 50s: 37

One-Day 100s: 10
Place in batting averages: 134th av. 26.56 (1985 61st av. 36.88)
1st-Class catches 1986: 13 (career: 161)
Parents: Mavis (father deceased)
Wife and date of marriage: Jane Elaine, 22 March 1975
Children: Philippa Jane, 30 May 1981
Education: Bushmead, Eaton Socon, Huntingdon
Jobs outside cricket: Farming
Family links with cricket: Father was umpire. Brother, Melvin, 'played for Bedford Town for many years.'
Overseas tours: England tour to Australia and India 1979–80
Cricketers particularly learnt from: Mushtaq Mohammad
Off-season 1986–87: Organising benefit year
Other sports played: Golf, football (currently with Buckingham and was on Notts County's books), squash
Relaxations: Gardening
Extras: With Peter Willey, received 2016 pints of beer (seven barrels) from a Northampton brewery as a reward for their efforts in Australia in 1979–80. Hat-trick for Northamptonshire v Combined Universities, Benson & Hedges Cup, 1980. Banned from English Test Cricket for three years for joining rebel tour of South Africa in 1982. Recalled to Test team 1986 but withdrew due to thumb injury
Injuries 1986: Missed start of season after football injury (2nd successive year). Broken thumb
Best batting performance: 252 Northamptonshire v Glamorgan, Cardiff 1983
Best bowling performance: 5-59 Northamptonshire v Worcestershire, Worcester 1984

LAST SEASON: BATTING

	I.	N.O.	R.	H.S.	AV.
TEST					
1ST-CLASS	29	4	664	86	26.56
INT					
JPL	8	1	246	92	35.14
NAT.W.	1	0	40	40	–
B & H					

LAST SEASON: BOWLING

	O.	M.	R.	W.	AV.
TEST					
1ST-CLASS					
INT					
JPL					
NAT.W.					
B & H					

CAREER: BATTING

	I.	N.O.	R.	H.S.	AV.
TEST	11	0	176	34	16.00
1ST-CLASS	512	31	16702	252	34.72
INT	6	0	84	34	14.00
JPL	174	13	4461	172*	27.70
NAT.W.	28	2	936	92*	36.00
B & H	48	3	1571	132	34.91

CAREER: BOWLING

	O.	M.	R.	W.	AV.
TEST					
1ST-CLASS	487.5	95	1644	39	42.15
INT	2	0	21	0	–
JPL	305.5	9	1505	54	27.87
NAT.W.	73.5	9	249	4	62.25
B & H	105.3	14	413	16	25.81

LAWRENCE, D. V.   Gloucestershire

Full Name: David Valentine Lawrence
Role: Right-hand bat, right-arm fast bowler, slip fielder
Born: 28 January 1964, Gloucester
Height: 6′ 3″ **Weight:** 15st 7lbs
Nickname: Syd, Bruno
County debut: 1981
County cap: 1985
1st-Class 5 w. in innings: 9
Place in batting averages: —
(1985 237th av. 12.33)
Place in bowling averages: 85th
av. 36.49 (1985 16th av. 24.62)
1st-Class catches 1986: 5 (career: 20)
Parents: Joseph and Joyce
Education: Linden School, Gloucester
Qualifications: 3 CSEs
Overseas tours: England B to Sri Lanka 1986
Overseas teams played for: Scarborough CC, Perth, Western Australia
Cricketers particularly learnt from: Michael Holding, Richard Hadlee, Dennis Lillee
Cricketers particularly admired: Viv Richards
Off-season 1986–87: Playing for Manley CC, Australia
Other sports played: Rugby football. 'Was offered terms to play professional rugby league winter 1985–86, but turned them down.'
Relaxations: 'Like listening to jazz, funk and dancing.'

LAST SEASON: BATTING

	I.	N.O.	R.	H.S.	AV.
TEST					
1ST-CLASS	25	5	198	34*	9.90
INT					
JPL	5	2	44	21*	14.66
NAT.W.	2	0	0	0	0.00
B & H	3	1	13	5	6.50

CAREER: BATTING

	I.	N.O.	R.	H.S.	AV.
TEST					
1ST-CLASS	90	19	677	41	9.53
INT					
JPL	9	5	75	21*	18.75
NAT.W.	6	2	2	1*	0.50
B & H	6	4	36	22*	18.00

LAST SEASON: BOWLING

	O.	M.	R.	W.	AV.
TEST					
1ST-CLASS	588.1	85	2299	63	36.49
INT					
JPL	31	1	176	1	–
NAT.W.	16	0	63	4	15.75
B & H	35	2	154	7	22.00

CAREER: BOWLING

	O.	M.	R.	W.	AV.
TEST					
1ST-CLASS	1911.4	281	7271	205	35.22
INT					
JPL	199	2	1115	38	29.34
NAT.W.	88.2	8	398	13	30.61
B & H	96	4	393	17	23.11

Best batting performance: 41 Gloucestershire v Nottinghamshire, Trent Bridge 1985
Best bowling performance: 7-48 Gloucestershire v Sussex, Hove, 1985

LENHAM, N. J. Sussex

Full Name: Neil John Lenham
Role: Right-hand bat, right-arm medium bowler
Born: 17 December 1965, Worthing
Height: 5′ 11″ **Weight:** 10st 7lbs
Nickname: Archie, Pin
County debut: 1984
1st-Class 50s scored: 6
One-Day 50s: 1
Place in batting averages: 176th av. 21.36 (1985 81st av. 33.79)
1st-Class catches 1986: 6 (career: 11)
Parents: Leslie John and Valerie Anne
Marital status: Single
Education: Broadwater Manor House Prep School; Brighton College
Qualifications: 5 O-levels, 2 A-levels, Advanced Cricket Coach

Jobs outside cricket: Teacher, grease monkey in a garage
Family links with cricket: Father, ex-Sussex county cricketer and now NCA National Coach
Cricketing superstitions: Adjusting all equipment to obtain comfort
Overseas tours: 1981 tour to Barbados with Sussex U-16; 1982 tour to Barbados with Sussex Young Cricketers; 1985 England Young Cricketers tour to West Indies (as captain)
Cricketers particularly learnt from: Les Lenham, John Spencer, Ralph Dellor
Cricketers particularly admired: Ken McEwan, Barry Richards
Other sports played: Hockey, squash, golf, snooker
Relaxations: Music, listening to Van Morrison, Fleetwood Mac; reading
Extras: Made debut for Young England 1983. Broke record for number of runs scored in season at a public school in 1984 (1534 av. 80.74). Youngest player to appear for County 2nd XI at 14 years old
Opinions on cricket: 'Over-rate fines should be looked into so they don't end up punishing attacking cricket.'
Injuries 1986: Broken finger

Best batting performance: 89 Sussex v Kent, Canterbury 1985
Best bowling performance: 4-88 Sussex v Leicestershire, Leicester 1986

LAST SEASON: BATTING

	I.	N.O.	R.	H.S.	AV.
TEST					
1ST-CLASS	29	4	544	77	21.76
INT					
JPL	1	1	7	7*	–
NAT.W.	1	0	6	6	–
B & H	3	0	121	82	40.33

LAST SEASON: BOWLING

	O.	M.	R.	W.	AV.
TEST					
1ST-CLASS	131	26	409	9	45.44
INT					
JPL	8	0	40	0	–
NAT.W.	9	0	48	1	–
B & H					

CAREER: BATTING

	I.	N.O.	R.	H.S.	AV.
TEST					
1ST-CLASS	46	6	1048	89	26.20
INT					
JPL	2	2	8	7*	–
NAT.W.	1	0	6	6	–
B & H	3	0	121	82	40.33

CAREER: BOWLING

	O.	M.	R.	W.	AV.
TEST					
1ST-CLASS	131	26	409	9	45.44
INT					
JPL	8	0	40	0	–
NAT.W.	9	0	48	1	–
B & H					

LE ROUX, G. S. Sussex

Full Name: Garth Sterling Le Roux
Role: Right-hand bat, right-arm
fast bowler, slip fielder
Born: 4 September 1955, Cape
Town, South Africa
Height: 6′ 3″ **Weight:** 15st 5lbs
Nickname: Rocky, Grumps
County debut: 1978
County cap: 1981
50 wickets in a season: 3
1st-Class 50s scored: 22
1st-Class 5 w. in innings: 32
1st-Class 10 w. in match: 3
One-Day 50s: 4
Place in batting averages: 105th
av. 29.80 (1985 73rd av. 35.08)
Place in bowling averages: 81st
av. 35.69 (1985 43rd av. 28.30)
1st-Class catches 1986: 6 (career: 73)
Parents: Pierre and Audrey
Wife and date of marriage: Martine, 19 February 1986
Education: Wynberg Boys' High School; Stellenbosch University
Qualifications: BA Physical Education
Overseas tours: World XI in World Series Cricket Tour 1978–79

Overseas teams played for: Western Province; South African XI
Cricketers particularly learnt from: Hylton Ackerman, Eddie Barlow
Cricketers particularly admired: Dennis Lillee, Graeme Pollock
Off-season 1986–87: Playing in South Africa
Other sports played: Golf, tennis, fishing
Relaxations: Cooking, sailing, reading
Extras: Played for Packer's World Series Cricket, 1978–79 in Australia. First player to get a hat-trick in the Rebel Series in South Africa (1985–86)
Opinions on cricket: 'Too much travelling and playing on the County Circuit.'
Injuries 1986: Broken right index finger
Best batting performance: 86 Western Province v Border, Cape Town 1985–86
Best bowling performance: 8-107 Sussex v Somerset, Taunton 1981

LAST SEASON: BATTING

	I.	N.O.	R.	H.S.	AV.
TEST					
1ST-CLASS	16	6	298	72*	29.80
INT					
JPL	10	2	113	41*	14.12
NAT.W.	1	1	39	39*	–
B & H	3	0	16	7	5.33

LAST SEASON: BOWLING

	O.	M.	R.	W.	AV.
TEST					
1ST-CLASS	302.2	66	928	26	35.69
INT					
JPL	76	4	287	13	22.07
NAT.W.	31.3	3	91	5	18.20
B & H	40.1	3	166	5	33.20

CAREER: BATTING

	I.	N.O.	R.	H.S.	AV.
TEST					
1ST-CLASS	248	69	4563	86	25.49
INT					
JPL	59	13	1091	88	23.71
NAT.W.	11	3	119	39*	14.87
B & H	22	6	376	50	23.50

CAREER: BOWLING

	O.	M.	R.	W.	AV.
TEST					
1ST-CLASS	5871.4	1300	15444	729	21.18
INT					
JPL	528.5	27	2232	107	20.85
NAT.W.	145.5	25	391	29	13.48
B & H	256.5	27	1014	42	24.14

104. Who was England's vice-captain on the 1986–87 tour of Australia?

LEVER, J. K. — Essex

Full Name: John Kenneth Lever
Role: Right-hand bat, left-arm fast-medium bowler
Born: 24 February 1949, Stepney
Height: 6′ 0″ **Weight:** 13st
Nickname: Jake, J.K., Stanley
County debut: 1967
County cap: 1970
Benefit: 1980 (£66,250)
Test debut: 1976–77
No. of Tests: 21
No. of One-Day Internationals: 22
50 wickets in a season: 16
1st-Class 50s scored: 3
1st-Class 5 w. in innings: 82
1st-Class 10 w. in match: 12
Place in batting averages: —
(1985 124th av. 13.79)
Place in bowling averages: 53rd
av. 28.42 (1985 23rd av. 25.91)
1st-Class catches 1986: 1 (career: 178)
Parents: Ken and Doris
Wife and date of marriage: Chris, 30 July 1983
Children: Jocelyn Jennifer, 9 January 1985
Education: Highlands Junior; Dane County Secondary School
Qualifications: 3 O-levels, 3 RSAs
Jobs outside cricket: Clerk with Access Social Club; Byron Shipping; Dominion Insurance
Cricketing superstitions: 'Too many to mention.'
Overseas tours: India, Sri Lanka and Australia, 1976–77; Pakistan and New Zealand, 1977–78; Australia, 1978–79 and 1979–80
Cricketers particularly learnt from: 'The Essex team.'
Cricketers particularly admired: Sir Gary Sobers
Off-season 1986–87: In England
Other sports played: Football, golf
Relaxations: Indian food, real ale
Extras: Took 10 wickets on his Test debut in 1976 v India at Delhi. Took 106 wickets at an average of 15.80 in 1978, and 106 wickets at an average of 17.30 in 1979, and 106 wickets at an average of 16.28 in 1983. President of Blythswood CC. Member of Ilford CC since the age of 14. Another of the renowned Essex comedians. Has reputation of 'not breaking down'. On the executive of the Cricketers' Association. Banned from Test Cricket for three years for joining rebel tour of South Africa in 1982. Recalled to England side

in 1986 after four-year absence

Opinions on cricket: 'I would like to see over-rate fines disappear from one-day cricket.'

Best batting performance: 91 Essex v Glamorgan, Cardiff 1970

Best bowling performance: 8-37 Essex v Gloucestershire, Bristol 1984

LAST SEASON: BATTING

	I.	N.O.	R.	H.S.	AV.
TEST	2	1	0	0*	–
1ST-CLASS	25	5	199	38	9.95
INT					
JPL	4	3	6	5*	–
NAT.W.	2	1	8	7	–
B & H	2	2	2	2*	–

LAST SEASON: BOWLING

	O.	M.	R.	W.	AV.
TEST	53	9	166	6	27.33
1ST-CLASS	585.1	145	1824	64	28.50
INT					
JPL	101.3	7	474	15	31.60
NAT.W.	21	4	95	0	–
B & H	53.1	8	186	10	18.60

CAREER: BATTING

	I.	N.O.	R.	H.S.	AV.
TEST	31	5	306	53	11.76
1ST-CLASS	476	183	3203	91	10.93
INT	11	4	56	27*	8.00
JPL	101	61	382	23	9.55
NAT.W.	24	16	90	15*	11.25
B & H	25	17	94	13	11.75

CAREER: BOWLING

	O.	M.	R.	W.	AV.
TEST	166.7 516.2	27 113	1951	23	26.72
1ST-CLASS	210.4 13102.4	40 2927	36866	1546	23.84
INT	33 148	5 15	713	24	29.71
JPL	1760.2	200	6430	344	18.69
NAT.W.	407.3	93	1087	62	17.53
B & H	759.5	147	2290	132	17.34

LILLEY, A. W. Essex

Full Name: Alan William Lilley
Role: Right-hand bat, cover fielder
Born: 8 May 1959, Ilford, Essex
Height: 6′ 2″ **Weight:** 14st
Nickname: Lil
County debut: 1978
County cap: 1986
1st-Class 50s scored: 14
1st-Class 100s scored: 1
One-Day 50s: 6
One-Day 100s: 2
Place in batting averages: 146th av. 25.16 (1985 176th av. 21.50)
1st-Class catches 1986: 6 (career: 29)
Parents: Min and Ron
Wife and date of marriage: Helen, 6 October 1984
Education: Caterham High School, Ilford

Family links with cricket: Father played for Osborne CC as a bowler for 18 years

Overseas teams played for: Perth CC, Western Australia, 1979–80

Cricketers particularly learnt from: Stuart Turner, Bill Morris

Off-season 1986–87: Working in a shipping office

Other sports played: Most

Extras: Was on MCC Young Pro staff at Lord's one season after leaving school. Scored century in second innings of debut v Nottinghamshire

Injuries 1986: Broken fingers

Best batting performance: 100* Essex v Nottinghamshire, Trent Bridge 1978

Best bowling performance: 2-11 Essex v Surrey, Chelmsford 1984

LAST SEASON: BATTING

	I.	N.O.	R.	H.S.	AV.
TEST					
1ST-CLASS	26	2	604	87	25.16
INT					
JPL	10	2	145	52	18.12
NAT.W.	2	0	118	113	59.00
B & H	2	0	33	18	16.50

CAREER: BATTING

	I.	N.O.	R.	H.S.	AV.
TEST					
1ST-CLASS	100	6	2295	100*	24.41
INT					
JPL	80	7	1149	60	15.73
NAT.W.	10	2	308	113	38.50
B & H	22	2	441	119	22.05

LAST SEASON: BOWLING

	O.	M.	R.	W.	AV.
TEST					
1ST-CLASS	18.3	1	104	2	52.00
INT					
JPL	1	0	1	0	–
NAT.W.					
B & H					

CAREER: BOWLING

	O.	M.	R.	W.	AV.
TEST					
1ST-CLASS	56.3	3	309	7	44.14
INT					
JPL	3.3	0	20	3	6.66
NAT.W.	8	3	33	2	16.50
B & H	1	0	4	1	–

---

105. How much should a regulation cricket ball weigh when new?

106. Which British Prime Minister was a fag to which English Test Captain at school?

LLOYD, C. H. Lancashire

Full Name: Clive Hubert Lloyd
Role: Left-hand bat, right-arm
medium bowler
Born: 31 August 1944, Georgetown,
Guyana
Height: 6′ 4½″ **Weight:** 14st
Nickname: Big C, Hubert
County debut: 1968
County cap: 1969
Testimonial: 1977 (£27,199)
Test debut: 1966–67
No. of Tests: 110
No. of One-Day Internationals: 87
1000 runs in a season: 10
1st-Class 50s scored: 171
1st-Class 100s scored: 74
1st-Class 200s scored: 5
One-Day 50s: 64
One-Day 100s: 12

Place batting averages: 8th av. 49.57 (1985 16th av. 52.00)
1st-Class catches 1986: — (career: 377)
Parents: Arthur Christopher and Sylvia Thelma
Wife and date of marriage: Waveney, 11 September 1971
Children: Melissa Monica Simone, 22 February 1974; Samantha Louise, 26 January 1976; Clive Jason Christopher, 15 June 1981
Education: Fountain AME School and Chatham High School, Georgetown, Guyana
Qualifications: Cricket Coaching Certificate
Jobs outside cricket: Civil servant, Guyana Ministry of Health
Family links with cricket: Cousin of Lance Gibbs of Warwickshire CCC and West Indies. 'My parents had no interest in sport.'
Overseas tours: India and Ceylon 1966–67; Australia and New Zealand 1968–69; England 1969, 1973, 1976, 1980 and 1984; Australia 1979–80 and 1984–85; Pakistan 1980–81; India 1983–84
Other sports played: Tennis, table tennis, squash, soccer, basketball. Was a schoolboy athletics champion
Relaxations: Coaching, charity work, TV, music
Extras: Offered terms by Warwickshire before signing for Lancashire. Played for Haslingden in Lancashire League in 1967. Played for Rest of the World XI in 1967, 1968, five matches in 1970 and two in 1971 and 1972. Has written articles for *Lancashire Evening Post* and *Bolton Express*. Has had knee injury problems since 1976. Was strong supporter of World Series Cricket. Published (by Stanley Paul) *Living for Cricket* in 1980. Eye-sight deteriorated

after he tried to separate two boys fighting, at age 12, and received a blow in the eye, and has worn spectacles ever since. Has scored 6 centuries v Yorkshire, a Lancashire record. Scored 201* in 120 minutes for West Indies v Glamorgan at Swansea, 1976, to equal record for fastest double century in first-class cricket. Captain of West Indies 1974–85. Captain of Lancashire 1981–83 and resumed 1985–86. Resigned from Test cricket and the West Indies captaincy in 1985. Became British citizen during 1986. Honorary degrees bestowed by Universities of West Indies, Manchester and Hull

Best batting performance: 242* West Indies v India, Bombay 1974–75
Best bowling performance: 4-48 Lancashire v Leicestershire, Old Trafford 1970

LAST SEASON: BATTING

	I.	N.O.	R.	H.S.	AV.
TEST					
1ST-CLASS	8	1	347	128	49.57
INT					
JPL	15	2	501	91*	38.53
NAT.W.	5	1	164	65	41.00
B & H	2	0	168	101	84.00

LAST SEASON: BOWLING

	O.	M.	R.	W.	AV.
TEST					
1ST-CLASS					
INT					
JPL					
NAT.W.					
B & H					

CAREER: BATTING

	I.	N.O.	R.	H.S.	AV.
TEST	175	14	7515	242*	46.67
1ST-CLASS	555	82	23717	217*	50.14
INT	69	19	1977	102	39.54
JPL	171	40	5198	134*	39.67
NAT.W.	41	6	1920	126	54.85
B & H	45	6	1338	124	34.30

CAREER: BOWLING

	O.	M.	R.	W.	AV.
TEST	39 234.0	6 69	622	10	62.20
1ST-CLASS	34 1263	7 302	3482	104	33.48
INT	3 55.4	0 7	210	8	26.25
JPL	221	16	935	36	25.97
NAT.W.	92.3	16	320	12	26.66
B & H	83.3	18	302	12	25.17

107. Who was Ray Illingworth's best man?

108. Which England cricketer was forbidden to use a blue bat at Lord's in 1973?

LLOYD, T. A.   Warwickshire

Full Name: Timothy Andrew Lloyd
Role: Left-hand bat, right-arm
off-break bowler
Born: 5 November 1956, Oswestry
Height: 5′ 10″ **Weight:** 11st 12lbs
Nickname: Teflon
County debut: 1977
County cap: 1980
Test debut: 1984
No. of tests: 1
No. of One-Day Internationals: 3
1000 runs in a season: 5
1st-Class 50s scored: 57
1st-Class 100s scored: 17
1st-Class 200s scored: 1
One-Day 50s: 34
One-Day 100s: 1
Place in batting averages: 122nd

av. 28.32 (1985 53rd av. 38.44)
1st-Class catches 1986: 6 (career: 98)
Marital status: Single
Education: Oswestry Boys' High School; Dorset College of Higher Education
Qualifications: O-levels, A-levels, HND Tourism, NCA Advanced Coach
Jobs outside cricket: Agent for Italian colour printer, book publishing, lorry
driver
Overseas tours: Derrick Robins' tour to South America 1979; Warwickshire
CCC to Zambia 1977; Warwickshire Wanderers to Barbados 1978
Overseas teams played for: Orange Free State, Zingari CC, Waverley CC
Cricketers particularly learnt from: Dennis Amiss
Cricketers particularly admired: Gary Sobers
Off-season 1986–87: Working in sporting promotions and sponsorship
Other sports: Soccer, golf, tennis, table-tennis, squash
Other sports followed: Most sports
Relaxations: 'Enjoying my home, drinking good wine and beer, eating various
cuisine.'
Extras: Scored 202* for Shropshire Schools v Worcestershire. Played for
Shropshire and Warwickshire 2nd XI, both in 1975
Opinions on cricket: 'Toss should be awarded to visiting captain in cham-
pionship cricket in an attempt to prevent home sides preparing pitches geared
to their advantage.'
Injuries 1986: Broken nose followed by chronic back condition
Best batting performance: 208* Warwickshire v Gloucestershire, Edgbaston
1983

Best bowling performance: 3-62 Warwickshire v Surrey, Edgbaston 1985

LAST SEASON: BATTING

	I.	N.O.	R.	H.S.	AV.
TEST					
1ST-CLASS	28	0	793	100	28.32
INT					
JPL	8	0	229	74	28.62
NAT.W.	2	0	48	44	24.00
B & H	4	0	25	22	6.25

LAST SEASON: BOWLING

	O.	M.	R.	W.	AV.
TEST					
1ST-CLASS	16	0	113	0	--
INT					
JPL	1	0	10	0	--
NAT.W.	6	0	43	1	--
B & H	2	0	20	0	--

CAREER: BATTING

	I.	N.O.	R.	H.S.	AV.
TEST	1	1	10	10*	--
1ST-CLASS	321	31	10435	208*	35.98
INT	3	0	101	49	33.66
JPL	97	11	2666	90	31.00
NAT.W.	18	3	573	81	38.20
B & H	29	3	817	137*	31.42

CAREER: BOWLING

	O.	M.	R.	W.	AV.
TEST					
1ST-CLASS	232	41	980	13	75.38
INT					
JPL	23.1	0	149	1	--
NAT.W.	9	1	47	2	23.50
B & H	15	1	76	0	--

LLOYDS, J. W.   Gloucestershire

Full Name: Jeremy William Lloyds
Role: Left-hand bat, right-arm
off-break bowler, close fielder
Born: 17 November 1954, Penang,
Malaya
Height: 5′ 11″ **Weight:** 11st 8lbs
Nickname: Jo'burg, J.J. or Jerry
County debut: 1979 (Somerset),
1985 (Gloucestershire)
County cap: 1982 (Somerset),
1985 (Gloucestershire)
1000 runs in a season: 1
1st-Class 50s scored: 34
1st-Class 100s scored: 7
1st-Class 5 w. in innings: 9
1st-Class 10 w. in match: 1
One-Day 50s: 1
Place in batting averages: 37th

av. 43.16 (1985 109th av. 30.30)
Place in bowling averages: 72nd av. 33.00 (1985 33rd av. 27.38)
1st-Class catches 1986: 21 (career: 131)
Parents: Edwin William and Grace Cicely
Marital status: Single
Education: St Dunstan's Prep School; Blundell's School

Qualifications: 10 O-levels, NCA Advanced Coach

Jobs outside cricket: Lloyds Bank, Taunton, for 1½ years. MCC Young Professionals at Lord's 1975 for four years

Family links with cricket: Father played Blundell's 1st XI 1932–35, selected for Public Schools Rest v Lord's Schools at Lord's 1935, Inter-State cricket in Malaya and Singapore 1950–55. Brother, Christopher Edwin Lloyds, played for Blundell's 1st XI 1964–66 and Somerset 2nd XI in 1966

Overseas tours: With Somerset to Antigua, 1981; with Gloucestershire to Barbados, 1985; Sri Lanka 1987

Overseas teams played for: St Stithian's Old Boys, Johannesburg, 1978–80; Toombul DCC, Brisbane, 1980–82; North Sydney District 1982–83; Orange Free State 1983–84

Cricketers particularly learnt from: Don Wilson, Derek Taylor, Brian Davison

Cricketers particularly admired: John Hampshire, Graeme Pollock

Other sports played: Rugby, soccer, golf, tennis, swimming, squash

Other sports followed: Watches motor-racing and American football

Off-season 1986–87: Training for 1987 season and perhaps coaching abroad

Relaxations: Music, cinema, driving, reading

Extras: Scored 132* and 102* for Somerset in same Championship match, June 1982. Took 30 catches in 1982 season for Somerset. Moved to Gloucestershire for 1985 season

Injuries 1986: Rib injury and left knee

Best batting performance: 132* Somerset v Northamptonshire, Northampton 1982

Best bowling performance: 7-88 Somerset v Essex, Chelmsford 1982

LAST SEASON: BATTING

	I.	N.O.	R.	H.S.	AV.
TEST					
1ST-CLASS	39	9	1295	111	43.16
INT					
JPL	9	1	95	45*	11.87
NAT.W.	1	0	1	1	–
B & H	2	0	9	6	4.50

LAST SEASON: BOWLING

	O.	M.	R.	W.	AV.
TEST					
1ST-CLASS	369.2	71	1221	37	33.00
INT					
JPL	27	0	138	3	46.00
NAT.W.	11.3	3	35	2	17.50
B & H	19.2	2	49	4	12.25

CAREER: BATTING

	I.	N.O.	R.	H.S.	AV.
TEST					
1ST-CLASS	235	36	6163	132*	30.96
INT					
JPL	50	10	477	45*	11.92
NAT.W.	9	2	146	40*	20.86
B & H	13	0	162	51	12.46

CAREER: BOWLING

	O.	M.	R.	W.	AV.
TEST					
1ST-CLASS	2047.4	470	6463	193	33.48
INT					
JPL	55.5	3	272	6	45.33
NAT.W.	20.3	4	53	2	26.50
B & H	21.2	2	55	4	13.75

LORD, G. J.   Warwickshire

Full Name: Gordon John Lord
Role: Left-hand bat, slow left-arm
bowler
Born: 25 April 1961, Birmingham
Height: 5′ 10″ **Weight:** 11st 10lbs
Nickname: Plod
County debut: 1983
1st-Class 50s scored: 2
1st-Class 100s scored: 1
One-Day 50s: 1
One-Day 100s: 1
Place in batting averages: —
(1985 130th av. 27.10)
1st-Class catches 1986: 2 (career: 6)
Parents: Michael David and
Christine Frances
Marital status: Single
Education: Warwick School;
Durham University
Qualifications: 7 O-levels, 4 A-levels, BA General Studies
Overseas tours: England U-19 tour Australia 1978–79 and West Indies
1979–80
Cricketers particularly learnt from: Allan Wilkins (school coach), R. N.
Abberley (2nd XI coach), Norman Graham (University coach)
Other sports played: Squash, tennis, swimming, running
Other sports followed: Watches rugby, athletics, boxing
Relaxations: All forms of music, particularly church organ music; astronomy,
reading, people
Extras: Released at end of 1986 season
Best batting performance: 199 Warwickshire v Yorkshire, Edgbaston 1985

LAST SEASON: BATTING

	I.	N.O.	R.	H.S.	AV.
TEST					
1ST-CLASS	6	1	63	24*	12.60
INT					
JPL	3	1	10	6	5.00
NAT.W.					
B & H	1	0	0	0	—

LAST SEASON: BOWLING

	O.	M.	R.	W.	AV.
TEST					
1ST-CLASS	1	0	6	0	—
INT					
JPL					
NAT.W.					
B & H					

CAREER: BATTING

	I.	N.O.	R.	H.S.	AV.
TEST					
1ST-CLASS	26	2	508	199	21.16
INT					
JPL	12	1	243	103	22.09
NAT.W.					
B & H	1	0	0	0	—

CAREER: BOWLING

	O.	M.	R.	W.	AV.
TEST					
1ST-CLASS	14	3	37	0	—
INT					
JPL					
NAT.W.					
B & H					

LOVE, J. D. — Yorkshire

Full Name: James Derek Love
Role: Right-hand bat, right-arm medium bowler
Born: 22 April 1955, Leeds
Height: 6′ 2″ **Weight:** 14st
Nickname: Jim
County debut: 1975
County cap: 1980
No. of One-Day Internationals: 3
1000 runs in a season: 2
1st-Class 50s scored: 45
1st-Class 100s scored: 13
One-Day 50s: 14
One-Day 100s: 3
Place in batting averages: 74th av. 34.62 (1985 42nd av. 40.74)
1st-Class catches 1986: 7 (career: 100)
Parents: Derek Oliver and Betty
Marital status: Divorced
Education: Brudenell County Secondary, Leeds
Jobs outside cricket: Civil servant for three years until left to become professional cricketer
Family links with cricket: Father played local cricket; brother Robert plays for Castleford CC in Yorkshire League
Overseas teams played for: Whitbread Scholarship to Mosman Middle Harbour and District CC in 1977–78; Scarborough CC, Perth, Western Australia, 1978–79; Mosman Middle Harbour and District CC 1982–83, 1984–85
Cricketers particularly learnt from: Doug Padgett, county coach

LAST SEASON: BATTING

	I.	N.O.	R.	H.S.	AV.
TEST					
1ST-CLASS	29	5	831	109	34.62
INT					
JPL	13	1	408	104*	34.00
NAT.W.	2	1	20	12	–
B & H	4	1	99	34*	33.00

LAST SEASON: BOWLING

	O.	M.	R.	W.	AV.
TEST					
1ST-CLASS	39.2	7	146	0	–
INT					
JPL	5	0	31	0	–
NAT.W.					
B & H					

CAREER: BATTING

	I.	N.O.	R.	H.S.	AV.
TEST					
1ST-CLASS	316	48	8637	170*	32.22
INT	3	0	61	43	20.33
JPL	114	13	2321	104*	22.98
NAT.W.	14	3	114	61*	10.36
B & H	29	7	841	118*	38.22

CAREER: BOWLING

	O.	M.	R.	W.	AV.
TEST					
1ST-CLASS	104.2	22	387	2	193.50
INT					
JPL	8	0	38	1	–
NAT.W.					
B & H					

Off-season 1986–87: Trying to find employment
Other sports played: Local football, golf
Relaxations: Shooting
Opinions on cricket: 'I wish employment could be found for more cricketers when the season ends.'
Best batting performance: 170* Yorkshire v Worcestershire, Worcester 1979

LYNCH, M. A. Surrey

Full Name: Monte Allan Lynch
Role: Right-hand bat, right-arm medium and off-break bowler
Born: 21 May 1958, Georgetown, Guyana
Weight: 12st
Nickname: Mont
County debut: 1977
County cap: 1982
1000 runs in a season: 5
1st-Class 50s scored: 44
1st-Class 100s scored: 24
One-Day 50s: 22
One-Day 100s: 3
Place in batting averages: 76th av. 34.27 (1985 17th av. 53.56)
1st-Class catches 1986: 38 (career: 174)
Parents: Lawrence and Doreen Austin
Marital status: Single

LAST SEASON: BATTING

	I.	N.O.	R.	H.S.	AV.
TEST					
1ST-CLASS	39	3	1234	152	34.27
INT					
JPL	14	0	276	78	19.71
NAT.W.	4	0	90	29	22.50
B & H	4	1	153	68*	51.00

CAREER: BATTING

	I.	N.O.	R.	H.S.	AV.
TEST					
1ST-CLASS	317	35	9837	152	34.88
INT					
JPL	110	13	2698	136	27.81
NAT.W.	18	3	402	129	26.80
B & H	29	1	686	85	24.50

LAST SEASON: BOWLING

	O.	M.	R.	W.	AV.
TEST					
1ST-CLASS	24.2	3	119	2	59.50
INT					
JPL					
NAT.W.	1	0	5	0	–
B & H					

CAREER: BOWLING

	O.	M.	R.	W.	AV.
TEST					
1ST-CLASS	204	34	828	17	48.70
INT					
JPL	43	0	41	0	–
NAT.W.	12	5	31	1	–
B & H					

Education: Ryden's School, Walton-on-Thames
Family links with cricket: 'Father and most of family played at some time or another.'
Other sports: Football, table-tennis
Extras: Hitting 141* for Surrey v Glamorgan at Guildford in August 1982, off 78 balls in 88 minutes, one six hit his captain's, Roger Knight's, car, denting it. Repeated trick in 1983 v Worcestershire in John Player Special League. Joined West Indies 'rebels' in South Africa 1983–84, although qualified for England
Best batting performance: 152 Surrey v Nottinghamshire, The Oval 1986
Best bowling performance: 3-6 Surrey v Glamorgan, Swansea 1981

MAHER, B. J. M.   Derbyshire

Full Name: Bernard Joseph Michael Maher
Role: Right-hand bat, wicket-keeper
Born: 11 February 1958, Hillingdon
Height: 5' 10" **Weight:** 11st 7lbs
Nickname: 'Tends to vary.'
County debut: 1981
1st-Class 50s scored: 7
1st-Class 100s scored: 1
Place in batting averages: 50th
av. 39.57 (1985 236th av. 12.50)
Parents: Francis J. and Mary Ann
Marital status: Single
Education: Abbotsfield
Comprehensive; Bishopsmalt
Grammar; Harrow College;
Loughborough University
Qualifications: 10 O-levels,

3 A-levels, BSc Hons in Economics
and Accountancy. NCA coaching award 1982. Gave up accountancy studies to play cricket
Jobs outside cricket: Accountant
Family links with cricket: Brother kept wicket for school; father followed Derbyshire CCC quite closely
Overseas tours: With the Middlesex Cricket League touring team to Trinidad and Tobago, 1978; Amsterdam with Loughborough University 1981
Overseas teams played for: Ellerslie CC, Auckland, New Zealand 1984–85; Kamo CC & Northland, New Zealand 1985–86

Cricketers particularly learnt from: Bob Taylor, Alan Knott
Cricketers particularly admired: Malcolm Marshall, Richard Hadlee, Gordon Greenidge, Graham Gooch, Ian Botham
Off-season 1986–87: Playing for Kamo CC & the Northland representative side. Also coaching Northern Districts B side – my main activity after Christmas
Other sports played: Badminton, rugby union (for Old Abbotsonians)
Other sports followed: Athletics, rugby, tennis, boxing
Relaxations: Scuba-diving, fishing, skiing, travel to foreign countries
Injuries 1986: Broken cheekbone in New Zealand – missed 1 week
Extras: Caught five catches in innings on debut v Gloucestershire
Opinions on cricket: 'One, I have spoken to American professional footballers and baseball players who could not believe how low the average county cricketers' wages are. In comparison to other sports, the game in England is not marketed at all, and it is not surprising that attendances are so low. We should play a one-day competition on Saturdays and Sundays even at the expense of three-day cricket. At these one-day games all the gimmicks of floodlights and coloured clothing should be used to get public and TV interest. If cricket authorities do not act now, televised matches and sponsorship will decline. Two, I would like to see a "transfer system" operate in professional cricket; it would allow players and clubs to make more money. Three, virtually nothing is done at school level to coach kids and organise competitions to stimulate their interest. Four, faster, harder pitches with consistent bounce should be produced to improve the standard of English players and encourage fast bowlers.'

LAST SEASON: BATTING

	I.	N.O.	R.	H.S.	AV.
TEST					
1ST-CLASS	24	5	752	126	39.57
INT					
JPL	7	1	120	45	20.00
NAT.W.					
B & H					

CAREER: BATTING

	I.	N.O.	R.	H.S.	AV.
TEST					
1ST-CLASS	79	21	1253	126	21.60
INT					
JPL	22	4	190	45	10.53
NAT.W.	1	0	0	0	–
B & H	2	2	2	2	–

LAST SEASON: WICKET-KEEPING

	C.	ST.		
TEST				
1ST-CLASS	23	–		
INT				
JPL	5	–		
NAT.W.				
B & H				

LAST SEASON: BOWLING

	O.	M.	R.	W.	AV.
TEST					
1ST-CLASS	33	2	151	3	50.33
INT					
JPL					
NAT.W.					
B & H					

CAREER: BOWLING

	O.	M.	R.	W.	AV.
TEST					
1ST-CLASS	33	2	151	3	50.33
INT					
JPL					
NAT.W.					
B & H					

CAREER: WICKET-KEEPING

	C.	ST.		
TEST				
1ST-CLASS	91	7		
INT				
JPL	17	6		
NAT.W.	–	–		
B & H	3	1		

Best batting performance: 126 Derbyshire v New Zealand, Derby 1986
Best bowling performance: 2-69 Derbyshire v Glamorgan, Abergavenney 1986

MAKINSON, D. J.   Lancashire

Full Name: David John Makinson
Role: Right-hand bat, left-arm fast-medium bowler
Born: 12 January 1961, Eccleston, Lancashire
Height: 6′ 4″ **Weight:** 13st
Nickname: Maki
County debut: 1984
1st-Class 50s scored: 1
1st-Class 5 w. in innings: 1
Place in batting averages: 232nd av. 12.00 (1985 101st av. 31.00)
Place in bowling averages: 79th av. 34.80 (1985 74th av. 33.72)
1st-Class catches 1986: 7 (career: 9)
Parents: Thomas Andrew and Rhoda
Wife and date of marriage: Susan, 9 April 1983
Education: St Mary's High School; Leyland Motors Technical College; Bolton Institute of Technology
Qualifications: 6 O-levels, ONC in Mechanical Engineering; HNC in Automobile Engineering. Qualified Engineering Technician
Jobs outside cricket: Draughtsman (Leyland Trucks)
Overseas tours: New York 1985 with Lancashire
Overseas teams played for: Maroochydore, Queensland, 1984–85
Cricketers particularly learned from: Clive Lloyd, Peter Lever
Cricketers particularly admired: Ian Botham
Off-season 1986–87: Playing for Maroochydore in Queensland
Other sports played: Football
Other sports followed: Rugby league
Relaxations: Sunbathing, swimming, eating out
Extras: Writes on cricket for Sunshine Coast newspaper in Queensland
Opinions on cricket: 'I think a four-day county championship would bring more results.'
Best batting performance: 58* Lancashire v Northamptonshire, Lytham 1985
Best bowling performance: 5-60 Lancashire v Derbyshire, Old Trafford 1985

	I.	N.O.	R.	H.S.	AV.
TEST					
1ST-CLASS	14	6	96	43	12.00
INT					
JPL	6	3	23	12*	7.66
NAT.W.	1	1	8	8*	–
B & H	1	1	0	0*	–

LAST SEASON: BOWLING

	O.	M.	R.	W.	AV.
TEST					
1ST-CLASS	325.1	65	1044	30	34.80
INT					
JPL	96.2	4	493	7	70.42
NAT.W.					
B & H	26	3	89	4	22.25

CAREER: BATTING

	I.	N.O.	R.	H.S.	AV.
TEST					
1ST-CLASS	40	17	486	58*	21.13
INT					
JPL	14	7	56	13	8.00
NAT.W.	2	1	25	17	–
B & H	3	2	5	5	–

CAREER: BOWLING

	O.	M.	R.	W.	AV.
TEST					
1ST-CLASS	584.1	150	2436	69	35.30
INT					
JPL	245.1	10	1154	35	32.97
NAT.W.	17	3	86	1	–
B & H	53	3	217	8	27.12

MALCOLM, D. E. Derbyshire

Full Name: Devon Eugene Malcolm
Role: Right-hand bat, right-arm fast-medium bowler
Born: 22 February 1963, Kingston, Jamaica
Height: 6′ 2″ **Weight:** 14st
County debut: 1984
1st-Class 5 w. in innings: 1
Place in bowling averages: 43rd av. 27.34 (1985 122nd av. 42.13)
1st-Class catches 1986: 2 (career: 6)
Parents: Albert and Brendale (deceased)
Marital status: Single
Education: St Elizabeth Technical High School; Richmond College
Qualifications: College certificates
Cricketers particularly admired: Michael Holding, Richard Hadlee
Other sports played: Football, table tennis
Relaxations: Reggae, funk and soul music
Best batting performance: 29* Derbyshire v Gloucestershire, Gloucester 1986
Best bowling performance: 5-42 Derbyshire v Gloucestershire, Gloucester 1986

	I.	N.O.	R.	H.S.	AV.
TEST					
1ST-CLASS	7	4	37	29*	12.33
INT					
JPL	1	0	16	16	–
NAT.W.					
B & H					

CAREER: BATTING

	I.	N.O.	R.	H.S.	AV.
TEST					
1ST-CLASS	16	5	77	29*	7.00
INT					
JPL	1	0	16	16	–
NAT.W.					
B & H					

LAST SEASON: BOWLING

	O.	M.	R.	W.	AV.
TEST					
1ST-CLASS	216.2	38	765	28	27.32
INT					
JPL	16	0	87	3	29.00
NAT.W.					
B & H					

CAREER: BOWLING

	O.	M.	R.	W.	AV.
TEST					
1ST-CLASS	389.4	64	1521	47	32.36
INT					
JPL	16	0	87	3	29.00
NAT.W.					
B & H					

MALLENDER, N. A.   Somerset

Full Name: Neil Alan Mallender
Role: Right-hand bat, right-arm
fast-medium bowler
Born: 13 August 1961, Kirk
Sandall, Nr Doncaster
Height: 6′ 1″ **Weight:** 12st 10lbs
Nickname: Ghostie
County debut: 1980
(Northamptonshire)
County cap: 1984 (Northamptonshire)
50 wickets in a season: 2
1st-Class 50s scored: 4
1st-Class 5 w. in innings: 9
1st-Class 10 w. in match: 1
Place in batting averages: 232nd
av. 11.90 (1985 175 av. 15.71)
Place in bowling averages: 83rd
av. 36.02 (1985 59th av. 31.29)
1st-Class catches 1986: 4 (career: 54)
Parents: Ron and Jean
Wife and date of marriage: Caroline,
1 October 1983
Education: Beverley Grammar School, East Yorkshire
Qualifications: 7 O-levels
Family links with cricket: Brother, Graham, used to play good representative
cricket before joining the RAF
Cricket superstitions: Left boot on first

Overseas tours: Young England tour to West Indies, 1980
Overseas teams played for: Belmont DCC, NSW, 1980–81; Bathurst, NSW, 1982–83; Otago and Kaikorai CC, New Zealand, 1983–86
Cricketers particularly learnt from: Peter Willey, Warren Lees
Off season 1986–87: Playing and coaching in Otago, New Zealand
Other sports played: Golf
Other sports followed: Rugby league (especially Hull RFC)
Relaxations: Watching most other sports
Extras: Signed a 3-year contract to play for Somerset in 1987
Best batting performance: 88 Otago v Central Districts, Otago 1985–86
Best bowling performance: 7-27 Otago v Auckland, Auckland 1984–85

LAST SEASON: BATTING

	I.	N.O.	R.	H.S.	AV.
TEST					
1ST-CLASS	20	10	119	37	11.90
INT					
JPL	4	2	5	2	2.50
NAT.W.	1	0	0	0	–
B & H	2	1	4	3	–

LAST SEASON: BOWLING

	O.	M.	R.	W.	AV.
TEST					
1ST-CLASS	611	137	1693	47	36.02
INT					
JPL	91.5	6	400	15	26.66
NAT.W.	12	0	44	1	–
B & H	43.4	6	148	8	18.50

CAREER: BATTING

	I.	N.O.	R.	H.S.	AV.
TEST					
1ST-CLASS	174	55	1628	88	13.68
INT					
JPL	31	15	152	22	9.50
NAT.W.	8	3	39	11*	7.80
B & H	8	3	23	7	4.60

CAREER: BOWLING

	O.	M.	R.	W.	AV.
TEST					
1ST-CLASS	3904.3	860	11575	389	29.75
INT					
JPL	534.5	34	2512	99	25.37
NAT.W.	164.4	26	472	26	18.15
B & H	202	24	737	27	27.29

109. How old was W. G. Grace when he first captained England: 22, 31 or 40?

MARKS, V. J.   Somerset

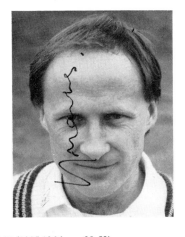

Full Name: Victor James Marks
Role: Right-hand bat, right-arm off-break bowler
Born: 25 June 1955, Middle Chinnock, Somerset
Height: 5′ 9″ **Weight:** 11st 8lbs
Nickname: Vic
County debut: 1975
County cap: 1979
Test debut: 1982
No. of tests: 6
No. of One-Day Internationals: 33
1000 runs in a season: 2
50 wickets in a season: 6
1st-Class 50s scored: 62
1st-Class 100s scored: 5
1st-Class 5 w. in innings: 30
1st-Class 10 w. in match: 4
One-Day 50s: 9
Place in batting averages: 30th av. 44.04 (1985 106th av. 30.52)
Place in bowling averages: 82nd av. 35.94 (1985 73rd av. 33.63)
1st-Class catches 1986: 8 (career: 112)
Parents: Harold and Joan
Wife and date of marriage: Anna, 9 September 1978
Children: Amy, 27 November 1979
Education: Blundell's School; Oxford University
Qualifications: MA Classics
Jobs outside cricket: Teaching – but not since March 1981
Family links with cricket: 'Father a dangerous village cricketer.'
Overseas tours: Derrick Robins' tour of Canada 1977; England in Australia and New Zealand 1982–83, New Zealand and Pakistan 1983–84, India and Australia 1984–85
Overseas teams played for: Grade cricket with Bayswater Morley CC in Perth, Western Australia, 1981–82
Cricketers particularly learnt from: Tom Cartwright, Arthur Milton
Cricketers particularly admired: Colin Dredge
Off-season 1986–87: Playing state cricket for Western Australia
Other sports played: Squash, golf
Extras: Half-blue for rugby fives at Oxford University. Debut for Oxford University CC 1975. Blue 1975–76–77–78. Captain 1976–77. Somerset vice-captain 1984. Author: *Somerset County Cricket Scrapbook* (1984); *Marks Out of XI* (1985)

Best batting performance: 134 Somerset v Worcestershire, Weston-super-Mare 1984
Best bowling performance: 8-17 Somerset v Lancashire, Bath 1985

LAST SEASON: BATTING

	I.	N.O.	R.	H.S.	AV.
TEST					
1ST-CLASS	36	12	1057	110	44.04
INT					
JPL	12	3	216	32*	24.00
NAT.W.	1	0	8	8	–
B & H	4	0	67	32	16.75

LAST SEASON: BOWLING

	O.	M.	R.	W.	AV.
TEST					
1ST-CLASS	744.5	198	2121	59	35.94
INT					
JPL	79.4	2	422	10	42.20
NAT.W.	24	5	75	1	–
B & H	41	4	133	3	44.33

CAREER: BATTING

	I.	N.O.	R.	H.S.	AV.
TEST	10	1	249	83	27.66
1ST-CLASS	386	67	9624	134	30.16
INT	24	3	285	44	13.57
JPL	99	26	1616	72	22.13
NAT.W.	20	6	392	55	28.00
B & H	38	8	756	81*	25.20

CAREER: BOWLING

	O.	M.	R.	W.	AV.
TEST	180.2	54	484	11	44.00
1ST-CLASS	7417	2033	20531	625	32.84
INT	295.2	28	1077	44	24.48
JPL	664.4	41	2651	103	25.73
NAT.W.	190.1	28	620	19	32.63
B & H	408.5	72	1194	40	29.85

MARPLES, C.   Derbyshire

Full Name: Christopher Marples
Role: Right-hand bat, wicket-keeper
Born: 3 August 1964, Chesterfield
Height: 6 ′ 0″ **Weight:** 12st 4lbs
Nickname: Jed
County debut: 1985
1st-Class 50s scored: 2
Place in batting averages: 173rd av. 22.19
Parents: Terence John and Patricia Ann
Marital status: Single
Family links with cricket: Father played a good standard of local cricket
Education: Tupton Hall Comprehensive
Qualifications: O-levels and CSEs, City and Guilds Roadworks
Jobs outside cricket: Plays professional football for Chesterfield; worked for Derbyshire County Council for four years
Overseas tours: Chesterfield to Barbados, 1981
Cricketers particularly learnt from: Bob Taylor

Cricketers particularly admired: Bob Taylor, Alan Knott
Off-season 1986–87: Playing football
Other sports played: Football
Relaxations: Listening to music, Prince and T. Rex
Extras: The first goalkeeper and wicket-keeper to play both sports at professional level
Best batting performance: 57 Derbyshire v Lancashire, Liverpool 1986

LAST SEASON: BATTING

	I.	N.O.	R.	H.S.	AV.
TEST					
1ST-CLASS	24	3	466	57	22.19
INT					
JPL	4	0	55	42	13.75
NAT.W.					
B & H					

LAST SEASON: BOWLING

	O.	M.	R.	W.	AV.
TEST					
1ST-CLASS	4	0	48	0	
INT					
JPL					
NAT.W.					
B & H					

CAREER: BATTING

	I.	N.O.	R.	H.S.	AV.
TEST					
1ST-CLASS	39	8	580	57	18.70
INT					
JPL	8	2	97	42	16.16
NAT.W.					
B & H					

CAREER: BOWLING

	O.	M.	R.	W.	AV.
TEST					
1ST-CLASS	4	0	48	0	–
INT					
JPL					
NAT.W.					
B & H					

LAST SEASON: WICKET-KEEPING

	C.	ST.		
TEST				
1ST-CLASS	31	4		
INT				
JPL	1	–		
NAT.W.				
B & H				

CAREER: WICKET-KEEPING

	C.	ST.		
TEST				
1ST-CLASS	54	5		
INT				
JPL	8	–		
NAT.W.				
B & H				

110. Which Australian fast bowler was no-balled 35 times playing in his first game in England in 1938?

MARSH, S. A.   Kent

Full Name: Steven Andrew Marsh
Role: Right-hand bat, wicket-keeper
Born: 27 January 1961, Westminster
Height: 6′ **Weight:** 12st
Nickname: Marshy
County debut: 1982
1st-Class 50s scored: 6
Place in batting averages: 100th
av. 30.60
Parents: Mel Graham and Valerie
Ann
Wife and date of marriage: Julie
27 September 1986
Education: Walderslade Secondary
School for Boys; Mid-Kent College
of Higher and Further Education
Qualifications: 6 O-levels,
2 A-levels, OND in Business Studies
Jobs outside cricket: Office clerk;
cricket coach
Family links with cricket: Father played local cricket for Lordswood
Cricketing superstitions: 'When batting, getting into double figures.'
Overseas tours: Barbados, 1979 with Lordswood CC, Kent
Cricketers particularly learnt from: 'Alan Igglesden – I have learnt to keep to
leg-side bowling.'
Cricketers particularly admired: Gary Sobers
Off-season 1986–87: Working for Bowater-Scott
Other sports played: Golf, snooker, horse-racing, soccer (striker) with Maidstone Utd

LAST SEASON: BATTING

	I.	N.O.	R.	H.S.	AV.
TEST					
1ST-CLASS	36	8	857	70	30.60
INT					
JPL	10	2	73	22*	9.12
NAT.W.	1	0	1	1	–
B & H	3	2	32	15	–

LAST SEASON: WICKET-KEEPING

	C.	ST.		
TEST				
1ST-CLASS	48	3		
INT				
JPL	15	–		
NAT.W.	2	–		
B & H	10	–		

CAREER: BATTING

	I.	N.O.	R.	H.S.	AV.
TEST					
1ST-CLASS	50	11	1037	70	26.58
INT					
JPL	12	3	76	32*	8.44
NAT.W.	1	0	1	1	–
B & H	3	2	32	15	–

CAREER: WICKET-KEEPING

	C.	ST.		
TEST				
1ST-CLASS	74	6		
INT				
JPL	18	–		
NAT.W.	2	–		
B & H	10	–		

Relaxations: Watching TV
Best batting performance: 70 Kent v Warwickshire, Folkestone 1986

MARSHALL, M. D. Hampshire

Full Name: Malcolm Denzil Marshall
Role: Right-hand bat, right-arm fast bowler
Born: 18 April 1958, Barbados
Height: 5′ 11″ **Weight:** 12st 4lbs
Nickname: Macko
County debut: 1979
County cap: 1981
Test debut: 1978/79
No. of Tests: 45
No. of One-Day Internationals: 71
50 wickets in a season: 6
1st-Class 50s scored: 25
1st-Class 100s scored: 4
1st-Class 5 w. in innings: 62
1st-Class 10 w. in match: 9
One-Day 50s: 1
Place in batting averages: 228th av. 12.52 (1985 149th av. 24.77)
Place in bowling averages: 1st av. 15.08 (1985 3rd av. 17.68)
1st-Class catches 1986: 5 (career: 92)
Parents: Eleanor
Children: Shelly, 24 November 1984
Education: Parkinson Comprehensive School, Barbados
Jobs outside cricket: Promoter of banks products
Family links with cricket: Cousin plays for Texaco as a fast bowler
Overseas tours: With West Indies to India and Sri Lanka 1978–79; Australia 1979–80, 1981–82, 1984–85; Pakistan 1980–81; India 1983–84; England 1980 and 1984; Zimbabwe 1981; New Zealand 1979–80
Overseas teams played for: Barbados (debut 1977–78)
Cricketers particularly learnt from: 'The West Indies team.'
Other sports played: Tennis, darts, pool, golf
Relaxations: Soul-music, reggae
Extras: Took nine wickets in debut match v Glamorgan in May 1979. Scored his first first-class century (109) in Zimbabwe, October 1981, for the West Indies against Zimbabwe. Most wickets in the Shell Shield Competition (25) by a Barbadian. Broke record of number of wickets taken in 22-match season (i.e. since 1969) with 133

Best batting performance: 116* Hampshire v Lancashire, Southampton 1982
Best bowling performance: 8-71 Hampshire v Worcestershire, Southampton 1982

LAST SEASON: BATTING

	I.	N.O.	R.	H.S.	AV.
TEST					
1ST-CLASS	23	2	263	58*	12.52
INT					
JPL	7	2	69	39*	13.80
NAT.W.	2	1	47	32	–
B & H	3	0	37	33	12.33

LAST SEASON: BOWLING

	O.	M.	R.	W.	AV.
TEST					
1ST-CLASS	656.3	171	1508	100	15.08
INT					
JPL	109	4	428	13	32.92
NAT.W.	24	5	62	2	31.00
B & H	24	5	67	2	33.50

CAREER: BATTING

	I.	N.O.	R.	H.S.	AV.
TEST	53	4	953	92	19.44
1ST-CLASS	234	28	4589	116*	22.27
INT	35	12	369	56*	16.04
JPL	49	13	618	46	17.16
NAT.W.	12	7	143	32	28.60
B & H	19	1	209	33	11.61

CAREER: BOWLING

	O.	M.	R.	W.	AV.
TEST	1646.4	349	4639	215	21.57
1ST-CLASS	5387.4	1544	13535	802	16.87
INT	633.3	71	2154	87	24.75
JPL	608.5	65	2095	86	24.36
NAT.W.	173.4	33	454	16	28.37
B & H	219	46	601	31	19.38

MARTINDALE, D. J. R.
Nottinghamshire

Full Name: Duncan John Richardson Martindale
Role: Right-hand bat, cover fielder
Born: 13 December 1963, Harrogate
Height: 5′ 11½″ **Weight:** 12st
Nickname: Bloers
County debut: 1985
1st-Class 50s scored: 2
1st-Class 100s scored: 1
Place in batting averages: —
(1985 121st av. 28.81)
1st-Class catches 1986: — (career: 6)
Parents: Don and Isabel
Marital status: Single
Family links with cricket: Father and grandfather played club cricket in Nottingham; great uncle played for Nottinghamshire 2nd XI
Education: Lymm Grammar School; Trent Polytechnic
Qualifications: 9 O-levels, 2 A-levels, HND Business Studies, NCA Coaching Award
Cricketers particularly learnt from: Everybody at Trent Bridge

Cricketers particularly admired: 'Geoff Boycott, Viv Richards, Richard Hadlee, to name three of many.'
Other sports played: All sports, particularly long-distance running and squash
Relaxations: Reading, listening to all types of music, watching TV
Extras: Scored century (104*) in fifth first-class innings. First one-day match was 1985 NatWest final
Best batting performance: 104* Nottinghamshire v Lancashire, Old Trafford 1985

LAST SEASON: BATTING

	I.	N.O.	R.	H.S.	AV.
TEST					
1ST-CLASS	4	0	115	88	28.75
INT					
JPL	1	0	4	4	–
NAT.W.					
B & H					

LAST SEASON: BOWLING

	O.	M.	R.	W.	AV.
TEST					
1ST-CLASS					
INT					
JPL					
NAT.W.					
B & H					

CAREER: BATTING

	I.	N.O.	R.	H.S.	AV.
TEST					
1ST-CLASS	18	3	324	104*	28.80
INT					
JPL	3	0	44	33	14.66
NAT.W.					
B & H					

CAREER: BOWLING

	O.	M.	R.	W.	AV.
TEST					
1ST-CLASS	2	0	8	0	–
INT					
JPL					
NAT.W.					
B & H					

MARU, R. G.   Hampshire

Full Name: Rajesh J. Govind Maru
Role: Right-hand bat, slow left-arm bowler, close fielder
Born: 28 October 1962, Nairobi
Height: 5′ 6″ **Weight:** 10st 7lbs
Nickname: Raj, Rat.
County debut: 1980 (Middlesex), 1984 (Hampshire)
50 wickets in a season: 1
1st-Class 50s scored: 1
1st-Class 5 w. in innings: 6
Place in batting averages: 113th av. 29.00 (1985 169th av. 22.70)
Place in bowling averages: 51st av. 27.83 (1985 25th av. 26.34)
1st-Class catches 1986: 13 (career: 64)
Parents: Jamnadass and Prabhavati

Qualifications: Cricket coach
Jobs outside cricket: Cricket coach
Family links with cricket: Brother has played for Middlesex 2nd XI
Cricketing superstitions: Nelsons: 111, 222 and 333
Overseas tours: Young England tour of West Indies 1980; NCA tour of Canada; Barbican International XI to Dubai; Middlesex to Zimbabwe 1980–81
Overseas teams played for: Blenheim CC, New Zealand, 1985–86
Cricketers particularly learnt from: Jack Robertson, Derek Underwood, David Graveney, Malcolm Marshall
Other sports played: Badminton, table-tennis, squash, swimming
Other sports followed: Football, rugby union
Relaxations: Music and wine bars
Extras: Played for Middlesex 1980–83
Best batting performance: 62 Hamsphire v Sussex, Portsmouth 1985
Best bowling performance: 7-79 Hampshire v Middlesex, Bournemouth 1984

LAST SEASON: BATTING

	I.	N.O.	R.	H.S.	AV.
TEST					
1ST-CLASS	10	6	116	23	29.00
INT					
JPL					
NAT.W.					
B & H					

LAST SEASON: BOWLING

	O.	M.	R.	W.	AV.
TEST					
1ST-CLASS	497.5	146	1336	48	27.83
INT					
JPL					
NAT.W.					
B & H					

CAREER: BATTING

	I.	N.O.	R.	H.S.	AV.
TEST					
1ST-CLASS	65	22	736	62	17.11
INT					
JPL	1	1	3	3*	–
NAT.W.					
B & H					

CAREER: BOWLING

	O.	M.	R.	W.	AV.
TEST					
1ST-CLASS	2031.2	553	5689	191	29.78
INT					
JPL	15	0	86	2	43.00
NAT.W.					
B & H					

111. Which two Leicestershire bowlers bowled unchanged through four consecutive county innings against three different counties?

MAYNARD, C.   Lancashire

Full Name: Christopher Maynard
Role: Right-hand bat, wicket-keeper
Born: 8 April 1958, Haslemere,
Surrey
Height 6' **Weight:** 12st
Nickname: Tosh
County debut: 1978 (Warwickshire),
1982 (Lancashire)
County cap: 1986 (Lancashire)
1st-Class 50s scored: 12
1st-Class 100s scored: 1
One-Day 50s: 1
Place in batting averages: 95th
av. 31.52 (1985 241st av. 12.09)
Parents: John and Joan
Wife and date of marriage: Kim,
14 January 1982
Education: Bishop Vesey's Grammar
School, Sutton Coldfield

Qualifications: 10 O-levels, 1 A-level, cricket coaching certificate
Jobs outside cricket: Has been salesman and has worked for jewellery firm.
Coaches schoolchildren for Manchester Education Committee

LAST SEASON: BATTING

	I.	N.O.	R.	H.S.	AV.
TEST					
1ST-CLASS	26	5	662	132*	31.52
INT					
JPL	14	6	150	49*	18.75
NAT.W.	3	0	41	22	13.66
B & H	4	0	52	22	13.00

CAREER: BATTING

	I.	N.O.	R.	H.S.	AV.
TEST					
1ST-CLASS	150	27	2541	132*	20.65
INT					
JPL	65	16	766	49*	15.63
NAT.W.	9	2	63	22	9.00
B & H	18	5	268	60	20.61

LAST SEASON: WICKET-KEEPING

	C.	ST.			
TEST					
1ST-CLASS	29	3			
INT					
JPL	7	2			
NAT.W.	3	1			
B & H	3	—			

LAST SEASON: BOWLING

	O.	M.	R.	W.	AV.
TEST					
1ST-CLASS					
INT					
JPL					
NAT.W.					
B & H					

CAREER: BOWLING

	O.	M.	R.	W.	AV.
TEST					
1ST-CLASS	2	0	8	0	—
INT					
JPL					
NAT.W.					
B & H					

CAREER: WICKET-KEEPING

	C.	ST.			
TEST					
1ST-CLASS	186	28			
INT					
JPL	62	11			
NAT.W.	6	3			
B & H	26	1			

Family links with cricket: Father and brother, Steve, used to play for Sutton Coldfield CC
Overseas tours: Australia with Derrick Robins' U-23 XI in 1979–80; Warwickshire to Zambia 1977; Lancashire to Barbados 1984; Clive Lloyd XI to New York 1985
Overseas teams played for: West Rand, Johannesburg, 1981–82
Off-season 1986–87: Coaching/playing golf
Other sports played: 'Golf, hockey – try anything.'
Relaxations: Reading, sleeping, gardening, being dragged by the dog
Extras: Was on Warwickshire staff for six years (only played 26 matches), making debut in 1979. Joined Lancashire in 1982
Best batting performance: 132* Lancashire v Yorkshire, Leeds 1986

MAYNARD, M. P. Glamorgan

Full Name: Matthew Peter Maynard
Role: Right-hand bat, right-arm medium bowler
Born: 21 March 1966, Oldham
Height: 5' 10½" **Weight:** 12st
Nickname: Walter
County debut: 1985
1000 runs in a season: 1
1st-Class 50s scored: 7
1st-Class 100s scored: 3
Place in batting averages: 85th av. 33.40
1st-Class catches 1986: 13 (career: 14)
Parents: Pat and Ken (deceased)
Wife and date of marriage: Susan, 27 September 1986
Education: Ysgol David Hughes, Anglesey
Jobs outside cricket: Sales rep for Bangor City FC; barman
Family links with cricket: Father pro'd for Duckinfield; brother played club cricket
Cricketing superstitions: Putting equipment on in a certain order
Overseas tours: Barbados with North Wales, 1982
Cricketers particularly learnt from: Colin Page, Bill Clutterbuck, John Steele
Cricketers particularly admired: Richard Hadlee, Ian Botham
Off-season 1986–87: Playing and coaching for St Joseph's CC, Whakatane, New Zealand

Other sports played: Football, rugby, golf, snooker, squash
Relaxations: Listening to Lionel Ritchie and George Benson and decorating
Extras: Scored century on debut v Yorkshire at Swansea. Also youngest centurion for Glamorgan. Scored 1000 runs in first full season
Opinions: 'I think that it is good to have an overseas player in a county side because it lifts the standard of play. I think there should be only one overseas player in a side at a time. I also think that the introduction of four-day county cricket would make the game more interesting and the wickets better.'
Best batting performance: 148 Glamorgan v Oxford University, Oxford 1986

LAST SEASON: BATTING

	I.	N.O.	R.	H.S.	AV.
TEST					
1ST-CLASS	34	4	1002	148	33.40
INT					
JPL	13	0	197	31	15.15
NAT.W.	2	0	16	9	8.00
B & H	1	0	0	0	–

LAST SEASON: BOWLING

	O.	M.	R.	W.	AV.
TEST					
1ST-CLASS	4	0	13	0	
INT					
JPL					
NAT.W.					
B & H					

CAREER: BATTING

	I.	N.O.	R.	H.S.	AV.
TEST					
1ST-CLASS	37	4	1200	148	36.36
INT					
JPL	16	0	228	31	14.35
NAT.W.	2	0	16	9	8.00
B & H	1	0	0	0	–

CAREER: BOWLING

	O.	M.	R.	W.	AV.
TEST					
1ST-CLASS	4.1	0	17	0	–
INT					
JPL					
NAT.W.					
B & H					

MAYS, C. S. Sussex

Full Name: Christopher Sean Mays
Role: Right-hand bat, right-arm
off-break bowler
Born: 11 May 1966, Brighton
Height: 5′ 9″
County debut: 1986
Place in bowling averages: 123rd
av. 54.30
Education: Lancing College
Overseas tours: To Holland with
NAYC 1983; West Indies with
Young England 1985
Off-season 1986–87: On five-
year course at Middlesex
Hospital Medical School
Extras: Has represented
England Schools and MCC Schools

Best batting performance: 8* Sussex v Gloucestershire, Bristol 1986
Best bowling performance: 3-77 Sussex v New Zealand, Hove 1986

LAST SEASON: BATTING

	I.	N.O.	R.	H.S.	AV.
TEST					
1ST-CLASS	6	2	19	8*	4.75
INT					
JPL					
NAT.W.					
B & H					

CAREER: BATTING

	I.	N.O.	R.	H.S.	AV.
TEST					
1ST-CLASS	6	2	19	8*	4.75
INT					
JPL					
NAT.W.					
B & H					

LAST SEASON: BOWLING

	O.	M.	R.	W.	AV.
TEST					
1ST-CLASS	212.5	45	706	13	54.30
INT					
JPL					
NAT.W.					
B & H					

CAREER: BOWLING

	O.	M.	R.	W.	AV.
TEST					
1ST-CLASS	212.5	45	706	13	54.30
INT					
JPL					
NAT.W.					
B & H					

McEWAN, S. M.   Worcestershire

Full Name: Steven Michael McEwan
Role: Right-hand bat, right-arm fast-medium bowler
Born: 5 May 1962, Worcester
Height: 6′ 1″ **Weight:** 13st
Nickname: Mac, Maciz
County debut: 1985
Place in bowling averages: 98th av. 39.87 (1985 102nd av. 39.69)
1st-Class catches 1986: 7 (career: 8)
Parents: Michael James and Valerie Jeanette
Marital status: Single
Education: Worcester Royal Grammar School
Education: 6 O-levels, 3 A-levels
Qualifications: Technician's certificate in building

Jobs outside cricket: Assistant buyer, building trade
Family links with cricket: Father and uncle played club cricket
Cricketers particularly learnt from: Dipak Patel, Basil D'Oliveira
Cricketers particularly admired: Richard Hadlee, Malcolm Marshall

Off-season 1986–97: Playing cricket in New Zealand with Birkenhead City, Auckland

Other sports played: Soccer, skittles, golf

Other sports followed: American football

Relaxations: Watching movies, reading, music

Extras: Took 10 wickets for 13 runs in an innings in 1983 for Worcester Nomads against Moreton-in-Marsh. Also broke school bowling record, 60 wickets, at WRGS, 1982

Injuries 1986: Bruised ligaments in left ankle, missed 2 weeks in early season

Best batting performance: 13* Worcestershire v Oxford University, Oxford 1985

Best bowling performance: 3-33 Worcestershire v Leicestershire, Worcester 1986

LAST SEASON: BATTING

	I.	N.O.	R.	H.S.	AV.
TEST					
1ST-CLASS	3	2	13	7	–
INT					
JPL	2	2	13	7*	–
NAT.W.					
B & H					

LAST SEASON: BOWLING

	O.	M.	R.	W.	AV.
TEST					
1ST-CLASS	180.1	31	638	16	39.87
INT					
JPL	42	2	209	8	26.12
NAT.W.					
B & H					

CAREER: BATTING

	I.	N.O.	R.	H.S.	AV.
TEST					
1ST-CLASS	11	7	38	13*	9.50
INT					
JPL	3	2	13	7*	–
NAT.W.					
B & H					

CAREER: BOWLING

	O.	M.	R.	W.	AV.
TEST					
1ST-CLASS	357.1	60	1273	32	39.78
INT					
JPL	74	2	385	13	29.61
NAT.W.					
B & H					

---

112. In 1977, Geoff Boycott and John Edrich both scored their 100th 100. On both occasions the same man was batting at the other end. Who was he?

Full Name: Neil Ralph Charter McLaurin
Role: Right-hand bat, right-arm medium pace bowler
Born: 22 March 1966, Welwyn Garden City
Height: 5′ 11″ **Weight:** 12st
County debut: 1986
1st-Class 50s scored: 1
1st-Class 5 w. in innings: 1
1st-Class catches 1986: — (career: 3)
Education: Malvern College
Off-season 1986–87: Playing cricket in Australia
Best batting performance: 56 Oxford University v Warwickshire, Oxford 1985
Best bowling performance: 2-25 Oxford University v Middlesex, Oxford 1986

LAST SEASON: BATTING

	I.	N.O.	R.	H.S.	AV.
TEST					
1ST-CLASS	5	1	9	4	2.25
INT					
JPL	2	0	3	3	1.50
NAT.W.					
B & H					

LAST SEASON: BOWLING

	O.	M.	R.	W.	AV.
TEST					
1ST-CLASS	26.5	5	89	2	44.50
INT					
JPL					
NAT.W.					
B & H					

CAREER: BATTING

	I.	N.O.	R.	H.S.	AV.
TEST					
1ST-CLASS	15	2	177	56	13.61
INT					
JPL	2	0	3	3	1.50
NAT.W.					
B & H					

CAREER: BOWLING

	O.	M.	R.	W.	AV.
TEST					
1ST-CLASS	87.2	15	318	3	106.00
INT					
JPL					
NAT.W.					
B & H					

113. How many times was Bradman out for a duck in Tests?

McMILLAN, B. M.   Warwickshire

Full Name: Brian Mervin McMillan
Role: Right-hand bat, right-arm
fast-medium bowler, slip fielder
Born: 22 December 1963, Welkom,
South Africa
Height: 6′ 3½″ **Weight:** 15st 3lbs
Nickname: Mac
County debut: 1986
1st-Class 50s scored: 10
1st-Class 100s scored: 4
One-Day 50s: 3
Place in batting averages: 5th
av. 58.76
Place in bowling averages: 114th
av. 47.52
1st-Class catches 1986: 11
(career: 23)

Marital status: Single
Education: Carleton Jones
High School; University|of Witwatersrand
Qualifications: A-levels, gave up in 3rd year at university
Cricketing superstitions: Put left pad on first and always put a protective box
on
Overseas teams played for: Transvaal
Cricketers particularly learnt from: Clive Rice, Graeme Pollock, Alan
Kourie and rest of Transvaal side
Off-season 1986–87: In South Africa
Other sports played: Squash, tennis, hockey, rugby union
Other sports followed: Football, golf

LAST SEASON: BATTING

	I.	N.O.	R.	H.S.	AV.
TEST					
1ST-CLASS	21	4	999	136	58.76
INT					
JPL	5	2	133	78*	44.33
NAT.W.	1	0	10	10	–
B & H	4	0	170	76	42.50

CAREER: BATTING

	I.	N.O.	R.	H.S.	AV.
TEST					
1ST-CLASS	40	5	1531	136	43.74
INT					
JPL	5	2	133	78*	44.33
NAT.W.	1	0	10	10	–
B & H	4	0	170	76	42.00

LAST SEASON: BOWLING

	O.	M.	R.	W.	AV.
TEST					
1ST-CLASS	220	34	808	17	47.52
INT					
JPL	36.2	3	177	7	25.28
NAT.W.	11.4	1	54	3	18.00
B & H	42	4	161	6	26.83

CAREER: BOWLING

	O.	M.	R.	W.	AV.
TEST					
1ST-CLASS	444.3	86	1520	41	37.07
INT					
JPL	36.2	3	177	7	25.28
NAT.W.	11.4	1	54	3	18.00
B & H	42	4	161	6	26.83

Relaxations: Videos, books (novels). Few drinks in pub
Opinions on cricket: 'Don't mix sport and politics.'
Best batting performance: 136 Warwickshire v Nottinghamshire, Trent Bridge 1986
Best bowling performance: 4-53 Transvaal B v Boland, Johannesburg 1984–85

MEDLYCOTT, K. T. Surrey

Full Name: Keith Thomas Medlycott
Role: Right-hand bat, slow left-arm bowler, short-leg fielder
Born: 12 May 1965, Whitechapel
Height: 5′ 11″ **Weight:** 12st 3lbs
Nickname: Medders, Max, C.D.F.
County debut: 1984
1st-Class 50s scored: 1
1st-Class 100s scored: 1
1st-Class 5 w. in innings: 3
1st-Class 10 w. in match: 1
Place in batting averages: 214th av. 14.07
Place in bowling averages: 55th av. 29.15
1st-Class catches 1986: 9 (career: 9)
Parents: Thomas Alfred and June Elizabeth
Marital status: Single

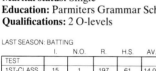

Education: Parmiters Grammar School; Wandsworth Comprehensive
Qualifications: 2 O-levels

LAST SEASON: BATTING

	I.	N.O.	R.	H.S.	AV.
TEST					
1ST-CLASS	15	1	197	61	14.07
INT					
JPL	1	0	0	0	–
NAT.W.					
B & H					

CAREER: BATTING

	I.	N.O.	R.	H.S.	AV.
TEST					
1ST-CLASS	24	7	336	117*	19.76
INT					
JPL	1	0	0	0	–
NAT.W.					
B & H					

LAST SEASON: BOWLING

	O.	M.	R.	W.	AV.
TEST					
1ST-CLASS	356.2	86	1166	40	29.13
INT					
JPL	2	0	21	0	–
NAT.W.					
B & H					

CAREER: BOWLING

	O.	M.	R.	W.	AV.
TEST					
1ST-CLASS	478.2	132	1391	48	28.97
INT					
JPL	2	0	21	0	–
NAT.W.					
B & H					

Family links with cricket: 'Father plays club cricket (not very well).'
Overseas teams played for: Oostelikes CC 1984–85; Harlequins CC 1985–86
Cricketers particularly learnt from: G. G. Arnold, T. Sheppard
Cricketers particularly admired: C. Waller, P. Edmonds
Off-season 1986–87: Coaching in S. Africa
Other sports played: Football
Extras: Scored 100 on debut (117*)
Best batting performance: 117* Surrey v Cambridge University, Banstead 1984
Best bowling performance: 6-63 Surrey v Kent, The Oval 1986

MENDIS, G. D. Lancashire

Full Name: Gehan Dixon Mendis
Role: Right-hand opening bat
Born: 24 April 1955, Colombo, Sri Lanka
Height: 5' 8" **Weight:** 10st 7lbs
Nickname: Mendo, Dix
County debut: 1974 (Sussex), 1986 (Lancashire)
County cap: 1980 (Sussex), 1986 (Lancashire)
1000 runs in a season: 7
1st-Class 50s scored: 64
1st-Class 100s scored: 23
1st-Class 200s scored: 2
One-Day 50s: 24
One-Day 100s: 6
Place in batting averages: 48th av. 40.08 (1985 23rd av. 47.46)
1st-Class catches 1986: 2 (career: 93)
Parents: Sam Dixon Charles and Sonia Marcelle
Children: Hayley, 11 December 1982
Education: St Thomas College, Mount Lavinia, Sri Lanka; Brighton, Hove & Sussex Grammar School; Bede College, Durham University
Qualifications: BEd Mathematics, Durham; NCA coaching certificate
Jobs outside cricket: Teacher at Rosemead School, Littlehampton, Sussex; Richard Ellis, Perth, Western Australia; City Sales & Marketing Ltd, London
Overseas tours: Maharaja Organisation XI to India 1980; Rohan Kanhai's Invitation XI to Pakistan 1981; numerous international teams to West Indies

Overseas teams played for: Maharaja Organisation XI in Sri Lanka 1980–81; Colombo CC; Sebastianites CC, and Mount Lawley CC, Western Australia; Nedlands CC, Perth

Cricketers particularly admired: Barry Richards, Richard Hadlee

Off-season 1986–87: In England earning a living

Other sports played: Table-tennis for Sussex at junior level

Other sports followed: Formula One motor racing

Relaxations: Music, cinema and wine bars

Extras: Played for TCCB XI in 1981. Has twice turned down invitations to play for Sri Lanka in order to be free to be chosen for England. Left Sussex at end of 1985 to join Lancashire

Opinions on cricket: 'Championship 16 four-day games Tuesday–Friday. B & H/NatWest to be played Sat/Mon. Sunday League to remain the same.'

Best batting performance: 209* Sussex v Somerset, Hove 1984

LAST SEASON: BATTING

	I.	N.O.	R.	H.S.	AV.
TEST					
1ST-CLASS	37	3	1363	108	40.08
INT					
JPL	15	0	287	66	19.13
NAT.W.	5	0	117	72	23.40
B & H	4	0	86	35	21.50

LAST SEASON: BOWLING

	O.	M.	R.	W.	AV.
TEST					
1ST-CLASS					
INT					
JPL					
NAT.W.					
B & H					

CAREER: BATTING

	I.	N.O.	R.	H.S.	AV.
TEST					
1ST-CLASS	400	36	12984	209*	35.67
INT					
JPL	124	12	3189	125*	28.47
NAT.W.	27	2	872	141*	34.88
B & H	41	1	1074	109	26.85

CAREER: BOWLING

	O.	M.	R.	W.	AV.
TEST					
1ST-CLASS	5.3	0	76	1	–
INT					
JPL					
NAT.W.					
B & H					

114. In how many overseas countries did Bradman play Test cricket?

METCALFE, A. A.   *Yorkshire*

Full Name: Ashley Anthony Metcalfe
Role: Right-hand bat
Born: 25 December 1963, Horsforth, Leeds
Height: 5' 9½" **Weight:** 11st 7lbs
County debut: 1983
County cap: 1986
1000 runs in a season: 1
1st-Class 50s scored: 11
1st-Class 100s scored: 8
One-Day 50s: 2
One-Day 100s: 1
Place in batting averages: 26th av. 45.07 (1985 177th av. 21.42)
1st-Class catches 1986: 10 (career: 17)
Wife and date of marriage: Diane, 20 April 1986
Parents: Tony and Ann
Education: Ladderbanks Middle School; Bradford Grammar School; University College, London
Qualifications: 9 O-levels, 3 A-levels, coaching certificate
Jobs outside cricket: Worked for Grattan Mail Order Co., Paul Madeley's DIY
Family links with cricket: Father played in local league; father-in-law Ray Illingworth (Yorkshire and England)
Overseas tours: NCA tour of Denmark 1981
Overseas teams played for: Ringwood CC, Melbourne 1985–86

LAST SEASON: BATTING

	I.	N.O.	R.	H.S.	AV.
TEST					
1ST-CLASS	41	1	1803	151	45.07
INT					
JPL	14	1	341	74*	26.23
NAT.W.	3	0	29	23	9.66
B & H	2	0	42	31	21.00

CAREER: BATTING

	I.	N.O.	R.	H.S.	AV.
TEST					
1ST-CLASS	68	1	2405	151	35.89
INT					
JPL	33	2	789	115*	25.45
NAT.W.	5	0	62	33	12.40
B & H	2	0	42	31	21.00

LAST SEASON: BOWLING

	O.	M.	R.	W.	AV.
TEST					
1ST-CLASS	18.1	4	75	0	–
INT					
JPL					
NAT.W.					
B & H					

CAREER: BOWLING:

	O.	M.	R.	W.	AV.
TEST					
1ST-CLASS	23.1	4	85	0	–
INT					
JPL					
NAT.W.					
B & H					

Cricketers particularly learnt from: Doug Padgett, Ray Illingworth, Don Wilson
Cricketers particularly admired: Barry Richards
Off-season 1986–87: Club cricket in Melbourne with Ringwood
Other sports played: Golf
Other sports followed: Most
Relaxations: 'Relaxing at home with my wife.'
Extras: 'I made 122 on my debut for Yorkshire against Nottinghamshire at Park Avenue in 1983. I was the youngest ever player to do so and it was the highest ever score on a debut.'
Opinions on cricket: 'Politics should not interfere with sport – South Africa should be eligible for Test Cricket.'
Best batting performance: 151 Yorkshire v Northamptonshire, Luton 1986

METSON, C. P. Middlesex

Full Name: Colin Peter Metson
Role: Right-hand bat, wicket-keeper
Born: 2 July 1963, Cuffley, Hertfordshire
Height: 5' 7" **Weight:** 10st 8lbs
Nickname: Dempster, Meto, Reggie
County debut: 1981
1st-Class 50s scored: 2
Parents: Denis Alwyn and Jean Mary
Marital status: Single
Education: Stanborough School, Welwyn Garden City; Enfield Grammar School; Durham University
Qualifications: 10 O-levels, 5 A-levels, BA Hons, Economic History, NCA Preliminary Coaching Award

Jobs outside cricket: Trainee accounts clerk
Family links with cricket: Father played good club cricket and for MCC; brother plays club cricket
Cricketing superstitions: 'Always put right pad on before left; try to use the same equipment right through the season if possible, especially wicketkeeping gloves.'
Cricketers particularly learnt from: 'Jack Robertson, Bob Taylor, my father.'

Cricketers particularly admired: Bob Taylor, Rod Marsh, Mike Brearley, Wayne Daniel
Other sports played: Football, hockey, tennis, squash, golf
Other sports followed: American football, football
Relaxations: Computers, sleeping
Extras: Young Wicketkeeper of the Year 1981; three Young England Tests v India 1981. Captain Durham University 1984, losing finalists in UAU competition. Beat Cambridge University twice. Middlesex 2nd XI Player of the Year 1984
Best batting performance: 96 Middlesex v Gloucestershire, Uxbridge 1984

LAST SEASON: BATTING

	I.	N.O.	R.	H.S.	AV.
TEST					
1ST-CLASS	4	0	29	15	7.25
INT					
JPL	1	1	4	4*	–
NAT.W.					
B & H					

LAST SEASON: WICKET-KEEPING

	C.	ST.			
TEST					
1ST-CLASS	3	–			
INT					
JPL	2	–			
NAT.W.					
B & H					

CAREER: BATTING

	I.	N.O.	R.	H.S.	AV.
TEST					
1ST-CLASS	31	9	426	96	19.36
INT					
JPL	8	5	53	15*	17.66
NAT.W.					
B & H					

CAREER: WICKET-KEEPING

	C.	ST.			
TEST					
1ST-CLASS	50	2			
INT					
JPL	11	2			
NAT.W.					
B & H					

115. What colour is the fox on the Leicestershire badge?

MIDDLETON, T. C.   Hampshire

Full Name: Tony Charles Middleton
Role: Right-hand bat, slow left-arm bowler
Born: 1 February 1964, Winchester
Height 5′ 11″ **Weight:** 11 st
Nickname: Roo, Midders, T.C.
County debut: 1984
1st-Class 50s scored: 1
Place in batting averages: 119th av. 28.72
1st-Class catches 1986: 7 (career: 7)
Parents: Peter and Molly
Marital status: Single
Education: Weeke Infants and Junior Schools; Montgomery of Alamein Comprehensive, Winchester; Peter Symonds Sixth Form College, Winchester
Qualifications: 1 A-level, 5 O-levels
Jobs outside cricket: Worked for two winters as an electrical engineer
Family links with cricket: Brother plays local club cricket in Hampshire
Cricketing superstitions: Always wear spikes to bat in
Overseas teams played for: Club cricket in South Africa, 1984–85 and 1985–86
Cricketers particularly learnt from: 'Too many to name.'
Cricketers particularly admired: Barry Richards, Gordon Greenidge
Off-season 1986–87: Working in England
Other sports played: Squash, football, badminton

LAST SEASON: BATTING

	I.	N.O.	R.	H.S.	AV.
TEST					
1ST-CLASS	14	3	316	68*	28.72
INT					
JPL					
NAT.W.					
B & H					

LAST SEASON: BOWLING

	O.	M.	R.	W.	AV.
TEST					
1ST-CLASS	8	1	39	1	—
INT					
JPL					
NAT.W.					
B & H					

CAREER: BATTING

	I.	N.O.	R.	H.S.	AV.
TEST					
1ST-CLASS	16	3	331	68*	25.46
INT					
JPL					
NAT.W.					
B & H					

CAREER: BOWLING

	O.	M.	R.	W.	AV.
TEST					
1ST-CLASS	8	1	39	1	—
INT					
JPL					
NAT.W.					
B & H					

Other sports followed: Football, rugby union
Relaxations: Watching and playing other sports
Extras: Played for England Schools 1981
Opinions on cricket: 'More care should be taken of spectators. An improvement and widening of their facilities would encourage them to watch county cricket.'
Best batting performance: 68* Hampshire v Somerset, Taunton 1986

MILLER, A. J. T.   Middlesex

Full Name: Andrew John Trevor Miller
Role: Left-hand opening bat, right-arm medium bowler, short-leg fielder
Born: 30 May 1963, Chesham
Height: 5′ 11″ **Weight:** 12st 7lbs
Nickname: Dusty, Wino
County debut: 1983
1st-Class 50s scored: 15
1st-Class 100s scored: 3
One-Day 50s: 3
One-Day 100s: 1
Place in batting averages: 98th av. 31.06 (1985 93rd av. 31.63)
1st-Class catches 1986: 13 (career: 19)
Parents: John Innes and Sheila Mary
Marital status: Single
Education: Belmont School; Haileybury; Oxford University
Qualifications: 10 O-levels, 3 A-levels; BA Hons Biochemistry
Jobs outside cricket: Stockbroker
Cricketing superstitions: 'I have a fixed order for putting on gear, which changes after failure.'
Overseas tours: Australia with Oxford and Cambridge Combined Universities 1985
Overseas teams played for: Adelaide University 1986
Cricketers particularly learnt from: Opening partners at Middlesex
Off-season 1986–87: Stockbroking
Other sports played: Rugby, squash
Relaxations: 'Drinking; sports of many kinds; playing brag and taking money off Jamie Sykes/Philip Tufnell.'

Extras: 'First Oxonian since 1975 to score a century in the Varsity Match. First century by Combined Universities batsman in Benson and Hedges competition. Got maiden first-class wicket in maiden over (4th ball).' Captain of Oxford University 1985. Scored 231 v Combined Services 1984

Opinions on cricket: 'We play too much cricket; fines for slow over rates in one-day cricket are very unfair. The best games are often slow in over rates, but does the public mind? I think not.'

Injuries 1986: Dislocated finger hampered pre-season training

Best batting performance: 128* Middlesex v Oxford University, Oxford 1984

LAST SEASON: BATTING

	I.	N.O.	R.	H.S.	AV.
TEST					
1ST-CLASS	35	4	963	111*	31.06
INT					
JPL	8	1	276	69	39.42
NAT.W.	2	0	69	35	34.50
B & H	2	0	64	37	32.00

LAST SEASON: BOWLING

	O.	M.	R.	W.	AV.
TEST					
1ST-CLASS	2	0	6	0	–
INT					
JPL					
NAT.W.					
B & H					

CAREER: BATTING

	I.	N.O.	R.	H.S.	AV.
TEST					
1ST-CLASS	98	12	2744	128*	31.90
INT					
JPL	8	1	276	69	39.42
NAT.W.	3	0	69	35	23.00
B & H	10	0	402	101	40.20

CAREER: BOWLING

	O.	M.	R.	W.	AV.
TEST					
1ST-CLASS	3	0	10	1	–
INT					
JPL					
NAT.W.					
B & H	7	1	30	1	–

MILLER, G. Essex

Full Name: Geoffrey Miller
Role: Right-hand bat, right-arm off-break bowler
Born: 8 September 1952, Chesterfield
Height: 6' 2" **Weight:** 11st 6lbs
Nickname: Dusty
County debut: 1973 (Derbyshire)
County cap: 1976 (Derbyshire)
Benefit: 1985
Test debut: 1976
No. of Tests: 34
No. of One-Day Internationals: 25
50 wickets in a season: 4
1st-Class 50s scored: 68
1st-Class 100s scored: 2
1st-Class 5 w. in innings: 36
1st-Class 10 w. in match: 6

One-Day 50s: 17
Place in batting averages: 179th av. 20.48 (1985 123rd av. 28.62)
Place in bowling averages: 103rd av. 41.80 (1985 115th av. 43.00)
1st-Class catches 1986: 12 (career: 244)
Parents: Gwen and Keith
Wife: Carol
Children: Helen Jane; Anna Louise; James Daniel
Education: Chesterfield Grammar School
Family links with cricket: Father played local cricket in Chesterfield. Brother plays for Chesterfield CC
Overseas tours: With England Young Cricketers to India 1970–71 and West Indies 1972; toured with England to India, Sri Lanka, Australia 1976–77; Pakistan and New Zealand 1977–78; Australia 1978–79 and 1979–80 but had to return December 1979 through injury; West Indies 1981; Australia and New Zealand 1982–83
Cricketers particularly learnt from: E. J. Barlow, R. Illingworth, F. Titmus
Other sports played: Golf, table-tennis, football
Relaxations: Crosswords, reading, television, family life. Watching Chesterfield FC particularly, and all sports in general
Extras: Became Captain of Derbyshire half-way through 1979 season, but relinquished it half-way through 1981 season in favour of Barry Wood. Declined to sign for Derbyshire for 1982 season, and was released. Negotiated with several other counties, but signed again. Eventually left at end of 1986 and joined Essex for 1987
Best batting performance: 130 Derbyshire v Lancashire, Old Trafford 1984
Best bowling performance: 8-70 Derbyshire v Leicestershire, Coalville 1982

LAST SEASON: BATTING

	I.	N.O.	R.	H.S.	AV.
TEST					
1ST-CLASS	27	2	512	65	20.48
INT					
JPL	10	3	170	73*	24.28
NAT.W.	1	1	32	32*	–
B & H	3	2	86	32	–

LAST SEASON: BOWLING

	O.	M.	R.	W.	AV.
TEST					
1ST-CLASS	634.2	187	1406	33	42.06
INT					
JPL	78	4	316	5	63.20
NAT.W.	12	2	30	2	15.00
B & H	40	8	132	5	26.40

CAREER: BATTING

	I.	N.O.	R.	H.S.	AV.
TEST	51	4	1213	98*	25.80
1ST-CLASS	418	70	9487	130	27.26
INT	18	2	136	46	8.50
JPL	137	28	2225	84	20.41
NAT.W.	16	4	305	59*	25.41
B & H	47	10	978	88*	26.43

CAREER: BOWLING

	O.	M.	R.	W.	AV.
TEST	280.1 484.4	79 140	1859	60	30.98
1ST-CLASS	256.2 7204.5	48 2064	19051	712	26.75
INT	13 194	1 19	813	25	32.52
JPL	809.1	56	3435	117	29.35
NAT.W.	194	47	507	18	28.16
B & H	466	92	1320	53	24.90

MOLES, A. J.   Warwickshire

Full Name: Andrew James Moles
Role: Right-hand opening bat,
right-arm medium bowler
Born: 12 February 1961, Solihull
Height: 5' 10" **Weight:** 13st
Nickname: Molar
County debut: 1986
1st-Class 50s scored: 5
1st-Class 100s scored: 2
One-Day 50s: 1
Place in batting averages: 14th
av. 49.20
1st-Class catches 1986: 4 (career: 4)
Parents: Stuart Francis and
Gillian Margaret
Marital status: Single
Education: Finham Park
Comprehensive, Coventry;
Henley College of Further
Education; Butts College of
Further Education

Qualifications: 3 O-levels, 4 CSEs, Toolmaker/Standard Room Inspector City
& Guilds 205 Pts I, II, III
Jobs outside cricket: Standard Room Inspector
Family links with cricket: Brother plays for Solihull in the Midland Championship
Cricketing superstitions: Puts left pad on first. Never looks back at stumps
after being bowled
Cricketers particularly learnt from: Dennis Amiss, Fred Gardner

LAST SEASON: BATTING

	I.	N.O.	R.	H.S.	AV.
TEST					
1ST-CLASS	18	3	738	102	49.20
INT					
JPL	8	2	142	85	23.66
NAT.W.	1	0	14	14	–
B & H					

LAST SEASON: BOWLING

	O.	M.	R.	W.	AV.
TEST					
1ST-CLASS	64.3	10	198	5	39.60
INT					
JPL	16	0	107	1	–
NAT.W.	6	0	27	0	–
B & H					

CAREER: BATTING

	I.	N.O.	R.	H.S.	AV.
TEST					
1ST-CLASS	18	3	738	102	49.20
INT					
JPL	8	2	142	85	23.66
NAT.W.	1	0	14	14	–
B & H					

CAREER: BOWLING

	O.	M.	R.	W.	AV.
TEST					
1ST-CLASS	64.3	10	198	5	39.60
INT					
JPL	16	0	107	1	–
NAT.W.	6	0	27	0	–
B & H					

Cricketers particularly admired: Dennis Amiss, Ian Botham, Richard Hadlee
Off-season 1986–87: Playing and coaching cricket in South Africa
Other sports played: Football, rugby, squash
Relaxations: Listening to music or a meal with friends
Best batting performance: 102 Warwickshire v Somerset, Weston 1986
Best bowling performance: 2-57 Warwickshire v Sussex, Edgbaston 1986

MONKHOUSE, G. Surrey

Full Name: Graham Monkhouse
Role: Right-hand bat, right-arm
fast-medium bowler, slip fielder
Born: 26 April 1955, Carlisle
Height: 6′ 1″ **Weight:** 13st 8lbs
Nickname: Farmer
County debut: 1981
County cap: 1984
50 wickets in a season: 1
1st-Class 50s scored: 3
1st-Class 100s scored: 1
1st-Class 5 w. in innings: 2
Place in batting averages: 182nd
av. 20.25 (1985 80th av. 33.83)
Place in bowling averages: 104th
av. 42.07 (1985 29th av. 26.70)
1st-Class catches 1986: 6 (career: 35)
Parents: James Chris and Nancy
Marital status: Single
Education: Penrith Queen Elizabeth Grammar School; Nottinghamshire
College of Agriculture
Qualifications: 'Various O-levels, ONC Business Studies, HND Agriculture.'
NCA Advanced Cricket Coach
Jobs outside cricket: Ex-professional footballer, representative for J. Bibby
Agriculture 1976, farm manager 1976–79
Family links with cricket: Father is chairman and ex-captain of Edenhall CC,
Cumberland Senior League, Division I
Overseas tours: McAlpine Tour to South Africa 1984; English Counties tour
to Zimbabwe 1985
Overseas teams played for: Oostelikes CC, South Africa, 1979–80, 1981–82;
Harlequins CC, 1982–83
Cricketers particularly learnt from: Surrey Cricket Manager, M. J. Stewart,
Roy Miles (Wimbledon CC)
Off-season 1986–87: Farming

Other sports played: Professional football with Workington AFC 4th Division. Other clubs: Carlisle United, Netherfield, Penrith AFC. Played county junior tennis, badminton at U-16 level, and when allowed plays football for Dennis Waterman 'Showbiz XI' in charity games in and around London. Plays club cricket for Wimbledon CC in the Surrey Championship League when not required by Surrey

Relaxations: Photography, reading, eating, sleeping

Extras: Youngest player to be capped by Cumberland in the Minor Counties. Retired from full-time cricket at end of 1986 to concentrate on farming in Cumbria. Intends 'to continue playing for Minor Counties, MCC and is available for any overseas tour!'

Opinions on cricket: 1) Cricketers and cricket teams should be allowed to play anywhere in the world of their choosing. 2) Too much cricket being played, which breeds mediocrity within the playing ranks

Injuries 1986: Broken knuckle and bone in right hand

Best batting performance: 100* Surrey v Kent, The Oval 1984

Best bowling performance: 7-51 Surrey v Nottinghamshire, The Oval 1983

LAST SEASON: BATTING

	I.	N.O.	R.	H.S.	AV.
TEST					
1ST-CLASS	12	4	162	51	20.25
INT					
JPL	6	3	54	24*	18.00
NAT.W.	2	0	35	18	17.50
B & H	1	1	2	2*	–

CAREER: BATTING

	I.	N.O.	R.	H.S.	AV.
TEST					
1ST-CLASS	86	33	1158	100*	21.84
INT					
JPL	29	14	205	27	13.66
NAT.W.	5	0	50	18	10.00
B & H	9	5	57	24*	14.25

LAST SEASON: BOWLING

	O.	M.	R.	W.	AV.
TEST					
1ST-CLASS	233.1	69	589	14	42.07
INT					
JPL	60.1	2	297	10	29.70
NAT.W.	19.5	5	89	5	17.80
B & H	43	6	159	6	26.50

CAREER: BOWLING

	O.	M.	R.	W.	AV.
TEST					
1ST-CLASS	1688.4	412	4682	173	27.06
INT					
JPL	393.3	20	1754	58	30.24
NAT.W.	121.2	14	440	18	24.44
B & H	152.2	15	594	23	25.82

116. What are the birds depicted on the Sussex badge and how many are there?

Full Name: Steven Monkhouse
Role: Right-hand bat, left-arm
fast medium bowler, outfielder
Born: 24 November 1962, Bury
Height: 6' 3" **Weight:** 13st 5lbs
Nickname: Bob, Millstone,
Monky
County debut: 1985 (Warwickshire)
Parents: Harold and May
Marital status: Single
Education: Derby Technical
Grammar School; Peel College
Qualifications: 7 O-levels,
BEC National Business Studies
Cert, NCA Coaching Certificate
Family links with cricket: Father
played in the Lancashire League
Cricketers particularly learnt from:
Murray Bennett, Anton Ferreira
Cricketers particularly admired: N. Radford, Andrew Moles
Off-season 1986–87: Playing and coaching in Tasmania
Other sports played: 'Quite a few but none seriously.'
Other sports followed: Anything on TV
Relaxations: Anything away from cricket especially the pub after a day in the field
Extras: Signed for Glamorgan at end of 1986 season
Opinions on cricket: '2nd XI's don't play enough games on county grounds but play nearly every game on club grounds.'
Best batting performance: 5 Warwickshire v Surrey, The Oval 1985

LAST SEASON: BATTING

	I.	N.O.	R.	H.S.	AV.
TEST					
1ST-CLASS	1	0	0	0	–
INT					
JPL					
NAT.W.					
B & H					

LAST SEASON: BOWLING

	O.	M.	R.	W.	AV.
TEST					
1ST-CLASS	10	4	34	1	–
INT					
JPL					
NAT.W.					
B & H					

CAREER: BATTING

	I.	N.O.	R.	H.S.	AV.
TEST					
1ST-CLASS	3	1	7	5	3.50
INT					
JPL					
NAT.W.					
B & H					

CAREER: BOWLING

	O.	M.	R.	W.	AV.
TEST					
1ST-CLASS	27	6	95	2	47.50
INT					
JPL					
NAT.W.					
B & H					

MORRIS, H. — Glamorgan

Full Name: Hugh Morris
Role: Left-hand bat, right-arm medium bowler
Born: 5 October 1963, Cardiff
Height: 5′ 8″ **Weight:** 12st
Nickname: 'H', Banacek
County debut: 1981
County cap: 1986
1000 runs in a season: 1
1st-Class 50s scored: 18
1st-Class 100s scored: 3
One-Day 50s: 9
One-Day 100s: 1
Place in batting averages: 68th av. 36.23 (1985 138th av. 26.79)
1st-Class catches 1986: 9 (career: 23)
Parents: Roger and Anne
Marital status: Single
Education: Blundell's School, South Glamorgan Institute
Qualifications: 8 O-levels, 3 A-levels, 1 AO-level, BA Physical Education, NCA Coaching Award
Family links with cricket: Brother played for Wales U-19 and Glamorgan U-19. Father played club cricket
Cricketing superstitions: 'Getting off "0" and "111". Put right pad on first.'
Overseas tours: With English Public Schoolboy tour to West Indies, 1980–81; to Sri Lanka 1982–83; to USA (Los Angeles) with Haverfordwest CC, 1984
Cricketers particularly learnt from or admired: Javed Miandad, Alan Jones, Tom Cartwright, Kevin Lyons
Off-season 1986–87: Playing overseas
Other sports played: Rugby, squash, golf
Other sports followed: Most sports
Relaxations: Music, watching movies
Extras: Highest schoolboy cricket average in 1979 (89.71), 1981 (184.6) and 1982 (149.2). Captain of England U-19 Schoolboys in 1981 and 1982. Played for Young England v Young West Indies 1982, and captained Young England v Australia. Won Gray-Nicholls 'Most Promising Schoolboy' Award 1981, and Young Cricketer of 1982. Played first-class rugby for Aberavon 1984–85 and South Glamorgan Institute scoring over 150 points. Appointed Glamorgan captain 1986 – the youngest ever for county. Scored most runs in Sunday League by a Glamorgan player – 586
Best batting performance: 128* Glamorgan v Kent, Maidstone 1986

	I.	N.O.	R.	H.S.	AV.
TEST					
1ST-CLASS	44	2	1522	128*	36.23
INT					
JPL	15	1	587	100	41.92
NAT.W.	2	0	75	48	37.50
B & H	4	1	79	51	26.33

CAREER: BATTING

	I.	N.O.	R.	H.S.	AV.
TEST					
1ST-CLASS	104	16	2901	128*	32.96
INT					
JPL	29	3	954	100	36.69
NAT.W.	5	0	192	75	38.40
B & H	5	1	89	51	22.25

LAST SEASON: BOWLING

	O.	M.	R.	W.	AV.
TEST					
1ST-CLASS	11	4	44	0	–
INT					
JPL					
NAT.W.					
B & H					

CAREER: BOWLING

	O.	M.	R.	W.	AV.
TEST					
1ST-CLASS	26.5	5	144	1	–
INT					
JPL					
NAT.W.					
B & H					

MORRIS, J. E. Derbyshire

Full Name: John Edward Morris
Role: Right-hand bat,
right-arm medium bowler
Born: 1 April 1964, Crewe
Height: 5′ 10″ **Weight:** 11st 8lbs
Nickname: Animal
County debut: 1982
1000 runs in a season: 1
1st-Class 50s scored: 17
1st-Class 100s scored: 8
One-Day 50s: 8
One-Day 100s: 1
Place in batting averages: 23rd
av. 47.00 (1985 125th av. 27.77)
1st-Class catches 1986: 8 (career: 21)
Parents: George (Eddie) and Jean
Marital status: Single
Education: Shavington Comprehensive
School; Dane Bank College of Further Education
Qualifications: O-levels
Jobs outside cricket: Worked as a carpet fitter
Family links with cricket: 'Father played for Crewe CC for many years as an opening bowler.'
Overseas teams played for: Umbilo CC, Durban, South Africa, 1982–83, 1983–84
Cricketers particularly learnt from: 'Tony Borrington, Phil Russell and my father.'

Other sports played: Football, basketball, snooker
Other sports followed: Watching athletics and motor-racing
Relaxations: Movies, music, good food
Best batting performance: 191 Derbyshire v Kent, Derby 1986

LAST SEASON: BATTING

	I.	N.O.	R.	H.S.	AV.
TEST					
1ST-CLASS	40	3	1739	191	47.00
INT					
JPL	14	1	293	66*	22.53
NAT.W.	2	1	12	12*	–
B & H	5	0	90	65	18.00

LAST SEASON: BOWLING

	O.	M.	R.	W.	AV.
TEST					
1ST-CLASS	44.4	5	245	1	–
INT					
JPL					
NAT.W.					
B & H					

CAREER: BATTING

	I.	N.O.	R.	H.S.	AV.
TEST					
1ST-CLASS	117	6	3788	191	34.12
INT					
JPL	46	4	1055	104	25.11
NAT.W.	5	1	39	12*	9.75
B & H	12	0	188	65	15.66

CAREER: BOWLING

	O.	M.	R.	W.	AV.
TEST					
1ST-CLASS	62.5	7	373	2	186.50
INT					
JPL					
NAT.W.					
B & H					

MORTENSEN, O. H.   Derbyshire

Full Name: Ole Henrik Mortensen
Role: Right-hand bat, right-arm
fast-medium bowler
Born: 29 January 1958, Vejle,
Denmark
Height: 6′ 4″ **Weight:** 14st 2lbs
Nickname: Stan (coined by Bob
Taylor after England footballer
Stan Mortenson), Blood-Axe
County debut: 1983
50 wickets in a season: 1
1st-Class 5 w. in innings: 5
1st-Class 10 w. in match: 1
Place in bowling averages: 23rd
av. 23.52 (1985 56th av. 31.09)
1st-Class catches 1986: 1 (career: 14)
Parents: Will Ernst and Inge Wicka
Wife: Jette Jepmond

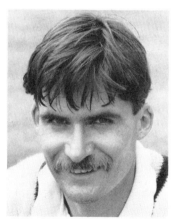

Children: Julie Jepmond, 30 August 1982
Education: Brondbyoster School; Avedore School
Jobs outside cricket: Worked as a tax assistant in Denmark
Family links with cricket: 'My small brother, Michael, used to play cricket. He

is now a professional tennis player, and has played in Davis Cup for Denmark.'

Overseas tours: Touring East Africa in 1976 with the Danish national side, and Scotland, Wales, Ireland and Holland

Overseas teams played for: Ellerslie, Auckland, New Zealand, 1983–84; Brighton CC, Melbourne 1985–86; Svanholm CC, Denmark

Cricketers particularly learnt from: Torben Jensen, Jorgen Janson, Peter Hargreaves and many others

Cricketers particularly admired: Dennis Lillee, Bob Taylor

Other sports played: Tennis, golf, football

Relaxations: Music, books, movies

Extras: *Derbyshire's Dane* by Peter Hargreaves, published 1984. Has played for Denmark

Best batting performance: 40* Derbyshire v Glamorgan, Derby 1984

Best bowling performance: 6-27 Derbyshire v Yorkshire, Sheffield 1983

LAST SEASON: BATTING

	I.	N.O.	R.	H.S.	AV.
TEST					
1ST-CLASS	17	9	69	31*	8.62
INT					
JPL	7	6	7	3*	–
NAT.W.	1	0	11	11	–
B & H	–	–	–	–	–

LAST SEASON: BOWLING

	O.	M.	R.	W.	AV.
TEST					
1ST-CLASS	416.2	111	1082	46	23.52
INT					
JPL	120	10	493	14	35.21
NAT.W.	10	1	47	1	–
B & H	50	9	133	9	14.77

CAREER: BATTING

	I.	N.O.	R.	H.S.	AV.
TEST					
1ST-CLASS	63	35	247	40*	8.82
INT					
JPL	18	14	19	5	4.75
NAT.W.	3	2	17	11	–
B & H	1	0	2	2	–

CAREER: BOWLING

	O.	M.	R.	W.	AV.
TEST					
1ST-CLASS	1487.2	349	4283	163	26.27
INT					
JPL	346.4	29	1422	52	27.34
NAT.W.	44.4	10	150	6	25.00
B & H	91.2	12	262	17	15.41

117. When was the last Gentlemen v Players match?

MOSELEY, E. A.   Glamorgan

Full Name: Ezra Alphonsa Moseley
Role: Right-hand bat, right-arm fast
medium bowler
Born: 5 January 1958, Barbados
Height: 5′ 11″ **Weight:** 12st 7lbs
Nickname: Alfie, Father Rat
County debut: 1980
1st-Class 50s scored: 1
1st-Class 5 w. in innings: 6
1st-Class catches 1986: —
(career: 14)
Parents: Mrs Muriel Edwards
Education: Christ Church High
School, Barbados
Jobs outside cricket: Stock clerk
and waiter
Family links with cricket: Related
to Hallam Moseley
Cricketers particularly learnt from:
Geoffrey Boycott, Dennis Lillee, John Snow, Fred Rumsey
Other sports played: Table-tennis
Relaxations: Horse-racing, volleyball, listening to music
Extras: Recommended to Glamorgan by Trevor Bailey and Reg Simpson
Best batting performance: 70* Glamorgan v Kent, Canterbury 1980
Best bowling performance: 6-23 Glamorgan v Australia, Swansea 1981

LAST SEASON: BATTING

	I.	N.O.	R.	H.S.	AV.
TEST					
1ST-CLASS	8	1	55	19	7.85
INT					
JPL					
NAT.W.	1	0	4	4	—
B & H	2	1	34	25	—

LAST SEASON: BOWLING

	O.	M.	R.	W.	AV.
TEST					
1ST-CLASS	124.3	14	447	11	40.63
INT					
JPL					
NAT.W.	7	1	12	0	
B & H	12	2	67	0	—

CAREER: BATTING

	I.	N.O.	R.	H.S.	AV.
TEST					
1ST-CLASS	71	14	1048	70*	18.38
INT					
JPL					
NAT.W.	2	0	6	4	3.00
B & H	8	3	51	25	10.20

CAREER: BOWLING

	O.	M.	R.	W.	AV.
TEST					
1ST-CLASS	1570.5	352	4579	194	23.60
INT					
JPL					
NAT.W.	30.2	8	70	4	17.50
B & H	70	13	207	8	25.87

MOXON, M. D. Yorkshire

Full Name: Martyn Douglas Moxon
Role: Right-hand bat, right-arm
medium bowler, slip fielder
Born: 4 May 1960, Barnsley
Height: 6′ 1″ **Weight:** 13st 7lbs
Nickname: Frog
County debut: 1981
County cap: 1984
Test debut: 1986
No. of Tests: 2
No. of One-Day Internationals: 5
1000 runs in a season: 2
1st-Class 50s scored: 27
1st-Class 100s scored: 14
One-Day 50s: 14
One-Day 100s: 1
Place in batting averages: 82nd
av. 33.86 (1985 39th av. 41.34)
1st-Class catches 1986: 13
(career: 69)
Parents: Audrey and Derek
Wife and date of marriage: Sue, October 1985
Education: Holgate Grammar School, Barnsley
Qualifications: 8 O-levels, 3 A-levels, HNC in Business Studies, NCA
Coaching Award
Jobs outside cricket: Bank clerk with Barclays Bank for two years before
turning professional full-time
Family links with cricket: Father and grandfather played local league cricket.
Father was coach to Wombwell Cricket Lovers' Society
Cricketing superstitions: Always put left pad on first
Overseas tours: Captain of North of England U-19 Tour of Canada, 1979;
with England to India and Australia 1984–85, England B tour to Sri Lanka
1986
Overseas teams played for: Griqualand West in South Africa 1982–83 and
1983–84
Cricketers particularly learnt from: Doug Padgett, Phil Carrick, Steve Old-
ham
Cricketers particularly admired: Viv Richards
Off-season 1986–87: Staying at home
Other sports played: Football in the local league in the winter and golf
Other sports followed: 'Am a keen supporter of Barnsley FC.'
Relaxations: Listening to most types of music, having a drink with friends
Extras: Captained Yorkshire Schools U-15s and North of England U-15s.

Played for Yorkshire Cricket Federation U-19s. Captained Yorkshire Senior Schools. Like Yorkshire colleagues, G. Stevenson and A. Sidebottom, he played for Wombwell Cricket Lovers' Society U-18 side which competes in the Joe Lumb U-18 Competition. Made the highest score by a player on his Yorkshire debut – 116 v Essex. First Yorkshire player to make centuries on his first two championship games in Yorkshire: 116 v Essex at Headingley; 111 v Derbyshire at Sheffield. Changed spectacles to contact lenses in 1981. Scored 153 in first 'Roses' innings. Picked for Lord's Test of 1984 and West Indies, but had to withdraw through injury and had to wait until 1986 to make debut

Injuries 1986: Several hand injuries
Best batting performance: 168 Yorkshire v Worcestershire, Worcester 1985
Best bowling performance: 3-26 D. B. Close's XI v Sri Lankans, Scarborough 1985

LAST SEASON: BATTING

	I.	N.O.	R.	H.S.	AV.
TEST	4	0	111	74	27.75
1ST-CLASS	29	4	871	147	34.84
INT					
JPL	8	1	177	48	25.28
NAT.W.	3	0	146	75	48.66
B & H	4	1	231	106*	77.00

CAREER: BATTING

	I.	N.O.	R.	H.S.	AV.
TEST	4	0	111	74	27.75
1ST-CLASS	170	9	5794	168	35.98
INT	5	0	132	70	26.40
JPL	38	5	944	86	28.60
NAT.W.	8	2	323	82*	53.83
B & H	15	1	593	106*	42.35

LAST SEASON: BOWLING

	O.	M.	R.	W.	AV.
TEST					
1ST-CLASS	35.4	10	113	2	56.50
INT					
JPL					
NAT.W.					
B & H					

CAREER: BOWLING

	O.	M.	R.	W.	AV.
TEST					
1ST-CLASS	267.4	42	972	17	57.17
INT					
JPL	31	0	197	3	65.66
NAT.W.	4	0	17	1	–
B & H	25	0	111	2	55.50

118. Which Irishman captained England and once offered to fight W. G. Grace at the wicket?

MUNTON, T. A. Warwickshire

Full Name: Timothy Alan Munton
Role: Right-hand bat, right-arm
fast-medium bowler
Born: 30 July 1965, Melton
Mowbray
Height: 6′ 5″
County debut: 1985
Place in bowling averages: —
52 av. 28.28
1st-Class catches 1986: 1 (career: 1)
Education: Sarson High School,
King Edward VII Upper School
Extras: Appeared for Leicestershire
2nd XI 1982–84
Best batting performance: 19
Warwickshire v Hampshire,
Portsmouth 1986
Best bowling performance: 4-60
Warwickshire v Kent, Edgbaston 1986

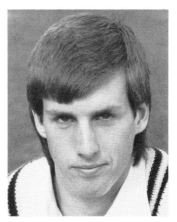

LAST SEASON: BATTING

	I.	N.O.	R.	H.S.	AV.
TEST					
1ST-CLASS	15	6	58	19	6.44
INT					
JPL	3	2	10	5*	–
NAT.W.					
B & H					

CAREER: BATTING

	I.	N.O.	R.	H.S.	AV.
TEST					
1ST-CLASS	15	6	58	19	6.44
INT					
JPL	3	2	10	5*	–
NAT.W.					
B & H	2	2	0	0*	–

LAST SEASON: BOWLING

	O.	M.	R.	W.	AV.
TEST					
1ST-CLASS	297.4	68	905	32	28.28
INT					
JPL	62	4	309	10	30.90
NAT.W.					
B & H	32	3	102	4	25.50

CAREER: BOWLING

	O.	M.	R.	W.	AV.
TEST					
1ST-CLASS	306.4	68	940	32	29.37
INT					
JPL	62	4	309	10	30.90
NAT.W.					
B & H	32	3	102	4	25.50

119. When was overarm bowling legalized: 1799, 1823, 1864?

MURPHY, A. J.   Lancashire

Full Name: Anthony John Murphy
Role: Right-hand bat,
right-arm medium bowler
Born: 6 August 1962, Manchester
Height: 6′ 0″ **Weight:** 14st
Nickname: Audi, Headless
County debut: 1985
1st-Class catches 1986: 2 (career: 2)
Parents: John Desmond and
Elizabeth Catherine
Marital status: Single
Education: Xaverian College,
Manchester; Swansea University
Qualifications: 9 O-levels, 4 A-levels
Jobs outside cricket: Computer
operator for Barclays Bank
Family links with cricket: Brother
plays club cricket
Overseas tours: Kenya 1986 with Minor Counties U-25s
Overseas teams played for: Central Districts & Taradale CC, New Zealand,
1985–86
Off-season 1986–87: Playing in New Zealand
Other sports played: Any
Other sports followed: American football
Relaxations: Sunbathing on foreign beaches
Injuries 1986: Shoulder and side injuries – out for two months
Best batting performance: 2* Lancashire v Leicestershire, Leicester 1985
Best bowling performance: 3-67 Lancashire v Nottinghamshire, Southport
1986

LAST SEASON: BATTING

	I.	N.O.	R.	H.S.	AV.
TEST					
1ST-CLASS	3	3	2	1*	
INT					
JPL	1	1	2	2*	
NAT.W.					
B & H					

CAREER: BATTING

	I.	N.O.	R.	H.S.	AV.
TEST					
1ST-CLASS	10	5	6	2*	1.20
INT					
JPL					
NAT.W.					
B & H					

LAST SEASON: BOWLING

	O.	M.	R.	W.	AV.
TEST					
1ST-CLASS	64	13	203	7	29.00
INT					
JPL	6	0	33	1	–
NAT.W.					
B & H					

CAREER: BOWLING

	O.	M.	R.	W.	AV.
TEST					
1ST-CLASS	185.5	45	600	19	31.57
INT					
JPL					
NAT.W.					
B & H					

NEALE, P. A.   Worcestershire

Full Name: Phillip Anthony Neale
Role: Right-hand bat, cover fielder
Born: 5 June 1954, Scunthorpe
Height: 5′ 11″ **Weight:** 11st 11lbs
County debut: 1975
County cap: 1978
100 runs in a season: 7
1st-Class 50s scored: 69
1st-Class 100s scored: 20
One-day 50s: 23
One-day 100s: 2
Place in batting averages: 66th
av. 36.55 (1985 32nd av. 44.09)
1st-Class catches 1986: 7 (career: 92)
Parents: Geoff and Margaret
Wife and date of marriage: Christine,
26 September 1976
Children: Kelly Joanne, 9 November 1979; Craig Andrew, 11 February 1982
Education: Frederick Gough Grammar School, Scunthorpe; John Leggot Sixth Form College, Scunthorpe; Leeds University
Qualifications: 10 O-levels, 2 A-levels, BA Hons Russian, Preliminary football and cricket coaching awards.
Cricketing superstitions: Always puts left pad on first
Cricketers particularly learnt from: Most county players – you learn by watching
Cricketers particularly admired: Basil D'Oliveira, Norman Gifford, Alan Ormrod
Off-season 1986–87: Teaching at Worcester Royal Grammar School (French, games and a little Russian); part-time soccer with Worcester City in Southern League, Premier Division
Other sports played: Squash, golf ('very badly')
Other sports followed: Most sports – mainly via TV
Relaxations: Reading, spending time with my family
Extras: Played for Lincolnshire 1973–74. Scored 100 runs before lunch v Warwickshire at Worcester, 1979. Captain 1983–. Testimonial season with Lincoln City 1984–85. Now retired from full-time football
Best batting performance: 163* Worcestershire v Nottinghamshire, Worcester 1979

	I.	N.O.	R.	H.S.	AV.
TEST					
1ST-CLASS	34	7	987	118*	36.55
INT					
JPL	15	2	230	49*	17.69
NAT.W.	3	0	79	42	26.33
B & H	4	0	133	53	33.25

LAST SEASON: BOWLING

	O.	M.	R.	W.	AV.
TEST					
1ST-CLASS					
INT					
JPL					
NAT.W.					
B & H					

CAREER: BATTING

	I.	N.O.	R.	H.S.	AV.
TEST					
1ST-CLASS	417	58	12912	163*	35.96
INT					
JPL	148	28	3423	102	28.52
NAT.W.	19	0	560	81	29.47
B & H	42	6	1135	128	31.52

CAREER: BOWLING

	O.	M.	R.	W.	AV.
TEST					
1ST-CLASS	42.4	3	201	1	–
INT					
JPL	8.2	0	50	2	25.00
NAT.W.					
B & H					

NEEDHAM, A.   Surrey

Full Name: Andrew Needham
Role: Right-hand bat, right-arm off-break bowler
Born: 23 March 1957, Calow, Derbyshire
Height: 5′ 10″ **Weight:** 10st 7lbs
Nickname: Needers
County debut: 1977
County cap: 1985
1000 runs in a season: 1
1st-Class 50s scored: 10
1st-Class 100s scored: 4
1st-Class 5 w. in innings: 5
One-day 50s: 3
Place in batting averages: 199th av. 17.06 (1985 55th av. 37.63)
Place in bowling averages: —
(1985 119th av. 44.22)
1st-Class catches 1986: 6 (career: 42)
Parents: Thomas Robin and Peggy
Wife and date of marriage: Jane Marion, 1 November 1984
Education: Ecclesbourne Grammar School, Derbyshire; Paisley Grammar School, Scotland; Watford Grammar School
Qualifications: 6 O-levels
Cricketing superstitions: Always puts left pad on first
Overseas tours: Antigua with Surrey Young Cricketers 1977–78; Hong Kong, Singapore and Bangkok with Surrey 1979–80; Bangladesh with MCC

1980–81; UAE with Barbican Touring Side 1983; South Africa with Alfred McAlpine 1983–84

Overseas team played for: Glenwood Old Boys, Durban 1979–80 and 1984

Cricketers particularly learnt from: Fred Titmus

Cricketers particularly admired: Barry Richards

Off-season 1986–87: Working with my father for Needham and Needham Ltd

Other sports played: Squash and snooker

Other sports followed: Watches Chesterfield (football), horse racing and American football

Relaxations: Horses, cards, music, learning about wines

Extras: Left Surrey after 1986 season in search of a new county

Injuries 1986: Damaged right knee sliding into an advertising hoarding at Worcester; groin injury later in season

Best batting performance: 138 Surrey v Warwickshire, The Oval 1985

Best bowling performance: 6-30 Surrey v Oxford University, The Oval 1983

LAST SEASON: BATTING

	I.	N.O.	R.	H.S.	AV.
TEST					
1ST-CLASS	17	2	256	52	17.06
INT					
JPL	7	1	111	49	18.50
NAT.W.	2	0	17	13	8.50
B & H	1	0	8	8	–

LAST SEASON: BOWLING

	O.	M.	R.	W.	AV.
TEST					
1ST-CLASS	109	39	227	1	–
INT					
JPL	59	3	268	11	24.36
NAT.W.	16	3	44	5	8.80
B & H	10	3	21	0	–

CAREER: BATTING

	I.	N.O.	R.	H.S.	AV.
TEST					
1ST-CLASS	132	17	2620	138	22.78
INT					
JPL	39	8	594	55	19.16
NAT.W.	3	0	43	26	14.33
B & H	6	1	106	30	21.20

CAREER: BOWLING

	O.	M.	R.	W.	AV.
TEST					
1ST-CLASS	1497.3	374	4429	104	42.58
INT					
JPL	134.3	7	697	22	31.68
NAT.W.	27	3	99	7	14.14
B & H	19	3	61	0	–

---

120. Which Somerset bowler had the following analysis in a John Player League game in 1969? 8–8–0–0?

NEWELL, M.   Nottinghamshire

Full Name: Michael Newell
Role: Right-hand opening bat,
occasional wicket-keeper
Born: 25 February 1965, Blackburn
Height: 5′ 8″ **Weight:** 11st 3lbs
Nickname: Sam, Judas, Mule or Dot
County debut: 1984
1st-Class 50s scored: 9
1st-Class 100s scored: 1
Place in batting averages: 43rd
av. 41.04 (1985 160th av. 23.77)
1st-Class catches 1986: 15
(career: 25)
Parents: Barry and Janet
Marital status: Single
Education: West Bridgford
Comprehensive
Qualifications: 8 O-levels, 3 A-levels.
Qualified coach
Jobs outside cricket: Part-time
barman; has worked in children's
home; packer at Gunn and Moore
Family links with cricket: 'Father chairman of local club for which my brother
Paul plays.'
Cricketing superstitions: Always puts right pad on first; always bats in short
sweater and long-sleeved shirt
Overseas tours: NCA U-19 tour to Holland 1983
Overseas teams played for: Nedland CC, Perth 1985–86

LAST SEASON: BATTING

	I.	N.O.	R.	H.S.	AV.
TEST					
1ST-CLASS	30	9	862	112*	41.04
INT					
JPL					
NAT.W.					
B & H					

CAREER: BATTING

	I.	N.O.	R.	H.S.	AV.
TEST					
1ST-CLASS	50	10	1280	112*	32.00
INT					
JPL					
NAT.W.					
B & H					

LAST SEASON: BOWLING

	O.	M.	R.	W.	AV.
TEST					
1ST-CLASS	2	0	19	0	–
INT					
JPL					
NAT.W.					
B & H					

CAREER: BOWLING

	O.	M.	R.	W.	AV.
TEST					
1ST-CLASS	18	2	95	1	–
INT					
JPL					
NAT.W.					
B & H					

Cricketers particularly learnt from: All the batsmen at Nottinghamshire, Mike Bore and Bob White
Cricketers particularly admired: Richard Hadlee and Graham Gooch
Other sports played: Football ('of a low standard')
Other sports followed: Watches rugby union and football
Relaxations: Good films, music and drinking
Best batting performance: 112* Nottinghamshire v Oxford University, Oxford 1986

NEWMAN, P. G. Derbyshire

Full Name: Paul Geoffrey Newman
Role: Right-hand bat, right-arm fast-medium bowler
Born: 10 January 1959, Leicester
Height: 6′ 2½″ **Weight:** 13st 7lbs
Nickname: Judge
County debut: 1980
50 wickets in a season: 1
1st-Class 50s scored: 3
1st-Class 100s scored: 1
1st-Class 5 w. in innings: 3
One-day 50s: 1
Place in batting averages: —
(1985 163rd av. 23.23)
Place in bowling averages: —
(1985 60th av. 31.31)
1st-Class catches 1986: 1 (career: 19)

Marital status: Single
Education: Alderman Newton's Grammar School, Leicester
Qualifications: 6 O-levels
Jobs outside cricket: Various temporary jobs
Cricketing superstitions: Always wears wrist bands to bowl. Puts left pad on first
Overseas tours: English Counties XI to Zimbabwe 1985
Overseas teams played for: Queensland Cricket Association Colts XI, 1981–82; Old Collegians and Pietermaritzburg, South Africa, 1983–84 and 1985–86
Other sports played: Golf, football, snooker, pool
Relaxations: Crosswords, Barry Manilow's music, TV, watching Leicester FC, keeping up scrapbooks and eating
Extras: Played for Leicestershire 2nd XI in 1978 and 1979, but was released.

As a schoolboy, was a wicket-keeper. Took 50 wickets in his first season with Derbyshire. Won Commercial Union U-23 Bowling Award for 1981. Won Whitbread Scholarship to Brisbane, Australia 1981–82

Best batting performance: 115 Derbyshire v Leicestershire, Chesterfield 1985
Best bowling performance: 7-104 Derbyshire v Surrey, The Oval 1984

LAST SEASON: BATTING

	I.	N.O.	R.	H.S.	AV.
TEST					
1ST-CLASS	4	2	62	34	31.00
INT					
JPL	2	0	24	23	12.00
NAT.W.	–	–	–	–	–
B & H	1	0	7	7	–

LAST SEASON: BOWLING

	O.	M.	R.	W.	AV.
TEST					
1ST-CLASS	73.1	16	198	9	22.00
INT					
JPL	16	1	72	3	24.00
NAT.W.	6	2	13	1	–
B & H	28.2	1	96	5	19.20

CAREER: BATTING

	I.	N.O.	R.	H.S.	AV.
TEST					
1ST-CLASS	102	18	1315	115	15.65
INT					
JPL	29	7	254	46	11.54
NAT.W.	4	1	69	35	23.00
B & H	12	6	145	56*	24.17

CAREER: BOWLING

	O.	M.	R.	W.	AV.
TEST					
1ST-CLASS	1953	351	6679	205	32.58
INT					
JPL	394	23	1734	63	27.52
NAT.W.	81.4	9	258	9	28.66
B & H	179.1	22	688	25	27.52

NEWPORT, P. J. — Worcestershire

Full Name: Philip John Newport
Role: Right-hand bat, right-arm fast-medium bowler, outfielder
Born: 11 October 1962, High Wycombe
Height: 6' 2" **Weight:** 13st 7lbs
Nickname: Newps, Spike, Schnozz
County debut: 1982
County cap: 1986
50 wickets in a season: 1
1st-Class 50s scored: 1
1st-Class 5 w. in innings: 9
1st-Class 10 w. in match: 1
Place in batting averages: 174th av. 21.92 (1985 179th av. 21.13)
Place in bowling averages: 30th av. 25.24 (1985 26th av. 26.39)
1st-Class catches 1986: 8 (career: 13)
Parents: John and Sheila Diana
Wife and date of marriage: Christine, 26 October 1985

Education: Royal Grammar School, High Wycombe; Portsmouth Polytechnic
Qualifications: 8 O-levels, 3 A-levels, BA (Hons) Geography, basic coaching qualification
Jobs outside cricket: Schoolmaster at Worcester Royal Grammar School 1985–86
Family links with cricket: 'Father is a good club cricketer, my younger brother Stewart plays with High Wycombe CC.'
Cricketing superstitions: 'Always put a 10p in left pocket when batting.'
Overseas tours: With NCA to Denmark 1981
Cricketers particularly admired: Richard Hadlee
Off-season 1986–87: Coaching and playing in New Plymouth, New Zealand
Other sports played: Soccer, rugby union
Other sports followed: American football, golf and athletics
Relaxations: Listening to music, reading; in New Zealand surfing, water-skiing, horse riding
Injuries 1986: Sprained left wrist
Extras: Had trial as schoolboy for Southampton FC. Played cricket for NAYC England Schoolboys 1981. Also for Buckinghamshire in Minor Counties in 1981. Minor Counties final 1982. Wears contact lens in left eye only
Opinions on cricket: 'Sponsored incentive schemes such as Webster's Yorkshire Bitter scheme for fast bowlers certainly add to a player's determination to do well. Schemes for run-scoring, boundary hitting, catches, etc., etc. are a great idea and I hope to see more introduced.'
Best batting performance: 68 Worcestershire v Derbyshire, Derby 1986
Best bowling performance: 6-48 Worcestershire v Hampshire, Worcester 1986

LAST SEASON: BATTING

	I.	N.O.	R.	H.S.	AV.
TEST					
1ST-CLASS	17	4	285	68	21.92
INT					
JPL	7	1	46	17*	7.66
NAT.W.	1	0	15	15	–
B & H	2	0	20	15	10.00

LAST SEASON: BOWLING

	O.	M.	R.	W.	AV.
TEST					
1ST-CLASS	632.3	90	2146	85	25.24
INT					
JPL	57	0	323	4	80.75
NAT.W.	36	5	114	4	28.50
B & H	26	0	91	1	–

CAREER: BATTING

	I.	N.O.	R.	H.S.	AV.
TEST					
1ST-CLASS	63	21	920	68	21.90
INT					
JPL	15	5	128	24	12.80
NAT.W.	3	1	44	25	22.00
B & H	2	0	20	15	10.00

CAREER: BOWLING

	O.	M.	R.	W.	AV.
TEST					
1ST-CLASS	1287.3	181	4405	161	27.36
INT					
JPL	150	1	759	18	42.16
NAT.W.	63.2	7	227	5	45.40
B & H	26	0	91	1	–

Full Name: Mark Charles Jefford Nicholas
Role: Right-hand bat, right-arm medium bowler, slip fielder
Born: 29 September 1957, London
Height: 5′ 11½″ **Weight:** 12st 7lbs
Nickname: Skip, Cappy, Leader, Busby
County debut: 1978
County cap: 1982
1000 runs in a season: 4
1st-Class 50s scored: 36
1st-Class 100s scored: 15
1st-Class 200s scored: 1
1st-Class 5 w. in innings: 1
One-day 50s: 15
One-day 100s: 1
Place in batting averages: 188th av. 18.80 (1985 50th av. 39.42)
1st-Class catches 1986: 13 (career: 115)
Parents: Anne
Marital status: Single
Education: Fernden Prep. School; Bradfield College
Qualifications: 9 O-levels, 3 A-levels
Jobs outside cricket: Worked in Classified Advertising for *The Observer*; sales for agencies; writing for papers and magazines; PR; publishing
Family links with cricket: Grandfather (F.W.H.) played for Essex as batsman and wicket-keeper and toured with MCC
Cricketing superstitions: 'Kit must fit.'
Overseas tours: Toured South Africa with Dragons (Public Schools team) 1976–77 as captain; with MCC to Bangladesh, February 1981; and to East and Central Africa, October 1981; Dubai with *Cricketer* International XI, November 1981; Dubai and Bahrain with 'England XI', March 1981; Sri Lanka with England B 1986 as captain
Overseas teams played for: Captain of Southern Lakes in Australia 1978–79 and Grosvenor/Fynnland, Durban, 1982–83, 1983–84
Cricketers particularly learnt from: Barry Richards, Mike Brearley, Graham Gooch
Other sports played: Regular football with Old Bradfieldians (Arthurian League)
Off-season 1986–87: Two tours to West Indies and Australia as courier for supporters' tour
Relaxations: Bruce Springsteen concerts

Injuries 1986: Back muscle tear – 10 days out
Extras: Appointed captain 1985
Opinions on cricket: 'Heavens above – do we have all night?!'
Best batting performance: 206* Hampshire v Oxford University, Oxford 1982
Best bowling performance: 5-45 Hampshire v Worcestershire, Southampton 1983

LAST SEASON: BATTING

	I.	N.O.	R.	H.S.	AV.
TEST					
1ST-CLASS	32	2	564	55	18.80
INT					
JPL	15	5	358	62*	35.80
NAT.W.	2	0	46	29	23.00
B & H	3	0	11	7	3.66

LAST SEASON: BOWLING

	O.	M.	R.	W.	AV.
TEST					
1ST-CLASS	64	13	198	3	66.00
INT					
JPL	42	0	254	10	25.40
NAT.W.	8	1	37	0	–
B & H	34	2	163	3	54.33

CAREER: BATTING

	I.	N.O.	R.	H.S.	AV.
TEST					
1ST-CLASS	293	33	8297	206*	31.91
INT					
JPL	86	15	1990	108	28.02
NAT.W.	19	1	391	63	21.72
B & H	27	1	544	74	20.92

CAREER: BOWLING

	O.	M.	R.	W.	AV.
TEST					
1ST-CLASS	640.4	140	2013	48	41.93
INT					
JPL	247	2	1354	49	29.63
NAT.W.	72.2	8	288	9	32.00
B & H	131	9	551	19	29.00

NORTH, P. D. Glamorgan

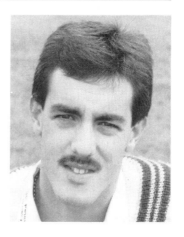

Full Name: Philip David North
Role: Right-hand bat, slow left-arm bowler
Born: 16 May 1965, Newport, Gwent
Height: 5' 6" **Weight:** 9st 7lbs
Nickname: Philge
County debut: 1986
Parents: Arthur and Audrey
Marital status: Single
Education: St Julian's Comprehensive; Nash College of Further Education
Qualifications: 5 O-levels, TEC Mechanical Engineering, qualified toolmaker.
Jobs outside cricket: Toolmaker with brake manufacturer (Lucas Girling in Cwmbran).
Gardener and window cleaner in Australia

Family links with cricket: Father played club cricket
Overseas teams played for: Southport CC, Brisbane 1985–86
Cricketers particularly learnt from: Alan Jones, Tom Cartwright
Cricketers particularly admired: Jim Pressdee
Off-season 1986–87: Playing in Australia for Penrith CC, Sydney
Other sports played: Snooker
Other sports followed: Soccer
Relaxations: Films, socialising, eating out
Injuries 1986: Tendonitis in shoulder (3 weeks), hamstring (2 weeks)
Extras: 'Nothing to do with cricket but when I was an apprentice with Lucas Girling I machined three or four disc brakes that were on Richard Noble's "Thrust II" world land speed record-breaking car.'
Opinions on cricket: 'Should play four-day cricket to ease travel and playing fatigue.'
Best batting performance: 17* Glamorgan v Lancashire, Lytham 1986
Best bowling performance: 4-49 Glamorgan v Lancashire, Lytham 1986

LAST SEASON: BATTING

	I.	N.O.	R.	H.S.	AV.
TEST					
1ST-CLASS	5	2	22	17*	7.33
INT					
JPL					
NAT.W.					
B & H					

LAST SEASON: BOWLING

	O.	M.	R.	W.	AV.
TEST					
1ST-CLASS	60.4	13	149	4	37.25
INT					
JPL					
NAT.W.					
B & H					

CAREER: BATTING

	I.	N.O.	R.	H.S.	AV.
TEST					
1ST-CLASS	6	3	22	17*	7.33
INT					
JPL					
NAT.W.					
B & H					

CAREER: BOWLING

	O.	M.	R.	W.	AV.
TEST					
1ST-CLASS	87.4	20	209	5	41.80
INT					
JPL					
NAT.W.					
B & H					

121. Who was England's first Test captain?

ONTONG, R. C.　　　　　　Glamorgan

Full Name: Rodney Craig Ontong
Role: Right-hand bat, right-arm
off-spin bowler
Born: 9 September 1955,
Johannesburg
County debut: 1975
County cap: 1979
1000 runs in a season: 5
50 wickets in a season: 5
1st-Class 50s scored: 69
1st-Class 100s scored: 17
1st-Class 200s scored: 1
1st-Class 5 w. in innings: 28
1st-Class 10 w. in match: 4
One-day 50s: 14
One-day 100s: 1
Place in batting averages: 171st
av. 22.54 (1985 21st av. 48.74)
Place in bowling averages: 48th
av. 27.71 (1985 37th av. 27.77)
1st-Class catches 1986: 8 (career: 142)
Education: Selbourne College, East London, South Africa
Overseas teams played for: Made debut in 1972–73 for Border in Currie Cup
Competition. Transferred to Transvaal for 1976–77 season, before returning
to Border
Extras: Took over Glamorgan captaincy during 1984, but resigned during
1986
Best batting performance: 204* Glamorgan v Middlesex, Swansea 1984

LAST SEASON: BATTING

	I.	N.O.	R.	H.S.	AV.
TEST					
1ST-CLASS	37	4	744	80*	22.54
INT					
JPL	15	4	268	35	24.36
NAT.W.	2	1	86	54*	–
B & H	4	1	145	58*	48.33

LAST SEASON: BOWLING

	O.	M.	R.	W.	AV.
TEST					
1ST-CLASS	606.4	153	1774	64	27.71
INT					
JPL	120	5	483	17	28.41
NAT.W.	20	3	94	3	31.38
B & H	34	6	112	1	–

CAREER: BATTING

	I.	N.O.	R.	H.S.	AV.
TEST					
1ST-CLASS	507	62	12983	204*	29.17
INT					
JPL	121	16	2468	100	23.50
NAT.W.	15	3	480	64	40.00
B & H	31	4	619	81	22.92

CAREER: BOWLING

	O.	M.	R.	W.	AV.
TEST					
1ST-CLASS	7332	1719	21359	721	29.62
INT					
JPL	796	42	3630	119	30.50
NAT.W.	141	24	548	12	45.66
B & H	285.4	53	876	42	20.85

Best bowling performance: 8-67 Glamorgan v Nottinghamshire, Trent Bridge 1985

O'SHAUGHNESSY, S. J.　　Lancashire

Full Name: Steven Joseph
O'Shaughnessy
Role: Right-hand bat, right-arm
medium bowler
Born: 9 September 1961, Bury
Height: 5' 10½"
County debut: 1980
County cap: 1985
1000 runs in a season: 1
1st-Class 50s scored: 15
1st-Class 100s scored: 5
One-day 50s: 9
One-day 100s: 1
Place in batting averages: 136th
av. 26.45 (1985 230th av. 13.09)
Place in bowling averages: —
(1985 77th av. 34.73)
1st-Class catches 1986: 5 (career: 37)
Education: Harper Green
Secondary School, Farnworth, Lancashire
Overseas tours: Canada 1979 with NCA U-19 XI; West Indies 1980 with England Young Cricketers
Relaxations: Snooker
Extras: Scored 100 in 35 minutes v Leicestershire, 11 September 1983 to equal

LAST SEASON: BATTING

	I.	N.O.	R.	H.S.	AV.
TEST					
1ST-CLASS	14	3	291	74	26.45
INT					
JPL	8	0	208	51	26.00
NAT.W.	4	1	120	62	40.00
B & H	3	0	31	14	10.33

CAREER: BATTING

	I.	N.O.	R.	H.S.	AV.
TEST					
1ST-CLASS	145	23	3292	159*	26.98
INT					
JPL	62	11	1165	101*	22.84
NAT.W.	14	4	264	62	26.40
B & H	20	0	477	90	23.85

LAST SEASON: BOWLING

	O.	M.	R.	W.	AV.
TEST					
1ST-CLASS	97	18	363	5	18.15
INT			1		
JPL	64	2	357	8	44.62
NAT.W.	46	3	228	3	76.00
B & H	16	1	95	0	—

CAREER: BOWLING

	O.	M.	R.	W.	AV.
TEST					
1ST-CLASS	1030.3	182	3592	103	34.87
INT					
JPL	391.1	13	1921	48	40.02
NAT.W.	135	13	563	13	43.30
B & H	157	29	548	24	24.33

fastest first-class century scored by Percy Fender in 1920 (the bowling to O'Shaughnessy was not of the highest standard)
Best batting performance: 159* Lancashire v Somerset, Bath 1984
Best bowling performance: 4-66 Lancashire v Nottinghamshire, Trent Bridge 1982

PALMER, G. V. Somerset

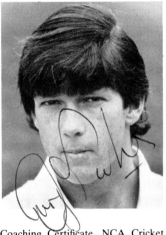

Full Name: Gary Vincent Palmer
Role: Right-hand bat, right-arm fast-medium bowler
Born: 1 November 1965, Taunton
Height: 6′ 1″ **Weight:** 11st 7lbs
Nickname: Pedlar
County debut: 1982
1st-Class 50s scored: 2
1st-Class 5 w. in innings: 1
One-day 50s: 1
Place in batting averages: —
(1985 184th av. 20.50)
1st-Class catches 1986: 1 (career: 26)
Parents: Kenneth Ernest and Joy Valerie
Marital status: Single
Education: North Town Junior School; Queen's College, Junior and Senior
Qualifications: SRA Part 1 Squash Coaching Certificate, NCA Cricket Coaching Award, GCEs
Jobs outside cricket: Squash coaching
Family links with cricket: Father, K. E. Palmer, played for Somerset and England. Toured Pakistan with Commonwealth team, 1963. Test Umpire. Coach at Somerset CCC in winter. Grandfather did the double for 13 consecutive seasons in club cricket, and scored 25 centuries for Devizes CC
Overseas tours: English Schools U-19 to Zimbabwe 1982–83; England Young Cricketers to West Indies 1984–85
Cricketers particularly learnt from: 'Learnt from my father from an early age.'
Cricketers particularly admired: Viv Richards, Joel Garner, Ian Botham
Other sports played: Squash
Relaxations: 'Listening to music – the up-to-date variety.'
Extras: Somerset U-19 Squash champion. Youngest professional ever; had summer contract with Somerset at 14. Captain of England U-15. English Schools U-16 Cricketer of the Year. Possibly youngest cricketer to play for

England U-19. Made debut for Somerset 1st XI at 16. Opened his first class career v Leicestershire by bowling two maidens
Best batting performance: 78 Somerset v Gloucestershire, Bristol 1983
Best bowling performance: 5-38 Somerset v Warwickshire, Taunton 1983

LAST SEASON: BATTING

	I.	N.O.	R.	H.S.	AV.
TEST					
1ST-CLASS	6	0	31	17	5.17
INT					
JPL	4	2	42	33	21.00
NAT.W.					
B & H	1	0	53	53	–

CAREER: BATTING

	I.	N.O.	R.	H.S.	AV.
TEST					
1ST-CLASS	52	7	646	78	14.35
INT					
JPL	18	9	179	33	19.88
NAT.W.	–	–	–	–	–
B & H	5	1	77	53	19.25

LAST SEASON: BOWLING

	O.	M.	R.	W.	AV.
TEST					
1ST-CLASS	81	9	290	5	58.00
INT					
JPL	28	0	177	8	22.12
NAT.W.					
B & H	6	1	20	2	10.00

CAREER: BOWLING

	O.	M.	R.	W.	AV.
TEST					
1ST-CLASS	794	126	2891	62	46.62
INT					
JPL	169.4	1	922	29	31.79
NAT.W.	20	0	102	1	–
B & H	57	4	260	7	37.14

PARKER, P. W. G.   Sussex

Full Name: Paul William Giles Parker
Role: Right-hand bat, right-arm leg-break bowler
Born: 15 January 1956, Bulawayo, Rhodesia
Height: 5′ 10½″ **Weight:** 12st
Nickname: Porky, Polly
County debut: 1976
County cap: 1979
Test debut: 1981
1000 runs in a season: 7
1st-Class 50s scored: 62
1st-Class 100s scored: 30
1st-Class 200s scored: 1
One-day 50s: 32
One-day 100s: 4
Place in batting averages: 29th
av. 44.30 (1985 78th av. 34.08)
1st-Class catches 1986: 18 (career: 164)
Parents: Anthony John and Margaret Edna
Wife and date of marriage: Teresa, 25 January 1980

Children: James William Ralph, 6 November 1980; Jocelyn Elizabeth, 10 September 1984
Education: Collyer's Grammar School; St Catharine's College, Cambridge
Qualifications: MA (Cantab.)
Jobs outside cricket: Winter employment with Messrs Laing & Cruickshank (Stockbrokers), London
Family links with cricket: Father played with Essex II. Uncle, David Green, played for Northamptonshire and Worcestershire. Two brothers, Guy and Rupert, 'very keen and active cricketers'. Father wrote *The Village Cricket Match* and was sports editor with ITN
Overseas tours: Combined Oxford & Cambridge XI tour of Australia 1979–80
Overseas teams played for: Sturt CC, Adelaide, Australia, 1979–80; Natal, South Africa, 1980–81
Cricketers particularly learnt from: J. Denman, Sussex CCC
Other sports played: Most ball games
Relaxations: Reading, crosswords, bridge, music
Extras: Was selected for Cambridge against Oxford rugby match in 1977 but had to withdraw through injury. Was first reserve for England in Australia tour 1979–80. Vice-captain of Sussex
Opinions on cricket: Advocates four-day cricket and the continuance of covered wickets
Best batting performance: 215 Cambridge University v Essex, Cambridge 1976
Best bowling performance: 2-21 Sussex v Surrey, Guildford 1984

LAST SEASON: BATTING

	I.	N.O.	R.	H.S.	AV.
TEST					
1ST-CLASS	43	7	1595	125	44.30
INT					
JPL	16	1	623	92	41.53
NAT.W.	5	1	151	85	37.75
B & H	5	0	60	20	12.00

LAST SEASON: BOWLING

	O.	M.	R.	W.	AV.
TEST					
1ST-CLASS	3	1	13	0	–
INT					
JPL					
NAT.W.					
B & H					

CAREER: BATTING

	I.	N.O.	R.	H.S.	AV.
TEST	2	0	13	13	6.50
1ST-CLASS	412	59	12651	215	35.83
INT					
JPL	132	20	3247	121*	28.99
NAT.W.	29	4	900	109	36.00
B & H	45	4	1052	77	25.65

CAREER: BOWLING

	O.	M.	R.	W.	AV.
TEST					
1ST-CLASS	140.3	24	566	10	56.60
INT					
JPL	5	0	20	2	10.00
NAT.W.	2	0	17	1	–
B & H					

PARKS, R. J.   Hampshire

Full Name: Robert James Parks
Role: Right-hand bat, wicket-keeper
Born: 15 June 1959, Cuckfield,
Sussex
Height: 5′ 7½″ **Weight:** 10st 7lbs
Nickname: Bobby
County debut: 1980
County cap: 1982
1st-Class 50s scored: 11
Place in batting averages: 162nd
av. 23.33 (1985 143rd av. 25.13)
Parents: James and Irene
Wife and date of marriage: Amanda,
30 January 1982
Education: Eastbourne Grammar
School; Southampton Institute of
Technology
Qaulifications: 9 O-levels, 1 A-level,
OND and HND in Business
Studies

Jobs outside cricket: Training in accountancy, working for Jardine Air Cargo
Family links with cricket: Father, Jim Parks, played for Sussex and England,
as did his grandfather, J. H. Parks. Uncle, H. W. Parks, also played for Sussex

LAST SEASON: BATTING

	I.	N.O.	R.	H.S.	AV.
TEST					
1ST-CLASS	23	5	420	80	23.33
INT					
JPL	2	2	14	10*	–
NAT.W.	1	0	6	6	–
B & H	1	0	16	16	–

CAREER: BATTING

	I.	N.O.	R.	H.S.	AV.
TEST					
1ST-CLASS	170	41	2342	89	18.15
INT					
JPL	31	17	290	36*	20.71
NAT.W.	8	3	67	25	13.40
B & H	18	6	109	16	9.08

LAST SEASON: BOWLING

	O.	M.	R.	W.	AV.
TEST					
1ST-CLASS	23	1	110	0	–
INT					
JPL					
NAT.W.					
B & H					

CAREER: BOWLING

	O.	M.	R.	W.	AV.
TEST					
1ST-CLASS	23	1	110	0	–
INT					
JPL					
NAT.W.					
B & H					

LAST SEASON: WICKET-KEEPING

	C.	ST.			
TEST					
1ST-CLASS	73	8			
INT					
JPL	12	4			
NAT.W.	3	2			
B & H	3	1			

CAREER WICKET-KEEPING

	C.	ST.			
TEST					
1ST-CLASS	382	47			
INT					
JPL	98	22			
NAT.W.	21	5			
B & H	34	5			

Cricketing superstitions: Left pad on first
Overseas tours: English Counties XI to Zimbabwe 1985
Cricketers particularly learnt from: A. Knott, J. Rice
Cricketers particularly admired: R. Taylor, N. Pocock
Other sports played: Squash, football, golf
Relaxations: Stamp collecting and cycling
Extras: Broke the Hampshire record for the number of dismissals in a match, against Derbyshire in 1982 (10 catches). Took over from Bob Taylor as stand-in wicket-keeper for England v New Zealand at Lord's after injury to Bruce French
Best batting performance: 89 Hampshire v Cambridge University, Cambridge 1984

PARSONS, G. J.   Warwickshire

Full Name: Gordon James Parsons
Role: Left-hand bat, right-arm medium bowler, outfielder
Born: 17 October 1959, Slough
Height: 6' 1" **Weight:** 13st 6lbs
Nickname: Bullhead, Triangle
County debut: 1978 (Leicestershire), 1986 (Warwickshire)
County cap: 1984 (Leicestershire)
50 wickets in a season: 2
1st-Class 50s scored: 15
1st-Class 5 w. in innings: 9
1st-Class 10 w. in match: 1
Place in batting averages: 201st av. 16.94 (1985 221st av. 14.17)
Place in bowling averages: 93rd av. 38.03 (1985 116th av. 43.91)
1st-Class catches 1986: 3 (career: 44)
Parents: Dave and Evelyn
Marital status: Single
Education: Woodside County Secondary School, Slough
Qualifications: 5 O-levels
Jobs outside cricket: Worked as clerk at T. L. Bennett, Ratby, Leicester
Family links with cricket: Father played club cricket
Overseas tours: Australasia with Derrick Robins' U-23 XI 1979–80; ESCA tour to India 1977–78; Zimbabwe with Leicestershire 1981
Overseas teams played for: Maharaja's in Sri Lanka, 1979, 1981–82, 1982–83; Boland, South Africa, 1983–84

Cricketers particularly learnt from: 'Alf Gover, Ken Higgs, Roger Tolchard and Andy Roberts have given me plenty of good advice. Plus too many to mention – particularly in the team.'

Cricketers particularly admired: Jonathan Agnew, Mike Garnham, David Allett

Other sports played: Golf

Extras: Played for Leicester 2nd XI since 1976 and also for Buckinghamshire in 1977. Left Leicestershire after 1985 season and joined Warwickshire

Best batting performance: 76 Boland v Western Province B, Cape Town 1984–85

Best bowling performance: 9-72 Boland v Transvaal B, Johannesburg 1984–85

LAST SEASON: BATTING

	I.	N.O.	R.	H.S.	AV.
TEST					
1ST-CLASS	24	5	322	58*	16.94
INT					
JPL	7	3	43	23	10.75
NAT.W.	3	0	15	7	5.00
B & H	4	1	43	20	14.33

LAST SEASON: BOWLING

	O.	M.	R.	W.	AV.
TEST					
1ST-CLASS	371.1	72	1179	31	38.03
INT					
JPL	77	4	340	14	24.28
NAT.W.	28	8	69	2	34.50
B & H	42.4	2	170	7	24.28

CAREER: BATTING

	I.	N.O.	R.	H.S.	AV.
TEST					
1ST-CLASS	201	44	2974	76	18.94
INT					
JPL	47	14	316	24*	9.57
NAT.W.	8	0	69	23	8.62
B & H	15	7	171	29*	14.25

CAREER: BOWLING

	O.	M.	R.	W.	AV.
TEST					
1ST-CLASS	3513.5	736	11147	367	30.37
INT					
JPL	591.2	30	2617	90	29.07
NAT.W.	132.5	20	502	12	41.83
B & H	277.3	30	983	38	25.86

122. Who captained South Africa in their last tour to England in 1965?

PATEL, D. N.   Worcestershire

Full Name: Dipak Narshi Patel
Role: Right-hand bat, right-arm off-break bowler
Born: 25 October 1958, Nairobi, Kenya
Height: 5' 11½" **Weight:** 10st 9lbs
Nickname: Dip
County debut: 1976
County cap: 1979
1000 runs in a season: 6
50 wickets in a season: 2
1st-Class 50s scored: 43
1st-Class 100s scored: 17
1st-Class 5 w. in innings: 14
One-day 50s: 11
One-day 100s: 1
Place in batting averages: 20th av. 47.85 (1985 133rd av. 26.72)
Place in bowling averages: 103rd av. 41.80 (1985 86th av. 36.59)
1st-Class catches 1986: 5 (career: 135)
Parents: Narshibhai and Laxmiben
Wife and date of marriage: Vina, 27 February 1983
Education: George Salter Comprehensive School, West Bromwich, West Midlands
Qualifications: 3 O-levels
Jobs outside cricket: Sales assistant, Oakfield Tile Co. Ltd., Worcester
Family links with cricket: Three uncles played for Kenya XI. Cousin, Harshad, was on Worcestershire staff
Cricketing superstitions: Left pad on first
Overseas tours: Zambia 1977 with Warwickshire; South America 1979 with Derrick Robins' XI; Australia with U-23 XI 1979–80; Trinidad and Tobago 1984 with World Invitation XI
Overseas teams played for: Hawthorn CC, Melbourne, on Whitbread Scholarship 1979–80; Birkenhead City CC, Auckland, 1980–86
Cricketers particularly learnt from: Norman Gifford, Glenn Turner, Kapil Dev, Basil D'Oliveira
Other sports played: Golf, squash, snooker, football
Other sports followed: Watching West Bromwich Albion FC
Relaxations: TV
Extras: Has lived in UK since 1967. Discovered by Basil D'Oliveira. Shared record JPL partnership of 224 with Alan Ormrod v Hampshire at Southampton, August 1982. Shared in first-class 6th wicket partnership record for

county, 227 with E. J. O. Hemsley v Oxford University at Oxford, 1976. Vice-captain 1985

Best batting performance: 197 Worcestershire v Cambridge University, Worcester 1984

Best bowling performance: 7-46 Worcestershire v Lancashire, Worcester 1982

LAST SEASON: BATTING

	I.	N.O.	R.	H.S.	AV.
TEST					
1ST-CLASS	30	9	1005	132*	47.85
INT					
JPL	14	2	315	48	26.25
NAT.W.	3	1	57	31*	28.50
B & H	4	0	85	76	21.25

LAST SEASON: BOWLING

	O.	M.	R.	W.	AV.
TEST					
1ST-CLASS	453.2	115	1254	30	41.80
INT					
JPL	68	2	370	9	41.11
NAT.W.	36	10	99	4	24.75
B & H	46	6	120	4	30.00

CAREER: BATTING

	I.	N.O.	R.	H.S.	AV.
TEST					
1ST-CLASS	381	32	10379	197	29.73
INT					
JPL	131	11	2523	125	21.02
NAT.W.	16	2	305	54	21.78
B & H	36	4	727	96*	22.71

CAREER: BOWLING

	O.	M.	R.	W.	AV.
TEST					
1ST-CLASS	5064.1	1326	14021	393	35.67
INT					
JPL	579.4	19	2841	91	31.21
NAT.W.	130.1	20	435	14	31.07
B & H	256.4	27	886	29	30.55

PATTERSON, B. P.   Lancashire

Full Name: Balfour Patrick Patterson

Role: Right-hand bat, right-arm fast bowler, outfielder

Born: 15 September 1961, Portland, Jamaica

Height: 6′ 2½″ **Weight:** 14st

Nickname: Balf, Pato

County debut: 1984

Test debut: 1985–86

No. of Tests: 5

No. of One-Day Internationals: 2

1st-Class 5 w. in innings: 8

1st-Class 10 w. in match: 2

Place in bowling averages: 42nd av. 27.27 (1985 38th av. 27.90)

1st-Class catches 1986: 4 (career: 14)

Parents: Maurice and Emelda

Marital status: Single

Education: Happy Grove High School; Wolmers High School for Boys

Qualifications: Jamaica School Certificates, O-levels

Jobs outside cricket: Accounts clerk
Family links with cricket: Father and grandfather played for parish in Jamaica
Overseas teams played for: Tasmania 1984–85
Cricketers particularly learnt from: Anderson Roberts
Cricketers particularly admired: Present West Indian team; Dennis Lillee
Off-season 1986–87: Playing for Jamaica in Shell Shield and West Indies in Pakistan
Other sports played: Basketball, football, squash and table-tennis for fitness and pleasure
Other sports followed: Watches football
Relaxations: Swimming, listening to music, watching television
Best batting performance: 22 Lancashire v Northamptonshire, Lytham 1985
Best bowling performance: 7-24 Jamaica v Guyana, Kingston 1985–86

LAST SEASON: BATTING

	I.	N.O.	R.	H.S.	AV.
TEST					
1ST-CLASS	15	5	54	12*	5.40
INT					
JPL					
NAT.W.					
B & H	1	1	3	3*	–

LAST SEASON: BOWLING

	O.	M.	R.	W.	AV.
TEST					
1ST-CLASS	391.4	70	1309	48	27.27
INT					
JPL					
NAT.W.					
B & H	20	3	74	3	24.66

CAREER: BATTING

	I.	N.O.	R.	H.S.	AV.
TEST	5	3	12	9	6.00
1ST-CLASS	52	16	143	22	3.97
INT	–	–	–	–	–
JPL	1	1	3	3*	–
NAT.W.	1	0	4	4	–
B & H	2	2	18	15*	–

CAREER: BOWLING

	O.	M.	R.	W.	AV.
TEST	118.1	18	426	19	22.42
1ST-CLASS	1319.5	214	4379	152	28.80
INT	22	1	85	4	21.25
JPL	1.2	0	6	0	–
NAT.W.	12	0	69	1	–
B & H	31	4	108	4	27.00

123. Did Sir Jack Hobbs ever captain England?

PAULINE, D. B.　　　　　　　Glamorgan

Full Name: Duncan Brian Pauline
Role: Right-hand bat, right-arm
medium bowler
Born: 15 December 1960, Aberdeen
Height: 5′ 10″ **Weight:** 12st 7lbs
Nickname: The Colonel
County debut: 1979 (Surrey),
1986 (Glamorgan)
1st-Class 50s scored: 16
1st-Class 100s scored: 1
1st-Class 5 w. in innings: 1
One-day 50s: 4
Place in batting averages: 169th
av. 22.75 (1985 157th av. 24.50)
Place in bowling averages: —
(1985 90th av. 35.44)
1st-Class catches 1986: 4 (career: 22)
Parents: Brian and Vivienne
Marital status: Single
Education: Ashley Road School, Aberdeen; Bishop Fox, East Molesey
Jobs outside cricket: Pop-corn maker
Family links with cricket: Father and uncle both played in Aberdeen
Overseas tours: Australia with Young England XI 1978; Surrey CCC Far
East Tour 1979; Barbados 1985
Overseas teams played for: Glenwood Old Boys, Durban; Waverley, Sydney
Other sports played: Golf, squash, snooker and pool
Extras: Played for Surrey Schools U-12 and U-15. Played for South-East
England U-15. England U-19 v West Indies and v Australia. Opening bat for
one of England's oldest clubs, East Molesey (founded 1730). Name is

LAST SEASON: BATTING

	I.	N.O.	R.	H.S.	AV.
TEST					
1ST-CLASS	20	0	455	97	22.75
INT					
JPL	2	0	26	22	13.00
NAT.W.					
B & H	3	0	50	31	16.66

LAST SEASON: BOWLING

	O.	M.	R.	W.	AV.
TEST					
1ST-CLASS	14	0	67	2	33.50
INT					
JPL					
NAT.W.					
B & H	1	0	18	0	—

CAREER: BATTING

	I.	N.O.	R.	H.S.	AV.
TEST					
1ST-CLASS	96	6	2258	115	25.08
INT					
JPL	23	4	516	92	27.15
NAT.W.	2	0	15	10	7.50
B & H	10	1	156	69*	17.33

CAREER: BOWLING

	O.	M.	R.	W.	AV.
TEST					
1ST-CLASS	187.4	36	662	18	36.77
INT					
JPL	84	1	433	13	33.30
NAT.W.	7	0	29	0	—
B & H	22	4	99	3	33.00

pronounced with the 'ine' to rhyme with 'keen' (Scottish). Left Surrey after 1985 season to join Glamorgan
Best batting performance: 115 Surrey v Sussex, The Oval 1983
Best bowling performance: 5-52 Surrey v Derbyshire, Derby 1985

PAYNE, I. R.   Gloucestershire

Full Name: Ian Roger Payne
Role: Right-hand bat, right-arm medium bowler
Born: 9 May 1958, Kennington
Height: 5' 10" **Weight:** 13st
Nickname: Clouseau, Freda, Inspector
County debut: 1977 (Surrey), 1985 (Gloucestershire)
1st-Class 5 w. in innings: 1
One-day 50s: 1
Place in batting averages: 219th av. 13.25
Place in bowling averages: 94th av. 38.40
1st-Class catches 1986: 7 (career: 41)
Parents: Richard John and Agnes Ross

Wife and date of marriage: Julie, 22 September 1979
Children: Nicola Mary, 17 August 1984
Education: Emanuel School, Wandsworth
Qualifications: 5 O-levels, Advanced Cricket Coach
Jobs outside cricket: Many varied jobs
Cricketing superstitions: 'Always changing them as they fail, which is very often.'
Overseas tours: Antigua 1978 with Surrey Young Cricketers; Far East 1979 with Surrey; Barbados 1985 with Gloucestershire
Overseas teams played for: Nedlands CC, Perth, 1980–81, 1982–83
Cricketers particularly learnt from: Craig Sarjeant, D. K. Lillee, B. D. Richards
Other sports played: Soccer, golf, squash
Other sports followed: All except horse-racing
Relaxations: Reading, music, travelling, TV and films; watching fifth repeat of 'Star Trek'
Extras: Released at end of 1984 by Surrey after making debut in 1977

Best batting performance: 43 Surrey v Essex, The Oval 1983
Best bowling performance: 5-13 Surrey v Gloucestershire, The Oval 1983

LAST SEASON: BATTING

	I.	N.O.	R.	H.S.	AV.
TEST					
1ST-CLASS	12	4	106	30*	13.25
INT					
JPL	9	1	30	12*	3.75
NAT.W.	2	0	35	23	17.50
B & H	3	1	59	40	29.50

LAST SEASON: BOWLING

	O.	M.	R.	W.	AV.
TEST					
1ST-CLASS	215.1	58	576	15	38.40
INT					
JPL	81	1	376	4	94.00
NAT.W.	12	3	35	0	–
B & H	35.3	6	132	5	26.40

CAREER: BATTING

	I.	N.O.	R.	H.S.	AV.
TEST					
1ST-CLASS	55	10	550	43	12.22
INT					
JPL	41	15	342	37	13.15
NAT.W.	8	3	198	56*	39.60
B & H	6	1	65	40	13.00

CAREER: BOWLING

	O.	M.	R.	W.	AV.
TEST					
1ST-CLASS	639.5	165	1917	45	42.60
INT					
JPL	347	11	1757	48	36.18
NAT.W.	67	11	218	8	27.25
B & H	73.3	12	263	13	20.23

PENN, C.   Kent

Full Name: Christopher Penn
Role: Left-hand bat, right-arm
medium bowler
Born: 19 June 1963, Dover
Height: 6′ **Weight:** 14st 3lbs
Nickname: Penny, Cliff
County debut: 1982
1st-Class 50s scored: 3
1st-Class 100s scored: 1
1st-Class 5 w. in innings: 1
Place in bowling averages: —
(1985 69th av. 33.29)
1st-Class catches 1986: 1 (career: 23)
Parents: Reg and Brenda
Wife and date of marriage: Caroline,
22 March 1986
Education: Dover Grammar School
Qualifications: 8 O-levels, 2 A-levels
Jobs outside cricket: Farm worker,
car cleaner for hire company
Family links with cricket: Father
played club cricket for Dover CC for 26 years
Overseas tours: NCA tour of Denmark 1981; Whitbread Scholarship to
Australia 1982–83

Overseas teams played for: Koohinore Crescents, Johannesburg, 1981–82 and 1983–84; West Perth 1982–83; Johannesburg Municipals 1983–84; Wits University 1984–85

Cricketers particularly learnt from: 'My father, Colin Page, Brian Luckhurst, Barney Lock and many others.'

Cricketers particularly admired: Alan Knott, Dennis Lillee

Off-season 1986–87: 'Trying very hard to find employment as a cricket coach.'

Other sports played: Rugby, football, golf, squash

Other sports followed: All sports

Relaxations: Music, art and art history, Indian food, Dutch dwarf rabbits

Extras: Played for Young England and England Schools. Took hat-trick in first 2nd XI match v Middlesex when 16 years old

Opinions on cricket: 'Possibly too much car travel which could lead to a serious accident.'

Best batting performance: 115 Kent v Lancashire, Old Trafford 1984

Best bowling performance: 5-65 Kent v Somerset, Maidstone 1986

LAST SEASON: BATTING

	I.	N.O.	R.	H.S.	AV.
TEST					
1ST-CLASS	7	2	95	84*	19.00
INT					
JPL	4	0	7	4	1.75
NAT.W.					
B & H	–	–	–	–	–

LAST SEASON: BOWLING

	O.	M.	R.	W.	AV.
TEST					
1ST-CLASS	117.3	24	407	14	29.07
INT					
JPL	32	1	126	4	31.50
NAT.W.					
B & H	8	2	23	2	11.50

CAREER: BATTING

	I.	N.O.	R.	H.S.	AV.
TEST					
1ST-CLASS	38	10	592	115	21.14
INT					
JPL	19	4	119	40	7.93
NAT.W.	1	0	5	5	–
B & H	5	2	36	17	12.00

CAREER: BOWLING

	O.	M.	R.	W.	AV.
TEST					
1ST-CLASS	527.5	91	1807	45	40.15
INT					
JPL	176	7	865	28	30.89
NAT.W.	12	1	34	1	–
B & H	43	4	147	6	24.50

124. Who was the last white man to captain the West Indies?

PHILLIPSON, C. P.   Sussex

Full Name: Christopher Paul
Phillipson
Role: Right-hand bat, right-arm
medium bowler, slip fielder
Born: 10 February 1952, Vrindaban,
India
Height: 6′ 2″ **Weight:** 13st 5lbs
Nickname: Phillipo, Log
County debut: 1970
County cap: 1980
Benefit: 1985
1st-Class 50s scored: 12
1st-Class 5 w. in innings: 4
One-day 50s: 4
1st-Class catches 1986: —
(career: 135)
Parents: Rev. Christopher Quentin
and Muriel Regina
Wife and date of marriage: Adell, 24 March 1979
Children: Kirstin Jane, 3 March 1981; Christopher Ross, 14 September 1983
Education: Prebendal School, Chichester; Ardingly College; Loughborough
College
Qualifications: Teacher's certificate (PE and geography), 2 A-levels, NCA
Coaching Certificate
Family links with cricket: 'My wife's mother's family (Dell) achieved fame in
the Eastern Cape in 1908 when they formed a cricket team in Bathurst made
up solely of their own family and played as such for several years.'
Other sports played: General fitness training, running, squash and swimming
in the off-season

LAST SEASON: BATTING

	I.	N.O.	R.	H.S.	AV.
TEST					
1ST-CLASS	1	0	6	6	–
INT					
JPL	10	5	137	27*	27.40
NAT.W.	–	–	–	–	–
B & H	–	–	–	–	–

LAST SEASON: BOWLING

	O.	M.	R.	W.	AV.
TEST					
1ST-CLASS					
INT					
JPL					
NAT.W.					
B & H					

CAREER: BATTING

	I.	N.O.	R.	H.S.	AV.
TEST					
1ST-CLASS	226	61	3052	87	18.49
INT					
JPL	113	44	1485	71	21.52
NAT.W.	19	7	301	70*	25.08
B & H	29	13	390	66*	24.37

CAREER: BOWLING

	O.	M.	R.	W.	AV.
TEST					
1ST-CLASS	1787	387	5213	153	34.07
INT					
JPL	458.4	29	2141	77	27.80
NAT.W.	64.4	6	261	9	29.00
B & H	122.3	7	532	15	35.46

Relaxations: Listening to contemporary music
Extras: Retired from county cricket at end of 1986 season
Best batting performance: 87 Sussex v Hampshire, Hove 1980
Best bowling performance: 6-56 Sussex v Nottinghamshire, Hove 1972

PICK, R. A. — Nottinghamshire

Full Name: Robert Andrew Pick
Role: Left-hand bat, right-arm fast-medium bowler
Born: 19 November 1963, Nottingham
Height: 5′ 10″ **Weight:** 13st
Nickname: Dad, Chirp
County debut: 1983
50 wickets in a season: 1
1st-Class 50s scored: 2
1st-Class 5 w. in innings: 3
1st-Class 10 w. in match: 1
Place in batting averages: 222nd av. 12.87 (1985 145th av. 25.00)
Place in bowling averages: 65th av. 31.40 (1985 111th av. 42.15)
1st-Class catches 1986: 5 (career: 11)
Parents: Bob and Lillian
Marital status: Single
Jobs outside cricket: Labourer
Family links with cricket: Father, uncles and cousins all play local cricket
Education: Alderman Derbyshire Comprehensive, High Pavement College
Qualifications: 6 O-levels, 1 A-level, coaching qualification
Overseas tours: Barbados with Keith Pont Benefit 1986
Overseas teams played for: Upper Hutt CC, New Zealand 1984–85
Cricketers particularly admired: Bob White, Mike Hendrick, Mike Harris
Off-season 1986–87: Coaching/playing in New Zealand with Taita District CC
Other sports: Football, basketball and fishing
Relaxations: 'As much fishing as possible and listening to a wide range of music.'
Extras: Played three Tests for Young England against Young Australia 1983
Injuries 1986: Ankle injury
Best batting performance: 63 Nottinghamshire v Warwickshire, Nuneaton 1983
Best bowling performance: 6-68 Nottinghamshire v Yorkshire, Worksop 1986

LAST SEASON: BATTING

	I.	N.O.	R.	H.S.	AV.
TEST					
1ST-CLASS	17	1	206	55	12.87
INT					
JPL	7	2	56	24	11.20
NAT.W.	2	1	16	9*	–
B & H	2	1	3	3*	–

LAST SEASON: BOWLING

	O.	M.	R.	W.	AV.
TEST					
1ST-CLASS	469.1	88	1570	50	31.40
INT					
JPL	101.4	0	546	18	30.33
NAT.W.	33	6	96	4	24.00
B & H	65	4	256	8	32.00

CAREER: BATTING

	I.	N.O.	R.	H.S.	AV.
TEST					
1ST-CLASS	50	13	636	63	17.18
INT					
JPL	14	6	91	24	11.37
NAT.W.	5	4	57	34*	–
B & H	3	2	6	3*	–

CAREER: BOWLING

	O.	M.	R.	W.	AV.
TEST					
1ST-CLASS	1137.4	208	3939	108	36.47
INT					
JPL	251.2	4	1338	39	34.30
NAT.W.	113	14	431	13	33.15
B & H	76	4	310	8	38.75

PICKLES, C. S. Yorkshire

Full Name: Christopher Stephen Pickles
Role: Right-hand bat, right-arm medium bowler
Born: 30 January 1966, Cleckheaton
Height: 6′ 1″ **Weight:** 13st
Nickname: Pick, Piccolo
County debut: 1985
1st-Class catches 1986: — (career: 3)
Parents: Ronald Albert and Christine Mary
Marital status: Single
Education: Whitcliffe Mount School
Qualifications: Qualified cricket coach
Jobs outside cricket: Work in textiles
Family links with cricket: Father and brother both play local league cricket
Overseas tours: Bermuda in 1985 with NCA U-19 team
Cricketers particularly learnt from: Ian Steen, Doug Padgett, Steve Oldham
Cricketers particularly admired: Geoff Boycott, Richard Hadlee
Off-season 1986–87: Going to New Zealand
Other sports played: Rugby union
Relaxations: 'Going out for a pint and then having some fish and chips.'
Injuries 1986: Tore muscle in right shoulder – out for 2 weeks

Best batting performance: 31* Yorkshire v Leicestershire, Bradford 1985
Best bowling performance: 2-31 Yorkshire v Kent, Scarborough 1985

LAST SEASON: BATTING

	I.	N.O.	R.	H.S.	AV.
TEST					
1ST-CLASS					
INT					
JPL	1	1	16	16*	—
NAT.W.					
B & H					

LAST SEASON: BOWLING

	O.	M.	R.	W.	AV.
TEST					
1ST-CLASS					
INT					
JPL	8	0	51	1	—
NAT.W.					
B & H					

CAREER: BATTING

	I.	N.O.	R.	H.S.	AV.
TEST					
1ST-CLASS					
INT					
JPL	7	4	48	16*	16.00
NAT.W.					
B & H					

CAREER: BOWLING

	O.	M.	R.	W.	AV.
TEST					
1ST-CLASS					
INT					
JPL	72	4	339	8	42.37
NAT.W.					
B & H					

PIERSON, A. R. K.   Warwickshire

Full Name: Adrian Roger Kirshaw
Pierson
Role: Right-hand bat, right-arm
off-break bowler
Born: 21 July 1963, Enfield,
Middlesex
Height: 6′ 4″ **Weight:** 12st
Nickname: Skirlog, Stick
County debut: 1985
Place in batting averages: —
(1985 234th av. 12.86)
1st-Class catches 1986: — (career: 3)
Parents: Patrick Blake Kirshaw
and Patricia Margaret
Marital status: Single
Education: Lochinver House
Primary; Kent College, Canterbury;
Hatfield Polytechnic

Qualifications: 2 A-levels, Advanced Coaching Certificate
Jobs outside cricket: Worked on light aircraft at Elstree Aerodrome, 1982
Cricketing superstitions: Always puts left pad on first
Overseas tours: Barbados 1985 with Dennis Amiss Testimonial XI
Cricketers particularly learnt from: Don Wilson and Warwickshire staff
Cricketers particularly admired: John Emburey, Phil Edmonds, Tony Greig

Off-season 1986–87: Coaching cricket
Other sports played: Hockey, golf
Other sports followed: All sports
Relaxations: Music, driving
Injuries 1986: Kept out for half the season with a back injury
Extras: On Lord's groundstaff 1984–85
Opinions on cricket: 'One-day cricket could be played in coloured clothing with each team having its own strip. One-day games to be fitted in at weekends.'
Best batting performance: 42* Warwickshire v Northamptonshire, Northampton 1986
Best bowling performance: 3-92 Warwickshire v Oxford University, Oxford 1985

LAST SEASON: BATTING

	I.	N.O.	R.	H.S.	AV.
TEST					
1ST-CLASS	2	2	42	42*	–
INT					
JPL	1	1	5	5*	–
NAT.W.					
B & H	2	0	11	11	5.50

LAST SEASON: BOWLING

	O.	M.	R.	W.	AV.
TEST					
1ST-CLASS	36	5	133	2	66.50
INT					
JPL	15	1	78	1	–
NAT.W.					
B & H	22	4	58	2	29.00

CAREER: BATTING

	I.	N.O.	R.	H.S.	AV.
TEST					
1ST-CLASS	16	9	132	42*	18.85
INT					
JPL	4	1	12	5*	4.00
NAT.W.	1	1	1	1*	–
B & H	2	0	11	11	5.50

CAREER: BOWLING

	O.	M.	R.	W.	AV.
TEST					
1ST-CLASS	191	35	720	10	72.00
INT					
JPL	50	3	232	2	116.00
NAT.W.	12	2	32	0	–
B & H	22	4	58	2	29.00

125. Who was the first captain of the West Indies?

PIGOTT, A. C. S.   Sussex

Full Name: Anthony Charles Shackleton Pigott
Role: Right-hand bat, right-arm fast bowler, slip fielder
Born: 4 June 1958, London
Height: 6′ 1″ **Weight:** 12st 6lbs
Nickname: Lester
County debut: 1978
County cap: 1982
Test debut: 1983–84
No. of Tests: 1
50 wickets in a season: 2
1st-Class 50s scored: 6
1st-Class 100s scored: 1
1st-Class 5 w. in innings: 13
1st-Class 10 w. in match: 1

Place in batting averages: 22nd av. 47.66
Place in bowling averages: 50th av. 27.81 (1985 70th av. 33.32)
1st-Class catches 1986: 4 (career: 46)
Parents: Tom and Juliet
Marital status: Divorced
Children: Elliott, 15 March 1983
Education: Harrow School
Qualifications: 5 O-levels, Junior Coaching Certificate
Jobs outside cricket: Sportsmaster at Claremont Prep. School, Hastings; just bought lease of squash courts on cricket ground
Family links with cricket: Father captained club side
Overseas tours: With Derrick Robins' XI to Australasia 1980; part of England tour to New Zealand 1983–84
Overseas teams played for: Waverley CC, Sydney, Australia, 1976–77, 1977–78, 1979–80; Whitbread Scholarship 1979–80; Wellington, New Zealand, 1982–83 and 1983–84; Claremont, Cape Town, 1980–81, 1981–82
Cricketers particularly learnt from: G. G. Arnold, Imran Khan
Cricketers particularly admired: I. T. Botham, Imran Khan
Off-season 1986–87: Looking after the squash courts
Other sports played: Squash, raquets, football, tennis, rugger
Relaxations: 'My son.'
Extras: Public Schools Raquets Champion 1975. Had operation on back, April 1981, missing most of season, and was told by a specialist he would never play cricket again. First three wickets in first-class cricket were a hat-trick. Postponed wedding to make Test debut when called into England party on

tour of New Zealand. Originally going to Somerset for 1984 season, but then remained with Sussex

Opinions on cricket: 'It seems strange that every year when I look at this space most cricketers put that they would like to see four-day cricket. Nothing ever seems to happen! I think it should at least be given a chance.'

Best batting performance: 104* Sussex v Warwickshire, Edgbaston 1986

Best bowling performance: 7-74 Sussex v Northamptonshire, Eastbourne 1982

LAST SEASON: BATTING

	I.	N.O.	R.	H.S.	AV.
TEST					
1ST-CLASS	18	6	572	104*	47.66
INT					
JPL	6	4	47	18*	23.50
NAT.W.	–	–	–	–	–
B & H	2	0	23	21	11.50

CAREER: BATTING

	I.	N.O.	R.	H.S.	AV.
TEST	2	1	12	8*	–
1ST-CLASS	122	28	1798	104*	19.12
INT					
JPL	31	13	235	49	13.05
NAT.W.	4	0	70	30	17.50
B & H	12	4	48	21	6.00

LAST SEASON: BOWLING

	O.	M.	R.	W.	AV.
TEST					
1ST-CLASS	390	48	1363	49	27.81
INT					
JPL	88.3	4	413	22	18.77
NAT.W.	16	3	71	2	35.50
B & H	44	7	192	8	24.00

CAREER: BOWLING

	O.	M.	R.	W.	AV.
TEST	17	7	75	2	37.50
1ST-CLASS	2453.5	431	8284	296	27.98
INT					
JPL	458.1	17	2179	103	21.15
NAT.W.	77.4	10	269	11	24.45
B & H	173	19	752	27	27.85

POCOCK, P. I.   Surrey

Full Name: Patrick Ian Pocock
Role: Right-hand bat, right-arm off-break bowler
Born: 24 September 1946, Bangor, Caernarvonshire
Height: 6′ 1½″ **Weight:** 13st
Nickname: Percy
County debut: 1964
County cap: 1967
Benefit: 1977 (£18,500)
Test debut: 1967–68
No. of Tests: 25
No. of One-Day Internationals: 1
50 wickets in a season: 16
1st-Class 50s scored: 1
1st-Class 5 w. in innings: 60
1st-Class 10 w. in match: 7
Place in batting averages: —
(1985 217th av. 15.25)

Place in bowling averages: 86th av. 36.50 (1985 75th av. 34.00)
1st-Class catches 1986: 7 (career: 186)
Parents: James Reginald and Cecelia Frances
Wife and date of marriage: Diane, 8 March 1966
Children: Samantha, 8 March 1971; Toby, 18 May 1973
Education: Merton C of E Secondary Boys' School; Wimbledon Technical School
Qualifications: MCC Advanced Coach
Jobs outside cricket: Various posts in sales and marketing. Has own company, Pat Pocock Sports Promotions Ltd
Family links with cricket: Brothers, Nigel and Tim, are very active members of Merton Cricket Club. 'W. G. Grace's mother was a Pocock, a relative of mine.'
Overseas tours: Toured Pakistan in 1966–67; West Indies 1967–68 and 1973–74; Sri Lanka and Pakistan 1968–69; India, Pakistan and Sri Lanka 1972–73; India 1984–85
Overseas teams played for: Northern Transvaal in 1971–72 Currie Cup Competition
Other sports played: Squash and golf
Relaxations: 'Holidays.'
Extras: Organised the Chubb World Double Wicket Championship at Wembley in April 1979, the first time a cricket competition has been televised indoors. Took four wickets in four balls, five in six, six in nine and seven in eleven v Sussex at Eastbourne in 1972. Responsible for the La Manga cricket development in Spain. Recalled to England side during 1984 after eight-year absence. Captained Surrey during 1986 and then retired from 1st-Class cricket
Best batting performance: 75* Surrey v Nottinghamshire, The Oval 1968
Best bowling performance: 9-57 Surrey v Glamorgan, Cardiff 1979

LAST SEASON: BATTING

	I.	N.O.	R.	H.S.	AV.
TEST					
1ST-CLASS	20	9	93	16*	8.45
INT					
JPL	3	3	4	2*	–
NAT.W.	3	2	13	9*	–
B & H	–	–	–	–	–

CAREER: BATTING

	I.	N.O.	R.	H.S.	AV.
TEST	37	4	206	33	6.24
1ST-CLASS	548	152	4661	75*	11.77
INT	1	0	4	4	–
JPL	104	38	492	22	7.45
NAT.W.	20	7	77	14	5.92
B & H	32	16	124	19	7.75

LAST SEASON: BOWLING

	O.	M.	R.	W.	AV.
TEST					
1ST-CLASS	394.5	107	1095	30	36.50
INT					
JPL	41	1	225	7	32.14
NAT.W.	42.4	11	112	6	18.66
B & H	35	8	123	4	30.75

CAREER: BOWLING

	O.	M.	R.	W.	AV.
TEST	1108.2	279	2976	67	44.42
1ST-CLASS	15662.1	4553	39672	1540	25.76
INT	10	1	20	0	–
JPL	1413	130	5795	213	27.20
NAT.W.	353.4	77	961	37	25.97
B & H	691.4	127	2168	76	28.52

Full Name: Ian Leslie Pont
Role: Right-hand bat, right-arm fast-medium bowler, outfielder
Born: 28 August 1961, Brentwood
Height: 6' 3" **Weight:** 14st
Nickname: Pud, Puck, Pike, Ponty
County debut: 1985
1st-Class 5 w. in innings: 1
1st-Class catches 1986: 1 (career: 2)
Parents: Duncan and Eileen
Marital status: Single
Education: Brentwood School, Essex
Qualifications: 7 O-levels, 3 A-levels, NCA Cricket Coach
Family links with cricket: Brother Keith at Essex
Overseas tours: Public Schools, India 1978–79 and Australia 1979–80; NCA Young Cricketers to Canada 1980
Overseas teams played for: Durban 1985–86
Cricketers particularly learnt from: Richard Hadlee, Bob White, John Lever
Cricketers particularly admired: Richard Hadlee
Other sports played: Hockey, darts, javelin, baseball
Other sports followed: Watches soccer, golf
Relaxations: Reading psychology books
Extras: Spent time on Nottinghamshire staff before joining Essex. Also appeared for Buckinghamshire. Took hat-trick in 2nd XI match v Gloucester-

LAST SEASON: BATTING

	I.	N.O.	R.	H.S.	AV.
TEST					
1ST-CLASS	6	3	73	43	24.33
INT					
JPL					
NAT.W.					
B & H					

LAST SEASON: BOWLING

	O.	M.	R.	W.	AV.
TEST					
1ST-CLASS	50.2	6	190	3	63.33
INT					
JPL					
NAT.W.					
B & H					

CAREER: BATTING

	I.	N.O.	R.	H.S.	AV.
TEST					
1ST-CLASS	20	6	169	43	12.07
INT					
JPL	–	–	–	–	–
NAT.W.	1	1	7	7*	–
B & H	2	1	18	13*	–

CAREER: BOWLING

	O.	M.	R.	W.	AV.
TEST					
1ST-CLASS	260	37	1039	27	38.48
INT					
JPL	49	0	222	7	31.72
NAT.W.	21	2	79	1	–
B & H	26.5	6	101	1	–

shire, 1985. Has come close to breaking world record for throwing the cricket ball. Took up javelin with coaching from Fatima Whitbread's mother. Has also had trials as a pitcher with New York Yankees baseball team
Best batting performance: 43 Essex v New Zealand, Chelmsford 1986
Best bowling performance: 5-103 Essex v Somerset, Taunton 1985

PONT, K. R. Essex

Full Name: Keith Rupert Pont
Role: Right-hand bat, right-arm medium bowler
Born: 16 January 1953, Wanstead
Height: 6′ 2″ **Weight:** 13st
Nickname: Monty, Plod, Ponty, Rodney Port, Vintage
County debut: 1970
County cap: 1976
Benefit: 1986
1st-Class 50s scored: 35
1st-Class 100s: 7
1st-Class 5 w. in innings: 2
One-day 50s scored: 5
Place in batting averages: 234th av. 11.83 (1985 153rd av. 24.50)
1st-Class catches 1986: 1 (career: 92)
Wife: Veronica
Education: Secondary school

Jobs outside cricket: Has been furniture representative, insurance clerk and in road haulage management
Family links with cricket: Younger brother Ian played for England U-19, and

LAST SEASON: BATTING

	I.	N.O.	R.	H.S.	AV.
TEST					
1ST-CLASS	13	1	142	36	11.83
INT					
JPL	5	2	101	34	33.66
NAT.W.	2	0	20	20	10.00
B & H	1	0	24	24	–

LAST SEASON: BOWLING

	O.	M.	R.	W.	AV.
TEST					
1ST-CLASS	35.5	8	102	4	25.50
INT					
JPL	37	1	177	6	29.50
NAT.W.	12	1	55	0	–
B & H					

CAREER: BATTING

	I.	N.O.	R.	H.S.	AV.
TEST					
1ST-CLASS	305	44	6558	125*	25.12
INT					
JPL	142	31	1968	53*	17.72
NAT.W.	22	2	265	39	13.25
B & H	14	10	648	60*	20.90

CAREER: BOWLING

	O.	M.	R.	W.	AV.
TEST					
1ST-CLASS	1087.4	214	3189	96	33.21
INT					
JPL	551.4	38	2533	96	26.38
NAT.W.	88.5	10	338	12	28.16
B & H	226.2	19	878	33	26.60

Nottinghamshire and now plays for Essex. Elder brother Kelvin was on MCC staff

Cricketing superstitions: 'None really, touch wood.'
Other sports played: Scuba-diving, golf
Other sports followed: Watches skiing
Extras: The first person to pedal on a bicycle from third man to third man whilst a first-class match is in progress, while playing for Essex. Released at end of 1986 season
Best batting performance: 125* Essex v Glamorgan, Southend 1983
Best bowling performance: 5-17 Essex v Glamorgan, Cardiff 1982

POTTER, L. Leicestershire

Full Name: Laurie Potter
Role: Right-hand bat, slow left-arm bowler, slip fielder
Born: 7 November 1962, Bexleyheath, Kent
Height: 6′ 1″ **Weight:** 14st
Nickname: Potts, Liz, Lounge
County debut: 1981 (Kent), 1986 (Leicestershire)
1st-Class 50s scored: 19
1st-Class 100s scored: 4
One-day 50s: 5
One-day 100s: 2
Place in batting averages: 183rd av. 20.18 (1985 196th av. 18.85)
Place in bowling averages: 66th av. 31.80 (1985 87th av. 36.76)
1st-Class catches 1986: 17 (career: 63)
Parents: Ronald Henry Ernest and Audrey Megan
Wife and date of marriage: Diana Frances, 28 September 1985
Education: Kelmscott Senior High School, Perth, Western Australia
Qualifications: Australian leaving exams
Overseas tours: With Australian U-19 team to Pakistan 1981
Overseas teams played for: Australia U-19 team, West Perth CC, 1977–82; Griqualand West, 1984–85 and 1985–86 as captain
Cricketers particularly learnt from: Norman O'Neill, Alan Beukas (Griqualand West), majority of senior players
Cricketers particularly admired: Derek Underwood, Alan Knott

Off-season 1986–87: 'At new home in Leicestershire with wife.'
Other sports played: Australian rules football, soccer, squash
Relaxations: Music, watching movies (cinema), reading, following sports
Injuries 1986: Broken toe
Extras: Captained Australia U-19 team to Pakistan 1981. Played for Young England v Young India 1981. Parents emigrated to Australia when he was 4. His mother wrote to Kent in 1978 asking for trial for him. Captained Young Australia as well as Young England. Decided to leave Kent after 1985 season and joined Leicestershire.
Best batting performance: 165* Griqualand West v Border, East London 1984–85
Best bowling performance: 4-52 Griqualand West v Boland, Stellenbosch 1985–86

LAST SEASON: BATTING

	I.	N.O.	R.	H.S.	AV.
TEST					
1ST-CLASS	30	3	545	81*	20.18
INT					
JPL	14	1	522	105	40.15
NAT.W.	3	0	36	24	12.00
B & H	4	0	151	112	37.75

CAREER: BATTING

	I.	N.O.	R.	H.S.	AV.
TEST					
1ST-CLASS	131	11	3259	165*	27.15
INT					
JPL	44	2	1099	105	26.16
NAT.W.	5	0	122	45	24.40
B & H	7	0	235	112	33.57

LAST SEASON: BOWLING

	O.	M.	R.	W.	AV.
TEST					
1ST-CLASS	113	31	318	10	31.80
INT					
JPL	33.5	1	179	4	44.75
NAT.W.	14	3	35	1	–
B & H	25	2	135	2	67.50

CAREER: BOWLING

	O.	M.	R.	W.	AV.
TEST					
1ST-CLASS	753.3	193	2075	62	33.46
INT					
JPL	93.5	4	424	19	22.31
NAT.W.	14	3	35	1	–
B & H	25	2	135	2	67.50

126. Who was the first captain of India?

PRICHARD, P. J.   Essex

Full Name: Paul John Prichard
Role: Right-hand bat,
cover/mid-wicket fielder
Born: 7 January 1965, Brentwood
Height: 5′ 10″ **Weight:** 11st 7lbs
Nickname: Digger, Pablo
County debut: 1984
County cap: 1986
1000 runs in a season: 1
1st-Class 50s scored: 21
1st-Class 100s scored: 2
One-day 50s: 4
One-day 100s: 1
Place in batting averages: 91st
av. 32.73 (1985 135th av. 25.97)
1st-Class catches 1986: 19
(career: 43)
Parents: Margaret and John
Education: Brentwood County High
School
Qualifications: NCA Senior
Coaching Award
Family links with cricket: Father played club cricket in Essex
Overseas tours: Kingfishers tour of South Africa, January 1981
Overseas teams played for: VOB Cavaliers, Cape Town, 1981–82; Sutherland
CC, Sydney 1985–86
Cricketers particularly learnt from: All at Essex
Cricketers particularly admired: 'Too many to mention.'
Other sports played: Football, golf

LAST SEASON: BATTING

	I.	N.O.	R.	H.S.	AV.
TEST					
1ST-CLASS	44	3	1342	147*	32.73
INT					
JPL	14	3	462	103*	42.00
NAT.W.	2	0	12	10	6.00
B & H	5	0	104	52	20.80

LAST SEASON: BOWLING

	O.	M.	R.	W.	AV.
TEST					
1ST-CLASS					
INT					
JPL					
NAT.W.					
B & H					

CAREER: BATTING

	I.	N.O.	R.	H.S.	AV.
TEST					
1ST-CLASS	107	9	3009	147*	30.70
INT					
JPL	20	3	563	103*	33.11
NAT.W.	6	0	173	94	28.83
B & H	9	1	203	52	25.37

CAREER: BOWLING

	O.	M.	R.	W.	AV.
TEST					
1ST-CLASS	1	0	5	0	–
INT					
JPL					
NAT.W.					
B & H					

Other sports followed: American football
Relaxations: 'Sailing my boat, listening to music.'
Best batting performance: 147* Essex v Nottinghamshire, Chelmsford 1986

PRIDGEON, A. P.　　　　Worcestershire

Full Name: Alan Paul Pridgeon
Role: Right-hand bat, right-arm medium bowler
Born: 22 February 1954, Wall Heath, Staffordshire
Height: 6′ 3″ **Weight:** 13st 2lbs
Nickname: Pridge
County debut: 1972
County cap: 1980
50 wickets in a season: 6
1st-Class 50s scored: 1
1st-Class 5 w. in innings: 9
1st-Class 10 w. in match: 1
Place in bowling averages: 24th av. 23.66
1st-Class catches 1986: 9 (career: 71)
Parents: Albert Ernest and Sybil Ruby
Wife and date of marriage: Jane, 7 October 1978
Children: Laura, 8 August 1983
Education: Summerhill Secondary Modern, Kingswinford, West Midlands
Qualifications: 6 CSEs, Qualified FA Coach; Qualified NCA Coach
Jobs outside cricket: Semi-professional footballer; salesman; has worked for Manpower Commission
Cricketing superstitions: 'Hate batting while Sylvester Clarke is bowling.'
Overseas tours: Worcestershire Club tour to Barbados 1980
Overseas teams played for: Howick and Pakuranga, New Zealand, 1983–84
Cricketers particularly learnt from: I. V. A. Richards, Dennis Lillee, Norman Gifford
Cricketers particularly admired: Steve Perryman
Other sports played: Semi-professional footballer for Dudley Town FC, West Midlands League; golf, snooker, tennis
Other sports followed: Horse-racing
Relaxations: Horse-racing, taking dog (Muffin) for walks
Best batting performance: 67 Worcestershire v Warwickshire, Worcester 1984
Best bowling performance: 7-35 Worcestershire v Oxford University, Oxford 1976

	I.	N.O.	R.	H.S.	AV.
TEST					
1ST-CLASS	10	3	44	10*	6.28
INT					
JPL	1	1	0	0*	–
NAT.W.	1	1	4	4*	–
B & H	1	1	1	1*	–

LAST SEASON: BOWLING

	O.	M.	R.	W.	AV.
TEST					
1ST-CLASS	536	134	1396	59	23.66
INT					
JPL	85.5	2	388	13	29.84
NAT.W.	43.1	6	94	3	31.33
B & H	46	6	189	7	27.00

CAREER: BATTING

	I.	N.O.	R.	H.S.	AV.
TEST					
1ST-CLASS	195	78	1076	67	9.16
INT					
JPL	49	27	143	17	6.50
NAT.W.	9	6	38	13*	12.66
B & H	17	9	71	13*	8.87

CAREER: BOWLING

	O.	M.	R.	W.	AV.
TEST					
1ST-CLASS	5344	1096	15636	477	32.77
INT					
JPL	877.2	42	4030	124	32.50
NAT.W.	148.2	25	441	11	40.09
B & H	351.2	38	1404	30	46.80

PRINGLE, D. R.   Essex

Full Name: Derek Raymond Pringle
Role: Right-hand bat, right-arm fast-medium bowler, 1st slip fielder
Born: 18 September 1958, Nairobi
Height: 6′ 5″ **Weight:** 15¾st
Nickname: Ignell, Suggs
County debut: 1978
County cap: 1982
Test debut: 1982
No. of Tests: 14
No. of One-Day Internationals: 13
50 wickets in a season: 3
1st-Class 50s scored: 25
1st-Class 100s scored: 7
1st-Class 5 w. in innings: 11
1st-Class 10 w. in match: 1
One-day 50s: 18
Place in batting averages: 175th 21.82 (1985 158th av. 24.22)
Place in bowling averages: 28th av. 24.07 (1985 46th av. 29.36)
1st-Class catches 1986: 14 (career: 92)
Parents: Donald James (deceased) and Doris May
Marital status: Single
Education: St Mary's School, Nairobi; Felsted School, Essex; Cambridge University (Fitzwilliam College)
Qualifications: 8 O-levels, 3 A-levels, MA Cantab.
Jobs outside cricket: T-shirt design

Family links with cricket: Father represented Kenya and East Africa (played in World Cup 1975)

Cricket superstitions: 'None now; too many ducks have seen to that.'

Overseas tours: With England Schools to India 1978–79; Oxbridge tour of Australia 1979–80; England to Australia and New Zealand 1982–83; England B tour to Sri Lanka 1986

Cricketers particularly learnt from: My father, Gordon Barker, 'Tonker' Taylor, Keith Fletcher

Off-season 1986–87: Grade cricket in Sydney

Other sports played: Squash, golf

Other sports followed: Watches rugby union

Relaxations: 'Modern music, especially The Smiths, New Order, Echo and the Bunnymen, photography, conchology, pub discussions over a pint of Adnams.'

Injuries 1986: Minor back spasm

Extras: 'Took all ten wickets for Nairobi Schools U-13½ v Up Country Schools U-13½. Captain of Cambridge 1982 season. Extra in *Chariots of Fire*. Once went shark hunting with Chris Smith of Hampshire (a recklessly brave fellow) in the Maldive Islands.'

Opinions on cricket: 'Format of 16 three-day games, present one-day fixtures but reduce B & H to 50 overs and Nat West to 55. It has often been a privilege to play against many of the overseas players; they bring a dimension of quality to the game. That can only improve those they play with and against, but one per county is enough. Counties should play a more active role in trying to help find opportunities in employment during the close season.'

Best batting performance: 127* Cambridge University v Worcestershire, Cambridge 1981

Best bowling performance: 7-32 Essex v Middlesex, Chelmsford 1983

LAST SEASON: BATTING

	I.	N.O.	R.	H.S.	AV.
TEST	8	0	166	65	20.75
1ST-CLASS	24	4	445	97	22.25
INT	4	2	105	49*	52.50
JPL	10	4	177	64	29.50
NAT.W.	2	0	55	33	27.50
B & H	5	2	217	65	72.33

LAST SEASON: BOWLING

	O.	M.	R.	W.	AV.
TEST	148.3	32	376	13	28.92
1ST-CLASS	358	96	972	43	22.60
INT	38.2	6	174	1	–
JPL	75.4	1	370	12	30.83
NAT.W.	19.5	2	83	4	20.75
B & H	54	3	221	6	36.83

CAREER: BATTING

	I.	N.O.	R.	H.S.	AV.
TEST	25	3	413	65	18.77
1ST-CLASS	214	43	4922	127*	28.78
INT	11	4	183	49*	26.14
JPL	52	15	1191	81*	32.18
NAT.W.	15	3	258	55	21.50
B & H	36	7	935	68	32.24

CAREER: BOWLING

	O.	M.	R.	W.	AV.
TEST	401.5	85	1128	29	38.89
1ST-CLASS	3422	835	9361	352	26.59
INT	120.2	11	575	13	44.23
JPL	467	20	2214	73	30.32
NAT.W.	164.3	35	494	23	21.47
B & H	359.3	42	1278	52	24.57

PRINGLE, N. J. — Somerset

Full Name: Nicholas John Pringle
Role: Right-hand bat, right-arm medium bowler, cover fielder
Born: 20 September 1966, Weymouth, Dorset
Height: 5′ 11″ **Weight:** 12st
Nickname: Pring
County debut: 1986
Parents: Marian and Guy Pease
Marital status: Single
Education: Priorswood Comprehensive, Taunton; Taunton School
Qualifications: 8 O-levels, 1 A-level
Cricketing superstitions: 'Throwing my bat, pads, gloves and kicking my coffin!'
Overseas tours: Taunton School to Sri Lanka 1983
Cricketers particularly learnt from: Martin Crowe, Don Wilson
Cricketers particularly admired: M. Crowe, R. Hadlee, V. Richards, G. Chappell
Off-season 1986–87: Grade cricket, Mosman CC, Sydney, New South Wales
Other sports played: Football
Other sports followed: Rugby, American football
Relaxations: 'Gardeners Arms, Taunton, Dire Straits, travelling.'
Injuries 1986: Dislocated shoulder, broken hand
Extras: On Lord's ground staff 1986. Called up from there by Somerset for his debut

LAST SEASON: BATTING

	I.	N.O.	R.	H.S.	AV.
TEST					
1ST-CLASS	2	0	21	11	10.50
INT					
JPL					
NAT.W.					
B & H					

LAST SEASON: BOWLING

	O.	M.	R.	W.	AV.
TEST					
1ST-CLASS	10	0	48	0	–
INT					
JPL					
NAT.W.					

CAREER: BATTING

	I.	N.O.	R.	H.S.	AV.
TEST					
1ST-CLASS	2	0	21	11	10.50
INT					
JPL					
NAT.W.					
B & H					

CAREER: BOWLING

	O.	M.	R.	W.	AV.
TEST					
1ST-CLASS	10	0	48	0	–
INT					
JPL					
NAT.W.					
B & H					

Opinions on cricket: 'I think that there should be cricket apprenticeships, similar to that of the Lord's groundstaff around the counties. This way young cricketers learn about other aspects of the game and perform duties that in years to come they can look back at, and not take things for granted, which these days, with all the money and sponsorship involved in cricket, is very easy to do.'

Best batting performance: 11 Somerset v Worcestershire, Worcester 1986

RADFORD, N. V.   Worcestershire

Full Name: Neal Victor Radford
Role: Right-hand bat, right-arm fast-medium bowler, gully fielder
Born: 7 June 1957, Luanshya, Zambia
Height: 5′ 11″ **Weight:** 12st 4lbs
Nickname: Radiz, Vic
County debut: 1980 (Lancashire), 1985 (Worcestershire)
County cap: 1985 (Worcestershire)
Test debut: 1986
No. of Tests: 2
50 wickets in a season: 2
1st-Class 50s scored: 3
1st-Class 5 w. in innings: 19
1st-Class 10 w. in match: 4

Place in batting averages: 217th av. 13.69 (1985 210th av. 17.00)
Place in bowling averages: 37th av. 26.71 (1985 17th av. 24.68)
1st-Class catches 1986: 12 (career: 55)
Parents: Edith Joyce and Victor Reginald
Wife: Lynne
Education: Athlone Boys High School, Johannesburg
Qualifications: Matriculation and university entrance, NCA Advanced Coach
Jobs outside cricket: Auditor
Family links with cricket: Brother Wayne pro for Gowerton (SWCA) and Glamorgan 2nd XI. Also Orange Free State in Currie Cup
Cricketing superstitions: 'Nelson and left pad on first.'
Overseas teams played for: Transvaal 1979–83; South African Schools XI; South African Army
Cricketers particularly admired: Vincent Van der Bijl

Off-season 1986–87: 'Playing cricket in the sun.'
Other sports played: Golf, squash
Other sports followed: All sports
Relaxations: Music, TV, films
Extras: Only bowler to take 100 first-class wickets in 1985
Opinions on cricket: 'Play too much cricket! A cut down will result in better standard all round. Have a day off for travelling as the majority of injuries and stiffness are caused by travelling hundreds of miles immediately after matches.'
Injuries 1986: Side injury (missed 2 matches); groin injury (missed 2 matches)
Best batting performance: 76* Lancashire v Derbyshire, Blackpool 1981
Best bowling performance: 9-70 Worcestershire v Somerset, Worcester 1986

LAST SEASON: BATTING

	I.	N.O.	R.	H.S.	AV.
TEST	3	1	13	12*	6.50
1ST-CLASS	13	2	165	30	15.00
INT					
JPL	10	7	89	37*	29.66
NAT.W.	1	0	0	0	–
B & H	4	2	45	29*	22.50

LAST SEASON: BOWLING

	O.	M.	R.	W.	AV.
TEST	63	7	219	3	73.00
1ST-CLASS	602.4	125	1945	78	25.32
INT					
JPL	75.3	4	351	12	29.25
NAT.W.	43	6	114	8	14.25
B & H	60	7	235	6	39.17

CAREER: BATTING

	I.	N.O.	R.	H.S.	AV.
TEST	3	1	13	12*	6.50
1ST-CLASS	133	33	1750	76*	17.50
INT					
JPL	36	19	347	48*	20.41
NAT.W.	6	2	45	16	11.25
B & H	9	3	77	29*	12.83

CAREER: BOWLING

	O.	M.	R.	W.	AV.
TEST	63	7	219	3	73.00
1ST-CLASS	3508.2	693	11248	421	26.71
INT					
JPL	328.2	19	1471	64	22.98
NAT.W.	121.3	20	359	20	17.95
B & H	123.2	17	465	11	42.27

127. Who was the first captain of Sri Lanka?

RADLEY, C. T.   Middlesex

Full Name: Clive Thornton Radley
Role: Right-hand bat, right-arm
leg-break bowler
Born: 13 May 1944, Hertford
Height: 5′ 10″ **Weight:** 12st
Nickname: Radders
County debut: 1964
County cap: 1967
Benefit: 1977 (£26,000) and 1987
Test debut: 1977–78
No. of Tests: 8
No. of One-Day Internationals: 4
1000 runs in a season: 16
1st-Class 50s scored: 136
1st-Class 100s scored: 45
1st-Class 200s scored: 1
One-Day 50s: 56
One-Day 100s: 7
Place in batting averages: 109th
av. 29.33 (1985 18th av. 52.89)
1st-Class catches 1986: 16 (career: 513)

Parents: Laura and late Arthur
Wife and date of marriage: Linda, 22 September 1973
Children: Louise, 18 September 1978; Paul Craig Thornton, 26 July 1980
Education: King Edward VI Grammar School, Norwich
Jobs outside cricket: Has coached in South Africa and Australia
Family links with cricket: Father played club cricket
Overseas tours: Pakistan and New Zealand 1977–78; Australia 1978–79

LAST SEASON: BATTING

	I.	N.O.	R.	H.S.	AV.
TEST					
1ST-CLASS	33	6	792	113*	29.33
INT					
JPL	12	3	365	78*	40.55
NAT.W.	2	0	96	67	48.00
B & H	7	3	289	62*	72.25

LAST SEASON: BOWLING

	O.	M.	R.	W.	AV.
TEST					
1ST-CLASS					
INT					
JPL					
NAT.W.					
B & H					

CAREER: BATTING

	I.	N.O.	R.	H.S.	AV.
TEST	10	0	481	158	48.10
1ST-CLASS	907	131	25587	200	32.97
INT	4	1	250	117*	83.33
JPL	246	26	6536	133*	29.70
NAT.W.	54	6	1514	105*	31.54
B & H	68	14	1825	121*	33.79

CAREER: BOWLING

	O.	M.	R.	W.	AV.
TEST					
1ST-CLASS	1 44	0 10	160	8	20.00
INT					
JPL	3.4	1	17	1	–
NAT.W.					
B & H					

Cricketers particularly learnt from: Ken Barrington
Cricketers particularly admired: Bob Willis
Other sports: Squash, golf
Extras: Played for Norfolk under former Middlesex and England player W. J. Edrich, who eased his way to Middlesex. Shared in the 6th wicket partnership record for Middlesex, 227 with F. Titmus v South Africa at Lord's in 1965. First fielder to hold 50 catches in JPL. Gold Award winner in 1983 Benson and Hedges Final
Best batting performance: 200 Middlesex v Northamptonshire, Uxbridge 1985
Best bowling performance: 2-38 Middlesex v Glamorgan, Cardiff 1985

RANDALL, D. W. Nottinghamshire

Full Name: Derek William Randall
Role: Right-hand bat, cover fielder
Born: 24 February 1951, Retford, Nottinghamshire
Height: 5′ 8½″ **Weight:** 11st
Nickname: Arkle, Rags
County debut: 1972
County cap: 1973
Benefit: 1983 (£42,000)
Test debut: 1976–77
No. of Tests: 47
No. of One-Day Internationals: 49
1000 runs in a season: 10
1st-Class 50s scored: 124
1st-Class 100s scored: 36
1st-Class 200s scored: 2
One-Day 50s: 46
One-Day 100s: 4
Place in batting averages: 161st
av. 23.47 (1985 16th av. 53.78)
1st-Class catches 1986: 14 (career: 274)
Parents: Frederick and Mavis
Wife and date of marriage: Elizabeth, September 1973
Children: Simon, June 1977
Education: Sir Frederick Milner Secondary Modern School, Retford
Qualifications: ONC Mechanical engineering, Mechanical draughtsman
Jobs outside cricket: Coaching
Family links with cricket: Father played local cricket, 'tried to bowl fast off a long run and off the wrong foot too!'

Overseas tours: India, Sri Lanka and Australia 1976–77; Pakistan and New Zealand 1977–78; Australia 1978–79; Australia and India 1979–80; Australia and New Zealand 1982–83; New Zealand and Pakistan 1983–84.
Overseas teams played for: North Perth, Australia
Cricketers particularly learnt from: Sir Gary Sobers, Tom Graveney (boyhood idol), Reg Simpson
Other sports played: Football, squash, golf
Relaxations: Listening to varied selection of tapes. Family man
Extras: Played in one John Player League match in 1971 for Nottinghamshire. Before joining Nottinghamshire staff, played for Retford Cricket Club in the Bassetlaw League, and helped in Championship wins of 1968 and 1969. One of the finest fielders in cricket. Scored 174 in Centenary Test v Australia 1977
Best batting performance: 209 Nottinghamshire v Middlesex, Trent Bridge 1979
Best bowling performance: 3-15 Nottinghamshire v MCC, Lord's 1982

LAST SEASON: BATTING

	I.	N.O.	R.	H.S.	AV.
TEST					
1ST-CLASS	22	1	493	101*	23.47
INT					
JPL	11	3	343	88	42.87
NAT.W.	3	1	63	53	31.50
B & H	6	1	209	82*	41.80

LAST SEASON: BOWLING

	O.	M.	R.	W.	AV.
TEST					
1ST-CLASS	3	0	17	0	–
INT					
JPL					
NAT.W.					
B & H					

CAREER: BATTING

	I.	N.O.	R.	H.S.	AV.
TEST	79	5	2470	175	33.37
1ST-CLASS	547	52	18834	209	38.04
INT	45	5	1067	88	26.68
JPL	171	22	4465	107*	29.96
NAT.W.	29	2	655	75	24.25
B & H	66	10	1932	103*	34.50

CAREER: BOWLING

	O.	M.	R.	W.	AV.
TEST	2	0	3	0	–
1ST-CLASS	69.5	5	380	12	31.66
INT	0.2	0	2	1	–
JPL	0.5	0	9	0	–
NAT.W.	1	0	3	0	–
B & H	2.5	0	5	0	–

128. Which are the only two English counties not to have produced an England captain since 1945?

REEVE, D. A.   Sussex

Full Name: Dermot Alexander Reeve
Role: Right-hand bat, right-arm
fast-medium bowler
Born: 2 April 1963, Hong Kong
Height: 6′ 0″ **Weight:** 11st 7lbs
Nickname: Ears
County debut: 1983
County cap: 1986
50 wickets in a season: 2
1st-Class 50s scored: 5
1st-Class 100s scored: 1
1st-Class 5 w. in innings: 4
Place in batting averages: 141st
av. 25.58 (1985 209th av. 17.00)
Place in bowling averages: 40th
av. 27.13 (1985 50th av. 29.67)
1st-Class catches 1986: 11
(career: 38)
Parents: Monica and Alexander
James
Wife and date of marriage: Julie, 20 December 1986
Education: King George V School, Kowloon, Hong Kong
Qualifications: 7 O-levels
Family links with cricket: Father captain of school XI, brother Mark an
improving club cricketer
Overseas tours: Hong Kong tour to Malaysia and Singapore 1980; Hong Kong
British Forces tour to Malaysia 1982; MCC tour to Holland and Denmark
1983
Overseas teams played for: Claremont-Cottesloe CC, Western Australia,
1982–83; Mount Lawley CC, Perth, 1985–86
Cricketers particularly learnt from: Don Wilson, David Clinton
Cricketers particularly admired: I. T. Botham, P. Willey, P. Parker, J.
Middleton (ex Hong Kong pace bowler)
Off-season 1986–87: Playing cricket in Perth, Western Australia, resting, and
large wedding celebrations
Other sports played: Golf, volleyball
Other sports followed: Football and most sports
Relaxations: Music, movies, sleeping in
Extras: Formerly on Lord's groundstaff. Represented Hong Kong in the ICC
Trophy competition June 1982. Hong Kong Cricketer of the Year 1980–81.
Hong Kong's Cricket Sports Personality of the Year 1981. Man of the Match
in 1986 NatWest final
Opinions on cricket: 'Believe four-day cricket should be introduced on

covered wickets, 100 overs/day, 16 matches. More one-day internationals in England.'
Injuries 1986: Slight groin and back strains
Best batting performance: 119 Sussex v Surrey, Guildford 1984
Best bowling performance: 5-22 Sussex v Cambridge University, Cambridge 1984

LAST SEASON: BATTING

	I.	N.O.	R.	H.S.	AV.
TEST					
1ST-CLASS	21	9	307	51	25.58
INT					
JPL	9	3	35	9	5.83
NAT.W.	2	1	2	1*	–
B & H	2	1	27	21*	–

CAREER: BATTING

	I.	N.O.	R.	H.S.	AV.
TEST					
1ST-CLASS	78	23	1155	119	21.00
INT					
JPL	21	10	118	19	10.72
NAT.W.	6	4	37	16*	18.50
B & H	7	1	65	21*	10.83

LAST SEASON: BOWLING

	O.	M.	R.	W.	AV.
TEST					
1ST-CLASS	525.5	127	1411	52	27.13
INT					
JPL	96.2	2	513	17	30.17
NAT.W.	45	13	112	8	14.00
B & H	34	3	155	4	38.75

CAREER: BOWLING

	O.	M.	R.	W.	AV.
TEST					
1ST-CLASS	2046.3	540	5488	197	27.85
INT					
JPL	319.1	10	1498	63	23.77
NAT.W.	100.5	24	266	15	17.73
B & H	108.4	11	490	11	44.54

RHODES, S. J.   Worcestershire

Full Name: Steven John Rhodes
Role: Right-hand bat, wicket-keeper
Born: 17 June 1964, Bradford
Height: 5′ 8″ **Weight:** 11st 9lbs
Nickname: Wilf, Bumpy
County debut: 1981 (Yorkshire), 1985 (Worcestershire)
1st-Class 50s scored: 6
Place in batting averages: 105th av. 29.94 (1985 138th av. 25.62)
Parents: Bill and Norma
Marital status: Single
Education: Bradford Moor Junior School; Lapage St Middle; Carlton-Bolling Comprehensive
Qualifications: 4 O-levels, cricket coaching certificate
Jobs outside cricket: Trainee manager in sports retailer in winters of 1980–81 and 1981–82

Family links with cricket: Father played for Nottinghamshire 1961–64
Cricketing superstitions: 'I like to make sure I am not last out of the changing room when fielding.'
Overseas teams played for: Past Brothers Cricket Club, Bundaberg, Queensland, Australia, 1982–83 and 1983–84, and Bundaberg Cricket Association
Cricketers particularly learnt from: 'Phil Carrick, Doug Padgett, Kapil Dev and my father.'
Cricketers particularly admired: Alan Knott ('seems to have lots of time with his keeping.')
Other sports played: Golf
Other sports followed: Rugby league (Bradford Northern)
Extras: Played for Young England against Young Australia in 1983. Youngest wicket-keeper to play for Yorkshire. Holds record for most victims in an innings for Young England. Played for England Schools U-15s. Released by Yorkshire to join Worcestershire at end of 1984 season
Best batting performance: 77* England B v Sri Lankan XI, Colombo 1985–86

LAST SEASON: BATTING

	I.	N.O.	R.	H.S.	AV.
TEST					
1ST-CLASS	27	10	509	71*	29.94
INT					
JPL	15	2	304	46	23.38
NAT.W.	3	2	46	32*	–
B & H	4	0	10	4	2.50

CAREER: BATTING

	I.	N.O.	R.	H.S.	AV.
TEST					
1ST-CLASS	73	28	1380	77*	30.66
INT					
JPL	28	5	518	46	22.52
NAT.W.	6	4	67	32*	33.50
B & H	8	2	67	27*	11.17

LAST SEASON: WICKET-KEEPING

	C.	ST.			
TEST					
1ST-CLASS	58	8			
INT					
JPL	12	7			
NAT.W.	5	–			
B & H	4	3			

LAST SEASON: BOWLING

	O.	M.	R.	W.	AV.
TEST					
1ST-CLASS					
INT					
JPL					
NAT.W.	1	0	1	0	–
B & H					

CAREER: BOWLING

	O.	M.	R.	W.	AV.
TEST					
1ST-CLASS					
INT					
JPL					
NAT.W.	1	0	1	0	–
B & H					

CAREER: WICKET-KEEPING

	C.	ST.			
TEST					
1ST-CLASS	124	14			
INT					
JPL	25	8			
NAT.W.	10	1			
B & H	11	4			

129. Which England captain scored a century on both his first and last first-class appearance?

RICE, C. E. B.　　　Nottinghamshire

Full Name: Clive Edward Butler Rice
Role: Right-hand bat, right-arm fast-medium bowler, slip fielder
Born: 23 July 1949, Johannesburg, South Africa
Height: 6′ 0″ **Weight:** 13st 3lbs
Nickname: Ricey
County debut: 1975
County cap: 1975
Benefit: 1982 (South Africa), 1985 (England)
1000 runs in a season: 12
50 wickets in a season: 4
1st-Class 50s scored: 117
1st-Class 100s scored: 39
1st-Class 200s scored: 3
1st-Class 5 w. in innings: 20
1st-Class 10 w. in match: 1
One-Day 50s: 56
One-Day 100s: 7

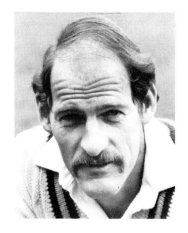

Place in batting averages: 27th av. 44.72 (1985 13th av. 55.76)
Place in bowling averages: 31st av. 25.25 (1985 57th av. 31.16)
1st-Class catches 1986: 27 (career: 339)
Parents: Patrick and Angela
Wife and date of marriage: Susan Elizabeth, 28 February 1975
Children: Jackie Elizabeth, 27 June 1981; Mark Richard, 11 August 1983
Education: St John's College and Damelin College, Johannesburg; Natal University, Pietermaritzburg
Jobs outside cricket: Director of companies
Family links with cricket: Grandfather, Phillip Syndercombe Bower, played for Repton and Oxford University. Brother, Richard Patrick Butler Rice, selected for Transvaal B but unavailable because of university exams. Brother, John Cromwell Rice, captain of school 1st XI
Cricket superstitions: '111, 222 or 333 on scoreboard.'
Overseas tours: World Team in World Series Cricket, Australia 1978–79
Overseas teams played for: World Series Cricket; Transvaal; Bedfordview CC, Johannesburg
Cricketers particularly learnt from: Don Mackay-Coghill, Ali Bacher, Graeme Pollock
Cricketers particularly admired: Mike Procter, Graeme Pollock, Richard Hadlee, Dennis Lillee
Off-season 1986–87: Playing in South Africa for Transvaal

Other sports followed: English football, rugby, motor-racing

Relaxations: Reading, listening to music, studying stock markets

Extras: Writes for local South African newspapers. Captain of Bedfordview CC, Johannesburg. Made debut for Transvaal in 1969. Professional for Ramsbottom in Lancashire League, 1973. Originally appointed captain of Nottinghamshire in 1978 but was at first relieved of his appointment after signing for World Series Cricket. Reappointed for 1979. Played three 'Supertests' for WSC. Was sponsored at 5 rands (£2.77) a run, 50 rands (£27) a wicket and 100 rands (£55) a catch in the 1980–81 Currie Cup competition in South Africa. Wisden Cricketer of the Year 1981. South African Players' Player 1985–86. Most runs in John Player League in a season: 814 in 1977 and equalled bowling record with 34 wickets. Highest score for Transvaal in Datsun Shield, 169 v Griqualand West. Highest score for Nottinghamshire in John Player League, 120 against Glamorgan. 1984 and 1985 winner of Silk Cut Challenge all-rounders competition. Hat-trick for South Africa v Australians 1985–86

Opinions on cricket: 'We need quality cricket and not quantity for England to perform better.'

Injuries 1986: Broken finger and broken foot

Best batting performance: 246 Nottinghamshire v Sussex, Hove 1976

Best bowling performance: 7-62 Transvaal v Western Province, Johannesburg 1975–76

LAST SEASON: BATTING

	I.	N.O.	R.	H.S.	AV.
TEST					
1ST-CLASS	31	6	1118	156*	44.72
INT					
JPL	15	4	571	94*	51.90
NAT.W.	3	1	31	15*	15.50
B & H	6	1	201	71	40.20

LAST SEASON: BOWLING

	O.	M.	R.	W.	AV.
TEST					
1ST-CLASS	413.2	115	1111	44	25.25
INT					
JPL	109.1	5	539	34	15.85
NAT.W.	30	4	83	1	–
B & H	64.2	1	287	8	35.87

CAREER: BATTING

	I.	N.O.	R.	H.S.	AV.
TEST					
1ST-CLASS	652	102	22571	246	41.03
INT					
JPL	169	29	5936	120*	42.40
NAT.W.	24	2	451	71	20.50
B & H	54	7	1685	130*	35.85

CAREER: BOWLING

	O.	M.	R.	W.	AV.
TEST					
1ST-CLASS	6749.4	1793	17777	800	22.22
INT					
JPL	861.3	51	3864	170	22.72
NAT.W.	180	23	620	26	23.84
B & H	429.2	58	1466	73	20.08

130. When were both captains in a Test Series Glamorgan players, and who were they?

RICHARDS, C. J.   Surrey

Full Name: Clifton James Richards
Role: Right-hand bat, wicket-keeper
Born: 10 August 1958, Penzance
Height: 5′ 11″ **Weight:** 11st 8lbs
Nickname: Jack
County debut: 1976
County cap: 1978
No. of One-Day Internationals: 3
1000 runs in a season: 1
1st-Class 50s scored: 27
1st-Class 100s scored: 4
One-Day 50s: 4
One-Day 100s: 1
Place in batting averages: 46th
av. 40.24 (1985 31st av. 44.33)
Parents: Clifton and Elizabeth June
Wife: Birgitta, 27 September 1980
Education: Humphrey Davy
Grammar School, Penzance
Qualifications: 7 O-levels

Jobs outside cricket: Trainee electrical engineer, apprentice draughtsman
Family links with cricket: Father a member of Penzance CC and Surrey CCC

LAST SEASON: BATTING

	I.	N.O.	R.	H.S.	AV.
TEST					
1ST-CLASS	34	9	1006	115	40.24
INT	1	0	8	8	–
JPL	15	4	373	55*	33.90
NAT.W.	4	2	95	53*	47.50
B & H	3	0	68	45	22.66

CAREER: BATTING

	I.	N.O.	R.	H.S.	AV.
TEST					
1ST-CLASS	303	75	6035	117*	26.46
INT	3	0	11	8	3.66
JPL	92	24	1113	55*	16.36
NAT.W.	16	5	308	105*	28.00
B & H	28	7	286	45	13.61

LAST SEASON: BOWLING

	O.	M.	R.	W.	AV.
TEST					
1ST-CLASS	5	0	34	1	–
INT					
JPL					
NAT.W.					
B & H					

CAREER: BOWLING

	O.	M.	R.	W.	AV.
TEST					
1ST-CLASS	43	3	198	5	39.60
INT					
JPL					
NAT.W.					
B & H					

LAST SEASON: WICKET-KEEPING

	C.	ST.
TEST		
1ST-CLASS	39	5
INT	1	–
JPL	13	5
NAT.W.	5	1
B & H	3	–

CAREER: WICKET-KEEPING

	C.	ST.
TEST		
1ST-CLASS	443	62
INT	2	–
JPL	78	33
NAT.W.	29	5
B & H	39	5

Cricketing superstitions: Always last out of the dressing room when fielding
Overseas tours: Australia with Derrick Robins' U-23 XI in 1979–80; Far East with Surrey CCC in 1978–79; England to India 1981–82
Overseas teams played for: Klaas Vervelde XI, 1981
Off-season 1986–87: Touring Australia with England
Other sports played: Tennis, golf, rugby, skiing, ice-skating, sailing
Other sports followed: Most sports, especially American and other foreign sports
Relaxations: Reading, television, driving
Best batting performance: 117* Surrey v Nottinghamshire, The Oval 1982
Best bowling performance: 2-42 Surrey v Somerset, The Oval 1985

RICHARDS, I. V. A. Somerset

Full Name: Isaac Vivian Alexander Richards
Role: Right-hand bat, right-arm off-break bowler
Born: 7 March 1952, St John's, Antigua
Height: 5′ 11″ **Weight:** 13st 7lbs
Nickname: Smokey, Viv, Vivvy
County debut: 1974
County cap: 1974
Benefit: 1982 (£56,440)
Test debut: 1974–75
No. of Tests: 82
No. of One-Day Internationals: 109
1000 runs in a season: 12
1st-Class 50s scored: 123
1st-Class 100s scored: 83
1st-Class 200s scored: 9
1st-Class 5 w. in innings: 1
One-Day 50s: 81
One-Day 100s: 19
Place in batting averages: 35th av. 43.48 (1985 1st av. 76.50)
1st-Class catches 1986: 18 (career: 353)
Parents: Malcolm and Gratel
Wife and date of marriage: Miriam, 24 March 1981
Children: Daughter Matara and son born on eve of 1983 NatWest final
Education: St John's Boys School; Antigua Grammar School
Jobs outside cricket: Worked as a waiter at D'Arcy's Bar and Restaurant, in St John's, Antigua. Apprentice mechanic. Assistant groundsman

Family links with cricket: Father played cricket for Antigua as fast-bowler and all-rounder. He also played soccer for Antigua. Half-brother Donald opened bowling for Antigua, and also played for Leeward Islands. Brother Mervyn has played both cricket and soccer for Antigua

Overseas tours: With West Indies to India, Sri Lanka and Pakistan 1974–75; Australia 1975–76, 1979–80, 1980–81, 1984–85; England 1976, 1980 and 1984; Pakistan 1980–81, 1986–87; India 1983–84

Overseas teams played for: Leeward Islands 1971–72; Queensland in 1976–77 Sheffield Shield Competition

Cricketers particularly learnt from: Father, Pat Evanson, Shandy Perera

Other sports played: Captained school soccer team as centre-half. Invited to go for a trial with Bath City, FC, the Southern League club, but no offer of terms followed. Played basket ball for The Knickerbockers in Antigua. Squash

Relaxations: Music, 'I sit for hours listening to my stereo.' Has large collection of LPs

Extras: Made debut 1971–72 for Leeward Islands. Has written autobiography with David Foot, entitled *Viv Richards*. Helps to sponsor young cricketers, footballers and basketball players in Antigua. Brother Mervyn appointed national soccer coach in Antigua. Attended Alf Gover's cricket school in 1972. Shared in 4th wicket partnership record for Somerset of 251 with P. M. Roebuck v Surrey at Weston-super-Mare in 1977. Record for most sixes hit in John Player League in one season, 26 in 1977. Took hat-trick v Essex in JPL at Chelmsford, 1982. Awarded honorary doctorate of letters by Exeter University in 1986. Captain of West Indies since 1985. Contract with Somerset not renewed after 1986 season and joined Rishton, the Lancashire League club

Opinions on cricket: 'I have never contemplated wearing a helmet. My personal view is that a helmet with a visor takes a little of the batsman's vision – and just a little of the challenge out of the game.'

Best batting performance: 322 Somerset v Warwickshire, Taunton 1985

Best bowling performance: 5-88 West Indies v Queensland, Brisbane 1981–82

LAST SEASON: BATTING

	I.	N.O.	R.	H.S.	AV.
TEST					
1ST-CLASS	28	1	1174	136	43.48
INT					
JPL	14	1	382	64	29.38
NAT.W.	2	1	56	50	–
B & H	4	0	85	29	21.25

LAST SEASON: BOWLING

	O.	M.	R.	W.	AV.
TEST					
1ST-CLASS	161	32	500	9	55.55
INT					
JPL	68.1	2	341	9	37.88
NAT.W.	24	3	62	3	20.66
B & H	17	4	47	0	–

CAREER: BATTING

	I.	N.O.	R.	H.S.	AV.
TEST	122	8	6220	291	54.56
1ST-CLASS	489	32	22313	322	48.82
INT	99	15	4600	189*	54.76
JPL	139	16	4745	126*	38.57
NAT.W.	31	3	1209	139*	43.17
B & H	39	6	1395	132*	42.27

CAREER: BOWLING

	O.	M.	R.	W.	AV.
TEST	17.1 465.5	2 132	1052	19	55.36
1ST-CLASS	26.3 2271.2	2 572	6632	158	41.97
INT	2 536	0 16	2402	63	38.12
JPL	387	14	1758	70	25.11
NAT.W.	133.1	15	478	16	29.87
B & H	67.4	14	225	7	32.14

RIPLEY, D.   Northamptonshire

Full Name: David Ripley
Role: Right-hand bat, wicket-keeper
Born: 13 September 1966, Leeds
Height: 5′ 11″ **Weight:** 11st
Nickname: Rippers, Rips, Spud
County debut: 1984
1st-Class 50s scored: 1
1st-Class 100s scored: 1
Place in batting averages: 104th
av. 30.10
Parents: Arthur and Brenda
Marital status: Single
Education: Woodlesford Primary
and Royds High, Leeds
Qualifications: 5 O-levels, NCA
Coaching Certificate
Family links with cricket: 'My Mum
once made the teas at Farsley CC.'
Jobs outside cricket: 'Any odds and ends jobs I can find.'
Cricketing superstitions: 'If having a good run will not have my hair cut; left
pad first. Like to be last out of changing room. The number 111.'
Overseas tours: To West Indies with England Young Cricketers 1984–85
Overseas teams played for: Poverty Bay Cricket Association, New Zealand,
1985–86
Cricketers particularly learnt from: Brian Reynolds, Jim Yardley, Ian Stein,
Billy Rhodes, Roy Wills
Cricketers particularly admired: Alan Knott, Bob Taylor, Roy Fredericks
Off-season 1986–87: Playing and coaching with Poverty Bay CA, New
Zealand

LAST SEASON: BATTING

	I.	N.O.	R.	H.S.	AV.
TEST					
1ST-CLASS	15	5	301	134*	30.10
INT					
JPL	3	2	44	36*	–
NAT.W.					
B & H	2	0	26	26	13.00

CAREER: BATTING

	I.	N.O.	R.	H.S.	AV.
TEST					
1ST-CLASS	50	12	665	134*	17.50
INT					
JPL	14	6	130	36*	16.25
NAT.W.	3	1	40	27*	20.00
B & H	2	0	26	26	13.00

LAST SEASON: WICKET-KEEPING

	C.	ST.		
TEST				
1ST-CLASS	12	4		
INT				
JPL	–	2		
NAT.W.				
B & H	3	1		

CAREER: WICKET-KEEPING

	C.	ST.		
TEST				
1ST-CLASS	59	20		
INT				
JPL	12	6		
NAT.W.	8	1		
B & H	3	1		

Other sports played: Soccer, golf, pool
Other sports followed: Soccer (Leeds United) and rugby league (Castleford)
Relaxations: Music, eating out
Best batting performance: 134* Northamptonshire v Yorkshire, Scarborough 1986

ROBERTS, B. Derbyshire

Full Name: Bruce Roberts
Role: Right-hand bat, right-arm medium bowler, slip fielder, occasional wicket-keeper
Born: 30 May 1962, Lusaka, Zambia
Height: 6' 1" **Weight:** 14st
County debut: 1984
1000 runs in a season: 1
1st-Class 50s scored: 17
1st-Class 100s scored: 3
One-Day 50s: 8
Place in batting averages: 170th av. 22.70 (1985 113rd av. 29.68)
1st-Class catches 1986: 16 (career: 67)
Parents: Arthur William and Sara Ann
Marital status: Single
Education: Ruzawi, Peterhouse; Prince Edward, Zimbabwe
Qualifications: O-levels
Family links with cricket: Father played for Orange Free State
Overseas teams played for: Transvaal B 1982–85
Cricketers particularly learnt from: 'My father and Ali Bacher.'
Cricketers particularly admired: Imran Khan, Michael Holding
Other sports followed: Rugby
Relaxations: Family
Best batting performance: 124* Derbyshire v Somerset, Chesterfield 1986
Best bowling performance: 4-32 Transvaal B v Orange Free State, Johannesburg 1982–83

LAST SEASON: BATTING

	I.	N.O.	R.	H.S.	AV.
TEST					
1ST-CLASS	37	3	772	124*	22.70
INT					
JPL	14	3	372	60*	33.81
NAT.W.	2	1	14	12	–
B & H	5	2	191	86*	63.66

CAREER: BATTING

	I.	N.O.	R.	H.S.	AV.
TEST					
1ST-CLASS	148	15	3763	124*	28.29
INT					
JPL	36	6	941	77*	31.36
NAT.W.	4	1	30	13	10.00
B & H	12	3	334	86*	37.11

LAST SEASON: BOWLING

	O.	M.	R.	W.	AV.
TEST					
1ST-CLASS	22	5	53	2	26.50
INT					
JPL	22	0	128	3	42.66
NAT.W.					
B & H					

CAREER: BOWLING

	O.	M.	R.	W.	AV.
TEST					
1ST-CLASS	559	99	2065	56	36.87
INT					
JPL	93.4	1	597	24	24.62
NAT.W.	16	1	84	2	42.00
B & H	30	2	151	4	37.75

LAST SEASON: WICKET-KEEPING

	C.	ST.		
TEST				
1ST-CLASS				
INT				
JPL				
NAT.W.	2	–		
B & H				

CAREER: WICKET-KEEPING

	C.	ST.		
TEST				
1ST-CLASS				
INT				
JPL				
NAT.W.	2	–		
B & H				

ROBERTS, M. L. — Glamorgan

Full Name: Martin Leonard Roberts
Role: Right-hand bat, wicket-keeper
Born: 12 April 1966, Mullion, Cornwall
Height: 6′ 1″ **Weight:** 11st 13lbs
Nickname: Mert
County debut: 1985
Parents: Len and Marian
Wife and date of marriage: Sue, 20 September 1986
Education: Helston Comprehensive School
Qualifications: 4 O-levels, 6 CSEs, Qualified Coach
Jobs outside cricket: Working at W. H. Smiths and helping out PE staff at Helston Comprehensive School
Family links with cricket: Father and brother both play
Cricketing superstitions: Always puts left pad on first

Overseas tours: Holland with Young England amateur side, 1983
Cricketers particularly learnt from: Bob Taylor, Andy Brassington, Terry Davies
Cricketers particularly admired: Bob Taylor, Alan Knott
Off-season 1986–87: Staying in Cardiff and looking for a job of any kind
Other sport played: Football, volleyball, golf
Other sports followed: Snooker, American football
Relaxations: Playing golf, watching films
Extras: England Schools U-19's 1983–1984. Played for Cornwall in Minor Counties
Opinions on cricket: 'I think fines in limited overs cricket should not be allowed. How is a captain able to set the correct field nearing the end of a game, when one man in the wrong position could be the losing of the match, if he is rushing through the overs so as not to be fined?'
Injuries 1986: Car accident early in the year. Did not fully recover until mid-season
Best batting performance: 8 Glamorgan v Northamptonshire, Northampton 1986

LAST SEASON: BATTING

	I.	N.O.	R.	H.S.	AV.
TEST					
1ST-CLASS	1	0	8	8	–
INT					
JPL	1	1	6	6*	–
NAT.W.					
B & H					

LAST SEASON: WICKET-KEEPING

	C.	ST.			
TEST					
1ST-CLASS	2	1			
INT					
JPL	1	–			
NAT.W.					
B & H					

CAREER: BATTING

	I.	N.O.	R.	H.S.	AV.
TEST					
1ST-CLASS	2	0	8	8	4.00
INT					
JPL	1	1	6	6*	–
NAT.W.					
B & H					

CAREER: WICKET-KEEPING

	C.	ST.			
TEST					
1ST-CLASS	2	1			
INT					
JPL	1	–			
NAT.W.					
B & H					

131. Which legendary cricket commentator wrote this verse about which cricket ground:
    'From the top of the hill-top pavilion
    The sea is a cheat to the eye,
    Where it secretly seeps into coast-line,
    Or fades in the yellow-grey sky . . .'

ROBINSON, P. E.   Yorkshire

Full Name: Phillip Edward Robinson
Role: Right-hand bat
Born: 3 August 1963, Keighley
Height: 5′ 10″ **Weight:** 13st
Nickname: Red Robbo, Billy
County debut: 1984
1st-Class 50s scored: 12
1st-Class 100s scored: 1
One-Day 50s: 6
Place in batting averages: 70th
av. 35.63 (1985 111th av. 30.00)
1st-Class catches 1986: 7 (career: 16)
Parents: Keith and Margaret Lesley
Wife: Jane
Education: Hartington Middle;
Greenhead Grammar
Qualifications: 2 O-levels
Family links with cricket: Father
played in Bradford League
Cricketing superstitions: 'Always put my left sock on first.'
Cricketers particularly learnt from: 'I learn from all cricketers.'
Cricketers particularly admired: Gary Sobers, Viv Richards
Off-season 1986–87: Abroad
Other sports played: Football, golf, squash
Relaxations: Watching TV, having a drink
Extras: Scored the highest score by a Yorkshire 2nd XI player of 233 in 1983 v
Kent at Canterbury
Best batting performance: 104* Yorkshire v Kent, Scarborough 1986

LAST SEASON: BATTING

	I.	N.O.	R.	H.S.	AV.
TEST					
1ST-CLASS	13	2	392	104*	35.63
INT					
JPL	11	1	340	76*	34.00
NAT.W.	2	0	66	66	33.00
B & H					

LAST SEASON: BOWLING

	O.	M.	R.	W.	AV.
TEST					
1ST-CLASS	11	0	115	0	–
INT					
JPL					
NAT.W.					
B & H					

CAREER: BATTING

	I.	N.O.	R.	H.S.	AV.
TEST					
1ST-CLASS	53	8	1598	104*	35.51
INT					
JPL	29	2	722	78*	26.74
NAT.W.	3	0	66	66	22.00
B & H	3	0	59	42	19.66

CAREER: BOWLING

	O.	M.	R.	W.	AV.
TEST					
1ST-CLASS	13	0	127	0	–
INT					
JPL					
NAT.W.					
B & H					

ROBINSON, R. T.　　Nottinghamshire

Full Name: Robert Timothy Robinson
Role: Right-hand opening bat, cover fielder
Born: 21 November 1958, Sutton-in-Ashfield, Nottinghamshire
Height: 6′ **Weight:** 12st 4lbs
Nickname: Robbo, Chop
County debut: 1978
County cap: 1983
Test debut: 1984–85
No. of Tests: 16
No. of One-Day Internationals: 10
1000 runs in a season: 4
1st-Class 50s scored: 54
1st-Class 100s scored: 21
1st-Class 200s scored: 1
One-Day 50s: 21
One-Day 100s: 2
Place in batting averages: 18th av. 48.20 (1985 8th av. 59.96)
1st-Class catches 1986: 15 (career: 88)
Parents: Eddy and Christine
Wife and date of marriage: Trisha, 2 November 1985
Education: Dunstable Grammar School; High Pavement College, Nottingham; Sheffield University
Qualifications: Honorary degree in Accounting and Financial Management
Jobs outside cricket: Trainee accountant
Family links with cricket: Father, uncle, cousin and brother played local cricket. Brother played for Nottinghamshire Schoolboys
Cricketing superstitions: Always puts left pad on first
Overseas tours: NCA U-19 tour 1976; England to India and Australia 1984–85 and West Indies 1986
Overseas teams played for: Durban Collegians, South Africa, 1980–81
Cricketers particularly learnt from: Clive Rice, Eddie Hemmings
Cricketers particularly admired: Geoff Boycott
Off-season 1986–87: Renovating the house
Other sports played: Soccer, golf, badminton
Other sports followed: Rugby
Relaxations: Driving, listening to all music, films, doing nothing
Extras: Played for Northants 2nd XI in 1974–75 and for Nottinghamshire 2nd XI in 1977. Had soccer trials with Portsmouth, Chelsea and QPR
Injuries 1986: Two broken fingers

Best batting performance: 207 Nottinghamshire v Warwickshire, Trent Bridge 1983

LAST SEASON: BATTING

	I.	N.O.	R.	H.S.	AV.
TEST	2	0	46	35	23.00
1ST-CLASS	32	5	1352	159*	50.07
INT					
JPL	12	0	297	67	24.75
NAT.W.	3	0	58	49	19.33
B & H	6	1	186	76*	37.20

LAST SEASON: BOWLING

	O.	M.	R.	W.	AV.
TEST					
1ST-CLASS	2	0	18	0	–
INT					
JPL					
NAT.W.					
B & H					

CAREER: BATTING

	I.	N.O.	R.	H.S.	AV.
TEST	28	3	1052	175	42.08
1ST-CLASS	262	33	9302	207	40.62
INT	10	0	175	55	17.50
JPL	83	8	2155	97*	28.73
NAT.W.	16	2	694	139	49.57
B & H	31	3	830	120	29.64

CAREER: BOWLING

	O.	M.	R.	W.	AV.
TEST	1	1	0	0	–
1ST-CLASS	18	0	120	2	60.00
INT					
JPL					
NAT.W.					
B & H					

ROEBUCK, P. M. Somerset

Full Name: Peter Michael Roebuck
Role: Right-hand bat, right-arm leg-break bowler, slip fielder
Born: 6 March 1956, Oxford
Height: 6′ 0″ **Weight:** 13st 5lbs
Nickname: Professor
County debut: 1974
County cap: 1978
1000 runs in a season: 6
1st-Class 50s scored: 71
1st-Class 100s scored: 18
1st-Class 200s scored: 1
1st-Class 5 w. in innings: 1
One-Day 50s: 22
One-Day 100s: 1
Place in batting averages: 21st av. 47.70 (1985 30th av. 44.82)
1st-Class catches 1986: 12 (career: 122)
Parents: James and Elizabeth
Marital status: Single
Education: Park School, Bath; Millfield School; Emmanuel College, Cambridge University
Qualifications: 1st Class Hons degree in law

Jobs outside cricket: Teaching and freelance journalism
Family links with cricket: Mother and sister both played for Oxford University Ladies. Young brother, Paul, played for ESCA U-15 and now Gloucestershire.
Cricketing superstitions: 'Just about conquered all of these now (I am 30!).'
Overseas tours: Toured in Australia with Combined Oxford & Cambridge XI 1979–80. 'Christians in Sport' Tour to India 1985
Overseas teams played for: Played in Perth, Australia, 1979–80; also in Corfu, Sydney and Fiji
Cricketers particularly learnt from: Viv Richards, Martin Crowe
Cricketers particularly admired: R. J. O. Meyer, K. Fletcher
Off-season 1986–87: Working as a journalist in Australia
Other sports played: Tennis
Other sports followed: Anything except American sports ('They shriek too much!')
Relaxations: 'Reading, music, sitting in a bath, telephone calls.'
Extras: Cambridge blue 1975–76–77. Plays in spectacles. Youngest Minor County cricketer, playing for Somerset 2nd XI at age of 13. Shared in 4th wicket partnership record for county of 251 with I. V. A. Richards v Surrey at Weston-super-Mare in 1977. Books: *Slice of Cricket*, *It Never Rains* and *It Sort of Clicks*. Articles in *Sunday Independent*, *Guardian,* 'and anyone else who asks'. Founder member of campaign for fair play. Appointed captain in 1986
Opinions on cricket: 'People seem to have forgotten that this is, above all else, an aesthetic game.'
Best batting performance: 221* Somerset v Nottinghamshire, Trent Bridge 1986
Best bowling performance: 6-50 Cambridge University v Kent, Canterbury 1977

LAST SEASON: BATTING

	I.	N.O.	R.	H.S.	AV.
TEST					
1ST-CLASS	35	8	1288	221*	47.70
INT					
JPL	12	1	405	75*	36.81
NAT.W.	2	0	41	41	20.50
B & H	4	0	51	26	12.75

CAREER: BATTING

	I.	N.O.	R.	H.S.	AV.
TEST					
1ST-CLASS	410	62	12533	221*	36.01
INT					
JPL	118	22	2961	105	30.84
NAT.W.	28	2	734	98	28.23
B & H	44	5	873	53*	22.38

LAST SEASON: BOWLING

	O.	M.	R.	W.	AV.
TEST					
1ST-CLASS	24	3	120	1	–
INT					
JPL					
NAT.W.					
B & H					

CAREER: BOWLING

	O.	M.	R.	W.	AV.
TEST					
1ST-CLASS	772.3	200	2189	43	50.90
INT					
JPL	12.3	0	65	2	32.50
NAT.W.					
B & H	8.2	1	23	2	11.50

ROMAINES, P. W. Gloucestershire

Full Name: Paul William Romaines
Role: Right-hand opening bat
Born: 25 December 1955, Bishop Auckland, Co Durham
Height: 6' 0" **Weight:** 12st 8lbs
Nickname: Canny, Human
County debut: 1975 (Northamptonshire), 1982 (Gloucestershire)
County cap: 1983 (Gloucestershire)
1000 runs in a season: 2
1st-Class 50s scored: 25
1st-Class 100s scored: 10
One-Day 50s: 17
One-Day 100s: 2
Place in batting averages: 178th av. 20.69 (1985 173rd av. 22.23)
1st-Class catches 1986: 4 (career: 42)
Parents: George and Freda
Wife and date of marriage: Julie Anne, 1979
Education: Leeholme School, Bishop Auckland
Qualifications: 8 O-levels, NCA Qualified Coach
Jobs outside cricket: Sales representative for L'Oreal
Family links with cricket: Father played local cricket and is still an avid watcher. Grandfather, W. R. Romaines, represented Durham in Minor Counties cricket, and played v Australia in 1926
Cricketing superstitions: 'Put left pad on first but during 1986 tried everything which offered the slightest hint of success!'
Cricketers particularly learnt from or admired: P. Willey, Zaheer Abbas,

LAST SEASON: BATTING

	I.	N.O.	R.	H.S.	AV.
TEST					
1ST-CLASS	27	4	476	67*	20.69
INT					
JPL	7	0	140	33	20.00
NAT.W.					
B & H	4	0	181	79	45.25

LAST SEASON: BOWLING

	O.	M.	R.	W.	AV.
TEST					
1ST-CLASS	21.1	0	152	0	—
INT					
JPL					
NAT.W.					
B & H					

CAREER: BATTING

	I.	N.O.	R.	H.S.	AV.
TEST					
1ST-CLASS	199	16	5400	186	29.50
INT					
JPL	56	3	1645	105	31.03
NAT.W.	12	1	324	82	29.45
B & H	13	1	530	125	44.16

CAREER: BOWLING

	O.	M.	R.	W.	AV.
TEST					
1ST-CLASS	36.4	2	211	3	70.33
INT					
JPL					
NAT.W.					
B & H					

Barry Dudleston, Graham Gooch, Clive Radley, Ian Botham, Richard Hadlee, Malcolm Marshall
Other sports played: Squash, golf, soccer
Other sports followed: Athletics
Relaxations: 'Listening to music, having a good pint, antiques, people.'
Extras: Debut for Northamptonshire 1975. Played Minor County cricket with Durham 1977–1981. Joined Gloucestershire in 1982
Injuries 1986: Broken finger
Best batting performance: 186 Gloucestershire v Warwickshire, Nuneaton 1982

ROSE, B. C. Somerset

Full Name: Brian Charles Rose
Role: Left-hand bat
Born: 4 June 1950, Dartford, Kent
Height: 6′ 1″ **Weight:** 13st 8lbs
Nickname: Harry
County debut: 1969
County cap: 1975
Benefit: 1983 (£71,863)
Test debut: 1977–78
No. of Tests: 9
No. of One-Day Internationals: 2
1000 runs in a season: 8
1st-Class 50s scored: 53
1st-Class 100s scored: 23
1st-Class 200s scored: 2
One-Day 50s: 29
One-Day 100s: 3
Place in batting averages: 34th av. 43.55 (1985 54th av. 24.50)
1st-Class catches 1986: 3 (career: 123)

Parents: Jean and Charles
Wife and date of marriage: Stevie, 16 March 1978
Children: Stuart Charles, 19 March 1979; Jamie Joseph, 14 December 1981
Education: Weston-super-Mare Grammar School; Borough Road College, Isleworth
Jobs outside cricket: Teacher
Overseas tours: Pakistan, New Zealand 1977–78; West Indies 1981
Overseas teams played for: Claremont-Cottesloe, Western Australia 1979–80

Off-season 1986–87: Golfing
Other sports played: Golf, squash
Relaxations: Gardening
Extras: Played for English Schools Cricket Association at Lord's in 1968. Plays in spectacles. Captain 1978–83
Opinions on cricket: 'There should be a 16-match championship.'
Injuries 1986: Broken wrist
Best batting performance: 205 Somerset v Northamptonshire, Weston 1977
Best bowling performance: 3-9 Somerset v Gloucestershire, Taunton 1975

LAST SEASON: BATTING

	I.	N.O.	R.	H.S.	AV.
TEST					
1ST-CLASS	23	5	784	129	43.55
INT					
JPL	10	0	239	66	23.90
NAT.W.	1	1	43	43*	
B & H	1	0	49	49	–

LAST SEASON: BOWLING

	O.	M.	R.	W.	AV.
TEST					
1ST-CLASS	11	0	57	2	28.50
INT					
JPL					
NAT.W.					
B & H					

CAREER: BATTING

	I.	N.O.	R.	H.S.	AV.
TEST	16	2	358	70	25.57
1ST-CLASS	428	48	12818	205	33.73
INT	2	0	99	54	49.50
JPL	160	21	3606	112*	25.94
NAT.W.	25	5	757	128	37.85
B & H	50	7	1342	137	31.20

CAREER: BOWLING

	O.	M.	R.	W.	AV.
TEST					
1ST-CLASS	70.1	6	289	8	36.12
INT					
JPL	34	0	152	7	21.71
NAT.W.					
B & H					

ROSE, G. D. Somerset

Full Name: Graham David Rose
Role: Right-hand bat, right-arm fast-medium bowler
Born: 12 April 1964, Tottenham
Height: 6′ 4″ **Weight:** 14½st
Nickname: Rosie
County debut: 1985 (Middlesex)
1st-Class 50s scored: 1
1st-Class 5w. in innings: 1
Parents: William and Edna
Marital status: Single
Education: Northumberland Park School, Tottenham
Qualifications: 6 O-levels, 4 A-levels
Family links with cricket: Father played club cricket in North London

Overseas tours: ESCA U-19 to Zimbabwe; Haringey Cricket College to West Indies 1986

Cricketers particularly learnt from: Jack Robertson, Ted Jackson, Father

Cricketers particularly admired: Dennis Lillee, Richard Hadlee, Wilf Slack

Off-season 1986–87: Playing for Freemantle CC, Perth, Western Australia

Other sports: Golf, squash

Other sports followed: 'Follow Spurs for my sins.'

Opinions on cricket: 'The County Championships should be revised to accommodate 16 four-day championship games during the week with the Benson & Hedges and NatWest played on the Saturdays with the Sunday game remaining.'

Extras: Played for Young England v Young Australia 1983; took 6 wickets on debut. Joined Somerset for 1987 season

Best batting performance: 52 Middlesex v Worcestershire, Worcester 1986

Best bowling performance: 6-41 Middlesex v Worcestershire, Worcester 1985

LAST SEASON: BATTING

	I.	N.O.	R.	H.S.	AV.
TEST					
1ST-CLASS	6	1	74	52	14.80
INT					
JPL	6	1	36	16	7.20
NAT.W.					
B & H					

LAST SEASON: BOWLING

	O.	M.	R.	W.	AV.
TEST					
1ST-CLASS	64	10	277	7	39.57
INT					
JPL	58	4	227	2	113.50
NAT.W.					
B & H					

CAREER: BATTING

	I.	N.O.	R.	H.S.	AV.
TEST					
1ST-CLASS	8	1	93	52	13.28
INT					
JPL	9	1	104	33	11.69
NAT.W.					
B & H	1	0	3	3	–

CAREER: BOWLING

	O.	M.	R.	W.	AV.
TEST					
1ST-CLASS	109.1	18	419	16	26.18
INT					
JPL	97	4	425	5	85.00
NAT.W.					
B & H	4	0	15	0	–

132. Who was the first Glamorgan player to play for England?

ROSEBERRY, M. A.   Middlesex

Full Name: Michael Anthony Roseberry
Role: Right-hand bat, right-arm slow-medium bowler, slip and silly point fielder
Born: 28 November 1966, Sunderland
Height: 6′ 0″ **Weight:** 14st
Nickname: Zorro
County debut: 1985
1st-Class 50s scored: 1
Place in batting averages: 151st av. 24.85
1st-Class catches 1986: 1 (career: 1)
Parents: Matthew and Jean
Marital status: Single
Education: Durham School
Qualifications: 5 O-levels, 1 A-level
Family links with cricket: Uncle, Peter Wyness, played for Royal Navy
Cricketing superstitions: 'Tend to put my front batting pad on first.'
Overseas tours: Young England to West Indies, 1985; Durham School 1st XI to Barbados, 1983
Cricketers particularly learnt from: Alec Coxon (ex-England and Yorkshire bowler), Don Wilson and Gordon Jenkins (MCC Indoor School)
Cricketers particularly admired: Ian Botham, Geoff Boycott
Other sports played: 'Rugby, squash, snooker and whatever takes my fancy.'
Other sports followed: 'Rugby, basketball, football.'
Relaxations: Snooker, music, watching movies
Extras: Won Lord's Taverners/MCC Cricketer of the Year 1983. Won Sunday Sun/Dixon Sport Cricketer of the Year 1983. Won Cricket Societies' Wetherall award 1983, 1984. Won Cricket Societies' award for best Young Cricketer of Year 1984 and Frank Morris memorial award 1984
Best batting performance: 70* Middlesex v Northamptonshire, Northampton 1986

LAST SEASON: BATTING

	I.	N.O.	R.	H.S.	AV.
TEST					
1ST-CLASS	8	1	174	70*	24.85
INT					
JPL	2	0	45	23	22.50
NAT.W.					
B & H					

CAREER: BATTING

	I.	N.O.	R.	H.S.	AV.
TEST					
1ST-CLASS	8	1	174	70*	24.85
INT					
JPL	3	0	60	23	20.00
NAT.W.					
B & H					

RUDD, C. F. B. P.   Derbyshire

Full Name: Christopher Francis
Baines Paul Rudd
Role: Right-hand bat, right-arm
off-spin bowler
Born: 9 December 1963, Sutton
Coldfield
Height: 5' 10½" **Weight:** 11st 12lbs
Nickname: Ruddy
County debut: 1986
Parents: Christopher Michael and
Christine Ann
Marital status: Single
Education: St Richards Prep
School, Herefordshire; Douai
School, Berkshire
Qualifications: 5 O-levels,
cricket coach
Family links with cricket: None
Overseas tours: Minor Counties U-25
to Kenya in 1986

Overseas teams played for: Newcastle University, Newcastle District, Australia
Cricketers particularly learnt from: Phil Russell, Bob Taylor
Cricketers particularly admired: Dennis Amiss
Off-season 1986–87: Player/coach, Newcastle University, New South Wales,
Australia
Other sports played: Golf, football, squash, rugby
Relaxations: Golf, music, meeting friends/people

LAST SEASON: BATTING

	I.	N.O.	R.	H.S.	AV.
TEST					
1ST-CLASS	1	0	1	1	–
INT					
JPL					
NAT.W.					
B & H					

LAST SEASON: BOWLING

	O.	M.	R.	W.	AV.
TEST					
1ST-CLASS	28.3	7	90	0	–
INT					
JPL					
NAT.W.					
B & H					

CAREER: BATTING

	I.	N.O.	R.	H.S.	AV.
TEST					
1ST-CLASS	1	0	1	1	–
INT					
JPL					
NAT.W.					
B & H					

CAREER: BOWLING

	O.	M.	R.	W.	AV.
TEST					
1ST-CLASS	28.3	7	90	0	–
INT					
JPL					
NAT.W.					
B & H					

Extras: Captain Devon U-19 1983. Played for Devon (Minor Counties) 1984–86

RUSSELL, P. E. Derbyshire

Full Name: Philip Edgar Russell
Role: Right-hand bat, right-arm medium bowler
Born: 9 May 1944, Ilkeston
Height: 5′ 11″ **Weight:** 11st 10lbs
County debut: 1965
County cap: 1975
50 wickets in a season: 3
1st-Class 50s scored: 4
1st-Class 5 w. in innings: 5
1st-Class catches 1986: —
(career: 124)
Wife: Phyllis
Children: Miles
Education: Ilkeston Grammar School
Jobs outside cricket: Works full-time for Derbyshire CCC as county coach
Family links with cricket: Father played local cricket
Cricketers particularly learnt from: Les Jackson, Derek Morgan
Cricketers particularly admired: Derek Shackleton
Other sports played: Most ball games
Extras: Not re-engaged after 1972 season but rejoined county in 1974. Retired from first-class cricket but re-appeared in 1985

LAST SEASON: BATTING

	I.	N.O.	R.	H.S.	AV.
TEST					
1ST-CLASS					
INT					
JPL	1	0	1	1	—
NAT.W.	—	—	—	—	—
B & H	1	1	6	6*	—

LAST SEASON: BOWLING

	O.	M.	R.	W.	AV.
TEST					
1ST-CLASS					
INT					
JPL	13	0	47	0	—
NAT.W.	9	2	20	0	—
B & H	7	0	26	1	—

CAREER: BATTING

	I.	N.O.	R.	H.S.	AV.
TEST					
1ST-CLASS	210	46	2929	72	12.32
INT					
JPL	75	30	541	47*	12.02
NAT.W.	7	1	53	27*	8.83
B & H	20	9	80	22*	7.27

CAREER: BOWLING

	O.	M.	R.	W.	AV.
TEST					
1ST-CLASS	4082.5	1227	10351	339	30.53
INT					
JPL	776.3	78	3214	154	20.87
NAT.W.	138.5	28	410	10	41.00
B & H	316.1	56	892	32	27.87

Best batting performance: 72 Derbyshire v Glamorgan, Swansea 1970
Best bowling performance: 7-46 Derbyshire v Yorkshire, Sheffield 1976

RUSSELL, R. C.   Gloucestershire

Full Name: Robert Charles Russell
Role: Left-hand bat, wicket-keeper
Born: 15 August 1963, Stroud
Height: 5' 8½" **Weight:** 9st 8lbs
Nickname: Jack
County debut: 1981
County cap: 1985
1st-Class 50s scored: 6
One-Day 50s: 1
One-Day 100s: 1
Place in batting averages: 133rd
av. 26.59 (1985 227th av. 13.32)
Parents: Derek John and Jenifer
Mary Anne
Wife and date of marriage: Aileen
Ann, 6 March 1985
Children: Stepson, Marcus Anthony
Education: Archway Comprehensive
School
Qualifications: 6 O-levels, 2 A-levels (Technical Drawing, Engineering)
Family links with cricket: Keen sporting family
Cricketing superstitions: 'The numbers 37 and 87. In general try to make
clothing and equipment last as long as possible.'
Overseas tours: Denmark with NCA Young Cricketers 1981; with Gloucestershire to Barbados 1985; Mendip Acorns Pacific tour 1984
Overseas teams played for: Takapuna CC, New Zealand, 1983–85
Cricketers particularly learnt from: Alan Knott, Bob Taylor, Andy
Brassington
Off-season 1986–87: Carpet fitting
Other sports played: Squash, snooker
Other sports followed: Football
Relaxations: 'Watching cricket videos, oil painting, films and comedy.'
Extras: Record for most dismissals in a match for first-class debut: eight (7
caught, 1 stumped) for Gloucestershire v Sri Lanka at Bristol, 1981. Youngest
wicket-keeper for Gloucestershire (17 years 307 days). Represented Young
England against Young West Indies in the Agatha Christie 'Test Match'
series, 1982. Played for Duchess of Norfolk's XI against West Indies at
Arundel in 1984. Joint holder of world record for hat-trick of catches (v

Surrey at The Oval 1986). Youngest wicket-keeper to score JPL hundred (v Worcestershire at Hereford 1986)
Best batting performance: 71 Gloucestershire v Surrey, The Oval 1986

LAST SEASON: BATTING

	I.	N.O.	R.	H.S.	AV.
TEST					
1ST-CLASS	31	9	585	71	26.59
INT					
JPL	11	3	294	108	36.75
NAT.W.	2	0	42	39	21.00
B & H	2	0	11	11	5.50

CAREER: BATTING

	I.	N.O.	R.	H.S.	AV.
TEST					
1ST-CLASS	120	30	1940	71	21.55
INT					
JPL	29	13	435	108	27.18
NAT.W.	8	2	101	39	16.83
B & H	9	2	79	36*	11.29

LAST SEASON: WICKET-KEEPING

	C.	ST.		
TEST				
1ST-CLASS	53	4		
INT				
JPL	5	4		
NAT.W.	1	2		
B & H	4	–		

CAREER: WICKET-KEEPING

	C.	ST.		
TEST				
1ST-CLASS	195	39		
INT				
JPL	28	9		
NAT.W.	8	4		
B & H	16	6		

SAINSBURY, G. E.   Gloucestershire

Full Name: Gary Edward Sainsbury
Role: Right-hand bat, left-arm medium bowler
Born: 17 January 1958, Wanstead, Essex
Height: 6′ 3″ **Weight:** 12st
Nickname: Sains, Noddy
County debut: 1979 (Essex), 1983 (Gloucestershire)
50 wickets in a season: 1
1st-Class 5 w. in innings: 7
Place in bowling averages: —
(1985 4th av. 17.82)
1st-Class catches 1986: —
(career: 11)
Parents: Gordon and Muriel
Wife and date of marriage: Karen Frances, 24 December 1985
Education: Beal Grammar School; Bath University
Qualifications: 11 O-levels, 3 A-levels, BSc (Hons) Statistics. First stage of the NCA Coaching Award
Jobs outside cricket: Computer programmer, C. E. Heath & Co. Ltd. Assis-

tant in Finance Section of Tower Hamlets Council's Social Services Department. Assistant in Research Department, Mortgages Services Department and Dealing Room for Bristol and West Building Society.

Overseas teams played for: Hamilton-Wickham CC, Newcastle, New South Wales, 1981–82

Cricketers particularly learnt from: Bill Morris (Ilford Cricket School), John Gray (Wanstead CC), Mike Denness, John Lever

Cricketers particularly admired: 'First childhood hero was Clive Lloyd, have since admired many cricketers.'

Off-season 1986–87: Resume with Bristol and West Building Society

Other sports played: Squash, badminton, golf

Other sports followed: Casual interest in most sports

Relaxations: Music (Todd Rundgren, Hall and Oates, Judy Tzuke, Phil Collins). Walking the dog. TV. Reading (Tolkien, Donaldson, Forsyth). Eating out (when I can afford it).

Extras: 'Played for Essex CCC 1977–1982. First-class appearances limited to three matches. In my last season with them I was named Young Player of the Year. I believe my claim to fame is taking the first 1st-Class wicket in England this decade (Essex v MCC).'

Opinions on cricket: 'County cricket clubs should be adopting a more professional approach to attracting sponsors. Cricket should be cashing in now on potential sponsors' current disenchantment with football. At the same time, all professional cricketers should recognise their responsibilities towards maintaining cricket's favourable image and keeping existing sponsors happy.'

Best batting performance: 14* Gloucestershire v Yorkshire, Bristol 1986

Best bowling performance: 7-38 Gloucestershire v Northamptonshire, Northampton 1985

LAST SEASON: BATTING

	I.	N.O.	R.	H.S.	AV.
TEST					
1ST-CLASS	3	2	28	14*	–
INT					
JPL	4	2	8	7*	4.00
NAT.W.					
B & H	1	0	4	4	–

CAREER: BATTING

	I.	N.O.	R.	H.S.	AV.
TEST					
1ST-CLASS	53	30	151	14*	6.56
INT					
JPL	12	6	28	7*	4.66
NAT.W.	2	1	5	3*	–
B & H	4	2	6	4	3.00

LAST SEASON: BOWLING

	O.	M.	R.	W.	AV.
TEST					
1ST-CLASS	169.1	46	498	12	41.50
INT					
JPL	92	3	396	14	28.28
NAT.W.					
B & H	3.2	1	14	1	–

CAREER: BOWLING

	O.	M.	R.	W.	AV.
TEST					
1ST-CLASS	1619.1	408	4780	153	31.24
INT					
JPL	334.4	21	1503	44	34.15
NAT.W.	54	14	180	6	30.00
B & H	75	12	237	12	19.75

SAXELBY, K.   Nottinghamshire

Full Name: Kevin Saxelby
Role: Right-hand bat, right-arm medium bowler
Born: 23 February 1959, Worksop
Height: 6′ 2″ **Weight:** 14st
Nickname: Sax
County debut: 1978
County cap: 1984
50 wickets in a season: 1
1st-Class 50s scored: 1
1st-Class 5 w. in innings: 5
1st-Class 10 w. in match: 1
Place in batting averages: 47th av. 41.33
Place in bowling averages: 77th av. 33.51 (1985 98th av. 38.47)
1st-Class catches 1986: 4 (career: 15)
Parents: George Kenneth and Hilda Margaret
Wife: Peta Jean Wendy
Children: Craig Robert, 6 June 1985
Education: Magnus Grammar School, Newark
Qualifications: 10 O-levels, 4 A-levels
Overseas teams played for: North Perth, Australia 1979–80; Durban Collegians, South Africa 1980–81; Alma-Marist, Cape Town 1982–83
Off-season 1986–87: Farming
Other sports played: Rugby union
Relaxations: Gardening
Injuries 1986: Shoulder injury

LAST SEASON: BATTING

	I.	N.O.	R.	H.S.	AV.
TEST					
1ST-CLASS	8	5	124	34	41.53
INT					
JPL	3	3	11	6*	–
NAT.W.	–	–	–	–	–
B & H	–	–	–	–	–

CAREER: BATTING

	I.	N.O.	R.	H.S.	AV.
TEST					
1ST-CLASS	92	28	873	59*	13.64
INT					
JPL	26	17	121	23*	13.44
NAT.W.	3	2	25	12	–
B & H	10	7	51	13*	17.00

LAST SEASON: BOWLING

	O.	M.	R.	W.	AV.
TEST					
1ST-CLASS	284	54	905	27	33.51
INT					
JPL	70	2	367	11	33.36
NAT.W.	19	2	65	3	21.66
B & H	11	0	61	1	–

CAREER: BOWLING

	O.	M.	R.	W.	AV.
TEST					
1ST-CLASS	2080.5	487	6513	211	30.86
INT					
JPL	450	13	2245	80	28.06
NAT.W.	108.5	18	347	18	19.27
B & H	214.2	25	803	29	27.68

Best batting performance: 59* Nottinghamshire v Derbyshire, Chesterfield 1982
Best bowling performance: 6-64 Nottinghamshire v Kent, Tunbridge Wells 1985

SCOTT, A. M. G. Sussex

Full Name: Alastair Martin Gordon Scott
Role: Right-hand bat, left-arm medium pace bowler
Born: 31 March 1966, Guildford
County debut: 1986
Height: 5′ 10″
1st-Class 5 w. in innings: 1
Place in bowling averages: 111th av. 45.22
1st-Class catches 1986: 4 (career: 7)
Education: Seaford Head Comprehensive School; Queens College Cambridge
Overseas tours: Combined Universities to Australia and Hong Kong 1985–86
Extras: Made debut for Cambridge University in 1985, topping the bowling averages. Blues 1985 and 1986. Represented Combined Universities 1986

LAST SEASON: BATTING

	I.	N.O.	R.	H.S.	AV.
TEST					
1ST-CLASS	9	6	29	8	9.67
INT					
JPL					
NAT.W.					
B & H	2	1	2	2	–

CAREER: BATTING

	I.	N.O.	R.	H.S.	AV.
TEST					
1ST-CLASS	16	10	41	8	6.83
INT					
JPL					
NAT.W.					
B & H	4	3	4	2*	–

LAST SEASON: BOWLING

	O.	M.	R.	W.	AV.
TEST					
1ST-CLASS	273	71	814	18	45.22
INT					
JPL					
NAT.W.					
B & H	32.1	5	122	2	61.00

CAREER: BOWLING

	O.	M.	R.	W.	AV.
TEST					
1ST-CLASS	516.3	105	1693	43	39.37
INT					
JPL					
NAT.W.					
B & H	66.1	8	259	4	64.75

Best bowling performance: 5-68 Cambridge University v Nottinghamshire, Cambridge 1986

SCOTT, C. W.   Nottinghamshire

Full Name: Christopher Wilmot Scott
Role: Right-hand bat, wicket-keeper
Born: 23 January 1964, Lincoln
Height: 5′ 9″ **Weight:** 11st
Nickname: George
County debut: 1981
1st-Class 50s scored: 2
Place in batting averages: 31st
av. 44.00
Parents: Kenneth and Kathleen
Marital status: Single
Education: Robert Pattinson
Comprehensive School
Qualifications: 4 O-levels, 2 CSEs,
cricket coach
Jobs outside cricket: Farming
Family links with cricket: Father and
elder brother play for Collingham CC.
Younger brother for Lincolnshire U-19s
Overseas teams played for: Poverty Bay CC, New Zealand 1983–84
Cricketers particularly learnt from: Everyone at Nottinghamshire
Other sports played: Rugby union, soccer
Relaxations: Watching films, listening to records

LAST SEASON: BATTING

	I.	N.O.	R.	H.S.	AV.
TEST					
1ST-CLASS	8	3	220	69*	44.00
INT					
JPL	1	0	10	10	–
NAT.W.					
B & H					

LAST SEASON: WICKET-KEEPING

	C.	ST.			
TEST					
1ST-CLASS	22	1			
INT					
JPL	3	1			
NAT.W.					
B & H					

CAREER: BATTING

	I.	N.O.	R.	H.S.	AV.
TEST					
1ST-CLASS	17	6	410	78	37.27
INT					
JPL	2	0	19	10	9.50
NAT.W.					
B & H					

CAREER: WICKET-KEEPING

	C.	ST.			
TEST					
1ST-CLASS	40	3			
INT					
JPL	3	1			
NAT.W.					
B & H					

Extras: One of the youngest players to play for Nottinghamshire in County Championship team – made debut at 17 years 157 days
Best batting performance: 78 Nottinghamshire v Cambridge University, Cambridge 1983

SCOTT, R. J. — Hampshire

Full Name: Richard James Scott
Role: Left-hand bat, right-arm medium pace bowler
Born: 2 November 1963, Poole, Dorset
Education: Queen Elizabeth School, Wimborne
Extras: Played Minor Counties Cricket for Dorset since 1981. Represented Minor Counties Cricket Association in 1985

LAST SEASON: BATTING

	I.	N.O.	R.	H.S.	AV.
TEST					
1ST-CLASS					
INT					
JPL	1	1	8	8*	–
NAT.W.					
B & H					

CAREER: BATTING

	I.	N.O.	R.	H.S.	AV.
TEST					
1ST-CLASS					
INT					
JPL	1	1	8	8*	–
NAT.W.					
B & H					

133. Who is the only batsman to have scored double centuries in both innings of the same first-class game?

SHARMA, R.   Derbyshire

Full Name: Rajesh Sharma
Role: Right-hand bat, right-arm
off-break bowler, slip or
short-leg fielder
Born: 27 June 1962, Kenya
Height: 6′ 3″ **Weight:** 13st
Nickname: Reg
County debut: 1985
1st-Class 50s scored: 2
Place in batting averages: 109th
av. 29.18
Place in bowling averages: 88th
av. 37.00
1st-Class catches 1986: 14
(career: 20)
Parents: M. R. and R. D.
Marital status: Single
Education: Parkland School for Boys
Qualifications: CSEs and
O-levels
Jobs outside cricket: Family
business (retail trade)
Family links with cricket: Younger brother has played 2nd XI cricket for Kent
Overseas teams played for: Mudgreeba, Queensland 1982–83; Helensvale,
Queensland 1983–84
Cricketers particularly learnt from: Ron Harland (played for Bexley CC)
Cricketers particularly admired: Viv Richards
Off-season 1986–87: Hoping to start own business
Other sports played: Snooker and golf

LAST SEASON: BATTING

	I.	N.O.	R.	H.S.	AV.
TEST					
1ST-CLASS	17	6	321	71	29.18
INT					
JPL	9	3	101	37	16.83
NAT.W.	1	0	9	9	–
B & H	1	0	2	2	–

CAREER: BATTING

	I.	N.O.	R.	H.S.	AV.
TEST					
1ST-CLASS	29	8	530	71	25.23
INT					
JPL	10	3	109	37	15.57
NAT.W.	1	0	9	9	–
B & H	1	0	2	2	–

LAST SEASON: BOWLING

	O.	M.	R.	W.	AV.
TEST					
1ST-CLASS	140.5	33	407	11	37.00
INT					
JPL	38	2	203	1	–
NAT.W.	20	4	52	4	13.00
B & H					

CAREER: BOWLING

	O.	M.	R.	W.	AV.
TEST					
1ST-CLASS	140.5	33	407	11	37.00
INT					
JPL	38	2	203	1	–
NAT.W.	20	4	52	4	13.00
B & H					

Other sports followed: Football and snooker
Relaxations: 'Spending lots of time with my dogs, Simba, Sable and Bruno.'
Opinions on cricket: 'I believe that overseas players have improved the standard of county cricket and their experience has helped younger players. However, I fail to understand the fairness of one county being allowed to have more overseas players than others. When each county is allowed an equal number of overseas players the standards will improve even more.'
Best batting performance: 71 Derbyshire v Warwickshire, Edgbaston 1986
Best bowling performance: 3-72 Derbyshire v Warwickshire, Edgbaston 1986

SHARP, K. Yorkshire

Full Name: Kevin Sharp
Role: Left-hand bat, right-arm off-break bowler
Born: 6 April 1959, Leeds
Height: 5′ 10″ **Weight:** 12st 9lbs
Nickname: Lambsy, Poodle
County debut: 1976
County cap: 1982
1000 runs in a season: 1
1st-Class 50s scored: 34
1st-Class 100s scored: 13
One-day 50s: 16
One-day 100s: 3
Place in batting averages: 58th av. 38.32 (1985 146th av. 25.00)
1st-Class catches 1986: 10 (career: 82)
Parents: Joyce and Gordon
Wife and date of marriage: Karen, 1 October 1983
Children: Amy Lauren, 28 December 1985
Education: Abbey Grange C of E High School, Leeds
Qualifications: CSE Grade I Religious Education. Coaching award
Jobs outside cricket: Plasterer's labourer, warehouseman, driver for film company
Family links with cricket: Father played with Woodhouse in Leeds League for many years. Young brother, David, now playing local cricket
Overseas tours: Derrick Robins' XI to Australasia 1980
Overseas teams played for: Subiaco Floreat CC, Perth, Australia; De Beers CC, Griqualand West, 1981–82
Cricketers particularly learnt from: Doug Padgett, Geoff Boycott, Phil Carrick

Cricketers particularly admired: Richard Hadlee, Malcolm Marshall
Off-season 1986–87: Coaching at home
Other sports played: Golf, squash
Other sports followed: Snooker and soccer
Relaxations: Decorating and maintaining the house
Injuries 1986: Broken big toe
Extras: 260* v Young West Indies 1977. Rested during latter part of 1980 season, on medical advice. Captain of England U-19 v West Indies U-19 1978 at Worcester. Winston Churchill Travelling Fellowship to Australia for two months, 1978. 'I took the first wicket of my career in 1984 – a feat I never thought possible.'
Opinions on cricket: 'Would like to see more Englishmen playing for England. Would like to see Graham Gooch and company left alone because of their contact with South Africa. Why should English players be made scapegoats when South Africans are left well alone?'
Best batting performance: 181 Yorkshire v Gloucestershire, Harrogate 1986
Best bowling performance: 2-13 Yorkshire v Glamorgan, Bradford 1984

LAST SEASON: BATTING

	I.	N.O.	R.	H.S.	AV.
TEST					
1ST-CLASS	31	6	958	181	38.32
INT					
JPL	11	0	328	94	29.81
NAT.W.	2	1	35	33*	–
B & H	4	1	136	105*	45.33

LAST SEASON: BOWLING

	O.	M.	R.	W.	AV.
TEST					
1ST-CLASS	29	4	192	3	64.00
INT					
JPL					
NAT.W.					
B & H					

CAREER: BATTING

	I.	N.O.	R.	H.S.	AV.
TEST					
1ST-CLASS	276	25	7953	181	31.68
INT					
JPL	98	9	2244	114	25.21
NAT.W.	9	2	129	33*	18.42
B & H	32	1	868	105*	28.00

CAREER: BOWLING

	O.	M.	R.	W.	AV.
TEST					
1ST-CLASS	158.1	37	602	11	54.72
INT					
JPL	0.1	0	1	0	–
NAT.W.	1	0	7	0	–
B & H					

---

134. Which current player has the nickname Teflon or Towser?

SHAW, C. Yorkshire

Full Name: Christopher Shaw
Role: Right-hand bat, right-arm fast-medium bowler
Born: 17 February 1964, Hemsworth
Height: 6′ **Weight:** 12st 7lbs
Nickname: Sandie
County debut: 1984
1st-Class 5 w. in innings: 2
Place in bowling averages: 44th av. 27.35 (1985 103rd av. 40.19)
1st-Class catches 1986: 2 (career: 7)
Parents: Brian and Betty
Marital status: Single
Education: Crofton High School
Qualifications: 5 CSEs, Qualified Cricket Coach
Jobs outside cricket: Electrician
Family links with cricket: Father good local league cricketer
Overseas tours: Holland with NCA U-19s North of England 1983; Barbados with Yorkshire Cricket Association 1984
Overseas teams played for: Epuni-Cambridge CC, New Zealand 1985–86
Cricketers particularly learnt from: Father, D. Padgett, S. Oldham, J. Lawrence
Cricketers particularly admired: D. Lillee, M. Holding
Off-season 1986–87: Playing and coaching in Wellington, New Zealand for Hutt Valley Cricket Association
Other sports played: Golf

LAST SEASON: BATTING

	I.	N.O.	R.	H.S.	AV.
TEST					
1ST-CLASS	10	4	57	21	9.50
INT					
JPL	1	1	4	4*	–
NAT.W.	2	0	2	2	1.00
B & H					

CAREER: BATTING

	I.	N.O.	R.	H.S.	AV.
TEST					
1ST-CLASS	28	11	146	21	8.58
INT					
JPL	11	4	85	26	12.14
NAT.W.	3	1	8	6*	4.00
B & H					

LAST SEASON: BOWLING

	O.	M.	R.	W.	AV.
TEST					
1ST-CLASS	300.1	64	848	31	27.35
INT					
JPL	50.4	2	205	4	51.25
NAT.W.	24	4	90	4	22.50
B & H					

CAREER: BOWLING

	O.	M.	R.	W.	AV.
TEST					
1ST-CLASS	770.5	164	2311	68	33.98
INT					
JPL	137.3	4	697	25	27.88
NAT.W.	34.1	7	104	5	20.80
B & H					

Other sports followed: Likes watching all sports; keen supporter of Feather-stone Rovers RLFC
Relaxations: Playing golf, listening to music
Extras: 'On debut at Lord's took 6-48 v Middlesex. Took 5-41 in my second JPL match v Hampshire at Bournemouth.'
Best batting performance: 21 Yorkshire v Leicestershire, Middlesbrough 1986
Best bowling performance: 5-38 Yorkshire v Northamptonshire, Scarborough 1986

SIDEBOTTOM, A.   Yorkshire

Full Name: Arnold Sidebottom
Role: Right-hand bat, right-arm fast-medium bowler, outfielder
Born: 1 April 1954, Barnsley
Height: 6' 2" **Weight:** 13st 10lbs
Nickname: Woofer, Red Setter, Arnie
County debut: 1973
County cap: 1980
Test debut: 1985
No. of Tests: 1
50 wickets in a season: 2
1st-Class 50s scored: 11
1st-Class 100s scored: 1
1st-Class 5 w. in innings: 15
1st-Class 10 w. in match: 2
One-day 50s: 1
Place in batting averages: —
(1985 156th av. 24.50)
Place in bowling averages: 39th av. 26.84 (1985 80th av. 35.23)
1st-Class catches 1986: 3 (career: 41)
Parents: Jack and Florence
Wife and date of marriage: Gillian, 17 June 1977
Children: Ryan Jay, 1978; Dale, 1980
Education: Barnsley Broadway Grammar School
Jobs outside cricket: Professional footballer with Manchester United for five years, Huddersfield Town for two years and Halifax Town
Family links with cricket: 'Father good cricketer.'
Overseas tours: Rebel England team to South Africa 1982
Cricketers particularly learnt from: Father, Doug Padgett, G. Boycott
Cricketers particularly admired: S. Oldham, D. Bairstow, G. Stevenson
Other sports played: Professional football, tennis, table-tennis, badminton
Other sports followed: Most sports
Relaxations: Watching television, horse-racing, playing with sons

Injuries 1986: Broken finger
Extras: Banned from Test cricket for three years for joining rebel team to South Africa in 1982. Injured toe during Test debut in 1985 and not picked for England again
Best batting performance: 124 Yorkshire v Glamorgan, Cardiff 1977
Best bowling performance: 7-18 Yorkshire v Oxford University, Oxford 1980

LAST SEASON: BATTING

	I.	N.O.	R.	H.S.	AV.
TEST					
1ST-CLASS	9	2	65	18	9.28
INT					
JPL	6	3	41	35*	13.66
NAT.W.	1	0	1	1	–
B & H	2	1	31	18*	–

CAREER: BATTING

	I.	N.O.	R.	H.S.	AV.
TEST	1	0	2	2	–
1ST-CLASS	186	45	3246	124	23.02
INT					
JPL	59	21	634	52*	16.68
NAT.W.	11	4	172	45	24.57
B & H	21	7	232	32	16.57

LAST SEASON: BOWLING

	O.	M.	R.	W.	AV.
TEST					
1ST-CLASS	226.1	37	671	25	26.84
INT					
JPL	68.3	0	292	12	24.33
NAT.W.	12	0	31	1	–
B & H	40	8	152	9	16.88

CAREER: BOWLING

	O.	M.	R.	W.	AV.
TEST	18.4	3	65	1	–
1ST-CLASS	3460.1	759	10066	414	24.31
INT					
JPL	721.5	29	3132	108	29.00
NAT.W.	161.2	18	477	26	18.34
B & H	345	51	1149	53	21.67

SIMMONS, J. Lancashire

Full Name: Jack Simmons
Role: Right-hand bat, right-arm off-break bowler, slip fielder
Born: 28 March 1941, Clayton-le-Moors, near Accrington
Height: 6' 2" **Weight:** 15st
Nickname: Simmo, Flat Jack
County debut: 1968
County cap: 1971
Benefit: 1980 (£128,000)
50 wickets in a season: 7
1st-Class 50s scored: 37
1st-Class 100s scored: 6
1st-Class 5 w. in innings: 35
1st-Class 10 w. in match: 5
One-day 50s: 6
Place in batting averages: 148th av. 25.00 (1985 199th av. 18.65)
Place in bowling averages: 9th av. 21.16 (1985 100th av. 38.57)

1st-Class catches 1986: 7 (career: 309)

Parents: Ada and Robert

Wife and date of marriage: Jacqueline, 23 March 1963

Children: Kelly Louise, 28 January 1979

Education: Accrington Technical School; Blackburn Technical College

Qualifications: 5 O-levels, ONC, City & Guilds in Quantities

Jobs outside cricket: Draughtsman with Accrington Brick & Tile Co Ltd, and Lancashire County Surveyors' Department. Partnership with Clive Lloyd as agents for cricketers, also partnership with Pat Pocock in managing cricket matches for club cricketers at La Manga in Spain. Director of Leisure Centre called 'Bowlers'; the largest indoor cricket and bowls centre in the world, situated in Trafford Park, Manchester

Family links with cricket: Father, Robert, played with Enfield, Lancashire League. Grandfather, Robert, also played for Enfield since 1887, 'giving 92 years' association with the same club.'

Cricketing superstitions: 'I always like to be last on the field. To do the same things again if successful once, i.e. clothes or eating habits.'

Overseas tours: Zimbabwe and South Africa with Whitbread Wanderers 1975; Mike Brearley Invitation XI to Calcutta 1981; New York 1985 with C. Lloyd Lancashire XI

Overseas teams played for: Tasmania 1972–79 (where he is 'a bit of a folk hero'). Captained Tasmania to Gillette Cup for first time in 1979, and when they first entered Sheffield Shield (1978)

Cricketers particularly learnt from: 'Coached by Clyde Walcott when I was a youngster. Learnt from Clive Lloyd with Lancashire. Jack Bond, Ray Illingworth, plus many more off-spinners.'

Cricketers particularly admired: 'Clive Lloyd (great team man), Viv Richards, Chappell brothers and great bowlers, Dennis Lillee and Michael Holding.'

Off-season 1986–87: Working at 'Bowlers' and taking two tours to watch England in Australia

Relaxations: Soccer, golf, horse-racing, 'plus eating, playing cards, watching television and going on holiday.'

Injuries 1986: Kicked ball with instep and was injured for 4 weeks

Extras: 'I didn't play for a couple of years because I broke my leg three times in ten months and the previous year broke my arm quite badly, all playing soccer – except one broken leg, which was broken going down to the football ground just after I had it out of plaster for the first time.' Made debut for 2nd XI in 1959. Hat-trick v Nottinghamshire (Liverpool) 1977, Director of Burnley FC. Published autobiography *Flat Jack* in 1986

Opinions on cricket: 'Would like to see lbw law changed for leg-spin bowlers. If pitched outside leg stump and would hit wicket, especially if batsman on back foot, he should be out.'

Best batting performance: 112 Lancashire v Sussex, Hove 1970

Best bowling performance: 7-59 Tasmania v Queensland, Brisbane 1978–79

	I.	N.O.	R.	H.S.	AV.
TEST					
1ST-CLASS	17	5	300	61	25.00
INT					
JPL	4	1	18	15	6.00
NAT.W.	2	1	15	9	–
B & H	4	3	40	16*	–

LAST SEASON: BOWLING

	O.	M.	R.	W.	AV.
TEST					
1ST-CLASS	230.5	52	762	36	21.16
INT					
JPL	92.4	5	456	16	28.50
NAT.W.	36	11	81	3	27.00
B & H	39	7	119	3	39.66

CAREER: BATTING

	I.	N.O.	R.	H.S.	AV.
TEST					
1ST-CLASS	501	126	8738	112	23.30
INT					
JPL	168	50	1865	65	15.80
NAT.W.	33	14	442	54*	23.26
B & H	47	18	602	64	20.75

CAREER: BOWLING

	O.	M.	R.	W.	AV.
TEST					
1ST-CLASS	446.2 9116.1	94 2088	24671	895	27.56
INT					
JPL	1657.2	130	6799	261	26.04
NAT.W.	555.5	103	1626	71	22.90
B & H	606.2	124	1677	68	24.66

SLACK, W. N. — Middlesex

Full Name: Wilfred Norris Slack
Role: Left-hand bat, right-arm medium bowler, short-leg fielder
Born: 12 December 1954, Troumaca, St Vincent, West Indies
Height: 6′ **Weight:** 13st
Nickname: Slacky
County debut: 1977
County cap: 1981
Test debut: 1985–86
No. of Tests: 3
No. of One-Day Internationals: 2
1000 runs in a season: 6
1st-Class 50s scored: 61
1st-Class 100s scored: 16
1st-Class 200s scored: 3
One-day 50s: 24
One-day 100s: 1
Place in batting averages: 59th
av. 38.25 (1985 15th av. 54.29)
1st-Class catches 1986: 19 (career: 145)
Parents: Grafton and Doreen
Education: Wellesbourne Secondary, High Wycombe
Qualifications: City & Guilds in Radio and TV mechanics, NCA Advanced Coach
Jobs outside cricket: Digital electronics test engineer

Overseas tours: To Pakistan with Rohan Kanhai's World XI in September 1981. England B to Sri Lanka 1986 and then joined England tour of West Indies 1986
Overseas teams played for: Played in Auckland, New Zealand, 1979–80; World XI in Pakistan 1981
Cricketers particularly learnt from: Don Bennett, Clive Radley
Off-season 1986–87: Touring Australia with England
Other sports played: Basketball for Bucks and Wycombe Pirates; tennis, squash, badminton, football, athletics
Relaxations: Building electronic projects. Relaxing in a sauna
Injuries 1986: Groin strain
Extras: Played for Buckinghamshire in 1976. At 16 played for Wycombe Colts. Played for Freith in Haigh Village Cricket Competition. Then joined High Wycombe; then Buckinghamshire in 1976; then Middlesex in 1977. Qualified to play both for West Indies and England
Best batting performance: 248* Middlesex v Worcestershire, Lord's 1981
Best bowling performance: 3-17 Middlesex v Leicestershire, Uxbridge 1982

LAST SEASON: BATTING

	I.	N.O.	R.	H.S.	AV.
TEST	2	0	19	18	9.50
1ST-CLASS	33	3	1205	106	40.16
INT					
JPL	10	1	327	101*	36.33
NAT.W.	2	0	45	27	22.50
B & H	7	0	195	65	27.85

LAST SEASON: BOWLING

	O.	M.	R.	W.	AV.
TEST					
1ST-CLASS	17	3	75	1	–
INT					
JPL	12	0	50	1	–
NAT.W.	2	0	14	0	–
B & H					

CAREER: BATTING

	I.	N.O.	R.	H.S.	AV.
TEST	6	0	81	52	13.50
1ST-CLASS	309	35	10821	248*	39.49
INT	2	0	43	34	21.50
JPL	75	9	1860	101*	28.18
NAT.W.	19	1	680	98	37.77
B & H	28	3	653	65	26.12

CAREER: BOWLING

	O.	M.	R.	W.	AV.
TEST					
1ST-CLASS	199.5	34	581	19	30.57
INT					
JPL	158.4	1	779	31	25.12
NAT.W.	81	6	290	8	36.25
B & H	7	0	34	0	–

135. Which current player has the nickname Zorro?

SMALL, G. C.   Warwickshire

Full Name: Gladstone Cleophas
Small
Role: Right-hand bat, right-arm
fast-medium bowler
Born: 18 October 1961, St George,
Barbados
Height: 5' 11" **Weight:** 12st
Nickname: Gladys
County debut: 1980
County cap: 1982
Test debut: 1986
No. of Tests: 2
50 wickets in a season: 4
1st-Class 50s scored: 1
1st-Class 5 w. in innings: 13
Place in batting averages: 205th
av. 16.00 (1985 219th av. 15.00)
Place in bowling averages: 17th
av. 23.12 (1985 31st av. 26.81)

1st-Class catches 1986: 4 (career: 38)
Parents: Chelston and Gladys
Marital status: Single
Education: Mosely School; Hall Green Technical College, Birmingham
Qualifications: 2 O-levels
Family links with cricket: Cousin, Milton Small, toured England with West
Indies in 1984
Overseas tours: With Young England to New Zealand 1979–80; Derrick
Robins' XI tour of Australia, Tasmania, New Zealand 1980; Rohan Kanhai
International XI tour of Pakistan 1981
Overseas teams played for: Balwyn CC, Melbourne 1982–83, 1984–85; South
Australia and West Torrens, Adelaide 1985–86
Cricketers particularly learnt from: David Brown (manager at Warwickshire)
Cricketers particularly admired: Dennis Lillee, Malcolm Marshall, Richard
Hadlee, Bob Willis
Off-season 1986–87: Touring Australia with England
Other sports played: Golf, tennis
Other sports followed: Athletics, golf, tennis, soccer
Relaxations: 'Playing a round of golf really relaxes me; listening to music and
relaxing with my fiancée.'
Extras: In 1980, became youngest bowler to take five JPL wickets in one
innings. Was called up for England Test squad v Pakistan at Edgbaston, July
1982, but did not play. Bowled 18-ball over v Middlesex in August 1982, with
11 no balls

Opinions on cricket: 'The introduction of four-day championship cricket would improve the first-class game in that teams would have to bowl out the opposition twice instead of relying on contrived results. For four-day cricket to be successful, clubs must be made to produce good hard cricketing wickets that would be beneficial to both batsmen and bowlers.'

Best batting performance: 57* Warwickshire v Oxford University, Oxford 1982

Best bowling performance: 7-68 Warwickshire v Yorkshire, Edgbaston 1982

LAST SEASON: BATTING

	I.	N.O.	R.	H.S.	AV.
TEST	2	1	14	12	–
1ST-CLASS	24	6	290	45*	16.11
INT					
JPL	5	1	36	23	9.00
NAT.W.	2	1	3	3*	–
B & H	3	1	9	5*	4.50

LAST SEASON: BOWLING

	O.	M.	R.	W.	AV.
TEST	64	20	134	4	33.50
1ST-CLASS	575.3	138	1647	73	22.56
INT					
JPL	83	8	317	15	21.13
NAT.W.	24	5	68	3	22.66
B & H	32.5	2	137	4	34.25

CAREER: BATTING

	I.	N.O.	R.	H.S.	AV.
TEST	2	1	14	12	–
1ST-CLASS	178	42	1806	57*	13.27
INT					
JPL	39	14	216	40*	8.64
NAT.W.	10	4	99	33	16.50
B & H	16	5	76	19*	6.90

CAREER: BOWLING

	O.	M.	R.	W.	AV.
TEST	64	20	134	4	33.50
1ST-CLASS	3625.5	695	11707	395	29.63
INT					
JPL	577.3	39	2691	122	22.05
NAT.W.	166.1	33	552	22	25.09
B & H	244.2	43	922	32	28.81

SMITH, C. L.   Hampshire

Full Name: Christopher Lyall Smith
Role: Right-hand bat
Born: 15 October 1958, Durban, South Africa
Height: 5' 11" **Weight:** 13st 7lbs
Nickname: Kippy
County debut: 1979 (Glamorgan), 1980 (Hampshire)
County cap: 1981 (Hampshire)
Test debut: 1983
No. of Tests: 8
No. of One-Day Internationals: 4
1000 runs in a season: 5
1st-Class 50s scored: 50
1st-Class 100s scored: 28
One-day 50s: 23
One-day 100s: 1
Place in batting averages: 17th av. 48.22 (1985 9th av. 57.14)

1st-Class catches 1986: 16 (career: 98)
Parents: John Arnold and Elaine Jessie
Marital status: Single
Education: Northlands High School, Durban, South Africa
Qualifications: Matriculation (2 A-level equivalents)
Jobs outside cricket: Chris Smith Promotions, sports marketing and promotions business
Family links with cricket: Grandfather, Vernon Lyall Shearer, played for Natal; brother, Robin, also plays for Hampshire
Overseas tours: Toured UK with Kingsmead Mynahs (Natal under-25s under another name) 1976; with England to New Zealand and Pakistan 1983–84; England B to Sri Lanka 1986
Overseas teams played for: Kingsmead Mynahs; Natal Schools 1975; South African Schools 1976; Natal B, debut 1978
Cricketers particularly admired: 'Barry Richards, Grayson Heath (my coach in South Africa).'
Other sports played: League squash, golf (handicap 15)
Other sports followed: Watches football (Southampton FC)
Relaxations: Walking in the countryside or lying on the beach. In winter, pheasant or partridge shooting at a friend's on Lulworth Estate
Extras: Made debut for Glamorgan in 1979. Played for Gorseinon in South Wales League in 1979. Made Hampshire debut 1980. Captained Hampshire 2nd XI in 1981. Became eligible to play for England in 1983
Best batting performance: 193 Hampshire v Derbyshire, Derby 1983
Best bowling performance: 3-35 Hampshire v Glamorgan, Southampton 1983

LAST SEASON: BATTING

	I.	N.O.	R.	H.S.	AV.
TEST	2	0	34	28	17.00
1ST-CLASS	28	8	1027	114*	51.35
INT					
JPL	8	2	224	75*	37.33
NAT.W.	2	0	26	25	13.00
B & H	2	0	88	67	44.00

LAST SEASON: BOWLING

	O.	M.	R.	W.	AV.
TEST					
1ST-CLASS	40	11	157	1	–
INT					
JPL					
NAT.W.					
B & H					

CAREER: BATTING

	I.	N.O.	R.	H.S.	AV.
TEST	14	1	392	91	30.15
1ST-CLASS	269	33	10012	193	42.42
INT	4	0	109	70	27.25
JPL	60	9	2037	95	39.94
NAT.W.	14	2	308	101*	25.66
B & H	15	2	416	82*	32.00

CAREER: BOWLING

	O.	M.	R.	W.	AV.
TEST	17	4	39	3	13.00
1ST-CLASS	567.5	109	2148	34	63.17
INT	6	0	28	2	14.00
JPL	3.3	1	10	2	5.00
NAT.W.	12	3	32	3	10.66
B & H					

SMITH, D. M. Worcestershire

Full Name: David Mark Smith
Role: Left-hand bat, right-arm
fast-medium bowler
Born: 9 January 1956, Balham
Height: 6′ 4″ **Weight:** 15st
Nickname: Smudger, Tom
County debut: 1973 (Surrey),
1984 (Worcestershire)
County cap: 1980 (Surrey),
1984 (Worcestershire)
Test debut: 1985–86
No. of Tests: 2
No. of One-Day Internationals: 1
1000 runs in a season: 4
1st-Class 50s scored: 40
1st-Class 100s scored: 16
One-day 50s: 21
One-day 100s: 3
Place in batting averages: 36th
av. 43.37 (1985 28th av. 46.38)
1st-Class catches 1986: 9 (career: 129)
Parents: Dennis Henry and Tina
Wife and date of marriage: Jacqui, 7 January 1977
Children: Sarah Jane Louise, 4 April 1982
Education: Battersea Grammar School
Qualifications: 3 O-levels
Jobs outside cricket: Two years with insurance company, one year with Harrods, one year spent in Zimbabwe, two years with building firm. Contracts manager, painting and decorating firm

LAST SEASON: BATTING

	I.	N.O.	R.	H.S.	AV.
TEST					
1ST-CLASS	28	4	1041	165*	43.37
INT					
JPL	9	1	272	64*	34.00
NAT.W.	4	0	101	62	25.25
B & H	5	2	191	90*	63.66

LAST SEASON: BOWLING

	O.	M.	R.	W.	AV.
TEST					
1ST-CLASS	11	3	35	2	17.50
INT					
JPL					
NAT.W.	2	1	5	1	–
B & H					

CAREER: BATTING

	I.	N.O.	R.	H.S.	AV.
TEST	4	0	80	47	20.00
1ST-CLASS	308	62	8582	189*	34.88
INT	1	1	10	10*	–
JPL	107	24	2154	87*	25.95
NAT.W.	23	5	942	109	52.33
B & H	40	7	1109	126	33.60

CAREER: BOWLING

	O.	M.	R.	W.	AV.
TEST					
1ST-CLASS	456	96	1520	30	50.66
INT					
JPL	124.5	6	606	12	50.50
NAT.W.	31	6	118	4	29.50
B & H	56	4	266	8	33.25

Family links with cricket: Father plays cricket for the BBC
Cricketing superstitions: 'No room for them all.'
Overseas tours: West Indies with England 1986
Overseas teams played for: Sydney University, Australia, 1980–81, 1982–83
Cricketers particularly learnt from: Mickey Stewart and Graham Roope
Cricketers particularly admired: Graham Gooch, Malcolm Marshall, Ian Botham
Other sports played: Football, motor-racing
Relaxations: 'I own my own racing car.'
Injuries 1986: Disc trouble and broken finger
Extras: Played for Surrey 2nd XI in 1972. Was not retained after 1977 but was re-instated in 1978. Top of Surrey first-class batting averages in 1982. 'Has a cocker spaniel called Winston.' Sacked by Surrey during 1983 season. Joined Worcestershire in 1984
Best batting performance: 189* Worcestershire v Kent, Worcester, 1984
Best bowling performance: 3-39 Surrey v Derbyshire, Ilkeston 1976

SMITH, G.   Northamptonshire

Full Name: Gareth Smith
Role: Right-hand bat, left-arm fast-medium bowler, mid-off or cover fielder
Born: 20 July 1966, Jarrow
Height: 6′ 1″ **Weight:** 12st
Nickname: 'Quite a few actually! – Happy, Hippy, Bob, Oz, Gelders, Smudger.'
County debut: 1986
1st-Class catches 1986: 1 (career: 1)
Parents: John and Patricia
Marital status: Single
Education: Boldon Comprehensive School; South Tyneside College
Qualifications: 6 O-levels. B/Tec ONC in computer studies. B/Tec OND in computer studies
Jobs outside cricket: Worked in sports shop in Newcastle
Family links with cricket: Father on selection committee at Boldon CC
Cricketing superstitions: If there is one, it is putting left pad on first
Cricketers particularly learnt from: Bob Carter (Northamptonshire CCC), Bob Cottam, Keith Judd
Cricketers particularly admired: Michael Holding

Off-season 1986–87: Looking for employment ('easier said than done living in the North-East')
Other sports played: Football, squash, golf, tennis
Relaxations: Listening to music, watching TV, reading
Injuries 1986: 'You name it! Pulled back muscle, knee strain, badly bruised finger, bruised and swollen instep.'
Extras: 'With only my 2nd ball in first class cricket got the wicket of S. M. Gavaskar (versus Indian tourists, 1986). Was part of a team of runners who ran 759 miles in a relay run from Headingley, via all the other 1st-Class county grounds to The Oval to raise money for Leukaemia Research.'
Opinions on cricket: 'At times I wish the stumps were twice the normal size (when bowling of course!). County clubs should do more to find or help find employment for players who stay at home as opposed to playing cricket abroad.'
Best batting performance: 4 Northamptonshire v India, Northampton 1986

LAST SEASON: BATTING

	I.	N.O.	R.	H.S.	AV.
TEST					
1ST-CLASS	2	0	7	4	3.50
INT					
JPL					
NAT.W.					
B & H					

CAREER: BATTING

	I.	N.O.	R.	H.S.	AV.
TEST					
1ST-CLASS	2	0	7	4	3.50
INT					
JPL					
NAT.W.					
B & H					

SMITH, I. Glamorgan

Full Name: Ian Smith
Role: Right-hand bat, right-arm medium bowler, slip fielder
Born: 11 March 1967, Consett
Height: 6' 3" **Weight:** 13st
Nickname: Smudga
County debut: 1985
1st-Class catches 1986: 1 (career: 2)
Parents: Jim and Mary
Marital status: Single
Education: Ryton Comprehensive School
Qualifications: 2 O-levels, CSE
Jobs outside cricket: Coach
Family links with cricket: Father NCA staff coach, brother league player
Overseas tours: England Young Cricketers in West Indies 1985

Cricketers particularly learnt from: Tom Cartwright, Alan Jones
Cricketers particularly admired: Ian Botham
Off-season 1986–87: Playing in New Zealand
Other sports played: Football, golf, snooker
Other sports followed: All sports
Relaxations: Music
Injuries 1986: Back injury
Extras: Played for Young England v Sri Lanka 1986. Represented county at football. Offered terms by Southampton, York City and Carlisle United. Now plays for Blyth Spartans
Best batting performance: 12 Glamorgan v Derbyshire, Derby 1985
Best bowling performance: 1-18 Glamorgan v Essex, Chelmsford 1986

LAST SEASON: BATTING

	I.	N.O.	R.	H.S.	AV.
TEST					
1ST-CLASS	2	0	0	0	0.00
INT					
JPL	2	1	3	3*	–
NAT.W.					
B & H	1	0	6	6	–

LAST SEASON: BOWLING

	O.	M.	R.	W.	AV.
TEST					
1ST-CLASS	24	3	111	1	–
INT					
JPL					
NAT.W.					
B & H	7	0	32	0	–

CAREER: BATTING

	I.	N.O.	R.	H.S.	AV.
TEST					
1ST-CLASS	7	0	27	12	3.85
INT					
JPL	4	1	8	3*	2.66
NAT.W.					
B & H	1	0	6	6	–

CAREER: BOWLING

	O.	M.	R.	W.	AV.
TEST					
1ST-CLASS	68.4	14	265	2	132.50
INT					
JPL					
NAT.W.					
B & H	7	0	32	0	–

136. Which current player has the nickname Dusty or Wino?

137. Which current player has the nickname Bumper or Wingnut?

138. Which current player has the nickname Kippy?

139. Which current player has the nickname Gladys?

SMITH, L. K.   Worcestershire

Full Name: Lawrence Kilner Smith
Role: Right-hand opening bat, occasional wicket-keeper
Born: 6 January 1964, Mirfield, Spen Valley, Yorkshire
Height: 5′ 8″ **Weight:** 9st
Nickname: Smithy, Smudge
County debut: 1985
1st-Class catches 1986: 1 (career: 1)
Parents: David Henry Kilner and Christine Sonia
Marital status: Single
Family links with cricket: Father played for Derbyshire and Orange Free State
Education: Stancliffe Hall, Derbyshire; CBC and St Andrew's, Welkom, South Africa; KES Johannesburg; Beachwood, Durban
Jobs outside cricket: Worked as a video electrician for a company operating video games
Overseas teams played for: Lived and played in South Africa for seven years. Played in Durban, Natal for Durban Collegians winning batting trophy in 1984–85 season
Cricketers particularly learnt from: 'My father particularly and since coming to Worcester, Basil D'Oliveira.'
Cricketers particularly admired: Geoff Boycott, David Gower
Other sports played: Squash, golf
Other sports followed: Motor sport, golf
Relaxations: Music, movies
Extras: Broke batting record, most runs in a season Stancliffe Hall 1977. First ever honours for cricket at St Andrew's Welkom. OFS schools side.
Best batting performance: 28 Worcestershire v Cambridge University, Cambridge 1985

LAST SEASON: BATTING

	I.	N.O.	R.	H.S.	AV.
TEST					
1ST-CLASS	2	0	4	2	2.00
INT					
JPL					
NAT.W.					
B & H					

CAREER: BATTING

	I.	N.O.	R.	H.S.	AV.
TEST					
1ST-CLASS	3	0	32	28	10.66
INT					
JPL	1	0	3	3	–
NAT.W.					
B & H					

SMITH, P. A. Warwickshire

Full Name: Paul Andrew Smith
Role: Right-hand bat, right-arm
fast-medium bowler, cover fielder
Born: 15 April 1964, Newcastle
Height: 6′ 2″ **Weight:** 12st
Nickname: Moonman, Smithy
County debut: 1982
County cap: 1986
1000 runs in a season: 2
1st-Class 50s scored: 31
1st-Class 100s scored: 2
One-day 50s: 3
Place in batting averages: 63rd
av. 37.70 (1985 157th av. 23.97)
Place in bowling averages: 124th
av. 57.15 (1985 117th av. 43.96)
1st-Class catches 1986: 7 (career: 34)

Parents: Kenneth and Joy
Marital status: Single
Education: Heaton Grammar School
Qualifications: 5 O-levels
Jobs outside cricket: Warehouseman 1985–86
Family links with cricket: Father played for Leicestershire and Northumberland. Both brothers played for Warwickshire
Cricketing superstitions: 'I have a long sleeved shirt which I wear all the time if I am scoring runs.'
Overseas teams played for: Florida, Johannesburg, 1982–83; Belgrano CC, Argentina 1983–84; Carlton, Melbourne, 1984–85
Cricketers particularly learnt from: D. Amiss, D. J. Brown, R. G. D. Willis
Cricketers particularly admired: Father and K. D. Smith
Off-season 1986–87: Finding work
Other sports played: Occasional squash
Relaxations: Listening to music
Injuries 1986: Hit on the head twice in 3 days, breaking helmets on each occasion but missed no cricket
Extras: Along with Andy Moles set a new world record for most consecutive 50+ partnerships in first 12 innings together
Opinions on cricket: 'I think we play far too much cricket and with the amount of time spent on motorways players are very tired before they bowl a ball or take guard. If Sunday matches become 50 overs it will make matters worse.'
Best batting performance: 119 Warwickshire v Worcestershire, Edgbaston 1986
Best bowling performance: 4-25 Warwickshire v Lancashire, Edgbaston 1985

	I.	N.O.	R.	H.S.	AV.
TEST					
1ST-CLASS	44	4	1508	119	37.70
INT					
JPL	12	2	131	28*	13.10
NAT.W.	3	0	109	79	36.33
B & H	4	0	83	35	20.75

CAREER: BATTING

	I.	N.O.	R.	H.S.	AV.
TEST					
1ST-CLASS	155	15	4204	119	30.03
INT					
JPL	52	16	790	50*	21.94
NAT.W.	9	2	220	79	31.42
B & H	14	3	205	37	18.63

LAST SEASON: BOWLING

	O.	M.	R.	W.	AV.
TEST					
1ST-CLASS	159	19	743	13	57.15
INT					
JPL	41	0	209	5	41.80
NAT.W.	17	1	57	2	28.50
B & H					

CAREER: BOWLING

	O.	M.	R.	W.	AV.
TEST					
1ST-CLASS	945	118	4105	90	45.61
INT					
JPL	214.1	4	1184	34	34.82
NAT.W.	43.4	1	189	7	27.00
B & H	38.1	1	184	5	36.80

SMITH, R. A. — Hampshire

Full Name: Robin Arnold Smith
Role: Right-hand bat
Born: 13 September 1963, Durban, South Africa
Height: 5′ 11½″ **Weight:** 15st
Nickname: Judge
County debut: 1982
County cap: 1985
1000 runs in a season: 2
1st-Class 50s scored: 27
1st-Class 100s scored: 10
One-day 50s: 11
One-day 100s: 3
Place in batting averages: 41st av. 41.23 (1985 37th av. 42.58)
1st-Class catches 1986: 21 (career: 54)
Parents: John Arnold and Elaine Jessie
Marital status: 'Halfway stage.'
Education: Northlands Boys High, Durban
Qualifications: 'Highly qualified with regard to my educational studies.'
Family links with cricket: Grandfather played for Natal in Currie Cup. Brother Chris plays for Hampshire, Natal and England.
Cricketing superstitions: 'Always have a big night out before a game.'
Overseas teams played for: Natal B, 1980–81; Natal A, 1981–82
Cricketers particularly admired: Barry Richards, Viv Richards, Graeme Pollock, Malcolm Marshall

Other sports played: Rugby, squash, golf
Other sports followed: Soccer, athletics
Relaxations: Backgammon, fishing, music and 'siestas'
Extras: Played rugby for Natal Schools, 1980. South Africa Schools Cricket, 1979–80. Still holds South African shot-putt and hurdles U-19 records
Opinions on cricket: 'I would like to see the 4-day game introduced into English county cricket.'
Best batting performance: 140* Hampshire v Derbyshire, Basingstoke 1985
Best bowling performance: 2-11 Hampshire v Surrey, Southampton 1985

LAST SEASON: BATTING

	I.	N.O.	R.	H.S.	AV.
TEST					
1ST-CLASS	38	8	1237	128*	41.23
INT					
JPL	14	5	629	95	69.88
NAT.W.	2	0	57	39	28.50
B & H	4	0	61	37	15.25

LAST SEASON: BOWLING

	O.	M.	R.	W.	AV.
TEST					
1ST-CLASS	48.4	6	217	3	72.33
INT					
JPL					
NAT.W.					
B & H					

CAREER: BATTING

	I.	N.O.	R.	H.S.	AV.
TEST					
1ST-CLASS	161	27	5108	140*	38.11
INT					
JPL	33	9	1241	104	51.70
NAT.W.	6	1	252	110	50.40
B & H	10	1	320	81	35.55

CAREER: BOWLING

	O.	M.	R.	W.	AV.
TEST					
1ST-CLASS	82.2	14	340	7	48.57
INT					
JPL					
NAT.W.	2.5	0	13	2	6.50
B & H					

140. Which current player has the nickname Stan?

141. Which current player has the nickname Tommy?

142. Which current player has the nickname Digger or Pablo?

143. Which current player has the nickname K.C.?

Full Name: Martin Peter Speight
Role: Right-hand bat, wicket-keeper
Born: 24 October 1967, Walsall
Height: 5′ 9½″ **Weight:** 10st 8lbs
Nickname: Speighty, Sprog
County debut: 1986
Parents: Peter John and Valerie
Marital status: Single
Education: Windmills, Hassocks; Hurstpierpoint College
Qualifications: 13 O-levels and 3 A-levels
Overseas tours: NCA U-19 South Tour to Bermuda, 1985; Hurstpierpoint College Tour to India, 1985–86

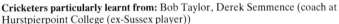

Cricketers particularly learnt from: Bob Taylor, Derek Semmence (coach at Hurstpierpoint College (ex-Sussex player))
Cricketers particularly admired: Viv Richards, Imran Khan, Malcolm Marshall
Off-season 1986–87: Going to Durham University to read joint honours in archaeology/ancient history
Other sports played: Hockey, squash, golf
Other sports followed: Football, rugby, snooker
Relaxations: Watching films and comedies, music, doing crosswords
Extras: Played for England Schools U-15 1983. Holds Hurstpierpoint College records for most runs in a season (1180 in 1986) and highest aggregate of runs

LAST SEASON: BATTING

	I.	N.O.	R.	H.S.	AV.
TEST					
1ST-CLASS	2	0	21	17	10.50
INT					
JPL	–	–	–	–	–
NAT.W.					
B & H					

CAREER: BATTING

	I.	N.O.	R.	H.S.	AV.
TEST					
1ST-CLASS	2	0	21	17	10.50
INT					
JPL	–	–	–	–	–
NAT.W.					
B & H					

LAST SEASON: WICKET-KEEPING

	C.	ST.		
TEST				
1ST-CLASS				
INT				
JPL	1	–		
NAT.W.				
B & H				

CAREER: WICKET-KEEPING

	C.	ST.		
TEST				
1ST-CLASS				
INT				
JPL	1	–		
NAT.W.				
B & H				

Opinions on cricket: 'Cricketers should be allowed to play in South Africa without fear of later punishment. There should not be an 18½-overs per hour rate because it forces bowlers (especially the quicker ones) to rush through their overs. To speed up the over rate to prevent the loss of money through fines. Four-day county matches (instead of three days) would be more inducive to gaining results. If 16 four-day matches were played during weekdays and one-day games at the weekends players would have more rest days and probably play better as well (e.g. time for a lower order (number 6, 7 or 8) batsman to build a long innings).'

Best batting performance: 17 Sussex v Nottinghamshire, Hove 1986

STANDING, D. K. Sussex

Full Name: David Kevin Standing
Role: Right-hand bat, right-arm off-break bowler
Born: 21 October 1963, Brighton, Sussex
Height: 5' 7" **Weight:** 11st
Nickname: Uppers, Theo, Gummy
County debut: 1983
1st-Class 50s scored: 3
Place in batting averages: 193rd av. 17.91
1st-Class catches 1986: 9 (career: 12)
Parents: David Eric and Valerie Mavis
Marital status: Single
Education: Tideway School, Newhaven; Brighton and Hove VI Form
Qualifications: 9 O-levels, 1 A-level, coaching certificate
Family links with cricket: Father local cricketer at good level
Overseas tours: West Indies with Sussex Young Cricketers as captain
Cricketers particularly learnt from: Paul Parker
Cricketers particularly admired: Greg Chappell
Other sports played: Football, golf, squash, snooker
Relaxations: Reading, music, drinking – anything other than cricket
Extras: Captained England Schools U-15. Played England Schools U-19
Opinions on cricket: 'Too much cricket played. Would like to see four-day county cricket.'

Best batting performance: 65 Sussex v Warwickshire, Edgbaston 1986
Best bowling performance: 2-28 Sussex v New Zealand, Hove 1986

LAST SEASON: BATTING

	I.	N.O.	R.	H.S.	AV.
TEST					
1ST-CLASS	26	3	412	65	17.91
INT					
JPL	2	1	12	8*	–
NAT.W.	2	2	1	1*	–

LAST SEASON: BOWLING

	O.	M.	R.	W.	AV.
TEST					
1ST-CLASS	195	37	536	4	134.00
INT					
JPL	20.1	1	91	3	30.33
NAT.W.	17	3	54	2	27.00

CAREER: BATTING

	I.	N.O.	R.	H.S.	AV.
TEST					
1ST-CLASS	38	7	674	65	21.74
INT					
JPL	2	1	12	8*	–
NAT.W.	2	2	1	1*	–
B & H					

CAREER: BOWLING

	O.	M.	R.	W.	AV.
TEST					
1ST-CLASS	199.3	37	568	4	142.00
INT					
JPL	20.1	1	91	3	30.33
NAT.W.	17	3	54	2	27.00
B & H					

STANWORTH, J. Lancashire

Full Name: John Stanworth
Role: Right-hand bat, wicket-keeper
Born: 30 September 1960, Oldham
Height: 5′ 10″ **Weight:** 10st 7lbs
Nickname: Stick
County debut: 1983
1st-Class 50s scored: 1
Parents: Robert and Freda
Wife and date of marriage: Dianne,
22 March 1986
Education: Chadderton Grammar
School; North Cheshire College,
Warrington
Qualifications: 8 O-levels, 1 A-level,
BEd Physical Education
Jobs outside cricket: Health and
fitness programmer, PE teacher
Overseas tours: Australia 1978,
playing and coaching in Grade cricket; West Indies 1981 with British Colleges
Sports Association
Cricketers particularly learnt from: 'Bob Blair (ex-New Zealand and Wellington) gave me a kick up the pants in my formative years.'
Cricketers particularly admired: Alan Knott, for his dedication, Bob Taylor
for his 'ease' behind the wicket

Off-season 1986–87: Teaching PE
Other sports played: Rugby
Relaxations: Car mechanics, TV, music and films
Injuries 1986: Thumb injury
Extras: Instigated pre-season training for the squad
Opinions on cricket: 'The view of the county cricketer should be given more importance in the making of decisions which directly affects his job.'
Best batting performance: 50* Lancashire v Gloucestershire, Bristol 1985

LAST SEASON: BATTING

	I.	N.O.	R.	H.S.	AV.
TEST					
1ST-CLASS	2	1	13	11*	–
INT					
JPL	–	–	–	–	–
NAT.W.	–	–	–	–	–
B & H					

LAST SEASON: WICKET-KEEPING

	C.	ST.			
TEST					
1ST-CLASS	4	–			
INT					
JPL					
NAT.W.	4	–			
B & H					

CAREER: BATTING

	I.	N.O.	R.	H.S.	AV.
TEST					
1ST-CLASS	28	8	191	50*	9.55
INT					
JPL	2	0	2	2	1.00
NAT.W.	–	–	–	–	–
B & H	1	1	8	8*	–

CAREER: WICKET-KEEPING

	C.	ST.			
TEST					
1ST-CLASS	28	4			
INT					
JPL	8	–			
NAT.W.	6	–			
B & H	1	–			

STEELE, J. F.   Glamorgan

Full Name: John Frederick Steele
Role: Right-hand bat, slow left-arm bowler
Born: 23 July 1946, Stafford
Height: 5′ 10½″ **Weight:** 11st 7lbs
Nickname: Steeley, Rustless
County debut: 1970 (Leicestershire), 1984 (Glamorgan)
County cap: 1971 (Leicestershire), 1984 (Glamorgan)
Benefit: With Leicestershire in 1983 (£33,470)
1000 runs in a season: 6
50 wickets in a season: 2
1st-Class 50s scored: 70
1st-Class 100s scored: 21
1st-Class 5 w. in innings: 16
One-day 50s: 14

One-day 100s: 1
Place in batting averages: 160th av. 23.50 (1985 96th av. 31.44)
Place in bowling averages: — (1985 133rd av. 52.82)
1st-Class catches 1986: 9 (career: 413)
Parents: Alfred and Grace
Wife and date of marriage: Susan, 16 April 1977
Education: Endon Secondary Modern, Staffordshire
Jobs outside cricket: Work study officer. Junior fireman, Staffordshire Fire Brigade
Family links with cricket: Younger brother of David Steele of Derbyshire and England, and cousin of former Northamptonshire player B. S. Crump. Uncle, Stan Crump, played as professional in Lancashire League
Overseas teams played for: Natal in 1973–74 and 1977–78 Currie Cup Competitions; Pinetown Cricket Club, Natal, S Africa
Other sports played: Golf
Relaxations: Music, reading
Extras: Was 12th man for England v Rest of the World at Lord's in 1970, only a month after making debut. Played for Leicestershire 1970–1983. Became responsible for Glamorgan coaching during 1986
Best batting performance: 195 Leicestershire v Derbyshire, Leicester 1971
Best bowling performance: 7-29 Natal B v Griqualand West, Umzinto 1973–74; 7-29 Leicestershire v Gloucestershire, Leicester 1980

LAST SEASON: BATTING

	I.	N.O.	R.	H.S.	AV.
TEST					
1ST-CLASS	17	5	282	41*	23.50
INT					
JPL	5	2	55	30*	18.33
NAT.W.	1	0	0	0	—
B & H	2	2	8	6*	—

LAST SEASON: BOWLING

	O.	M.	R.	W.	AV.
TEST					
1ST-CLASS	156	27	583	9	64.77
INT					
JPL	70	0	314	8	39.25
NAT.W.	11	1	32	3	110.66
B & H	22	4	78	4	19.50

CAREER: BATTING

	I.	N.O.	R.	H.S.	AV.
TEST					
1ST-CLASS	605	85	15054	195	28.95
INT					
JPL	140	38	1911	92	18.73
NAT.W.	22	4	452	106*	25.11
B & H	54	8	1138	91	24.73

CAREER: BOWLING

	O.	M.	R.	W.	AV.
TEST					
1ST-CLASS	6547	2044	15793	584	27.04
INT					
JPL	1219.2	95	4871	199	24.47
NAT.W.	228	45	679	25	27.16
B & H	591	96	1808	67	26.98

144. Who wrote 'Batters Castle'?

145. Who wrote 'Brightly Fades the Don'?

146. Who wrote in 1986 'The Game Is Not the Same'?

STEPHENSON, J. P.   Essex

Full Name: John Patrick Stephenson
Role: Right-hand opening bat,
right-arm medium bowler
Born: 14 March 1965, Stebbing
Height: 6′ 1″ **Weight:** 12st
Nickname: Stanley
County debut: 1985
1st-Class 50s scored: 4
One-day 50s: 1
Place in batting averages: 131st
av. 26.95
1st-Class catches 1986: 5 (career: 6)
Parents: Patrick and Eve
Marital status: Single
Education: Felstead Preparatory
School; Felstead Senior School;
Durham University
Qualifications: 7 O-levels,
3 A-levels, NCA Coaching Award
Family links with cricket: 'Father
member of Rugby Meteors Cricketer Cup winning side in 1973. Three
brothers in Felstead 1st XI. Guy played for Essex 2nd XI and Paul
terrorised me in back field with short-pitched bowling.'
Overseas tours: Zimbabwe 1982–83 with ESCA U-19s; Barbados with K.
Pont Benefit 1986
Overseas teams played for: Fitzroy CC, Melbourne 1983–84
Cricketers particularly learnt from: All the Essex players
Off-season 1986–87: Doing 3rd year of degree course at university
Other sports played: Squash, football, hockey, snooker, golf

LAST SEASON: BATTING

	I.	N.O.	R.	H.S.	AV.
TEST					
1ST-CLASS	25	1	647	85	26.95
INT					
JPL	3	1	93	45	46.50
NAT.W.	1	0	55	55	–
B & H					

LAST SEASON: BOWLING

	O.	M.	R.	W.	AV.
TEST					
1ST-CLASS	2	0	5	0	–
INT					
JPL					
NAT.W.					
B & H					

CAREER: BATTING

	I.	N.O.	R.	H.S.	AV.
TEST					
1ST-CLASS	27	1	661	85	25.42
INT					
JPL	3	1	93	45	46.50
NAT.W.	1	0	55	55	–
B & H					

CAREER: BOWLING

	O.	M.	R.	W.	AV.
TEST					
1ST-CLASS	2	0	5	0	–
INT					
JPL					
NAT.W.					
B & H					

Relaxations: 'Music, keep fit, running, the odd pint, cleaning my car.'
Injuries 1986: 'Recurring problem with right shoulder dislocation.'
Extras: Awarded 2nd XI cap in 1984 when he was leading run-scorer with Essex 2nd XI. Young player of the year 1985 for Essex CCC. Captained Durham University to victory in UAU Competition 1986
Best batting performance: 85 Essex v Worcestershire, Southend 1986

STEVENSON, G. B.   Northamptonshire

Full Name: Graham Barry Stevenson
Role: Right-hand bat, right-arm fast-medium bowler
Born: 16 December 1955, Hemsworth, Yorkshire
Height: 6' **Weight:** 13st
Nickname: Moonbeam
County debut: 1973 (Yorkshire)
County cap: 1978 (Yorkshire)
Test debut: 1979–80
No. of Tests: 2
No. of One-Day Internationals: 4
50 wickets in a season: 5
1st-Class 50s scored: 16
1st-Class 100s scored: 2
1st-Class 5 w. in innings: 18
1st-Class 10 w. in match: 2
One-day 50s: 2
1st-Class catches 1986: — (career: 73)
Wife and date of marriage: Angela, 29 October 1977
Children: Christopher George, 9 January 1982
Education: Minsthorpe High School, where they did not play cricket
Jobs outside cricket: Clerk at Foster Wheeler Power Products Ltd, Snaith, near Goole
Family links with cricket: Two uncles, Keith and Jack Stevenson, both played local league cricket
Overseas tours: Australia 1979–80; West Indies 1981
Cricketers particularly learnt from: Geoff Boycott
Other sports played: Member of local club snooker team, golf
Relaxations: Watching Sheffield Wednesday FC
Extras: Toured Australia with England 1979–80, being called in after return to England through injury of Mike Hendrick. Vice-President Townville CC. Steve Oldham was his best man. Batting No. 11 made 115* in a record

stand of 149 for Yorkshire v Warwickshire, May 1982, with Geoff Boycott, beating previous Yorkshire record for last wicket by one run, set by Lord Hawke and David Hunter in 1898. Released by Yorkshire at end of 1986. Joined Northamptonshire in 1987

Best batting performance: 115* Yorkshire v Warwickshire, Edgbaston 1982
Best bowling performance: 8-57 Yorkshire v Northamptonshire, Leeds 1980

LAST SEASON: BATTING

	I.	N.O.	R.	H.S.	AV.
TEST					
1ST-CLASS	1	1	58	58*	–
INT					
JPL	3	2	26	22*	–
NAT.W.					
B & H	3	1	58	27*	29.00

CAREER: BATTING

	I.	N.O.	R.	H.S.	AV.
TEST	2	1	28	27*	–
1ST-CLASS	225	33	3935	115*	20.49
INT	4	3	43	28*	–
JPL	116	16	1275	81*	12.75
NAT.W.	13	1	190	34	15.83
B & H	28	6	234	36	10.63

LAST SEASON: BOWLING

	O.	M.	R.	W.	AV.
TEST					
1ST-CLASS	29	8	75	2	37.50
INT					
JPL	16	1	77	2	38.50
NAT.W.					
B & H	36	2	148	7	21.14

CAREER: BOWLING

	O.	M.	R.	W.	AV.
TEST	52	7	183	5	36.60
1ST-CLASS	4375.3	978	13825	481	28.74
INT	32	3	125	7	17.86
JPL	1023.1	76	4641	186	24.95
NAT.W.	193.3	36	612	30	20.40
B & H	413.3	55	1567	74	21.17

STEWART, A. J.   Surrey

Full Name: Alec James Stewart
Role: Right-hand bat, right-arm medium bowler, occasional wicket-keeper
Born: 8 April 1963, Wimbledon
Nickname: Stewie
Height: 5′ 11″ **Weight:** 12st
County debut: 1981
County cap: 1985
1000 runs in a season: 2
1st-Class 50s scored: 25
1st-Class 100s scored: 5
One-day 50s: 5
Place in batting averages: 24th av. 46.25 (1985 95th av. 31.53)
1st-Class catches: 15 (career: 80)
Parents: Michael James and Sheila Marie Macdonald
Marital status: Single

Education: Tiffin Grammar School

Qualifications: 4 O-levels

Family links with cricket: Father played for England (1962–64) and Surrey (1954–72). Brother Neil plays club cricket and Surrey 2nd XI; sister, Judy, plays for Malden Wanderers Ladies XI

Overseas tours: 1980–81 tour of Australia with Surrey U-19

Cricketers particularly learnt from: Geoff Arnold, Mickey Stewart and Kevin Gartrell

Cricketers particularly admired: Geoff Boycott, Tony Mann

Off-season 1986–87: Cricket in Perth, Western Australia, with Midland-Guildford, as has done since 1981

Other sports played: All sports

Relaxations: 'Music, Perth beaches, eating out.'

Opinions on cricket: 'That all, or at least as many 2nd XI games as possible should be played on first-class grounds rather than club pitches which are a lot lower standard and slower than most county pitches. That all championship matches be played over four days, therefore meaning more "results", and also it would prepare the players better for a 5-day Test Match.'

Best batting performance: 166 Surrey v Kent, The Oval 1986

LAST SEASON: BATTING

	I.	N.O.	R.	H.S.	AV.
TEST					
1ST-CLASS	39	3	1665	166	46.25
INT					
JPL	14	0	236	59	16.85
NAT.W.	4	0	59	31	14.75
B & H	4	1	108	63*	36.00

CAREER: BATTING

	I.	N.O.	R.	H.S.	AV.
TEST					
1ST-CLASS	117	14	3804	166	36.93
INT					
JPL	44	6	799	86	21.02
NAT.W.	17	1	249	34	15.56
B & H	10	1	159	63*	17.66

LAST SEASON: BOWLING

	O.	M.	R.	W.	AV.
TEST					
1ST-CLASS	5	0	55	0	–
INT					
JPL					
NAT.W.					
B & H					

CAREER: BOWLING

	O.	M.	R.	W.	AV.
TEST					
1ST-CLASS	11	0	98	0	–
INT					
JPL	0.3	0	4	0	–
NAT.W.					
B & H					

147. Who wrote 'That Test Match'?

148. Who was, in fiction, an England Test cricketer by day and a burglar by night?

STORIE, A. C.   Warwickshire

Full Name: Alastair Caleb Storie
Role: Right-hand bat, right-arm medium bowler
Born: 25 July 1965, Glasgow
Height: 25 July 1965, Glasgow
Height: 5′ 8″ **Weight:** 9st 11lbs
Nickname: Ally, Wolf, Archie
County debut: 1985 (Northamptonshire)
1st-Class 50s scored: 3
1st-Class 100s scored: 1
Place in batting averages: 208th av. 15.54 (1985 49th av. 40.70)
1st-Class catches 1986: 3 (career: 6)
Parents: Hank and Jenny
Marital status: Single
Education: St Stithians College, Johannesburg; UNISA Correspondence University
Qualifications: JMB Matriculation
Family links with cricket: Father played club cricket in Glasgow and Johannesburg
Cricketing superstitions: Always puts left pad on first
Overseas teams played for: Transvaal Schools 1978–83; Transvaal B 1985
Cricketers particularly learnt from: Willie Watson, Peter Stringer, Richard Lumb
Cricketers particularly admired: Clive Rice, Graham Gooch, Graeme Pollock
Off-season 1986–87: Coaching abroad

LAST SEASON: BATTING

	I.	N.O.	R.	H.S.	AV.
TEST					
1ST-CLASS	11	0	171	38	15.54
INT					
JPL					
NAT.W.					
B & H					

LAST SEASON: BOWLING

	O.	M.	R.	W.	AV.
TEST					
1ST-CLASS					
INT					
JPL					
NAT.W.					
B & H					

CAREER: BATTING

	I.	N.O.	R.	H.S.	AV.
TEST					
1ST-CLASS	23	2	578	104	27.52
INT					
JPL					
NAT.W.					
B & H					

CAREER: BOWLING

	O.	M.	R.	W.	AV.
TEST					
1ST-CLASS	18	6	51	0	–
INT					
JPL					
NAT.W.					
B & H					

Other sports played: Represented South Africa U-19 hockey team 1982–83
Other sports followed: Football, rugby union
Relaxations: Music, reading
Injuries 1986: Broken nose and six stitches fielding at short leg; five stitches in chin batting
Extras: First Northamptonshire batsman to score a 100 on first-class debut. Left to join Warwickshire for 1987 season
Opinions on cricket: '2nd XI wickets and umpiring are generally of a low standard and thus do not simulate conditions in first-class cricket.'
Best batting performance: 106 Northamptonshire v Hampshire, Northampton 1985

STOVOLD, A. W.   Gloucestershire

Full Name: Andrew Willis-Stovold
Role: Right-hand bat, wicket-keeper
Born: 19 March 1953, Bristol
Height: 5' 7" **Weight:** 12st 4lbs
Nickname: Stumper, Squeak, Stov, Stovers, Stubble
County debut: 1973
County cap: 1976
Benefit: 1987
1000 runs in a season: 7
1st-Class 50s scored: 85
1st-Class 100s scored: 17
1st-Class 200s scored: 1
One-day 50s: 31
One-day 100s: 2
Place in batting averages: 116th av. 28.79 (1985 188th av. 19.83)
1st-Class catches 1986: 9 (career: 267)
Parents: Lancelot Walter and Dorothy Patricia
Wife and date of marriage: Kay Elizabeth, 30 September 1978
Children: Nicholas, 18 June 1981; Neil, 24 February 1983
Education: Filton High School; Loughborough College of Education
Qualifications: Certificate of Education
Jobs outside cricket: Teacher at Tockington Manor Prep School
Family links with cricket: Father played local club cricket for Old Down CC. Brother, Martin, also played county cricket for Gloucestershire
Cricketing superstitions: 'Keeping the same routine until I have a bad run, then trying something else. Always prepare for batting in the same order.'

Overseas tours: England Schools to India, 1970–71; England Young Cricketers to West Indies 1972
Overseas teams played for: Orange Free State, 1974–76
Cricketers particularly admired: M. J. Proctor, B. A. Richards, R. J. Hadlee
Off-season 1986–87: Supply teaching and organising benefit
Other sports played: Football, golf
Other sports followed: Rugby, hunting, horse racing
Relaxations: Gardening, walking
Extras: Writes a weekly article for *Gloucestershire Echo*
Opinions on cricket: 'Worried about the sudden increase in player "transfers". We must not let it get too much like football.'
Best batting performance: 212* Gloucestershire v Northamptonshire, Northampton 1982

LAST SEASON: BATTING

	I.	N.O.	R.	H.S.	AV.
TEST					
1ST-CLASS	43	4	1123	118	28.79
INT					
JPL	4	0	94	35	23.50
NAT.W.	2	0	69	58	34.50
B & H	4	1	79	72*	26.33

LAST SEASON: BOWLING

	O.	M.	R.	W.	AV.
TEST					
1ST-CLASS	27	2	132	2	66.00
INT					
JPL					
NAT.W.					
B & H					

CAREER: BATTING

	I.	N.O.	R.	H.S.	AV.
TEST					
1ST-CLASS	530	30	15109	212*	30.21
INT					
JPL	156	20	3293	98*	24.21
NAT.W.	25	2	708	82	30.78
B & H	51	7	1669	123	37.93

CAREER: BOWLING

	O.	M.	R.	W.	AV.
TEST					
1ST-CLASS	52.3	8	218	4	54.50
INT					
JPL					
NAT.W.					

LAST SEASON: WICKET-KEEPING

	C.	ST.			
TEST					
1ST-CLASS					
INT					
JPL					
NAT.W.					
B & H					

CAREER: WICKET-KEEPING

	C.	ST.			
TEST					
1ST-CLASS	267	45			
INT					
JPL					
NAT.W.					
B & H					

149. Which Nottinghamshire player wrote a cricketing novel called 'Willow the King'?

150. Who wrote the novel 'Pip' which contains a lot of cricket?

151. Which Somerset player wrote the novel 'A Village Match and After'?

Full Name: Peter Mark Such
Role: Right-hand bat, right-arm off-break bowler
Born: 12 June 1964, Helensburgh, Scotland
Height: 6′ 1″ **Weight:** 11st 7lbs
Nickname: Suchy
County debut: 1982 (Nottinghamshire)
1st-Class 5 w. in innings: 5
Place in bowling averages: 32nd av. 25.72 (1985 83rd av. 36.00)
1st-Class catches 1986: 3 (career: 29)
Parents: John and Margaret
Marital status: Single
Education: Harry Carlton Comprehensive
Qualifications: 9 O-levels, 3 A-levels. Qualified Cricket Coach (Senior)
Jobs outside cricket: Van driver
Family links with cricket: Father and brother village cricketers
Overseas teams played for: Kempton Park CC, South Africa 1982–83; Bathurst CC, New South Wales 1985–86
Cricketers particularly learnt from: Bob White, Eddie Hemmings
Cricketers particularly admired: Richard Hadlee
Off-season 1986–87: Working for an electroplating firm
Other sports played: Hockey and golf
Other sports followed: American football
Relaxations: Music, TV, films

LAST SEASON: BATTING

	I.	N.O.	R.	H.S.	AV.
TEST					
1ST-CLASS	4	0	9	6	2.25
INT					
JPL					
NAT.W.					
B & H	–	–	–	–	–

CAREER: BATTING

	I.	N.O.	R.	H.S.	AV.
TEST					
1ST-CLASS	50	17	72	16	2.18
INT					
JPL	1	1	0	0*	–
NAT.W.					
B & H	–	–	–	–	–

LAST SEASON: BOWLING

	O.	M.	R.	W.	AV.
TEST					
1ST-CLASS	231.3	69	566	22	25.72
INT					
JPL					
NAT.W.					
B & H	22	0	101	1	–

CAREER: BOWLING

	O.	M.	R.	W.	AV.
TEST					
1ST-CLASS	1408.4	385	4159	141	29.49
INT					
JPL	15	0	116	2	58.00
NAT.W.					
B & H	33	1	151	4	37.75

Extras: Played for Young England v Young Australia in three 'Tests' in 1983. Represented TCCB v New Zealand 1986. Left Nottinghamshire at end of 1986 season. Joined Leicestershire for 1987 season
Best batting performance: 16 Nottinghamshire v Middlesex, Lord's 1984
Best bowling performance: 6-123 Nottinghamshire v Kent, Trent Bridge 1983

SWALLOW, I. G.   Yorkshire

Full Name: Ian Geoffrey Swallow
Role: Right-hand bat, right-arm off-break bowler, cover or slip fielder
Born: 18 December 1962, Barnsley
Height: 5′ 7″ **Weight:** 10st
Nickname: Chicken or Swal
County debut: 1983
Place in batting averages: 144th av. 25.33 (1985 249th av. 11.22)
Place in bowling averages: —
(1985 135th av. 55.83)
1st-Class catches 1986: —
(career: 14)
Parents: Joyce and Geoffrey
Marital status: Single
Education: Hayland Kirk, Balk, Comprehensive School; Barnsley Technical College
Qualifications: 3 O-levels
Jobs outside cricket: Storeman

LAST SEASON: BATTING

	I.	N.O.	R.	H.S.	AV.
TEST					
1ST-CLASS	11	5	152	43*	25.33
INT					
JPL					
NAT.W.					
B & H					

CAREER: BATTING

	I.	N.O.	R.	H.S.	AV.
TEST					
1ST-CLASS	34	12	408	43*	18.54
INT					
JPL	1	0	2	2	–
NAT.W.					
B & H	3	2	18	10*	–

LAST SEASON: BOWLING

	O.	M.	R.	W.	AV.
TEST					
1ST-CLASS	172	37	510	6	85.00
INT					
JPL					
NAT.W.					
B & H					

CAREER: BOWLING

	O.	M.	R.	W.	AV.
TEST					
1ST-CLASS	656.5	153	1882	35	53.77
INT					
JPL	4	0	31	0	–
NAT.W.					
B & H	36	4	151	2	75.50

Family links with cricket: Father and brother both played for Elsecar Village CC, where he also started his career at the age of 10 years
Cricketing superstitions: Always puts left pad on first
Cricketers particularly learnt from: D. Padgett, P. Carrick, S. Oldham
Off-season 1986–87: Playing cricket in Melbourne, Australia
Other sports played: Football and most sports for fun
Other sports followed: Barnsley FC
Relaxations: Sports in general
Extras: Took hat-trick v Warwickshire 2nd XI 1984. Figures: 4-3-2-4
Best batting performance: 43* Yorkshire v Hampshire, Bournemouth 1986
Best bowling performance: 4-52 Yorkshire v Kent, Tunbridge Wells 1984

SYKES, J. F. Middlesex

Full Name: James Frederick Sykes
Role: Right-hand bat, right-arm off-break bowler, slip or gully fielder
Born: 30 December 1965, Shoreditch
Height: 6′ 2″ **Weight:** 13st 7lbs
Nickname: Eric, Sykesy
County debut: 1983
1st-Class 50s scored: 1
1st-Class 100s scored: 1
Place in batting averages: —
(1985 127th av. 27.50)
Place in bowling averages: —
(1985 120th av. 44.23)
1st-Class catches 1986: —
(career: 10)
Parents: James and Kathleen
Education: Bow Comprehensive
Qualifications: 1 O-level
Overseas tours: England U-19 to West Indies, 1984–85
Cricketers particularly learnt from: John Emburey, Don Bennett
Cricketers particularly admired: Clive Radley
Other sports played: Squash, golf
Other sports followed: Most sports
Relaxations: Girls, soul music
Best batting performance: 126 Middlesex v Cambridge University, Cambridge 1985
Best bowling performance: 4-102 Middlesex v Essex, Chelmsford 1986

	I.	N.O.	R.	H.S.	AV.
TEST					
1ST-CLASS	4	1	63	26	21.00
INT					
JPL	1	0	6	6	–
NAT.W.					
B & H					

LAST SEASON: BOWLING

	O.	M.	R.	W.	AV.
TEST					
1ST-CLASS	43.3	5	161	5	32.20
INT					
JPL	30	1	129	4	32.25
NAT.W.					
B & H					

CAREER: BATTING

	I.	N.O.	R.	H.S.	AV.
TEST					
1ST-CLASS	18	4	342	126	24.42
INT					
JPL	6	1	49	25	9.80
NAT.W.					
B & H					

CAREER: BOWLING

	O.	M.	R.	W.	AV.
TEST					
1ST-CLASS	256.2	53	790	19	41.57
INT					
JPL	56	1	214	6	35.66
NAT.W.					
B & H					

TAVARÉ, C. J. Kent

Full Name: Christopher James Tavaré
Role: Right-hand bat, right-arm bowler, slip fielder
Born: 27 October 1954, Orpington
Height: 6′ 1½″ **Weight:** 12st 8lbs
Nickname: Tav, Rowdy
County debut: 1974
County cap: 1978
Benefit: 1988
Test debut: 1980
No. of Tests: 30
No. of One-Day Internationals: 29
1000 runs in a season: 10
1st-Class 50s scored: 92
1st-Class 100s scored: 30
One-Day 50s: 38
One-Day 100s: 8
Place in batting averages: 86th

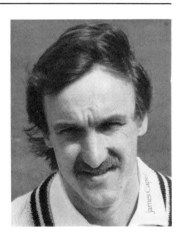

av. 33.34 (1985 69th av. 36.03)
1st-Class catches 1986: 21 (career: 269)
Parents: Andrew and June
Wife and date of marriage: Vanessa, 22 March 1980
Education: Sevenoaks School; Oxford University
Qualifications: Studied zoology
Family links with cricket: Father, uncle Jack Tavaré, and uncle, Derrick Attwood, all played school and club cricket, father and Uncle Jack at

Chatham House, father and Uncle Derrick at Bickley Park CC. Elder brother, Stephen, and younger brother, Jeremy, both play cricket

Overseas teams played for: University of Western Australia, Perth, 1977–78; West Perth CC for half a season 1978–79

Off-season 1986–87: As an agent for Schroder Financial Management Ltd, East Kent Branch

Other sports followed: 'Take an interest in most sports, especially American football in winter.'

Relaxations: Music, zoology, films, gardening, woodwork, golf

Extras: Played for England Schools v All-India Schools at Birmingham in 1973, scoring 124*. Oxford University cricket blue 1975–76–77. Whitbread Scholarship to Perth, Australia, 1978–79. Suffers from asthma and hay-fever. Was top-scorer with 82* and Man of the Match, on debut for England in 55-over match v West Indies at Headingley, May 1980. Captain of Kent 1983–84

Best batting performance: 168* Kent v Essex, Chelmsford 1982

LAST SEASON: BATTING

	I.	N.O.	R.	H.S.	AV.
TEST					
1ST-CLASS	42	4	1267	123	33.34
INT					
JPL	13	2	376	88	34.18
NAT.W.	2	1	48	48*	–
B & H	7	1	136	68	22.66

LAST SEASON: BOWLING

	O.	M.	R.	W.	AV.
TEST					
1ST-CLASS	27	6	107	2	53.50
INT					
JPL					
NAT.W.					
B & H					

CAREER: BATTING

	I.	N.O.	R.	H.S.	AV.
TEST	55	2	1753	149	33.07
1ST-CLASS	419	48	14199	168*	38.27
INT	28	2	720	83*	27.69
JPL	129	19	3612	136*	32.83
NAT.W.	30	3	871	118*	32.25
B & H	60	3	1544	143	27.08

CAREER: BOWLING

	O.	M.	R.	W.	AV.
TEST	6	3	11	0	–
1ST-CLASS	72.4	10	389	4	97.25
INT					
JPL					
NAT.W.					
B & H					

152. Whom did Bradman rate the two finest bowlers he had ever seen at any speed?

153. Which British Prime Minister played for the MCC on an overseas tour?

TAYLOR, J. P.   Derbyshire

Full Name: Jonathan Paul Taylor
Role: Left-hand bat, left-arm
fast-medium bowler
Born: 8 August 1964, Ashby-
de-la-Zouch, Leicestershire
Height: 6′ 2″ **Weight:** 12st 10lbs
Nickname: Arthur, Nasty
County debut: 1984
1st-Class catches 1986: 1 (career: 3)
Parents: Roland Derek and Janet
Elizabeth
Marital status: Single
Education: Pingle School,
Swadlincote
Qualifications: 6 O-levels
Jobs outside cricket: Mining craft
apprentice for National Coal Board
Family links with cricket: Father

and brother played local league cricket
Cricketers particularly learnt from: John Lever, Bob Taylor
Other sports played: Basketball, squash, badminton, football, swimming
Best batting performance: 11 Derbyshire v Middlesex, Derby 1984
Best bowling performance: 4-81 Derbyshire v Gloucestershire, Derby 1986

LAST SEASON: BATTING

	I.	N.O.	R.	H.S.	AV.
TEST					
1ST-CLASS	5	2	18	9*	6.00
INT					
JPL	–	–	–	–	–
NAT.W.					
B & H					

CAREER: BATTING

	I.	N.O.	R.	H.S.	AV.
TEST					
1ST-CLASS	7	2	29	11	5.80
INT					
JPL	3	0	5	4	1.66
NAT.W.					
B & H					

LAST SEASON: BOWLING

	O.	M.	R.	W.	AV.
TEST					
1ST-CLASS	87	12	299	8	37.37
INT					
JPL	9	0	44	3	14.66
NAT.W.					
B & H					

CAREER: BOWLING

	O.	M.	R.	W.	AV.
TEST					
1ST-CLASS	136.2	18	487	10	48.10
INT					
JPL	40	1	216	8	27.00
NAT.W.					
B & H					

TAYLOR, L. B.   Leicestershire

Full Name: Leslie Brian Taylor
Role: Right-hand bat, right-arm
fast-medium bowler
Born: 25 October 1953, Earl Shilton,
Leicestershire
Height: 6′ 3½″ **Weight:** 14st 7lbs
Nickname: Les
County debut: 1977
County cap: 1981
Test debut: 1985
No. of Tests: 2
One-Day Internationals: 2
50 wickets in a season: 4
1st-Class 5 w. in innings: 15
1st-Class 10 w. in match: 1
Place in bowling averages: 62nd
av. 29.96 (1985 11th av. 22.93)
1st-Class catches 1986: 3 (career: 41)
Parents: Peggy and Cyril
Wife and date of marriage: Susan, 12 July 1973
Children: Jamie, 24 June 1976; Donna, 10 November 1978; Suzy, 3 June 1981
Education: Heathfield High School, Earl Shilton
Qualifications: Qualified carpenter and joiner
Family links with cricket: Relation of the late Sam Coe, holder of highest
individual score for Leicestershire, 252* v Northamptonshire at Leicester in
1914
Overseas tours: South America with Derrick Robins' XI in 1978–79; West
Indies with England 1986

LAST SEASON: BATTING

	I.	N.O.	R.	H.S.	AV.
TEST					
1ST-CLASS	15	6	48	13	5.33
INT	1	1	1	1*	–
JPL	5	3	16	14*	8.00
NAT.W.	1	1	6	6*	–
B & H	–	–	–	–	–

LAST SEASON: BOWLING

	O.	M.	R.	W.	AV.
TEST					
1ST-CLASS	280.3	66	809	27	29.96
INT	7	1	30	0	–
JPL	87.1	2	447	8	55.87
NAT.W.	31	4	107	5	21.40
B & H	30	3	71	5	14.20

CAREER: BATTING

	I.	N.O.	R.	H.S.	AV.
TEST	1	1	1	1*	–
1ST-CLASS	155	68	823	47	9.45
INT	1	1	1	1*	–
JPL	26	20	91	15*	15.16
NAT.W.	6	5	18	6*	–
B & H	7	3	11	5	2.75

CAREER: BOWLING

	O.	M.	R.	W.	AV.
TEST	63.3	11	178	4	44.50
1ST-CLASS	4325	1082	12053	497	24.25
INT	14	3	47	0	–
JPL	694.4	57	2960	146	20.27
NAT.W.	146.1	23	496	30	16.53
B & H	267.2	53	862	44	19.59

Overseas teams played for: Natal 1982–84
Other sports: Swimming and football
Relaxations: Game-shooting and fox-hunting with the Atherstone Hunt
Extras: Was banned from Test cricket for three years for joining rebel England tour of South Africa in 1982
Opinions on cricket: Should not be subjected to over-rate fines in one-day cricket
Best batting performance: 47 Leicestershire v Derbyshire, Derby 1983
Best bowling performance: 7-48 Leicestershire v Derbyshire, Leicester 1981

TAYLOR, N. R. Kent

Full Name: Neil Royston Taylor
Role: Right-hand bat, right-arm off-break bowler, outfielder
Born: 21 July 1959, Farnborough, Kent
Height: 6′ 1″ **Weight:** 13st 10lbs
Nickname: Map
County debut: 1979
County cap: 1982
1000 runs in a season: 4
1st-Class 50s scored: 29
1st-Class 100s scored: 15
One-Day 50s: 9
One-Day 100s: 3
Place in batting averages: 97th av. 31.10 (1985 26th av. 46.83)
1st-Class catches 1986: 10 (career: 70)

Parents: Leonard and Audrey
Wife and date of marriage: Jane Claire, 25 September 1982
Children: Amy Louise, 7 November 1985
Education: Cray Valley Technical High School
Qualifications: 8 O-levels, 2 A-levels, NCA Coaching Certificate
Jobs outside cricket: Insurance broker, and working in Civil Service
Family links with cricket: Brother Colin played for Kent U-19s
Cricketing superstitions: Always put batting gear on in same order
Overseas tours: With England Schools Team to India 1977–78; Kent to Vancouver 1979
Overseas teams played for: Randburg, Johannesburg, South Africa, 1980–86; Coach at St Stithians College 1981–86
Cricketers particularly learnt from: Bob Woolmer, Mark Benson

Off-season 1986–87: 'Lazing around.'
Other sports played: Rugby – played for Kent U-21 XV – golf, 'try and play anything.'
Relaxations: Listening to records, reading
Extras: Made 110 on debut match for Kent CCC v Sri Lanka, 1979. Won four Man of the Match awards in first five matches. Scored highest score by Kent player in Benson and Hedges cricket: 121 v Sussex and Somerset
Best batting performance: 155* Kent v Glamorgan, Cardiff 1983
Best bowling performance: 2-20 Kent v Somerset, Canterbury 1985

LAST SEASON: BATTING

	I.	N.O.	R.	H.S.	AV.
TEST					
1ST-CLASS	42	5	1151	106	31.10
INT					
JPL	11	2	326	75*	36.22
NAT.W.	2	0	47	26	23.50
B & H	7	1	223	68	37.17

LAST SEASON: BOWLING

	O.	M.	R.	W.	AV.
TEST					
1ST-CLASS	77.3	9	252	3	84.00
INT					
JPL					
NAT.W.	9	3	19	0	–
B & H					

CAREER: BATTING

	I.	N.O.	R.	H.S.	AV.
TEST					
1ST-CLASS	226	33	6609	155*	34.24
INT					
JPL	50	4	1218	75*	26.47
NAT.W.	10	0	233	51	23.33
B & H	20	1	786	121	41.36

CAREER: BOWLING

	O.	M.	R.	W.	AV.
TEST					
1ST-CLASS	221.3	37	760	14	54.28
INT					
JPL					
NAT.W.	9	3	19	0	–
B & H					

154. Where was the first Test Match played in 1877?

155. When did Lord's cricket ground move to its present site?

156. When were the first laws of cricket drawn up, 1645, 1744 or 1843?

157. Who was vice-captain of Australia at the start of the series against England in 1986–87?

TAYLOR, N. S.   Somerset

Full Name: Nicholas Simon Taylor
Role: Right-hand bat, right-arm
fast-medium bowler, outfielder
Born: 2 June 1963, Holmfirth,
Yorkshire
Height: 6′ 3″ **Weight:** 14st
Nickname: Bond, Harry, Don
County debut: 1982 (Yorkshire),
1984 (Surrey), 1986 (Somerset)
1st-Class 5 w. in innings: 2
Place in batting averages: —
(1985 247th av. 11.40)
Place in bowling averages: 105th
av. 42.13 (1985 66th av. 32.17)
1st-Class catches 1986: 2 (career: 7)
Parents: Kenneth and Avril
Marital status: Single
Education: Gresham's School, Holt,
Norfolk
Qualifications: 7 O-levels, 3 A-levels
Jobs outside cricket: Squash coach, builder, gym instructor
Family links with cricket: Father, Ken, played for Yorkshire and England
Cricketing superstitions: 'Always hold the ball in left hand when starting to
run in to bowl.'
Overseas teams played for: Hawthorn, Melbourne, 1982–83; Wangari, New
Zealand, 1983–84; Springs, South Africa, 1984–84; St Mary's CC, Australia
1985–86
Cricketers particularly learnt from: Dennis Lillee, Geoff Arnold and father

LAST SEASON: BATTING

	I.	N.O.	R.	H.S.	AV.
TEST					
1ST-CLASS	18	6	107	24*	8.91
INT					
JPL	4	1	31	28	10.33
NAT.W.	1	1	1	1*	–
B & H	2	0	10	9	5.00

LAST SEASON: BOWLING

	O.	M.	R.	W.	AV.
TEST					
1ST-CLASS	342.2	62	1222	29	42.13
INT					
JPL	88.5	3	422	19	22.21
NAT.W.	21.1	3	68	5	13.60
B & H	25.5	1	111	5	22.20

CAREER: BATTING

	I.	N.O.	R.	H.S.	AV.
TEST					
1ST-CLASS	33	11	180	24*	8.18
INT					
JPL	5	2	40	28	13.33
NAT.W.	1	1	1	1*	–
B & H	4	0	12	9	3.00

CAREER: BOWLING

	O.	M.	R.	W.	AV.
TEST					
1ST-CLASS	766.4	143	2775	79	35.12
INT					
JPL	100.5	3	486	20	24.30
NAT.W.	21.1	3	68	5	13.60
B & H	44.3	4	195	6	32.50

Other sports: Squash (played in British Open U-19s), swimming, tennis, gym, pool
Relaxations: Fly fishing, shooting, books, making money, going abroad
Extras: Released by Yorkshire 1983 and joined Surrey for 1984. Released at end of 1985 and joined Somerset
Best batting performance: 24* Somerset v Gloucestershire, Taunton 1986
Best bowling performance: 7-44 Surrey v Cambridge University, Cambridge 1985

TENNANT, L. Leicestershire

Full Name: Lloyd Tennant
Role: Right-hand bat, right-arm medium bowler
Debut: 9 April 1968, Walsall
Height: 5′ 11″
County debut: 1986
Education: Shellfield Comprehensive School
Off-season 1986–87: Young England tour to Sri Lanka
Best batting performance: 12* Leicestershire v Sussex, Leicester 1986

LAST SEASON: BATTING

	I.	N.O.	R.	H.S.	AV.
TEST					
1ST-CLASS	2	1	13	12*	–
INT					
JPL	1	1	2	2*	–
NAT.W.					
B & H					

LAST SEASON: BOWLING

	O.	M.	R.	W.	AV.
TEST					
1ST-CLASS	8	1	35	0	–
INT					
JPL	33	2	145	6	24.17
NAT.W.					
B & H					

CAREER: BATTING

	I.	N.O.	R.	H.S.	AV.
TEST					
1ST-CLASS	2	1	13	12*	–
INT					
JPL	1	1	2	2*	–
NAT.W.					
B & H					

CAREER: BOWLING

	O.	M.	R.	W.	AV.
TEST					
1ST-CLASS	8	1	35	0	–
INT					
JPL	33	2	145	6	24.17
NAT.W.					
B & H					

TERRY, V. P.   Hampshire

Full Name: Vivian Paul Terry
Role: Right-hand bat, right-arm
medium bowler, slip or cover
fielder
Born: 14 January 1959, Osnabruck,
West Germany
Height: 6′ 0″ **Weight:** 13st
County debut: 1978
County cap: 1983
Test debut: 1984
No. of Tests: 2
1000 runs in a season: 3
1st-Class 50s scored: 30
1st-Class 100s scored: 11
One-Day 50s: 10
One-Day 100s: 5
Place in batting averages: 124th
av. 28.00 (1985 85th av. 32.92)
1st-Class catches 1986: 17
(career: 94)
Parents: Michael and Patricia
Wife and date of marriage: Bernadette, 4 June 1986
Education: Durlston Court, Barton-on-Sea, Hampshire; Millfield School,
Somerset
Qualifications: 8 O-levels, 1 A-level
Jobs outside cricket: Worked in a fish factory, apple picker, estate agent
Overseas tours: ESCA tour to India 1977–78; Gordon Greenidge benefit
tour to Paris and Isle of Wight; English Counties tour to Zimbabwe 1985

LAST SEASON: BATTING

	I.	N.O.	R.	H.S.	AV.
TEST					
1ST-CLASS	36	4	896	80	28.00
INT					
JPL	15	2	472	142	36.30
NAT.W.	2	0	9	8	4.50
B & H	4	0	124	41	31.00

CAREER: BATTING

	I.	N.O.	R.	H.S.	AV.
TEST	3	0	16	8	5.33
1ST-CLASS	168	20	5114	175*	34.55
INT					
JPL	73	13	1848	142	30.80
NAT.W.	13	1	440	165*	36.66
B & H	20	0	462	72	23.10

LAST SEASON: BOWLING

	O.	M.	R.	W.	AV.
TEST					
1ST-CLASS	1	1	0	0	–
INT					
JPL					
NAT.W.					
B & H					

CAREER: BOWLING

	O.	M.	R.	W.	AV.
TEST					
1ST-CLASS	14.5	5	39	0	–
INT					
JPL					
NAT.W.					
B & H					

Overseas teams played for: Sydney 1978–79; in New Zealand 1980–81; Durban Collegians 1982–83
Cricketers particularly learnt from: Chris Smith
Cricketers particularly admired: Gordon Greenidge, Chris Smith, Viv and Barry Richards, Malcolm Marshall, Gary Sobers
Off-season 1986–87: Playing in Perth
Other sports played: Golf, squash, soccer
Relaxations: Music, sport
Best batting performance: 175* Hampshire v Gloucestershire, Bristol 1984

THOMAS, D. J. Surrey

Full Name: David James Thomas
Role: Left-hand bat, left-arm fast-medium bowler
Born: 30 June 1959, Solihull, Warwickshire
Height: 6′ 0″ **Weight:** 13st 4lbs
Nickname: Teddy
County debut: 1977
County cap: 1982
50 wickets in a season: 2
1st-Class 50s scored: 7
1st-Class 100s scored: 2
1st-Class 5 w. in innings: 6
1st-Class 10 w. in match: 1
One-Day 50s: 6
Place in batting averages: 125th av. 27.75 (1985 233rd av. 12.89)
Place in bowling averages: 117th av. 49.00 (1985 89th av. 37.06)
1st-Class catches 1986: 1 (career: 44)
Parents: Howard James and Heather
Wife and date of marriage: Miranda, 20 February 1982
Children: Christopher James Owen, 4 May 1986
Education: Licensed Victuallers' School, Slough
Jobs outside cricket: Salesman for Securicor Communications
Family links with cricket: Father played for RAF. Brother, Howard, played for Bucks U-19 and now club cricket
Overseas tours: Surrey CCC tour of the Far East and Antigua; *Cricketer* International in Dubai: Whitbread Scholarship in Australia 1982–83
Overseas teams played for: Northern Transvaal 1980–81; Natal 1983–84
Cricketers particularly learnt from or admired: Mike Procter, Robin Jackman, Imran Khan, Graham Monkhouse

Off-season 1986–87: PR for Europa Communications Ltd (car 'phones)
Other sports played: Golf, squash
Relaxations: Theatre, pubs, watching Chelsea FC
Extras: Played for England U-19 v West Indies U-19, and for Derrick Robins' XI v New Zealand U-25 XI
Injuries 1986: Hernia operation followed by splitting pubic bone
Best batting performance: 119 Surrey v Nottinghamshire, The Oval 1983
Best bowling performance: 6-36 Surrey v Somerset, The Oval 1984

LAST SEASON: BATTING

	I.	N.O.	R.	H.S.	AV.
TEST					
1ST-CLASS	12	4	222	47*	27.75
INT					
JPL	7	2	88	37*	17.60
NAT.W.	2	0	77	65	38.50
B & H					

LAST SEASON: BOWLING

	O.	M.	R.	W.	AV.
TEST					
1ST-CLASS	166.3	29	588	12	49.00
INT					
JPL	37	3	190	6	31.66
NAT.W.	19	2	97	3	32.33
B & H					

CAREER: BATTING

	I.	N.O.	R.	H.S.	AV.
TEST					
1ST-CLASS	172	36	2724	119	20.02
INT					
JPL	67	14	1015	72	19.15
NAT.W.	16	5	279	65	25.36
B & H	11	1	75	19	7.50

CAREER: BOWLING

	O.	M.	R.	W.	AV.
TEST					
1ST-CLASS	3156.5	680	10011	296	33.82
INT					
JPL	584.5	35	2720	83	32.70
NAT.W.	189.5	22	703	21	33.47
B & H	143.3	24	510	13	39.23

THOMAS, J. G.   Glamorgan

Full Name: John Gregory Thomas
Role: Right-hand bat, right-arm fast bowler
Born: 12 August 1960, Trebanos, Swansea
Height: 6′ 3″ **Weight:** 14st
County debut: 1979
Test debut: 1985–86
No. of Tests: 5
No. of One-Day Internationals: 2
1st-Class 50s scored: 5
1st-Class 5 w. in innings: 6
1st-Class 10 w. in match: 1
Place in batting averages: 150th av. 24.90 (1985 193rd av. 19.14)
Place in bowling averages: 95th av. 38.80 (1985 63rd av. 31.59)
1st-Class catches 1986: 7 (career: 44)

Parents: Illtyd and Margaret
Marital status: Single
Education: Cwmtawe Comprehensive School; South Glamorgan Institute of Higher Education
Qualifications: Qualified teacher, advanced cricket coach
Family links with cricket: Father played village cricket
Cricketing superstitions: The number 111
Overseas tours: West Indies with British Colleges 1982; West Indies with England 1986
Overseas teams played for: Border Cricket Union, South Africa
Off-season 1986–87: In Australia, coaching and playing
Other sports followed: Watches rugby
Relaxations: Any sport, music
Extras: Bowling award for 4 wickets or more most times in 1983
Best batting performance: 84 Glamorgan v Surrey, Guildford 1982
Best bowling performance: 5-56 Glamorgan v Somerset, Cardiff 1984

LAST SEASON: BATTING

	I.	N.O.	R.	H.S.	AV.
TEST	2	0	38	28	19.00
1ST-CLASS	25	6	485	70	25.52
INT					
JPL	13	3	121	24	12.10
NAT.W.	2	0	20	19	10.00
B & H	4	0	13	9	2.25

LAST SEASON: BOWLING

	O.	M.	R.	W.	AV.
TEST	43	5	140	2	70.00
1ST-CLASS	435.5	72	1606	43	37.34
INT					
JPL	101	8	449	16	28.06
NAT.W.	21	3	74	0	–
B & H	33	6	133	3	44.33

CAREER: BATTING

	I.	N.O.	R.	H.S.	AV.
TEST	10	4	83	31*	13.83
1ST-CLASS	108	15	1617	84	17.38
INT	2	1	0	0*	–
JPL	46	11	483	37	13.80
NAT.W.	5	1	61	24	15.25
B & H	10	0	50	17	5.00

CAREER: BOWLING

	O.	M.	R.	W.	AV.
TEST	129	18	504	10	50.40
1ST-CLASS	2071.5	386	7411	240	30.87
INT	15	2	85	1	–
JPL	340.1	21	1685	67	25.14
NAT.W.	39	5	163	5	32.60
B & H	98.3	14	378	15	25.20

158. What was the surname of three brothers who all played in one Test Match, England v South Africa, two for England and one for South Africa?

159. Who scored the first 100 for England after the Second World War?

160. Who announced his retirement from Test cricket in an interview with his brother?

THORNE, D. A.   Warwickshire

Full Name: David Anthony Thorne
Role: Right-hand bat, left-arm medium bowler
Born: 12 December 1964, Coventry
Height: 5′ 11″ **Weight:** 12st
Nickname: Strop, Thorney
County debut: 1983
1st-Class 50s scored: 12
1st-Class 100s scored: 2
1st-Class 5 w. in innings: 1
Place in batting averages: 115th av. 28.82 (1985 20th av. 49.94)
Place in bowling averages: 122nd av. 53.72
1st-Class catches 1986: 4 (career: 22)
Parents: Dennis and Barbara
Marital status: Single
Education: Bablake School, Coventry; Keble College, Oxford

Qualifications: 10 O-levels, 3 A-levels, BA (2.1) in Modern History
Jobs outside cricket: Components packager for Quinton Hazell car components. Worked as a labourer on building site pre-season 1983
Family links with cricket: Father is a qualified coach in Warwickshire area. Brothers, Robert and Philip, both played for Warwickshire Schools. Mother played for Hinckley Ladies
Cricketing superstitions: 'Always left pad on first. If I get runs I try to wear the same shirt and trousers no matter how dirty until I fail again.'
Overseas tours: Oxbridge to Hong Kong and Australia 1985–86
Cricketers particularly learnt from: 'Dennis Amiss and above all my Father.'
Off-season 1986–87: Playing and coaching abroad
Other sports played: Rugby, football, golf
Other sports followed: 'Any sports except horse-racing.'
Relaxations: Listening to music, reading
Extras: 'Was hit for 26 in my 3rd over in my first John Player League game by Trevor Jesty. Was out first ball for 0 in my first-class debut v Oxford University. Once took 7 for 7 in a school's first XI match including a hat-trick and all 7 bowled. Secretary OUCC 1985, captain 1986; scoring unbeaten 100 in Varsity Match lost off last ball to a leg-bye
Opinions: 'There is too much cricket played and the new proposals of a 50-over game on Sundays only adds to this. There are far too many contrived games and false declarations gained by using "joke" bowlers. Perhaps four-day cricket is the answer. There is too much travelling in a season.'
Injuries 1986: Groin strain mid-June. Poisoned arm early July

Best batting performance: 124 Oxford University v Zimbabwe, Oxford 1985
Best bowling performance: 5-39 Oxford University v Cambridge University, Lord's 1984

LAST SEASON: BATTING

	I.	N.O.	R.	H.S.	AV.
TEST					
1ST-CLASS	21	4	490	104*	28.82
INT					
JPL	3	1	55	24	27.50
NAT.W.	2	0	42	21	21.00
B & H	4	1	53	36*	17.66

LAST SEASON: BOWLING

	O.	M.	R.	W.	AV.
TEST					
1ST-CLASS	239.3	70	591	11	53.72
INT					
JPL	14	0	66	1	–
NAT.W.	1	0	4	0	–
B & H	20.3	1	73	0	–

CAREER: BATTING

	I.	N.O.	R.	H.S.	AV.
TEST					
1ST-CLASS	64	13	1707	124	33.47
INT					
JPL	16	4	189	42	15.75
NAT.W.	2	0	42	21	21.00
B & H	12	2	157	36*	15.70

CAREER: BOWLING

	O.	M.	R.	W.	AV.
TEST					
1ST-CLASS	683.5	152	2009	41	49.00
INT					
JPL	91.5	1	548	11	49.81
NAT.W.	1	0	4	0	–
B & H	56.3	4	230	1	–

TOMLINS, K. P.　　　　Gloucestershire

Full Name: Keith Patrick Tomlins
Role: Right-hand bat, short-leg fielder
Born: 23 October 1957, Kingston-upon-Thames
Height: 5′ 9½″ **Weight:** 11st 9lbs
Nickname: Tommo
County debut: 1977 (Middlesex), 1986 (Gloucestershire)
County cap: 1983 (Middlesex)
1st-Class 50s scored: 17
1st-Class 100s scored: 4
One-Day 50s: 6
Place in batting averages: 114th av. 29.00 (1985 141st av. 25.29)
1st-Class catches 1986: 1 (career: 64)
Parents: Royston John and Joan Muriel
Marital status: Single
Education: St Benedict's School, Ealing; College of St Hilda and St Bede, Durham University
Qualifications: 5 O-levels, 3 A-levels

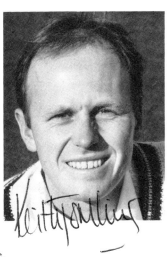

Jobs outside cricket: Stage-hand at Richmond Theatre. Sports and music management with Williams Maloney Associates. Ship hand with BP on survey ship

Family links with cricket: Father and 2 brothers play for Wycombe House CC in Osterley, Middlesex

Overseas tours: South America with Derrick Robins' XI in 1983; West Indies with British Colleges 1978 and Ealing CC 1982; Zimbabwe with Middlesex CCC 1984

Overseas teams played for: Greenpoint CC, Cape Town, 1979–80, 1983–84; Merewether DCC, Newcastle, New South Wales, 1981–82; Parnell CC, Auckland, 1985–86

Cricketers particularly learnt from: Mike Brearley

Cricketers particularly admired: Graham Gooch and John Emburey

Off-season 1986–87: At home in Thornbury

Other sports played: Golf

Other sports followed: Rugby

Relaxations: Reading, gardening, crosswords, fly fishing

Extras: Left Middlesex after 1985 season and joined Gloucestershire

Opinions on cricket: 'Over rate fines wrong, particularly in one day cricket when the setting of fields is so vital and bound to be a bit time consuming. I don't think spectators feel cheated by below normal over rates in these circumstances. It is an unavoidable part of the game. Certain respected umpires should be on the England selection panel as these people are "closer to the pulse" of the current form and abilities of the players.'

Best batting performance: 146 Middlesex v Oxford University, Oxford 1982

Best bowling performance: 2-28 Middlesex v Kent, Lord's 1982

LAST SEASON: BATTING

	I.	N.O.	R.	H.S.	AV.
TEST					
1ST-CLASS	29	5	696	75	29.00
INT					
JPL	10	3	230	45	32.85
NAT.W.	1	0	8	8	–
B & H	1	0	1	1	–

CAREER: BATTING

	I.	N.O.	R.	H.S.	AV.
TEST					
1ST-CLASS	152	19	3579	146	26.90
INT					
JPL	54	11	824	59	19.16
NAT.W.	6	0	201	80	33.50
B & H	7	0	104	40	14.86

LAST SEASON: BOWLING

	O.	M.	R.	W.	AV.
TEST					
1ST-CLASS	6	0	34	0	–
INT					
JPL	5	0	30	0	–
NAT.W.	1	0	10	0	–
B & H					

CAREER: BOWLING

	O.	M.	R.	W.	AV.
TEST					
1ST-CLASS	102.3	21	360	4	90.00
INT					
JPL	67	2	337	11	30.63
NAT.W.	1	0	10	0	–
B & H					

TOPLEY, T. D.   Essex

Full Name: Thomas Donald Topley
Role: Right-hand bat, right-arm
fast-medium bowler
Born: 25 February 1964, Canterbury
Height: 6' 3" **Weight:** 13st 8lbs
Nickname: Toppers
County debut: 1985
1st-Class 5 w. in innings: 2
Place in batting averages: 127th
av. 12.55
Place in bowling averages: 20th
av. 23.25
1st-Class catches 1986: 8 (career: 10)
Parents: Tom and Rhoda
Marital status: Single
Education: Royal Hospital School,
Holbrook, Suffolk
Qualifications: 6 O-levels, NCA
Senior Coach
Jobs outside cricket: Cricket coach; exporting to the Gulf States
Family links with cricket: Brother, Peter, played for Kent (1972–75). Father
played for Royal Navy
Overseas tours: Keith Pont Benefit Tour to Barbados 1986
Overseas teams played for: Natal Midlands & Noodsburg, S. Africa 1985–86
Cricketers particularly learnt from: Don Wilson, and all at Essex
Cricketers particularly admired: John Lever, Richard Hadlee and anyone
who gives 100 per cent
Off-season 1986–87: Playing and coaching abroad
Other sports played: Rugby, football, badminton and all ball sports

LAST SEASON: BATTING

	I.	N.O.	R.	H.S.	AV.
TEST					
1ST-CLASS	11	2	113	45	12.55
INT					
JPL	2	2	8	8*	–
NAT.W.					
B & H	–	–	–	–	–

CAREER: BATTING

	I.	N.O.	R.	H.S.	AV.
TEST					
1ST-CLASS	15	4	128	45	11.63
INT					
JPL	2	2	8	8*	–
NAT.W.	2	0	10	9	5.00
B & H	–	–	–	–	–

LAST SEASON: BOWLING

	O.	M.	R.	W.	AV.
TEST					
1ST-CLASS	249.4	55	744	32	23.25
INT					
JPL	52	2	235	9	26.11
NAT.W.					
B & H	22	3	74	2	37.00

CAREER: BOWLING

	O.	M.	R.	W.	AV.
TEST					
1ST-CLASS	410.5	82	1208	49	24.65
INT					
JPL	60	3	261	11	23.72
NAT.W.	23	1	81	3	27.00
B & H	22	3	74	2	37.00

Relaxations: Photography
Extras: Spent three years prior to joining Essex on the MCC Young Professionals at Lord's. As 12th man held famous Test match 'catch' England v West Indies at Lord's. Also appeared for Surrey during 1985
Opinions on cricket: 'Abolish over rate during three-day cricket.'
Best batting performance: 45 Essex v New Zealanders, Chelmsford 1986
Best bowling performance: 5-52 Essex v Sussex, Ilford 1986

TREMLETT, T. M.   Hampshire

Full Name: Timothy Maurice Tremlett
Role: Right-hand bat, right-arm medium bowler
Born: 26 July 1956, Wellington, Somerset
Height: 6' 2" **Weight:** 13st 7lbs
Nickname: Hurricane, Trooper, R2
County debut: 1976
County cap: 1983
50 wickets in a season: 3
1st-Class 50s scored: 17
1st-Class 100s scored: 1
1st-Class 5 w. in innings: 8
Place in batting averages: 110th av. 29.27 (1985 112th av. 30.00)
Place in bowling averages: 58th av. 29.37 (1985 7th av. 21.60)
1st-Class catches 1986: 2 (career: 62)
Parents: Maurice Fletcher and Melina May
Wife and date of marriage: Carolyn Patricia, 28 September 1979
Children: Christopher Timothy, 2 September 1981; Alastair Jonathan, 1 February 1983; Benjamin Paul, 2 May 1984
Education: Bellemoor Secondary Modern; Richard Taunton Sixth-Form College
Qualifications: 5 O-levels, 1 A-level. Advanced Coaching Certificate
Jobs outside cricket: 'One winter spent labouring on building site for muscle-building (did not seem to work).' Furrier
Family links with cricket: Father played for Somerset and England 1947–48 against West Indies in the West Indies. Captained Somerset 1958–60. Younger brother plays in local club cricket for Deanery CC
Cricketing superstitions: 'I always like to be the last to leave the dressing room when taking the field.'

Overseas tours: English Counties tour to Zimbabwe 1985; England B to Sri Lanka 1986

Overseas teams played for: Oudtshoorn Teachers' Training College, Western Cape, South Africa, 1978–79

Cricketers particularly learnt from: 'My father, and in general watching and listening to other cricketers, first-class or club players.'

Cricketers particularly admired: Vincent Van der Bijl, Mike Hendrick, Malcolm Marshall

Other sports played: Golf (7 handicap), table-tennis, squash, swimming and badminton

Relaxations: Collecting cricket books and records, gardening, cinema

Extras: Member of local cricket club, Deanery. Batted in almost every position for Hants in batting order from 1 to 11 in 1979. Captained both his school and sixth-form college at cricket

Best batting performance: 102* Hampshire v Somerset, Taunton 1985

Best bowling performance: 6-82 Hampshire v Derbyshire, Portsmouth 1983

LAST SEASON: BATTING

	I.	N.O.	R.	H.S.	AV.
TEST					
1ST-CLASS	23	12	322	59*	29.27
INT					
JPL	4	3	15	4*	–
NAT.W.	2	1	28	28*	–
B & H	2	2	43	36*	–

LAST SEASON: BOWLING

	O.	M.	R.	W.	AV.
TEST					
1ST-CLASS	453.4	110	1263	43	29.37
INT					
JPL	104.5	1	468	26	18.00
NAT.W.	22	2	77	2	38.50
B & H	35	1	136	6	22.66

CAREER: BATTING

	I.	N.O.	R.	H.S.	AV.
TEST					
1ST-CLASS	209	52	3337	102*	21.25
INT					
JPL	46	20	285	35	10.96
NAT.W.	12	3	99	28*	11.00
B & H	21	8	191	36*	14.69

CAREER: BOWLING

	O.	M.	R.	W.	AV.
TEST					
1ST-CLASS	3459	1002	8274	337	24.55
INT					
JPL	746.3	33	3453	135	25.57
NAT.W.	193.2	35	587	23	25.52
B & H	274.5	41	900	40	22.50

---

161. Who is the only Lancashire player to have scored 100 for England at Old Trafford?

162. Who was the youngest man ever to captain England and at what age?

163. Which first-class county did F. S. Trueman play for, as well as Yorkshire?

TUFNELL, P. C. R.   Middlesex

Full Name: Philip Clive Roderick Tufnell
Role: Right-hand bat, slow left-arm spinner
Born: 29 April 1966, Hadley Wood, Hertfordshire
Height: 6′ 0″ **Weight:** 11st 8lbs
Nickname: Tuffers, Brucie
County debut: 1986
1st-Class catches 1986: 1 (career: 1)
Parents: Sylvia and Alan
Wife and date of marriage: Alison Jane, 5 October 1986
Education: Highgate School; Southgate School
Qualifications: O-level in Art; City & Guilds Silversmithing
Jobs outside cricket: Silversmith, mini cabbing
Overseas tours: Young England tour to the West Indies 1985
Cricketers particularly learnt from: Alan Gorden, Don Wilson
Cricketers particularly admired: Clive Radley
Off-season 1986–87: Working as silversmith/mini cab driver
Other sports played: Football, snooker
Other sports followed: American football
Relaxations: 'Taking Alison and her friend Elaine shopping.'
Opinions on cricket: 'Tea should be longer.'
Injuries 1986: Slight knee injury

LAST SEASON: BATTING

	I.	N.O.	R.	H.S.	AV.
TEST					
1ST-CLASS	7	1	32	9	5.33
INT					
JPL					
NAT.W.					
B & H					

LAST SEASON: BOWLING

	O.	M.	R.	W.	AV.
TEST					
1ST-CLASS	148	32	479	5	95.80
INT					
JPL					
NAT.W.					
B & H					

CAREER: BATTING

	I.	N.O.	R.	H.S.	AV.
TEST					
1ST-CLASS	7	1	32	9	5.33
INT					
JPL					
NAT.W.					
B & H					

CAREER: BOWLING

	O.	M.	R.	W.	AV.
TEST					
1ST-CLASS	148	32	479	5	95.80
INT					
JPL					
NAT.W.					
B & H					

Best batting performance: 9 Middlesex v Worcestershire, Worcester 1986
Best bowling performance: 2-47 Middlesex v Warwickshire, Uxbridge 1986

TURNER, D. R. Hampshire

Full Name: David Roy Turner
Role: Left-hand bat, right-arm
medium bowler, cover fielder
Born: 5 February 1949, Corsham,
near Chippenham, Wiltshire
Height: 5′ 6″ **Weight:** 11st 8lbs
Nickname: Birdy, Fossil
County debut: 1966
County cap: 1970
Benefit: 1981 (£23,011)
1000 runs in a season: 7
1st-Class 50s scored: 72
1st-Class 100s scored: 24
One-Day 50s: 52
One-Day 100s: 3
Place in batting averages: 67th
av. 36.30 (1985 120th av. 28.86)
1st-Class catches 1986: 2

(career: 176)
Parents: Robert Edward and Evelyn Peggy
Wife and date of marriage: Henriette, 18 February 1977
Children: Nicola Marianna, 15 March 1984
Education: Chippenham Boys' High School
Qualifications: 5 O-levels
Jobs outside cricket: Player-coach for the Paarl Cricket Club, South Africa
1972–80, 1982–85
Overseas tours: With Derrick Robins' XI to South Africa 1972–73
Overseas teams played for: Western Province in the winning 1977–78 Currie
Cup Competition side
Cricketers particularly learnt from: Roy Marshall
Cricketers particularly admired: Mike Procter
Off-season 1986–87: Becoming involved in the shoe business
Cricket records: Shared in an unbeaten partnership of 283 with C. G.
Greenidge, a record in any one-day competition, in Benson & Hedges Cup,
Hampshire v Minor Counties South at Amersham in 1973
Other sports played: Golf, football, athletics
Relaxations: Chess, gardening, reading, television, watching war films
Extras: Played for Wiltshire in 1965. Took a hat-trick in a Lambert & Butler

7-a-side floodlit tournament at Ashton Gate (Bristol) on 17 September 1981 against Glamorgan. Captained his school at soccer, rugger and cricket. Also ran for school in cross-country and athletics. Played in school hockey team
Opinions on cricket: 'I would like the cricket authorities to try for one season, 16 4-day Championship matches, coupled with a Saturday 60-overs limited cricket league, along with the usual Sunday John Player League. There should be tighter controls on overseas players.'
Injuries 1986: Recurring split webbing between middle fingers of left hand during 2nd half of season
Best batting performance: 181* Hampshire v Surrey, The Oval 1969
Best bowling performance: 2-7 Hampshire v Glamorgan, Bournemouth 1981

LAST SEASON: BATTING

	I.	N.O.	R.	H.S.	AV.
TEST					
1ST-CLASS	14	1	472	96*	36.30
INT					
JPL	8	1	181	40*	25.85
NAT.W.	1	0	17	17	–
B & H	4	2	62	40*	31.00

LAST SEASON: BOWLING

	O.	M.	R.	W.	AV.
TEST					
1ST-CLASS	3	1	6	0	–
INT					
JPL					
NAT.W.					
B & H					

CAREER: BATTING

	I.	N.O.	R.	H.S.	AV.
TEST					
1ST-CLASS	604	56	16109	181*	29.39
INT					
JPL	214	20	5657	114*	29.15
NAT.W.	31	3	803	86	28.67
B & H	62	10	1828	123*	35.15

CAREER: BOWLING

	O.	M.	R.	W.	AV.
TEST					
1ST-CLASS	99.4	27	338	9	37.55
INT					
JPL	1.3	0	11	0	–
NAT.W.	1	0	4	0	–
B & H	0.2	0	4	0	–

164. Who was out first ball when the Australians scored 721 in a day v Essex in 1948?

165. Who almost achieved the double of 100 wickets and 1000 runs in 1971, and how near did he get?

166. What was unusual about Peter Judge's two innings for Glamorgan v India in 1946?

167. What Gloucestershire player was sacked two weeks after being awarded his county cap in 1979?

TURNER, M. S.   Somerset

Full Name: Murray Stewart Turner
Role: Right-hand bat, right-arm
medium bowler, close fielder
Born: 27 January 1964, Shaftesbury,
Dorset
Height: 6' 5" **Weight:** 13st 7lbs
Nickname: Ziggy
County debut: 1984
Place in batting averages: —
(1985 83rd av. 23.83)
Place in bowling averages: —
(1985 127th av. 49.85)
1st-Class catches 1986: — (career: 2)
Parents: John and Kathleen
Marital status: Single
Education: Huish Grammar School,
Taunton
Qualifications: 3 O-levels
Jobs outside cricket: Service
reception in a main Ford dealer
Cricketing superstitions: Wears a floppy white hat whenever possible
Overseas tours: Barbados with Somerset 1985
Cricketers particularly admired: Dennis Lillee, Michael Holding, Joel Garner, David Joseph (Taunton CC)
Other sports played: Football, darts, snooker, pool, golf
Other sports followed: Football (Crystal Palace)
Relaxations: Rock/pop concerts (especially David Bowie); good films
Extras: Bowls right-arm seamers and also left-arm spin. Scored 101* and took

LAST SEASON: BATTING

	I.	N.O.	R.	H.S.	AV.
TEST					
1ST-CLASS	–	–	–	–	–
INT					
JPL	2	1	23	22*	–
NAT.W.					
B & H					

LAST SEASON: BOWLING

	O.	M.	R.	W.	AV.
TEST					
1ST-CLASS	15	3	55	2	27.50
INT					
JPL	22	0	176	4	44.00
NAT.W.					
B & H					

CAREER: BATTING

	I.	N.O.	R.	H.S.	AV.
TEST					
1ST-CLASS	14	6	144	24*	18.00
INT					
JPL	7	2	49	22*	9.80
NAT.W.					
B & H	3	1	42	19	21.00

CAREER: BOWLING

	O.	M.	R.	W.	AV.
TEST					
1ST-CLASS	229.5	41	788	15	52.53
INT					
JPL	67	2	421	10	42.10
NAT.W.					
B & H	41.5	4	156	4	39.00

8-35 in same game in 1984 season.' Left staff after 1985 season, but played on a match contract basis in 1986
Best batting performance: 24* Somerset v Warwickshire, Taunton 1985
Best bowling performance: 4-74 Somerset v Warwickshire, Taunton 1985

TURNER, S.   Essex

Full Name: Stuart Turner
Role: Right-hand bat, right-arm fast-medium bowler
Born: 18 July 1943, Chester
Height: 6′ 0½″ **Weight:** 12st 7lbs
Nickname: Stu
County debut: 1965
County cap: 1970
Benefit: 1979
50 wickets in a season: 6
1st-Class 50s scored: 41
1st-Class 100s scored: 4
1st-Class 5 w. in innings: 27
1st-Class 10 w. in match: 1
One-Day 50s: 11
1st-Class catches 1986: —
(career: 217)
Parents: Arthur Leonard and Alice
Wife and date of marriage: Jacqueline Linda, 9 April 1966
Children: Jeremy Paul, 12 February 1968; Emma Louise, 21 January 1970
Education: Epping Junior School; Epping Secondary Modern
Qualifications: Advanced Cricket Coach
Jobs outside cricket: Insurance claims broker. Coaching cricket both in South Africa and England
Overseas tours: Toured West Indies 1974 with Derrick Robins' XI; South Africa 1975 with Derrick Robins' XI
Overseas teams played for: Natal in Currie Cup and Gillette Cup Competitions 1976–77–78. Won both in 1976–77
Cricketers particularly learnt from: 'Learnt from so many – one never stops learning.'
Cricketers particularly admired: 'G. Sobers – a great privilege to play against him.'
Cricket records: First player to take 200 wickets and score 2000 runs in the John Player League
Other sports played: Golf, squash, occasional football, enjoys as many sports as possible, watching and playing

Relaxations: 'Reading, playing records, watching television, driving, doing anything that takes my fancy and just enjoying life.'

Extras: A century before lunch against Kent (108 mins) 3 May 1979, Chelmsford. Hat-trick against Surrey at The Oval, 4 May 1971. Spent 1966 and 1967 out of the game, returning in 1968. Retired from 1st class cricket at end of 1986 season

Best batting performance: 121 Essex v Somerset, Taunton 1970

Best bowling performance: 6-26 Essex v Northamptonshire, Northampton 1977

LAST SEASON: BATTING

	I.	N.O.	R.	H.S.	AV.
TEST					
1ST-CLASS	4	1	72	32	24.00
INT					
JPL	1	0	24	24	–
NAT.W.					
B & H	3	0	43	41	14.33

LAST SEASON: BOWLING

	O.	M.	R.	W.	AV.
TEST					
1ST-CLASS	40	11	138	2	69.00
INT					
JPL	33	1	193	2	96.50
NAT.W.					
B & H	53	9	221	6	36.83

CAREER: BATTING

	I.	N.O.	R.	H.S.	AV.
TEST					
1ST-CLASS	513	101	9411	121	22.84
INT					
JPL	205	44	3165	87	19.65
NAT.W.	29	4	449	50*	17.96
B & H	56	17	651	55*	16.69

CAREER: BOWLING

	O.	M.	R.	W.	AV.
TEST					
1ST-CLASS	8899	2277	21351	821	26.00
INT					
JPL	1766.5	169	7231	303	23.86
NAT.W.	354.5	70	1027	50	20.54
B & H	750.2	132	2222	107	20.76

168. How many editions of the Cricketer's Who's Who have now been produced?

169. Which is the only Test ground to have had three triple centuries hit on it, and by whom?

170. Who scored over 2000 runs every season between 1922 and 1935?

171. Who succeeded John Hampshire as captain of Yorkshire?

TWIZELL, P. H. — Gloucestershire

Full Name: Peter Henry Twizell
Role: Right-hand bat, right-arm fast medium bowler
Born: 18 June 1959, Rothbury, Northumberland
Height: 6′ 3½″ **Weight:** 14st 7lbs
Nickname: Big Hen, H.F.T.
County debut: 1985
Parents: Sylvia Rose Daykin
Marital status: Single
Education: Ponteland High School
Qualifications: 9 CSEs
Jobs outside cricket: Steel erector, welder
Overseas tours: Gloucestershire to Barbados 1985
Overseas teams played for: Mangere CC, Auckland, New Zealand, 1985–86

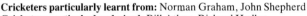

Cricketers particularly learnt from: Norman Graham, John Shepherd
Cricketers particularly admired: Bill Athey, Richard Hadlee
Off-season 1986–87: Playing abroad or seeking employment
Other sports played: Squash, football
Other sports followed: Rugby, boxing
Relaxations: Watching TV, music, cards, backgammon
Extras: Released at end of 1986 season
Best bowling performance: 2-65 Gloucestershire v Zimbabweans, Bristol 1985

LAST SEASON: BATTING

	I.	N.O.	R.	H.S.	AV.
TEST					
1ST-CLASS	1	0	0	0	–
INT					
JPL	1	0	4	4	–
NAT.W.					
B & H					

LAST SEASON: BOWLING

	O.	M.	R.	W.	AV.
TEST					
1ST-CLASS	11.1	3	38	0	–
INT					
JPL	29	0	168	6	28.00
NAT.W.					
B & H					

CAREER: BATTING

	I.	N.O.	R.	H.S.	AV.
TEST					
1ST-CLASS	1	0	0	0	–
INT					
JPL	1	0	4	4	–
NAT.W.	1	1	9	9*	–
B & H					

CAREER: BOWLING

	O.	M.	R.	W.	AV.
TEST					
1ST-CLASS	39.1	9	136	2	68.00
INT					
JPL	31	0	191	7	27.18
NAT.W.	12	1	45	1	–
B & H					

UNDERWOOD, D. L.   Kent

Full Name: Derek Leslie Underwood
Role: Right-hand bat, slow left-arm bowler
Born: 8 June 1945, Bromley, Kent
Height: 5′ 11″ **Weight:** 12st
Nickname: Deadly, Unders
County debut: 1963
County cap: 1964
Benefit: 1975 (£24,114), 2nd benefit 1986
Test debut: 1966
No. of Tests: 86
No. of One-Day Internationals: 26
50 wickets in a season: 22
1st-Class 50s scored: 2
1st-Class 100s scored: 1
1st-Class 5 w. in innings: 156
1st-Class 10 w. in match: 47
Place in batting averages: 235th av. 11.57
Place in bowling averages: 35th av. 26.36 (1985 32nd av. 26.90)
1st-Class catches 1986: 2 (career: 258)
Parents: Leslie (deceased) and Evelyn
Wife and date of marriage: Dawn, 6 October 1973
Children: Heather, 7 February 1976; Fiona, 22 November 1977
Education: Beckenham & Penge Grammar School
Jobs outside cricket: Company representative, cricket coach, PE schoolmaster. Director of company of Law Stationers
Family links with cricket: 'I played with my father and brother for a local village team, Farnborough. I played for Beckenham with my brother until I played for the Kent 1st XI. My brother now plays for Orpington CC.'
Overseas tours: Pakistan 1966–67; Sri Lanka and Pakistan 1968–69; Australia and New Zealand 1970–71 and 1974–75; India, Sri Lanka and Pakistan 1972–73; West Indies 1973–74; India, Sri Lanka and Australia 1976–77; Australia and India 1979–80
Other sports played: Occasional golf
Relaxations: Photography, philately, coarse fishing, gardening
Extras: Second youngest player to receive county cap. Played World Series Cricket 1978–79. Youngest player ever to take 100 wickets in debut season. Banned from Test cricket for three years for joining rebel team from England to South Africa. Writes articles for *Cricketer International* magazine. Top of Kent first-class bowling averages in 1982, 1983 and 1984. Awarded MBE. Scored maiden century in 1984 in 618th first-class innings

Best batting performance: 111 Kent v Sussex, Hastings 1984
Best bowling performance: 9-28 Kent v Sussex, Hastings 1964

LAST SEASON: BATTING

	I.	N.O.	R.	H.S.	AV.
TEST					
1ST-CLASS	26	5	243	29	11.57
INT					
JPL	8	5	16	6*	5.33
NAT.W.	1	1	2	2*	
B & H	2	1	1	1*	–

CAREER: BATTING

	I.	N.O.	R.	H.S.	AV.
TEST	116	35	937	45	11.56
1ST-CLASS	574	156	4060	111	9.71
INT	13	4	53	17	5.89
JPL	98	41	382	22	6.70
NAT.W.	33	12	156	28	7.42
B & H	44	19	190	27	7.60

LAST SEASON: BOWLING

	O.	M.	R.	W.	AV.
TEST					
1ST-CLASS	638.1	259	1371	52	26.36
INT					
JPL	97.2	9	391	18	21.72
NAT.W.	19	6	36	0	–
B & H	66	14	251	7	35.85

CAREER: BOWLING

	O.	M.	R.	W.	AV.
TEST	542.2 2920.4	142 1097	7674	297	25.84
1ST-CLASS	390.5 18587.1	85 7416	41024	2123	19.32
INT	6 205	0 26	734	32	22.93
JPL	1559.3	197	5779	344	16.79
NAT.W.	559.3	149	1659	67	24.76
B & H	777.2	167	2179	97	22.46

VAREY, D. W.   Lancashire

Full Name: David William Varey
Role: Right-hand opening bat, occasional right-arm off-break bowler
Born: 15 October 1961, Darlington
Height: 6′ 2″ **Weight:** 13st
Nickname: Wilbur, D-Dubs, Dubsy, Hoorah Henry
County debut: 1984
1st-Class 50s scored: 9
1st-Class 100s scored: 3
Place in batting averages: 81st av. 33.87
1st-Class catches 1986: 5 (career: 24)
Parents: Bill (deceased) and Monica
Marital status: Single
Education: Birkenhead School; Pembroke College, Cambridge
Qualifications: BA Hons French and German
Family links with cricket: Brother, John, is an Oxford Blue

Overseas teams played for: South Hobart CC, Tasmania, 1984–86
Cricketers particularly learnt from: Peter Lever, Mick Bowyer, Mike Fell, Dave Ewing
Cricketers particularly admired: Clive Lloyd, Viv Richards, Ian Botham
Other sports played: Rugby, snooker
Other sports followed: Rugby, soccer (Everton)
Relaxations: Disco dancing, body-popping, reading, watching TV, music
Extras: Played for Cheshire 1977, Lancashire 2nd XI debut 1980. Blues in 1982 and 1983. Secretary CUCC 1983
Best batting performance: 156* Cambridge University v Northamptonshire, Cambridge 1982

LAST SEASON: BATTING

	I.	N.O.	R.	H.S.	AV.
TEST					
1ST-CLASS	10	2	271	83	33.87
INT					
JPL	1	0	3	3	–
NAT.W.					
B & H					

LAST SEASON: BOWLING

	O.	M.	R.	W.	AV.
TEST					
1ST-CLASS					
INT					
JPL					
NAT.W.					
B & H					

CAREER: BATTING

	I.	N.O.	R.	H.S.	AV.
TEST					
1ST-CLASS	100	11	2437	156*	27.38
INT					
JPL	1	0	3	3	–
NAT.W.					
B & H	5	0	58	27	11.60

CAREER: BOWLING

	O.	M.	R.	W.	AV.
TEST					
1ST-CLASS	1	0	4	0	–
INT					
JPL					
NAT.W.					
B & H					

172. Who scored the only Test century at Bramall Lane?

173. Which batsman has scored most centuries for Middlesex?

174. Who succeeded Chris Old as captain of Yorkshire?

175. Which player left Surrey CCC because they would not award him his county cap, although he had an England cap, and when?

176. Who was Fred Trueman's last Test victim?

WALKER, A.   Northamptonshire

Full Name: Alan Walker
Role: Left-hand bat, right-arm fast-medium bowler, outfielder
Born: 7 July 1962, Emley, Nr Huddersfield
Height: 5′ 11″ **Weight:** 12st 7lbs
Nickname: Arthur Scargill
County debut: 1983
1st-Class 5 w. in innings: 1
Place in batting averages: 194th av. 17.40 (1985 223rd av. 13.83)
Place in bowling averages: 97th av. 39.81 (1985 76th av. 34.17)
1st-Class catches 1986: 6 (career: 19)
Parents: Malcolm and Enid
Wife and date of marriage: Janice, 17 September 1983
Education: Emley Junior School; Kirkburton Middle School; Shelley High School
Qualifications: 2 O-levels, 4 CSEs
Jobs outside cricket: Miner
Overseas tours: Denmark, with NCA U-19s North of England 1980
Overseas teams played for: Uitenhage, South Africa 1984–85
Cricketers particularly learnt from: David Steele
Cricketers particularly admired: Dennis Lillee, Richard Hadlee
Other sports played: Football
Other sports followed: Rugby league, any sport on TV
Relaxations: 'Watching TV, listening to music, DIY, having a pint.'

LAST SEASON: BATTING

	I.	N.O.	R.	H.S.	AV.
TEST					
1ST-CLASS	15	10	87	40*	17.40
INT					
JPL	1	1	9	9*	–
NAT.W.	1	0	3	3	–
B & H	1	1	3	3*	–

CAREER: BATTING

	I.	N.O.	R.	H.S.	AV.
TEST					
1ST-CLASS	48	25	242	40*	10.52
INT					
JPL	7	3	41	13	10.25
NAT.W.	1	0	3	3	–
B & H	1	1	3	3*	–

LAST SEASON: BOWLING

	O.	M.	R.	W.	AV.
TEST					
1ST-CLASS	422	76	1314	33	39.81
INT					
JPL	105.4	3	546	19	28.73
NAT.W.	11	1	53	0	–
B & H	44	3	197	2	98.50

CAREER: BOWLING

	O.	M.	R.	W.	AV.
TEST					
1ST-CLASS	1148.1	209	3796	105	36.15
INT					
JPL	291.4	14	1335	54	24.72
NAT.W.	48.5	5	198	5	39.60
B & H	75.5	4	346	9	38.44

Best batting performance: 40* Northamptonshire v Indians, Northampton 1986
Best bowling performance: 6-50 Northamptonshire v Lancashire, Northampton 1986

WALSH, C. A.   Gloucestershire

Full Name: Courtney Andrew Walsh
Role: Right-hand bat, right-arm fast bowler
Born: 30 October 1962, Kingston, Jamaica
Height: 6′ 5½″ **Weight:** 13st 7lbs
Nickname: Mask, Walshy
County debut: 1984
County cap: 1985
Test debut: 1984–85
No. of Tests: 7
No. of One-Day Internationals: 13
50 wickets in a season: 2
1st-Class 50s scored: 1
1st-Class 5 w. in innings: 26
1st-Class 10 w. in match: 6
Place in batting averages: 230th av. 12.27 (1985 174th av. 15.75)
Place in bowling averages: 5th av. 18.17 (1985 5th av. 20.07)
1st-Class catches 1986: 7 (career: 27)
Parents: Joan Wollaston and Erick
Marital status: Single

LAST SEASON: BATTING

	I.	N.O.	R.	H.S.	AV.
TEST					
1ST-CLASS	24	6	221	52	12.27
INT					
JPL	7	1	37	35	6.16
NAT.W.	2	1	26	25*	–
B & H	2	1	10	8	–

CAREER: BATTING

	I.	N.O.	R.	H.S.	AV.
TEST	8	4	47	18*	11.75
1ST-CLASS	99	26	767	52	10.50
INT	1	1	7	7*	–
JPL	13	2	65	35	5.90
NAT.W.	6	2	57	25*	14.25
B & H	2	1	10	8	–

LAST SEASON: BOWLING

	O.	M.	R.	W.	AV.
TEST					
1ST-CLASS	789.5	193	2145	118	18.17
INT					
JPL	89.1	6	420	15	28.00
NAT.W.	19	2	51	3	17.00
B & H	40	5	162	4	40.50

CAREER: BOWLING

	O.	M.	R.	W.	AV.
TEST	204.2	40	610	21	29.04
1ST-CLASS	2598.5	417	8004	367	21.80
INT	117	3	521	10	52.10
JPL	182.3	14	810	28	28.92
NAT.W.	47	6	158	6	26.33
B & H	61.3	8	274	8	28.00

Education: Excelsior High School
Qualifications: GCE and CXL
Overseas tours: To England 1984, Australia 1984–85, Pakistan 1986, with West Indies
Overseas teams played for: West Indies, Jamaica
Other sports played: Football
Other sports followed: Basketball and track and field events
Relaxations: Music and watching TV
Extras: Took record 10-43 in Jamaican school cricket in 1979
Best batting performance: 52 Gloucestershire v Yorkshire, Bristol 1986
Best bowling performance: 9-72 Gloucestershire v Somerset, Bristol 1986

WARD, D. M. Surrey

Full Name: David Mark Ward
Role: Right-hand bat, right-arm off-spin bowler, gully fielder
Born: 10 February 1961, Croydon
Height: 6′ **Weight:** 13st 2lbs
Nickname: Cocker, Wardy, Jaws, Gnasher
County debut: 1985
1st-Class 100s scored: 1
One-Day 50s: 1
Place in batting averages: —
(1985 49th av. 39.86)
1st-Class catches 1986: 1 (career: 3)
Parents: Dora Kathleen and Thomas
Marital status: Single
Education: Haling Manor High School; Croydon Technical College
Qualifications: 2 O-levels, City and Guilds in Carpentry and Joinery
Jobs outside cricket: Carpenter
Family links with cricket: 'Grandad played for the Tamworth Arms.'
Cricketing superstitions: Marks across corner of non-striking crease with bat
Overseas tours: Barbados 1985 with Surrey
Overseas teams played for: Caulfield CC 1984–85 and 1985–86
Cricketers particularly learnt from: G. G. Arnold, G. Clinton, G. Howarth, M. Lynch, C. Walker, M. Stewart
Cricketers particularly admired: G. Gooch, I. T. Botham, I. V. A. Richards
Off-season 1986–87: Playing in Australia for Caulfield CC
Other sports played: Football, snooker, table-tennis

Relaxations: Eating out, watching TV, movies, jazz
Opinions on cricket: 'Avoid the politics and get on with the game!'
Best batting performance: 143 Surrey v Derbyshire, Derby 1985

WARD, T. R.   Kent

Full Name: Trevor Robert Ward
Role: Right-hand opening bat
Born: 18 January 1968,
Farningham, Kent
Height: 5′ 11″ **Weight:** 13st
Nickname: Zippy
County debut: 1986
Parents: Robert Henry and Hazel
Ann
Marital status: Single
Education: Hextable
Comprehensive
Qualifications: 6 O-levels
Family links with cricket: Father
played a little village cricket
with Farningham
Overseas tours: Bermuda with
NCA
Cricketers particularly learnt from: Alan
Ealham, Derek Aslett
Cricketers particularly admired: Viv Richards, Alan Ealham, Graham
Gooch
Off-season 1986–87: Playing in Perth, Australia
Other sports played: Football, golf, squash
Other sports followed: American football
Relaxations: Watching films, playing golf, fishing
Best batting performance: 29 Kent v Hampshire, Southampton 1986

	I.	N.O.	R.	H.S.	AV.
TEST					
1ST-CLASS	2	0	41	29	20.50
INT					
JPL					
NAT.W.					
B & H					

CAREER: BATTING

	I.	N.O.	R.	H.S.	AV.
TEST					
1ST-CLASS	2	0	41	29	20.50
INT					
JPL					
NAT.W.					
B & H					

WARING, I. C. Sussex

Full Name: Ian Charles Waring
Role: Left-hand bat, right-arm fast-medium bowler
Born: 6 December 1963, Chesterfield
Height: 6′ 1″ **Weight:** 13st 10lbs
Nickname: Eddie
County debut: 1985
1st-Class catches 1986: 1 (career: 1)
Parents: Jack and Dorothy
Marital status: Single
Education: Tupton Hall
Qualifications: 7 O-levels, Coaching Certificate
Overseas tours: Gibraltar 1980 with Sheffield Cricket Lovers
Overseas teams played for: Pretoria High School Old Boys 1983–84; Alma Marist, Cape Town, 1984–85; Bishops School, Cape Town, 1985–86

LAST SEASON: BATTING

	I.	N.O.	R.	H.S.	AV.
TEST					
1ST-CLASS	–	–	–	–	–
INT					
JPL					
NAT.W.					
B & H					

CAREER: BATTING

	I.	N.O.	R.	H.S.	AV.
TEST					
1ST-CLASS	–	–	–	–	–
INT					
JPL	–	–	–	–	–
NAT.W.					
B & H					

LAST SEASON: BOWLING

	O.	M.	R.	W.	AV.
TEST					
1ST-CLASS	22	6	45	1	–
INT					
JPL					
NAT.W.					
B & H					

CAREER: BOWLING

	O.	M.	R.	W.	AV.
TEST					
1ST-CLASS	22	6	45	1	–
INT					
JPL	11	0	58	0	–
NAT.W.					
B & H					

Cricketers particularly learnt from: Tony Pigott, Tony Borrington and Les Lenham
Cricketers particularly admired: Barry Richards, Imran Khan, Peter Kirsten
Other sports played: Football, swimming, baseball and anything outdoors
Other sports followed: All sports on TV
Relaxations: Listening to music, reading autobiographies and photography
Extras: Took wicket with first ball at Lord's
Best bowling performance: 1-18 Sussex v Cambridge University, Hove 1986

WARNER, A. E. Derbyshire

Full Name: Allan Esmond Warner
Role: Right-hand bat, right-arm fast bowler, outfielder
Born: 12 May 1959, Birmingham
Height: 5' 8" **Weight:** 10st
Nickname: Esis
County debut: 1982 (Worcestershire), 1985 (Derbyshire)
1st-Class 50s scored: 9
1st-Class 5 w. in innings: 2
One-Day 50s: 1
Place in batting averages: 132nd av. 26.95 (1985 204th av. 17.44)
Place in bowling averages: 107th av. 42.85 (1985 112th av. 42.21)
1st-Class catches 1986: 6 (career: 18)
Parents: Edgar and Sarah
Children: Alvin, 6 September 1980
Education: Tabernacle School, St Kitts, West Indies
Qualifications: CSE Maths. Bricklaying
Cricketers particularly learnt from: John Browny, Henry Benjamin
Cricketers particularly admired: M. Marshall and M. Holding
Other sports played: Football, table-tennis
Other sports followed: Football, boxing and athletics
Relaxations: Watching movies; music (soul, reggae and calypso)
Extras: Released by Worcestershire (debut 1982) at end of 1984 and joined Derbyshire
Best batting performance: 91 Derbyshire v Leicestershire, Chesterfield 1986
Best bowling performance: 5-27 Worcestershire v Glamorgan, Worcester 1984

449

	I.	N.O.	R.	H.S.	AV.
TEST					
1ST-CLASS	28	6	593	91	26.95
INT					
JPL	9	3	121	68	20.17
NAT.W.	1	0	6	6	–
B & H	1	1	17	17*	–

LAST SEASON: BOWLING

	O.	M.	R.	W.	AV.
TEST					
1ST-CLASS	349.1	67	1200	28	42.85
INT					
JPL	96	1	520	18	28.88
NAT.W.	6	0	49	0	–
B & H	23.4	1	150	5	30.00

CAREER: BATTING

	I.	N.O.	R.	H.S.	AV.
TEST					
1ST-CLASS	87	17	1387	91	19.81
INT					
JPL	30	9	213	68	10.14
NAT.W.	3	0	25	17	8.33
B & H	10	4	78	29*	13.00

CAREER: BOWLING

	O.	M.	R.	W.	AV.
TEST					
1ST-CLASS	1214.2	213	4160	113	36.81
INT					
JPL	273.5	6	1388	50	27.76
NAT.W.	37.3	3	178	3	59.33
B & H	170.3	10	523	19	27.52

WATERTON, S. N. V. Northamptonshire

Full Name: Stuart Nicholas Varney Waterton
Role: Right-hand bat, wicket-keeper
Born: 6 December 1960, Dartford
Height: 5′ 11½″ **Weight:** 12st
Nickname: Buck, Twatters
County debut: 1980 (Kent), 1986 (Northamptonshire)
1st-Class 50s scored: 2
Place in batting averages: 156th av. 24.25
Parents: Barry and Olive
Marital status: Single
Education: St George's Church of England School; Gravesend School for Boys; London School of Economics, London University
Qualifications: 10 O-levels, 3 A-levels, BSc Hons Economics, NCA Coaching Award
Jobs outside cricket: Civil servant, winter 1979–80, building labourer, cricket coach
Family links with cricket: 'Father was a magnificent back garden bowler and avid watcher.'
Cricketing superstitions: 'I always cross myself before going onto the field.'
Overseas teams played for: Goudstad Onderwyskollege, Johannesburg, 1984–85; Florida Park CC 1985

Cricketers particularly learnt from: Alan Knott, Bob Taylor, George Baker
Cricketers particularly admired: Bob Taylor, Alan Knott, Glenn Turner, Viv Richards
Off-season 1986: Playing and coaching for Combined Colleges in Johannesburg
Other sports played: Golf, road-running and cross-country
Other sports followed: Athletics
Relaxations: Music, TV, reading, cinema
Extras: Second wicket-keeper from Gravesend School to play for Kent CCC – David Nicolls being the other. Record individual score for Kent Schools Player, 163 v Sussex Schools 1979. Record number of runs aggregated in a season for Gravesend School, 983 runs at average of 75 in 1979. England Young Wicket-keeper of the Year 1980. Played for UAU 1981–83 (captain 1983 but did not take the field due to bad weather). Made NatWest debut in 1984 final. Member (with Laurie Potter) of Ashford CC side which won the Courage Kent League in 1985. Batting average in 2nd XI of 59.86 in 1985. Left Kent after 1985 season to further career
Opinions on cricket: '1) Working life after cricket is not adequately allowed for by players, especially younger ones, who do not seem to be given useful advice regarding the acquisition of a trade or work experience by their clubs. 2) There should be a reduction in the amount of three-day cricket played in favour of more financially viable competitions. 3) County clubs should do more to help young cricketers to find employment in winters.'
Injuries 1986: 'Mystery virus (diagnosed initially as glandular fever) which incapacitated me from mid-July.'
Best batting performance: 58* Middlesex v Worcestershire, Northampton 1986

LAST SEASON: BATTING

	I.	N.O.	R.	H.S.	AV.
TEST					
1ST-CLASS	17	4	314	58*	24.15
INT					
JPL	3	1	43	28	21.50
NAT.W.	1	1	4	4*	–
B & H					

LAST SEASON: WICKET-KEEPING

	C.	ST.			
TEST					
1ST-CLASS	31	5			
INT					
JPL	6	3			
NAT.W.					
B & H	1	1			

CAREER: BATTING

	I.	N.O.	R.	H.S.	AV.
TEST					
1ST-CLASS	45	9	700	58*	19.44
INT					
JPL	6	3	64	28	21.33
NAT.W.	2	1	5	4*	–
B & H					

CAREER: WICKET-KEEPING

	C.	ST.			
TEST					
1ST-CLASS	74	15			
INT					
JPL	6	3			
NAT.W.					
B & H	2	1			

WATKIN, S. L.   Glamorgan

Full Name: Steven Llewellyn Watkin
Role: Right-hand bat, medium fast right-arm bowler
Born: 15 September 1964, Duffrun Rhondda, Nr Port Talbot
Height: 6' 3" **Weight:** 12st 8lbs
Nickname: Watty
County debut: 1986
Parents: John and Sandra
Marital status: Single
Education: Cymer Afan Comprehensive; South Glamorgan Institute of Higher Education
Qualifications: 8 O-levels, 2 A-levels. Presently studying Degree in Human Movement Studies.
Cricketers particularly learnt from: Tom Cartwright, Allan Jones
Cricketers particularly admired: Richard Hadlee, Dennis Lillee
Off-season 1986–87: Student in 3rd year at SGIHE and touring West Indies with British Colleges
Other sports played: Football, tennis, rugby, basketball
Relaxations: Watching TV, listening to music, a quiet pint
Opinions on cricket: 'The qualifying rules in cricket are about right. In other sports it's a joke that people like Zola Budd can be made British literally overnight.'
Best bowling performance: 2-74 Glamorgan v Worcestershire, Worcester 1986

LAST SEASON: BATTING

	I.	N.O.	R.	H.S.	AV.
TEST					
1ST-CLASS	–	–	–	–	–
INT					
JPL	1	0	7	7	–
NAT.W.					
B & H					

LAST SEASON: BOWLING

	O.	M.	R.	W.	AV.
TEST					
1ST-CLASS	16	1	82	2	41.00
INT					
JPL	12	0	59	1	–
NAT.W.					
B & H					

CAREER: BATTING

	I.	N.O.	R.	H.S.	AV.
TEST					
1ST-CLASS	–	–	–	–	–
INT					
JPL	1	0	7	7	–
NAT.W.					
B & H					

CAREER: BOWLING

	O.	M.	R.	W.	AV.
TEST					
1ST-CLASS	16	1	82	2	41.00
INT					
JPL	12	0	59	1	–
NAT.W.					
B & H					

WATKINSON, M.   Lancashire

Full Name: Michael Watkinson
Role: Right-hand bat, right-arm
medium or off-spin bowler
Born: 1 August 1961, Westhoughton
Height: 6' 1½" **Weight:** 13st
Nickname: Winker
County debut: 1982
1st-Class 50s scored: 9
1st-Class 100s scored: 1
1st-Class 5 w. in innings: 5
One-Day 50s: 1
Place in batting averages: 287th
av. 19.45 (1985 150th av. 24.71)
Place in bowling averages: 119th
av. 50.08 (1985 62nd av. 31.49)
1st-Class catches 1986: 14
(career: 29)
Parents: Albert and Marian
Wife and date of marriage: Susan,
12 April 1986
Education: Rivington and Blackrod High School, Horwich
Qualifications: 8 O-levels, HTC Civil Engineering
Jobs outside cricket: Draughtsman
Overseas teams played for: Woder Valley CC, Canberra, 1984–85
Cricketers particularly learnt from: Paul Allott, Steve O'Shaughnessy
Cricketers particularly admired: Clive Lloyd, Imran Khan
Off-season 1986–87: Playing and coaching in Canberra, Australia
Other sports played: Football

LAST SEASON: BATTING

	I.	N.O.	R.	H.S.	AV.
TEST					
1ST-CLASS	24	4	389	58*	19.45
INT					
JPL	11	7	87	34*	21.75
NAT.W.	3	2	29	15*	–
B & H	4	0	42	19	10.50

CAREER: BATTING

	I.	N.O.	R.	H.S.	AV.
TEST					
1ST-CLASS	102	15	1917	106	18.08
INT					
JPL	36	18	340	34*	18.88
NAT.W.	6	1	101	56	20.20
B & H	10	1	84	34	9.33

LAST SEASON: BOWLING

	O.	M.	R.	W.	AV.
TEST					
1ST-CLASS	504.4	87	1753	35	50.08
INT					
JPL	99	4	417	10	41.70
NAT.W.	55.2	1	199	5	39.80
B & H	39	2	167	1	–

CAREER: BOWLING

	O.	M.	R.	W.	AV.
TEST					
1ST-CLASS	1616.2	327	5184	139	37.29
INT					
JPL	344	20	1565	53	29.52
NAT.W.	131.5	12	498	9	54.22
B & H	164.1	14	690	25	27.60

Extras: Played with Cheshire CCC in Minor Counties, and NatWest Trophy (v Middlesex) 1982
Injuries 1986: Broken bone in wrist
Best batting performance: 106 Lancashire v Surrey, Southport 1985
Best bowling performance: 6-39 Lancashire v Leicestershire, Leicester 1984

WELLS, A. P. Sussex

Full Name: Alan Peter Wells
Role: Right-hand bat, right-arm medium bowler, cover fielder
Born: 2 October 1961, Newhaven, Sussex
Height: 6' 0" **Weight:** 12st 4lbs
Nickname: Morph, Bomber
County debut: 1981
1000 runs in a season: 1
1st-Class 50s scored: 17
1st-Class 100s scored: 4
One-Day 50s: 9
Place in batting averages: 89th av. 33.00 (1985 165th av. 23.08)
1st-Class catches 1986: 10 (career: 46)
Parents: Ernest William Charles and Eunice Mae
Marital status: Single
Education: Tideway Comprehensive, Newhaven
Qualifications: 5 O-levels, NCA Coaching Certificate
Jobs outside cricket: Laboratory assistant. Coached in South Africa
Family links with cricket: Father played for many years for local club. Eldest brother, Ray, plays club cricket. Brother of C. M. Wells of Sussex
Cricketing superstitions: 'Have to put bat at junction of return and popping crease at the end of each over. Never stand inside the return crease when backing up. When repairing wicket count how many times I tap ground. Double whirl of arms with bat when going in to bat. Plus many more.'
Overseas tours: NCA U-19 tour of Canada, 1979
Cricketers particularly learnt from: Father, Chris Waller, Roger Marshall, Les Lenham
Other sports played: Table-tennis, squash, darts, snooker, tennis
Relaxations: Listening to music, eating out, drinking in country pubs
Extras: Played for England Young Cricketers v India 1981
Best batting performance: 150* Sussex v Nottinghamshire, Hove 1986

454

	I.	N.O.	R.	H.S.	AV.
TEST					
1ST-CLASS	34	7	891	150*	33.00
INT					
JPL	16	2	352	63	25.14
NAT.W.	3	0	28	21	9.33
B & H	2	0	38	21	19.00

	O.	M.	R.	W.	AV.
TEST					
1ST-CLASS	13	2	44	1	–
INT					
JPL	1.1	0	11	1	–
NAT.W.					
B & H					

	I.	N.O.	R.	H.S.	AV.
TEST					
1ST-CLASS	146	28	3512	150*	29.76
INT					
JPL	60	11	1245	71*	25.40
NAT.W.	10	2	79	24	9.88
B & H	14	2	372	62	31.00

	O.	M.	R.	W.	AV.
TEST					
1ST-CLASS	25	3	86	1	–
INT					
JPL	2.1	0	16	1	–
NAT.W.	1	0	1	0	–
B & H	2.1	1	17	1	–

WELLS, C. M. Sussex

Full Name: Colin Mark Wells
Role: Right-hand bat, right-arm medium bowler
Born: 3 March 1960, Newhaven, Sussex
Height: 6′ 0″ **Weight:** 12st 10lbs
Nickname: Bomber
County debut: 1979
County cap: 1982
No. of One-Day Internationals: 2
1000 runs in a season: 4
50 wickets in a season: 1
1st-Class 50s scored: 33
1st-Class 100s scored: 11
1st-Class 200s scored: 1
1st-Class 5 w. in innings: 2
One-Day 50s: 14
One-Day 100s: 1
Place in batting averages: 61st av. 37.86 (1985 103rd av. 30.97)
Place in bowling averages: 90th av. 37.10 (1985 96th av. 38.34)
1st-Class catches 1986: 5 (career: 44)
Parents: Ernest William Charles and Eunice Mae
Wife and date of marriage: Celia, 25 September 1982
Education: Tideway Comprehensive School, Newhaven
Qualifications: 9 O-levels, 2 CSEs, 1 A-level, MCC Intermediate Coaching Certificate

Jobs outside cricket: Working as a cellular telephone salesman for F. Smith & Co. of Horsham

Family links with cricket: Father, Billy, had trials for Sussex and played for Sussex Cricket Association. Both brothers play cricket and youngest brother, Alan, played for England Schools and toured Canada with NCA 1979, and plays for Sussex

Cricketing superstitions: Left boot and left pad put on first

Overseas tours: With England to Sharjah 1985

Overseas teams played for: Border, 1980–81; Western Province, 1984–85

Other sports played: Football, rugby, hockey, basketball, tennis, table-tennis

Relaxations: Sea-angling, philately, listening to music

Extras: Played in three John Player League matches in 1978. Was recommended to Sussex by former Sussex player, Ian Thomson. Highest 4th wicket partnership of 256 for Sussex v Glamorgan with Imran Khan

Opinions on cricket: 'Strongly believe that we cram in too much cricket, which must have a detrimental effect on all, especially the fast bowlers, particularly long term.'

Injuries 1986: Groin strain, originally incurred early in 1985 season

Best batting performance: 203 Sussex v Hampshire, Hove 1984

Best bowling performance: 5-25 Sussex v Kent, Hastings 1984

LAST SEASON: BATTING

	I.	N.O.	R.	H.S.	AV.
TEST					
1ST-CLASS	38	9	1098	106	37.86
INT					
JPL	14	4	308	68	30.80
NAT.W.	4	2	110	45*	55.00
B & H	4	2	76	27*	38.00

LAST SEASON: BOWLING

	O.	M.	R.	W.	AV.
TEST					
1ST-CLASS	458.2	102	1373	37	37.10
INT					
JPL	77	2	295	11	26.81
NAT.W.	47	7	127	4	31.75
B & H	14	2	53	2	26.50

CAREER: BATTING

	I.	N.O.	R.	H.S.	AV.
TEST					
1ST-CLASS	259	42	7216	203	33.25
INT	2	0	22	17	11.00
JPL	94	16	2080	104*	26.66
NAT.W.	17	2	362	76	24.13
B & H	29	3	662	80	25.46

CAREER: BOWLING

	O.	M.	R.	W.	AV.
TEST					
1ST-CLASS	2379.4	588	6855	203	33.76
INT					
JPL	500.4	35	1900	75	25.33
NAT.W.	128.4	21	340	10	34.00
B & H	137	22	471	20	23.55

177. Who was the last man to take 15 wickets in one day in a Test Match?

178. Name in chronological order the first-class sides of which Raymond Illingworth was captain?

WESTON, M. J.   Worcestershire

Full Name: Martin John Weston
Role: Right-hand bat, right-arm
medium bowler
Born: 8 April 1959, Worcester
Height: 6′ 1″ **Weight:** 14st 7lbs
Nickname: Wesso, Shag
County debut: 1979
County cap: 1986
1st-Class 50s scored: 18
1st-Class 100s scored: 3
One-Day 50s: 6
One-Day 100s: 1
Place in batting averages: 202nd
av. 16.70 (1985 117th av. 29.14)
Place in bowling averages: —
(1985 107th av. 40.90)
1st-Class catches 1986: 3 (career: 41)
Parents: John Franklyn and Sheila
Margaret
Marital status: Single
Education: St George's C of E Junior; Samuel Southall Secondary Modern
Qualifications: City & Guilds and Advance Crafts in Bricklaying
Overseas tours: 1980 tour to Barbados with Worcestershire CCC
Cricketers particularly learnt from: Basil D'Oliveira
Other sports played: Football, squash
Relaxations: Horse-racing
Best batting performance: 145* Worcestershire v Northamptonshire, Worcester 1984

LAST SEASON: BATTING

	I.	N.O.	R.	H.S.	AV.
TEST					
1ST-CLASS	12	2	167	49	16.70
INT					
JPL	13	3	169	47	16.95
NAT.W.	1	1	44	44*	–
B & H	5	0	94	42	18.80

CAREER: BATTING

	I.	N.O.	R.	H.S.	AV.
TEST					
1ST-CLASS	162	9	3776	145*	24.67
INT					
JPL	64	7	1104	109	19.36
NAT.W.	8	2	148	44*	24.66
B & H	20	0	415	56	20.75

LAST SEASON: BOWLING

	O.	M.	R.	W.	AV.
TEST					
1ST-CLASS	135	37	376	5	75.20
INT					
JPL	83.1	4	385	10	38.50
NAT.W.	9	1	20	0	–
B & H	34	5	96	4	24.00

CAREER: BOWLING

	O.	M.	R.	W.	AV.
TEST					
1ST-CLASS	659.4	158	1913	46	41.58
INT					
JPL	208	6	987	31	31.83
NAT.W.	47.5	7	176	5	35.20
B & H	63.0	7	218	8	27.25

Best bowling performance: 4-44 Worcestershire v Northamptonshire, Wellingborough 1984

WHITAKER, J. J.   Leicestershire

Full Name: John James Whitaker
Role: Right-hand bat, right-arm off-break bowler
Born: 5 May 1962, Skipton, Yorkshire
Height: 6′ 0″ **Weight:** 13st
County debut: 1983
County cap: 1986
1000 runs in a season: 3
1st-Class 50s scored: 20
1st-Class 100s scored: 9
1st-Class 200s scored: 1
One-Day 50s: 6
One-Day 100s: 3
Place in batting averages: 2nd av. 66.34 (1985 71st av. 35.38)
1st-Class catches 1986: 18 (career: 48)
Parents: John and Anne
Education: Uppingham School
Qualifications: 7 O-levels
Jobs outside cricket: Employee of Whitakers Chocolates Ltd; groundsman, Adelaide 1982–83; cricket coach and farmer, Tasmania 1983
Family links with cricket: Father plays club cricket

LAST SEASON: BATTING

	I.	N.O.	R.	H.S.	AV.
TEST					
1ST-CLASS	32	9	1526	200*	66.34
INT					
JPL	9	0	145	73	16.11
NAT.W.	1	0	25	25	–
B & H	4	0	61	30	15.25

LAST SEASON: BOWLING

	O.	M.	R.	W.	AV.
TEST					
1ST-CLASS	5.2	0	47	1	–
INT					
JPL					
NAT.W.	1	1	0	0	–
B & H					

CAREER: BATTING

	I.	N.O.	R.	H.S.	AV.
TEST					
1ST-CLASS	114	18	4031	200*	41.98
INT					
JPL	34	5	1000	132	34.48
NAT.W.	5	0	268	155	53.60
B & H	14	2	282	73*	23.50

CAREER: BOWLING

	O.	M.	R.	W.	AV.
TEST					
1ST-CLASS	15.2	2	135	1	–
INT					
JPL	0.2	0	4	0	–
NAT.W.	2	1	5	0	–
B & H					

Overseas tours: Australia 1981–82 with Uppingham School
Overseas teams played for: Glenelg CC, Adelaide, 1982–83; Old Scotch CC, Tasmania, 1983–84; Somerset West, South Africa, 1984–85
Cricketers particularly learnt from: Maurice Hallam (coach at Uppingham) and Brian Davison
Cricketers particularly admired: Geoff Boycott, Dennis Amiss
Off-season 1986–87: Touring Australia with England
Other sports played: Rugby, hockey, tennis, golf, squash
Relaxations: Discos, videos, music, reading
Injuries 1986: Broken fingers (out for 5 weeks)
Best batting performance: 200* Leicestershire v Nottinghamshire, Leicester 1986

WHITTICASE, P.　　　　Leicestershire

Full Name: Philip Whitticase
Role: Right-hand bat, wicket-keeper
Born: 15 March 1965, Birmingham
Height: 5′ 8″ **Weight:** 10st 7lbs
Nickname: Jasper, Tracy, Roland
County debut: 1984
1st-Class 50s scored: 6
Place in batting averages: 92nd av. 32.58
Parents: Larry Gordon and Ann
Marital status: Single
Education: Buckpool Secondary; Crestwood Comprehensive
Qualifications: 5 O-levels, 4 CSEs
Jobs outside cricket: Inland Revenue, Linkbronze Ltd
Family links with cricket: Grandfather and Father club cricketers (both wicket-keepers)
Overseas teams played for: South Bunbury, Western Australia, 1983, 1985
Cricketers particularly learnt from: D. Collins (Stourbridge CC), members of Leicestershire staff
Cricketers particularly admired: Bob Taylor, Alan Knott, Phillip DeFreitas
Off-season 1986–87: Working for Linkbronze Ltd, getting fit!
Other sports played: Football, table-tennis, golf (used to be on schoolboy forms with Birmingham City FC)
Relaxations: Football, golf, listening to music. 'I'm interested in most sports.

Playing cards is amusing especially when Les Taylor and John Agnew are involved.'

Extras: Played for MCC v Scotland 1985. Took two catches in P. Clift's hat-trick v Derby at Chesterfield 1985

Opinions on cricket: 'I would like to see four-day cricket brought in during the week, and have the weekends for two one-day competitions, which I feel would be more entertaining for the public.'

Injuries 1986: Torn thigh muscle, broken finger

Best batting performance: 67* Leicestershire v Somerset, Leicester 1986

LAST SEASON: BATTING

	I.	N.O.	R.	H.S.	AV.
TEST					
1ST-CLASS	21	4	554	67*	32.58
INT					
JPL	7	2	65	29*	13.00
NAT.W.	1	0	32	32	–
B & H	2	1	32	19*	–

CAREER: BATTING

	I.	N.O.	R.	H.S.	AV.
TEST					
1ST-CLASS	35	·7	738	67*	26.35
INT					
JPL	8	3	70	29*	14.00
NAT.W.	1	0	32	32	–
B & H	2	1	32	19*	–

LAST SEASON: WICKET-KEEPING

	C.	ST.			
TEST					
1ST-CLASS	23	1			
INT					
JPL	12	2			
NAT.W.	3	–			
B & H	4	–			

CAREER: WICKET-KEEPING

	C.	ST.			
TEST					
1ST-CLASS	50	1			
INT					
JPL	13	2			
NAT.W.	3	–			
B & H	4	–			

WILD, D. J.   Northamptonshire

Full Name: Duncan James Wild
Role: Left-hand bat, right-arm medium bowler, cover fielder
Born: 28 November 1962, Northampton
Height: 6' 0" **Weight:** 12st 7lbs
Nickname: Oscar, Wildy
County debut: 1980
County cap: 1986
1st-Class 50s scored: 8
1st-Class 100s scored: 3
One-Day 50s: 2
Place in batting averages: 83rd av. 33.77 (1985 117th av. 29.17)
Place in bowling averages: 54th av. 28.60
1st-Class catches 1986: 2 (career: 15)
Parents: John and Glenys

Marital status: Single
Education: Cherry Orchard Middle; Northampton School for Boys
Qualifications: 7 O-levels
Jobs outside cricket: Law costs draughtsman
Family links with cricket: Father played for Northamptonshire
Overseas tours: England Young Cricketers to West Indies 1980
Cricketers particularly learnt from: Wayne Larkins, Bob Carter
Cricketers particularly admired: David Gower
Off-season 1986–87: 'Relaxing.'
Extras: Played for England Young Cricketers v Young India in 3-Test series 1981. Also for Young England v Young West Indies, 1982
Best batting performance: 144 Northamptonshire v Lancashire, Southport 1984
Best bowling performance: 4-4 Northamptonshire v Cambridge University, Cambridge 1986

LAST SEASON: BATTING

	I.	N.O.	R.	H.S.	AV.
TEST					
1ST-CLASS	21	3	608	85	33.77
INT					
JPL	9	1	95	35*	11.87
NAT.W.	1	0	0	0	–
B & H	5	3	57	38	28.50

LAST SEASON: BOWLING

	O.	M.	R.	W.	AV.
TEST					
1ST-CLASS	132.3	17	429	15	28.60
INT					
JPL	59.1	2	303	15	20.20
NAT.W.	7	0	32	0	–
B & H	34	3	117	5	23.40

CAREER: BATTING

	I.	N.O.	R.	H.S.	AV.
TEST					
1ST-CLASS	94	14	2391	144	29.88
INT					
JPL	39	12	449	63*	16.62
NAT.W.	6	0	23	11	3.83
B & H	11	6	139	48	27.80

CAREER: BOWLING

	O.	M.	R.	W.	AV.
TEST					
1ST-CLASS	475.5	74	1742	36	48.38
INT					
JPL	289.1	8	1388	54	25.70
NAT.W.	74	9	272	9	30.22
B & H	42	4	158	5	31.60

179. Who was the first man to do the double of 100 wickets and 1000 runs in an English season?

180. Who was the last player to hit 100 before lunch on the first day of the season?

181. Which England Test cricketer once held the world long-jump record?

WILLEY, P.

Leicestershire

Full Name: Peter Willey
Role: Right-hand bat, right-arm
off-break bowler
Born: 6 December 1949, Sedgefield,
County Durham
Height: 6′ 1″ **Weight:** 13st
Nickname: Chin, Will
County debut: 1966
(Northamptonshire), 1984
(Leicestershire)
County cap: 1971
(Northamptonshire), 1984
(Leicestershire)
Benefit: 1981 (£31,400)
with Northamptonshire
Test debut: 1976
No. of Tests: 25
No. of One-Day Internationals: 26
1000 runs in a season: 7
50 wickets in a season: 3
1st-Class 50s scored: 79
1st-Class 100s scored: 37
1st-Class 200s scored: 1
1st-Class 5 w. in innings: 25
1st-Class 10 w. in match: 3
One-Day 50s: 56
One-Day 100s: 8
Place in batting averages: 28th av. 44.68 (1985 29th av. 46.14)
Place in bowling averages: — (1985 41st av. 28.25)
1st-Class catches 1986: 7 (career: 187)
Parents: Oswald and Maisie
Wife and date of marriage: Charmaine, 23 September 1971
Education: Secondary School, Seaham, County Durham
Jobs outside cricket: Has worked as a groundsman, labourer and in a shoe factory. Coached in South Africa 1978–79
Family links with cricket: Father played local club cricket in County Durham
Overseas tours: Toured Australia with England 1979–80; West Indies, 1981 and 1986
Overseas teams played for: Eastern Province, South Africa
Other sports played: Golf, shooting
Other sports followed: All sports
Relaxations: Reading, taking Irish Setter for long walks and shooting
Extras: With Wayne Larkins, received 2016 pints of beer (seven barrels) from

a brewery in Northampton as a reward for their efforts in Australia with England in 1978–79. Hit a six off his first ball v Middlesex in JPL, 26 July 1981. Shared in 4th wicket partnership record for county, 370 with R. T. Virgin v Somerset at Northampton in 1976. Youngest player ever to play for Northamptonshire CCC at 16 years 180 days v Cambridge in 1966. Banned from Test cricket for three years for joining England rebel tour of South Africa in 1982. Left Northamptonshire at end of 1983 (debut 1966, cap 1971) and moved to Leicestershire as vice-captain. Appointed Leicestershire captain for 1987

Injuries 1986: Returned early from West Indies tour with knee injury. Operation meant missing early part of season

Best batting performance: 227 Northamptonshire v Somerset, Northampton 1976

Best bowling performance: 7-37 Northamptonshire v Oxford University, Oxford 1975

LAST SEASON: BATTING

	I.	N.O.	R.	H.S.	AV.
TEST	2	0	86	44	43.00
1ST-CLASS	28	5	1031	172*	44.82
INT					
JPL	9	0	223	59	24.77
NAT.W.	3	1	139	101	69.50
B & H					

LAST SEASON: BOWLING

	O.	M.	R.	W.	AV.
TEST					
1ST-CLASS	176.2	49	418	7	59.71
INT					
JPL	55.3	1	269	8	33.62
NAT.W.	36	5	92	2	46.00
B & H					

CAREER: BATTING

	I.	N.O.	R.	H.S.	AV.
TEST	50	6	1184	102*	26.90
1ST-CLASS	693	98	18563	227	31.19
INT	24	1	538	64	23.39
JPL	214	17	5587	107	28.36
NAT.W.	38	5	1082	101	32.78
B & H	53	9	1327	88*	30.16

CAREER: BOWLING

	O.	M.	R.	W.	AV.
TEST	181.5	49	456	7	65.14
1ST-CLASS	32.6 7972.1	13 2210	19010	647	29.38
INT	171.5	9	659	13	50.69
JPL	1249.2	110	5030	191	26.33
NAT.W.	369.3	56	1094	29	37.72
B & H	485.4	82	1316	34	38.71

182. Which two England Test players have also won full England soccer caps since 1945?

183. Who scored the most centuries ever, and how many?

184. Who succeeded Ray Illingworth as captain of Yorkshire?

185. Which Australian Test captain had 16 children?

WILLIAMS, N. F.   Middlesex

Full Name: Neil Fitzgerald Williams
Role: Right-hand bat, right-arm fast-medium bowler
Born: 2 July 1962, Hopewell, St Vincent, West Indies
Height: 5′ 11″ **Weight:** 11st 7lbs
Nickname: Joe
County debut: 1982
County cap: 1984
50 wickets in a season: 2
1st-Class 50s scored: 5
1st-Class 5 w. in innings: 4
1st-Class 10 w. in match: 1
Place in batting averages: —
(1985 170th av. 22.24)
Place in bowling averages: —
(1985 54th av. 30.76)
1st-Class catches 1986: —
(career: 24)

Parents: Alexander and Aldreta
Marital status: Single
Education: Cane End Primary School, St Vincent; Acland Burghley School, Tufnall Park
Qualifications: School Leavers Certificate, 6 O-levels, 1 A-level
Family links with cricket: 'Uncle Joe was 12th man for St Vincent and plays 1st Division cricket.'
Overseas tours: English Counties to Zimbabwe 1985
Overseas teams played for: Windward Islands 1983; Tasmania 1983–84
Cricketers particularly learnt from: Wilf Slack, Roland Butcher, Wayne Daniel
Cricketers particularly admired: Viv Richards, Andy Roberts, Michael Holding, Dennis Lillee, Malcolm Marshall, Laurence Rowe
Off-season 1986–87: Recuperating/rehabilitation training with RAF in Surrey
Other sports followed: Most
Relaxations: Relax to sound of reggae, soca, soul, cinema
Extras: Was on stand-by for England in New Zealand and Pakistan 1983–84
Injuries 1986: Back strain
Best batting performance: 67 Middlesex v Cambridge University, Cambridge 1985
Best bowling performance: 7-55 English Counties XI v Zimbabwean XI, Harare 1984–85

	I.	N.O.	R.	H.S.	AV.
TEST					
1ST-CLASS	4	1	51	23*	17.00
INT					
JPL	1	0	6	6	—
NAT.W.					
B & H	1	0	8	8	—

CAREER: BATTING

	I.	N.O.	R.	H.S.	AV.
TEST					
1ST-CLASS	98	23	1522	67	20.29
INT					
JPL	21	8	152	31*	11.69
NAT.W.	6	2	28	10	7.00
B & H	9	3	112	29*	18.66

LAST SEASON: BOWLING

	O.	M.	R.	W.	AV.
TEST					
1ST-CLASS	79.3	9	264	10	26.40
INT					
JPL	8	0	28	0	—
NAT.W.					
B & H	30	3	108	3	36.00

CAREER: BOWLING

	O.	M.	R.	W.	AV.
TEST					
1ST-CLASS	2309.1	423	7588	255	29.75
INT					
JPL	263.3	7	1200	43	27.90
NAT.W.	77	11	277	11	25.18
B & H	181.3	22	685	22	31.13

WILLIAMS, R. G.   Northamptonshire

Full Name: Richard Grenville Williams
Role: Right-hand bat, right-arm off-break bowler
Born: 10 August 1957, Bangor, Caernarvonshire
Height: 5' 6" **Weight:** 12st
Nickname: Chippy
County debut: 1974
County cap: 1979
1000 runs in a season: 6
1st-Class 50s scored: 41
1st-Class 100s scored: 15
1st-Class 5 w. in innings: 7
One-Day 50s: 16
Place in batting averages: —
(1985 97th av. 31.43)
Place in bowling averages: —
(1985 105th av. 40.79)
1st-Class catches 1986: 1 (career: 76)
Parents: Gordon and Rhianwen
Wife and date of marriage: Helen Laura, 24 April 1982
Education: Ellesmere Port Grammar School
Jobs outside cricket: Qualified carpenter
Family links with cricket: Father played for Caernarvonshire
Overseas tours: Australasia in February and March 1980 with Derrick Robins'

U-23 XI; West Indies with England Young Cricketers 1976; Zimbabwe with English Counties 1985

Overseas teams played for: Stockton CC and Belmont CC in Sydney, Australia, on Whitbread Scholarship. Also played in New Zealand

Relaxations: Fly fishing and shooting

Extras: Debut for 2nd XI in 1972 aged 14 years 11 months. Made maiden century in 1979 and then scored four centuries in five innings. Hat-trick v Gloucestershire, at Northampton, 1980. Was first player to score a century against the 1980 West Indies touring team. Was stand-by for England in India, 1981

Best batting performance: 175* Northamptonshire v Leicestershire, Leicester 1980

Best bowling performance: 7-73 Northamptonshire v Cambridge University, Cambridge 1980

LAST SEASON: BATTING

	I.	N.O.	R.	H.S.	AV.
TEST					
1ST-CLASS	7	0	161	93	23.00
INT					
JPL	2	0	21	12	10.50
NAT.W.					
B & H					

LAST SEASON: BOWLING

	O.	M.	R.	W.	AV.
TEST					
1ST-CLASS	74	22	190	3	63.33
INT					
JPL	8	0	28	1	–
NAT.W.					
B & H					

CAREER: BATTING

	I.	N.O.	R.	H.S.	AV.
TEST					
1ST-CLASS	338	40	9092	175*	30.51
INT					
JPL	107	18	2029	82	22.79
NAT.W.	21	4	444	94	26.12
B & H	26	7	602	83	31.68

CAREER: BOWLING

	O.	M.	R.	W.	AV.
TEST					
1ST-CLASS	3351.4	865	7588	255	29.75
INT					
JPL	363.4	24	1716	58	29.58
NAT.W.	118	16	363	18	20.16
B & H	134	23	421	11	38.27

---

186. What have the following got in common: Ashley Metcalfe, Alan Lilley, Derek Aslett and Martyn Moxon?

187. Which player since 1945 has hit the highest score on his first-class debut?

188. Who captained the winning Manchester United team in the FA Cup Final, and played cricket and soccer for his country?

WINTERBORNE, G.   Surrey

Full Name: Gary Winterborne
Role: Right-hand bat, right-arm medium bowler
Born: 26 June 1967, Hammersmith
Height: 6′ 1″ **Weight:** 11st
Nickname: Wincey, Gazza
County debut: 1986
Parents: Alexander William and Irene Patricia
Marital status: Single
Education: St Bedes Middle School; George Abbot Comprehensive
Qualifications: 5 O-levels, 1st Year National Certificate
Jobs outside cricket: Trainee accountant
Cricketing superstitions: Left glove before right, left pad before right
Cricketers particularly learnt from: G. Arnold, M. Edwards, M. Stewart
Cricketers particularly admired: G. Gooch, I. Botham
Off-season 1986–87: Working on building site
Other sport played: Boxing
Relaxations: Listening to music

LAST SEASON: BATTING

	I.	N.O.	R.	H.S.	AV.
TEST					
1ST-CLASS	–	–	–	–	–
INT					
JPL					
NAT.W.					
B & H					

LAST SEASON: BOWLING

	O.	M.	R.	W.	AV.
TEST					
1ST-CLASS	20	5	47	0	–
INT					
JPL					
NAT.W.					
B & H					

CAREER: BATTING

	I.	N.O.	R.	H.S.	AV.
TEST					
1ST-CLASS	–	–	–	–	–
INT					
JPL					
NAT.W.					
B & H					

CAREER: BOWLING

	O.	M.	R.	W.	AV.
TEST					
1ST-CLASS	20	5	47	0	–
INT					
JPL					
NAT.W.					
B & H					

WOOD, L. J.   Derbyshire

Full Name: Lindsay Jonathan Wood
Role: Left-hand bat, left-arm
orthodox bowler
Born: 12 May 1961, Ruislip,
Middlesex
Height: 6' 2" **Weight:** 12st 10lbs
Nickname: Chopper, Woody
County debut: 1981 (Kent),
1986 (Derbyshire)
Parents: Denis John and Joan Edna
Education: Wye Primary School;
Simon Langton Boys' Grammar School;
King Alfred College, Winchester
Qualifications: 2 A-levels,
5 O-levels, BEd degree in PE
Jobs outside cricket: Teacher;
farm labourer
Family links with cricket: Father
played for Kings Hall CC, Wembley
Cricketing superstitions: Number 111
Overseas tours: British Colleges to West Indies, 1982
Cricketers particularly learnt from: 'Don Wilson, Derek Underwood and
Colin Page and anyone else who has been kind enough to offer any advice, no
matter what!'
Other sports played: Football, rugby
Relaxations: Angling and music – and perhaps a good book. 'Watching
opposing left-armer get hit for six.'
Extras: On Kent staff 1981–85, but did not play in 1983, 1984 or 1985 seasons

LAST SEASON: BATTING

	I.	N.O.	R.	H.S.	AV.
TEST					
1ST-CLASS	2	0	7	5	3.50
INT					
JPL					
NAT.W.					
B & H					

LAST SEASON: BOWLING

	O.	M.	R.	W.	AV.
TEST					
1ST-CLASS	39	10	95	2	47.50
INT					
JPL					
NAT.W.					
B & H					

CAREER: BATTING

	I.	N.O.	R.	H.S.	AV.
TEST					
1ST-CLASS	4	0	12	5	3.00
INT					
JPL					
NAT.W.					
B & H					

CAREER: BOWLING

	O.	M.	R.	W.	AV.
TEST					
1ST-CLASS	94	22	277	6	46.16
INT					
JPL					
NAT.W.					
B & H					

WRIGHT, A. J.　　　Gloucestershire

Full Name: Anthony John Wright
Role: Right-hand bat, right-arm
off-spin bowler, short-leg/slip
fielder
Born: 27 July 1962, Stevenage
Height: 6′ 0″ **Weight:** 13st 7lbs
Nickname: Billy, Horace
County debut: 1980
1st-Class 50s scored: 14
1st-Class 100s scored: 1
One-Day 50s: 2
Place in batting averages: 163rd
av. 23.19 (1985 192nd av. 19.15)
1st-Class catches 1986: 13
(career: 34)
Parents: Patricia and Michael
Wife and date of marriage: Rachel,
21 December 1986
Education: Alleyn's School,
Stevenage
Qualifications: 6 O-levels
Jobs outside cricket: Plasterer's labourer, wine waiter, working for Gray
Nicholls (Australia)
Overseas tours: Barbados 1980, 1985 and 1986 with Gloucestershire
Overseas teams played for: Port Melbourne 1981–82, 1982–83, 1984–85
Cricketers particularly learnt from: John Childs, Barry Duddleston, Andy
Brassington
Cricketers particularly admired: Zaheer Abbas, Vivian Richards, Ian
Botham

LAST SEASON: BATTING

	I.	N.O.	R.	H.S.	AV.
TEST					
1ST-CLASS	26	0	603	87	23.19
INT					
JPL	4	0	19	11	4.75
NAT.W.	2	0	94	51	47.00
B & H					

LAST SEASON: BOWLING

	O.	M.	R.	W.	AV.
TEST					
1ST-CLASS	1	0	10	0	–
INT					
JPL					
NAT.W.					
B & H					

CAREER: BATTING

	I.	N.O.	R.	H.S.	AV.
TEST					
1ST-CLASS	117	10	2602	139	24.31
INT					
JPL	26	4	223	52	10.13
NAT.W.	3	0	108	51	36.00
B & H					

CAREER: BOWLING

	O.	M.	R.	W.	AV.
TEST					
1ST-CLASS	2	0	13	0	–
INT					
JPL					
NAT.W.					
B & H					

Off-season 1986–87: Working in Bristol
Other sports played: Rugby, golf, soccer
Relaxations: Eating out, drinking socially, listening to music
Extras: Played twice in John Player League in 1980. Did not play in 1981
Opinions on cricket: 'Clubs should attempt to give assistance to players seeking winter employment. Like to see more ex-pro's serving on committees instead of people who know absolutely nothing about professional cricket.'
Injuries 1986: Slight rib injury
Best batting performance: 139 Gloucestershire v Surrey, Cheltenham 1984

WRIGHT, J. G.   Derbyshire

Full Name: John Geoffrey Wright
Role: Left-hand bat
Born: 5 July 1954, Darfield, New Zealand
Height: 6′ 1″ **Weight:** 12st 7lbs
Nickname: Shake
County debut: 1977
County cap: 1977
Test debut: 1977–78
No. of Tests: 49
No. of One-Day Internationals: 86
1000 runs in a season: 6
1st-Class 50s scored: 90
1st-Class 100s scored: 41
One-Day 50s: 29
One-Day 100s: 4
Place in batting averages: 94th
av. 32.47 (1985 10th av. 56.93)
1st-Class catches 1986: 1
(career: 156)
Parents: Geoff and Helen
Wife: Susan
Education: Christ's College, Christchurch, New Zealand; University of Otago, Dunedin, New Zealand
Qualifications: BSc in Biochemistry
Family links with cricket: 'Father played first-class cricket.'
Cricketing superstitions: 'Ironed shirts are bad luck.'
Overseas tours: With New Zealand to England 1978, 1986; Australia 1980 –81; Sri Lanka and Pakistan 1984–85; West Indies 1985
Overseas teams played for: Northern Districts, Canterbury, New Zealand
Cricketers particularly learnt from: Eddie Barlow, David Steele

Cricketers particularly admired: 'Cutter' Curtayne
Other sports played: Horse-racing, tennis, rugby
Relaxations: Music
Extras: Holds record of 7 centuries for Derbyshire in a season – beating record of 6 held by Peter Kirsten in previous season, after record of 5 had stood for 49 years. Vice-captain of New Zealand 1984
Best batting performance: 190 Derbyshire v Yorkshire, Derby 1982

LAST SEASON: BATTING

	I.	N.O.	R.	H.S.	AV.
TEST	6	1	191	119	38.20
1ST-CLASS	16	0	491	96	30.68
INT	2	0	60	39	30.00
JPL					
NAT.W.					
B & H					

LAST SEASON: BOWLING

	O.	M.	R.	W.	AV.
TEST					
1ST-CLASS	4	1	13	0	
INT					
JPL					
NAT.W.					
B & H					

CAREER: BATTING

	I.	N.O.	R.	H.S.	AV.
TEST	86	4	2635	141	32.13
1ST-CLASS	385	28	15148	190	42.43
INT	85	1	2087	84	24.84
JPL	91	6	2170	108	31.88
NAT.W.	12	2	555	87*	55.50
B & H					

CAREER: BOWLING

	O.	M.	R.	W.	AV.
TEST	5	1	5	0	–
1ST-CLASS	46.4	5	221	2	110.00
INT	4	1	8	0	–
JPL					
NAT.W.					
B & H					

WYATT, J. G. Somerset

Full Name: Julian George Wyatt
Role: Right-hand bat, right-arm medium bowler
Born: 19 June 1963, Paulton, Somerset
Height: 5' 10" **Weight:** 11st 10lbs
Nickname: Jules, Earp
County debut: 1983
1st-Class 50s scored: 8
1st-Class 100s scored: 3
Place in batting averages: —
(1985 98th av. 31.38)
1st-Class catches 1986: —
(career: 16)
Parents: Christopher Hedley and Dinah Ruby
Marital status: Single
Education: Wells Cathedral School, Somerset

Qualifications: 5 O-levels, NCA Senior Coaching Certificate
Jobs outside cricket: Brandon Tool Hire 1980–83
Cricketing superstitions: Right pad always put on first
Overseas tours: Barbados with Somerset 1985
Overseas teams played for: Kew CC, Melbourne, 1984–85
Cricketers particularly admired: B. Rose, P. Denning, C. Dredge, T. Gard
Off-season 1986–87: Cricket in Melbourne
Other sports played: Squash, football, tennis
Other sports followed: Rugby
Relaxations: 'Socialising at local pubs.'
Opinions on cricket: 'I'm not sure if cricket matters are worthy of being taken seriously. However, I would like to see four-day cricket in operation and less one-day, for blockers like myself.'
Injuries 1986: Broken arm
Best batting performance: 145 Somerset v Oxford University, Oxford 1985

LAST SEASON: BATTING

	I.	N.O.	R.	H.S.	AV.
TEST					
1ST-CLASS	6	0	81	40	13.50
INT					
JPL	2	1	86	48*	–
NAT.W.					
B & H					

LAST SEASON: BOWLING

	O.	M.	R.	W.	AV.
TEST					
1ST-CLASS					
INT					
JPL					
NAT.W.					
B & H					

CAREER: BATTING

	I.	N.O.	R.	H.S.	AV.
TEST					
1ST-CLASS	72	2	1915	145	27.35
INT					
JPL	9	2	142	48*	20.28
NAT.W.	2	0	3	3	1.50
B & H	4	0	39	22	9.75

CAREER: BOWLING

	O.	M.	R.	W.	AV.
TEST					
1ST-CLASS	13	1	63	2	31.50
INT					
JPL					
NAT.W.					
B & H					

189. Who was the undergraduate at Oxbridge to score a century for England?

190. Which was the last county to join the county championship and when?

191. Who are the only father and son both to have scored 100s on their Test debut?

192. Who has taken the most hat-tricks in first-class cricket, and how many?

YOUNIS AHMED　　　　　Glamorgan

Full Name: Mohammed Younis
Ahmed
Role: Left-hand bat, left-arm
medium bowler
Born: 20 October 1947, Lahore,
Pakistan
Height: 5' 10" **Weight:** 12st
Nickname: Yoon
County debut: 1965 (Surrey), 1979
(Worcestershire), 1985 (Glamorgan)
County cap: 1969 (Surrey), 1979
(Worcestershire),
1985 (Glamorgan)
Test debut: 1969–70
No. of Tests: 2
1000 runs in a season: 13
1st-Class 50s scored: 141
1st-Class 100s scored: 43
1st-Class 200s scored: 1
One-Day 50s: 47
One-Day 100s: 5
Place in batting averages: 47th av. 40.23 (1985 6th av. 64.59)
1st-Class catches 1986: 4 (career: 239)
Parents: Father, Inaitullah; mother, Shamin
Wife and date of marriage: Gloria Ahmed, 15 September 1972
Children: Samir Ahmed, 2 January 1975; Yasmine Ahmed, 16 January 1979
Education: Moslem High School, Lahore; Government College, Lahore
Qualifications: Matriculation, BA degree
Jobs outside cricket: Runs coaching clinics in Melbourne. Owns and runs own
travel agency
Family links with cricket: Younger brother of Saeed Ahmed who played for
Pakistan
Overseas tours: West Indies 1970; Commonwealth tour to Kuwait, 1971;
South Australia 1972–73; South Africa 1973–74; International XI to
Rhodesia 1974–75
Overseas teams played for: Pakistan Inter Board Schools, South Australia in
1972–73 Sheffield Shield; Universal Club, Rhodesia, 1974–75–76–77
Cricketers particularly learnt from or admired: Saeed Ahmed (brother), Sir
Gary Sobers, Sir Don Bradman
Other sports: Squash, tennis
Relaxations: Reading cricket books, theatre
Extras: Debut in 1962 at age of 14 years 4 months for Pakistan School v South
Zone (counts as first-class). Debut for Surrey in 1965, cap 1969. Is now

eligible to play for England. Suffers from hay fever. Sacked by Worcestershire in 1983 season. Joined Glamorgan in 1985

Best batting performance: 221* Worcestershire v Nottinghamshire, Trent Bridge 1979

Best bowling performance: 4-10 Surrey v Cambridge University, Cambridge 1975

LAST SEASON: BATTING

	I.	N.O.	R.	H.S.	AV.
TEST 1ST-CLASS	23	2	845	105*	40.23
INT					
JPL	6	0	121	50	20.16
NAT.W.	2	0	33	31	16.50
B & H					

CAREER: BATTING

	I.	N.O.	R.	H.S.	AV.
TEST	4	0	89	62	22.25
1ST-CLASS	742	114	25299	221*	40.28
INT					
JPL	221	23	5897	113	29.78
NAT.W.	28	2	768	87	29.53
B & H	57	7	1434	115	28.68

LAST SEASON: BOWLING

	O.	M.	R.	W.	AV.
TEST 1ST-CLASS	20	4	82	0	–
INT					
JPL	6	0	28	2	14.00
NAT.W.					
B & H					

CAREER: BOWLING

	O.	M.	R.	W.	AV.
TEST					
1ST-CLASS	108.5 552.3	11 142	1899	41	46.31
INT					
JPL	138.3	0	663	19	34.89
NAT.W.	46	4	149	4	37.25
B & H	51	2	208	9	23.11

---

193. Who kept wicket for England v Australia in the first Test at Brisbane in 1986?

194. Who scored more first-class centuries, Brian Close or Ted Dexter, and how many?

195. Who scored two separate centuries in a match most times?

196. Who has the highest first-class batting average of all time, and what is it?

197. Who scored the most first-class runs of all time, and how many?

BIRD, H. D.

Full Name: Harold Dennis Bird
Role: Right-hand opening bat
Born: 19 April 1933, Barnsley
Height: 5′ 10½″ **Weight:** 11st 6lbs
Nickname: Dickie
Counties: Yorkshire, Leicestershire
County debut: 1956 (Yorkshire), 1960 (Leicestershire)
County cap: 1960 (Leicestershire)
1000 runs in a season: 1
1st-Class 50s scored: 14
1st-Class 100s scored: 2
1st-Class catches: 20
Best batting performance: 181* Yorkshire v Glamorgan, Bradford 1959
Appointed to 1st-Class list: 1969
Appointed to Test panel: 1972
No. of Tests umpired: 36
No. of One-Day Internationals umpired: 61
Education: Raley School, Barnsley
Jobs outside cricket: 'Cricket is my life.'
Off-season 1986–87: Umpiring One-Day Internationals in Sharjah
Parents: James Harold and Ethel
Marital status: Bachelor
Other sporting interests: Football
Relaxations: 'Listening to Barbra Streisand and Diana Ross records.'
Opinions on cricket: 'I would like to see an experimental law where we do away with leg-byes, because it is difficult to know whether a batsman has played a genuine shot or not.'
Extras: Awarded MBE, June 1986. Only man to umpire in three World Cup Finals, 1975, 1979 and 1983. Voted Yorkshire Personality of the Year, 1977. Umpired Centenary Test Match, England v Australia, 1980. Umpired Queen's Silver Jubilee Test Match, England v Australia, Lord's 1977. Author of *Not Out* (1978), *That's Out* (1985).

CAREER: BATTING

	I.	N.O.	R.	H.S.	AV.
TEST					
1ST-CLASS	170	10	3314	181*	20.71
INT					
JPL					
NAT.W.	2	0	9	7	4.50
B & H					

CAREER: BOWLING

	O.	M.	R.	W.	AV.
TEST					
1ST-CLASS	8	2	22	0	—
INT					
JPL					
NAT.W.					
B & H					

BIRKENSHAW, J.

Full Name: Jack Birkenshaw
Role: Left-hand bat, right-arm off-break bowler
Born: 13 November 1940, Rothwell, Leeds
Height: 5′ 9″ **Weight:** 11st
Nickname: Birky
Counties: Yorkshire, Leicestershire, Worcestershire
County debut: 1958 (Yorkshire), 1961 (Leicestershire), 1981 (Worcestershire)
County cap: 1965 (Leicestershire)
Test debut: 1972
No. of Tests: 5
Benefit: 1974 (£13,100)
50 wickets in a season: 8
1st-Class 50s scored: 53
1st-Class 100s scored: 4
1st-Class catches: 318
1st-Class 5 w. in innings: 44
1st-Class 10 w. in match: 4
One-day 50s: 6
One-day 100s: 1
Best batting performance: 131 Leicestershire v Surrey, Guildford 1969
Best bowling performance: 8-94, Leicestershire v Somerset, Taunton 1972
Appointed to 1st-Class list: 1982
Appointed to Test panel: 1986
Parents: John and Edith
Wife: Gloria
Children: Mark, 9 December 1962
Education: Rothwell Grammar School
Qualifications: Qualified coach
Jobs outside cricket: 'Everything from the bakehouse to promotional work, plus coaching for Leicestershire County Cricket Club.'
Overseas tours: India, Pakistan and Sri Lanka 1972–73; West Indies 1973–74
Cricket records: Shared in seventh wicket partnership record for county, 206 with B. Dudleston v Kent at Canterbury, 1969
Other sports played: Squash, table-tennis
Relaxations: Coaching young people, music, gardening, wine-making
Extras: Played for Yorkshire 1958–60. Joined Leicestershire in 1961. Released at end of 1980 season by Leicestershire, but signed for Worcestershire

CAREER: BATTING

	I.	N.O.	R.	H.S.	AV.
TEST	7	0	148	64	21.14
1ST-CLASS	658	123	12632	131*	23.61
INT					
JPL	89	16	1344	79	18.41
NAT.W.	19	3	290	101*	18.13
B & H	17	4	197	35*	15.15

CAREER: BOWLING

	O.	M.	R.	W.	AV.
TEST	169.3	33	469	13	36.08
1ST-CLASS	11362.4	3060	28803	1060	27.18
INT					
JPL	285.4	20	1147	52	22.05
NAT.W.	106	18	335	14	23.93
B & H	166	21	574	16	35.88

CONSTANT, D. J.

Full Name: David John Constant
Role: Left-hand bat, slow left-arm bowler
Born: 9 November 1941, Bradford-on-Avon, Wiltshire
Counties: Kent 1961–63, Leicestershire 1965–68
County debut: 1961 (Kent), 1965 (Leicestershire)
1st-Class 50s scored: 6
1st-Class catches: 33
Best batting performance: 80 Leicestershire v Gloucestershire, Bristol 1966
Appointed to 1st-Class list: 1969
Appointed to Test panel: 1971

CAREER: BATTING					
	I.	N.O.	R.	H.S.	AV.
TEST					
1ST-CLASS	93	14	1517	80	19.20
INT					
JPL					
NAT.W.	1	0	5	5	–
B & H					

CAREER: BOWLING				
	O.	M.	R.	W.	AV.
TEST					
1ST-CLASS	12.3	3	36	1	–
INT					
JPL					
NAT.W.					
B & H					

COOK, C.

Full Name: Cecil Cook
Role: Slow left-arm bowler
Born: 23 August 1921, Tetbury, Gloucestershire
Height: 5′ 9½″ **Weight:** 12st
Nickname: Sam
County: Gloucestershire
County debut: 1946
County cap: 1946
Test debut: 1947
No. of Tests: 1
50 wickets in a season: 17
1st-Class 5 w. in innings: 99
1st-Class 10 w. in match: 15
Best batting performance: 35* Gloucestershire v Sussex, Hove 1957
Best bowling performance: 9-42 Gloucestershire v Yorkshire, Bristol 1947
1st-Class catches: 153
Appointed to 1st-Class list: 1971
Education: Church of England
Jobs outside cricket: Plumber
Wife and date of marriage: Daisy Ann, 8 July 1946

Children: Carol Ann, 12 January 1947; Pauline Yvonne, 23 April 1948; Sally Jayne, 18 May 1961
Family links with cricket: Father and brother played for Tetbury
Other sports interests: 'All sports.'
Relaxations: Watching television, gardening
Extras: 'I took a wicket with the first ball I bowled in first-class cricket.' Retired after 1986 season
Opinions on cricket: 'Too much cricket played today. If Sunday cricket is here to stay I would like to see it played with more than 40-over matches which at the present time is getting players into bad habits. Also make the wickets uncovered to bring the spinners back into the game. Discipline has got worse over the years, due I think to the big money prizes of today. The bowling of bouncers is part of the fast-bowlers' armoury and should be kept under control by the umpires. Politics should be kept out of sport and South Africa welcomed back to Test cricket.'

CAREER: BATTING

	I.	N.O.	R.	H.S.	AV.
TEST	2	0	4	4	2.00
1ST-CLASS	610	248	1961	35*	5.41
INT					
JPL					
NAT.W.					
B & H					

CAREER: BOWLING

	O.	M.	R.	W.	AV.
TEST	30	4	127	0	–
1ST-CLASS	17689.5	6643	36451	1782	20.45
INT					
JPL					
NAT.W.					
B & H					

DUDLESTON, B.

Full Name: Barry Dudleston
Role: Right-hand bat, slow left-arm bowler
Born: 16 July 1945, Bebington, Cheshire
Height: 5' 9" **Weight:** 11st 8lbs
Nickname: Danny
Counties: Leicestershire, Gloucestershire
County debut: 1966 (Leicestershire), 1981 (Gloucestershire)
County cap: 1969 (Leicestershire)
Benefit: 1980 (£25,000)
1000 runs in a season: 8
1st-Class 100s scored: 31
1st-Class 200s scored: 1
1st-Class catches: 234
One-day 50s: 21
One-day 100s: 4
Best batting performance: 202 Leicestershire v Derbyshire, Leicester 1979
Best bowling performance: 4-6 Leicestershire v Surrey, Leicester 1972

Appointed to 1st-Class list: 1984
Parents: Percy and Dorothy Vera
Wife and date of marriage: Lindsey Vivien Stratford, 5 April 1980
Children: Sharon Louise, 29 October 1968
Education: Stockport School
Qualifications: O-levels. Junior Coaching Certificate. Shell marketing exams
Jobs outside cricket: Retail and commercial representative for Shell
Overseas tours: With Derrick Robins' XI to Rhodesia
Overseas teams played for: Played for Rhodesia from 1966–67 to 1979–80 in Currie Cup Competition
Cricketers particularly learnt from: Vinoo Mankad
Cricket records Leicestershire CCC 1st wicket record of 390, 7th wicket record of 206, with Jack Birkenshaw v Kent at Canterbury in 1969. Fastest to 1000 runs in Currie Cup ever for Rhodesia, 2nd fastest of all time in Currie Cup. Highest score by overseas player on debut in South Africa, 142 v Western Province
Relaxations: Bridge and philately, watching all sports
Extras: England Under-25. Has suffered badly from broken fingers. Broke fingers on same hand three times in 1978. Made debut for Leicestershire in 1966, gaining county cap in 1969. Released by Leicestershire at end of 1980 season and made debut for Gloucestershire 1981
Opinions on cricket: 'Now we are playing on covered wickets I should like to see a championship programme of 16 four-day games, two one-day matches and a day off per week, which would then be a balanced programme.'

CAREER: BATTING

	I.	N.O.	R.	H.S.	AV.
TEST					
1ST-CLASS	501	47	14747	202	32.48
INT					
JPL	123	8	2490	152	24.41
NAT.W.	18	1	586	125	34.47
B & H	42	5	1171	90	31.65

CAREER: BOWLING

	O.	M.	R.	W.	AV.
TEST					
1ST-CLASS	406	87	1365	47	29.04
INT					
JPL	1	0	4	0	–
NAT.W.	3	0	14	0	–
B & H					

EVANS, D. G. L.

Full Name: David Gwillim Lloyd Evans
Role: Right-hand bat, wicket-keeper
Born: 27 July 1933, Lambeth
County: Glamorgan
County debut: 1956
County cap: 1959
Benefit: 1969 (£3,500)
Best batting performance: 46* Glamorgan v Oxford University, Oxford 1961
Appointed to 1st-Class list: 1971
Appointed to Test panel: 1981

CAREER: BATTING

	I.	N.O.	R.	H.S.	AV.
TEST					
1ST-CLASS	364	91	2875	46*	10.53
INT					
JPL					
NAT.W.	2	0	9	8	4.50
B & H					

CAREER: BOWLING

	O.	M.	R.	W.	AV.
TEST					
1ST-CLASS	3	0	9	0	–
INT					
JPL					
NAT.W.					
B & H					

CAREER: WICKET-KEEPING

	C.	ST.			
TEST					
1ST-CLASS	503	55			
INT					
JPL					
NAT.W.	4	–			
B & H					

HAMPSHIRE, J. H.

Full Name: John Harry Hampshire
Role: Right-hand bat, right-arm leg-break bowler
Born: 10 February 1941, Thurnscoe
Height: 6′ **Weight:** 13½st
Nickname: Hamps (not Jackie)
Counties: Yorkshire, Derbyshire
County debut: 1961, 1982
County cap: 1963, 1982
Test debut: 1969
No. of Tests: 8
1000 runs in a season: 15
1st-Class 50s scored: 142
1st-Class 100s scored: 43
1st-Class catches: 445
1st-Class 5 w. in innings: 1
One-day 50s: 39
One-day 100s: 7
Best batting performance: 183* Yorkshire v Sussex, Hove 1971
Best bowling performance: 7-52 Yorkshire v Glamorgan, Cardiff 1963
Appointed to 1st-Class list: 1985
Education: Oakwood Technical High School, Rotherham
Off-season 1986–87: Manager, Redball, Yorkshire Indoor Cricket Centre, Sheffield
Wife and date of marriage: Judith, 5 September 1964
Children: Ian, 6 January 1969; Paul, 12 July 1972
Family links with cricket: Father played pre-war for Yorkshire CCC
Other sports played: Golf

Relaxations: Gardening, reading
Extras: Scored 107 in his first Test Match v West Indies at Lord's, 1969

CAREER: BATTING

	I.	N.O.	R.	H.S.	AV.
TEST	16	1	403	107	26.67
1ST-CLASS	908	111	27063	183*	33.96
INT	3	1	48	25*	24.00
JPL	172	20	4994	119	32.85
NAT.W.	33	5	930	110	33.21
B & H	45	6	1091	85*	27.97

CAREER: BOWLING

	O.	M.	R.	W.	AV.
TEST					
1ST-CLASS	16.6 402.5	1 85	1637	30	54.57
INT					
JPL	4	1	22	1	–
NAT.W.	2	0	4	0	–
B & H					

HARRIS, J. H.

Full Name: John Humphrey Harris
Role: Left-hand bat, right-arm fast-medium bowler
Born: 13 February 1936, Taunton
County: Somerset
County debut: 1952 (at 16 years 99 days)
1st-Class catches: 6
Best batting performance: 41 Somerset v Worcestershire, Taunton 1957
Best bowling performance: 3-29 Somerset v Worcestershire, Bristol 1959
Appointed to 1st-Class list: 1983
Extras: Played for Suffolk 1960–62 and Devon 1975

CAREER: BATTING

	I.	N.O.	R.	H.S.	AV.
TEST					
1ST-CLASS	18	4	154	41	11.00
INT					
JPL					
NAT.W.					
B & H					

CAREER: BOWLING

	O.	M.	R.	W.	AV.
TEST					
1ST-CLASS	217.2	42	619	19	32.57
INT					
JPL					
NAT.W.					
B & H					

HARRIS, M. J.

Full Name: Michael John Harris
Role: Right-hand bat, wicket-keeper, right-arm leg-break bowler
Born: 25 May 1944, St Just-in-Roseland, Cornwall
Height: 6′ 1″ **Weight:** 15st
Nickname: Pasty
Counties: Middlesex, Nottinghamshire
County debut: 1964 (Middlesex), 1969 (Nottinghamshire)

County cap: 1970 (Nottinghamshire)
Benefit: 1977
1000 runs in a season: 11
1st-Class 50s scored: 98
1st-Class 100s scored: 40
1st-Class 200s scored: 1
Parents: Winnie and Dick
Wife and date of marriage: Danielle Ruth, 10 September 1969
Children: Jodene, Elizabeth, Richard
Education: Gerrans C/P
Qualifications: MCC Advanced Coach. SRA Squash Coach
Jobs outside cricket: Squash club manager
Family links with cricket: Father and uncles on both sides played top village cricket
Cricketing superstitions: Left boot and pad go on first
Overseas tours: With Derrick Robins' XI to West Indies 1974. With International Wanderers to South Africa and Rhodesia in 1974
Overseas teams played for: Eastern Province in 1971–72 Currie Cup Competition. Wellington in New Zealand Shell Shield Competition 1975–76
Appointed to 1st-Class list: On reserve list
Cricket records: Scored nine centuries in 1971 to equal county record. Shared in first wicket partnership record for Middlesex of 312 with W. E. Russell v Pakistan, Lord's 1967
Cricketers particularly learnt from: Eric Russell of Middlesex
Other sports played: Squash, golf, football
Extras: Made debut for Middlesex in 1964. Left staff after 1968 to join Nottinghamshire in 1969. Scored 2,238 at an average of 50.86 in 1971. Scored two centuries in a match twice in 1971, 118 and 123 v Leicestershire at Leicester, and 107 and 131* v Essex at Chelmsford

CAREER: BATTING

	I.	N.O.	R.	H.S.	AV.
TEST					
1ST-CLASS	581	58	19196	201*	36.70
INT					
JPL	139	31	3303	104*	30.58
NAT.W.	25	1	579	101	24.13
B & H	34	7	925	101	34.26

CAREER: BOWLING

	O.	M.	R.	W.	AV.
TEST					
1ST-CLASS	1047.5	229	3459	79	43.78
INT					
JPL	6.4	1	41	3	13.67
NAT.W.					
B & H	9	0	46	1	–

HENDRICK, M.

Full Name: Michael Hendrick
Role: Right-hand bat, right-arm fast-medium bowler
Born: 22 October 1948, Darley Dale, Derbyshire
Height: 6′ 3″

Nickname: Hendo
Counties: Derbyshire, Nottinghamshire
County debut: 1969 (Derbyshire), 1982 (Nottinghamshire)
County cap: 1972 (Derbyshire)
Benefit: 1980 (£36,060)
Test debut: 1974
No. of Tests: 30
No. of One-Day Internationals: 10
50 wickets in a season: 8
1st-Class 5 w. in innings: 29
1st-Class 10 w. in match: 3
1st-Class catches: 176
Best batting performance: 46 Derbyshire v Essex, Chelmsford 1973
Best bowling performance: 8-45 Derbyshire v Warwickshire, Chesterfield 1973
Appointed to 1st-Class list: On reserve list
Jobs outside cricket: Has worked for Electricity Board, Leicester, and as labourer
Family links with cricket: Father was fast bowler
Overseas tours: West Indies 1973–74; Australia, New Zealand 1974–75; Pakistan, New Zealand 1977–78; Australia 1978–79 and 1979–80, but returned early through injury. Declined tour of West Indies 1980–81
Other sports played: Shooting, fishing, golf
Extras: Left Derbyshire at his own request at end of 1981 season. Joined Nottinghamshire in 1982. Banned from Test cricket for 3 years for touring South Africa 1981–82. Retired from 1st-class cricket due to recurring injury at end of 1984 season

CAREER: BATTING

	I.	N.O.	R.	H.S.	AV.
TEST	35	15	128	15	6.40
1ST-CLASS	267	109	1601	46	10.13
INT	10	5	6	2*	1.20
JPL	58	27	299	21	9.64
NAT.W.	10	3	64	18	9.14
B & H	19	9	130	32	13.00

CAREER: BOWLING

	O.	M.	R.	W.	AV.
TEST	226.6 732.2	42 207	2248	87	25.84
1ST-CLASS	246.2 5696.5	64 1647	13537	683	19.82
INT	36 160	2 34	681	35	19.45
JPL	946.2	125	3249	149	21.80
NAT.W.	224.1	51	588	33	17.81
B & H	463.1	108	1125	36	14.81

HOLDER, J. W.

Full Name: John Wakefield Holder
Role: Right-arm fast bowler
Born: 19 March 1945, Barbados
Height: 6′ **Weight:** 13½st

Nickname: Benson, Hod
County: Hampshire
County debut: 1968
50 wickets in a season: 1
1st-Class 5 w. in innings: 5
1st-Class 10 w. in match: 1
1st-Class catches: 12
Best batting performance: 33 Hampshire v Sussex, Hove 1971
Best bowling performance: 6-49 and 7-79 in same match Hampshire v Gloucestershire, Gloucester 1972
Appointed to 1st-Class list: 1983
Parents: Charles and Carnetta
Wife: Glenda
Children: Christopher, 1968; Nigel, 1970
Education: Combermere High School, Barbados
Qualifications: 3 O-levels. MCC Advanced Coach
Jobs outside cricket: Part-time cricket coach
Family links with cricket: 'Both my sons play for Royton in the Central Lancashire League. They want to play county cricket.'
Off-season 1986–87: Part-time cricket coach. Training to become a driving instructor
Other sports played: Weight-training in winter
Other sports followed: Manchester United
Relaxations: Watching documentaries about wildlife. Would like to become an accomplished after-dinner speaker
Extras: Holds best bowling performance ever for Rothmans International Cavaliers cricket matches. Playing for Hampshire Cavaliers, took 6-7 at Tichbourne Park, 1968. Would love to spend a winter in Australia, coaching and playing. Between 1974 and 1982, played professional league cricket in Lancashire and Yorkshire. One first-class hat-trick, Hampshire v Kent, 1972
Opinions on cricket: 'Until pitches and interest at school and club level improves, England will not produce enough top-class young players. Coaching in comprehensive schools is poor or non-existent. At club level and higher, coaches must not stick too rigidly to the coaching book. After all, it is only a guideline.'

CAREER: BATTING

	I.	N.O.	R.	H.S.	AV.
TEST					
1ST-CLASS	49	14	374	33	10.68
INT					
JPL	21	7	87	25	6.21
NAT.W.	2	0	4	3	2.00
B & H	3	1	23	14	11.50

CAREER: BOWLING

	O.	M.	R.	W.	AV.
TEST					
1ST-CLASS	1183	229	3415	139	24.56
INT					
JPL	237	14	984	38	25.89
NAT.W.	47	10	144	5	28.80
B & H	26	4	85	3	28.33

JAMESON, J. A.

Full Name: John Alexander Jameson
Role: Right-hand bat, occasional right-arm off-break bowler
Born: 30 June 1941, Bombay
Height: 6′ **Weight:** 15½st
Nickname: Tub
County: Warwickshire
County debut: 1960
County cap: 1964
Test debut: 1971
No. of Tests: 4
No. of One-Day Internationals: 3
1000 runs in a season: 11
1st-Class 50s scored: 90
1st-Class 100s scored: 31
1st-Class 200s scored: 2
One-day 50s: 20
One-day 100s: 6
1st-Class catches: 255
Best batting performance: 240* Warwickshire v Gloucestershire, Edgbaston 1974
Best bowling performance: 4-22 Warwickshire v Oxford University, Oxford 1971
Appointed to 1st-Class list: 1984
Parents: John James and Florence Sylvia
Education: Cathedral School Bombay; Sherwood College, Naini Tal; Taunton School, Taunton
Qualifications: 6 O-levels
Wife and date of marriage: Angela, 1967
Children: Alexandra, 1974; Victoria, 1977
Family links with cricket: Father played for Bombay State Police
Other sports played: Hockey, rugby
Relaxations: Watching all sport, photography
Extras: Holds world record for 2nd wicket partnership of 465 (unbroken) with Rohan Kanhai, Warwickshire v Gloucestershire, Edgbaston 1974. Achieved first-class hat-trick v Gloucestershire, 1965

CAREER: BATTING

	I.	N.O.	R.	H.S.	AV.
TEST	8	0	214	82	26.75
1ST-CLASS	603	43	18727	240*	33.44
INT	3	0	60	28	20.00
JPL	108	6	3077	123*	30.17
NAT.W.	31	2	758	100*	26.13
B & H	25	0	580	94	23.20

CAREER: BOWLING

	O.	M.	R.	W.	AV.
TEST	7	2	17	1	–
1ST-CLASS	1208.3	251	3765	88	42.78
INT	2	0	3	0	–
JPL	80.3	4	477	24	19.87
NAT.W.	36.1	5	138	6	23.00
B & H	46	9	135	6	22.50

JONES, A. A.

Full Name: Allan Arthur Jones
Role: Left-arm fast bowler
Born: 9 December 1947, Horley, Surrey
Height: 6′ 3½″ **Weight:** 14st
Nickname: Jonah, Buckets
Counties: Sussex, Somerset, Middlesex, Glamorgan
County debut: 1966 (Sussex), 1970 (Somerset), 1976 (Middlesex), 1980 (Glamorgan)
County cap: 1972 (Somerset), 1976 (Middlesex)
50 wickets in a season: 4
1st-Class 5 w. in innings: 23
1st-Class 10 w. in match: 3
1st-Class catches: 50
Best batting performance: 33 Middlesex v Kent, Canterbury 1978
Best bowling performance: 9-51 Somerset v Sussex, Hove 1976
Appointed to 1st-Class list: 1985
Parents: Leslie and Hazel
Wife and date of marriage: Marilyn, 1979
Children: Clare Michelle, 4 July 1979
Education: St John's College, Horsham
Qualifications: 5 O-levels. MCC 'A' coach, NCA staff coach
Jobs outside cricket: None at present
Family links with cricket: None
Off-season 1986–87: Coach at Kingswood School Grahamstown, South Africa
Other sports followed: 'All sports.'
Relaxations: Horse racing, cinema, reading
Opinions on cricket: 'I think there is too much one-day cricket played at present. Although it has its place and has brought money into the game, one-day cricket has undoubtedly lowered the standard of cricket as a whole. Also I am of the opinion that overseas players should be banned completely, or only allowed to play one-day cricket. That way we might be able to find more than just a dozen decent players in this country. As for cricket correspondents, most of them should take a look at their own knowledge of

CAREER: BATTING

	I.	N.O.	R.	H.S.	AV.
TEST					
1ST-CLASS	216	68	799	33	5.40
INT					
JPL	56	27	90	18*	3.10
NAT.W.	9	6	13	5*	4.33
B & H	18	8	51	14	5.10

CAREER: BOWLING

	O.	M.	R.	W.	AV.
TEST					
1ST-CLASS	4994.1	997	15414	549	28.08
INT					
JPL	952.1	99	3995	187	21.36
NAT.W.	167	14	658	29	22.68
B & H	352.2	60	1115	65	17.15

the game, and be seen to be watching, rather than just copying the scorecards. Also it might be good if they stuck to writing about cricket, and not cricketers.'

JULIAN, R.

Full Name: Raymond Julian
Role: Right-hand bat, wicket-keeper
Born: 23 August 1936, Cosby, Leicestershire
Height: 5' 11" **Weight:** 11st 4lbs
Nickname: Julie
County: Leicestershire
County debut: 1953
County cap: 1961
1st-Class 50s scored: 2
1st-Class catches: 382
Best batting performance: 51 Leicestershire v Worcestershire, Worcester 1962
Parents: George Ernest and Doris
Wife and date of marriage: Ruth Ann, 30 April 1958
Children: Peter, 1 February 1958; John, 13 October 1960; David, 15 October 1963; Paul, 22 September 1967
Education: Wigston Secondary Modern School
Jobs outside cricket: Painter and decorator, cricket kit salesman
Family links with cricket: Father and 2 brothers all played local club cricket
Off-season 1986–87: Cricket coaching at LCCC. Painting and decorating
Other sports played: Ex-1st-Class football referee (local), linesman on Southern League for four seasons, refereed one FA Cup match
Relaxations: Gardening, listening to Johnny Mathis records
Extras: Youngest player to make debut age 15 for Leicestershire v Gloucestershire, Bristol 1953. Gave 8 lbw decisions on the trot, Glamorgan v Sussex, Cardiff 1986. Played for Army 1955–57. Three Benson & Hedges Semi-Finals, one Gillette Cup Semi-Final
Opinions on cricket: 'Not allowed to comment due to contract.'

CAREER: BATTING

	I.	N.O.	R.	H.S.	AV.
TEST					
1ST-CLASS	288	23	2581	51	9.73
INT					
JPL					
NAT.W.	3	0	6	4	2.00
B & H					

CAREER: WICKET-KEEPING

	C.	ST.		
TEST				
1ST-CLASS	381	40		
INT				
JPL				
NAT.W.	—	—		
B & H				

KITCHEN, M. J.

Full Name: Mervyn John Kitchen
Role: Left-hand bat, right-arm medium bowler
Born: 1 August 1940, Nailsea, Somerset
County: Somerset
County debut: 1960
County cap: 1966
Benefit: 1973 (£6000)
1000 runs in a season: 7
1st-Class 50s scored: 68
1st-Class 100s scored: 17
One-day 50s: 22
One-day 100s: 1
1st-Class catches: 157
Best batting performance: 189 Somerset v Pakistan, Taunton 1967
Appointed to 1st-Class list: 1982
Education: Backwell Secondary Modern, Nailsea

CAREER: BATTING

	I.	N.O.	R.	H.S.	AV.
TEST					
1ST-CLASS	612	32	15230	189	26.25
INT					
JPL	111	10	2069	82	20.48
NAT.W.	27	1	815	116	31.34
B & H	25	1	504	70	21.00

CAREER: BOWLING

	O.	M.	R.	W.	AV.
TEST					
1ST-CLASS	30.1	7	109	2	54.50
INT					
JPL	17.5	0	89	4	22.25
NAT.W.	3	2	8	1	–
B & H					

LEADBEATER, B.

Full Name: Barrie Leadbeater
Role: Right-hand bat, right-arm medium bowler
Born: 14 August 1943, Harehills, Leeds
County: Yorkshire
County debut: 1966
County cap: 1969
Benefit: 1980 (£33,846 shared with G. A. Cope)
1st-Class 50s scored: 27
1st-Class 100s scored: 1
One-day 50s: 11
1st-Class catches: 82
Best batting performance: 140* Yorkshire v Hampshire, Portsmouth 1976
Appointed to 1st-Class list: 1981
Education: Harehills Secondary Modern

	I.	N.O.	R.	H.S.	AV.
TEST					
1ST-CLASS	241	29	5373	140*	25.34
INT					
JPL	68	14	1423	86*	26.35
NAT.W.	9	0	155	76	17.22
B & H	21	5	601	90	37.56

	O.	M.	R.	W.	AV.
TEST					
1ST-CLASS	5	1	5	1	–
INT					
JPL	8.5	0	38	2	19.00
NAT.W.					
B & H					

LLOYD, D.

Full Name: David Lloyd
Role: Left-hand opening bat
Born: 18 March 1947, Accrington, Lancashire
Height: 6′ **Weight:** 12½st
Nickname: Bumble
County: Lancashire
County debut: 1965
County cap: 1968
Test debut: 1974
No. of Tests: 9
No. of One-Day Internationals: 8
1000 runs in a season: 11
1st-Class 50s scored: 93
1st-Class 100s scored: 37
1st-Class 200s scored: 1
1st-Class 5 w. in innings: 5
1st-Class 10 w. in match: 1
One-day 50s: 41
One-day 100s: 7
1st-Class catches: 334
Best batting performance: 214* England v India, Edgbaston 1974
Best bowling performance: 7-38 Lancashire v Gloucestershire, Lydney 1966
Appointed to 1st-Class list: 1987
Parents: David and Mary
Wife and date of marriage: Susan, 30 March 1968
Children: Graham, 1969; Sarah, 1971; Steven, 1980; Ben, 1984
Education: Accrington Secondary Technical School
Other sports played: Soccer ('just hung up my boots – the linesman keeps passing me!')
Relaxations: Fly fishing
Extras: Played for Cumberland in Minor Counties

	I.	N.O.	R.	H.S.	AV.
TEST	15	2	552	214*	42.46
1ST-CLASS	637	72	18717	195	33.12
INT	8	1	285	116*	40.72
JPL	171	27	4653	103*	32.31
NAT.W.	42	7	1207	121*	34.49
B & H	48	3	1474	113	32.76

	O.	M.	R.	W.	AV.
TEST	4	0	17	0	–
1ST-CLASS	6.6 2584.1	2 719	9155	237	30.19
INT	2	1	3	1	–
JPL	77	2	420	17	24.70
NAT.W.	48.5	5	155	3	51.66
B & H	63.2	10	220	13	16.93

LYONS, K. J.

Full Name: Kevin James Lyons
Role: Right-hand bat, right-arm medium bowler
Born: 18 December 1946, Cardiff
County: Glamorgan
County debut: 1967
1st-Class 50s scored: 8
1st-Class catches: 27
Best batting performance: 92 Glamorgan v Cambridge University, Cambridge 1976
Appointed to 1st-Class list: 1985
Education: Lady Mary's High School, Cardiff

CAREER: BATTING

CAREER: BOWLING

	I.	N.O.	R.	H.S.	AV.
TEST					
1ST-CLASS	99	14	1673	92	19.68
INT					
JPL	24	3	205	56	9.76
NAT.W.	3	1	29	16	14.50
B & H	5	1	102	40	25.50

	O.	M.	R.	W.	AV.
TEST					
1ST-CLASS	69	10	252	2	126.00
INT					
JPL	14	0	94	2	47.00
NAT.W.					
B & H	23.5	0	104	7	14.85

MEYER, B. J.

Full Name: Barrie John Meyer
Role: Right-hand bat, wicket-keeper
Born: 21 August 1932, Bournemouth
Height: 5' 10½" **Weight:** 12st 7lbs
Nickname: B.J.
County: Gloucestershire
County debut: 1957
County cap: 1958
1st-Class 50s scored: 11
Best batting performance: 63 Gloucestershire v India, 1959; Gloucestershire v Oxford University, 1962; Gloucestershire v Sussex, 1964

Appointed to 1st-Class list: 1973
Appointed to Test panel: 1978
No. of Tests umpired: 18
No. of One-Day Internationals umpired: 15
Wife and date of marriage: Gillian, 4 September 1965
Children: Stephen, Christopher, Adrian
Education: Boscombe Secondary, Bournemouth
Jobs outside cricket: Salesman
Other sports played: Ex-professional footballer, golf (7 handicap)

CAREER: BATTING

	I.	N.O.	R.	H.S.	AV.
TEST					
1ST-CLASS	569	190	5367	63	14.16
INT					
JPL					
NAT.W.	9	2	69	21	9.86
B & H					

CAREER: BOWLING

	O.	M.	R.	W.	AV.
TEST					
1ST-CLASS	5	1	28	0	–
INT					
JPL					
NAT.W.					
B & H					

CAREER: WICKET-KEEPING

	C.	ST.			
TEST					
1ST-CLASS	708	117			
INT					
JPL					
NAT.W.	16	3			
B & H					

OSLEAR, D. O.

Full Name: Donald Osmund Oslear
Born: 3 March 1929, Cleethorpes
Height: 5′ 11″ **Weight:** 13st 6lbs
Appointed to 1st-Class list: 1975
Appointed to Test panel: 1980
No. of Tests umpired: 5
No. of One-Day Internationals umpired: 9
Parents: John Osmund and Violet Maude
Marital status: Divorced
Date of marriage: 1965
Children: Sara Elizabeth, 25 February 1970
Education: Elliston Street Secondary
Qualifications: Member of General Council ACU. Training Officer of ACU. Member of TCCB Electronic Aids Committee
Jobs outside cricket: Fishing Industry in Grimsby. Lecturing to umpires overseas
Family links with cricket: Father and brother, very good club cricketers

491

Off-season 1986–87: Lecture tour of Zimbabwe
Other sports followed: Anything which England are engaged in
Relaxations: The study of cricket law and the changes in the laws over the years. Reading cricket books
Extras: The only English umpire to have 'stood' in Test Matches, who has not played county cricket. Played soccer for Grimsby and ice-hockey for Grimsby and an England Select side
Opinions on cricket: 'I feel that a trial should be given to four days for matches in the County Championship.'

PALMER, K. E.

Full Name: Kenneth Ernest Palmer
Role: All-rounder: right-hand bat, right-arm fast-medium bowler
Born: 22 April 1937, Winchester
Height: 5' 10" **Weight:** 13st
Nickname: Pedlar
County: Somerset
County debut: 1955
County cap: 1958
Test debut: 1965
No. of Tests: 1
1000 runs in a season: 1
50 wickets in a season: 6
1st-Class 50s scored: 27
1st-Class 100s scored: 2
1st-Class 5 w. in innings: 46
1st-Class 10 w. in match: 5
1st-Class catches: 156
Best batting performance: 125* Somerset v Northamptonshire, Northampton 1961
Best bowling performance: 9-57 Somerset v Nottinghamshire, Trent Bridge 1963
Appointed to 1st-Class list: 1972
Appointed to Test panel: 1978
No. of Tests umpired: 14
No. of One-Day Internationals umpired: 7
Parents: Harry and Cecilia
Wife and date of marriage: Joy Valerie, 6 September 1962
Children: Gary, 1 November 1965
Jobs outside cricket: Coached cricket for Somerset for some time
Family links with cricket: Son Gary professional cricketer with Somerset. Brother umpire on first-class list and also played for Somerset

Other sports played: Squash

Relaxations: 'I enjoy watching my son play cricket on the rare occasions that I get the opportunity.'

Extras: Toured with Commonwealth side to Pakistan, 1962. West Indies with Denis Compton's team January 1963. 'I had the opportunity to see him score 100 in great style with a straw hat on!' Umpired in two Benson & Hedges Finals and two NatWest Finals. Also twice on World Cup panel in England. Won Carling Single Wicket Champion in 1961. Did the 'double' in 1961: 114 wickets and 1036 runs. Batting with former Australia and Somerset cricketer (and former Test umpire) Bill Alley, holds 6th wicket partnership record for Somerset. Wife, Joy, is a PE teacher

CAREER: BATTING

	I.	N.O.	R.	H.S.	AV.
TEST	1	0	10	10	–
1ST-CLASS	480	105	7751	125*	20.66
INT					
JPL	6	1	28	14	5.60
NAT.W.	13	4	109	35	12.11
B & H					

CAREER: BOWLING

	O.	M.	R.	W.	AV.
TEST	63	7	189	1	–
1ST-CLASS	7260.4	1767	18304	865	21.16
INT					
JPL	59	6	282	11	25.64
NAT.W.	163.3	35	451	23	19.60
B & H					

PALMER, R.

Full Name: Roy Palmer
Role: Right-hand bat, right-arm fast-medium bowler
Born: 12 July 1942, Devizes, Wiltshire
County: Somerset
County debut: 1965
50 wickets in a season: 1
1st-Class 50s scored: 1
1st-Class 5 w. in innings: 4
1st-Class catches: 25
Best batting performance: 84 Somerset v Leicestershire, Taunton 1967
Best bowling performance: 6-45 Somerset v Middlesex, Lord's 1967
Appointed to 1st-Class list: 1980
Education: Southbroom Secondary Modern
Extras: Brother Ken played for Somerset and is also a first-class umpire

CAREER: BATTING

	I.	N.O.	R.	H.S.	AV.
TEST					
1ST-CLASS	110	32	1037	84	13.29
INT					
JPL	19	2	168	25	9.88
NAT.W.	9	2	30	11	4.28
B & H					

CAREER: BOWLING

	O.	M.	R.	W.	AV.
TEST					
1ST-CLASS	1697.1	336	5439	172	31.62
INT					
JPL	220	14	963	37	26.03
NAT.W.	148.1	19	532	30	17.73
B & H					

PLEWS, N. T.

Full Name: Nigel Trevor Plews
Born: 5 September 1934, Nottingham
Height: 6′ 6½″ **Weight:** 16st 12lbs
Appointed to 1st-Class list: 1982
Appointed to Test panel: 1986 (one-day panel)
No. of One-Day Internationals umpired: 1
Parents: Parents deceased
Wife and date of marriage: Margaret, 1956
Children: Elaine, 1961; Douglas, 1964
Education: Mundella Grammar School, Nottingham
Qualifications: School Certificate, Royal Society Arts in Book-keeping
Jobs outside cricket: Nottingham City Police for 25 years as a Det. Sgt in Fraud Squad
Family links with cricket: None
Off-season 1986–87: Employed off season by international chartered accountants – Spicer and Pegler in insolvency work
Other sports played: Rugby, table tennis, swimming
Relaxations: Hill walking, reading, travel
Extras: Did not play first-class cricket. Was a policeman in Fraud Squad

RHODES, H. J.

Full Name: Harold James Rhodes
Role: Right-hand bat, right-arm fast bowler
Born: 22 July 1936, Hadfield, Derbyshire
Height: 6′ 2″ **Weight:** 14st
Nickname: Dusty
County: Derbyshire
County debut: 1953
County cap: 1958
Test debut: 1959
No. of Tests: 2
50 wickets in a season: 11
1st-Class 5 w. in innings: 42
1st-Class 10 w. in match: 4
1st-Class catches: 86
Best batting performance: 48 Derbyshire v Middlesex, Chesterfield 1958
Best bowling performance: 7-38 Derbyshire v Warwickshire, Edgbaston 1965
Appointed to 1st-Class list: On reserve list 1985 and 1986
Parents: Bert and Vera

Wife and date of marriage: Barbara 17 September 1960
Children: Marcus, 31 May 1961; Julie, 26 September 1962; Simon, 9 March 1968; Jonathan, 24 August 1969
Education: Vernon High School, Derby
Jobs outside cricket: Mortgage manager – Abbey Life Assurance Co.
Family links with cricket: Father was 1st-Class and Test umpire
Off-season 1986–87: Mortgage manager full-time
Other sports played: Rugby, cricket coach MCC Indoor School, Lord's
Relaxations: Reading, gardening
Extras: Top of 1st-Class bowling averages 1965 – 119 wickets, av. 11.09. Test career ruined by throwing controversy, cleared 1968 after eight years of deliberations. Autobiography published March 1987

CAREER: BATTING

	I.	N.O.	R.	H.S.	AV.
TEST	1	1	0	0*	–
1ST-CLASS	398	142	2427	48	9.48
INT					
JPL	11	5	23	6*	3.83
NAT.W.	10	6	84	26*	21.00
B & H	5	2	17	8*	5.66

CAREER: BOWLING

	O.	M.	R.	W.	AV.
TEST	74.5	10	244	9	27.11
1ST-CLASS	9128.4	2425	20901	1064	19.64
INT					
JPL	242.4	32	933	38	24.55
NAT.W.	173.4	41	435	22	19.77
B & H	98	18	302	11	27.45

SHEPHERD, D. R.

Full Name: David Robert Shepherd
Role: Right-hand bat, right-arm medium bowler
Born: 27 December 1940, Bideford, Devon
County: Gloucestershire
County debut: 1965
County cap: 1969
Benefit: 1978 (shared with J. Davey)
1000 runs in a season: 2
1st-Class 50s scored: 55
1st-Class 100s scored: 12
One-day 50s: 18
One-day 100s: 2
1st-Class catches: 95
Best batting performance: 153 Gloucestershire v Middlesex, Bristol 1968
Appointed to 1st-Class list: 1981
Appointed to Test panel: 1985
Education: Barnstaple GS; St Luke College, Exeter
Extras: Superstitious enough to stand on one leg when the score is on a 'Nelson'

CAREER: BATTING

	I.	N.O.	R.	H.S.	AV.
TEST					
1ST-CLASS	476	40	10672	153	24.47
INT					
JPL	118	9	2274	100	20.86
NAT.W.	24	3	457	72*	21.76
B & H	30	5	580	81	23.20

CAREER: BOWLING

	O.	M.	R.	W.	AV.
TEST					
1ST-CLASS	32.4	4	106	2	53.00
INT					
JPL	1	0	6	0	–
NAT.W.	0.2	0	4	0	–
B & H					

THOMPSETT, D. S.

Full Name: Donald Stanley Thompsett
Born: 8 April 1935, Piltdown, Sussex
Height: 6′ 1″ **Weight:** 13st
Appointed to 1st-Class list: On reserve list 1985
Parents: John and Dorothy
Wife and date of marriage: Valerie, 10 October 1957
Children: Glen, Clifford, Steven, Debbie and Linzie
Education: Secondary
Jobs outside cricket: Poultry farmer
Family links with cricket: Sons Cliff and Steve play club cricket for Chippenham in Western League
Other sports played: Bowls, football
Relaxations: Walking, gardening and reading
Extras: No first-class playing experience. Played local club cricket from the age of 11 years. Umpired at club level since 1974. Appointed to Minor Counties umpires list in 1978. Appointed to 1st-Class reserve list 1985. Umpired 2nd XI 1st-Class Championship matches since 1979. Debut in 1st-Class Championship Essex v Derbyshire, Colchester 1985
Opinions on cricket: 'Like many people I do feel that we have opened the floodgates for too many overseas players, therefore depriving us of some 25 or 30 places for youngsters coming into the game throughout the country.'

WHITE, R. A.

Full Name: Robert Arthur White
Role: Left-hand bat, right-arm off-break bowler
Born: 6 October 1936, Fulham
Height: 5′ 9½″ **Weight:** 12st 4lbs
Nickname: Knocker

Counties: Middlesex, Nottinghamshire
County debut: 1958 (Middlesex), 1966 (Nottinghamshire)
County cap: 1963 (Middlesex), 1966 (Nottinghamshire)
1000 runs in a season: 1
50 wickets in a season: 2
1st-Class 50s scored: 50
1st-Class 100s scored: 5
1st-Class 5 w. in innings: 28
1st-Class 10 w. in match: 4
1st-Class catches: 190
Best batting performance: 116* Nottinghamshire v Surrey, The Oval 1967
Best bowling performance: 7-41 Nottinghamshire v Derbyshire, Ilkeston 1971
Appointed to 1st-Class list: 1982
Wife: Janice
Children: Robin, Vanessa
Education: Chiswick Grammar School
Jobs outside cricket: Self employed agent
Other sports followed: 'All sports.'
Relaxations: Theatre goer, among others

CAREER: BATTING

	I.	N.O.	R.	H.S.	AV.
TEST					
1ST-CLASS	642	105	12452	116*	23.19
INT					
JPL	78	28	844	86*	16.88
NAT.W.	20	1	284	39	14.95
B & H	21	9	251	52*	20.92

CAREER: BOWLING

	O.	M.	R.	W.	AV.
TEST					
1ST-CLASS	7946	2219	21138	693	30.50
INT					
JPL	607	54	2448	103	23.76
NAT.W.	147	15	488	14	34.86
B & H	234.5	32	800	19	42.11

WHITEHEAD, A. G. T.

Full Name: Alan Geoffrey Thomas Whitehead
Role: Left-hand bat, slow left-arm bowler
Born: 28 October 1940, Butleigh, Somerset
County: Somerset
County debut: 1957
1st-Class 5 w. in innings: 3
1st-Class catches: 20
Best batting performance: 15 Somerset v Hampshire, Southampton 1959
Best bowling performance: 6-74 Somerset v Sussex, Eastbourne 1959
Appointed to 1st-Class list: 1970
Appointed to Test panel: 1982
No. of Tests umpired: 2

CAREER: BATTING

	I.	N.O.	R.	H.S.	AV.
TEST					
1ST-CLASS	49	25	137	15	5.71
INT					
JPL					
NAT.W.					
B & H					

CAREER: BOWLING

	O.	M.	R.	W.	AV.
TEST					
1ST-CLASS	846.4	250	2306	67	34.42
INT					
JPL					
NAT.W.					
B & H					

WIGHT, P. B.

Full Name: Peter Bernard Wight
Role: Right-hand bat, right-arm off-break bowler
Born: 25 June 1930, Georgetown, British Guyana
County: Somerset
County debut: 1953
County cap: 1954
Benefit: 1963 (£5000)
1000 runs in a season: 10
1st-Class 50s scored: 207
1st-Class 100s scored: 26
1st-Class 200s scored: 2
1st-Class 5 w. in innings: 1
1st-Class catches: 204
Best batting performance: 222* Somerset v Kent, Taunton 1959
Best bowling performance: 6-29 Somerset v Derbyshire, Chesterfield 1957
Appointed to 1st-Class list: 1966
Family links with cricket: Brother G. L. played for West Indies. Brothers H. A. and N. played for British Guyana

CAREER: BATTING

	I.	N.O.	R.	H.S.	AV.
TEST					
1ST-CLASS	590	53	17773	222*	33.10
INT					
JPL					
NAT.W.	6	0	56	38	9.33
B & H					

CAREER: BOWLING

	O.	M.	R.	W.	AV.
TEST					
1ST-CLASS	789.1	224	2262	68	33.26
INT					
JPL					
NAT.W.					
B & H					

ANSWERS

Q. 1. Dermot Reeve of Sussex.

Q. 2. Kevan James.

Q. 3. Lancashire and Hampshire.

Q. 4. 1969.

Q. 5. Jack Simmons of Lancashire.

Q. 6. £19,000 for the winners. £9,500 for the losers.

Q. 7. Garth Le Roux of Sussex.

Q. 8. It was for the first Test century ever by a New Zealander at The Oval.

Q. 9. 26.

Q. 10. Stuart Turner of Essex.

Q. 11. H. D. (Dickie) Bird.

Q. 12. B. H. Valentine.

Q. 13. Phil Mead of Hampshire and England.

Q. 14. Hungerford Town.

Q. 15. Peter West.

Q. 16. Pilling, Farrimond and Duckworth.

Q. 17. Walter Hammond of Gloucestershire and England, aged 31.

Q. 18. Paynter, 216 not out at Trent Bridge. Hammond 240 at Lord's. Hutton 364 at The Oval. (Leyland's 187 at The Oval also beat the pre-1938 record by Mead of 182 not out.)

Q. 19. Dick Collinge, 116.

Q. 20. 20.

Q. 21. Wimbledon, Hendon, Corinthian Casuals and Charlton.

Q. 22. Alan Hill of Derbyshire.

Q. 23. John Morris of Derbyshire.

Q. 24. Alf and George Powley were twins.

Q. 25. Tom Lowry.

Q. 26. 'South of the Border, Down Mexico Way.'

Q. 27. Limited Overs.

Q. 28. Dennis.

Q. 29. G. O. 'Gubby' Allen.

Q. 30. Both matches were tied.

Q. 31. G. O. Allen, M. Brearley, F. G. Mann, F. T. Mann, R. W. V. Robins, T. C. O'Brien, G. T. S. Stevans, A. E. Stoddart and P. F. Warner.

Q. 32. D. A. Allen in 1966.

Q. 33. Sir George Oswald Browning Allen.

Q. 34. It was his 115th Test, beating M. C. Cowdrey's record of 114.

Q. 35. 19.

Q. 36. Bruce French, Bill Athey, Bob Taylor and Bobby Parks.

Q. 37. Zimbabwe (winners) and The Netherlands.

Q. 38. Jack Simmons of Lancashire and Tasmania.

Q. 39. 1975.

Q. 40. George Mann of Middlesex.

Q. 41. Alec Stewart of Surrey.

Q. 42. John Bracewell (110), Evan Gray (50) and Derek Stirling (26).

Q. 43. W. G. Grace.

Q. 44. Graham Gooch v India at Lord's, 5 June 1986.

Q. 45. It was his highest Test score, and first Test 50.

Q. 46. Chris Old, Yorkshire, Warwickshire and England.

Q. 47. Derek Pringle, Essex and England.

Q. 48. Phil Edmonds, Middlesex and England.

Q. 49. F. J. Titmus of Middlesex, in both innings.

Q. 50. J. W. H. T. Douglas of Essex.

Q. 51. When a batsman is out for 0 in two successive innings.

Q. 52. Sunil Gavaskar of India.

Q. 53. Cornhill Insurance.

Q. 54. A kind of dried fish.

Q. 55. It was Vengsarkar's third successive century in successive Tests for India at Lord's.

Q. 56. Henry Blofeld.

Q. 57. J. W. H. T. Douglas of Essex.

Q. 58. J. C. Laker and W. J. Edrich.

Q. 59. Yorkshire where he was born and began his career by playing in the Bradford League; Surrey where he played most of his first-class cricket; and Essex where he played his last seasons.

Q. 60. True.

Q. 61. Frank Tyson of Northamptonshire and England.

Q. 62. True.

Q. 63. Trustee of the South Australian Cricket Association, and a member of its ground and finance committee.

Q. 64. Tony Brown.

Q. 65. Gloucestershire in 1977 and Essex in 1986.

Q. 66. They all made centuries in their first Test against Australia.

Q. 67. Mark Nicholas of Hampshire.

Q. 68. Kim Barnett of Derbyshire.

Q. 69. Clive Rice of Nottinghamshire.

Q. 70. Bruce French.

Q. 71. Balfour Patrick Patterson.

Q. 72. Surrey, Worcestershire and Glamorgan.

Q. 73. Hutton (Captain), Bailey, May, Graveney, Laker, Lock, Trueman, Edrich, Bedser, Compton, Evans, Wardle (12th man).

Q. 74. R. E. Foster of Worcestershire and England, 1878–1914.

Q. 75. Herbert Sutcliffe of Yorkshire and England christened his son, who captained Yorkshire, William Herbert Hobbs Sutcliffe, after Sir Jack Hobbs.

Q. 76. He scored a century in his first first-class match – the only Glamorgan player to do so since Frank Pinch in 1921.

Q. 77. Knott's slow off-break killed a butterfly in flight.

Q. 78. Lawrence, Walsh, Curran, Davison and Lloyds.

Q. 79. W. Bestwick (see 'Crusoe on Cricket').

Q. 80. Coe was the first man in first-class cricket out to a googly, bowled by B. J. T. Bosanquet.

Q. 81. Alfred Tennyson, Poet Laureate, Lord Tennyson of Hampshire and England.

Q. 82. Sir C. Aubrey Smith of Sussex, Hollywood and England.

Q. 83. George Gunn. Gunn was fielding in a topee. Constantine skied a ball to him in the deep. He held out his topee in his left hand at full stretch. It looked as though he was about to break Law 41.

Then he caught the ball with his right hand.

Q. 84. Gower pulled it for 4.

Q. 85. They have all scored over 1000 runs against all other counties.

Q. 86. Right-hand, slow leg-break.

Q. 87. Sammy Woods.

Q. 88. Herbert Sutcliffe and Percy Holmes.

Q. 89. Wilfred Rhodes of Yorkshire and England.

Q. 90. K. S. Ranjitsinhji of Cambridge University, Sussex and England.

Q. 91. The two Nawabs of Pataudi. The father for England, the son for India. The father also captained India.

Q. 92. Lord Hawke, 1860–1938. Born in Lincolnshire.

Q. 93. C. E. M. Wilson and E. R. Wilson, both of Yorkshire and England.

Q. 94. Allan Watkins.

Q. 95. 1948.

Q. 96. John (Jack) Cornish White, 1891–1961 of Somerset and England.

Q. 97. Sir Pelham Francis Warner (Plum) 1873–1963.

Q. 98. S. M. J. (Sammy) Woods, 1867–1931. Cambridge, Somerset, Australia and England.

Q. 99. Rodney Hogg.

Q. 100. Ian Chappell of Australia.

Q. 101. Australia, 1970.

Q. 102. David Gower.

Q. 103. Victor Trumper.

Q. 104. John Emburey.

Q. 105. 5½–5¾ozs.

Q. 106. Winston Churchill for F. S. Jackson at Harrow.

Q. 107. Brian Close.

Q. 108. Graham Roope of Surrey and England.

Q. 109. 40.

Q. 110. E. L. McCormick.

Q. 111. G. Geary and H. A. Smith in 1935, against Worcestershire, Gloucestershire and Northamptonshire.

Q. 112. Graham Roope. With Boycott v Australia at Headingley. With Edrich, for Surrey v Derbyshire.

Q. 113. Seven.

Q. 114. Only one; England.

Q. 115. Gold.

Q. 116. Six martlets.

Q. 117. 1962.

Q. 118. Sir Timothy O'Brien of Middlesex, Ireland and England.

Q. 119. 1864.

Q. 120. Brian Langford.

Q. 121. James Lillywhite of Sussex.

Q. 122. Peter Van Der Merwe.

Q. 123. Yes. In Australia. 4th Test, 1926.

Q. 124. F. C. M. 'Gerry' Alexander.

Q. 125. R. K. Nunes.

Q. 126. C. K. Nayudu.

Q. 127. B. Warnapuru.

Q. 128. Hampshire and Nottinghamshire.

Q. 129. A. C. Maclaren.

Q. 130. Tony Lewis for England and Majid Khan for Pakistan, during England's tour of Pakistan 1972–73.

Q. 131. John Arlott on Swansea.

Q. 132. Maurice Turnbull, 1930 v New Zealand.

Q. 133. Arthur Fagg, for Kent v Essex, 1938; 244, and 202 not out.

Q. 134. Andy Lloyd of Warwickshire and England.

Q. 135. M. A. Roseberry of Middlesex.

Q. 136. A. J. T. Miller of Middlesex.

Q. 137. Bill Athey of Gloucestershire, Yorkshire and England.

Q. 138. Chris Smith of Hampshire and England.

Q. 139. Gladstone Small of Warwickshire and England.

Q. 140. O. H. Mortensen of Derbyshire.

Q. 141. S. N. Hartley of Yorkshire.

Q. 142. P. J. Prichard of Essex.

Q. 143. Kevin Curran of Gloucestershire.

Q. 144. Ian Peebles of Middlesex and England.

Q. 145. Jack Fingleton of Australia.

Q. 146. Alan McGilvray of New South Wales, and Australian commentating team.

Q. 147. Sir Home Gordon.

Q. 148. A. J. Raffles in the novels of that name by E. W. Hornung.

Q. 149. J. C. Snaith.

Q. 150. Ian Hay.

Q. 151. M. O. Lyon.

Q. 152. S. F. Barnes of England and Bill O'Reilly of Australia.

Q. 153. Lord Home (then Lord Dunglass).

Q. 154. Melbourne.

Q. 156. 1815.

Q. 156. 1744.

Q. 157. David Boon.

Q. 158. Hearne (A. and G. G. for England; F. for South Africa).

Q. 159. Joe Hardstaff.

Q. 160. Greg Chappell.

Q. 161. Geoff Pullar v India, 1959.

Q. 162. M. P. Bowden, 23 years and 144 days, in 1888.

Q. 163. Derbyshire.

Q. 164. Keith Miller.

Q. 165. Peter Sainsbury of Hampshire: 107 wickets, and 959 runs.

Q. 166. He was out for 0 in successive balls (last out in Glamorgan's first innings and first out when they followed on).

Q. 167. Jim Foat.

Q. 168. Eight.

Q. 169. Leeds: 2 by Bradman; 1 by J. H. Edrich.

Q. 170. Herbert Sutcliffe of Yorkshire and England.

Q. 171. Chris Old.

Q. 172. Clem Hill.

Q. 173. Patsy Hendren.

Q. 174. Raymond Illingworth.

Q. 175. Bob Willis, in 1972.

Q. 176. Richard Collinge of New Zealand.

Q. 177. Johnny Briggs, England v South Africa, 1888–89.

Q. 178. Yorkshire, Leicestershire, England, Yorkshire.

Q. 179. W. G. Grace.

Q. 180. Chris Broad in 1980 for Gloucestershire v Oxford.

Q. 181. C. B. Fry.

Q. 182. Arthur Milton (Gloucestershire) and Willie Watson (Yorkshire and Leicestershire).

Q. 183. J. B. Hobbs, 197.

Q. 184. David Bairstow.

Q. 185. D. W. Gregory.

Q. 186. They all made 100s on their first-class debut.

Q. 187. G. H. G. Doggart of Cambridge, Sussex and England, 215 not out, Cambridge University v Lancashire, 1948.

Q. 188. Noel Cantwell of Ireland.

Q. 189. P. B. H. May.

Q. 190. Glamorgan, 1921.

Q. 191. L. and S. Armanath for India.

Q. 192. D. V. P. Wright of Kent and England.

Q. 193. Jack Richards of Surrey and England.

Q. 194. Brian Close, 52. Ted Dexter 51.

Q. 195. Zaheer Abbas, 8 times.

Q. 196. D. G. Bradman, 95.14.

Q. 197. Sir Jack Hobbs; 61,237; from 1905 to 1934.

NOTES/AUTOGRAPHS